Social Problems

Social Problems

Third Edition

A Canadian Perspective

Lorne Tepperman
& Josh Curtis

OXFORD
UNIVERSITY PRESS

OXFORD

UNIVERSITY PRESS

8 Sampson Mews, Suite 204, Don Mills, Ontario M3C 0H5
www.oupcanada.com

Oxford University Press is a department of the University of Oxford.
It furthers the University's objective of excellence in research, scholarship,
and education by publishing worldwide in

Oxford   New York

Auckland   Cape Town   Dar es Salaam   Hong Kong   Karachi
Kuala Lumpur   Madrid   Melbourne   Mexico City   Nairobi
New Delhi   Shanghai   Taipei   Toronto

With offices in

Argentina   Austria   Brazil   Chile   Czech Republic   France   Greece
Guatemala   Hungary   Italy   Japan   Poland   Portugal   Singapore
South Korea   Switzerland   Thailand   Turkey   Ukraine   Vietnam

Oxford is a trade mark of Oxford University Press
in the UK and in certain other countries

Published in Canada
by Oxford University Press

Library and Archives Canada Cataloguing in Publication

Tepperman, Lorne, 1943–
Social problems : a Canadian perspective/Lorne Tepperman & Josh Curtis.—3rd ed.

Includes bibliographical references and index.
ISBN 978-0-19-543239-8

1. Social problems—Textbooks. 2. Canada—Social conditions—
Textbooks. I. Curtis, Josh II. Title.

HN103.5.T46 2010   361.1   C2010-904919-5

Cover image: © Matt Child/Alamy

This book is printed on permanent (acid-free) paper ∞.

Printed and bound in the United States of America.

2 3 4 — 14 13 12 11

Contents

Each chapter includes, at the beginning, Learning Objectives, and, at the end, Questions for Critical Thought, Recommended Readings, and Recommended Websites.

PART 1 INTRODUCTION   1

PART 2 INEQUALITIES   29

PART 3   OUTCOMES   173

9 Health Issues   232

10 War and Terrorism   259

PART 4 DOMAINS   287

11 Families   288

12 Workplaces   318

13 Schools   346

14 Populations, Cities, and Neighbourhoods   374

PART 5 THE FUTURE   435

Preface

Welcome to the third edition of *Social Problems: A Canadian Perspective*. We were very pleased with the reception readers gave the first two editions and we have tried to make this new edition even better.

In this text we assume there is such a thing as a 'social problem'. A social problem is any circumstance that many people experience and that has both social causes and social consequences. The social problem in each case actually exists. We can verify that fact with our own eyes and with the measurement tools of social science. Yet the social problem is also socially constructed, in the sense that people think it exists and tend to agree on this. They define it as a social problem. The condition in question has become a problem for people, and if they did not think it was a problem, it would cease being one, at least at the level of consciousness, social definition, and social action.

Because of this socially constructed aspect of social problems, we can trace historically the rise and fall of social problems over time. We can study when people came to share the understanding that it was a problem. To take a simple example, few people in Canada today consider the so-called promiscuity of young women to be a social problem, although this was not the case in the past. Likewise, few Canadians today are troubled by what used to be called 'miscegenation'—couples from two different races having sexual relations—although in earlier times many people considered this a serious social problem.

Sociologists study why certain behaviours, and not others, come to occupy our concern and evoke the label of 'social problem'. This takes us into the areas of changing morality and moral panics—sudden, intense, widespread, and often fleeting concerns about the immorality of one particular group. Also of interest to sociologists, though, are social problems that can be shown to do major harm to our quality of life but that only a few people see as a problem and that government and other powerful agencies are doing little to address.

The social problems that are longest lasting and evoke concern among the largest numbers of people are those that are not merely socially constructed and, in that sense, are not simply problems 'in people's minds'. They are also serious matters of health, and of life and death. Poverty, racial discrimination, bad working conditions, domestic violence—these are all serious social problems because, at the extremes, they hurt or kill people. In less extreme circumstances, they increase illness and reduce people's well-being and quality of life. Increasingly, we live in what Ulrich Beck (1992) has called a 'risk society', in which we are all, always, in danger of harm from sources that are often hidden from view and beyond human control. Often these risks are a result of human activity, especially the applications of science and technology to the natural environment. Often they are a result of what we are taught to regard fondly as 'progress'.

So apart from the perceived immorality, injustice, or unfairness of the problems we will discuss in this book, serious social problems cost our society many human lives and many days lost from work and family life, as well as shattered families, workplace conflict, and destroyed hopes. These problems are not merely 'in people's minds'. In fact, the job of the sociologist, in these cases, is to bring them to people's conscious attention.

To summarize to this point, we are particularly interested in issues that are both potentially and actually social problems: they cause people trouble and are seen as causing trouble. We will pay no attention whatever to the more pleasant sides of life—making this a somewhat dark-hued book. Moreover, we will pay only passing attention to issues that people may briefly consider problems but, in the end, prove not to be. Actual and potential problems that lurk below the consciousness of most people will make intermittent appearances in this book, especially in the final chapter.

Sometimes people are unaware of the risks surrounding them because they have been disciplined to view the harmful as safe, the inhumane and dangerous as normal. To some degree, we are all victims of techniques of management and moral regulation that some, following Michel Foucault (2000), have called 'governmentality'. Our trained unawareness and secret but effective regulation ensure that we will usually abide by the rules of society, thus protecting the advantage of those in power.

Social science has a poor batting average in solving human problems. It has not done well at bringing about change, as we will see. The problem here is in part the complexity of the roots of social problems and in part the will and ability (or lack thereof) of society's agencies of power to address the problems. Yet we, as authors of this book, believe that the purpose of sociology today, just as in the nineteenth century when sociology began, is to use knowledge to improve social life. Thus, our goal in a book like this is to aid the understanding of the roots of social problems, their health consequences for individuals and society as a whole, and how these can be addressed. For this task, it is important to explore facts and theories concerning how problems develop and are maintained, and how they are interrelated. We believe that these theories help us organize our facts and help us work towards solving our problems.

We should say a few final words about the purpose of a book as general as this one. This text duplicates some of what students may have learned in an Introduction to Sociology course. The duplication is intentional. We want to refresh your memory of the basic principles of sociology before proceeding to a close discussion of social problems. Some instructors may even find that this book can substitute for a book that introduces first-time students to the field of sociology. In addition, this book covers a variety of problems, each briefly. This brevity is also intentional. We want to get students thinking in a particular way so that they can study these same problems, new problems, or changed problems on their own. We do not offer the last word on any social problem presented here—only the beginnings of a discussion informed by sociological principles.

We do not offer sociology as a cure-all. We emphasize how very difficult many social problems have been to solve and how little has been done about some of them. Like many of our colleagues in sociology, we understand the concerns of postmodernity. The 'project' of modernization that engaged thinkers and social practitioners for much of the last three centuries has taken a new turn. The horrors of the twentieth century shook our faith in reason and in the power of humans to build a better world using science and technology, social legislation, mass media, higher education, and secular values. No one who spends a few moments thinking about the Holocaust, the two world wars, the terrorism of September 2001 and the ensuing wars in Afghanistan, Iraq, Pakistan, Sri Lanka, and Israel, not to mention recurring crises in Darfur and the Congo and other parts of Africa, environmental degradation in many parts of the world, and continued practices of imperialist domination will readily indulge fantasies about the perfection, or even the perfectibility, of human societies. Part of the reason for this is that the solutions to social problems are often complex and costly. Another reason is that the solutions are political matters requiring strong commitment from society's elites.

In this respect, one of sociology's three founders was particularly prescient. Sociologist Max Weber saw the nightmare of modern society coming. His eyes were open to the 'iron cage' of modernity, especially to how bureaucracies and governments can enslave and torment humans more effectively than had ever been known before. Weber believed that bureaucracies would become all-powerful in society, and that their elites would end up largely serving their own interests, very often contrary to the interest of average people. Only those problems and solutions seen as important by powerful interests would be addressed in societies of the future (that is, in our time now).

Another founder of sociology, Karl Marx, believed that communism would solve all problems of the human condition. He appears to have been wrong, although some still argue that his theories have never been put to a proper test in any society. Émile Durkheim was, of sociology's three leading figures during its developing years, the most optimistic, and therefore the most wrong about the twentieth century. He believed that societies change in a progressive direction, solving social problems over time through the differentiation and specialization of tasks, with modest negative side effects of anomie, or alienation, on the part of individuals because of the processes of social change.

Yet, despite having been shaken by the twentieth century and its horrors, we persist in our efforts. As long as we live, most of us strive to build a better world for our children, our community, and ourselves. It is in the hopes of continuing this optimistic effort that we, the authors, have written this book. We believe that social problems really do exist and do great harm. Furthermore, we believe that knowledge and purposeful informed action may still improve human life. This, then, is where we begin our study of social problems.

HOW THIS BOOK IS ORGANIZED

We will see that sociologists, like other social scientists, have a variety of theories about society and its social problems. Throughout this book, we will return to three sociological theories—structural functionalism, conflict theory, and symbolic interactionism—as well as to two other important perspectives for understanding problems in society—feminism, which varies in its analysis and solutions from liberal to radical points of view, and social constructionism, an outgrowth of symbolic interactionism that posits that groups of people create and recreate their own realities. Each contributes important elements to our understanding of society and social problems. None rules out the validity or contribution of any other. Each of the theories approaches social life from a different standpoint, asking different questions and looking at different kinds of evidence. Therefore, each pays off for our understanding of social problems, in different ways. These approaches compete for our attention and loyalty. Sociologists tend to prefer and attach themselves to one approach rather than another. At the same time, applied sociologists go about analyzing and solving real-life problems in families, workplaces, organizations, and societies by combining insights from all of these perspectives.

We also employ an additional perspective—the population health perspective—in each chapter. This perspective focuses attention on the physical and psychological harm caused by social problems to individuals and, thereby, on the harm caused to society. This perspective also emphasizes the social sources and consequences of people's illness and health. The population health perspective complements the other perspectives: it not so much contradicts them as it adds to and extends them. It simply has a more explicit focus on the issues of the health of individuals and societies. All of the theoretical approaches will be discussed in further detail in the Introduction (Chapter 1) and in the ensuing chapters.

We have organized this book to reflect our assumptions about social problems. We begin each chapter with a brief general introduction to the problem at hand. We then follow with a section containing some facts about the problem, setting the stage for our understanding of it. This section is not meant to replace other information about the problem from, for example, academic reports, newspapers, magazines, or television reportage. Facts in books such as this one must be somewhat selective, and they tend to age quickly. We therefore urge the reader to seek additional facts about all of the problems discussed in this book from other sources.

Next, in each chapter, we review a range of theoretical approaches to the problem under discussion. We show how these approaches ask different questions and come to different conclusions. These theories help us organize our understanding of the problem. Since the theory sections are invariably brief, we urge the reader to explore further the assumptions and implications of the different approaches, as with much else in this book. Critical thinking questions at the end of each chapter will help the reader do this.

After the theoretical approaches follows, in each chapter, a section on the social consequences of the social problem in question. As we shall see throughout this book (often by way of mild repetition), most of the social problems we discuss are connected to one another, some more closely than others. For example, there is no adequate way to discuss work and unemployment without discussing poverty, no way to discuss family problems without also considering aging, gender inequality, and sexual orientation, and no way to discuss ageism without discussing stereotypes. A few general principles related to social inequality and social exclusion return time and again to inform our discussion.

Many serious social problems share a similar range of consequences. Problems such as exploitation, discrimination, and exclusion tend to impoverish people, isolate them, and give them less stake in the future of the community. The results of some social problems also commonly include crime, violence, addiction, stress, mental illness (for example, depression), and physical illness. We view these consequences as problems in their own right, and our goal would be for societies to solve them or at least reduce their prevalence. We therefore need to deal with the root causes of the social problems. These root causes are very much social in nature. As sociologists, we need to explain what occurs and why, and suggest how this situation might be improved. As citizens, we should try to understand the problems and their roots, and do what we can to improve the situation—for ourselves and for future generations.

NEW TO THIS EDITION

Two new chapters—on education and environment—have been added. We have reorganized the order of chapters, updated the examples and references, and made the book's layout more attractive by adding a new photo program and colour to the interior design. We have added new boxed materials and beefed up the discussion of social constructionism and claims-making. Yet, for all this, the book has remained the same in its fundamental approach.

A number of pedagogical features have been incorporated into the text to make it a more effective learning tool for students. Each chapter includes the following components:

- learning objectives;
- an introduction that sets the contents of the chapter in a wider context;
- theme boxes that reinforce chapter material:
    — Back in History boxes discuss periods of and incidents in history that relate to chapter material.
    — Classic Works boxes cite important research and scholarship of past sociologists.
    — International Comparisons boxes present sociological issues, debates, and practices in various parts of the world.
    — Personal Stories boxes highlight the struggles and experiences of individuals as they relate to chapter material.
    — Policy Debates boxes present differing viewpoints on contentious issues such as poverty, education, and social stratification.
    — Public Issues boxes discuss relevant and current social issues that affect Canadians.
- a margin glossary in each chapter and a compiled glossary at the back of the book;
- a conclusion that summarizes key points discussed in the chapter;
- questions for critical thought;
- annotated recommended readings;
- annotated recommended websites.

The text's well-developed art program is designed to make the book more accessible and engaging. Fifty-three photographs, 48 figures and charts, 27 tables, and 44 boxed inserts covering the full range of subject matter help clarify important concepts and make the subject come alive.

In addition, this text is accompanied by an impressive ancillary package.

- A Test Bank is available to instructors adopting the text. Each chapter in the Test Bank contains the following: 20 multiple-choice questions, 10 true/false questions, 10 short-answer questions, and 10 discussion questions.

- An Instructor's Manual is also available to adopters. Each chapter in the Instructor's Manual contains the following: chapter table of contents, summary, 5–10 learning objectives, 10 key concepts, and 10 audiovisual materials and teaching aids.
- PowerPoint Slides reiterate chapter material and act as a useful study tool for students and a helpful lecture tool for instructors.

Instructors should contact their Oxford University Press representative regarding ancillary materials.

ACKNOWLEDGEMENTS

Our first thank you is to the outstanding University of Toronto undergraduate students who helped us research this book. They include (in alphabetical order): Balsam Attarbashi, Pamela Bautista, Roxy Chis, Anita Feher, Nina Gheiman, Hilary Killam, Len Liu, Cathy Long, Brianna Sykes, Adam Whisler, and Cindy Yi. It's been a privilege and a pleasure to work with these talented young people—one of the two best parts of working on this book.

The other best part of this project was working with the people at Oxford University Press and their associates. Jennifer Mueller performed the difficult, even astonishing, task of reducing our original manuscript by about 30 per cent. (Yes, you can have too much of a good thing!) This she did with great intelligence and sensitivity, preserving the most important material we had put together. Thank you, Jennifer. Richard Tallman followed up, with his usual astute and insightful copy-editing, always forcing us to clarify the unclear statement, finish the incomplete thought, and defend vague or questionable assertions. So, thank you, too, Richard.

We also want to thank our anonymous reviewers and undergraduate students in Sociology 382 and SSC 199 who have read and responded to material in the first two editions. They have all given us new ideas about what to discuss and how to discuss it most effectively. We've learned a lot writing this book, and it's been fun, too. So, read the book and let us know what you think. We want this book to make your world clearer and more meaningful. If you have some ideas about how we can do that better in the next edition, send us an e-mail at: <lorne.tepperman@utoronto.ca>.

Finally, we would like to acknowledge the following reviewers, along with those reviewers who chose to remain anonymous, whose thoughtful comments and suggestions have helped to shape the third edition of *Social Problems*.

Professor Pearl Crichton, Concordia University
Professor Ineke Lock, University of Alberta
Professor Susan Miller, University of Manitoba
Professor Sylvia Peacock, University of Guelph
Professor Erin Steuter, Mount Allison University
Professor Victor Ujimoto, University of Guelph
Professor Sobia Zaman, Humber College

Lorne Tepperman
Josh Curtis
July 2010

PART 1

Introduction

CHAPTER 1

What Are Social Problems?

iStockphoto.com/dundamin

LEARNING OBJECTIVES

- To understand what a social problem is.
- To learn how sociologists think about the sociological imagination.
- To find out how sociologists think about social change.
- To recognize the importance of the historical context of social problems.
- To discover the value of information as a social resource.
- To learn the competing theories that clarify aspects of social problems.

WHAT IS A 'SOCIAL PROBLEM'?

When you hear the words social problem do you think of juvenile delinquents? Drug addicts? Homeless people? Sex workers? Or do you think about insider trading? Tax fraud? Arms sales? The mass marketing of junk food? How about witchcraft? Devil worship? Interplanetary abduction? Celebrity sex scandals? The secret lives of powerful people? The label *social problem* is applied to each of these topics and to hundreds more.

Today, there is no shortage of social problems in what Staeheli (2008) calls the 'terrains of political claims-making'. We see struggles everywhere over issues and inequalities (Wilkinson and Pickett, 2007), from rallies against Free Trade in Canada or in support of Mexican immigrants in the US, to parades featuring lesbian, gay, bisexual, transgendered, and queer communities in Sweden or Israel. These rallies do not merely represent identities and personal interests; they are efforts to change broader social, political, and economic relationships. Our society is saturated with problems and protests, with claims of importance and demands for consideration and dignity. The political terrain is jammed full—clogged—with political actors and activists trying to influence our views and political lives (Taft, 2009).

Such jostling for attention complicates our singling out of the most important problems, those most deserving of our notice. We cannot work for every cause; yet we want to support the right causes. But how can we tell truth from falsehood, fact from exaggeration or deception? At the same time, this competition for attention gives us a sense that our views matter—and they do! We all need to understand the social problems and political controversies about problems that are laying claim on our attention. We can have a say in how these problems will be solved.

That's where sociology comes in. As the systematic study of societies, sociology is well-equipped to help us inform ourselves about current problems and their possible solutions. No field is more likely than sociology to force us to make connections—among problems, and among levels of analysis—in seeking answers to the problems that face ordinary Canadians.

SOCIAL PROBLEM
A social condition or pattern of behaviour that is believed to warrant public concern and collective action.

SOCIOLOGY AND THE STUDY OF SOCIAL PROBLEMS

The study of social problems is at least as old as the study of sociology itself (McMullin, 2004). In fact, much of early sociology was the study of social problems. Marx, Durkheim, and Weber all were concerned with social problems, although they spoke about them in different ways.

More precisely, sociology has always been about social change, social conflict, and social cohesion—and all of these are connected to social problems. The rise of sociology itself—like the rise of the study of social problems—coincided with the rise of 'modern' societies in the nineteenth century. During this formative period, Western Europe and North America shared a deep confidence in the idea of 'progress'. At that time, 'progress' included industrialization and urbanization; inventions and scientific discovery; and exposure to new and different ideas and cultures. 'Progress' also meant the possibility of social improvement or social 'amelioration'.

Most sociologists then, like most social reformers, believed that social life could be improved through the systematic study of social issues: by applying knowledge and expelling ignorance, superstition, prejudice, and blind custom. They believed deeply in the value of social research as the means for diagnosing social problems and for inventing and evaluating solutions. They believed that social change could be directed to good ends; that social conflict could be resolved in just ways; and that the social order could be re-established around new principles of organization.

Sociologists today still struggle to see and record the patterns of social life that cause what we will call 'social problems'. We are not—cannot be—omniscient narrators, as in a novel by Dickens or Steinbeck. We do not see everything and know everything. Yet, as socially conscious members of our society, we want to take part in a struggle against these problems—if only by clarifying them. To do so—imperfectly, but as well as possible—we need to learn and to use the knowledge collected by expert researchers. This book is an introductory collection and explanation of the sociological knowledge we have today.

We will examine a variety of social problems using sociological concepts to understand them, sociological tools to measure them, and sociological theories to link them. Certain master themes or narratives will emerge; these reflect a variety of different ways of viewing reality.

We will pass over many topics and themes, only because space doesn't permit us to address them. What we discuss is treated briefly and points students to further research. We must ignore the variety of non-sociological approaches to the same social problems. For example, genetic, chemical, biological, and psychological factors influence such social problems as health, addiction, and crime. Nor can there be any doubt that cultural, political, and economic factors influence other social problems we discuss: for example, wars, environmental degradation, populations, and workplaces.

As we cannot delve into every possible topic or examine every possible approach, the reader is urged to seek a 'second opinion' on everything we have to say by reading widely in the social sciences.

Objective and Subjective Elements

Social problems have at least two aspects that sometimes seem contradictory: what we will call objective and subjective elements.

OBJECTIVE ELEMENTS
The measurable features of a negative social condition. Such a condition might include crime, poverty, or alcohol abuse and can be considered an objective reality.

Objective elements are the measurable features of a negative social condition. The condition in question—for example, crime, poverty, or alcohol abuse—can be considered an objective reality. Systematic measurements show that the condition exists and that it harms people. We can study its causes and effects without making a moral judgment and without judging it as 'serious' or 'trivial'. Sexual abuse, environmental pollution, and racially motivated hate crimes are examples of such problems. To a large extent, we can count and measure their incidence. We can study changes in social life that cause the numbers or rates of these events to increase and decrease. And we can make and test theories about their changing rates of occurrence.

This activity is based on a philosophical premise, sometimes called 'positivism', of a material reality we can perceive with our senses; and what we call 'science' is the systematic attempt to find and test natural laws through measurements of this reality. (Science is slightly more complex than our definition, but this is the gist of it.)

Subjective elements are people's *evaluations* of objective conditions and the processes that influence their evaluations. They include the moral labels ('wrong', 'immoral', 'sick', and so on) people apply to particular acts or situations, and the accounts they give for these acts and situations. These moral or aesthetic judgements reflect people's beliefs and tastes. They are a social reality in their own right; if people believe, for example, that smoking marijuana is evil, that multiculturalism is good, that homosexuals are sick, or that old people are incompetent, then these beliefs are aspects of social realities. Beliefs set in motion actions that have social consequences (legislation, for example), as we will see repeatedly throughout the book.

Note that an objective of sociology is also to find and test natural laws about these subjective beliefs and their consequences. Often, these phenomena are harder to measure and harder to explain than other things we study; so our theories about them are often less developed. Still, these 'subjective realities' are just as important among social issues that can be studied.

These 'subjective' aspects of social problems affect and reflect our emotional reactions to information we receive about the world. We do not like to hear about young children dying of malnutrition or suffering the effects of industrial water pollution. Hearing of such things reminds us—at least according to the values and beliefs generally shared by sociologists and some others in our culture—that global health inequality and corporate environmental negligence are worthy of social concern. Second, our 'subjective' or emotional responses often lead to what we call the 'social construction' of social problems—including a search for villains, moral panic, crusades for better behaviour, a demand for improved laws, and so on. A central feature in the social construction of social problems is called 'claims-making'—a process by which people try to capture attention and mobilize public opinion around particular problems and their solutions.

As we will see, our formulation of social problems is influenced both by changes in measurable reality and by changes in our *perceptions* of measurable reality. As sociologists, we are particularly well-suited to studying social problems, because we know how to measure changes in measurable reality and we know how to measure changes in people's perceptions. By bringing together the objective and subjective elements, we can define a *social problem* as both a condition—an empirically observed condition that threatens the well-being of a significant part of society—and a process—the sequence of events by which members of society come to see a condition as a social problem that warrants and needs collective remedial action.

SOCIAL PROBLEMS AND THE SOCIOLOGICAL IMAGINATION

According to sociologist C. Wright Mills (1959), the **sociological imagination** is the ability to see connections between one's own life (micro-events), the social world in which one lives (macro-events), and between personal or private troubles and public issues. This

SUBJECTIVE ELEMENTS People's evaluations of objective conditions and the processes that influence their evaluations. They include the moral labels that people apply to particular acts or situations, and the accounts they give for these acts and situations.

SOCIOLOGICAL IMAGINATION A term used by sociologist C. Wright Mills in his 1959 book, *The Sociological Imagination*, that describes the sociologist's ability to connect seemingly impersonal and remote historical forces to the most basic incidents of an individual's life. The sociological imagination enables people to distinguish between personal troubles and public issues.

macro–micro link between close-to-home aspects of social life and broad social trends is the subject matter of sociology. Further, this core relationship is our key to understanding how social problems affect our lives.

To use Mills's example, unemployed people may view their lack of a job as a private trouble involving only them, their immediate family members, and their friends. But this view is shortsighted. In fact, widespread unemployment—the source of private troubles for thousands or millions of people—often is caused by such factors as economic recession, corporate downsizing, and advances in technology that replace people with machines. Today's plant closings and the resulting unemployment are part of a centuries-old workplace struggle between workers and the people who own and manage workplaces, and such struggles involve the people who buy the manufactured products and the government they elect that regulates (or fails to regulate) the corporations. Present unemployment results in part from so-called 'globalization', a process that sends high-wage Canadian jobs to low-wage countries. Thus, unemployment is not merely a private or personal trouble; it is a public issue. The same is true of other social problems—crime and victimization, family violence, poverty, drug addiction, environmental pollution, racism, and so on. The sociological imagination makes a connection between the conditions of our personal lives and the larger social context in which we live.

Sociologists make these connections by closely analyzing reality at two levels, micro and macro. Microsociology, or *micro-level analysis*, focuses on the interactions between individuals in small groups. This approach studies people's understanding and experience of social problems at the local, personal level (Fine and Fields, 2008). Macrosociology, or *macro-level analysis*, focuses on the societal level. It explores the ways that social trends occurring within major bureaucratic organizations and social institutions, such as the economy or the government, affect the population as a whole (Krejci, 1994).

We need both levels of analysis for a proper understanding of social problems and to see that many private troubles are essentially public issues. Take the case of street youth, or homeless youth, written about in a classic work of sociology by John Hagan and Bill McCarthy (see Box 1.1). Hagan and McCarthy (1998) take a purely objective, positivistic approach to the study of homeless youth. They show no doubt whatever that (1) there are identifiable homeless youth they can study; (2) they can find out all the necessary facts about the lives of these homeless youth; and (3) they can devise explanations or theories about the reasons these young people live on the streets. This is sociology in the traditional, scientific manner.

An alternative approach might be to ask the youth to give personal accounts of their homelessness, then analyze and compare their narratives to understand why some youth accounted for homelessness in one way, while others did so in another way. This is called a post-modern approach. Finally, Hagan and McCarthy might have carried out the study a different way: to determine the reasons why few people consider youth homelessness a major social issue, despite the efforts by some to raise public awareness about this issue. This is called a subjectivist or constructionist approach. As you can see, each approach would involve collecting and analyzing different kinds of information.

PUBLIC ISSUES

Box 1.1 Living on the Streets

If someone has ever approached you asking for money, or offering to squeegee your (perfectly clean) car window, you may have wondered why people are begging on Canadian streets. In fact, you may have wondered why many seemingly healthy young Canadians *live* on the streets, in shelters, or other temporary accommodations.

Sociologists have found that many street youth are 'runaways'. Most street youth come from families that suffer serious emotional, mental, or substance abuse problems. Unlike street children in developing countries, Canadian youth rarely are on the street for reasons of family poverty, though family financial difficulties increase the likelihood of physical abuse, and abuse increases the likelihood of young people running away. Sexual abuse is another frequent element in the stories of homeless youth.

The classic work in this area is *Mean Streets: Youth, Crime and Homelessness* (1998) by Canadian sociologists John Hagan and Bill McCarthy. To do their study, they gathered data from 400 high school youth to compare the backgrounds of youth who live at home with those who live on the street.

They found that, compared to school youth, the majority of homeless youth come from dysfunctional families. As well, a disproportionate number of street kids come from homes where there is family violence and sexual abuse. Once on the street, youth's lives are characterized by a daily search for food, shelter, income, and companionship. If you hold all background variables constant, including prior involvement in crime, one factor consistently increases involvement in crime: lack of the necessities of life (i.e., food, shelter, or source of income). Crime, for street youth, clearly is a practical response to need. The influence of peers is another factor that increases street youth's involvement in crime.

Once they arrive on the street, youth become increasingly immersed in networks of other street youth and street adults, many of whom are heavily involved in crime. Employment is a turning point in the lives of street youth. While involvement in the street network encourages crime, involvement in paid work discourages it. Employment comes to have an important effect on street youth's involvement in crime and other dangerous activities characteristic of street life. Most street youth are in and out of employment, not chronically unemployed. Street youth who find stable, long-term employment are less involved in several types of crime and spend less time hanging out on the street.

SOCIAL PROBLEMS RESEARCH AS A MORAL ENTERPRISE

As you probably learned in an introductory course, sociology is an engaged, progressive, and optimistic discipline founded on the notion that we can improve society through research and the application of research-based knowledge (Zazar, 2008). So, many sociologists—like Hagan and McCarthy—do research aimed directly at reducing poverty, violence, injustice, and inequality, for example.

Paradoxically, however, our human efforts to improve society sometimes backfire. Modernization itself and its associated features, such as the free-market system and bureaucratic organization, not only leave primary problems unresolved, they fail to ensure that we preserve a decent quality of life (Morgan et al., 2006). The costs of our wrong-headed efforts can include homelessness, discrimination, recurrent warfare, mass deaths, and even genocide—realities throughout the twentieth century. As others have remarked, modernization itself carries heavy costs—for the natural environment, for example. No other century in human history combined as much technological progress with as much organized killing and environmental destruction as the twentieth century (Tippelt, 2009).

Undeterred by this record of destruction and despair, sociologists soldier on. Those sociologists who study social problems often think of themselves as engaged in a moral enterprise whose goal is to improve human societies through social change. Therefore, much of the sociological research on social problems is guided by seven value preferences (Alvarez, 2001):

- life over death;
- health over sickness;
- knowing over not knowing;
- co-operation over conflict;
- freedom of movement over physical restraint;
- self-determination over direction by others;
- freedom of expression over restraint of communication.

These values, we can agree, are desirable and worth achieving; but most societies fall far short of achieving them. As a result, much of the research on social problems simply criticizes the existing social order. Much of the social problems literature aims at change society, to protect the vulnerable and redress the injustices done them.

In this effort, we are often opposed and undermined by the myths, ideologies, and stereotypes that perpetuate harmful conditions. Too often, we find the media turning 'public issues' into 'private troubles'. Then, the victims are blamed and stigmatized for having these problems. For example, homeless youth may be blamed for running away from home, dropping out of school, committing petty crimes, using drugs, and so on. And they may indeed be guilty on all charges. Yet, there are reasons *why* they ran away from home, dropped out of school, and so on—those are the underlying causes we need to address.

Consider mental illness, a widespread and growing public health problem today (including on college campuses). Depressions, for example, cause severe suffering for the people affected and their families, leading to higher risks of death, disability, and secondary illness. Mental illness of every kind is a growing problem in our society—whether in the form of depression, anxiety, obsessive/compulsive disorder, panic, addiction, or other—and its prevalence points to significant strains and pressures throughout society (Moore et al., 2009). We are mistaken in blaming the sufferers of mental illness for a problem that is claiming ever more victims. How can the problem be 'personal' if it is shared by a huge and growing fraction of the Canadian population?

Sociologists identify the social-structural conditions that make people vulnerable to these so-called personal troubles. For example, many mentally ill people suffer from inadequate social support (Edwards, 2009). Durkheim, over a century ago in his classic study, *Suicide*, pointed out that a lack of social integration and social control are likely to cause great mental distress. Nowhere is this more evident than among homeless people, another vulnerable

The Canadian Press/ Peter Bregg

Margaret Trudeau on a mission with WaterCan, an Ottawa charity that places fresh water wells in East Africa. In 2006, Margaret Trudeau went public with her battle with bipolar disorder and has raised awareness about mental illness through speaking engagements.

population with too few social supports. They typically also suffer from unemployment, poverty, physical weaknesses, substance abuse, and mental illness (Caan, 2009; Weir-Hughes, 2009).

Sociologists also identify social-structural factors that increase the likelihood of problem behaviours—indeed, sequences or cascades of problem behaviours. For example, risky sexual behaviour in adolescence may lead to teenage parenthood, which reduces the likelihood of school completion and increases the likelihood of financial dependence (Domenico and Jones, 2007). Dropping out of school early also significantly increases the risk of early parenthood, as do low socio-economic status, low academic achievement, and social isolation (Westcott, 2005). As sociologists, we need to study these problems and find ways of preventing them—controlling them at their source—since efforts to correct them later have proved largely unsuccessful. As the data in Figure 1.1 show, school dropouts are much less likely to find employment than school graduates of the same age.

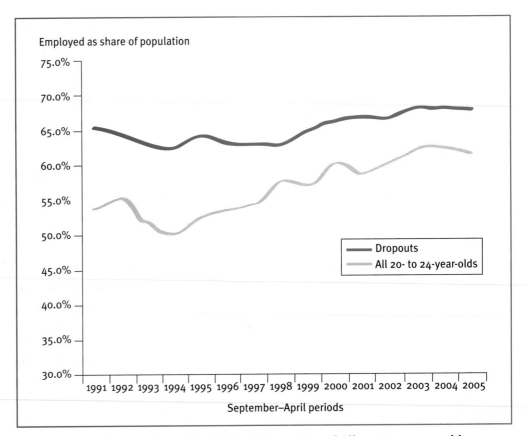

Figure 1.1 Employment Rates, High School Dropouts and All 20- to 24-year-olds, Canada, 1990–1 to 2004–5

Source: 'Good news: Canada's high-school dropout rates are falling', December 16, 2005. Canadian Council on Learning. Reproduced with permission.

SOCIAL CONSTRUCTION

All social reality is conditional and temporary. As sociologists, we know that social 'reality' in general is a social construct—a set of ideas, beliefs, and views that is (almost) infinitely flexible and always open to interpersonal influence (Searle, 2006). This is the central finding of social science research on religion, culture, ideology, mass communication, propaganda, and the like. The widely varying ways people think about reality are amply clear in historical and cross-national research on any topic.

As we know, people invent all kinds of 'stories' about reality. These stories—however imaginary—lead to actions that are real in their consequences. This observation usually is attributed to the early American sociologist W.I. Thomas, who stated the so-called Thomas dictum: when people define a situation as real, the situation will be real in its effects. Stated another way, people's subjective view of reality—not reality itself—shapes their behaviour.

Consider a prominent example: through the mass media, we have all become familiar with the work of professional 'spin doctors'—in politics, advertising, and elsewhere—whose job it is to promote a self-interested concern, belief, or wish, often at the expense of the truth. Lying has become full-time professional work for many of the most financially successful people in our society. Only the most naive people would believe everything they hear or read.

So, it takes no stretch of the imagination to realize that at least some of the supposed social problems we will discuss are not real problems—they are merely 'social constructions'. Though some people view them as social problems, other people do not. But bear in mind, these social constructions can have important social effects (Ajdukovic, 2008).

An approach to understanding the subjective aspect of reality is called **social construction-ism** and it rests on a sociological theory of knowledge stated by Peter L. Berger and Thomas Luckmann in their book *The Social Construction of Reality* (1966). Often, the social construction of reality involves the work of **moral entrepreneurs**—elites, interest groups, or even community leaders, who stereotype and classify some situations as problems. Constructing problems also involves **claims-making**, a procedure that describes, explains, and blames people who are involved with the problem, often labelling them as deviants or wrongdoers.

The goal of social constructionism as a sociological enterprise is to examine the ways people interact to create a shared social reality. Berger and Luckmann argue that *all* knowledge—including the most taken-for-granted knowledge of everyday life—is created, preserved, and spread by social interaction. According to the social constructionist approach, any idea, however natural or obvious it may seem to the people who accept it, is an invention of a particular culture or society. How, among the plethora of ideas, do some ideas become widely accepted as 'true' and compelling?

The answer to this question grows out of symbolic interactionism and the early twentieth-century work of George Herbert Mead (1934), who wrote that children learn to interact with others by learning a system of **symbols**, including language, which allows them to share and negotiate meanings among those who share the system. Using shared meanings, they can play together, perform complementary **roles**, and relate to the social group as a 'generalized other'. For Mead, this ability is the basis of all social order. Shared meanings (including shared symbols) make social interaction possible, and interaction allows people to co-operate and influence one another. Social life, for Mead, is the sharing of meanings—that is, the co-operative (social) construction of reality.

A generation later, another symbolic interactionist, Erving Goffman (1959), proposed that we can usefully think of society as a theatre in which people compose and perform social scripts together. We come to believe in the truth of the roles we play; often, we become the person people we pretend to be. Social life is a set of scripted, directed performances. Inside our social roles we find and express (or hide and protect) our 'true' identities.

In the view of social constructionists, human beings react not to physical objects and events themselves, but to the shared meanings of these objects and events. The shared meanings are not essential features of the objects and events, but are socially imposed or constructed meanings. In our society, for example, a red rose is considered 'beautiful', while a daisy is construed as 'simple' and a cabbage as 'ugly'. Though 'merely' social constructions, such shared meanings are powerful, nonetheless. (If you doubt the social power of this construction, give your loved one a dozen cabbages on Valentine's Day. But don't forget the French term of endearment, 'mon petit chou'—'my little cabbage'!) Thus, the meaning of

SOCIAL CONSTRUCTIONISM A sociological research approach that examines the ways people interact to create a shared social reality.

MORAL ENTREPRENEURS Term coined to describe people who 'discover' and attempt to publicize deviant behaviours. Moral entrepreneurs are crusading reformers who are disturbed by particular types of evil they see in the world and who will not rest until something is done to correct the problem.

CLAIMS-MAKING Claims-making involves the promotion of a particular moral vision of social life and, thus, is anything people do to propagate a view of who or what is a problem and what should be done about it.

SYMBOLS Gestures, artifacts, and words that represent something else.

ROLES The specific duties and obligations expected of those who occupy a specific social status.

anything, including a social problem, is the product of the dominant cultural and symbolic practices in a group or society.

Nowhere is this so readily obvious—at least to modern eyes—as in the social construction of witchcraft during the Middle Ages. The persecution of midwives and wise women as 'witches' shows how a social panic can emerge, that is, can be socially constructed (Box 1.2).

Burr (1995) identifies four basic assumptions of the social constructionist position, all of which we can apply to an understanding of the witch craze:

- *The world does not present itself objectively to the observer* but is known through human experience, which is largely influenced by language. That is, we use language and images to create emotional responses—for example, hostile reactions towards suspected witches.

BACK IN HISTORY

Box 1.2 The Social Construction of Witchcraft

The discriminatory treatment of women has spanned centuries and continents. Consider the notorious 'witch craze'. Referred to during its period as 'the Burning Times'—approximately the fifteenth to the seventeenth centuries—large numbers of European women were accused, principally by the Church, of witchcraft and condemned to death by burning. Although the numbers killed were smaller than some have suggested—roughly 60,000, not millions, and some men as well as women were put to death, about 80 per cent of those accused were women. The men killed were most often associated with women condemned as witches—their fathers, sons, husbands, or men who tried to defend them.

This craze of witch-burning led to and simplified the segregation and control of women. When the witch craze began, women were active in the public sphere, as farmers, traders, craftspeople, midwives, and folk-healers. The theology of the times made this witch craze possible, although the 'witch hunt' was conducted by civil authorities as well as by the churches, so it is unjust to blame the churches alone for this persecution.

Malleus Maleficarum, translated into German, French, Italian, and English, expressed the view of a vengeful hunter of witches, Heinrich Kramer, originally dismissed by his bishop as senile, who worked his way into a position as an inquisitor of the Church for his efforts against witches and witchcraft. His book, perhaps co-authored by Jacob Sprenger, was greatly furthered by the recent invention by Gutenberg of the printing press; it was extensively quoted in later witch-hunting manuals, and soon spread into civil law. Misogyny is evident throughout the *Malleus Maleficarum*. The book singles out women as specifically inclined to witchcraft, claiming they are vulnerable to demonic temptations because of their more sexual natures and diverse weaknesses. It accuses the witches of infanticide, cannibalism, casting evil spells to harm their enemies, and having the power to steal men's penises. The book gives supposed accounts of witches committing these crimes; it provides a detailed instruction for magistrates' legally prosecuting women, including torture, through to condemnation as accused witches.

Today, some analyses of the witch craze still do not mention the intense misogyny instilled by some late medieval Christian doctrines, or the determined suppression of folk religious practices among women of the period. Sometimes, the witch craze is portrayed as quaint, belonging to the past, and irrelevant to modern society. Many, however, point out that the effects of the witch craze period persist in images of older women, troublesome women, and disobedient women as 'witches'.

Source: Adapted from www.psy.dmu.ac.uk/michael/soc_con_disc.htm and en.wikipedia.org/wiki/Malleus_Maleficarum

- *Historical and cultural specificity is recognized.* The language categories used to classify things emerge from the social interactions within a group of people at a particular time and in a particular place. So, for example, the witch craze takes place within a social framework in which scientific proof is absent from the rule of law. The notion of witchcraft as a practice that could pose a real threat to the society existed then in a way that is not the case in North American society today. However, there are cultures extant that believe in the efficacy of witchcraft and similar systems of belief.
- *Knowledge is sustained by social process.* How reality is understood at a given moment is determined by the conventions of communication in force at that time. So, for example, the formal pronouncements of religious leaders about witches, combined with superstition and fear, were sufficient in the late medieval period in Europe to claim legitimacy as 'knowledge'.
- *Knowledge and social action go together.* Within a **social group** or culture, reality is defined by complex and organized patterns of ongoing actions. We cannot really understand the meaning people attached to witchcraft in the burning times without understanding their politics, religion, and gender relations.

SOCIAL GROUP
A set of people, defined by formal or informal criteria of membership, who feel unified or are bound together in stable patterns of interaction.

In short, when people interact, they share their views of reality and act on these shared views. Through discussion, debate, and bargaining, people construct a shared common-sense knowledge of the world. Social constructionism looks at the ways people create and institutionalize social reality. And when people act on their shared knowledge of this 'reality', they reinforce it or lock it in. To think in those terms becomes habitual and seems natural, even unavoidable.

Throughout this book, we will have to repeatedly ask ourselves, about any particular problem, is this a real problem or is it merely (or in large part) a social construction? We will have several reasons for doing this. First, as sociologists, we need to have the clearest possible understanding of reality, even if our own understanding challenges 'common sense', prevailing wisdom, or the dominant ideology on a given issue. Second, as sociologists, we need to learn as much as we can about the social processes by which real social problems, and imagined social problems, come into being. We need to be able to make theories about these historical or developmental processes, and by doing so we learn a great deal about how society works. Most importantly, we need to know which social problems require immediate, concerted action and which ones can be ignored for the time being.

So, we will need to keep asking, is X a 'real' problem or just a 'socially constructed' problem? More precisely, we will have to ask, to what degree is problem X 'real' and to what degree is it 'socially constructed'? And, even if X is a real problem, in what ways do the usual techniques of social construction help to put the problem on the public agenda for discussion, debate, and legislative action?

A useful variation of this social constructionist approach is institutional ethnography, a mode of inquiry designed by feminist sociologist Dorothy Smith and intended to help researchers explore the social organization of everyday knowledge. The purpose of this approach is to make the familiar strange and call into question taken-for-granted assumptions about social organization that, unexplored, serve the interests of the dominant groups in society. In this respect, the method is intended to shift sociological research away from the interests of the most powerful to better serve people who are subject to the administration of power. The result would be knowledge useful to anyone in challenging relations of domination.

A central means of performing this analytical exercise is by questioning the ways in which knowledge is used to manage institutional life—by defining the categories and conceptual frameworks of administration we all learn to use. Often, these categories and conceptual frameworks are not only inappropriate for most people's everyday lives, they promote ideas about social order that serve the dominant institutions and not ordinary people. Nowhere is this more evident than in the realm of public discourse.

So, for example, when the Prime Minister of Canada decides to hinder and hide public discussion of public issues he prorogues the Parliament. By using the formal and traditional language of governmental procedure in calling it 'proroguing', he makes it sound more complicated or justifiable than if his action simply were called 'suppression of dissent', or 'crushing the justifiable opposition', or 'wanting to enjoy the Vancouver Winter Olympics and the photo ops it provides without political pressure'. Likewise, during the administration of George W. Bush, torture of war prisoners was called 'enhanced interrogation'—a term intended to legitimate the action and sound 'professional'. By far the most elegant linguistic obfuscation was accomplished by 'extraordinary rendition' and 'irregular rendition', terms used by the US government to describe the illegal kidnapping and transfer of real or imagined US enemies from one state to another, where they might be legally (and even more secretly) tortured.

The first job of institutional ethnography, then, is to deconstruct the language used to confuse and obscure public understanding of reality. Second, institutional ethnography aims to shine a light on taken-for-granted relations of power, to demystify the relations of ruling, and to point out ways that ruling relations can be modified to better serve ordinary people in everyday life.

Warnings, Panics, and Claims

One goal of ruling classes is to generate social and moral concern about behaviours, such as dissent, they want to control. This means they are likely to use claims-making strategies to provoke intense feelings of pity, concern, and even fear.

To bring a perceived problem onto the public agenda, claims-makers usually rely on common rhetorical idioms and styles that reflect core cultural values. Often, the rhetoric used invokes certain types of risk avoidance as pre-eminent goals (Krinsky, 2008). For example, political and other leaders often call on people to take action to protect their homeland, their families, and their 'way of life'. Particular images may be used to sway public opinion: images of little children crying or houses destroyed, or of young children in attitudes of prayer with the Stars and Stripes fluttering in the background.

The media play a large part in shaping the public perception of a problem. In fact, popular perceptions today are more often shaped by media depictions than by firsthand experience; how the media depict a problem plays a crucial part in how the public will respond. For example, the media can influence public opinion by putting stories about a given 'problem' on the agenda for repeated discussion in news reports. As well, they can portray the alleged problem in sensational ways, with heroes and villains. Some media manipulation is more subtle, as brought to public attention in television 'talk' shows. From these shows, we are meant to infer community standards of behaviour—what is deemed by the talk show host to be 'deviant' and 'normal', 'praiseworthy' and 'shocking' is reinforced by the applause of the studio audience. Here, the hosts are moral entrepreneurs and claims-makers, but the audience in the studio and in the home becomes the 'court of public opinion'.

Sometimes, ordinary people begin the claims-making process. We all learn how to tell stories that describe or explain problems, and how to blame others for these problems; and some people learn these skills especially well (Bockman, 1991). For example, high school debaters learn how to take both sides of an argument, express ideas with which they do not necessarily agree, and present powerful if sometimes questionable evidence for those opinions. This process teaches them how to engage in social problem debate and trains them for moral entrepreneurship.

Sometimes, organization insiders (for example, in the nuclear power or tobacco industries) aid in claims-making (Ding, 2009). **Whistle-blowers** are unusual claims-makers who gain credibility for speaking out contrary to their own immediate interests and those of their employer; but they lack the organizational power to promote their definitions of the social problem. A few prominent whistle-blowers, blacklisted in their industries, have had to turn to social movements for employment.

WHISTLE-BLOWERS Employees in a bureaucratic organization who bring forward valid information about wrongdoing or illegal conduct by their organization and who are often punished for doing so.

Framing a social problem in a particular way is especially important for influencing public opinion. Consider, for instance, the attempts of the organization FARM (Farm Animal Reform Movement) to influence public opinion. Its goal was to eliminate the use of cows, pigs, and chickens as human food, a goal it could not achieve. Even its short-term goal, which was to reduce the suffering of farm animals by closing down factories that use modern intensive farming techniques, failed. Claims about the suffering of animals did not persuade the public, so FARM reframed the problem in the early 1990s, to focus attention on health, longevity, and environmental endangerment instead. These efforts gained wider support for the organization.

Some issues grow slowly and hold the public interest for a long time, two examples being domestic violence or school violence (Tanner, 2009). Others grow quickly, peak, and quickly lose public interest, for example, the alleged devil worship and satanic ritual that produced a flurry of concern in the 1990s. Sociologists refer to such short-lived, intense periods of concern as **moral panics**, and to the people responsible for these sensed threats as *folk devils* (Cohen, 1972). Though moral panics, like fads, are short-lived, they sometimes leave a legacy of laws, stereotypes, cultural beliefs, or changed attitudes.

MORAL PANICS Public expressions of feeling and attitude typically based on false or exaggerated perceptions that some cultural behaviour or group of people (frequently a minority group) is dangerously deviant and poses a menace to society.

Since our perception of social problems arises out of claims-making, and since claims-making is a social activity occurring within a specific historical context, we must understand social problems, and their construction, within their historical context.

HOW TO TELL IF A SOCIAL PROBLEM IS 'REAL'

A social arrangement can cause problems for people without having been recognized (yet) as a social problem. Some would say problems only become *social* problems when claims-makers and moral entrepreneurs succeed in drawing public attention to them. However, we can apply various standards to a stated problem, to decide how serious we think the problem may be. These standards apply especially to the problems of inequality we will study in the middle portion of this book, but they apply more generally, in slightly varying ways, to all the problems discussed here.

To understand the definitional dilemma, consider race relations and ask why, or under what conditions, *racism* might represent a social problem for Canadian society (Reitz, 2007a). Various problems might be linked to race relations. First, we might want to discuss unjust differences and inequalities between groups, and the fact that some groups exclude other groups from employment, housing, or social participation (Reitz, 2007b). These inequalities and exclusions are, if nothing else, a moral issue for Canadians, because they cause income inequalities, poverty, and demoralization. So, whenever we study a social inequality (like racism) and ask whether it is a social problem, we will want to decide whether it is exclusionary and the source of unjust differences.

Second, the lack of intergroup contact, due to exclusion and racism, produces problems of isolation and limited information flow. Excluded people will be 'out of the loop', separated from mainstream society. This limits their knowledge about and access to good jobs. It also reduces the development of *familiarity* between members of the different groups—a source of friendship and mutual understanding known to reduce conflict. Thus, we may want to consider racism a social problem because it encourages separation, segregation, ignorance, fear, and conflict between groups.

Third, problems associated with race relations might include second-order outcomes of segregation, exclusion, prejudice, and discrimination such as self-hate. People who suffer exclusion and stigmatization may feel inferior, since they are treated in an inferior manner. This we can view as a form of psychological disability—a way the host society disables various members of society, making them unwilling or unable to compete effectively for the 'rewards' of income, power, authority, and prestige (Moran, 2008).

Health consequences may follow. As the data in Figure 1.2 show, compared to non-Aboriginal Canadians, off-reserve Aboriginal Canadians are less likely to be in excellent or very good health at every age, and the differences get wider as people get older. This situation suggests a serious social problem for Canada, whether the larger society chooses to recognize it or not.

Of course, not all social problems show up in the form of poor physical health. As we will learn from Merton's theory of anomie, people react differently to social disadvantage. Many of the disadvantaged will suffer from reduced happiness and life satisfaction; they will feel frustrated, defeated, and depressed. Some will suffer from mental illness—depression, for example. Others will take action into their own hands, seeking to erase their disadvantage by criminal or revolutionary means. Others will retreat from life, into suicide, addiction, or blind, purposeless conformity to minimalist social expectations.

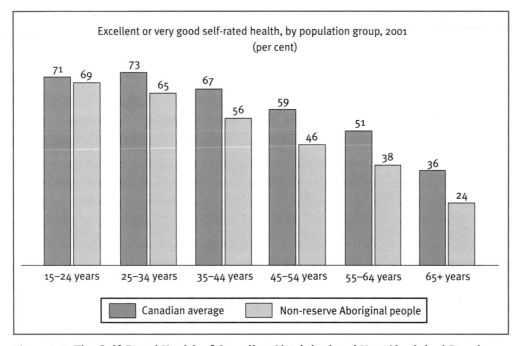

Figure 1.2 The Self-Rated Health of Canadian Aboriginal and Non-Aboriginal People
Source: **HRSDC (2010).**

Thus, race relations and racialization may be a problem for Canadian society if we can show, with data, that they produce any or all of these outcomes. To put our findings in context, we also need to ask ourselves whether Canada's problems of racism are worse than those found in other societies, and if so, why? Are these problems unmanageable and getting worse, or manageable and getting better? Can these problems be avoided, and if so are Canadians taking suitable steps to avoid them?

These same kinds of questions need to be asked about all the types of inequality we discuss in this book: income and class inequality, racial and ethnic inequality, gender inequality, and age inequality. Indeed, we can ask these questions about all the problems we discuss: crime, drugs, poverty, and so on. We need to understand why we think something is a social problem before we take the trouble to study and explain its causes and effects.

Consider the lengthy debate (in Box 1.3 on page 18) about the existence of a 'culture of poverty'. This debate keeps resurfacing in discussions about welfare recipients, homeless people, and even the chronically unemployed. One's position on this debate will greatly affect the social policies one chooses to support.

THEORETICAL PERSPECTIVES ON SOCIAL PROBLEMS

Though our goal in this book is to focus mainly on sociological approaches to problems in society, social problems are not the exclusive domain of sociologists. For this reason, we will

POLICY DEBATES

Box 1.3 The Culture of Poverty and Uneven Distribution of Resources

Poor families are especially common in certain social groups, for example, among Canadian Aboriginal peoples. Some have suggested that culture and poverty are linked, and that some people are perpetually economically disadvantaged because they have learned 'bad values' that limit their ability to improve their lives.

The scientific concept of a 'culture of poverty' arose first in the work of anthropologist Oscar Lewis. Lewis described how people can become trapped by their culture. Capitalism could not have arisen without hard work and the concept of investment; but, said Lewis, not all cultures espouse views that are in line with these values. Lewis considered that the people he studied—Mexican peasants, among others—held values that were not consistent with the need to change their farming practices to more profitable ones. They were not innovative; they valued the family over the individual; they were unwilling to place trust in people outside the family; and they viewed anybody who did get ahead as unfairly taking other people's shares of the village economic pie. Lewis saw these traits as cultural, rather than as individual. People learned them as children when they were socialized into the culture. The major problems of underdevelopment, Lewis concluded, were cultural. This analysis would lead to the policy conclusion that government needs to promote and reward education and value change as a means of eliminating poverty.

But what if, instead, we view poverty as the result of an uneven distribution of resources within society? After all, in a poor neighbourhood, many factors unrelated to culture hinder a person's chances to rise out of poverty. For example, female-headed households may be poorer due to the earning gap between men and women. Many blue-collar workers may be poor because many manufacturing jobs left the country, leaving the workers unemployed and without the skills or education to find another job. Poor people may not be able to work because they are sick, and this illness may be caused by their poverty due to lack of sanitation, improper nutrition, pests, lack of heating, or lead poisoning (lead paint is common in old low-rental units). They may also lack transportation and easy access to jobs.

As well, children in poor neighbourhoods may have to deal with under-equipped classrooms, crowded home conditions, lack of a place to study, or even hunger during the day, all of which prevent children from giving full attention to their classwork.

Like rich people, some poor people have 'bad' values and some don't. Rather than looking to changes in values for a solution, we can look to poverty reduction and changing the ways poor people are treated by officials and authorities, what rules are made concerning their employment, and how much they can earn before deduction of benefits, what labels are applied to them by officialdom, and what barriers (e.g., racist attitudes) specific groups or people encounter in trying to pursue their goals. Through taxation and social programs, some societies (notably the Scandinavian countries) attempt to combat poverty by distributing resources in a fairer, more equitable manner.

Taking this approach leads us to social policies that will stimulate job creation and provide social supports that enable poor people to complete their education and compete for jobs on a level playing field.

briefly take note of the somewhat different approaches that other fields of study have taken. In fact, both the natural and social sciences have brought their own unique understandings and perspectives to the study of social problems. It is important for the student of sociology (and of any other academic field) to note that, when we are seeking the truth, disciplines are not competing with one another. We will not find the contributions made by psychologists are 'right' while those by anthropologists are 'wrong'. Both disciplines are useful, according to

Table 1.1 The Main Sociological Approaches

Theory	Main Ideas
Structural Functionalism	• Elements in society are interconnected and interrelated. • Well-functioning societies require value consensus, social cohesion, and social control. • Social change or inequality may create social disorganization and strain, and lead to deviance and crime. • Social problems occasionally strengthen social cohesion by renewing commitment to social boundaries.
Conflict Theory	• Conflict and change are basic features of social life. • Social problems are a result of inequality, conflict, and change. • Conflicting groups, classes, and individuals routinely struggle for domination over others. • The conflict between men and women is a basic feature of all societies.
Symbolic Interactionism	• Society is a product of continuous face-to-face interactions. • Social problems are socially constructed. • Problematic behaviours are socially learned and practised in social settings. • Socialization and labelling shape deviant identities and subcultures.
Population Health Perspective	• Population health is a sensitive global measure of how well a society is working. • All common social inequalities have significant health consequences. • Social problems are revealed by declines in population health. • The goal in dealing with social problems is always to avoid and reduce harm.

their own designs and self-imposed limits. Both approaches can further our understanding of the problems we are considering.

Thus, the study of social problems is best understood as a complementary, multi-level co-operative activity. The findings of one field or discipline can be expected to confirm and elaborate on the research of the others. With this in mind, consider three of the more prominent contributors to the theories of social problems: biology, psychology, and sociology.

Biological Perspectives

Biologists who study social problems try to uncover the biological bases for socially harmful behaviour. To this end, they focus on individuals and on the genetic, hormonal, neurological, and physiological factors that contribute to their dysfunction in society.

An example is biology's contribution to understanding violence in society. A proponent of the biological approach might cite evidence showing that increases in the levels of a hormone (for example, testosterone) or neurotransmitter (for example, serotonin) are associated with increased aggression in both human and animal subjects (McAndrew, 2009). Other biologists might point to a genetic or evolutionary aspect to violence, noting that many primate species, including chimpanzees, our closest evolutionary relatives, typically 'go to war against one another' over limited assets or according to position on the social dominance hierarchy.

These insights are useful because we humans are, of course, animals with close genetic, chemical, and neurological links to primates and other mammals. Occasionally, biologists provide us with provocative new ways of thinking about the human condition. However, since they focus on (assumed) universal human traits, their theories are not helpful for explaining historical and cross-national variations.

Psychological Perspectives

Like biological perspectives, psychological perspectives centre on individuals. Unlike biologists, however, psychologists are concerned mainly with cognitive, perceptual, and affective (emotional) processes.

Much of the contribution psychology makes to understanding social problems comes from *social* psychologists, who study the ways in which social, cognitive, and emotional factors influence social action. Social psychologists distinguish themselves from sociologists by limiting their research to the thoughts and personalities of individuals as they are influenced by and represented in a social context. Methodologically, they tend to use experiments to study the influence of particular variables. This focus on experimentation, rather than on surveys or field studies, is another defining difference between sociologists and psychologists. For example, a social-psychological approach to the Holocaust might study how an authority figure, using personal charisma or scientific legitimacy, can induce unwavering obedience in subordinates. Such an experiment might help to explain why Nazi guards would carry out the atrocities ordered by Adolf Hitler against the Jews in concentration camps. Notice how this perspective places emphasis on the individual soldier and his thinking, rather than on the entire National Socialist (Nazi) Party as a social group or the political and social organization of German society.

These insights are useful because we are influenced by cognitive, perceptual, and affective factors. Nowhere is this recognized more clearly than in the symbolic interactionist and social constructionist approaches to social problems. However, psychological studies—typically carried out in laboratories using undergraduate subjects—tend to overlook the broad mix of social, cultural, and other contextual factors within which humans actually make their social decisions. The laboratory setting is chosen in hopes of controlling and/or testing one factor at a time, but it is far from natural.

By contrast, sociological researchers focus on group relations and culture. Some prefer macroanalysis at the societal level and others concentrate on microanalysis at the small-group level. The two major macroanalytical approaches in sociology are the structural-functional and conflict perspectives, while the major microanalytical approach is the symbolic inter-actionist perspective.

Sociological Perspectives

Structural Functionalism

Structural functionalism views society as a set of interconnected elements that work together to preserve the overall stability and efficiency of the whole. Individual social institu-tions—families, the economy, government, education, and others—contribute to the func-tioning of the entire society. Families, for instance, work to reproduce and nurture members of society, while the economy regulates the production, distribution, and consumption of goods and services.

Robert Merton (1968), a key figure in developing this perspective, argued that social insti-tutions perform both manifest and latent functions. Manifest functions are intended and easily recognized; while latent functions are unintended and often hidden from partici-pants. Education, for example, is intended to provide students with the knowledge, skills, and cultural values that will help them to work effectively in society. Both the school and its participants formally recognize these roles. At a latent level, however, education also works as an institutional 'babysitter' for young children and teenagers, keeping them safe and off the streets during the daytime, while their parents are at work. It also works as a 'matchmaker', giving older high school and university students a place to meet and socialize with potential future lovers or marriage partners.

These latent functions are important to society and carried out with great success. How-ever, they are considered latent because they are not the results imagined and programmed by designers of the educational system, nor do school administrators, students, or parents acknowledge them publicly.

According to functionalists, the cause of most social problems is a failure of institutions to fulfill their roles during times of rapid change. This *social disorganization* view of social problems holds that sudden cultural shifts disrupt traditional values and common ways of doing things. French sociologist Émile Durkheim (see, e.g., 1964 [1893], 1951 [1897], 1965 [1912]) introduced the term *anomie*, or *normlessness*, to reflect this condition in which social norms are weak or come into conflict with one another. For example, during the industrial-ization and urbanization in Western Europe and North America after 1850, crime, poverty, unsanitary living conditions, environmental pollution, and other forms of social disorgan-ization increased sharply.

As traditional norms and relations break down, social control declines and people feel less tied to one another; and as a result they become more likely to engage in non-conforming, devi-ant types of behaviour (crime, drug use, and so on). The general solution to social problems, according to this perspective, is to strengthen social norms and slow the pace of social change.

Conflict Theory

Conflict theory has its roots in the basic division between the 'haves' and the 'have-nots'. Conflict theorists criticize the structural-functionalist explanation of social problems,

STRUCTURAL FUNCTIONALISM A theoretical paradigm emphasizing the way each part of society functions to fulfill the needs of the society as a whole; also called 'functionalism'; a macrosociological approach that focuses on the societal, as opposed to the individual, level.

LATENT FUNCTIONS Hidden, unstated, and sometimes unintended consequences of activities in an organization or institution.

MANIFEST FUNCTIONS The visible and intended goals, consequences, or effects of social structures and institutions.

NORMS The rules and expectations of the society pertaining to appropriate behaviours under various social circumstances. Norms regulate behaviour in different situations and large-scale norm violation often is viewed as a social problem—a problem occurs when traditionally normative behaviour is violated.

CONFLICT THEORY A theoretical paradigm, derived from the writings of Marx and Engels, that emphasizes conflict and change as the regular and permanent features of society; a macrosociological research approach that focuses on processes within the whole society.

especially its assumption of consensus among members of society and its limited attention to power struggles and competing interests. The conflict perspective instead views society as a collection of varied groups—especially, social classes—locked in struggle over a limited supply of assets and power.

Conflict theory originates from the works of German economic-political philosopher Karl Marx (see, e.g., Marx and Engels, 1998 [1848]; Marx, 1990 [1862–3]: 89) and others. Marx notes that in an industrialized, capitalist system, two broad groups emerge: the *bourgeoisie*, the elite owners of the means of production, and the *proletariat*, the working class, who must sell their labour power in exchange for a livable wage. The capitalists use their great economic power and political influence to ensure that they remain in a position of dominance over the workers.

Conflict theories argue that social problems stem mainly from the economic inequalities that exist between competing groups—especially, between social classes. For the capitalist

The Canadian Press/Francis Vachon

The image above, of a homeless man in downtown Toronto in April 2010, illustrates one of the many social problems that arise, according to conflict theory, from economic inequalities between social classes.

class to uphold its wealthy, privileged status, it must ensure that those below it in power do not have the opportunity—and if possible, even the desire—to encroach on bourgeois power. However, for the bourgeoisie to reap so much economic gain from the system, sizable minorities must live in abject poverty. This poverty of the working and unemployed classes produces conflict and despair. It also leads to many other social problems, including crime, drug use, homelessness, environmental pollution, domestic violence, and racism, as well as physical and mental health problems.

Conflict theorists also contend that workers in a capitalist system feel alienated from the processes and products of their labour, which are fragmented and specialized. Because they are powerless and stuck in narrowly defined jobs, they are unable to control or change the conditions of their work. In every sense, they are alienated—estranged—from their work, their fellow workers, the products of their work, and even from themselves. Moreover, they are alienated because they are exploited: denied a fair and just payment for the value they produce through their labour.

Critics of the Marxian conflict theory approach have noted that, historically, communist societies founded on Marxism have failed either to prosper or to erase inequality. As well, non-Marxist conflict theories argue that many social conflicts are based on non-class-based interests, values, and beliefs. They point out that the Marxist approach has overemphasized the importance of economic inequality at the expense of other types of inequality and social injustice based on race, gender, age, or other factors linked to inequality. While they recognize the value people place on differences in income and social class, proponents of these perspectives believe that other divergent interests and characteristics can also lead to conflict and oppression.

Symbolic Interactionism

While the structural-functionalist and conflict perspectives focus on social institutions and major demographic groups, symbolic interactionism focuses on small-group interactions. The symbolic interactionist sees society as made up of the shared meanings, definitions, and interpretations held by interacting individuals. In studying social problems, followers of this perspective analyze how certain behaviours and conditions come to be defined or framed as social problems and how people learn to engage in such activities.

One of the forerunners of the interactionist approach was the German sociologist Georg Simmel (1976), who studied the effects of urbanization on group relations at the community level. He found the urban lifestyle to be relentless and alienating, with inhabitants limiting the openness of their contact with others to cope with the excessive stimulation that city life offered. As a result, the fragmentation of urban life leads to a decrease in shared experience. It is within such a framework of distinct, isolated, and isolating experiences that urban people must work out their social lives together.

Labelling theory, a major social theory originating in the symbolic interactionist tradition, rests on the premise that a given activity is viewed as a social problem if groups of people define it as such. In this sense, labelling theory is a close cousin of the social constructionist viewpoint discussed earlier. Howard Becker (1963), for example, argued that moral entrepreneurs

SYMBOLIC INTERACTIONISM
A theoretical paradigm that studies the process by which individuals interpret and respond to the actions of others and that conceives of society as the product of this continuous face-to-face interaction; a microsociological approach that focuses on individuals and small groups.

extend their own beliefs about right and wrong into social rules and norms. People who violate these rules are labelled 'deviant' and their actions are defined as social problems.

Consistent with the basic premise of labelling theory, Herbert Blumer (1971) proposed that social problems develop in stages. The first stage is *social recognition*, the point at which a given condition or behaviour—say, drug use—is first identified as a social concern. Second, *social legitimating* takes place when society and its various institutional elements formally recognize the social problem as a serious threat to social stability. With drug use, this stage might occur, for example, when high-profile drug-related deaths make news headlines or when public officials discover a connection between drug abuse and crime and violence. The third stage is termed *mobilization for action*, marking the point at which various social organizations begin planning strategies for remedial action. The final stage is the *development and implementation of an official plan*, such as a government-sanctioned 'war on drugs'.

Critics of the symbolic interactionist perspective argue that social problems may exist even when they are not recognized as problems. Date rape and wife battering, for example, were not considered social problems more than a few decades ago, but they still hurt their victims, regardless of an absence of public attention and labelling.

Population Health Perspective

Keeping the victims of date rape and wife battering in mind, without denying the subjective aspect of social problems, it would be useful to devise objective criteria that could be used to settle what is and what is not a social social problem, for social policy purposes.

Increasingly, social scientists have noted that many social problems are associated with harmful health outcomes. From these observations has emerged the *population health perspective*, a broad approach to health with goals of improving the health of the entire population and reducing health inequalities between social groups (Raphael, 2004). According to *The Chief Public Health Officer's Report on the State of Public Health in Canada* (Butler-Jones, 2009), 'determinants of health' include income and social factors, social support networks, education, employment, working and living conditions, physical environments, social environments, biology and genes, health practices, stress, coping skills, quality of life, childhood development, health services, gender, and culture, among other factors. Furthermore, these determinants interact and overlap with one another in a complex web that describes overall health.

As we will see in on the chapter on health and health care, some researchers also have suggested changing the notion of 'disease' to admit that views of health vary with historical and cultural contexts. A new definition should recognize biological, environmental, and socioeconomic factors. Social gradients in health status are 'surprisingly independent of diagnostic categories of illness, tending to persist across shifts in disease pattern and in hazardous exposures over time, and across societies' (Frank, 1995: 162).

Because of complex interactions among the determinants of health, the population health perspective employs a multidisciplinary approach to theory and research. To do this, it combines insights from various government divisions, such as health, justice, education, social services, finance, agriculture, and environment, with input from such academic fields as medicine, social work, psychology, cultural anthropology, and sociology.

SOLUTIONS TO SOCIAL PROBLEMS

C. Wright Mills, in his classic work *The Sociological Imagination* (1959), claimed 'knowledge can be power'—if individuals choose to act on it. When we know what is going on in society, then act suitably and in our best interests, we stand a chance of improving our opportunities. Using individual-level solutions, we can act to 'work the system' to our benefit.

However, people who act in groups and organizations actually *make history*. The chapters that follow will show this many times over for different areas, especially around social policy changes. Consider, for example, the changes in family law (discussed in Chapter 8) that have been forced by reform groups. Yet, this strategy of political action through groups and organizations can be a long, slow road. And many journeys have been unsuccessful. The analyses in this book will show that dominant groups tend to oppose solutions to certain social problems that are not in their short-term interests.

CHAPTER SUMMARY

The goal of sociology today, just as it was two centuries ago when the discipline began, is to use knowledge to improve social life. Sociologists are concerned about all the social problems that harm people—especially, those that can be shown to do major harm to our health and quality of life. Often, the government and other powerful agencies are doing too little to address these problems. So, one job of sociology is to issue a wake-up call.

Our goal here is to create an understanding of the roots of social problems, their health outcomes for individuals and society as a whole, and how these can be addressed. For this task, it is important to explore facts and theories about how problems develop and are preserved and about how problems are interrelated. After all, this bridge between private troubles and public issues is at the heart of sociological study.

As we will see, the individual social institutions—families, the economy, government, education, and others—each contribute to the larger functioning of society. Often, the cause of social problems is a failure of institutions to fulfill their roles during times of rapid change, as functionalists suggest. However, sociologists who support competing explanatory approaches hotly debate this view. In particular, conflict theorists insist that social inequalities are the key to understanding social problems. Accordingly, we have organized this book around this insight. The central section of this book is concerned with identifying important social inequalities of class, race, gender, and so on and their social effects.

The controversial search for suitable explanations and solutions for each problem makes the study of social problems fascinating to newcomers and professional sociologists alike. The great harm caused by many social problems and their continuing threat—to individuals and society—give this area of study a pressing importance.

QUESTIONS FOR CRITICAL THOUGHT

1.   If there are so many different sociological views about any particular social problem—so many approaches, so many theories—and some people may not even
view an issue as a 'problem', why do we spend so much time and money studying
the 'problem' and trying (often unsuccessfully) to fix it?

2.   What difficulties do we encounter trying to measure the true extent of a social
problem and its human consequences? Will we ever be able to overcome these difficulties? In answering, focus on one particular problem of interest: for example, on
poverty, sexism, or drug addiction.

3.   What factors affect the 'claims-making process' and its effectiveness? For example,
how effective would you be if you tried publicly to promote the idea that Canadian
colleges and universities deaden students' minds rather than stimulate them?
What strategies might you use to increase the effectiveness of post-secondary
education?

4.   What social factors influence people's willingness to line up for tickets or buses,
and are they the same factors that influence people's civility more generally (for
example, their politeness, etiquette, and table manners)?

5.   If the manifest function of this social problems course (and this textbook) is to
teach you about social problems, what is its latent function and how can you tell if
this latent function is being achieved?

6.   Why are so many people unwilling to join groups to protest inequality or to remedy
the social problems discussed in this book?

RECOMMENDED READINGS

Collins, Randall. 2008. *Violence: A Micro-Sociological Theory*. Princeton, NJ: Princeton University
Press. Violence comes neither easily nor automatically; according to Collins, it occurs only when
ways around the barrier to violence are apparent. Only a few individuals are truly competent at
violence, whether as genocidal atrocities against the weak or secret acts of terrorism and murder.

Kadison, Richard, and Theresa Foy Digeronimo. 2004. *College of the Overwhelmed: The Campus Mental Health Crisis and What to Do About It*. San Francisco: Jossey-Bass. The authors identify stressors
and developmental issues facing students. These include academic pressures, competition, parental
expectations, financial worries, and social fears. Unhealthy coping responses include depression,
sleep disorders, substance abuse, anxiety disorders, eating disorders, and even suicide.

Laub, John H., and Robert Sampson. 2003. *Shared Beginnings, Divergent Lives: Delinquent Boys to Age
70*. Cambridge, MA: Harvard University Press. Laub and Sampson follow 500 delinquent boys
through age 70 in a pioneering achievement. Both qualitative and quantitative data are used to
identify patterns of crime and profiles of criminal careers.

McKnight, David. 2002. *From Hunting to Drinking: The Devastating Effects of Alcohol on an Australian Aboriginal Community*. London and New York: Routledge. This book reveals the devastating effects that alcohol has had over a period of 30 years on people in Mornington Island, off the North Queensland coast in Australia. Drinking has become the main social activity and the amount of alcohol consumed per year has reached a disturbing level. Suicide and homicide rates are extremely high and people are drinking so much that alcohol-related illness is rife.

Rapping, Elayne. 2003. *Law and Justice as Seen on TV*. New York: New York University Press. Law-related television shapes the way the American public perceives justice, criminals, courts, and the law in general. However, since the late 1940s, there has been a gradual shift from generally liberal attitudes towards a more conservative perspective. This reflects a change in social consciousness—especially, a growing fear of 'criminals' and sympathy for the law enforcement officers and prosecutors who chase and imprison them.

Seidman, Steven. 2004. *Beyond the Closet: The Transformation of Gay and Lesbian Life*. New York: Routledge. This book, based on the close qualitative study of 30 gays and lesbians, explores the experience of living 'in the closet' and coming 'out of the closet'. The findings show differences in experiences from gays and lesbians of different generations, races, and classes. They also show changes in the 'closet' as social changes have occurred in society.

RECOMMENDED WEBSITES

Centre for Addiction and Mental Health

www.camh.net

The Centre for Addiction and Mental Health (CAMH) is the leading Canadian addiction and mental health teaching hospital. CAMH provides information, assistance, and treatment as well as mental health promotion programs across Ontario through its 26 branches.

Public Safety Canada

www2.ps-sp.gc.ca/policing/organized_crime/FactSheets/org_crime_e.asp

'Facts about Organized Crime in Canada', a brief summary of the issues surrounding organized crime in Canada, is from the archives of Public Safety Canada. The site provides basic information on government policy regarding policing and prevention, and is a useful introduction to the topic of Canadian organized crime.

Canadian Centre for Justice Statistics

dsp-psd.tpsgc.gc.ca/Collection-R/Statcan/85-551-XIE/0009985-551-XIE.pdf

Created by a subsidiary of Statistics Canada, this is a thorough review of the issues surrounding hate crime in Canada. Not only does this document, 'Hate Crime in Canada: An Overview of Issues and Data Sources', provide a literature review and an overview of legal policies regarding hate crimes, but it also provides a lengthy bibliography for further research.

Health Canada—Alcohol and Drug Prevention Publications

www.hc-sc.gc.ca/hl-vs/pubs/adp-apd/index-eng.php

Health Canada provides free, government-funded reports on alcohol and drug abuse in Canadian society. While some of the reports are myopic in focus, most relate to a specific aspect of alcohol or drug abuse, such as the affect of substance abuse on youths, Aboriginals, or seniors.

National Runaway Switchboard (USA)

www.1800runaway.org

The National Runaway Switchboard is a privately run American institution dedicated to aiding 'at-risk youth'. The site provides a modest, though interesting, mélange of links, publications, and research materials on the topic of runaway children in America.

Prostitute Research and Education

www.prostitutionresearch.com

Prostitute Research and Education is an NGO with the mandate to organize prostitutes and provide alternatives to the current forms of prostitution that exist in the United States. The website informs viewers as to laws, trafficking trends, and the latest research in prostitution.

Part 2
Inequalities

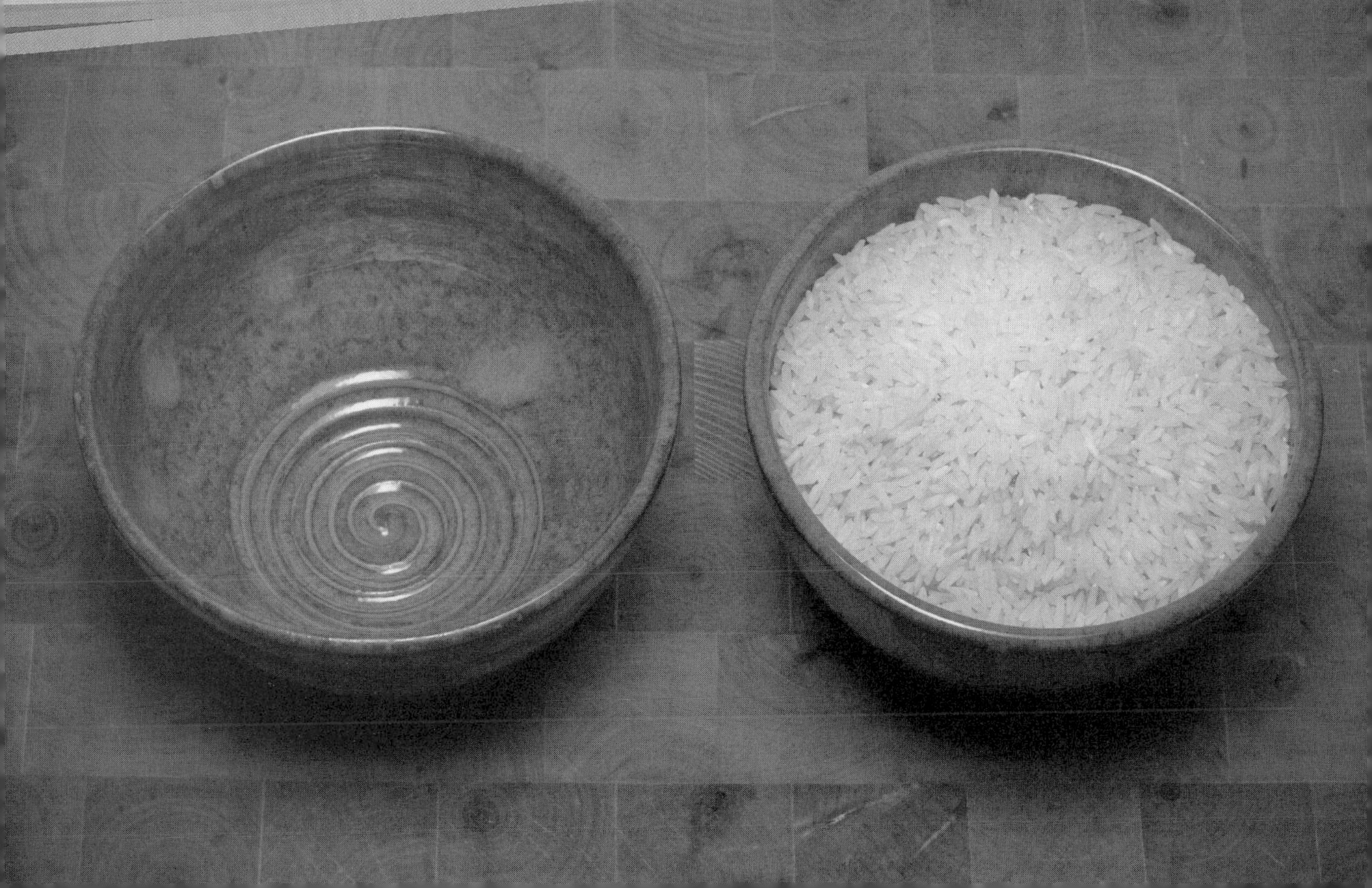

Class, Poverty, and Economic Inequality

iStockphoto.com/dblight

LEARNING OBJECTIVES

- To understand the sociological concepts of social class and inequality.
- To describe the difference between 'relative' and 'absolute' poverty.
- To discover different measures of poverty, including LICOs and poverty lines.
- To examine poverty and income inequality in Canada and around the world.
- To recognize the concentration of wealth that exists in capitalist societies today.
- To see how social inequality is related to other social problems.
- To know the effects of poverty on children, youth, and the elderly.
- To understand homelessness and urban poverty, and their effects on health.
- To learn about the different theoretical perspectives on economic inequality.
- To examine various solutions to the problems of poverty and economic inequality.

INTRODUCTION

Economic inequality includes large differences in income and wealth across individuals and groups, and large differences in the economic power of nations. The sociological take on this is that poverty and inequality are important public issues (Morgan et al., 2006); and they become named problems, with supposed causes and effects, through the efforts of claims-makers. It takes only a 'sociological imagination' to see how we can connect poverty and inequality to each other, and to issues of ideology, governance, and power. Karl Marx provided this sociological imagination in developing the notion of 'social class'.

In the nineteenth century, Marx first introduced the notion of social class and its relation to poverty and inequality in his social, economic, and philosophical works. Marx stressed that people always organize oppositionally around their relation to the means of production. Some own it, and the others do not. Those who do will enjoy the greatest power. In a capitalist industrial society, those who own the capital and productive technology will control the available jobs. The rest—proletarians—will have to sell their time and labour power to capitalists, to earn wages that allow them to survive. The capitalists, to maximize their profits, will pay the workers as little as possible and sell the product for as high a price as possible (Marx and Engels, 1972 [1848]).

'Classes', in sociological thinking, are groups of people who share a common economic condition, interest, or, as Marx described it, relationship to the means of production (that is, to technology and capital). In Marx's logic there are two main classes: the people who own the means of production, and the people who work for those who own the means of production. This binary—have and have-not—is fundamental to all social relations, since these two classes are forever locked in conflict.

The relationship of people to the 'means of production' is critical to this way of thinking. This dividing line separates those who must sell their work, their time, or labour power to earn wages so they can survive from those who buy this work and gain profits from the goods and services that workers produce. The profit gained by the second group depends mainly on the price of the manufactured product minus the cost of labour. As a result, profit-making depends on keeping prices high and wages (and other costs of production) low. But high prices, low wages, and poor working conditions are not good for workers; so workers struggle—through unions, co-operatives, legislation, and other means—to improve their wages, working conditions, job security, and the prices they have to pay for food, shelter, and health care.

People in the same relation to the means of production ought to have an interest in banding together: the workers to protect their wages and working conditions, the employers to protect their profit and control. But for this to happen, people in the same class must develop an awareness of their common interest, commit themselves to working together for common goals, and come to see their individual well-being as connected to the collective well-being of their class. Developing class awareness and class consciousness, however, is harder than it sounds. Many factors interfere with it.

This capitalist class system will have a long-range tendency to produce monopolies of wealth and ever-increasing inequality, globalization and imperialism, overproduction and

ECONOMIC INEQUALITY
Large differences in income and wealth across individuals and groups within a society; differences in the economic power of nations.

recurrent financial crises. Those at the bottom will be impoverished, desperate, and willing to do almost anything to survive.

In this system, employers may take steps to prevent the formation of unions or discussions of worker concerns. Legislators sympathetic to the interests of owners may make laws that give employers more power or workers less power in the event of a conflict. The police or military may be used to break strikes. Workers themselves may be reluctant to share a common cause with people of different racial or ethnic groups. Or, the unions and workers' representatives may not agree on how best to promote workers' interests. The workers may suffer from what is sometimes called 'false consciousness': an acceptance of the discourse and values of the dominant class, and thus a willingness to believe arguments that promote individualistic solutions to problems, or that blame the poor and unemployed for their problems. Workers may also be so 'alienated' from politics and from one another that they cannot put their trust in the collective enterprise of unionization and class conflict.

So workplaces, where the classes meet, are 'contested terrains', in the words of economist Richard Edwards. Here workers and bosses struggle for control, devising first one strategy and then another to overcome opposition.

Of course, this sounds very mechanical—almost automatic. Yet it is far from automatic. Marx didn't think inequality was inevitable—that's why he attempted to promote a revolutionary overthrow of capitalism and the formation of a communist (egalitarian) society. However, he realized, too, that the critical element was a development of class awareness and class consciousness. Oppressed classes can bring about change only after they become aware of their position in relation to the ruling class and their historic role (Marx and Engels, 1972 [1848]). So, in his correspondence with socialist leaders in various countries, Marx often discussed the practicalities of class formation: How should the working classes organize in reaction to exploitation? What kinds of revolutionary strategies will likely work, and what stands in the way of success?

This portrayal is far too simple for today's class structure. First, it is no longer necessary to own a business to control the means of production. Second, today the working class is international, a result of global ownership and economic competition. This introduces an even larger difficulty into the mass mobilization of workers.

Some sociologists have argued that the inequalities in a modern, democratic society are chiefly based on the agreement about the value of different jobs and social roles. The so-called 'functional theory of stratification' credited to Kingsley Davis and Wilbert Moore maintains that most people in most industrial societies agree about the relative social value of particular roles. They agree, for example, that a doctor, judge, or scientist is worth more to society than, say, an unskilled labourer, door-to-door salesman, or store clerk. Therefore, people are willing to see the first group receive higher salaries (also more respect and authority) than the second group. As a society, we can replace store clerks more easily than we can replace doctors, so we 'agree' to reward the doctors more to ensure a continued flow of recruits into medical training.

Some research supports this argument. It has shown that popular ratings of different occupations—their prestige and social value—tend to be stable over time and vary little from one industrial society to another. (Of course, non-industrial societies with different value systems that put a high premium, for example, on warfare or religion will rank jobs differently.) This means that inequalities of wealth, authority, and respect are to some degree based on shared values.

However, this functional theory fails to consider several facts. First, it cannot explain why the difference between top-paid and bottom-paid workers is wide or narrow—why, for example, the range of salaries in major American manufacturing companies was roughly tenfold in 1980, but three-hundredfold in 2008. Nor does it explain why the range of salaries is much wider in one capitalist society, the US, than it is in others, such as Germany, France, or Japan. Nor does such a theory of functional value address why some people get high salaries regardless of whether they confer a social benefit—consider, for example, movie stars, sports stars, professional criminals, auto executives, and bank executives. In fact, sometimes the public knows very little about the amount these people are paid or the reasons for this payment.

All we can say for certain is that not all inequality in Canada or the US is due to exploitation in the form that Marx imagined. Some of it is a result of unregulated market forces, such as inadequate laws governing the finance industry. Some is a result of the tax structure, which enables more or less wealth to be redistributed from poor to rich, or rich to poor. In turn, this redistribution is a result of the connection between the state and the ruling class, and the extent to which rich, powerful people can rely on elected politicians to serve their interests.

Marx recognized that, in general, all classes rest on inequality and that all inequality rests on social differentiation. However, not all differentiation leads to inequality, and inequality doesn't necessarily result in class formation. For revolutionary purposes, class formation required the growth of class consciousness, which in turn demanded four important changes in the thinking of workers: (1) identifying themselves as members of an exploited class; (2) seeing that the owners of the means of production are their enemy; (3) realizing that everything is at stake in the battle for equality; and (4) recognizing that societal change is possible through conflict.

As John Porter showed in *The Vertical Mosaic* (1965), there is some opportunity for people to cross class lines at the highest occupational levels. People from humble backgrounds—having performed very well at university and risen through the organizational ranks into positions of ever-increasing authority—may acquire the opportunity to work and socialize with people who have inherited their wealth and power. The professions of engineering, management, accounting, and law are especially good ladders of upward mobility. And at the elite levels of society, people in the highest union positions, political positions, and civil service positions are sometimes able to work and socialize with people in the highest economic positions of society; again, this can happen regardless of their class of origin.

That said, **social mobility** in capitalist societies has its limits. There is little chance of entering the 'upper class'—say, the top 1 per cent of income earners or wealth-holders—from below. Similarly, there is little chance of escaping the 'poorest class', say the bottom 1 per cent. There is more opportunity to enter the top income decile (that is, the top 10 per cent) and more opportunity to escape the bottom income decile, though such movements are still rare.

SOCIAL MOBILITY The movement of individuals from one social class to another during the course of one's lifetime.

In the middle of the income distribution, among the middle 80 per cent of all income earners, there is plenty of intergenerational mobility, both upward and downward, in income and occupational prestige. What makes this movement possible is higher education. In our society, educational credentials are the key to social mobility.

People who are more socially mobile are more likely to gain opportunities to interact with people of higher social classes. In fact, educated people are also more likely to interact with people of *lower* social classes. Research shows that people with more education have larger, more diverse social networks. They know more people by name and can link indirectly with a larger number of people through networks of friendship and acquaintance. This is partly through their exposure to many people in institutions of higher education and through their exposure to many people in their professional and managerial work. But it is also because educated people know many other people who also know many people.

MEASURING POVERTY

ABSOLUTE POVERTY Lack of the basic necessities (food, shelter, medicine) for basic survival. Starvation is an example of absolute poverty.

Sociologists agree that people who live in poverty have much less than the average standard of living (Defina and Thanawala, 2009). However, we can view poverty in two ways: as absolute and as relative. People who live in **absolute poverty** do not have enough of the basic requirements—food, shelter, and access to essential health care, for example—for physical survival. By contrast, people who live in **relative poverty** can survive, but their living standards are far below the general living standards of the society or social group to which they belong (Sarlo, 2007).

RELATIVE POVERTY Survival, but far below the general living standards of the society or social group in which the poor live; affects people's lives in dramatic ways.

Researchers disagree about how to measure poverty. Although you may think that it is easy to decide whether a lifestyle qualifies as 'poor', in practice, deciding what makes up poverty is difficult. Cross-national evidence from the United States, Great Britain, Canada, and Australia shows the **poverty line** is elastic, responding both to changes in real income and to the success of advocates fighting to increase social welfare by redefining or remeasuring poverty (Fisher, 1998).

POVERTY LINE It represents a usual standard of living and differs across countries. The definition of poverty varies by society, within societies, and also over time.

Until recently, Statistics Canada, the primary data-gathering agency for all of Canada, has relied on two different measurement strategies when compiling statistical data on poverty: LICOs and LIMs. The first method, **low-income cut-offs** (LICOs), is based on the percentage of income devoted to daily necessities such as food, shelter, and clothing. Although some consider LICOs to be equivalent to poverty lines, Statistics Canada stresses that they are not. Low-income cut-offs (LICOs) are income thresholds, determined by analyzing family expenditure data, below which families will devote a larger share of income to the necessities of food, shelter, and clothing than the average family would (Statistics Canada, 2009a). To take into account differences in the costs of necessities among different community and family sizes, LICOs are defined for five categories of community size and seven of family size (Sarlo, 2006). These cut-offs vary with the size of the family and the size of the community of residence because of geographic differences in the cost of living for families of different sizes. Thus, LICOs are higher in a large city than in a rural area and higher for a large family than for a small one. In a community with a population of 500,000 or more, if 'the average family' of four spends 35 per cent of its income on food, shelter, and clothing, then any four-person

LOW-INCOME CUT-OFFS (LICOs) A formal definition used by Statistics Canada for measuring relative poverty based on the percentage of income devoted to daily necessities (food, shelter, clothing) and determined both regionally and by population (size of city or rural).

household that spends 55 per cent or more of its income on these necessities is considered 'low-income' (Diekmeyer, 2001).

The second method used by Statistics Canada has been the low-income measures (LIMs)—a set of figures representing 50 per cent of the median 'adjusted family income', which is based on a consideration of the varying needs of families of differing sizes. Each family's actual income is compared with the corresponding LIM for their particular family size; those that fall below are considered 'low-income'. LIMs are strictly relative measures of low income, set at 50 per cent of adjusted median family income. These measures are categorized according to the number of adults and children present in families, reflecting the economies of scale inherent in family size and composition (Kirkpatrick and Tarasuk, 2003).

A third, alternative measure, the market-basket measure, was years in the making—a result of work by the Federal/Provincial/Territorial Working Group on Social Development Research and Information—and was designed to define and measure poverty in absolute, not relative, terms. This working group proposed a preliminary market-basket measure (MBM) of poverty based on an imaginary basket of market-priced goods and services. This measure, then, is based on the income needed to purchase the items in the basket (Watson, 2003).

The MBM measure signals a change in our perceived obligations to the poor because it replaces a relative (or comparative) measure of poverty—the LICO—with an absolute market-basket measure. Human Resources and Development Canada (HRDC) officials were instructed by politicians to create a measure 'related to changes in the cost of consumption rather changes in income' (HRDC, Mar. 1998, cited in Shillington, 1999). Implicit in the market-basket approach is the idea that our obligations to low-income people consist of a particular basket of goods, not a share of Canada's wealth. Notably, what goes into the 'basket' is not determined by those who must try to survive on it but by bureaucrats or right-leaning think-tanks, and some MBMs exclude such 'necessities' as transportation and a minimal amount of expenditure on entertainment.

MEASURING WELL-BEING AND INEQUALITY

Poverty as measured by income in these ways is only a pale reflection of people's well-being. Other socio-economic variables also contribute to well-being. The United Nations Development Program (2005), for example, monitors social and economic progress through a broad measure known as the Human Development Index (HDI). The HDI is a combined measure of achievement in three basic areas: a long and healthy life, as measured by life expectancy at birth; knowledge, as measured by adult and youth literacy; and standard of living, as measured by the natural logarithm of the gross domestic product (GDP) per capita.

However, even the HDI may not accurately reflect the extent of important differences among the world's most developed countries, which all score similarly high in the three dimensions of the index. So, for these nations, population well-being is measured by the second variant of the human poverty index (HPI-2). The HPI-2 assesses relative *deprivation* in these same dimensions: vulnerability to premature death, as measured by the likelihood at birth of not surviving to age 60; exclusion from reading and communications, as measured

LOW-INCOME MEASURES (LIMs) A set of figures representing 50 per cent of the median 'adjusted family income'. Actual incomes are compared with LIMs to determine whether or not a family can be considered 'low-income'.

MARKET-BASKET MEASURE (MBM) A way of measuring income and poverty that was added in 2003 to Statistics Canada's methods of measuring income and poverty. It is based on an imaginary basket of market-priced goods and services and on the income needed to purchase the items in the basket. The determination of what goes into this imaginary basket tends to exclude all but the absolute essentials of bare survival.

HUMAN DEVELOPMENT INDEX (HDI) A combined measure of achievement in three basic areas of human development— life expectancy at birth; literacy; and GDP per capita—used by the United Nations Development Program to monitor social and economic progress across countries.

by adult illiteracy; a deprived standard of living, as measured by the percentage of the population living below the income poverty line; and social exclusion, as measured by the rate of long-term unemployment.

When this measure is used, Canada's ranking falls to ninth in the world. Although our country provides a very high average standard of living, this standard of living is not equally distributed across all levels of society (UNDP, 2005). This suggests that social inequality—and relative poverty—may be at least as important for people's well-being as absolute poverty. We will see later that social inequality has a dramatic effect on people's physical (as well as mental) health, as demonstrated in the classic Whitehall studies.

Therefore, we need systematic measures of social inequality as well as poverty. A widely accepted measure of income inequality is the Gini coefficient. A perfect score of 0 on this index reflects total income equality across a society, while a score of 1 reflects total income inequality. To illustrate this, imagine distributing $1,000 among 1,000 people. If every person received $1, the Gini Index would be 0. If one person received $1,000 and the remaining 999 people received 0, the Gini Index would be 1.

Canada currently has a Gini index score of 0.32 or 0.33. This is far lower than the highest scores on record. To put it in context, the Gini index for the US, depending on whether we use a UN or CIA estimate, is 0.41 or 0.45, respectively. The Gini index for Sweden, again depending on which estimate we use, is 0.25 or 0.23. In general, the highest Gini index scores—in the range of 0.5–0.6—are found in the least developed nations of Africa and South America, and typically, the greatest poverty is found in continents and countries with the greatest inequality. By contrast, the countries of North America, Europe, and the rest of the developed world are relatively richer (on average), more equal, and have fewer desperately poor people (McMullin, 2004).

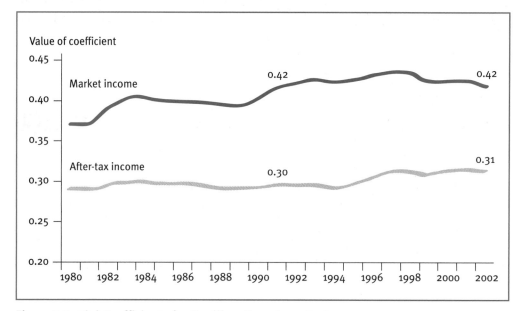

Figure 2.1 **Gini Coefficients for Families, Canada, 1980 to 2002**
Source: **Adapted from Statistics Canada (2004: Chart 7.4).**

As mentioned, the exact measurement of poverty is complicated and politically controversial. Errors can make a huge difference to needy people, taxpayers, and program administrators.

POVERTY IN CANADA

The face of poverty and economic inequality in Canada has been described as 'racialized, destitute, and young' (Curry-Stevens, 2004). In addition, poverty is on the rise in urban areas, in some cities more than others. Cities in Quebec tend to have the highest rates of poverty, while those in southern Ontario have the lowest.

Poverty is also more common among racial minorities, both non-white visible minority immigrants and Aboriginal communities. Racial minorities earn much less on average than their white counterparts and are also more likely to experience unemployment and

The Canadian Press/Darryl Dyck

Robert Bonner hangs a sign on a mock Olympic torch while preparing for a demonstration to announce the Poverty Olympics and torch relay near the Vancouver 2010 Winter Olympics countdown clock in Vancouver, BC. Social awareness groups held a Poverty Olympics event and torch relay in February 2010 to raise awareness about poverty and homelessness in Vancouver.

underemployment (Reitz, 2007a). Recent immigrants who arrived in Canada within the past five years earn much less than their Canadian-born counterparts, often because they are unable to gain acceptance of their foreign credentials (degrees, diplomas, and training experiences). Over time, this gap between immigrants and native-born Canadians narrows, but not by much; and some groups never reach equity (Reitz, 2007b).

The disadvantaged social and economic status of Aboriginals in Canada is also well documented. For example, the median pre-tax income of all people indicating Aboriginal identity during the 2001 census was $13,526, or 61 per cent of the national average (CCSD, 2003). At 1.5 per cent of Canada's urban population but 3.4 per cent of the urban poor, they are over-represented among the nation's impoverished urban populations. On reserves, the situation is equally bad, if not worse. A lack of employment opportunities combined with a sense of cultural isolation has resulted in economic, social, and health conditions that are in some instances as bad as or worse than those found in the least developed countries of the world.

The immediate cause of Aboriginal poverty is joblessness. Two forms of joblessness are particularly important. Unemployment can be understood as out of work but seeking employment. Many other Canadians, however, are out of work while *not* seeking employment, often because no opportunities exist. Unemployment rates among Aboriginals range from 1 per cent in Quebec to nearly 62 per cent in the Northwest Territories. On average, unemployment rates among Aboriginals have reached nearly 25 per cent in recent years. Within some communities, however, unemployment rates are nearly 80–90 per cent. Not surprisingly, rates of unemployment among Aboriginal communities are significantly higher than for the rest of the Canadian population because many of these communities are in remote areas with few job opportunities. This employment and income disparity likely explains the higher incidence of substance abuse, high rates of imprisonment and of such diseases as diabetes, as well as early mortality among Aboriginal people.

Poverty, wherever we find it, is in many ways self-perpetuating. Structural mechanisms ensure the poorest Canadians remain poor. The poorest of the poor lose proportionally the most during economic recessions and gain the least during times of prosperity. Curry-Stevens (2004) estimates that upward of 90 per cent of the total income of the poorest tenth of the Canadian population comes from Employment Insurance, welfare, and other government transfers, which are usually among the first social programs to see reductions in benefits during economic slowdowns.

However, chronic, continuing (absolute) poverty is a minority experience in Canada. In fact, large numbers of Canadians move in and out of poverty. Poverty is a widespread, common experience for many; but unrelenting poverty in Canada is relatively rare. This gives us two reasons to view it as a social problem: for the few who are chronically, desperately poor, only a change in social policies can save them. On the other hand, the many who at some point have experienced poverty will readily see the merit in fixing a system that is so patently unjust.

POVERTY AS AN URBAN PROBLEM

The incidence of urban poverty in Canada is rising. One of the most serious problems associated with urban poverty is the lack of affordable housing for low-income families and individuals. Economists argue that, as a rule, housing is 'affordable' if either the monthly rent or mortgage payments consume no more than one-third of household income.

Currently, affordable housing is scarce in many major Canadian cities. There are several reasons for this scarcity. First, the ownership of rental housing is being concentrated in the hands of a few property owners. Second, developers stand to make larger profits by investing in housing solely for the middle and upper classes. As a result, upscale homes are abundant for people who can afford them, while low-income housing remains scarce (Wratten, 2010).

When affordable housing is available, it is often found in city neighbourhoods that are economically stagnant and physically decayed. In these areas, rates of crime, violence, and drug use are typically higher than anywhere else in the city. People who are unable to afford even the most modest places to live increasingly come to rely on urban shelters for places to sleep at night. Although 'the poor' are often stereotyped as shiftless and unattached, two-parent families with children are the most rapidly increasing category of shelter-using poor (Reese, 2009). Still, as desperate and humbling as reliance on shelters may be for poor people, the alternative—homelessness—is even worse.

The Homeless

Connected with the shortage of affordable housing in cities is homelessness, one of Canada's most pressing social problems. Most low-income families are renters, not homeowners. Thus, when rent prices increase or owners change rental units into owner-occupied condominiums, many families are forced onto the streets and into shelters, while others must live in crowded conditions with parents, other relatives, or friends (Davis, 2008).

The exact number of homeless people in Canada is unknown, but some have tried to estimate the size of the problem. A study published in 2007 reports that:

> Canada's homeless population is somewhere between 200,000 and 300,000 people, while another 1.7 million residents struggle with 'housing affordability issues'. . . . In a report . . . from the Calgary-based Sheldon Chumir Foundation for Ethics in Leadership, journalist and author Gordon Laird argues homelessness is now chronic and is quickly becoming one of the country's defining social issues. He makes a case for a national housing strategy and a more robust income security program. Citing statistics from a wide range of organizations, Laird says poverty is the leading cause of homelessness in Canada, not substance abuse or mental illness. 'Roughly half of all Canadians live in fear of poverty, and 49 per cent polled believe they might be poverty stricken if they missed one or two paycheques', he writes. (CBC News, 2007)

A 2005 study of homelessness in Toronto, commissioned by the Wellesley Institute, an organization concerned about urban health problems in relation to social vulnerability, noted that homelessness 'has been growing . . . almost six times faster than the overall population.' This study reported:

BOYZ N THE HOOD

John Singleton's 1991 debut is a penetrating look at teenagers' lives in Los Angeles' desperately poor and violent South Central region.

Homelessness has a devastating impact on Toronto. More than 30,000 women, men and children crowd into the city's homeless shelters annually. Many thousands more sleep on the streets or join the ranks of the 'hidden homeless'. There are about 70,000 households on Toronto's social housing waiting list. And, on the brink of homelessness, are 150,000 households paying more than half their income on shelter. Homelessness and insecure housing are triggering a health crisis: The lack of safe, affordable housing leads to increased illness and premature death. But it's not just the homeless and inadequately housed who are suffering. Toronto's affordable housing crisis is disrupting neighbourhoods and threatening the city's competitiveness in the international economy. It is costing taxpayers $159 million annually just for homeless shelters and services. (The Wellesley Institute, 2006)

The homeless are a varied mix of single men and women, young people, families, Aboriginal people, and some individuals with serious health problems (such as HIV/AIDS). Many are able-bodied, free from substance or alcohol abuse, and willing to work. Some even have jobs but lack enough income to pay the rent on the cheapest city apartment.

In large cities, many of the homeless are young people who have run away from home because they would rather live on the street than under the same roof with an abusive parent. Most street youth are from families suffering serious emotional, mental, or substance abuse problems. These youth are not essentially on the street because of socio-economic pressures, though family financial difficulties increase the chance of physical abuse (Aratani,

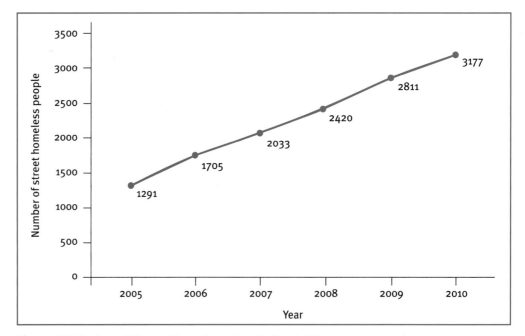

Figure 2.2 Projected Street Homeless Population in Vancouver, 2005–10
Source: **Pivot Legal Society (2006).**

2009). Research shows that runaways overlap, in experience and background, with a variety of other social types.

Repeatedly, research has shown that families of runaways tend to give their children less support, supervision, and acceptance than other families. Evidence also suggests the parents of runaways themselves had a history of running away from home when they were children. Runaways run a heightened risk of suicide attempts: in one study (ibid.), 30 per cent of runaways report having tried suicide in the past. Suicide attempts by runaway youth are most commonly a result of trouble at home, arguments, disappointments, humiliations, trouble at school, assault, and sexual abuse.

Thus, a principal reason that runaways remain on the street, refusing to return home or try foster care, is their stated belief that family conflict is inevitable. Runaways develop their own substitute families on the street, among other street people, rather than risk further rejection or abuse. Many chronic runaways grow up to be homeless adults. As a result, homeless adults with higher than average rates of criminal behaviour, substance abuse, and other forms of deviant behaviour tend to report more abusive and deprived childhoods (*The Nation*, 2009).

THEORETICAL PERSPECTIVES ON POVERTY

Table 2.1 Theoretical Perspectives

Theory	Main Points
Structural Functionalism	• Inequality and poverty serve important functions in society. • Poverty motivates people to work harder to improve their life conditions. • Those who invest the most time and effort receive the best-paying jobs and working conditions (e.g., physicians). • Such a view is most applicable in situations where effort corresponds with rewards.
Conflict Theory	• A structural power imbalance exists between capitalists and employees. • Employees depend on wages for survival and are therefore vulnerable to exploitation. • By exploiting workers through poor working conditions and poor pay, owners amass more wealth for themselves.
Symbolic Interactionism	• This approach focuses on the labels attributed to the 'wealthy' and the 'poor'. • Labels attached to the poor, such as 'lazy', are often unjustified stereotypes. • However, widespread subscription to these stereotypes makes them real in their consequences.

Structural Functionalism

The sociological perspective or approach called structural functionalism argues that society consists of a connected network of groups, organizations, and institutions that work together to maintain the survival of that society. In the eyes of a structural-functionalist, everything in a society has a purpose or function that, when fulfilled, allows society to continue, or 'survive', in its present form, largely resisting change.

The structural-functionalist perspective, therefore, argues that poverty and inequality may serve important functions in society. For example, poverty (or the threat of poverty) motivates people to work harder to move up the ladder. Jobs at the top of this ladder need much more investment in education and effort, but they also carry greater rewards. This motivates people to stay in school, get more education, and work harder for longer to get the top rewards (Mooney et al., 2001). Thus, inequality promotes economic growth.

CLASSIC WORKS

Box 2.1 Marx and Engels, *The Communist Manifesto* (1848)

Karl Marx was born in 1818 to well-off parents in Prussia. He studied at Bonn and in Berlin, where he was involved first with the Young Hegelians and later discovered the writings of Feuerbach. In 1843 he married Jenny von Westphalen and moved to Paris shortly thereafter where he met Friedrich Engels. They both joined the Communist League and agreed to write the 'Manifesto of the Communist Party' after the League in 1848 decided to put its ideas into writing. This sparked a short revolutionary burst across Europe, which was ultimately unsuccessful, and both Marx and Engels moved to London. Marx's views continued to get him both admiration and persecution for the remainder of his life, especially following the Paris Commune in 1870. Though Marx was influential in communist movements, he was rarely a direct leader and stayed away from large gatherings and even debate with other academics.

Friedrich Engels, born in 1820, was the son of a factory owner in Barmen (Prussia). He was well educated and harboured a secret passion for revolutionary thought, kept hidden from the more moderate views of his parents. In 1842 he was converted to communism, mainly through the efforts of Moses Hess. This new ideology led him to live parts of his life with working families so he would be able to understand their conditions. He published his experiences in the 1845 book, *The Condition of the Working Class in England*. The unity of their views soon brought Marx and Engels together

in a lifelong companionship, and they jointly published *The German Ideology* in 1845 and *The Communist Manifesto* in 1848.

In *The Communist Manifesto*, Marx and Engels proclaim the inevitable collapse of the capitalist system of production and consequently the end to social inequality and social strife.

The *Manifesto* is divided into four parts of which the first is the most theoretically interesting. In it, they show how the capitalist system of production continually splits society into two opposing classes: the bourgeoisie and the proletariat. 'By bourgeoisie is meant the class of modern capitalists, owners of the means of social production and employers of wage labour. By proletariat, the class of modern wage labourers who, having no means of production of their own, are reduced to selling their labour power in order to live' (Marx and Engels, 1955 [1848]: 3). This antagonism will result in the downfall of the bourgeoisie and the end of all class conflict. There are several stages to this argument.

Though the history of the world has always been a struggle between the oppressed and their oppressors, the relation between bourgeoisie and proletariat is markedly different and the last of such struggles, for three main reasons. First, whereas previous ruling classes needed to conserve the existing modes of production to stay in power, the bourgeoisie 'cannot exist without constantly revolutionizing the instruments of production, and thereby the relations of production, and with them the whole relations of society.' The owners of the means of production do this by expanding across the globe and exploiting existing areas more thoroughly. The two tactics either polarize class division in new areas or increasingly polarize the division in already industrialized areas, which inevitably is a self-defeating tactic. The rich will exploit the poor to a greater degree and so, too, will rich nations exploit poor nations. The entire world becomes similar and of a piece, both with regard to material production and intellectual production.

Second, in capitalist production, the worker increasingly becomes an appendage to a machine and all individual character of work is lost; thus, the cost of work is restricted only to that which ensures the worker's continued existence. The more monotonous the work, the lower the wage, and everything related to the production process moves in this direction in order to continue the existence of the bourgeoisie. Previous production regimes, such as feudalism, rationalized exploitation with religious or other reasons, but the bourgeoisie are naked in their quest for individual profit so that their increasing exploitation cannot help but affront the worker. Individual profit, individual property, is therefore the key. When the worker owns nothing, when all private property is in the hands of the bourgeoisie, when workers no longer compete, the worker has nothing to lose and can see that private property is really just bourgeoisie property.

Third, for these reasons, only abolishing private property will end class conflict. The proletariat have no property to secure. Its abolition, in and of itself, will end oppression and class divisions. Marx and Engels prominently declare this the end of history.

The second part of the *Manifesto* makes the communist program explicit and addresses many of the critiques raised against it. Ultimately, the Communist Party wishes the defeat of the bourgeois class by the proletariat, which is accomplished through the abolition of private property (Marx and Engels, 1955 [1848]: 14).

The Communist Manifesto is generally critiqued and praised on two major points: its materialist conception of history and its prophetic ability. The materialist conception of history is both revolutionizing and hotly contested. Certainly, this materialistic interpretation of history and society has been, if not disproved, consistently challenged by historians and sociologists—starting first with Max Weber.

One of the most obvious prophecies is the inevitability of the revolution due to the polarization of the populace into a working class and a bourgeoisie of dwindling size. This did not happen with any lasting success in the Western world. Although there is currently some evidence of the middle class being 'hollowed out', for the most part, beyond the early and dirty years of industrial capitalism, a large middle-income class with more skilled jobs was created to a greater extent than the ever-more mechanized work that Marx and Engels foresaw for the proletariat. Marx and Engels, however, were correct in their prediction of globalization and the homogenization it entails, as well as the accompanying exploitations of poor countries by the rich countries. They also predicted the cyclical crisis of capitalism, but not the Keynesian regulating state that resulted from these.

Conflict Theory

The conflict theory of poverty and inequality relies heavily on ideas first developed by Karl Marx and Max Weber.

As we saw earlier, according to Marxist theory, the bourgeoisie or capitalists own the means of production. As owners of the factories and other business establishments, the bourgeoisie can set the terms of employment for the other, less powerful class of society, the proletariat. This latter group, lacking the means to produce and sell goods on their own, must resort to selling the only commodity they possess: their labour power (Marx and Engels, 1955 [1848]).

The bourgeoisie, recognizing the proletariat's dependence on the wages earned from work, exploit the labour of the working class as a means to gaining wealth for themselves. They keep wages low to ensure that their workers remain dependent on them for economic survival. By manipulating the schools and mass media, they ensure that popular thinking, sometimes called ideology, will continue to support the unequal distribution of wealth and power (Marx and Engels, 1955 [1848]).

This practice continues in the present era, this theory argues. Today, multinational corporations—or, more precisely, the powerful executives who run them—continue to build up huge annual profits that are grossly out of line with the payments offered to their employees. In developed nations, owing to the influence of unions and labour legislation, employers are more likely to pay workers a reasonable wage for work done under safe conditions. In developing nations, however, employers are less constrained (Calvano, 2008). The result of this process is continued and increasing inequality—indeed, class polarization, with an ever-widening gap in wealth between rich and poor. Another result is alienation.

In an early work, Marx identified four types of alienation in labour under capitalism: alienation of the worker from his or her 'species essence' as a human being rather than a machine; alienation between workers, since capitalism reduces labour to a commodity to be traded on the market, rather than a social relationship; alienation of the worker from the product, since this is appropriated by the capitalist class, and so escapes the worker's control; and alienation from the act of production itself, such that work comes to be a meaningless activity, offering little or no intrinsic satisfactions.

Conflict theorists also recognize the biased nature of laws and policies that favour the rich, such as low-interest government loans to bail out failing businesses and tax breaks to corporations. As might be expected, conflict theories are more likely to discuss the types of social-structural and cultural causes of continued poverty that we discussed in the introductory chapter. Many of the mechanisms of exclusion and suppression that create economic inequality are familiar to conflict theorists.

Symbolic Interactionism

In relation to poverty, symbolic interactionists focus on the ways that people compose the labels 'wealthy' and 'poor' through social interaction. The typical though unspoken stereotype of a poor person in North American society runs as follows: a lazy, irresponsible, undeserving, freeloading ethnic minority (probably black, Latino, or Aboriginal) who would rely on welfare and social assistance rather than find a steady job to support himself or herself; a person who probably dabbles in petty crime and spends much of his or her money on alcohol and drugs; possibly a violent and dangerous threat, and a nuisance to society.

On the other hand, the stereotyped depiction of a rich person is this: greedy, shallow, snobbish, egotistical, callous, wasteful, and probably white; has no qualms about stepping on others for personal gain; born with a silver spoon in his or her mouth and used to living a life of sheltered privilege; inherited the already sizable wealth of mommy or daddy, and therefore has not had to expend any personal effort to build or increase the family fortune; and willing to take advantage of an unjust economic and social system that favours the privileged few at the expense of the disadvantaged many.

Like all stereotypes, these ones are exaggerations. Still, even if such labels are arbitrary and unfounded, their effects are real enough. Being labelled 'poor' creates many problems that contribute to further poverty. Employers, mindful of these stereotypes, are less likely to offer poor people well-paying, stable jobs. Poor people are more likely to be the targets of unwarranted police scrutiny and harassment. Members of the public will see any reliance on government assistance by the poor as proving the truth of the applied stereotype.

SOCIAL CONSEQUENCES OF POVERTY AND ECONOMIC INEQUALITY

Work and Unemployment

Both poverty and wealth are closely tied to employment, the main source of money for most people. Today in Canada, most families have trouble living comfortably on a single income (Defina and Thanawala, 2009). To avoid poverty, many households are becoming increasingly reliant on two or more incomes, compared to previous generations. Yet even this is no guarantee of prosperity. Often, even the gainfully employed live on the edge of poverty.

Many work lives are characterized by periods of employment followed by stretches of unwanted idleness. This is particularly the case when people work in the secondary sector of the dual-labour market. Jobs such as unskilled labourer, cab driver, and salesperson generally are characterized by poor pay, low status, low job security, high turnover, and easy entry. At the same time, low wages prevent many people from saving part of their income to provide a safety net during times of unemployment (Breau, 2007). As a result, many must rely on social assistance programs, such as Employment Insurance, welfare, and workfare. These programs, though helpful and well intentioned, help the poor survive but rarely help them improve their lives (Poliakova and Reut, 2008).

Crime and Violence

Many believe the poor, desperate to improve their financial state, are more likely than other people to commit opportunistic crimes, such as petty theft, muggings, or burglary. Research often bears out this belief (Braun, 1995; Hagan, 1994; Kennedy et al., 1998). After all, the poor have fewer legitimate opportunities to achieve the economic and social goals our culture teaches us to value. Consequently, rises in the crime rate may reflect desperation or even an increase in self-destructive attitudes among those who are poor; or they may reflect a decrease in community social cohesion (Baron, 2006).

Still, this is only half of the story. The poor do not commit all of society's crimes. As a later chapter will point out, violations of the law committed by the wealthy—so-called corporate crimes and white-collar crimes—are equally challenging and may harm many more people's lives. However, such crimes are rarely reported or punished.

Drug and Alcohol Abuse

Another result of poverty and inequality is the excessive use of alcohol and drugs, whether for pleasure or to dull pain (Gallupe and Baron, 2009). This behaviour, like crime, is found in all social classes and is not limited to the poor. Nor is it caused only by social inequality.

However, the desperately poor, deprived of conventional opportunities to achieve wealth and success, are more likely to use alcohol and drugs. They do so to deal with what Robert Merton (1957: 131–60), and before him Émile Durkheim, called 'anomie', the gap between what they have been taught to want and what they are able to get. Rhonda Jones-Webb and colleagues (1997), for instance, found that people living in poor neighbourhoods are more likely to suffer from alcoholism. Not only does poverty affect the use of drugs and alcohol, it also increases the influence of drug and alcohol use on people's lives.

One study found that poverty accounts for 69 per cent of the variance in the cocaine and opiate overdose mortality rates in New York City (Marzuk et al., 1997). So, by far the single best predictor of death from a drug is the poverty of the drug user. Drugs do their worst harm when people are already leading lives stressed by low income, poor health, bad nutrition, and inadequate housing. All of these conditions reduce the immunity to disease that helps us survive, and they also reduce a person's will to live.

Children and Poverty

Poverty is also age-related in most societies. People without an income (e.g., children) or with a fixed income (e.g., elderly people) are more susceptible to the risks of poverty and inequality than other members of society. They are also the most blameless victims of poverty in any society (National Advisory Council on Aging, 2005).

Research on children who grow up poor leads to three conclusions about poverty. First, raising the incomes of poor families, even just barely above the poverty line, will improve the learning ability and performance of young children. Second, raising the educational status of poor parents will have a similar effect. Third, raising both the income and the education of poor parents will have the greatest positive effect (Smith et al., 1999). However, it may be easier to raise family incomes (for example, through transfer payments) than to raise parental education levels (Prus, 2007).

Children are particularly vulnerable to dire and degrading consequences of poverty. One of the world's most serious threats to healthy child development is the underground trafficking of minors, for cheap labour and especially for the purposes of commercial sexual exploitation. The illegal sex trade is a shadowy business and reliable statistics about the extent of the problem are hard to find. However, the International Labour Organization (ILO, 2008) has conservatively estimated that human trafficking, defined as the illegal transport of persons across national borders, affects at least 1.2 million children per year.

The purpose and extent of underage human trafficking vary from one region to another. In East Asia, for instance, trafficked children, the vast majority of whom are girls, are used largely as child prostitutes. Tourists mainly coming from wealthy neighbouring and Western nations create the demand. In Europe, minors are trafficked from east to west (e.g., from Poland to England) across the open borders of the European Union for similar purposes.

In South Asia and West and Central Africa, too, children are recruited to take part in the exploitative child labour market, though many are still destined for the sex trade. Often, debt bondage—where children are forced to work off money given to their parents—is the route by which children enter the downward spiral of exploitation (UNICEF, 2005). In African nations experiencing civil or tribal conflicts, children may also be abducted and forced to fight in militias.

Many girls and women who live in poverty in the developing world are limited to a few tough choices: domestic subservience, sex work, forced labour, an unwanted marriage, or a handful of other grim options. One way to break the cycle of exploitation and poverty, then, is to empower women rather than marginalize them.

INTERNATIONAL COMPARISONS

Box 2.2 Girls' Education in Afghanistan

In North America and other developed regions, the extent to which international education is available to women has, to a certain degree, been much overlooked—if not entirely taken for granted. The women's movement has taken many progressive steps forward during the past two centuries, yet the availability of education for women has not been under as immense scrutiny since the late nineteenth century as other areas of concern, such as voting rights, representation in Parliament, and even labour force participation. Though women all over the world have had to claim their place in the education system at many times throughout history, education has never been as valued as it is at present. Considering the role of education in the modern world, both for employment and for self-actualization, it has been increasingly important for both men and women to have varying levels of education available to them. Though this has not been a problem for the world's most recent generations of young adults in developed nations, youth of many developing nations are facing a sad reality in which they are being deprived of such an opportunity. This is especially true for females: most educationally deprived youth in developing nations are girls and young women. In 2009 the United Nations Girls' Education Initiative (UNGEI) published a book by researcher Roshan Chitrakar, who investigated the barriers to girls' education and gender inequality in South Asia. One country in which the barriers to girls' education have been under much public attention on a global scale is Afghanistan, the first on the list of countries that Chitrakar examines (other countries discussed in the report are Bangladesh, Bhutan, India, Maldives, Nepal, Pakistan, and Sri Lanka). In her report, Chitrakar writes:

> The long-standing war in Afghanistan prior to and during the Taliban regime stalled not only the education of girls but also the entire process of development for many decades. The consequence of the war history looms large in present-day Afghanistan with the education sector facing massive challenges. Lack of female teachers and basic infrastructure are among the key obstacles to girls' education. With the advent of democratic government in the country in 2001, promoting girls' education has become a priority development agenda. Afghanistan's constitution recognizes the education of girls as their fundamental right. The first 5-year National Education Strategic Plan has attempted to uphold this constitutional provision through priority programs for a speedy promotion of girls' education. The challenges of promoting girls' education are massive, hence concerted efforts will need to be made for many more years to come. Special measures such as incentive packages are essential to bring more girls to school and narrow the gender gap. The incentive for girls to pursue higher education is even more critical to ensure that they are motivated not only to enrol in basic education but also to complete it and acquire further qualifications. . . . Enhanced capacity of stakeholders at macro- and micro-levels to carry out gender audits and meet gender-related targets will be a significant step forward. With a secure and violence-free environment at and on the way to school, the enrolment of rural Afghan girls in school can be multiplied many-fold. However, the state will be required to accept the high cost involved in raising the status and level of educational attainment of girls in the country. (Chitrakar, 2009)

HEALTH CONSEQUENCES OF POVERTY AND ECONOMIC INEQUALITY

Poverty and Health

Poverty directly hinders secure access to food of high quality—food that contains essential nutrients, vitamins, minerals, and so on—and this lack of access then leads to poorer health (Kirkpatrick and Tarasuk, 2003).

It has been estimated that because of poor nutrition, one-quarter of children under the age of five who live in the developing world—more than 150 million children—are underweight. Chronic hunger leads to serious health problems, including rickets, scurvy, intestinal infections or damage, a depressed immune system, and impaired cognitive development. As well, hungry children are more likely to be hyperactive, have problems concentrating in school, and have other serious behavioural problems (Raphael, 2004).

Poverty is also likely to worsen health problems through the social problems to which it is related, such as crime, depression, and substance abuse. These other problems can also lead to poverty and the health problems that poverty entails (Heflin and Iceland, 2009). We discuss the specific health consequences of these other social problems in their respective chapters.

ANGELA'S ASHES

This 1999 film, based on the best-selling book, shows the extraordinary health and lifestyle deprivations found within Limerick's poorest classes.

PUBLIC ISSUES

Box 2.3 Guaranteed Annual Income: Can It Eliminate Poverty?

In the midst of a recession, housing crisis, and an ever-widening gap between the rich and poor, what policies would be most effective in lowering poverty in Canada? Currently, one of the more talked about possible solutions in the ongoing poverty debate is the guaranteed annual income (GAI). Under a system of GAI, all families, households, or persons are given a continuous basic minimal income, which ideally is sufficient to live on. How much a person would get will depend on various factors, including family size and age and other sources of income. Certain requirements, such as citizenship, would need to be met in order to receive GAI.

The idea of GAI in Canada is nothing new. The first official proposal was by the Castonguay-Nepveu Commission, which argued for a three-tiered income security program in Quebec in 1971. That same year, the Special Senate Committee on Poverty proposed a uniform system for lower-income Canadians. The most widely known recommendation was that of Donald Macdonald, chair of the Royal Commission on the Economic Union and Development Prospects for Canada, in his 1985 report. Numerous reports and proposals have been

made since, and the debate continues. Conservative Senator Hugh Segal, a long-time advocate of GAI, sparked new debate with his 2005 report.

Supporters of GAI argue that current social welfare implementations are highly inefficient. David Croll, who unsuccessfully proposed GAI to Prime Minister Pierre Trudeau in 1972, described Canada's welfare system in 1972 as 'pouring billions of dollars every year into a . . . system that merely treats the symptoms of poverty but leaves the disease itself untouched.' Implementation of GAI, proponents say, would streamline the welfare system, putting less burden on the judicial system, as well as eliminating duplicate services and maximizing labour productivity. In addition, Segal's 2005 report for the National Council of Welfare states that welfare recipients in Canada are worse off than they were in the 1980s. Segal further argues that 'based on the current allowances provided by the welfare system, I also refuse to accept that people purposely choose to avoid employment in order to subsist on such a paltry income', and that individuals choose to collect welfare as a last resort. David Croll suggested in his 1972 report that GAI would actually increase the incentive to work because, since it would not be taxed, 'those who work will receive and keep more income than those who do not.' In current systems, any extra income earned outside of welfare is heavily taxed. Supporters such as Segal also make morality-based arguments that everyone has a fundamental right to the basic necessities of food, clothing, and shelter, and that GAI would inspire hope and boost confidence.

Critics of GAI attack the hefty price tag that would come with an ambitious GAI system. Trudeau, although recognizing the 'good theory' behind Croll's 1972 proposal, rejected it as 'unaffordable'. The concept of GAI has also been attacked on the basis that it may encourage recipients to choose not to work, and instead sit at home collecting GAI payments, leading to possible labour shortages. As John Stapleman says, 'People don't like the idea of entitlement, when they hear guarantees they think of rights without responsibilities.' The other big question is exactly how much GAI to give. What is the right amount? Even if a GAI system were implemented, setting the level of income too low would not leave people any better off. Ken Battle of the Caledon Institute for Social Policy argues that while guaranteed basic income sounds like a good idea, the 'one-size-fits-all' solution systematically ignores the plight of the disabled, seniors, children, and recent immigrants. Battle argues that instead of introducing GAI, a better option would be to build on existing programs, proposing a higher minimum wage and raising the national child benefit.

While the merits of GAI have been debated, proposed, and recommended for over three decades, a fully integrated GAI system of welfare has yet to be implemented. Part of the reason for this resistance, according to Segal, may be because of the supposed stigma placed on welfare recipients.

Sources: Monsebraaten (2007); Campion-Smith (2008).

Effects of Inequality

Inequality—like poverty—is bad for our health. Research shows that being at the bottom end of a hierarchy—no matter how affluent that hierarchy may be—leads to health problems (Sanmartin, 2009).

The world's poorest populations—whether they live in Sudan or Canada—experience worse health than people within the same country who are not so poor. In less developed countries like Sudan, the causes of ill health are obvious: a lack of clean water, famine, infectious disease, and so forth. In more developed countries like Canada, however, these conditions are not significant health threats except in some northern Aboriginal communities (Trovato, 2001). Something else, therefore, is at the root of much of the disparity in health outcomes in Canada, and this 'something' appears to be inequality itself. Relative poverty, not absolute poverty, is the problem.

Much research has focused on the **relative income hypothesis**, which proposes that income inequality alone (as opposed to absolute deprivation) is enough to bring on various health problems, including premature mortality, within a population (Gravelle and Sutton, 2009). This theory argues that the fact of inequality itself has real and measurable health outcomes for people at the lower end of the hierarchy. One influential study (Wilkinson, 1994) found a correlation between life expectancy and the proportion of income received by the poorest 70 per cent of the population. The author showed that the greater the difference in income distribution between the least well-off 70 per cent and the most well-off 30 per cent, the higher the levels of early mortality in an entire society or community.

RELATIVE INCOME HYPOTHESIS Proposal that income inequality alone (as opposed to absolute deprivation) is enough to bring on various health problems, including premature mortality, within a population.

The Canadian Press/Winnipeg Free Press-Ruth Bonneville

The Barkman family, from the Garden Hill First Nation, poses for a photo in Winnipeg in March 2009. The Barkmans, parents of a six-month-old boy who died of meningitis, are pushing for a complete overhaul of health care on native reserves.

The best-known investigations of the relationship between inequality and health are the so-called Whitehall studies, which involved 18,000 male British civil servants in the late 1960s and the 1970s. A major finding was that mortality rates, especially from coronary heart disease (CHD), were three times higher among workers in the lowest civil service positions (messengers, doorkeepers, and so on) than among workers in the highest positions (such as top administrators). This difference remained even after taking into account risk factors such as obesity, smoking habits, amount of leisure time and physical activity, other illnesses, baseline blood pressure, and height (Marmot et al., 1984).

One explanation of this variation in CHD mortality is the difference in control and support that workers experience at different levels of the job hierarchy (Marmot et al., 1987). In short, people in low-status jobs have less control over their work; this lack of control produces more stress; and more stress appears to produce higher blood pressure and higher risks of heart disease.

A second Whitehall study was conducted in 1985, involving more than 10,000 male and female British civil servants. It confirmed that, indeed, low work control—characteristic of low-status occupations such as clerical and office support workers—increases the risk of developing CHD (Bosma et al., 1997). Even those working *near* the top of the civil service hierarchy had poorer health outcomes than people working at the *very top*. Not surprisingly, low levels of work control are associated with more frequent absences from work (North et al., 1996).

Further evidence showing the importance of relative—not absolute—deprivation comes from the finding that GNP (gross national product) per capita is correlated with health only up to a boundary of $5,000 GNP per capita per year. Beyond this threshold, increases in standard of living have little effect on a population's health. Thus, in developed countries, people's disadvantage *in relation to others*, rather than their absolute deprivation, leads to health inequalities. As Daniels, Kennedy, and Kawachi (2000: 9) note, 'the health of a population depends not just on the size of the economic pie but on how the pie is shared. . . . Differences in health outcomes among developed nations cannot be explained by the absolute deprivation associated with low economic development.'

Thus, social inequality contributes directly to poor health and social problems, for two reasons: it increases social inequality and decreases social cohesion. Social inequality, in the form of relative disadvantage, increases the experience of stress. As well, for various reasons, it reduces access to health information and health-care services.

Social integration plays an important part in dealing with stresses associated with inequality. Robert Putnam (2000), for example, finds in many studies a link between social cohesion and social connectedness, on the one hand, and health and longevity, on the other. People with higher levels of social involvement are healthier and live longer. As well, communities with more social integration have better health and mortality records. Finally, cross-national comparisons find better health experiences and greater longevity in the countries with higher social integration (De Looper, 2009; Putnam, 2000; Wilkinson, 1996).

SOLVING THE PROBLEMS OF POVERTY AND ECONOMIC INEQUALITY

For centuries, people have debated possible solutions to the problems of poverty and inequality. The proposed solutions fall into two main categories—individual and collective (Bradley and Cole, 2002). Individuals, usually in their own interest, can undertake individual solutions. But collective solutions require the co-operation of many individuals for their mutual benefit. Let us begin by considering some of the ways that individuals deal with their own personal experience of poverty and/or inequality.

Individual Solutions

For an individual seeking an escape from or avoidance of poverty, there is no better investment than higher education. However, racial and ethnic discrimination continue to limit people's economic opportunities, despite a higher education (Reitz, 2007a, 2007b). For example, members of groups that suffer discrimination may not do as well economically in work settings controlled by people from other ethnic groups as they would by remaining within their own ethnic community, even with less education. The decision to be made here—and it is a complex one—depends on several factors: the actual extent of discrimination against your ethnic or racial group; the chance of a significant reduction in that discrimination during your lifetime; the range of attractive occupational opportunities within your own racial or ethnic community; and the chance of a significant increase in these opportunities during your lifetime.

Often, people seeking to escape from poverty need to change the way they think about themselves—not an easy task, but one that a great many people manage to accomplish. This is partly what the major social movements of our time—for example, feminism, Native rights, and gay rights—are all about. People learn more about the history of their oppression as members of a despised or belittled group, discuss this problem with others, and find mentors and role models within the community who have done what the majority society would have them think cannot be done.

People trying to escape from poverty can also build and make use of social networks. That is how people find good jobs—the size and variety of one's network of acquaintances can be improved by getting to know people who have larger and 'better' networks. People who are themselves mobile and widely acquainted, who are (typically) higher in status, or who operate within institutions that encourage interpersonal contact are valuable people to know (Bradley and Cole, 2002).

They should also seek out social institutions that break down traditional gender, class, and ethnic barriers to interpersonal contact; these include colleges, universities, and government. Thus, higher education and involvement in civic affairs are doubly beneficial: they allow self-improvement and they encourage contact with others. However, both activities leave less time for participation in one's own community. Here, wrong choices are potentially costly. Thus, one should try to become a 'cosmopolitan' member of her or his community, with feet in both camps (Merton, 1957: 387–420). This connects the individual and the community into the larger networks of influence and opportunity beyond (Myers, 2005).

Collective Solutions

The chief actors in a large, modern society are groups and organizations, not individuals. That is why we must look beyond individuals for adequate solutions to inequality.

Reducing Material Inequality

Karl Marx and Friedrich Engels contended in *The Communist Manifesto* that a revolution that would eliminate ruling classes forever by eliminating private property—by putting the means of production in the hands of the state—would bring better conditions for all. With the eventual 'withering away' of the state, communism would end history as we have known it, for it would end social classes and class conflict.

There are two problems with this formulation. First, a reading of history shows that every society of any size has had a class structure and a ruling class. This would not lead sociologists to the confident conclusion that a society with no class structure and no ruling class is truly possible. Rather, it would lead in the opposite direction—in the direction most often associated with the name of Robert Michels (1962 [1916]), who stated the 'iron law of oligarchy'.

Michels's principle, based on a socialist's study of the German socialist party—a sympathetic observer studying a radically democratic organization—holds that in every social grouping a dominant group will struggle to perpetuate its power, whatever its original ideology. That is, inequality is inevitable in human groupings, whatever their size or their members' ideology.

Michels's 'iron law' has not proven completely unbreakable. For example, a sociological study of the International Typographical Union, a democratic printers' union in the United States and Canada, found some of the conditions that prevent or minimize oligarchy (Lipset et al., 1963). So, not every organization must be oligarchic. Yet oligarchic organizations in our own society and elsewhere far outnumber the democratic organizations. There is no evidence of a society that has broken the hold of oligarchy. At best, there is only a slim chance that Marx was right about the possibility of a fully democratic society.

Second, the premise that history can end with a democratic, class-free society is far from supported by empirical evidence. History does not show that communist revolutions have succeeded in bringing about either equality or democracy. In the century and a half since Marx and Engels's *Communist Manifesto*, a number of groups in different countries have experimented with communism. Some attempts have been Utopian or anarchistic, based in a small community or region (see Hobsbawm, 1959; Kanter, 1972).

But, except for Cuba, the Israeli kibbutzim, and Hutterite communities, these have all failed, for various reasons. Some have been forcibly overturned; others have lacked a sufficient material base; still others have suffered from demographic pressures from within and attack from without. Even the relatively successful kibbutzim and Hutterite communities have suffered serious losses of population, as native-born members deserted. For its part, Cuba's revolution has produced neither prosperity nor democracy.

Other Group Remedies

Wherever opportunity is limited, any wholly individual remedies are no more than quick fixes with temporary effects. In the long run, the chance of getting more opportunity is greater for a group working together than for an individual working alone. But if we rule out the revolutionary option, what remains? Again, what follows is merely schematic. It would be impossible to encompass all remaining scenarios within the scope of this book.

Two group remedies to exclusion are truly possible: legislation and group action. To bring this about requires banding together with others who suffer discrimination, joining forces across ethnic, class, gender, and regional boundaries where necessary. It also means electing sympathetic legislators to push for changes. If successful, the result will be a more assimilated, less discriminatory society (Addison et al., 2009).

A second remedy is to mobilize within one's own group—whether class, ethnic, religious, or regional—to increase community organization. This has the effect of discriminating in one's own favour to counter the discrimination of the larger society. Many groups use this tactic today, notably class-based political parties, unions, lobbies, and associations (Hills et al., 2009).

Group mobilization carries the risks of increasing inter-group conflict without eliminating the underlying conditions that gave rise to it. By pitting one group against another—women against men, blacks against whites, gays against heterosexuals—this tactic increases the risk of misunderstanding and injustice. A society torn by such disputes is no further ahead than a society marked by smouldering resentment. Events in the Balkans, Somalia, Israel, and Northern Ireland, however, show that civil war is considerably worse than smouldering resentment (Addison et al., 2009).

The benefits of slow, incremental individual change are much more limited (Kanter, 1977). For example, a sole woman given the opportunity to 'model' executive abilities in a large organization is under unusual pressures to succeed 'on behalf of all women' and is judged by criteria quite unlike those applied to men. Confusion will arise between the unique characteristics of the individual and the 'type' she represents. Consequently, we really do not learn what excluded groups can do until we see many group members performing in common, emotionally neutral situations.

Achieving this requires legislation that ensures inclusion for as many representatives of a social 'type' as may seek it. Laws against discrimination not only break down traditional patterns of exclusion, they also repudiate a dominant ideology in our society that blames poor and vulnerable people—society's victims—for the problems they suffer. Again, governments will not pass and enforce such laws without group mobilization.

CHAPTER SUMMARY

Poverty has many definitions. Typically, governments decide where to draw the poverty line, so the meaning of poverty varies by society and, within societies, varies over time.

Some think that poverty is caused by the continuation of economically damaging cultural habits (this is the **culture of poverty** approach), while others believe it is simply caused by an unfair distribution of resources (the conflict approach). Functionalists believe that economic rewards are merit-based and inequality and poverty are mostly inevitable. It is not clear, however, from this standpoint, why women and ethnic minorities have the most poverty.

Widespread poverty is evident in Canada and throughout the world. For this country in 2008, Statistics Canada (2009b) classified 9.2 per cent of the population (3 million people) as living in a 'low-income' situation. Even though this is the lowest low-income rate since Statistics Canada began measuring it in 1976, it is not a constant figure. Since the recession of 2009 this rate has likely increased. As a result of such shifts in the economy, many people move in and out of poverty. Longer durations of poverty produce more harmful outcomes, and children who are continuously poor have higher rates of anti-social behaviour than transiently poor or non-poor children. Sometimes, poor health is a cause of poverty, not vice versa. However, for most people, the reverse is true. Poverty and inequality will be continuing problems they cannot handle on their own.

As we have seen, both inequality and poverty are thorny issues—not merely conditions of economic insufficiency, but also causes of physical and mental health problems. Further, lower income means a higher probability of dying relatively young. These patterns make it especially important—for individuals and for society—that we attempt to lessen economic inequality and try to discover ways of unlinking health and death from income level. Much of the research discussed in the remainder of this book is directed to these two ends.

CULTURE OF POVERTY Theory developed by Oscar Lewis characterizing the urban poor as having a distinct set of values and norms, including short-sightedness, impulsiveness, and a tendency to accept their marginalized status in society, and as remaining poor because they pass on these values to future generations.

QUESTIONS FOR CRITICAL THOUGHT

1. What type of policies do you think would effectively alleviate economic and class inequality?

2. How have the concept and perception of social class changed from the 1800s to the present day?

3. In your opinion, do the mass media have an impact on how the poor are perceived? Explain.

4. Explain the reasons why you think minority immigrants earn less income than whites in Canada.

5. What future trends do you see happening with regard to class and inequality in Canada?

6. Compare and contrast the economic issues faced by youth and the elderly.

RECOMMENDED READINGS

Davies, Matt, and Magnus Ryner, eds. 2006. *Poverty and the Production of World Politics: Unprotected Workers in the Global Political Economy*. London: Palgrave Macmillan. Global poverty and 'the underclass' are essential dimensions of world politics, yet analyses of how the global poor intervene in world politics are scarce. This book examines debates about migration, human rights, the feminization of labour markets, and the rise of the informal economy in innovative and provocative ways. The editors and contributors show how production and power relations frame world politics, and help us to understand the politics of production in the Third World, including migration, prostitution, the 'clash of civilizations', and union internationalism.

DiFazio, William. 2006. *Ordinary Poverty: A Little Food and Cold Storage*. Philadelphia: Temple University Press. At a soup kitchen in the Bedford-Stuyvesant section of Brooklyn, over a thousand people line up for food five days a week. The author shows how poverty has become 'ordinary', a fact of life for millions of Americans and for the thousands of social workers, volunteers, and everyday citizens who still think poverty ought to be wiped out. He argues that only a true program of living wages is the solution to poverty. DiFazio also argues for a true poor people's movement that links the interests of all social movements with the interests of ending poverty.

Handler, Joel F., and Yeheskel Hasenfeld. 2007. *Blame Welfare, Ignore Poverty and Inequality*. New York: Cambridge University Press. This book challenges the conventional wisdom that welfare reform worked. Bringing to bear a wealth of data on poverty, inequality, and welfare policy, the authors argue that welfare reform was built around 'myths' about the individual deviance of the poor. Instead, they argue that conditions in society and the economy are the underlying sources of poverty and inequality and must be addressed with new policy solutions. They also provide an excellent exposition of the internal workings of welfare bureaucracies as well as the many reasons welfare programs create widespread public opposition but rarely achieve their intended goals.

Kendall, Diana. 2005. *Framing Class: Media Representations of Wealth and Poverty in America*. Lanham, MD: Rowman & Littlefield. This book examines the significance of class representations in the media and shows how biased media framing of stories about wealth and poverty may influence many people. Through an analysis of newspaper articles and television shows, *Framing Class* illustrates how the media perpetuate negative stereotypes about the working class and the poor while glorifying the material possessions and privileged status of the upper classes. It explores how myths and negative stereotypes about the working class and the poor construct a reality that seemingly justifies the superior position of the upper-middle and upper classes, and shows them as entitled to the privileged position in the class system.

Kilty, Keith M., ed. 2006. *The Promise of Welfare Reform: Political Rhetoric and the Reality of Poverty in the Twenty-First Century*. Binghamton, NY: Haworth Press. This book presents articles from 23 community practitioners and welfare researchers who challenge the shift in the view of public aid from a right to a privilege. Examining the history of welfare reform, its connection to poverty and family issues, and the impact of racism on poverty and on the treatment of the poor, this book explores the social, political, and economic context of welfare reform, including the elimination of poverty as a societal goal, how racial and ethic groups have been targeted, popular stereotypes about the poor and their work ethic, anti-immigrant hostility, the struggles of single mothers with children, domestic violence, and marriage as a realistic escape from poverty.

Ross, Robert J.S. 2004. *Slaves to Fashion: Poverty and Abuse in the New Sweatshops*. Ann Arbor: University of Michigan Press. This book exposes the dark side of the apparel industry and its exploited workers, both in the US and abroad. Ross explains the new sweatshops as a product of unregulated global capitalism and associated deregulation, union erosion, and exploitation of undocumented workers. After a brief 35 years of fair practices, the US apparel business has once again sunk to shameful abuse and exploitation. *Slaves to Fashion* is a study of how the media portray sweatshops; an analysis of the fortunes of the current anti-sweatshop movement; and a study of the global South–southern US competition that sends wages and working conditions plummeting towards the bottom.

Wagner, David. 2008. *Ordinary People: In and Out of Poverty in the Gilded Age*. Boulder, CO: Paradigm. The author explores the lives of poor people in the final three decades of the nineteenth century, using biographies of people who were inmates in a large almshouse, as well as genealogical and other official records to follow their later lives. *Ordinary People* shows the fluid picture of poverty as people's lives change over time. The lives documented here help us to understand that many individuals living in poverty make inventive, bold moves to escape it. They were more than just victims, but people who asserted themselves and often managed to build their own lives.

Recommended Websites

International Labour Organization (ILO)

www.ilo.org

The ILO is a UN agency that promotes and establishes workplace standards and rights around the world. It advances social justice and human rights, creating decent jobs and better working conditions for everyone.

Human Resources and Skills Development Canada (HRSDC)

www.hrsdc.gc.ca

This government department aims to develop policies and create programs to help Canadians in the work environment, such as establishing healthy workplaces and improving leadership skills among workers. This website has information on a variety of topics in relation to work and social class in Canada, including data on labour. Related to this site is the federal Department of Labour, with more useful links. Visit it at: <www.hrsdc.gc.ca/eng/labour/index.shtml>.

Canadian Centre for Occupational Health and Safety (CCOHS)

www.ccohs.ca

CCOHS's mission is to inform about and improve workplace health and safety issues in Canada and to prevent work-related injuries and illnesses. The organization works through the Minister of Labour.

Ontario Ministry of Labour

www.labour.gov.on.ca

The purpose of this ministry is to develop and enforce labour legislation in Ontario, establishing safe workplaces for Canadians. It creates employment standards, health and safety regulations, and positive relations among workers and between workers and managers or bosses.

Canadian Labour Congress (CLC)

canadianlabour.ca

The CLC is the 'largest democratic and popular organization in Canada with over three million members'. This umbrella organization brings together Canadian provincial, territorial, national, and even some international unions and labour councils to ensure workers have the advantage of fair wages and safe working conditions, as well as various other benefits.

Canadian Committee on Labour History

www.cclh.ca

This website promotes the working class and its labour history in Canada. It outlines topics such as culture, ethnicity, family life, gender, migration, and politics, and also encourages the teaching of labour history in schools. It offers links to other resources, including recommended books, workshops, and a Labour History portal at: <www.workinghistories.ca>, which is a great link to international labour history. Here you'll find information on museums, archives, articles, documents, clips, and more. The CCLH also publishes an academic journal, *Labour/Le Travail*.

CHAPTER 3

Race and Ethnic Relations

iStockphoto.com/Lachlan Currie

LEARNING OBJECTIVES

- To learn that social distance is maintained between different ethnic and racial groups.
- To understand how racial and ethnic conflict occurs in Canada.
- To recognize the varying intensities of prejudice.
- To understand the process of chain migration.
- To know what is meant by the 'vertical mosaic'.
- To understand different theoretical perspectives on ethnic and racial inequality.
- To discover the social and health effects of racial and ethnic inequality.
- To identify possible solutions to problems of race and ethnic relations.

INTRODUCTION

Most people view racial prejudice as unfair; and Canadians tend to look for remedies to injustice (Wockner, 2004). Moreover, since it is unfair, prejudice creates conflicts in our society—between minorities and the majority, and between people who are prejudiced and people who are not. Finally, prejudice and its outcomes—discrimination, conflict, exclusion, hatred, distrust—are politically and economically wasteful because they neglect certain human resources and thus hinder our society's potential for prosperity. Therefore, obviously, no matter how we define the causes and allocate the blame, racialization and racial inequality are a problem for Canadian society.

RACE

Is race a social construction? People who have the most difficulty accepting other races believe that race is a biological—and therefore unassailable—fact. For them, race is an essential and permanent feature of any human being. They see each 'race' as having unique physiological characteristics, based in genetic differences that are specific to a certain race; they are likely to believe that certain cultural or personality dispositions are genetically based as well. People who take this approach believe there are at least three categories of people in the human species—Negroid ('black'), Caucasoid ('white'), and Mongoloid ('yellow')—from which all racial groups are derived (Omi and Winant, 2009).

However, scientists increasingly reject this view of race because of growing genetic evidence showing the so-called human races are more alike than different. For example, the Human Genome Project has shown that only a tiny fraction of humanity's genetic makeup varies by characteristics typically associated with 'race'. Indeed, 85 per cent of the genetic variability that exists within the entire human species can be found within a single local population (Barbujani et al., 1997). Thus, there could be as much or more genetic difference between two randomly selected Cambodians than between a Cambodian and a Norwegian. Besides, the physical features commonly associated with race—skin colour, hair texture, and eye colour, for example—are not genetically associated. That is, the pieces of DNA that control a person's skin colour are inherited separately from the pieces that control whether that person's hair is curly or straight.

Yet, many continue to believe that people can be usefully distinguished by race and that important human differences are biologically determined. Therefore, although many people reject racism in principle, many others continue to behave as though the idea of race is significant (Blatz and Ross, 2009). Thus, from a sociological perspective, race is significant. Race may be a social construction, but as long as large numbers of people continue to think race does make a difference, the idea of race will continue to influence the social order and social inequality.

ETHNICITY

Some people believe that 'race' and 'ethnicity' are, if not the same, closely related: 'One race, one ethnicity—biologically Negroid, therefore culturally African'. To be sure, a broad and

generalized understanding of ethnicity has some value. Cultural differences certainly exist between groups of people, and when they are sharpened by clear differences in skin colour, height, and other physical features, cultural differences seem more prominent and somehow significant.

The physical features supposedly shared by members of one race are a supposed result of collective evolutionary adaptation to specific environmental conditions—for example, the darkening of skin colour where strong sunlight shines most of the time, as it does near the equator (Baran, 2008). However, race and ethnicity are not necessarily connected. People who differ in appearance may share the same cultural values, whereas people who look the same may not.

The cultural features people share, as members of an ethnic group, are usually a result of collective experiences that are interpreted in a certain way given a particular historical and regional background. Differences do exist between members of different ethnic groups—for example, between Poles and Ukrainians, or Chinese and Koreans—and there are historical reasons for these differences (Steinberg, 1981).

The most useful way to think about ethnic groups is to see them as created by social interactions. We form ethnic groups relationally, through processes of exclusion and inclusion around symbols of real or imagined common descent, such as a common language, common

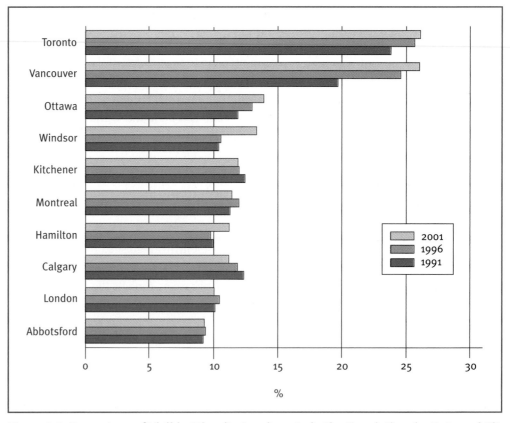

Figure 3.1 Percentage of Visible Minority Immigrants in the Population, by Date and City
Source: Statistics Canada, at www.statcan.gc.ca/pub/81-004-x/200410/chrt/immi2.gif.

rituals, and common folklore. As these are social and cultural in nature, they can be learned. As well, ethnic boundaries may be made and unmade over time (Fleras and Elliott, 2009).

Social scientists used to define culture as an inventory of visible characteristics. Today, they understand **culture** as the values and practices that frame people's lives (Ruffin, 2009). From this perspective, culture is not something constant or permanent. Most anthropologists would deny a fixed pattern of Chinese culture, for example, that is learned and enacted uniformly across generations and contexts by Asian people throughout the world. We can neither deduce people's ethnic affiliations from their skin colour, language, religion, or other markers used to place group members, nor can we assume that being Chinese today is similar to what it was in the past. For this reason and others, ethnicity is constantly changing.

CULTURE The way of life of a society that includes dress, language, norms of behaviour, foods, tools, beliefs, and folklore. This framework of values and practices adapts to the changing socio-historical context.

MULTICULTURALISM IN CANADA

As is evident in Figure 3.1, immigrants—people who migrate from other countries, usually for permanent residence—today constitute a large fraction of the population of Canada's cities. According to recent Statistics Canada data, for example, by 2031 it is expected that 63 per cent of Toronto's population will be from visible minority communities (Javed, 2010). It is clear that immigration has been important throughout Canadian history, making multiculturalism an important political issue.

Canada's multicultural policy was first set up in 1971, and many factors—political as well as sociological—influenced its introduction (Fujiwara, 2008). The 1960s had been marked by ever more stormy relations between English and French speakers, especially in Quebec. The Royal Commission on Bilingualism and Biculturalism, established in 1963, did original research—some of it by sociologists—and held hearings across Canada; and in 1969, the Official Languages Act was voted into law (Forgues, 2007).

During these proceedings, the Commissioners heard about other problems that could not be ignored. Spokespersons for ethnic minority groups across Canada argued that, given the current discussions of biculturalism, the old policy of cultural assimilation was unjust. They argued that immigrants and their children had made great sacrifices, during the Depression and the world wars, just as other Canadians had done. Therefore, they deserved the same respect and the same benefits of Canadian citizenship. Although they were not of English or French heritage, they were just as worthy of inclusion as Canada's so-called 'charter groups', as John Porter had called them (Porter, 1965).

Therefore, they urged the adoption of a new model of citizen participation that included all the ethnic groups in Canada on an equal footing. Against the melting pot model of the United States, they favoured a 'cultural mosaic', with distinct parts fitting together in a single society. In short, they opposed assimilation and demanded that government policy recognize their group distinctness and the right to group survival.

The Royal Commission agreed, recommending that the government recognize the value of cultural pluralism and encourage Canadian institutions to reflect the value of pluralism in their policies and programs. The policy was supported and promoted by then Prime Minister Pierre Elliott Trudeau. Many have said this was a political strategy on his part to win immigrant and ethnic-minority votes for the Liberal Party—and if so, it succeeded. It may also have been intended to weaken the effect of demands by Quebec nationalists for unique rights within Confederation, a principle that Trudeau rejected, as he believed it would fragment the federal state (Haque, 2007).

When first announced, the policy proposed that multiculturalism operate within a bilingual framework, affirming English and French as the two official languages. However, it also declared ethnic pluralism a goal worth preserving and nurturing in Canadian society. Provinces followed the federal lead by introducing their own multiculturalism policies in their own areas of jurisdiction. In 1971, multiculturalism became official federal policy with the passage of the Multiculturalism Act and the creation of a junior cabinet position for multiculturalism (now subsumed within the Department of Canadian Heritage); in 1982, the desire to preserve and enhance 'the multicultural heritage of Canadians' was entrenched in the Constitution (section 27 of the Constitution Act, 1982); and in 1988, a new Canadian Multiculturalism Act became law.

Today, Canada prides itself on its multicultural makeup. Yet, as multiculturalism is a complicated notion, Canadians have found it useful to distinguish between traditional, or liberal, multiculturalism and modern multiculturalism.

Traditional multiculturalism, or pluralism, is concerned with protecting the rights of individuals. It protects the rights of minority people through, for example, provincial human rights codes. By contrast, *modern multiculturalism* is concerned with the survival of diverse cultural groups. In this case, the individual is treated as the member of an ethnic or racial group, and the group—not the individual—is protected by law (Fleras and Elliott, 2009).

The difference between these two approaches is important. With its focus on fostering civil liberties, traditional multiculturalism protects individual job-seekers against bias. In contrast, modern multiculturalism supports blanket preferences, such as employment equity, to promote the hiring of disadvantaged group members (Reitz and Banerjee, 2007).

This policy is closely tied to employment equity (known in the US as affirmative action), which—other things being equal—gives *preference* to members of the specifically protected groups (for example, females, visible minorities, disabled people) over otherwise blameless males, white people, and the able-bodied. As certain groups are advantaged under such policies while other groups are disadvantaged, people may begin to argue about whom to include under the label 'visible minority' or 'disabled person'.

Some criticize the federal policy of multiculturalism (and employment equity) for highlighting group differences, encouraging different value systems, and building isolated communities rather than promoting common interests and objectives (Abu-Laban and Gabriel, 2004). Their argument is that as long as Canada preserves diverse cultures it will never build a national identity. In this nation of separate (and occasionally hostile) ethnic groups, racism is only one negative result. For some, treating minority groups in a special way violates the former Canadian norm of equal treatment. Without the social differences promoted by multiculturalism, there might be less exclusion, prejudice, or discrimination based on ethnic or cultural differences.

As Box 3.1 shows, high rates of immigration and the non-assimilationist policy implied by multiculturalism have sometimes led to nasty conflicts between people from different ancestral backgrounds.

PUBLIC ISSUES

Box 3.1 Racism at York University

Hundreds of students filled the York University student centre today for a rally against racism, but the meeting quickly degenerated into attacks on the government of Ontario, the state of Israel, and the new president of the university.

The rally was in response to the discovery Tuesday of racist graffiti on the doors of the York University Black Students' Alliance office and two washrooms adjacent to the office. The graffiti read, 'All Niggers must die' and 'Niggas go back to Africa'.

The rally began with speakers calling for the York community to unite to combat racism on campus. The first speakers described the graffiti as an attack on them, their space, and their safety.

As other speakers took the microphone, however, they turned the focus to attacks upon Israel as a 'racist and apartheid state', Premier Dalton McGuinty, and York University President Mamdouh Shoukri.

McGuinty was blamed for the 'racist actions' of the government for denying entry last summer to Malik Shabazz, the leader of the US New Black Panther Party.

The strongest attacks were saved for Shoukri. At the microphone, one of the rally organizers criticized Shoukri for 'not caring about students', claiming that Shoukri was not at the rally, and that by not being at the rally to address students, he was being silent in the face of racism.

Shoukri was in fact present and in the crowd, and in response to this criticism, he moved towards the stage. When he reached the front, he was seen speaking to the organizers. He was seen asking for the opportunity to address the assembled students but was apparently refused, after which he walked away. One of the organizers yelled that the rally was about 'African issues' and for 'Africanized people' to speak out against marginalization. Shoukri, whose undergraduate degree is from Cairo University, was born in Egypt.

Organizers then demanded that the media leave, accusing reporters of looking to sensationalize the story and 'looking for the picture of an angry person for [their] front pages'.

After the rally, York students explained to a reporter that they felt Shoukri should have spoken out immediately following the discovery of the graffiti, and that some of what happened at the rally was an expression of frustration at an alleged slow response from the university.

'The hateful graffiti is a reminder that even at an institution of higher learning, we are not immune from hate', Shoukri told reporters after the rally. 'We must work together, each of us, to find ways to ensure this never happens again.' . . .

Source: Abridged from Coleman (2008).

THE VERTICAL MOSAIC

Despite historically high rates of immigration, Canada has not always been as welcoming towards immigrants as one might imagine. Repeatedly, the majority group has excluded and devalued immigrant groups, with minority newcomers experiencing less-than-average access to better occupations and higher income. These facts led John Porter (1965) to describe Canadian society as a **vertical mosaic** in which English and French Canadians are at the top of a patchwork hierarchy, with other ethnic minorities positioned below.

Porter traced this stratification pattern to Canada's historical reliance on selective immigration that fulfilled specific workforce needs during industrialization. Gradually, as Canada industrialized, a close relationship between ethnicity and social class developed. Ethnic groups took and held onto the best available roles in society, leaving the less desirable roles for other ethnic groups—especially, for more recent immigrants.

VERTICAL MOSAIC
Coined by John Porter, a socio-economic hierarchy in which French and English Canadians live at the top and other ethnic minorities are positioned below.

Here is how the process worked: with each decade, fewer of the desired kinds of immigrants—Northern European Protestants—were available for migration. Canada's new, hard, and dangerous jobs—such as mining in northern Ontario—required new 'kinds' of immigrants, from Europe and then from Asia, the Caribbean, and countries in the southern hemisphere. New immigrants would arrive to find Canada's best jobs taken and they had to settle for those typically lower in the social hierarchy (Reitz, 2001).

With few exceptions, their children and grandchildren were unable to move up the hierarchy because mechanisms for upward mobility—especially, institutions of higher education—were largely inaccessible. Therefore, from generation to generation, particular ethnic groups remained stuck in their **entrance status**: the status attained when their group first arrived in Canada (Reitz et al., 2009). As the data in Figure 3.2 show, many immigrants who arrived over the past 25 years came as economic immigrants, to fill particular economic roles.

ENTRANCE STATUS The occupational status a group enters when it first immigrates to Canada.

However, immigrants today do not permanently retain their entrance status, as Porter claimed in 1965. By now, thanks to the continued expansion of educational opportunities, many of Canada's minority groups have moved out of low-status entrance jobs. Discrimination and a lack of educational opportunities have continued to make it difficult for the Canadian-born children of some ethnic minority immigrants to climb the economic ladder (Reitz, 2007a; Reitz, 2007b). This has left a stable base of labourers on which the dominant English/French group could perch. 'Ethnic differences', Porter concluded, 'have been

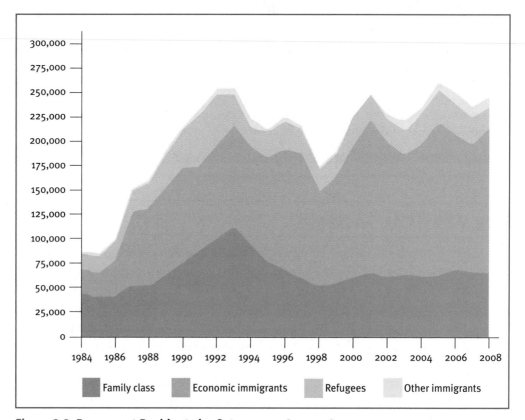

Figure 3.2 Permanent Residents by Category, 1984–2008

Source: Citizenship and Immigration Canada, at: www.cic.gc.ca/english/pdf/research-stats/facts2008.pdf.

important in building up the bottom layer of the stratification system in both agricultural and industrial settings' (1965: 73).

The vertical mosaic persisted not only because of exclusionary practices by the dominant English–French majority, but also because of the migration patterns and self-organization practices of the ethnic groups. Let us examine each of these briefly.

Chain Migration into the Mosaic

For most ethnic groups, the process of migration to Canada has been gradual. Some immigrants came to escape war, bad living conditions, or an absence of human rights—so-called 'push factors'. Others came in hope of finding better jobs and education for their children—so-called 'pull factors' (Costigan et al., 2009).

Typically, immigrants arrived generation after generation as links in a **chain migration** process. Family members would come, one or two at a time, set up a home, get work, and send for spouses, siblings, and children, gradually creating a chain (or sequence) of linked migrations. Eventually, these chains would extend outward to include relatives and even acquaintances. Many immigrants spent their first Canadian years in large old houses packed

CHAIN MIGRATION The successful migration of one family member creates a chain for the kin and community network. Migration is not random but is increasingly about networks, rational choices, and kinship relations.

The Canadian Press/Francis Vachon

An example of institutional completeness is the Toronto Chinatown, an ethnic enclave in downtown Toronto with a high concentration of ethnic Chinese residents and businesses extending along Dundas Street West and Spadina Avenue.

with family members who had just arrived and were looking for a foothold (Moya and Bjerg, 1999).

This pattern of chain migration is common throughout the world. Not only influenced by distance and economic opportunity, like many other social processes, migration relies on information flow. People generally migrate to nearby places they know about, usually through people they knew at home. This use of social networks explains why some immigrants who, in the same given year, left a particular town in Poland (or Italy or Vietnam) ended up living in Winnipeg, while others ended up living in Montreal, Boston, Capetown, or Sydney.

Institutional Completeness

With each arrival, the immigrant community becomes larger and more differentiated, containing a wider variety of communal institutions. As Raymond Breton (1964, 1978; Breton et al., 1980) has written, the growing communities often develop **institutional completeness**: they build schools, churches, newspapers, lending societies, shops, and so on. In turn, by increasing the numbers of those who carry out most of their activities within the ethnic group and preserve ethnic culture and ethnic social ties, community solidarity and cohesion is strengthened (Landry et al., 2007).

With unfairly restricted access to economic opportunities, new immigrants are sometimes forced to use their ethnic membership and assert their ethnic pride as a matter of economic and cultural survival. People who try to assimilate socially may find themselves marginalized—that is, accepted by neither the ethnic community nor the host culture.

This is a particular problem for the children of immigrants, as sociologists W.I. Thomas and Florien Znaniecki (1971 [1919]) first pointed out in their classic work, *The Polish Peasant in Europe and America*. Often, intergenerational value conflicts arise in immigrant families. Immigrants' grandchildren find themselves fully accepted into the society; immigrants' children—their parents—are only partly accepted; and the immigrants themselves, often limited in education, language skills, and social capital, are least accepted of all. Therefore, members of the same extended family can have very different experiences of the same society.

Diasporas

Viewed from within our own society, immigrant groups are either included or excluded. Viewed internationally, immigrant groups such as the Arabs of Montreal or the Sikhs of Edmonton are often the members of a much larger community: the global Arab or Sikh community to which they belong.

Originally, the word 'diaspora' described the scattering of the tribes of Israel and, in modern times, Jewish communities outside the state of Israel, especially as they were forced to flee the persecution of Nazi Germany. Today, we use **diaspora** to mean the global spread of migrants of any ethnic group or nationality and their culture. It is used as well to describe

INSTITUTIONAL COMPLETENESS A measure of the degree to which an immigrant ethnic group gives its own members the services they need through its own local institutions.

DIASPORA The dispersal of any group of people throughout the world; originally applied to the tribes of Israel. Almost any migrant community with some degree of international heritage is referred to as diasporic.

the global dispersion of any historically victimized minority, such as the Roma (gypsies) or Armenians, or visible and potentially victimized minorities (for example, Arabs in Africa and Chinese people in Indonesia). Almost any migrant community—especially a community made up mainly of refugees, deportees, or former slaves—is now referred to as 'diasporic' (Moghissi et al., 2009), and, with modern revolutions in communication and travel, these diasporic communities have developed transnational identities that transcend the specific geographic location of any single part of the community (Faist, 2000).

DISTRICT 9

This 2009 mega-hit tied together issues of diaspora and xenophobia in a metaphorical tale of alien settlements in modern-day South Africa.

THEORETICAL PERSPECTIVES ON RACE AND ETHNICITY

Table 3.1 Theoretical Perspectives	
Theory	**Main Points**
Structural Functionalism	• Ethnic identity provides social connectedness in an individualistic society. • Ethnocultural diversity provides a wide range of opinions, perspectives, and values that enrich society. • Ethnocultural conflict enforces boundaries, which give groups more cohesion and a sense of identity.
Conflict Theory	• Majority groups benefit from excluding and marginalizing minority groups. • Corporate leaders benefit by hiring minorities at low wages to secure shareholder profits. • Racial tension divides workers by setting up competition among them, diverting their anger from the exploitive capitalists.
Symbolic Interactionism	• Ethnic differentiation is constructed by a labelling process. • Racial slurs further undermine the inferior status of minority groups. • Racial labels and slurs can shape the way groups view themselves. • Constant awareness of race (racial socialization) in daily social interaction increases the likelihood of racial conflict.
Structural Theory	• Minorities that are more visible are streamed into the secondary labour market and rarely into the primary market. • Job markets sometimes exclude people on the grounds of race or ethnicity. • A general bias against hiring non-whites has made many visible minority immigrants become 'middlemen'.

Structural Functionalism

According to functionalists, even the inequality between racial or ethnic groups has a social purpose. As we noted, functionalists stress that social inequality provides incentives in the form of status and material rewards that prompt people to take on the most important social roles. For this reason, functionalists may see exclusion, prejudice, and discrimination as providing benefits for society as a whole. They point out the value of maintaining distinct ethnic identities in a pluralistic society such as Canada. Doing so helps to socially integrate people into their own distinct community.

Ethnic identity provides people with roots and social connectedness in an otherwise individualistic, fragmented society. As well, ethno-racial diversity benefits society as a whole. It allows for the discussion of a wider range of opinions, perspectives, and values, and for the development of a wider range of skills. Even social conflict has value (see, e.g., Coser, 1965). By drawing and enforcing boundaries, conflict intensifies people's sense of identity and belonging and gives groups more cohesion and a heightened sense of purpose.

Conflict Theory

Unlike functionalists, conflict theorists focus on how one group benefits more than another from differentiation, exclusion, and institutional racism. They explore, for instance, how economic competition results in the creation and preservation of racial stereotypes and institutionalized racism. Conflict theory proposes that majority groups seek to dominate minorities to reinforce their superiority, especially when they feel threatened by the minority, as was the case in British Columbia in the early twentieth century when the white majority saw Chinese and South Asian workers as a threat to their jobs and their way of life.

Feminist Theory

Some feminist theorists believe that giving ethnic minorities special rights ignores the rights of women and furthers female subordination and oppression (Okin, 1998). Arguing against multiculturalism, feminist theorists suggest that oppression occurs when certain minority groups—who are led by traditional values and come from traditionally oppressive cultures—are granted rights that are at odds with gender equality. With these rights, groups then have coercive and sometimes sexist authority over their members.

This form of 'strong multiculturalism' occurs when groups and not individuals are given enforceable rights against discrimination. Although the liberal state should support autonomy and equality, feminists believe there are times when the state should refrain from doing so (Okin, 1998). For instance, in 2005 Muslims living in Ontario proposed the application of *shariah* law—typically associated with the subordination of women—to settle certain familial disputes(Moghissi et al., 2009). This proposal was not passed, despite a government-commissioned report by former provincial Attorney General Marion Boyd that spoke favourably about some aspects of the proposal.

Most Canadian minorities are not given the right to exercise formal power over their members. In theory, Canada's form of multiculturalism rejects internal restrictions and permits only certain external protections (Adams, 2007). Through what Spinner-Halev (2001) terms 'integrative multiculturalism', ethnic minorities are granted non-threatening rights that enable them to maintain their culture (i.e., freedom of religion and the right to claim public funding for cultural festivals). At times, additional rights are granted, such as extra representation in political bodies and exemption from certain laws; multicultural theorists believe these special policies further facilitate integration into mainstream society (ibid). Despite such allowances, ethnic minorities are expected to integrate into Canadian society and abide by national laws (Adams, 2007).

Still, some feminists believe this lesser form of multiculturalism allows immigrant families to discriminate against their daughters, and liberal individual laws are useless when women are taught gender subordination at home (Okin, 1998). In contrast, others downplay the existence of extreme gender subordination, underlining that Canada takes in more educated immigrants who are more liberal-minded (Adams, 2007). Nonetheless, the feminist solution to the battle between the old and new world is the national enforcement of respect, and even self-respect, for women(Okin, 1998).

In theory, self-respect seems to be a plausible solution, but the liberal state cannot 'take upon itself the role of guardian for self-respect, since there are so many . . . ways to try to ensure self-respect' (Spinner-Halev, 2001).The state may be seen as the oppressor and resented if force is used to integrate and control minorities. Instead, theorists argue that the sole way to overturn generations of patriarchy is to allow groups to change from within (ibid). Many point to the natural process of education and interaction with the host culture (ibid.; Boyd, 2002). Observing the 1996 census, Boyd (2002) found that over the previous 10-year period more and more people identified themselves as Canadian. This trend may result from each subsequent generation retaining less of their culture.

Feminist scholars also indicate that certain groups of women, especially ethnic minorities, experience more discrimination than others. For instance, those who hold numerous minority statuses—for example, Aboriginal women living off the reserve or married to non-Natives (Green, 2001)—are likely to be isolated both from their own society and that of the mainstream. Like those of other ethnic minorities, certain Aboriginal practices discriminate against women and go against the Canadian Constitution. Often, these practices are legitimized through the evocation of tradition—a powerful method of resisting colonialism (ibid.), but also a source of danger to women's rights.

Symbolic Interactionism

Symbolic interactionists focus on microsociological aspects of race and discrimination, such as the ways people construct ethnic differences and racial labels to subordinate minority groups.

Many slang terms for race are used, sometimes casually, sometimes with cruel intent. Not only do such terms usually imply condescension intended to degrade, they also can create a self-fulfilling prophecy. If people come to believe slurs against their ethnic or national group—thinking themselves as actually stupid, lazy, cheap, underhanded, and so forth—they may behave according to the negative labels, and even come to hate themselves and reject their own group.

Interactionists also point to *racial socialization* as another factor that contributes to continuing racial conflicts in society (McKown and Strambler, 2009). Racial socialization is a process of social interaction that exposes people to the beliefs, values, cultural history, language, and social and economic realities of their own and other people's racial or ethnic identities (Scottham and Smalls, 2009). In other words, it is the process of learning 'what it means' socially and culturally to be a Jew, a Chinese person, a Ukrainian, and so on.

As already noted, 'race' is a social construct; we imagine it and then enact it. Likewise, the supposed attributes of race—for example, racial intelligence or virtue or instinct—also are socially constructed. For similar reasons, Ezeonu (2006) argues that even racial violence is socially constructed. He notes that public concern about crime and criminal victimization may be shaped by the operation of what Joel Best (1989) calls the 'social problem marketplace'. In the competition over how a social problem is defined, people whose definitions win public support or attract the sympathy of policy bureaucrats are most able to influence the making of social policies to control the problem.

The goal of claims-making is to influence social policies in particular ways. Claims-makers may call for new laws, new programs, or particular forms of government intervention in dealing with particular problems, and sometimes policy-makers respond to typifications used in making claims about particular policies. In other words, social policies often are products of competing claims-making among interest groups about how particular social problems are conceived, and about how to deal with such problems (Burns, 2002).

A constant awareness of race (or ethnicity) in daily social interaction increases the likelihood of racial conflict, which, in turn, promotes society's focus on race and racism (Lalonde et al., 2008). Box 3.2 raises questions about the ways race and racism may have shaped events in New Orleans following Hurricane Katrina and media depiction of those events.

Structural Theory

Structural theory particularly helps us understand the experiences of racial and ethnic minorities in economic life. People who are most similar—racially, culturally, and educationally—to members of the host society will enjoy the easiest, most rapid assimilation into the labour market. They will be able to compete more successfully for the better jobs, especially during economic growth. In recessionary times, everyone's assimilation will be slower and more conflictual. People's experiences will usually reflect the characteristics of the economy more than anything they do or believe (Kashefi, 2004).

The sorting of people into jobs in Canada usually begins in schools. Through the deliberate application of subtle and complex procedures like tracking and grade weighting, some students are encouraged while others are discouraged, reducing the opportunities of the latter group following high school graduation. On entering the workforce, people of 'different kinds' are streamed into some types of jobs and away from others. For example, far

PERSONAL STORIES

Box 3.2 Post-Katrina Racial Crimes in New Orleans

Television news reports are casting new light on the violence that flourished in New Orleans in the anarchic days after Hurricane Katrina in 2005.

The reports—broadcast Thursday by WTAE TV in Pittsburgh and WDSU in New Orleans—focus on two unsolved crimes: the near-fatal shooting of Donnell Herrington, who was allegedly attacked by a group of white vigilantes in the Algiers Point neighbourhood, and the murder of Henry Glover, whose charred remains were discovered on a Mississippi River levee. Both victims are African American.

At the centre of the news reports is a disturbing and grisly amateur video shot by a pair of private investigators in September 2005 and obtained recently by WTAE journalist Jim Parsons. (Full disclosure: This reporter was interviewed for the WTAE and WDSU stories.)

The private detectives, Mike Orsini and Istvan Balogh, are Pennsylvanians who travelled to New Orleans to volunteer in the wake of the storm. Orsini is a former police officer, while Balogh is an ex-corrections officer. They spent nearly two weeks camped out in Algiers Point, a middle class, largely white enclave nestled on the west bank of the Mississippi River.

On the video, a former Algiers Point resident talks calmly about shooting people. That man, Paul Gleeson, claimed that he and his fellow gunmen shot 38 people and said that the victims were looters. Asked if any of the shooting victims died, Gleeson replied, 'Who cares? I don't (expletive) know. Who cares? What does it (expletive) matter?'

The Algiers Point shootings, which have prompted an intensifying civil rights probe by the Federal Bureau of Investigation, were exposed late last year in stories published by *The Nation* and ProPublica. While the neighbourhood gunmen say that they were simply defending the community against thieves, other witnesses say that the group targeted black men and spewed racial epithets.

Orsini and Balogh say that they saw as many as five corpses lying around the neighbourhood, which did not flood and suffered only minor wind damage. Orsini told WTAE, 'Nobody took care of these bodies, and these were all individuals who had been shot.' The men videotaped one of the corpses, which was lying beneath a sheet of corrugated metal.

Orsini and Balogh have turned over their video over to the FBI.

In an off-camera interview with WTAE, Gleeson's ex-wife, Nicole Geraci, said that she didn't believe Gleeson was capable of murder. Just how credible Gleeson's claims are may be difficult to determine; Gleeson, an Irish citizen, was deported several years ago.

Another Algiers Point local, Cathy Carmack, told WTAE that the Algiers Point gunmen instructed her not to talk about the violence: 'They told me to keep my (expletive) mouth shut and I'd be afraid. I mean, I don't want them coming after me.'

Source: Abridged and adapted from Thompson (2009).

more women and visible minorities are streamed into the secondary labour market, and far more white men into the primary labour market, than could have occurred by chance. However, even within these markets, there are important differences among jobs. For example, although teachers and doctors both are in the primary labour market, few teachers feel they have the sort of benefits and opportunities that doctors do. Therefore, it is of interest to sociologists to know according to what criteria people become teachers or doctors.

Some job markets exclude or discourage people because of race, ethnicity, or gender, though this is becoming less common. One fact remains, however: immigration tends to level the playing field, whatever the immigrant's race or ethnicity, credentials, or background experience. Whatever their origins, new immigrants routinely hold similar positions in the labour market, and these are usually the lowest entrance statuses. In big cities, especially,

Table 3.2   Median Earnings, in 2005 Constant Dollars, of Male and Female Recent Immigrant Earners and Canadian-Born Earners Aged 25 to 54, with or without a University Degree, Canada, 1980 to 2005

	Recent immigrant earners[1]				Canadian-born earners[1]				Recent immigrant to Canadian-born earnings ratio			
	With a university degree		With no university degree		With a university degree		With no university degree		With a university degree		With no university degree	
	Males	Females	Males	Females	Males	Females	Males	Females	Males	Females	Males	Females
Year	2005 constant dollars								Ratio			
1980	48,541	24,317	36,467	18,548	63,040	41,241	43,641	21,463	0.77	0.59	0.84	0.86
1990	38,351	25,959	27,301	17,931	61,332	41,245	40,757	23,267	0.63	0.63	0.67	0.77
2000	35,816	22,511	25,951	16,794	61,505	43,637	39,902	25,622	0.58	0.52	0.65	0.66
2005	30,332	18,969	24,470	14,233	62,566	44,545	40,235	25,590	0.48	0.43	0.61	0.56

1. The numbers refer to all earners, whether or not they worked on a full-time basis for a full year. Individuals with self-employment income are included while those living in institutions are excluded.

Source: Adapted from Statistics Canada, censuses of population, 1981, 1991, 2001, and 2006. Table 8 from Earnings and Incomes of Canadians Over the Past Quarter Century. Accessed June 30, 2009 at: www12.statcan.ca/english/censuso6/analysis/income/pdf/97-563-XIE2006001.pdf

immigrants with a variety of advanced degrees—such as doctors, engineers, social workers, and nurses—can be found driving taxis or providing low-paid personal services. Even when they earn good wages, recent immigrants earn relatively less than native-born Canadians with equivalent education and experience (Reitz, 2001). This would account for the marked income differences shown in Table 3.2.

Many immigrants respond by starting their own businesses. Research on middleman minorities finds the following typical pattern: a culturally or racially distinct group immigrates and suffers discrimination (Godwyn, 2009). Members of the group come to see themselves as 'strangers' in the country and, to protect themselves, settle in the larger towns and cities. There, they become self-employed as wholesalers, small merchants (e.g., shopkeepers), or even professionals. As a result, they come into competition with local capitalists of the dominant ethnic group. Their economic and social survival depends on thrift, a high degree of education and organization, and the use of family and community ties in business. By these means, the group achieves a middle-class standard of living (Yamamoto, 2009).

RACISM AND PREJUDICE: SOCIAL PROBLEMS

Defining and Measuring Racial Prejudice

PREJUDICE A hostile or aversive attitude towards a person who belongs to a particular group, simply because of that person's membership in the group.

Psychologist Gordon Allport (1954: 7) defined **prejudice** as 'an aversive or hostile attitude toward a person who belongs to a group, simply because he belongs to that group, and is therefore presumed to have the objectionable qualities ascribed to the group.'

Racial discrimination has been characterized by the United Nations Office of the High Commissioner for Human Rights as 'any distinction, exclusion, restriction, or preference based on race, colour, descent, or national or ethnic origin which has the purpose or effect of nullifying or impairing the recognition, enjoyment or exercise, on an equal footing, of human rights and fundamental freedoms in the political, economic, social, cultural or any other field of public life' (Office for the High Commissioner for Human Rights, 1969).

Racism appears in society at multiple levels. Most broadly, **institutional (structural) racism** is any systemic bias embedded in an existing social structure, policy, or process that deprives some groups of equal access to goods, services, and rights because of their ethnic or racial membership (Kent, 2009). Examples of institutional racism include rental housing markets that try to keep 'undesirable' ethnic groups out of certain communities, and banks and insurance companies that deny loans to people in certain neighbourhoods based on crude economic (and racially tinged) criteria, a practice known as 'redlining' (Morris, 2008).

These actions result in unequal educational opportunities for some minority groups and an unequal distribution of material wealth in society by ethnic status. Eventually, this

RACIAL DISCRIMINATION 'Any distinction, exclusion, restriction, or preference based on race, colour, descent, or national or ethnic origin that has the purpose or effect of nullifying or impairing the recognition, enjoyment of exercise . . . of human rights and fundamental freedoms' (Office of the High Commissioner for Human Rights, 1969).

INSTITUTIONAL (STRUCTURAL) RACISM Any form of racism that occurs specifically from within an institution, such as public government bodies and private business corporations. This form of racism is considered to be 'built into' these prominent structures.

The Canadian Press/Jeff McIntosh

An example of individual racism can be found in the actions of an Aryan Guard supporter, who salutes at a White Pride rally as he yells at anti-racism supporters in Calgary, 21 March 2009.

translates into an under-representation of visible minorities in political offices, corporate boardrooms, and other positions of power. Policies such as employment equity seek to offset the effects of institutional racism on vulnerable groups (Thompson, 2008).

Individual racism is the classic form of prejudice, in which a person makes groundless assumptions about the motives and abilities of another based on a stereotypical understanding of the person's racial or ethnic group characteristics. Its epitome is the dangerous and unrepentant bigot—the Ku Klux Klan member, say, or the neo-Nazi. However, it would be wrong (and dangerous) to suppose that the practice of racism is limited to these extremist groups. As we shall see, research has found that subtle expressions of racism persist among a majority of people (e.g., Gaertner and Dovidio, 2000; Reitz and Breton, 1999; Devine and Elliot, 1995).

Perhaps the most destructive form of racism is **internalized racism**, where members of an ethnic or racial group come to believe the stereotypes that others have imposed on them (Cort et al., 2009). This tragic consequence of institutional and individual racism leads people to devalue their own worth, compromise their life goals, and passively accept the racial barriers that carry on the cycle of oppression and inequality (Bryant, 2009).

Unfortunately, no academic consensus exists on the best method for measuring people's levels of racial and ethnic bias. Asking people direct questions about the prejudices they hold against a particular ethnic or cultural group is unlikely to yield accurate results (Cea D'Ancona, 2009). People have a hard time admitting their biases to themselves, let alone to others, and may feel pressured to respond in a socially approved (i.e., non-prejudicial) way. Thus, social scientists often use indirect measures instead.

One way to do this is to measure the **social distance** between ethnic groups, which E.S. Bogardus did in 1928. By asking respondents whether they would accept certain ethnic groups in a variety of proximities such as kinship, club membership, or as neighbours, Bogardus found that people feel varying comfort levels when interacting with members of other cultures under different conditions. Generally, people are more willing to have close (e.g., kinship) relations with people they judge to be culturally and racially similar to themselves, though they may be willing to have only distant relations—if any at all—with people they view as different.

However, this distance preference is not symmetrical: people are more likely to accept their daughter marrying a distant 'higher status' group member than an equally distant 'lower status' group member. Finally, distance preferences are cumulative: groups a respondent would accept as close relations would also be accepted as workmates, friends, and neighbours. Groups a respondent would reject as citizens or even visitors would surely be rejected as workmates, friends, or neighbours (Zhang and Van Hook, 2009).

Through this scale, sociologists have learned that people who place other groups at a distance from themselves often hold prejudices about those other groups. They also sometimes act on those prejudices and practise discrimination at work and in the wider community. This creates hardship for members of minority groups so named, not only because they are few but because they are relatively powerless.

Other measures of racial prejudice are based on social psychological principles. By the 1980s, with the growing rejection of overt discrimination, many thought racist attitudes were

INDIVIDUAL RACISM
'Classic' form of prejudice in which a person makes unfounded assumptions about the motives and abilities of another based on a stereotypical understanding of the person's racial or ethnic group characteristics.

INTERNALIZED RACISM
When members of an ethnic or racial group accept and sometimes behave according to imposed stereotypes.

SOCIAL DISTANCE
Feelings of aloofness and inapproachability often felt between members of different social strata or of different ethnic or 'racial' origins.

declining. To test this assumption, the Modern Racism Scale (MRS) was designed as another way of indirectly tapping into respondents' prejudices about various ethnic groups (McConahay, 1981, 1986). The MRS shows that although adherence to explicitly racist notions (such as support for segregation or slavery) is considered socially unacceptable by almost everyone, racial ambivalence and prejudice persist in more subtle forms.

For example, so-called **aversive racists** sympathize with the victims of past injustice; support public policies that, in principle, promote racial equality and reduce the harm of racism; identify more generally with a liberal political agenda; and view themselves as non-prejudiced and non-discriminatory. However, they still harbour negative feelings about the members of other races: 'The negative affect that aversive racists have for blacks is not hostility or hate. Instead, this negativity involves discomfort, uneasiness, disgust, and sometimes fear, which motivate avoidance rather than intentionally destructive behaviours' (Gaertner and Dovidio, 2000: 289–90).

Researchers have developed the Implicit Association Test (IAT) as a cognitive measure of racial bias (Greenwald et al., 1998). In this procedure, two types of test stimuli are displayed in rapid succession on a computer screen—photographs of the faces of blacks and whites posed with neutral facial expressions, and positive and negative words, such as 'peace' and 'happy' or 'nasty' and 'failure'. Subjects are asked to quickly group each stimulus object into one of two headings, which are either consistent (i.e., 'black faces/negative words' and 'white faces/positive words') or inconsistent (i.e., 'black faces/positive words' and 'white faces/negative words') with popular racial stereotypes.

A fast response is interpreted as a sign of a stronger mental association between the stimulus object and the category heading, and therefore an implicit cognitive bias. That is, according to the test, racial prejudice may be signalled by a faster response time in assigning a photograph of a black person to the 'black faces/negative words' category than to the 'black faces/positive words' category. Conversely, it may show a faster response time in assigning a negative word to the 'black faces/negative words' category than to the 'white faces/negative words' category.

Although the IAT quickly became popular for its ease of administration, it also attracted much criticism from other academic circles (e.g., Arkes and Tetlock, 2004; Rothermund and Wentura, 2004; Ottaway et al., 2001).

Racialization

Racism is the everyday outcome of a historic process called **racialization**, the tendency in a community to introduce racial distinctions into situations that can be understood and managed without such distinctions (Abu-Laban and Bakan, 2008). Thus, race becomes a substitute for distinctions that otherwise would be based on class, education, age, or job experience, for example. In this way, race sometimes becomes the basis for decisions about hiring, buying, renting, befriending, and respecting others. Such changes of practice towards racialization can happen easily unless people take pains to avoid them.

In the police and judicial systems, racial profiling—a tendency to expect and interpret the acts of individuals differently based on their race—is all too common. For example, police

AVERSIVE RACISTS
Those who sympathize with the victims of past injustice and support public policies that promote racial equality but who, nonetheless, hold prejudicial views towards other races.

RACIALIZATION
The tendency in a community to introduce racial distinctions into situations that can be understood and managed without such distinctions, in other words, the way social institutions impose racial identities on minorities.

may pull over cars driven by young black or Aboriginal men but not by young white men in the expectation of finding alcohol, drugs, weapons, or other grounds for arrest there (Parmar, 2007).

SOCIAL CONSEQUENCES OF RACE AND ETHNICITY

Gender

The interaction of gender and racism leads to unique problems for women of some minority groups. Women continue to be given a lesser status within almost all immigrant groups, with a higher degree of oppression in certain groups. This oppressiveness creates further conflict when new immigrants find their notions of proper gender relations clashing with those generally accepted in North America (Hong, 2008).

The combination of a racial identity and a 'subordinate' gender means many immigrant women have to cope with society's clear racism, alongside the sometimes hidden sexism of a patriarchal social structure.

Work and Unemployment

As we have already noted, discrimination in the workplace may be directed along racial and ethnic lines. Aboriginal people, members of visible minority groups, and recent immigrants to Canada all experience lower employment and pay rates in almost every region of Canada. Differences in income between various immigrant and ethnic minorities also result from differences in human capital, such as education, experience, credentials, and scarce expertise (Rodlandt, 1996).

For some time after immigrating, visible minorities continue to fall behind in employment and income levels despite their high educational attainment when compared to non-racialized groups; foreign-born visible minorities experience even greater disadvantages (Picot et al., 2007). Those with a university degree are often forced into jobs that are below their credentials. In a longitudinal survey, Statistics Canada (2003) found that six out of 10 immigrants to Canada did not work in their original field of work after their arrival, and this circumstance is exacerbated during difficult economic times. In brief, highly trained immigrant visible minorities are the last hired and the first fired, and many recent immigrants find that their educational and work credentials are not recognized in the Canadian employment system.

Race continues to play a role in people's work experiences. In a set of field experiments, Frances Henry and Effie Ginzberg (1985; Henry, 1999) graphically showed how this occurs in Toronto. In one study, two equally qualified applicants, one black and the other white, applied for the same advertised jobs. With the results, Henry and Ginzberg created an Index of Discrimination and found that 'whites have three job prospects for every one that blacks have' (1985: 308).

This study and others like it (e.g., Beck et al., 2002; Austin and Este, 2001) prove that racial discrimination is common, not a result of the behaviour of a few bigoted employers. Also, even after members of minority groups find suitable employment, they sometimes are faced with discrimination when competing for promotions. Compared to non-visible minorities, members of visible racial groups and Aboriginal people with a university degree are less likely to enter managerial or professional positions. For those who do, more than half are self-employed, compared to only one-third in non-minority groups.

Poverty and Wealth

Although most of the people who live in poverty in Canada and the United States are white, higher *proportions* of minority groups are impoverished. Immigrants, visible minorities, and Aboriginal people are over-represented at the bottom of the income scale, while other Canadian-born non-racialized groups are under-represented (Gee and Prus, 2000; Hou and Balakrishnan, 1996). In contrast, among the top 20 per cent of income earners, Aboriginal people and visible minorities are under-represented while non-visible (ethnic) minorities are over-represented.

Studies have shown that Aboriginals living off-reserve are one of the least residentially concentrated groups and thus, with less social capital, endure greater economic difficulties compared to residentially concentrated groups, such as the Chinese and Jewish populations in Canada (Adams, 2007: 55). In recent years, however, Native Canadians have made economic progress. According to a 2008 Statistics Canada report, the employment rate of Natives between 25 and 45 years old living off-reserve was 70 per cent, about 12 per cent lower than that of non-Aboriginals (Statistics Canada, 2008).

Much of the disparity between Aboriginals and the general population stems from the historical injustices they suffered. One of the largest violations was residential schools, which removed young people from their cultural roots and where many Aboriginals endured physical and sexual abuse. In 2008, Prime Minister Stephen Harper apologized for the forced assimilation that took place in residential schools. In a momentous speech, Harper said, 'Today, we recognize that this policy of assimilation was wrong, has caused great harm, and has no place in our country' (Fenlon, 2008). With the apology, the government created a $4 billion compensation and healing package.

Social exclusion can take the form of geographic segregation, and although less advanced than in the US, some racial segregation is evident in Canada. In 1981, only three visible minority neighbourhoods—defined as census tracts in which at least 30 per cent of the population belongs to a single visible minority group—were identified. However, a 2001 Statistics Canada report showed this number had risen to 254. These communities are more likely than average to feature low household incomes and high rates of unemployment. An 'isolation index', which measures the extent to which minority group members meet only one another within their neighbourhoods, shows that segregation and concentration of ethnic minorities has increased (Hou and Picot, 2004). Many are concerned that, without policy interventions, the segregation will continue to rise to a dangerous level. Box 3.3 indicates how these ethnic and racial factors influence the allocation of housing in a region near Toronto.

RABBIT-PROOF FENCE

This critically acclaimed 2002 Australian film brought the story of the forced residential schooling of First Nations people to a mass audience.

POLICY DEBATES

Box 3.3 Race May Shorten Housing Wait

Should you have to wait longer for social housing because you're not Italian or Muslim? On the other hand, how would you feel if you found yourself slotted into a home where you didn't fit in?

With more than 6,000 people on the waiting list for social housing in York Region, two local housing providers have asked to be able to restrict who is eligible for their subsidized units.

It's an issue that goes to the heart of Canada's multicultural ethos, Richmond Hill Regional Councillor Brenda Hogg said. 'It would prolong the time other people must wait. . . . You would be jumping the queue. It sends a message to the public we are going to allow specific groups to self-impose segregation', she said.

'That's not the Canada I'm part of', the former community services and housing committee chairperson said.

But there is a very different perspective at Vaughan's Friuli Terrace, where 145 seniors live in supportive housing. 'We can't service the group we were meant to service', director of social services Elizabeth Anthony said.

Friuli Terrace was built in 1989 for Italian seniors and 78 of its units are subsidized, with rent geared to income.

The province once encouraged housing providers to serve ethnic and religious communities, but that changed with the passing of the Social Housing Reform Act in 2000. Responsibility was downloaded to municipalities and while private homes can do what they want, York Region administers a central list of subsidized units, prioritized chronologically.

Italian is the lingua franca at Friuli Terrace and everything from meals to entertainment is geared towards that.

'We've always encouraged multiculturalism. We're not like the Americans with their "melting pot",' Ms Anthony said.

Slots at Friuli Terrace open relatively rarely but when they do it is Ms Anthony's job to see who is next on the region's list.

Housing someone who is not Italian and who has requested to be somewhere else both dilutes the flavour of the building and makes it hard for that tenant to fit in, Ms Anthony said. 'It's not just that we don't want them. They also don't want to be here.' . . .

She would like to see a return to the old system where people are properly slotted rather than having to take the first person that comes up, regardless of where or what it is.

The same situation can be found at Richmond Hill's Jubilee Gardens, a 100-townhome neighbourhood in which three-quarters of the units are subsidized. It was built to meet the needs of the South Asian Ismaili community and now its owners would like to ensure subsidized units go to Shia Imami Ismaili Muslims.

A report by the Ontario Human Rights Commission, that should include comments on social housing, is expected soon, Ms Hogg said. In the meantime she would like to see public money continue to go to members of the public most in need, regardless of their ethnicity.

Ms Anthony countered that her tenants are all taxpayers too.

Regional staff recommended approving the mandates with the understanding the region can terminate the agreements at any time and that the region is indemnified from any costs resulting from litigation. The region would not be protected from costs of other remedies resulting from a decision by the Human Rights Commission, however.

Even more worrisome, staff acknowledged someone denied housing because of their ethnicity could make a court challenge under the Canadian Charter of Rights and Freedoms. . . .

Source: **Adapted and abridged from Fleischer (2009).**

Crime and Violence

As we will see in a later chapter, blacks and Aboriginal people are over-represented in the North American criminal justice system, both as perpetrators and as victims. Explanations of these statistics include unemployment, poverty, and substance abuse. There also is evidence of discrimination at the bail and sentencing stages (Roberts and Doob, 1997). Further, evidence suggests that law enforcement officers may racialize and stereotype ethnic minorities, especially when dealing with street gangs (Symons, 1999).

Although Aboriginal adults make up only 2 per cent of the Canadian population, they represented 15 per cent of all the people sentenced to provincial custody and 17 per cent of those sent to federal penitentiaries in 1997–8 (Reed and Roberts, 1999; see also Frideres and Robertson, 1994). Comparably, in the United States, although blacks account for only 13 per cent of the population, they represent 30 per cent of those people arrested and roughly half of those imprisoned. In short, disadvantage and poverty increase the likelihood of law-breaking by racial and ethnic minorities, while prejudice and discrimination increase the likelihood of arrest, conviction, and imprisonment (Gabbindon, 2010).

HEALTH CONSEQUENCES OF RACE AND ETHNICITY

Effects of Disadvantage

Disadvantaged groups lead different lives from the rest of the population. In Canada, though regional inequalities in health status are lessening, the life expectancy of Aboriginal Canadians is still significantly shorter than that of other groups (D'Arcy, 1998; see also Waldram et al., 1996; Rodney and Copeland, 2009). Similarly, in the US, of all racial groups, American blacks live the fewest years and they live a higher proportion of those years with chronic health problems (Hayward and Heron, 1999).

Studies of race and ethnicity as determinants of health have led to three different types of explanations: biological explanations based on genetic differences; cultural explanations that link differences in disease prevalence to cultural factors (such as diet); and socio-economic explanations that focus on the association between poor health, minority status, and economic disadvantage (Spencer, 1996). However, the link between poor health, material disadvantage and socio-economic status is clear (Farmer and Ferraro, 1999; Fenton et al., 1995). Racial and ethnic differences in physical and mental health shrink significantly when we control for education and other factors related to income (Williams et al., 1997).

Effects of Immigration

Though institutional racism creates economic hardships with bad health outcomes, Canadian research has found that neither the health status of immigrants nor their use of health services differs much from those of the Canadian-born population (Laroche, 2000).

However, immigration can have harmful health effects besides those due to poverty and discrimination. In fact, on arrival, new immigrants typically have better health than the host population, largely due to strict immigration selection criteria. Yet within a generation or two, this health advantage disappears for many ethnic minorities, and some groups even experience worse health status than the native-born.

As noted earlier, immigrants often find employment in lower-end and lower-paying jobs; there they are often exposed to higher-than-average health risks. Second, immigrants often experience a lack of access to health-care information and services, sometimes hesitating to use health services because of a low level of English- or French-language literacy.

Problems with their personal lives may also have health consequences. For example, 80 per cent of refugees to Quebec from Africa and Latin America had experienced or were experiencing separations (averaging three years) from their partners or children (Moreau et al., 1999). Such separations, often associated with traumatic events, can cause emotional distress and hinder the process of adapting to a new country.

In addition, immigrants may suffer from loneliness, boredom, and post-migration anxieties about discrimination. People who have been displaced by war are even worse off than people who are impoverished, for they suffer over and above their material disadvantage. The trauma of displacement often results in fear, disorientation, and distrust—conditions that are not easily relieved (Segura Escobar, 2000).

Access to Health Care

Research shows that, on the whole, Canadian immigrants, visible minorities, and Aboriginal populations are able to access adequate general care to meet their overall health needs (e.g., Quan et al., 2006; Wardman et al., 2005; Wu et al., 2005; Wen et al., 1996).

However, these same studies also find evidence of systemic barriers in accessing specialized health-care services, such as surgery, emergency room visits, and dental care. Obstacles include a lack of knowledge about where to find suitable help, language barriers between medical staff and patients, concerns about meeting institutional racial discrimination, and, for rural Aboriginal communities, a shortage of professionals and facilities. Researchers have called on governments and health-care practitioners to address these systemic barriers, for example, by ensuring availability of language interpreters (Tang, 1999).

Different cultures also have different views about health and illness. As a result, every culture provides its members with a culturally relevant diagnosis or cause and a framework for appropriate intervention. Ethnic groups living in a Western culture often find that non-Western health-care alternatives are scarce. So, when forced to seek help from the only available caregiver—the modern hospital—they are hesitant and worry that it will worsen the illness.

The Health Effects of Racism

Both racial discrimination and socio-economic discrimination contribute to the poor health of minorities. Some of the effects are obvious: discrimination, by increasing stress, increases the likelihood of psychiatric symptoms and unhealthy addictions, such as cigarette-smoking (Landrine and Klonoff, 1996).

To these, one must add the stress-related health effects of discrimination itself (Krieger et al., 1993). The experiences of racial discrimination and resulting family stress also reduce the well-being of minority people. Other factors, such as alienation, poverty, inequality at work, and worries about unemployment, all contribute to the poor health of minority people. Shelly Harrell (2000: 45–6) has identified six sources of racism-related stress:

- acute, intense, but relatively rare 'racism-related life events', such as police harassment or discrimination in the workplace;
- 'vicarious racism experiences', including the transmission of specific incidents of prejudice and discrimination experienced by family and friends, or through the news media;
- 'daily racism micro-stressors', which are subtle and frequent reminders of one's subordinate status in society, such as being ignored or overly scrutinized by sales staff;
- 'chronic contextual stress', which arises from the need to adapt to the broad racial and ethnic inequalities in social/political/economic structure;
- 'collective experiences', which reflect 'the idea that cultural-symbolic and sociopolitical manifestations of racism can be observed and felt by individuals' and which include the 'economic conditions of members of one's racial/ethnic group, the lack of political representation, or stereotypic portrayals in the media'; and
- 'transgenerational transmission', or the historical context in which modern racial and ethnic discrimination has been bred and preserved, such as the experiences of current refugees.

The health outcomes of racism-related stress can be severe. Several researchers have found, for instance, the resentment and distrust bred by racial victimization can raise a person's blood pressure (Franklin, 1998). Stress can also erode the mental health status, adversely affect a person's sense of self-worth, lead to substance abuse, and other chronic physical health problems (Rollock and Gordon, 2000; Malin, 2000).

CLAIMS-MAKING IN STUDIES OF RACE AND ETHNICITY

Constructionist views of ethnicity and race go back some time in sociological and political science literature. In particular, political sociology has long had an interest in understanding ethnic identities, sometimes with the goal of understanding where and why ethno-nationalist conflicts erupt.

In this field, views of ethnicity have varied from 'primordialist' positions that hold that ethnicity is an immutable, tangible quality to 'instrumentalist' positions that acknowledge the important role played by ethnic elites in selectively producing an ethnic history with the goal of uniting the nation. More nuanced constructivist positions hold that ethnopolitics are both real and imagined (Robertson, 1997).

The construction of race as tied to class, national origin, culture, and language, some argue, may amount to a type of 'ethnoracism' that persists in a climate of 'colourblind' racism (Aranda and Rebollo-Gil, 2004).

Constructionist views on race have had substantial impact in sociology. Indeed, this chapter has presented evidence on the socially constructed nature of race. However, it is easy to lose sight of this notion and uncritically accept race as an uncomplicated idea. This is especially true in the case of survey-based research, but it can also occur in qualitative work

(Morris, 2008). Thus, the constructionist viewpoint reminds us of the complexity of race as a concept, and a care on the part of researchers to avoid unwittingly reproducing racial inequalities in their research of it.

GOVERNMENTAL AND ORGANIZATIONAL SOLUTIONS TO PREJUDICE AND RACISM

The Employment Equity Act, passed in 1986, applies to the federal public service, Crown corporations and agencies, and private companies employing 100 employees or more, and it is intended to ensure the proportion of visible minorities, Aboriginal people, women, and people with disabilities hired in the workplace reflects the proportion of these groups who are applying for work. To ensure that hiring practices are equitable, employers are obliged to file annual reports on their employees to the federal government. Data from these reports are then made public (Lamarche et al., 2006).

As well, employers are obliged to identify and to make an effort to remove the barriers facing members of under-represented groups by planning initiatives to increase their representation. Employment equity is intended to tackle what many sociologists believe to be the cause of racial and ethnic inequality, that is, structural barriers erected by the dominant majority to support their advantage.

The Canadian Multiculturalism Act of 1988 required all federal institutions and employers to act in accordance with the country's stated multicultural policy when making their economic, social, cultural, and political policies. Although this process is not flawless, UNESCO (the United Nations Educational, Scientific and Cultural Organization) has cited Canada's approach to multiculturalism as the ideal model to be followed by other countries.

Canada's Charter of Rights and Freedoms (s. 15[1]) declares that 'Every individual is equal before and under the law and has the right to the equal protection and equal benefit of the law without discrimination and, in particular, without discrimination based on race, national or ethnic origin, colour, religion, sex, age or mental or physical disability.' In addition, the Criminal Code provides for strict enforcement against racist acts known as 'hate crimes'. However, to be effective, these commitments must be supported by sustained efforts to protect the rights of all ethnic groups.

CHAPTER SUMMARY

People often try to justify racist beliefs and behaviour by repeating misinformed views about a minority group's physical, psychological, and cultural inferiority. These views often rest on the flawed belief that 'racial groups' bear similar genetic or inherent characteristics.

However, research has shown us increasingly that the physical traits by which people are grouped into racial categories are not at all intrinsic; they reflect a particular way of dividing up people that depends on time and place. Ethnic groups, similarly, have common cultural traits and believe they are distinct. In different ways, both racial and ethnic groups are 'imagined communities'.

As we have seen, 'prejudice' refers to biased beliefs about individuals based on their presumed membership in a particular racial or ethnic group. Prejudice always starts with stereotyping. Some argue that prejudice is learned through socialization, while others highlight its economic benefits. Sometimes it is a strategy practised by a dominant group to preserve its dominance.

We are a long way from achieving the society Durkheim imagined a century ago, built on organic solidarity and a value for diversity. Today Canada needs immigrants more than ever—to make up for declining fertility, provide tomorrow's workers and taxpayers, link us to the rest of the world, and provide us with innovations. This means that we are likely to keep grappling with issues of racial and ethnic inequality, and with the topic of immigration. It is in Canada's national interest to solve these issues of inequality quickly and fairly.

QUESTIONS FOR CRITICAL THOUGHT

1. Which of the various consequences of racialization—health, social, economic, or other—do you find the most unacceptable or harmful? Why is that type of consequence more harmful than others?

2. Some African Americans have said that US President Barack Obama is 'not black enough'. What does this say about the social construction of race? What does it mean to be 'black enough'? White enough? South Asian enough?

3. Do you believe that racism has increased or decreased over the past century? How should sociologists measure the phenomenon of racism? For example, would increasing numbers of Caribbean Canadians filling corporate executive positions indicate a decrease in the racism that occurs here?

4. In what ways have rising urban crime rates been racialized? Do you feel that looking at the race of individual criminals provides fruitful understanding of the larger social problem?

5. Compare the treatment of Native peoples by the government of Canada with the treatment of blacks in South Africa during apartheid. What similarities do you see? How did both situations contribute to the social construction of the group that lacked agency and power?

6. Which form of multiculturalism—traditional or modern—do you think contributes more to the functioning of Canadian society? If you were a legislator, how would you approach the issue of multiculturalism within Canadian law?

RECOMMENDED READINGS

Anderson, Benedict. 1983. *Imagined Communities: Reflections on the Origin and Spread of Nationalism*. London: Verso. This classic work discusses the spread of nationalism as a result of European colonialism in Latin America and Asia. Anderson's work marked the beginning of a new socio-logical subject. A key issue examined is what social factors make people nationalistic, willing to risk everything in the name of their nations.

Gracia, Jorge J.E., ed. 2007. *Race or Ethnicity? On Black and Latino Identity*. Ithaca, NY: Cornell University Press. This collection of essays explores the relation between race and ethnicity and their connection to social identity, as well as issues such as racism, assimilation, exploitation, justice, law, and public policy.

Henry, Frances, and Carol Tator. 2005. *The Colour of Democracy: Racism in Canadian Society*, 3rd edn. Toronto: Thomson Nelson. This critique of racism in Canadian policies and institutions examines the contradictions of multiculturalism and democratic racism in contemporary Canadian society.

Loury, Glenn C. 2002. *The Anatomy of Racial Inequality*. Cambridge, MA: Harvard University Press. This book looks at the origins, consequences, and implications of the state of black society in North America. Writing from the viewpoint of a political economist, he highlights the connection of social underdevelopment of blacks to stigmatizing, racial thinking.

Murji, Karim, and John Solomos. 2005. *Racialization: Studies in Theory and Practice*. Oxford: Oxford University Press. Murji and Solomos present a thorough analysis of how racialization came to be within sociological discourse, and how theorists view the concept today.

Nelson, Camille A., and Charmaine A. Nelson. 2004. *Racism, eh? A Critical Interdisciplinary Anthology of Race and Racism in Canada Today*. Concord, ON: Captus Press. This book addresses issues of race and racism in contemporary Canada, focusing more specifically on race and nationality in this extremely diverse country. It was written in response to a lack of comprehensive knowledge on this subject within Canada.

Porter, John. 1965. *The Vertical Mosaic: An Analysis of Social Class and Power in Canada*. Toronto: University of Toronto Press. This is the first Canadian study of race and ethnicity in Canada, and remains highly influential. It asks how and why ethnicity is related to a group's position in the economic structure, and examines the role of education in fostering social mobility in society. Porter's study set the stage for future studies of race and ethnicity in Canada.

Satzewich, Vic, and Nikolaos Liodakis. 2007. *'Race' and Ethnicity in Canada: A Critical Introduction*. Toronto: Oxford University Press. This book is part of a series of works on important sociological topics with a specific emphasis on Canadian issues. It is an excellent and thorough introduction to concepts such as immigration, Aboriginal/non-Aboriginal relations, French–English relations, notions of racial and ethnic identity, sociological explanations for racism, and other race- and/or ethnicity-related issues in Canada. It encourages critical thinking when examining these topics.

Wade, Peter, ed. 2007. *Race, Ethnicity, and Nation: Perspectives from Kinship and Genetics*. New York: Berghahn Books. This book links the concepts of race and ethnicity with that of family and genetics, in the context of an ever-diversifying society. On one hand, it examines topics like transnational adoption, mixed-race unions and families, and identity politics. On the other, it looks into the genetic basis of race distinctions, linking this question to broad social issues.

RECOMMENDED WEBSITES

Multicultural Canada

www.multiculturalcanada.ca

This site contains a wealth of information about the history of immigration to Canada and how it has impacted people from diverse backgrounds. It includes newspapers, photographs, book references, legal documents, audio files, pamphlets, and other materials, most of which are in languages other than English.

Citizenship and Immigration Canada

www.cic.gc.ca

> CIC includes a great deal of useful information on immigration and citizenship in Canada on its site. This federal department publishes reports that include statistics, figures, tables, and other information. Here you can find out about the point system, immigration criteria, citizenship laws and policies, and more.

Canadian Heritage

www.pch.gc.ca

> Canadian Heritage is the federal ministry 'responsible for national policies and programs that promote Canadian content, foster cultural participation, active citizenship and participation in Canada's civic life', and aims to encourage communication and learning among our diverse population. It works in partnership with cultural institutions and different groups in the population, including Aboriginals and youth, aiding their cultural and civic initiatives.

First People's Heritage Language and Cultural Council

www.fphlcc.ca

> FPHLCC is a BC-based organization that works to promote Aboriginal culture and language and improve the well-being of Aboriginal peoples. It works in conjunction with the First People's Cultural Foundation as well as First Voices, organizations that 'raise awareness and funding for Aboriginal language revitalization'. Both also have interactive and informative websites. Visit www.fpcf.ca and www.firstvoices.com for more information.

Multicultural History Society of Ontario (MHSO)

www.mhso.ca

> MHSO is a 'not-for-profit educational institution and heritage centre' founded by Professor Robert F. Harney in 1976. Ontario has had a rich history of multiculturalism and this website provides information about cultural issues and links to publications and exhibit information at the Oral History Museum in Toronto.

Global Gathering Place

www.mhso.ca/ggp

> Related to the MHSO, Global Gathering Place is an interactive site that aims to educate Canadians about the diversity of Canadian people through documents, images, videos, and audio material. It has information about immigration, ethnicity, community and family life, labour, and Canadian citizenship.

Toronto's Mosaic: A Reality Check

www.cbc.ca/toronto/features/diversity/index.html

> This is a CBC feature about diversity in Toronto, one of Canada's principal immigrant destination cities (along with Vancouver and, to a somewhat lesser degree, Montreal). It is a series, and includes sections on ethnic enclaves, integration, leadership, and an audio archive where you can listen to all the clips online. The goal of this feature is to 'explore the current state of Toronto's cultural mosaic and the role it plays in both bringing us together and pulling us apart'.

Race: The Power of an Illusion

www.pbs.org/race/000_General/000_00-Home.htm

This exceptional site is about the concept of 'race'. It is interactive and informative, and allows you to explore the historical framework that created this concept. It is a supplementary resource to a television series by PBS, and includes features like 'Background Readings', 'Ask the Experts', and 'Is Race for Real?', where you can learn interesting facts about race and ethnicity. Each section has links to further information.

Understanding Prejudice

www.understandingprejudice.org

This website helps teachers, students, and others who are interested in the causes and consequences of social prejudice. Over 2,000 links are provided to improve one's understanding of discrimination, stereotyping, and prejudice.

Durban Review

www.un.org/durbanreview2009

The World Conference on Racism website provides a brief backdrop to the events leading up to the 2009 conference in Geneva. At this conference, progress was assessed in regard to the goals set by the conference in Durban, South Africa, in 2001.

National Association for the Advancement of Colored People

www.naacp.org

The NAACP fights to ensure that the voices of African Americans are heard in the larger society. For nearly a century, this group has been a catalyst for social justice in the United States, specifically striving for social, economic, political, and educational equality of coloured Americans.

Anti-Defamation League

www.adl.org

Originally formed to fight anti-Semitism in the early twentieth century, the Anti-Defamation League now fights all forms of bigotry, seeking fair democratic treatment and civil rights for all persons. The organization creates materials, programs, and services that can help bridge the gap between socially disparate groups.

Canadian Race Relations Foundation

www.crr.ca

An excellent authority on the movement to eliminate racism in Canada, the CRRF seeks to provide a framework from which the Canadian government, and its citizenry, can reduce and eliminate racist acts and attitudes in Canada.

Stop Racism

www.stopracism.ca/

This site tracks and monitors hate-group activity. It also provides information on how youths can leave hate groups, and how to legally combat the activity of hate groups.

Gender Relations

LEARNING OBJECTIVES

- To distinguish between sex and gender.
- To be able to define 'sexism' and 'gender inequality'.
- To know about factors that reinforce gender inequality.
- To recognize the significance of the 'glass ceiling'.
- To know what is meant by the 'feminization of poverty'.
- To understand feminist movements and become aware of gender stereotypes.
- To understand the different theoretical approaches to gender inequality.
- To discover the social, psychological, and health effects of gender inequality.
- To be able to propose possible solutions to gender inequality.

INTRODUCTION

Sex—the biological distinction between male and female—is a universal and ancient basis of social differentiation. We know of no human society now or in the past that does not divide work and status along the lines of sex. This social demarcation has some basis in biology and the fact that women alone can bear and nurse offspring. Women, on average, are physically smaller and weaker than men and, therefore, less suited for hunting and combat and certain types of work. Child-bearing makes women vulnerable and more dependent for extended periods. These biological realities have led to the widespread social practices of men's roles as protectors/breadwinners and women's roles as procreators/caregivers.

However, this simple distinction varies from one society to another. History and anthropology show us that women can be breadwinners and protectors; men, though they cannot be procreators, can be caregivers. What's more, in societies with low fertility, this male–female distinction fades in importance, since in these societies women spend relatively little time in reproduction and much of their lives breadwinning.

Societies differ in the extent and ways they dramatize this sex-based difference; that is, in the ways they 'enact' gender roles and gender differences. Some societies enlarge these differences, while others diminish them. In other words, societies vary in the degree to which they make sex differences *seem* large or small, important or unimportant. There is also much variation in how they rationalize their enactment of these differences. Some invoke religious edicts (Biblical commandments, for example), others draw on secular principles like the moral commitment to equality; still other societies rely on scientific or pseudo-scientific theories (for instance, ideas about evolutionary selection) to justify differences in how men and women are treated.

Although half of all humans are women and the other half men, the study of gender relations had almost no presence in sociology before the mid-twentieth century. Before 1900, there was little exploration of gender by any of the major European sociologists. Gender and gender roles were assumed.

During the Middle Ages and Renaissance a few women were as well-educated as the best-educated men: nun and abbess, Hildegard of Bingen; Queen Elizabeth I; and Sir Thomas More's four daughters, who received the same education as his son. Olympe de Gouges in France and Mary Wollstonecraft in England were among the outstanding women writers of the late eighteenth-century Enlightenment period who supported equality for women, including education. Nonetheless, women generally were not admitted to university until the late nineteenth century; before the twentieth century, few women were university-educated, and before mid-century they rarely taught in universities. We should not be surprised, then, that until relatively recently, women have enjoyed little social standing and almost no institutional support for their intellectual ambition.

In the late nineteenth and early twentieth centuries, women became more visible as thinkers about social matters, especially about poverty. This was especially obvious among the Fabians in England, where Beatrice Webb worked alongside her husband Sydney Webb; and in the United States, where church-promoted and social service research delved into problems in the growing cities, led by women like Jane Addams. Perhaps more important, the growing feminist movement continued to press for gender equality and related social

ORLANDO

Based on Virginia Woolf's novel, this 1992 film's eponymous lead (Tilda Swinton) lives out historical debates over women's autonomy and education.

concerns (for example, abstinence from alcohol). It's worth noting the early feminist movement was mainly concerned with women's suffrage; the right to vote was achieved in Canada, the US, and Britain in the early decades of the twentieth century.

Tellingly, until the early 1970s, no sociologist seemed to notice that housework was work of economic value, not just an outpouring of family affection. It was only in 1974 that English sociologist Ann Oakley published her seminal book on the sociology of housework, which drew needed attention to domestic inequality and its relation to other forms of gender inequality (see Box 4.1). The arrival of a full-fledged sociology of gender relations coincided with, and was promoted by, the large-scale entry of women into higher education throughout the West. It took women's contributions, and the third wave of the women's movement, to bring gender inequality and gender relations to full sociological attention. The third feminist wave arose as a response to the 'failures' of, or backlash against, various initiatives established by the second feminist wave. The third feminist wave embraced racial and class diversity and accommodated differences in nationality and cultural background (Tong, 2009), where the second wave largely had been a white, middle-class movement.

With a few exceptions—notably J.S. Mill and Friedrich Engels—the failure by major male sociologists and theorists, from Marx, Weber, and Durkheim onward, to contribute to gender issues tells us something interesting about the connection between social structure (especially the social distribution of power) and the propagation of knowledge: only the powerful get noticed, studied, and discussed. Therefore, to put gender issues on the list of research topics, women needed access to power. Once powerful, the next step was to draw attention to topics that concerned them directly, and that had been neglected by male scholars.

In fact, then, we can see that the subject matter of sociology itself is a measure of a society's equality, openness, self-awareness, and social concern. Changes in sociology reflect changes in the distribution of power. These changes are achieved largely through changes in the intellectual class and the institutionalization of knowledge, of peer review, research funding, and journal publication. The 'discovery' of gender relations as a field of study was a necessary (though not big enough) step towards addressing some of the problems we will now consider.

THE BATTLE OVER GENDER TODAY

Since this chapter is about issues associated with gender, we will discuss some of the disadvantages associated with being a *man* in our society. Indeed, as we will see, norms of masculinity are as much an impediment to men as norms of femininity are to women—especially if those men are elderly or disabled. However, the principal focus here is on the disadvantages associated with being a *woman* in our society. Historically, women have suffered more disadvantages than men at school, in the workplace, and in the public realm (Knudson-Martin and Mahoney, 2009). To a large degree, Canadian women have overcome these disadvantages in the past two decades. For example, formally, Canadians support rules that make it illegal for employers to limit or separate their employees by sex. Informally, however, many Canadians still discriminate against women or in favour of men. As we will see, gender stereotyping and discrimination hinder women far more than they do men, and often they do so in almost invisible but no less consequential ways (Bloom, 2009).

For the last 30 or so years, sociologists—especially feminist sociologists—have given a great deal of attention to the competing claims of social constructionism and biological essentialism in explanations of sexual inequality (D'Souza, 2007). Perhaps it would be truer to say that they have given their time to denying the claims of essentialism and enforcing the assertion that only social construction and socialization can account for the observed differences (and inequalities) associated with men and women in a given society.

Yet, to judge from recent comments by respected feminist scholars, this stage of analysis may be about to end. It may be permissible to talk once again about innate male–female differences without the fear that doing so will unleash justifications for gender inequality. Social critic Naomi Wolf recently reviewed the evidence of biologists, evolutionary psychologists, and anthropologists to reach the conclusion that this war may be about to end. So, for example, in discussing the work of a neurobiology consultant, Michael Gurian's *What Could He Be Thinking?*, Wolf (2009) notes that:

> Men's brains can feel invaded and overwhelmed by too much verbal processing of emotion, so that men's need to zone out or do something mechanical rather than emote is often not a rejection of their spouses, but a neural need. [Gurian] even posits that the male brain can't 'see' dust or laundry piling up as the female brain often can—which explains why men and women tend to perform household tasks in different ways. Men often can't hear women's lower tones, and their brains, unlike women's, have a 'rest' state (sometimes, he *is* thinking about 'nothing').

Wolf also notes that, according to Dr Gurian, men are inclined to socialize children differently from women—also for hardwired (neurological) reasons. In doing so, they encourage more risk-taking and independence than women. He believes that if women accept and work around these biological differences, men in relationships are likely to respond positively. What is needed is better understanding and better communication around recognized differences. Most important, Wolf asserts that such recent scientific research does not 'imply that men (or women) are superior, much less justify invidious discrimination. But it does suggest that a more pluralistic society, open to all kinds of differences, can learn, work, and love better.' So we need to make a new start on understanding the varied bases of gender difference and gender inequality, and the problems to which they give rise.

DEFINING SEXISM AND GENDER INEQUALITY

Sexism includes discrimination and insulting attitudes and beliefs that stereotype people because of their gender (Lillian, 2007). Sexism and gender stereotyping can be problems for either men or women. However, since males have traditionally occupied the dominant roles in Canadian society, sexism has harmed women more than men. **Gender inequality** is any difference between men and women in gaining access to valued societal rewards. It can grow out of structural arrangements, interpersonal discrimination, or cultural beliefs (McMullin, 2004).

SEXISM Discrimination and derogatory attitudes and beliefs that promote stereotyping of people because of their gender. Sexism and gender stereotyping are two problems for both men and women, and are most often experienced in institutions and social relationships.

GENDER INEQUALITY The differential success of men and women in gaining access to valued rewards. This tends to stem from structural arrangements, interpersonal discrimination, and cultural beliefs.

Sex and Gender

Sex is a biological concept. From a purely biological standpoint, the Y chromosome must be present for the embryonic sex glands to develop maleness. Further, a preponderance of particular hormones must be present in both sexes to reach sexual maturity. Most people are (mainly) male or (mainly) female from the moment of conception, with biological differences between the sexes that are anatomic, genetic, and hormonal.

However, research has not revealed any simple split between the sexes or any direct link between genetics and the behaviour of each sex. Also, current thinking is that 'male' and 'female' are not discrete biological categories. It would be more accurate to view them as opposite poles along a continuum of sexual variation. The value of such subtle thinking is obvious when we consider unusual cases. For example, consider the rare condition known as adrenogenital syndrome, in which an XX (46-chromosome) individual is exposed in the womb to abnormally high levels of androgens, a family of hormones that usually predominates in the development of masculine features (Crooks and Baur, 1999). The result is an intersexed appearance, with normal internal genitalia (ovaries, uterus, inner vagina) and an external phallus that is intermediate in size between a clitoris and a penis. Male or female? For practical purposes, the answer is socially determined, through socialization and social interaction (Sunden, 2002).

Moreover, whatever biological differences that exist between men and women have few (if any) unavoidable effects on modern-day social life. Men and women have different reproductive functions, but there is no scientific proof there are biologically based psychological differences (such as a 'maternal instinct') between human males and females. And as women spend less and less of their lives bearing children, the reproductive difference becomes less socially relevant to a definition of people's roles.

Gender refers to culturally learned notions of masculinity and femininity (Thetela, 2002). From a social standpoint, gender is the social enactment of a biological difference. Males are treated as men because they play masculine roles, and females are treated as women because they play feminine roles. All known societies have distinguished between male and female roles in some way. However, the precise distinctions made between men and women, and the resulting divisions of labour, have varied through time and across cultures. Gender distinctions are by definition socially constructed (Staudt, 2009). They work within social institutions to decide the roles that men and women can enter and the kinds of experiences they will have within these roles. So what begins as a biological difference between sexes assumes a vast importance through the social construction of gender roles. Sociologists use the term 'gender' when referring to these sex-based social constructions, a practice that suggests that biology is largely irrelevant to understanding the social distinctions people make between males and females.

Masculinity/Femininity

Views of the inherent difference between males and females are captured in a neat dichotomy found in our culture—and most others—that distinguishes masculinity and femininity.

SEX A biological concept that differentiates female and male. Most people are (mainly) male or (mainly) female from the moment of conception, with biological differences between the sexes that are anatomic, genetic, and hormonal.

GENDER A social division referring to the social and psychosocial attributes by which humans are categorized as 'male' or 'female'. Biology is deemed somewhat irrelevant to understanding social distinctions between males and females. Gender encompasses the shared understandings of how women and men, girls and boys, should look and act. It is a label that subsumes a large assortment of traits, beliefs, values, and mannerisms, and defines how we should practise social interactions.

Not only is this dichotomy an oversimplification of the real differences between people, but it is also the source of many problems for both men and women.

Gender roles are learned patterns of behaviour that a society expects of men or women, and they are a widespread aspect of social life (Astor, 2010). By **masculinity**, then, we mean that package of qualities that people in our society expect to find in a typical man. By **femininity**, we mean the various qualities that people expect to find in a typical woman.

People learn their gender-based habits of behaviour through **gender socialization** (Rodriguez-Dominguez et al., 2009). The socialization process links gender to personal identity—in the form of *gender identity*—and to distinctive activities—in the form of gender roles. The major agents of socialization—family, peer groups, schools, and the mass media—all serve to reinforce cultural definitions of masculinity and femininity.

Men suffer from gender stereotypes as well. Just as the stereotype of women as sex objects undermines women's pursuit of respect and opportunity, so the stereotype of men as aggressive and as protectors of frail femininity causes men to think twice about displaying their emotional, creative, or artistic dimensions (McNeill, 2007). Besides reducing men's opportunities to live as they wish, this stereotyping can have serious effects for mental health and social relations.

Men also are more likely to commit violent crimes and to be victimized in violent crimes (Kaukinen, 2002). They are more likely to work in dangerous work settings and more likely to be victims of occupational accidents. In our society, as in many others, male anti-social behaviours simply are associated with striving for a masculine self-image. Further, social practices that undermine men's health are signifiers of masculinity and as appropriate instruments men use to negotiate social power and status (Courtenay, 2000).

As a result, Canadian men suffer more severe chronic health conditions; have higher death rates for all leading causes of death; and die, on average, nearly five years younger than women (Keyfitz, 1988). Even the experience and expression of illness are gendered. Though men and women have similar overall rates of mental disorder, women more often develop symptoms of depression and anxiety, while men more often develop symptoms of alcoholism, drug abuse, and social withdrawal (Hankin, 1990).

FACTORS THAT REINFORCE GENDER INEQUALITY

Sociologically, the most important difference between the sexes is that most women can and do bear children, while men can't and don't. Gender researcher Nancy Chodorow, in the often-cited work, *Reproduction of Mothering* (1978), even explains women's subordination by the fact that women mother. If women and men shared equally in parenting, gender inequality would diminish, she argued. Today, gender inequality remains, as does motherhood.

To some degree, this basic difference between men and women is played out differently in different societies. In most, however, mothers carry the main burden of child care and housekeeping, which, in turn, has enormous effects on other aspects of their lives. Until the recent past, this burden has limited women's education, work, income, political representation, and legal rights.

GENDER ROLES The patterns of behaviour that a society expects of males and females and that all members of the society learn, to a greater or lesser extent, as part of the socialization process.

MASCULINITY A socially constructed idea of how boys and men should act; qualities that people in our society expect to find in a typical man.

FEMININITY A socially constructed idea of how girls and women should act, or the various qualities that people expect to find in a typical female.

GENDER SOCIALIZATION The process by which people learn their gender-based behaviour. The socialization process links gender to personal identity in the form of gender identity and to distinctive activities in the form of gender roles. The major agents of socialization all serve to reinforce cultural definitions of masculinity and femininity.

At Home

Reproduction and child-rearing continue to be mainly female activities in Canadian society. Women's genes and hormones make child-bearing possible. However, child-bearing is no longer unavoidable. Effective birth control, by reducing the risk of unwanted pregnancy, has made the outcome of sexual intercourse more predictable and controllable than at any other time in history (Abbasi-Shavazi et al., 2009). As a result, men and women can lead more similar lives than ever before. Today, women spend less time bearing and raising children than they did in the past. Other parts of their lives—especially education, work, career, and marital companionship—are more important than they once were. Even sexual practices and sexual ideas, like the traditional double standard, have changed because of this contraceptive revolution (Schoijet, 2007).

However, the family household remains a workplace for women more than for men. Before industrial capitalism, it was men's workplace, too, but the separation of home and paid work largely brought this to an end (Tilly and Scott, 1987).

Under this system, though each family has its own particular division of labour, what is remarkable is how similar this division is across families and even across nations. Domestic labour, in short, is gendered labour. We still expect adult women to carry out more of the work than men, daughters to do more of the work than sons. This pattern also persists in caregiving. The primary caregiver is usually the wife, mother, or daughter. Women do more of the domestic work even if they engage in paid employment outside the home and are parenting infants, and even when they are taking care of sick or disabled family members (Berg and Woods, 2009).

Of course, families do vary. In some studies, for example, remarried couples report a less complete or weaker version of gendered inequality than first-time married couples (Ishii-Kuntz and Coltrane, 1992). Couples who become parents in their twenties are more traditional in their gendering of domestic work than couples who make this transition in their thirties (Coltrane and Ishii-Kuntz, 1990). Women who cohabit do much less household work than women who are legally married (Shelton and John, 1993). And dual-career couples often renegotiate their domestic division of labour as outside work duties change (Gregson and Lowe, 1994).

Table 4.1 Participation in and Time Spent on Paid Work, Housework, and Other Unpaid Work, Canada, 1986–2005

	Men 25 to 54				Women 25 to 54			
	1986	1992	1998	2005	1986	1992	1998	2005
	Average hours per day (population)[1]							
Total paid and unpaid	**8.3**	**8.6**	**8.9**	**8.8**	**8.1**	**8.4**	**8.5**	**8.8**
Paid work and related	6.1	6.1	6.3	6.3	3.3	3.6	4.0	4.4
Work	4.9	5.1	5.1	5.3	2.8	3.0	3.2	3.7
Related activities	0.7	0.6	0.6	0.4	0.3	0.3	0.4	0.3
Commute	0.5	0.5	0.5	0.6	0.3	0.3	0.3	0.4

Continued

Table 4.1 Participation in and Time Spent on Paid Work, Housework, and Other Unpaid Work, Canada, 1986–2005—*Continued*

	Men 25 to 54				Women 25 to 54			
	1986	1992	1998	2005	1986	1992	1998	2005
Average hours per day (population)[1]								
Housework	1.0	1.4	1.4	1.4	2.8	2.9	2.6	2.4
Core	0.4	0.5	0.7	0.7	2.5	2.3	2.2	1.9
Non-core	0.6	0.9	0.7	0.7	0.3	0.6	0.5	0.5
Other unpaid	1.1	1.1	1.2	1.1	2.0	1.9	2.0	1.9
Child care	0.4	0.4	0.5	0.5	0.9	1.0	1.0	1.0
Shopping and services	0.7	0.6	0.7	0.6	1.1	0.9	1.0	0.9
Average hours per day (participants)[1]								
Total paid and unpaid	**8.7**	**8.9**	**9.1**	**9.2**	**8.3**	**8.5**	**8.6**	**8.9**
Paid work and related	9.0	9.4	9.5	9.7	7.6	8.0	8.2	8.5
Work	7.7	8.1	8.1	8.5	6.7	6.9	7.1	7.5
Related activities	1.4	1.2	1.3	1.1	1.1	1.0	1.0	1.1
Commute	0.9	0.8	0.9	1.0	0.7	0.7	0.8	0.9
Housework	1.9	2.0	1.8	2.1	3.1	3.1	2.8	2.8
Core	1.1	1.0	1.0	1.2	2.9	2.6	2.4	2.3
Non-core	2.2	2.3	2.2	2.5	1.3	1.6	1.4	1.8
Other unpaid	2.4	2.1	2.1	2.2	2.9	2.8	2.8	2.9
Child care	1.5	1.6	1.8	1.8	2.1	2.2	2.3	2.5
Shopping and services	2.3	1.8	1.7	1.9	2.4	2.0	1.9	2.0
Participation (%)								
Total paid and unpaid	**94**	**96**	**98**	**96**	**98**	**99**	**99**	**98**
Paid work and related	68	65	67	65	44	45	48	51
Work	64	63	63	62	41	43	46	49
Related activities	46	48	51	39	29	33	36	30
Commute	61	57	59	58	39	40	43	46
Housework	54	67	77	69	90	93	94	89
Core	40	52	69	59	88	91	92	85
Non-core	26	38	36	31	23	37	42	35
Other unpaid	46	51	56	49	69	68	71	66
Child care	23	28	30	27	44	44	43	39
Shopping and services	32	33	39	31	45	47	51	45

1. Time averaged over seven days; numbers may not add due to rounding.

Sources: Statistics Canada, General Social Survey; K. Marshall, Canadian Economic Observer, 2006.

The Arrival of Children

With most women in the paid workforce, who looks after their children? Some families rely on daycare provided by professional caregivers. More, however, rely on babysitters who come to the parents' houses, on small-scale child-care operations, or on family members' voluntary care.

Most babysitters are female and most non-household family members who 'help' with child care are female. When researchers ask parents how they divide the responsibility of the household, they find women taking much more responsibility for the events or tasks of child care (Doucet, 2000; Tremblay, 2001). While men might take children to doctor's appointments, most often women will have made the appointments.

Women's lives become much more complicated with the arrival of children. Helena Willen and Henry Montgomery (1996) refer to this fact as the 'Catch-22' of marriage: wishing and planning for a child increases marital happiness, but achieving this wish reduces that happiness. The birth of a child and the resulting intense mother–child relationship strain marital relations (Erel and Burman, 1995). New parents are less happy with each other and experience more frequent, sometimes violent, conflicts with each other after the baby arrives (Crohan, 1996). For some, the conflict may begin even before the baby arrives.

The radical shift from spousal (adult-centred) activities to parenting (child-centred) activities creates an emotional distance the partners find hard to bridge. Romance and privacy decline. Sleepless nights increase. Mothers, the main providers of child care, change their time use much more than fathers. Especially after the birth of a first child, marital quality and quantity of time together decline immediately. Mothers report feeling angrier and more depressed than before the child arrived (Monk et al., 1996; Cowan and Cowan, 1995).

The transition to parenthood increases gender inequality between partners (Fox, 2001). The social relationship between husband and wife changes. Wives, as mothers, devote more time to their infants and less time to their husbands. Husbands often resent this change, and wives may adopt a new, subservient way of dealing with husbands to reduce the resentment and conflict. This role change produces resentment on the wife's side.

Typically, marital satisfaction, which decreases with the arrival of children, reaches an all-time low when the children are teenagers. The presence of children in the household, though pleasing in many respects, also increases the domestic workload for parents and increases conflict. Once the children leave home, creating what some sociologists have called an 'empty nest', many marriages improve to near-newlywed levels of satisfaction (Lupri and Frideres, 1981; Wadsby and Sydsjo, 2001).

In part, this return to marital satisfaction is due to the decline in parental and other work responsibilities (Orbach et al., 1996). Many couples rediscover each other because they have more leisure time in which to become reacquainted. Thus, older couples show much less distress, less desire for change in their marriage, and a more accurate understanding of the needs of their partners than do younger married couples (Rabin and Rahav, 1995).

PROBLEMS OF STRUCTURAL SEXISM

Problems of *structural sexism*—that is, the ways social institutions outside the home treat men and women differently—and the problems that this different, unequal treatment poses for men and women reinforce one another. It would be hard to get rid of one without getting rid of them all.

CLASSIC WORKS

Box 4.1 Ann Oakley's *Sociology of Housework* (1974)

Ann Oakley was born in London in 1944, the only child of a social worker mother and influential architect father. Oakley is credited with introducing the term 'gender' into academic as well as everyday use, contributing substantially to future women's studies, since this discipline needed a distinction between biological sex and socialized gender. In 1974 Oakley published her most famous work, *The Sociology of Housework*. She argued that the social sciences were ignorant when it came to housework and other issues socially constructed to be solely women's concern. She also emphasized the importance of considering culture as a backdrop to social phenomena.

Oakley's housework research was based on a small sample of working-class and middle-class homemakers. Social class, in her sample, made little difference: both middle-class and working-class women reported similar negative attitudes about housework and a similar high degree of identification with their role. Both middle-class and working-class women found housework unpleasant. But in spite of this dislike, the role of homemaker was central to their identity. They perceived themselves to be the authority figures (only) in the household, while tending to the home and children. Most of these women accepted their dissatisfaction with the monotony, isolation, and low social status of homemaking, especially compared with higher-status occupations.

Oakley concludes that women are both disempowered and imprisoned by their beliefs about the proper role of women, and especially mothers, in a modern society. Despite their unhappiness, they feel obliged by our culture to play a fundamentally alienating and frustrating role. They are socialized by a patriarchal gender ideology into accepting servitude in marriage and motherhood. Housework is the visible symbol of this submission. Oakley has strong views on this topic. Consider a few of her more pointed observations about marriage as a gendered institution:

- Society has a tremendous stake in insisting on a woman's natural fitness for the career of mother: the alternatives are all too expensive.
- Families are nothing other than the idolatry of duty.
- Housework is work directly opposed to the possibility of human self-actualization.
- If love means that one person absorbs the other, then no real relationship exists any more. Love evaporates; there is nothing left to love. The integrity of self is gone.
- There are always women who will take men on their own terms. If I were a man, I wouldn't bother to change while there are women like that around.

Oakley called our attention to the neglected topic of housework. Thanks to her insight, we are more aware of its relation to gender inequality, and of the necessity for sensitive qualitative methods to explore this problem.

Work

Throughout most of the twentieth century, women still were expected to be homemakers (see Box 4.1). Therefore, they were discouraged from taking on jobs that would prevent them from fulfilling their household duties. However, many women needed or wanted to work; and many companies wanted to hire women who wanted to work. One attractive feature, for employers, was that women could be paid less than men for the same work (Crespo, 2007).

However, the range of available jobs in the paid workforce was narrow. During the first half of the twentieth century, women could find work as teachers, nurses, retail salespersons, or as domestic servants in higher-class homes. This was significantly interrupted by World War II, which allowed record numbers of women to enter factory jobs to replace men who were away at war. These jobs—hard, dirty, often unsafe and unhealthy—required women to work 60 or more hours per week, nearly double the working week today. Then, with war's end, the returning servicemen expected their jobs to be waiting for them, and women, therefore, were expected to leave these jobs at which they had worked so hard and so well. Many did just that, and were happy to return to the male breadwinner/female homemaker family model, especially since for a span of about 25 years a growing economy and increased workplace benefits made this possible. But a precedent had been set, and many women sought to continue working as well (Vallee, 2002).

Much has changed since then. We now understand that by excluding women from the most important jobs, we significantly limit the country's supply of human capital. Today, in many parts of the industrialized world, discrimination against women is illegal. Both women and men are encouraged to follow their educational and occupational talents to the maximum, in whatever field they have chosen. Statistics Canada shows that women accounted for nearly half of the total national labour force for the year 2009 (Statistics Canada, 2010).

Unfortunately, however, women continue to suffer inequalities in the workplace. If we look at the distribution of occupations, we still find fewer women than men in high-paying positions, and, on average, full-time working women still earn about 70 cents for every dollar earned by men in similar employment. Some men might say this is because women are perceived to be more transient—more likely to quit their job for family reasons, especially during the child-bearing years. The data below show there is some support for this assertion.

In many workplaces, women do have an equal opportunity. However, in many others, they still hit a **glass ceiling** when they strive to advance. This term points to the fact that women face nearly hidden obstacles when it comes to advancing into the highest-status jobs. Women are less often hired into these jobs, in part because of an 'old boys' club' mentality and a belief (sometimes) that women are inferior (Barreto et al., 2009). The gendering of work opportunities is far narrower and stricter in developing countries, like Bangladesh, as described in Box 4.2.

Feminization of Poverty

Women are over-represented among the poor people of the world. Researchers have labelled this development the **feminization of poverty**. High rates of female poverty are usually the result of (1) women's occupational disadvantage in society, (2) women's overall subordinate position to men, and (3) women's economic difficulties following abandonment, divorce, or widowhood (Angeles, 2009).

Fully up-to-date statistics on the feminization of poverty are hard to find. Over a decade ago the National Anti-Poverty Organization (NAPO, 1999) calculated that 41 per cent of non-elderly unattached women in Canada live in poverty, while 35 per cent of non-elderly unattached men are poor. Not only are the women who head poor families affected by their impoverished state, but their children feel the results of poverty as well. Roughly one-sixth of Canada's children, or 1.2 million people under 18, live in poverty (Campaign 2000, 2005), which, of course, means their parents do, too. Gender differences also increase with age. Older women are poorer and sicker, have less satisfactory housing and access to private transport, and are more likely to experience widowhood, disability, and institutionalization than are older men (Gibson, 1996).

IN THE COMPANY OF MEN

This 1997 art-house hit discusses issues of misogyny in the workplace, as two men plot to manipulate the emotions of a female co-worker.

GLASS CEILING Women can have considerable success, but can rarely reach and enter the topmost positions.

FEMINIZATION OF POVERTY Women are clearly over-represented among the impoverished people of the world. In the West, economic liberalization and the dominance of the market have meant that those with the least earning power—single mothers with children—have suffered most.

INTERNATIONAL COMPARISONS

Box 4.2 Women's Advancement up the Economic Ladder in Bangladesh

It is no big secret that female workers in developing countries live under less than stellar conditions. According to one author, though, there are signs that things may get better. In the first chapter of economist Jeffrey Sachs's best-selling *The End of Poverty: Economic Possibilities of Our Time* (2005), he discusses the progress that working women in Bangladesh have made in recent times, thanks to a burgeoning garment industry and micro-financing initiatives.

Sachs notes that during his visit to the city of Dhaka, in the poorest neighbourhoods Bangladesh's flourishing garment industry is dominated by young female workers, hard at work at the sewing machines. The women often get little to no break time, and are constantly under risk of sexual harassment by male bosses and co-workers. The lives of these women are far from glamorous, and extreme poverty still ravages the country, but Sachs argues that the Bangladeshi women have at least gotten a foothold on the first rung of the modern economic ladder out of poverty. This is still an improvement over no job at all, a point that sweatshop protestors, Sachs says, conveniently fail to point out.

On one particular morning in Bangladesh, Sachs picked up an English newspaper and read an article of interviews with female garment workers. The Bangladeshi women in the article repeatedly expressed that working was a great opportunity for them, despite the long hours, lack of labour rights, and threats of harassment. They had grown up in a poverty-stricken, male-dominated society, with little or no say in what they wanted, often being forced into arranged marriages and the raising of families. Now, these women are able to save a small surplus, manage their income, live in their own rooms, choose whom they want to date and marry, choose when to have children, and use their savings to go to school. Though these benefits of work are rather meagre by the standards of the developed Western world, Sachs argues that the Bangladeshi women have made great strides in their quest for personal liberation.

On another visit to the same city in 2003, Sachs met a group of women who were involved in microfinanced small-scale commercial activities. Thanks to the Bangladeshi Rural Advancement Committee (BRAC), these women were able to get small loans for financing micro businesses, something previously unheard of due to the women's lack of credit history. (Indeed, the concept of microfinance for small, female-run businesses originated in 1976 in Bangladesh with the Grameen Bank, originally a research project begun by a university professor, Muhammad Yunus.) The majority of the women also had only one or two children, indicating that they were no longer forced into having children and had some new-found personal autonomy in their lives. Sachs argues that reduced fertility has helped fuel the rise in incomes and literacy of Bangladeshi women, since there is more money left over to invest in the health and education of each individual in a household.

Women overall, and single mothers in particular, are more likely to be impoverished than any other demographic group (Albelda and Tilly, 1997). Various health consequences trouble women who are economically deprived, including increased vulnerability to infectious and other disease, arthritis, stomach ulcers, migraines, clinical depression, stress, vulnerability to mental illness, self-destructive coping behaviours, and increased risk of heart disease (Morris, 2000). The most comprehensive, up-to-date figures are presented in Box 4.3.

SUFFRAGE MOVEMENT
The central aim of many in the 'first wave' of the women's movement in the late nineteenth and early twentieth centuries was the right for women to vote in elections. With women's suffrage (i.e., voting rights), other goals—social reform, legal rights—would then be more readily attainable.

WOMEN'S RIGHTS AND THE FEMINIST MOVEMENT IN CANADA

The **suffrage movement**, or the 'first wave' of feminism, made important gains for women's rights in Canada through the late nineteenth and early twentieth centuries. Early feminists, represented nationally by the Woman's Christian Temperance Union, the Young

PUBLIC ISSUES

Box 4.3 Women and Poverty

A newborn child, just because she happens to be born female, is more likely to grow up to be poor as an adult. Women form the majority of the poor in Canada. One in seven (2.4 million) Canadian women is living in poverty today. The following statistics help us to understand the extent to which the poverty of women is a significant social problem.

- *Women raising families by themselves*: 51.6 per cent of lone-parent families headed by women are poor. With many of these families, financial support agreements with the non-custodial parent (usually the father) are either not in place or are in arrears.
- *Senior women*: Almost half (41.5 per cent) of single, widowed, or divorced women over 65 are poor. While the poverty rates for all seniors have improved, there is still a large gap between men and women. The poverty rate for all senior women is 19.3 per cent, while that for senior men is 9.5 per cent.
- *Women on their own*: Thirty-five per cent of women on their own under 65 live in poverty.
- *Women with disabilities*: More women than men live with disabilities in Canada. Aboriginal people have twice the national disability rate. Of all women with disabilities living in a household rather than an institution, and who had any income at all, those aged 35–54 had the highest incomes: an average of $17,000, which is 55 per cent of men with disabilities in that age range. Women with disabilities under 35 had an average income of $13,000, and women with disabilities over 55 had an average income of under $14,000. The more severe a woman's disability, the lower her income.
- *Aboriginal women*: The average annual income of Aboriginal women is $13,300, compared to $18,200 for Aboriginal men and $19,350 for non-Aboriginal women. Forty-four per cent of the Aboriginal off-reserve population live in poverty, but things are worse on reserve: almost half (47 per cent) of Aboriginal persons on reserve have an income of less than $10,000. Aboriginal women are also more likely than Aboriginal men to be trapped in low-paying jobs, and because of the continuing effects of the Indian Act, they face insecurities related to housing, access to services, and abuse both on and off reserve.
- *Women of colour*: Thirty-seven per cent of women of colour are low-income, compared with 19 per cent of all women. The average annual income for a woman of colour in Canada is $16,621, almost $3,000 less than the average for other women ($19,495) and almost $7,000 less than that of men of colour ($23,635). Women of colour also are over-represented in precarious (part-time and temporary) work and often have to live in substandard, segregated housing. They are more vulnerable to violence and other health risks.
- *Immigrant women*: Education does not reduce the income gap between immigrant women and Canadian-born women. New immigrant women between the ages of 25–44 who have a university degree and who worked full-year, full-time earn $14,000 less than Canadian-born women. This is partly because of overt racism, but also the structural racism of lack of recognition of foreign credentials and experience. New immigrant women, suffering from abuse, may have few options to escape this abuse if they are financially dependent on their male relative sponsors in Canada.
- *Lesbians*: There is little information about the economic status of lesbians. We only have isolated pieces of information to go by, such as a Winnipeg study that found that 14 per cent of gay men over 65 reported incomes below the poverty line, compared with 42 per cent of lesbian seniors.
- *Migrant women*: Migrant women, who often are refugees or foreign domestic workers, are particularly at risk of poverty and exploitation, as they are often forced to work in unregulated or hidden employment. Women make up the majority of migrant workers from Asia, many of whom work here to sustain their families back home. They are paid low wages, and despite the fact that they contribute significantly to the Canadian economy, they are not entitled to many benefits such as EI.
- *Low-wage earners*: In Canada it is not enough to have a job to keep you out of poverty. Most poor people do work full- or part-time. Poverty-level wages are a particular problem for women. Women and youth account for 83 per cent of Canada's minimum-wage workers; 37 per cent of lone mothers with paid employment must raise a family on incomes of less than $10 per hour.

Source: **Canadian Research Institute for the Advancement of Women (CRIAW)**, at: www.criaw-icref.ca/factSheets/Women%20and%20Poverty/Poverty%20Fact%20sheet_e.htm

Women's Christian Association, the National Council of Women of Canada, and the Federated Women's Institutes, focused mainly on three sets of issues—political rights, legal rights, and social reform. These early feminists fought to place the 'woman's role on a more secure material footing' rather than attempt to shatter the traditional gender myths that considered the man to be the provider and the woman to be the nurturer (Brooks, 2007: 426).

True to these goals, the tactics Canadian feminists employed were cautious and moderate, and were successful in bringing women the right to vote. Only in the last 35 years of the twentieth century did the 'second wave' of feminism begin its attacks on the cultural and social bases of inequality. Without this questioning of gender roles, as the women's movement has done over several decades, it is unlikely that women would have made strides towards social and economic equality.

Granting women's demands in one area led to granting demands in other areas. After the right to vote in federal elections was granted in 1918, five determined suffragists—the so-called Famous Five—pushed for changes to the British North America Act that would deem women to be legal 'persons' who qualified for appointment to the Senate. In 1929, the declaration of personhood for women by the Judicial Committee of the Privy Council increased the likelihood that further rights would be forthcoming.

A turning point in gender equalization was the Royal Commission on the Status of Women, which began in 1967 and heard the concerns of individuals and organizations across the country. As well as considering the specifics of women's lives, the Commission also looked at some of the underlying causes of women's inequality. One outcome of the Royal Commission's work was the establishment of Status of Women Canada as a government agency, now subsumed within the Department of Canadian Heritage. Since the Commission, women have continued to push for changes that would bring equality closer to reality (Van Wingerden, 1999).

Feminist ideology, or *feminism*, is a form of political activism that tries to change the conditions under which men and women lead their lives. Feminism, then, has an emancipatory goal—it aims to free people from oppression. If gender relations always reflect the larger pattern of social relations in a society, then changing gender relations requires changing those social relations as well. Feminism is one of the social movements that—alongside the anti-war, civil rights, gay rights, anti-racism, and environmental movements—have reshaped modern politics in the last 40 years (Lengermann et al., 2001).

GENDER STEREOTYPES IN THE MEDIA

Despite major advances in women's opportunities and rights during the twentieth century, portrayals of girls and women in the mass media, especially in television, keep harmful gender stereotypes alive. In this way, they continue to keep women from achieving full equality with men at home or at work (Das and Das, 2009).

In the mass media, we still see gendered images of women and men, boys and girls. These gendered images are paralleled in media advertisements for consumer items—toys, clothes,

Despite the gender stereotyping associated with Barbie dolls, they remain a popular toy among girls. Angelica Pupo plays with a Barbie doll during the seventh annual Hot Toys for the Holidays from the Canadian Toy Association on 2 November 2009 in Toronto.

cars, beer, and deodorant. This level of culture—commerce—assumes what male people and female people will typically want to do, producing a self-fulfilling prophecy—our children turn out to be how these others expect them to.

Consider Saturday morning children's television: cartoon shows interspersed with commercials. Advertisers aim the commercials directly at girls or boys, typically matched to the show—Barbie dolls (or the equivalent) for girls, droids or Transformers (or the equivalent) for boys. These programs entertain children, but they also teach them which toys are for them, how we expect them as girls or boys to behave, and what we expect them, as gendered beings, to want in our society.

Some socially conscious agencies are trying to use commercial media (for example, television advertisements) to promote change. We will occasionally see, for example, male sports stars talking about problems of violence against women and trying to promote models of masculinity that are concerned, caring, and nurturing though strong. However, the idea of a rapid direct imitative influence of media images on viewers, and therefore on society, may be too simplistic. The media may reflect and reinforce culture more than they are able to easily change culture and society (Royo Vela y Otros, 2005).

The mass media may not be the main cause of gender inequality in Canada, but they do play a major role in creating and upholding gender stereotypes. In this way, they help to perpetuate existing inequalities between men and women.

THEORETICAL PERSPECTIVES ON GENDER RELATIONS AND INEQUALITY

Table 4.2   Theoretical Perspectives

Theory	Main Points
Structural Functionalism	• Elements in society are interrelated. • Inequality rewards effectiveness and efficiency. • Inequality is based on value consensus. • Gender inequality stems from what was at one time an effective household arrangement, which has failed to develop with the times.
Conflict Theory	• Gender inequality results from struggle for economic and social power. • Capitalists benefit from gender inequality. • Gender inequality forces women to maintain the workforce without pay.
Symbolic Interactionism	• Socialization and labelling shape gender identities. • Most variations between men and women are cultural and learned. • A gendered self develops out of a process of gradual socialization, at all levels of social life: women learn to do women's jobs and see themselves as suited for these tasks. • Media, religion, and language help maintain gender differences. • Double standards are considered normal.
Feminist Theory	• Gender inequality is almost universal. • This inequality is a result of patriarchal values and institutions. • Gender inequality favours men over women.
Social Constructionism	• The creation of gender equality is a social process. • It usually requires leadership and organization. • Some social periods are more conducive to equalization than others.

Structural Functionalism

Remember that structural functionalists ask of every social arrangement: *What function* does it perform for society as a whole? In this case, how does gender inequality contribute to the well-being of society as a whole? Functionalist theorists starting with Talcott Parsons (1951) would say that a gendered division of labour is the most effective and efficient way to carry out society's tasks. It may even have evolutionary survival value for the human race. Mothers, by their early attachment to the child (via pregnancy and breast-feeding), are well-suited to raising the family's children. Since they are at home with the children anyway, mothers are also well-suited to caring for the household while the husband is at work outside the home.

Conflict and Feminist Theories

Conflict theorists and feminist theorists, by contrast, always ask the question: *Who benefits* from a particular social arrangement? In this case, who is best served by gender inequality? Marxists would tend to answer this question by class relations: capitalism requires the low-cost social reproduction of a workforce from one generation to the next. Families are the best and cheapest way to raise new workers. Mothers have the job of keeping all the family earners and earners-to-be healthy and well fed, housed, and cared for emotionally. They do this at no cost to capitalists who will benefit from the surplus value workers produce.

The Marxist approach assumes that working-class men and women are on the same side, both equally victims of the capitalist class. By contrast, the feminist approach assumes that women have a different experience from men and may be exploited by men of their own class, as well as by capitalists. Therefore, they see gender inequality as mainly serving the interests of men who, by lording it over their girlfriends, wives, and daughters, at least have someone subservient to them just as they are to their own bosses. The theory of patriarchy—that men are the main and universal cause of women's oppression—is compatible with Marxist analyses that view working-class women as being the victims of both class and gender oppression (Knudson-Martin and Mahoney, 2009).

Symbolic Interactionism

Symbolic interactionists, for their part, ask: *How* is an arrangement *symbolized*? For example, how is gender inequality negotiated, symbolized, and communicated in our society? The presumption is that inequalities arise where social differences have been symbolized, communicated, and negotiated—that is, made into something that is 'taken for granted' by the population at large. From this standpoint, people are always trying to understand and normalize social interaction through shared meanings. Thus, symbolic interactionists are concerned with the ways that gender differences become gender inequalities—for example, the ways that young women become 'objectified' and turned into sex *objects*. They would also want to understand how the double sexual standard, which has allowed men more sexual freedom than women, has been 'negotiated' so that many women go along with an agenda that, it would seem to many people, benefits males more than females.

Social Constructionism

Related to this approach, social constructionists always ask the question: *When and how* did the arrangement *emerge*? When, for example, did gender inequality begin to emerge in a particular society, what events preceded this emergence, and what individuals or groups were especially instrumental in this process of 'moral entrepreneurship'? This approach is much more historically oriented than the symbolic interactionist approach to which it is related. So, for example, a social constructionist would note that gender equality began to increase (a second time) in the 1960s and 1970s, largely because of the actions of the women's movement.

The women's movement was especially successful because social protest against many things—the rich, imperialists, and racists, for example—was prevalent throughout the Western world. The baby boom had ended and there was less desire for child-bearing. However, there was now a desire for two family incomes, and therefore a need for more education for women. This new agenda—getting women out of the homes and into the work-world—was aided significantly by the development of reliable birth control that made it possible for people to have sex without having babies. Cutting the links between gender, sexuality, and child-bearing was central to the emergence of women as contenders in the working world of men. It also helped gay and lesbian people stake a claim to full social inclusion, for similar reasons.

Notably, all these explanations are compatible with one another. Each focuses on a different aspect of the rise of gender equality. However, by far the most influential approach to studying gender issues has been the feminist approach, and that approach has shaped this chapter.

SOCIAL CONSEQUENCES OF GENDER INEQUALITY

As one would expect, issues of gender are involved in most if not all aspects of Canadian social life. We have already discussed issues associated with education, work, and income that pose particular problems for women. In this section, we consider crime, violence, and self-esteem.

Crime and Violence

Using data from the General Social Survey, Statistics Canada reported in 2005 that 'While overall rates of violent victimization did not differ between men and women, men were at greater risk of physical assault. Women were at higher risk of sexual assault' (Statistics Canada, 2005c).

Although men are sometimes the victims of rape and sexual assault, these vicious crimes are mainly directed towards women. Rape is devastating for the victim not only because of the physical and psychological violations, but also because the victim must come to terms with the fact that she was attacked solely because of her gender. Rape offenders, who are usually male, typically harbour misogynistic, sadistic attitudes towards their victims.

According to the Ontario Women's Directorate (2009), 83 per cent of all sexual assault victims in Canada are females while 17 per cent are males. A report on family violence in 2005 showed that women are more than twice as likely to be injured in episodes of spousal violence, three times more likely to fear for their life, and twice as likely to be the targets of repetitive abuse (Statistics Canada, 2005a). The report also showed that rates of spousal violence were highest among those aged 15–24 (in many instances these individuals were victims of date rape), those in a relationship of three years or less, those who had been recently separated, and those living in common-law unions.

Statistics Canada reported in 2005 that, 'As in previous years, most homicides in 2004 were committed by someone known to the victim. Among solved homicides, half were committed by an acquaintance, one-third by a family member, and 15 per cent by a stranger' (Statistics Canada, 2005b). Though Canada's spousal homicide rate has generally been declining since the mid-1970s, women remain much more likely to be killed by their spouse than are men.

In our society, violence against women runs the gamut from verbal and psychological harassment to physical assault, sexual assault, and homicide. Research on criminal victimization in Canada (Sacco and Johnson, 1990: 21) shows that 'rates of personal victimization are highest among males, the young, urban dwellers, those who are single or unemployed . . . . Risk of personal victimization is also greater among Canadians who often engage in evening activities outside the home and among heavier consumers of alcohol.' Most recorded victimization is male victimization in public, but this is not the *female* experience of crime or of victimization.

Women as well as men commit violent acts (Weizmann-Henelius et al., 2009). However, data indicate the chances of injury for males and females differ significantly. Since men usually are stronger than women, wives are more often injured than are husbands, even when both partners are acting violently.

While women are slightly more likely to start a violent episode—usually by slapping, kicking, or throwing an object—men are more likely to respond with more devastating force— beating, choking, or threatening to use (or actually using) a knife or gun. As a result, nearly half of women (49 per cent) who report being abused by a previous spouse in the past five years in Canada suffered physical injury, compared with less than a quarter (21 per cent) of men. Of these women, 19 per cent received injuries severe enough to need medical attention; only 5 per cent of men required medical attention. In retrospect, 48 per cent of female victims and 13 per cent of male victims feared for their lives during the ordeal (Statistics Canada, 2001: 40). In 2007, nearly 40,200 cases of spousal violence were reported to police. The prevalence of violence, however, has decreased in Canada by 15 per cent since 1998. Still, women are disproportionately the victims of spousal violence (Statistics Canada, 2009).

One survey of self-reported domestic violence in Canada shows that (1) younger people are more violent to their spouses than are older people; (2) unemployed people are more violent than employed people; but (3) people with less education and lower income are no more violent than those who are highly educated and who have higher incomes. There is also a relationship between a belief in patriarchy and wife-battering. Husbands who believe men ought to rule women are more likely than other husbands to beat their wives. In turn, a belief in patriarchy depends on educational and occupational level (Lupri et al., 1994; Lupri, 1993).

THELMA & LOUISE

Ridley Scott's 1991 film discusses hypocrisies regarding gender and violence, as two women, who kill a man in self-defense, must subsequently flee the law.

Ethnicity is also a factor here. Some cultures in multicultural Canada and elsewhere are more patriarchal than others. Specifically, other things being equal, patriarchal beliefs appeal to lower-status, less-educated men, perhaps because they have so little control over other aspects of their lives (Tichy et al., 2009).

The most revealing finding is that high rates of domestic violence are associated with high levels of domestic stress. That is, the more stressful events a person reports experiencing in the previous year, the more violence will have taken place within the household. Still, even if stress and frustrations result in violence, they do not excuse it. The real problem underlying violence is not stress or frustration but the fact that some men find it acceptable to channel their frustrations into violence towards family members.

Date Rape and Sexual Inequality

Most instances of forced sex occur between people who are friends, acquaintances or even relatives. (Estrich, 2007). The result, too often, is that women blame themselves for the experience. Because they know the assailant, they may react passively to the sexual assault. Because they react passively, they blame themselves for not reacting more forcefully. A few even continue in an abusive dating relationship (Humphreys and Herold, 1996).

Historically, women who faced violence from intimates could not rely on police protection. Because the larger community saw domestic violence as a private matter, police were trained to respond accordingly. In doing so, they reflected the expectation of the community and the criminal justice system that officers should be involved in only the most extreme cases. Police were taught to either defuse the situation quickly and leave, or try to mediate the 'dispute'. This reinforced a view of the victim and assailant as equal parties with equal power over each other's behaviour. Victims were left feeling confused and at fault. Having turned to the police for help, they were left blaming themselves for bothering to call.

Only recently have we come to understand that domestic violence is usually uneven. Even if men do not introduce the physical violence during an argument, once it is launched they tend to use more physical force than women do. Further, men and women often have different goals in using force. Women are more likely to leave an unsatisfactory relationship, while men are more likely to use force to prevent the partner from leaving. Women will use violence mainly to protect themselves. Men will also use violence to compel partners to give them sex. Only recently have law enforcement agencies and the public come to accept spousal rape as a criminal offence. In the past, many considered such behaviour, like spousal abuse, to be a private matter between husband and wife (Hovmand et al., 2009).

Harassment

SEXUAL HARASSMENT
Any unwanted physical or verbal conduct directed towards a person that is sexually offensive or humiliating.

Another problem that women sometimes must deal with is **sexual harassment** in the workplace. In fact, according to Status of Women Canada, in 2000 women represented 78 per cent of all reported cases of criminal harassment (National Day of Remembrance, 2005).

Harassment may involve a single incident or several incidents over the course of time. This creates a negative work environment that may interfere with job performance; it may also result in women being refused a desirable job, promotion, or training opportunity. The harasser may be a supervisor, a co-worker, or someone who provides service, such as a clerk in a government department (MacDonald, 2007).

It is impossible to know the full extent of gender-based harassment in Canada today, since much of it likely goes unreported (Clancy, 1994). Harassment comes in at least two forms. First, sexual harassment may be the open demand by employers for sexual favours in exchange for promotion opportunities, salary increases, and preferential treatment, in other words, **quid pro quo sexual harassment**. The second type of harassment is subtler, fostering a hostile and unpleasant work environment through sexist remarks, jokes, and insults. This second type of harassment is least likely to be reported.

QUID PRO QUO SEXUAL HARASSMENT The blatant demand by employers for sexual favours in exchange for promotion opportunities, salary increases, and preferential treatment.

Stalking

A rarer but more menacing form of harassment is stalking. Recently, stalking has emerged as a new form of criminal deviance in our society. This crime has gained much attention because it is common and is associated with gendered abuse and violence.

Stalking is a form of relationship abuse that may evolve into violent physical, psychological, and sexual forms. In the year 2003, nine in 10 female victims of stalking in Canada were stalked by men (METRAC, 2003). In all US stalking cases for the year of 1997, stalkers made overt threats to about 45 per cent of victims; spied on or followed about 75 per cent of victims; vandalized the property of about 30 per cent of victims; and threatened to kill or killed the pets of about 10 per cent of victims (Tjaden, 1997).

Stalking often follows a relationship breakup or a rejection in a proposed relationship. Most stalkers are former or imagined, rather than current, intimates. Many stalking victims must resort to help from the authorities and seek restraining orders to protect themselves from the emotional abuse and prevent the stalking from intensifying into violence.

Self-Esteem Issues

Gender discrimination also carries social-psychological costs. For women, decreased self-esteem, increased depression, and other psychological problems often result from derogation by men, awareness of their subordinate status in society, or a failure to achieve the stereotypical ideal female body (Foster, 2009).

As we have already noted, one area in which this limitation occurs is in the choice of careers. Women are often reluctant to enter professions that involve dangerous, physically demanding work, such as firefighting or the military. By contrast, men are informally, and sometimes directly, cautioned against entering professions that 'undermine their masculinity', such as early childhood education or nursing.

To protect their self-esteem, women sometimes attribute negative criticisms made to them about their work or their abilities to prejudice by male evaluators, whether the men actually believe in gender stereotypes or not (Crocker and Park, 2003). This defensive strategy, although understandable, may lead some people to see prejudice where none exists. This becomes a problem when it leads a person to imagine that every member of the opposite sex (or of a different 'race', ethnic group, age cohort, etc.) is the 'enemy'. Sometimes, workplace criticism is just criticism.

Body Image and Appearance Issues

Like it or not, people *do* judge books by their covers and strangers by their appearance. In judging appearance, people often look for points of likeness and familiarity that make them feel secure. Beyond that, they look for evidence of the cultural ideal. People admire others who look prosperous, healthy, and attractive, according to society's standards. Appearance features that approximate the ideal—not merely the familiar—are important because individuals want to fit in and be accepted. Such ideal features make up what we consider 'appearance norms'.

Society's dependence on and need for social norms—even appearance norms—teach us about deeper cultural ideals of beauty, propriety, and worth. Scarcity alone lends value to *some* physical qualities—for example, perfect facial features or flawless white teeth—but far from all. Our cultural ideals are manifested by the plentiful photos and media images that glorify so-called ideal men and women. To judge from these images of 'beautiful people', our culture idealizes youth, a slender toned body, and symmetrical, delicate facial features. Departures from these norms suggest poor genes, poor grooming, or a lack of self-discipline and self-worth (Jung and Peterson, 2007). The media spotlight on body image is far more intense for women than for men. As a result, women tend to experience more insecurities about their bodies than men, and are much more likely to starve their bodies into attempted perfection through anorexia or bulimia.

In 1983, eating disorders finally received media attention with the death of singer Karen Carpenter from cardiac complications caused by anorexia nervosa. This was the first time the media focused attention on the life-threatening results of eating disorders and stopped viewing them as simply a group of 'benign' psychiatric illnesses. Anorexia and bulimia came to be seen as a result of women over-conforming to norms of slenderness and sacrificing their health for unattainable cultural goals of 'perfect' thinness (Harrison et al., 2006).

Fertility and Abortion Issues

Adolescent fertility is another big problem for women in North America (Benokraitis, 2008). Factors predicting non-marital teenage pregnancy include two proximate determinants of pregnancy—contraceptive use and frequency of intercourse—as well as a history of school problems, drug use, fighting, living with parents, length of relationship with boyfriends, and best friends experiencing pregnancies (Gillmore et al., 1997). In short, young women without long-term goals and stable, cordial relationships are more likely to produce children in adolescence. The results are regrettable, for the children as well as for the mother: an end to the mother's education; a limit to the child's economic future; or, all too often, abortion, which effectively has become contraception of last resort. In 2005, for example, 30,534 pregnancies were recorded for young women ages 15–19, and of these, 15,217, or almost 50 per cent, were terminated by abortion (Statistics Canada, 2005d).

Patriarchy is, by its nature, pro-natal; it views women's primary responsibility as bearing and raising children. Many societies press women to bear as many children as they can, stigmatizing them if they are childless (Inhorn, 1998). Yet, high rates of pregnancy often result in high rates of illness and mortality. Each year around the world, half a million women die needlessly from pregnancy-related complications, worsened by poverty and remoteness (WHO, 2007). Many women, especially in developing countries, die during pregnancy and childbirth (and as result of botched abortions).

The figure is high in developing nations (450 deaths/100,000 live births, compared with 9/100,000 in developed countries), and is unsurprisingly highest in the least developed countries (1,000 deaths/100,000 live births). Overall, a woman's lifetime risk of maternal death in developing countries is 1 in 75, while it is 1 in 7,300 in developed countries (ibid.). These figures are even more striking if they are examined country by country. For example, in 2005 Niger had the highest estimated lifetime risk for women dying from pregnancy and childbirth-related problems with 1 woman out 7 dying, while Ireland had the lowest risk of 1 in 48,000 (ibid.). World Health Organization reported that in 2000, 529,000 women died from pregnancy-related causes, and for each of these women, 20 more—a total of 10 million women—were left seriously injured or disabled (WHO, 2000). These deaths, injuries, and disabilities are preventable, and they are symptomatic of women's vulnerability and the violation of their human rights. This fact turns women's health issues into a matter of social justice.

Limitations on women's child-bearing and enforced abortion, as in China, for example, also create serious problems. An experiment in one province in China found that permitting couples two children—rather than the usual one—led to a drastic drop in the abortion rate, equal acceptance of female children, happier parents, and a better-integrated society (Schiller, 2010).

CLAIMS-MAKING IN GENDER RELATIONS AND SEXISM

Social constructionism has had considerable success in the sociological study of gender, which, by its very focus on socialization and institutions, undermines notions of biological determinism. Indeed, constructionism has probably become the dominant view of gender in sociology, with some arguing that attempts on the part of 'value-free' science to discover biological gender differences constitute unwitting (or sometimes intentional) efforts to legitimate sexism and gender inequality (Risman, 2001).

Of import to discussions of gender is the backlash against women's rights movements found in conservative counter-movements. These groups have an interest in framing societal trends in certain ways, for example, describing divorce as a 'problem' associated with moral decline, even as divorce rates have dropped or stabilized (Coltrane and Adams, 2003).

In thinking about claims-making with regard to gender relations, we should also briefly discuss *men's rights movements* (or men's rights activists, known as MRAs). These groups vary in values and tactics, but men who are anti-feminist in orientation clearly have an interest in making particular claims about gender roles and the state of relations between men and women in society. For instance, the Promise Keepers are a Christian men's movement that has been characterized as anti-gay and anti-feminist (Heath, 2003). Such groups may hold

POLICY DEBATES

Box 4.4 Gender Debate Continues Over Women's Ski Jumping at Vancouver 2010

Female ski jumpers want equality. Leading up to the 2010 Winter Olympic Games in Vancouver, an ongoing political and court challenge sought to have women's ski jumping included as an event. The International Olympics Committee (IOC), who voted in 2006 to keep the event off the 2010 events program, argued that the event falls short of basic standards for inclusion as an Olympic event. Yet men's ski jumping events are included in Olympic competition. Deedee Corradini, former mayor of Salt Lake City, called for Canadian politicians to put pressure on the IOC to change its policies. Indeed, David Emerson, the federal minister in charge of the 2010 Olympics, as well as New Democrat member Harry Bains both spoke in favour of a policy change to allow female ski jumpers to compete.

In April 2009, a group of 15 ski jumpers, including world champion Lindsey Van, sued the Vancouver Olympic organizing committee (VANOC), charging that excluding women's ski jumping is a violation of the Canadian Charter of Rights and Freedoms. VANOC defended itself by stating that the Charter does not apply to the Olympic Games, which is not a government activity. VANOC further stated that it had supported the inclusion of the event, providing facilities and resources whenever possible but that, unfortunately, the IOC ultimately decides which events are included or not included.

IOC member Dick Pound of Canada says that the sport is just not practised widely enough by women on an international scale to be included, in spite of the fact that 100 women from 16 countries currently compete in a global circuit. That is not enough, said the IOC, which stated that the sport requires two world competitions (women's ski jumping only has one) in order to qualify. However, in the past, bobsledding has been included as an Olympic event despite similarly having only one world competition. In addition, the group of plaintiffs pointed out that women's ski cross, a less developed event, is included. This is because of an IOC rule that mandated that every new event added after 1991 must have events for both genders. However, ski jumping had been an Olympic event long before that.

In July of 2009, the BC Supreme Court ruled in favour of the defendant, citing that although the Canadian government has a degree of control over VANOC, it does not have control over the organization's day-to-day operations. Furthermore, VANOC ultimately is under the control of the IOC, which runs outside the jurisdiction of the Charter of Rights and Freedoms, and thus, the Supreme Court cannot order VANOC to hold a women's event. The BC Supreme Court judge presiding over the case, Lauri Ann Fenlon, acknowledged that the women were being discriminated against on account of their gender; however, not all discrimination is a violation of the Charter. VANOC CEO John Furlong expressed desire to help develop and expand the sport further in hopes that it would be included in future Winter Games. As it turned out—of course—the women ski jumpers were grounded in Vancouver.

Sources: Adapted from: CTV, at: www.ctv.ca/servlet/ArticleNews/story/CTVNews/20080105/ski_jump_080105?s_name=&no_ads=; www.wsj2010.com/; CBC, at: www.cbc.ca/sports/amateur/story/2009/04/22/sp-skijumping-olympic-women.html; CTVOlympics, at: www.ctvolympics.ca/ski-jumping/news/newsid=12786.html; *Toronto Star*, at: www.thestar.com/comment/columnists/article/664482; BBC, at: news.bbc.co.uk/2/hi/americas/8009464.stm

that the 'pendulum has swung too far' in the direction of women's rights, and thus claim that they, and not feminists, represent a sensible 'middle ground' of equality. However, studies suggest that such backlash claims may only reinforce gender inequalities. Heath (ibid.), in discussing the Promise Keepers, suggests that social movements on the part of privileged groups are often attempts to reform or rehabilitate that privilege. In other words, antifeminist MRAs are involved in a process of claims-making with the goal of defending male privilege against feminist claims to gender equality.

The Canadian Press/Toronto Star-Tony Bock

David Sweet, leader of the Canadian Promise Keepers, is shown in this recent photo. Promise Keepers says about 900 churches have already signed on and thousands of Canadian men believe in the million-dollar, men-only, Bible-based Christian organization.

Gender relations are not constructed by social movements, but by people in their everyday lives. One study of male university students found that they saw current gender relations as empowering for women and disempowering for men (Gough and Peace, 2000). The idea that women are already in a favourable position seems to rule out change of the status quo. Thus, quite apart from the actual state of gender inequality as discussed in this chapter, the ways in which gender relations are perceived and constructed by men and women are important in their own right.

POLICY AND INSTITUTIONAL SOLUTIONS TO GENDER INEQUALITY

Many institutional policies are designed to protect women in their private lives and remove barriers that prevent women (and other marginal groups) from taking part fully in public life. For example, discrimination in the workplace based on sex or gender is no longer tolerated in Canadian society, either by the judicial system or by most public opinion.

However, policies are not yet in place that would give women the same occupational freedom that men enjoy. For example, we know that many women—as employees, wives, and mothers—have been affected by lack of high-quality, inexpensive child care. Analysis suggests that policies to increase the supply of child care or to lower its cost could increase the female labour supply substantially, with an even greater rise among women most at risk of poverty and reliance on public assistance (Mason and Kuhlthau, 1989).

Finally, employment discrimination remains a problem. More effective workplace sexual harassment policies would likely improve women's work lives by preventing sexism from impeding a woman's career ambitions. Canada's Employment Equity Act protects all workers in federal employment (and all people who work for an employer that employs 100 or more employees on or in connection with federal work) against discriminatory hiring procedures, whatever their gender, race, ethnicity, disability status, or sexual orientation, by ensuring that employee composition reflects the diversity of society.

In specific relation to gender, this means the workforces of large companies and federal employees must have a roughly equal number of men and women in all levels of employment, at least in theory. In practice, the division is not nearly as exact, although the gap is closing.

The process of finding and implementing solutions will continue to be difficult, as society overcomes its inertia and undergoes the painful process of unlearning centuries of outmoded gender socialization. The system has been skewed in favour of men for generations. In trying to correct this problem, having some policies that temporarily favour the marginalized group may be necessary until the playing field has been levelled. In patriarchal communities and societies, a resistance to changes such as reduced fertility, new family forms, more education for women, and gender equality at work and in politics may create a social crisis that could even lead to political violence (Fargues, 1977).

Cross-national research makes clear that women's long-held concerns must be transformed into well-understood social problems before policy proposals are drafted and passed. Around the world, women have worked to place issues such as equal pay, affirmative action, educational equality, child care, abortion, domestic violence, and sexual harassment on the policy agenda. They have done so most directly and effectively in countries such as Norway, Sweden, and Finland, where women play a key role in politics and in the legislative process, largely through a history of effective mobilization in unions, social movements, and political parties (Bacchi, 1999; Tyyska, 1994). Canada has also made impressive progress, yet much more work remains to be done.

CHAPTER SUMMARY

Are gender inequality and sexism in Canadian society 'real' problems or merely socially constructed problems? On the one hand, there can be little doubt that 'moral entrepreneurship' by the leaders of the women's movement was critical in calling public attention to many of the issues associated with gender inequality—poverty, violence, discrimination, and so on.

However, gender inequality was and is not merely a manufactured issue. It did exist prior to the first and second waves of the women's movement. And although there has been considerable improvement in Canada over the past two generations, gender inequality is still a fact of life for many women. We have seen that women suffer the material, psychological, and emotional outcomes of inequality and discrimination. They even suffer significant health problems—our touchstone for measuring the 'reality' of a social issue.

As we have seen, gender inequality is a social phenomenon. Gender discrimination and gender inequality are not due to the intrinsic or biological inferiority of one or the other sex. Instead, they are the result of political, economic, and ideological structures. Women have increasingly entered the workforce in both developed and less developed countries. Despite this, women are still subject to discrimination within the workforce. This discrimination often takes the form of sexual harassment and the 'glass ceiling'. Women who work for pay are also likely to face the double shift—heavy workloads both at the workplace and at home. Within the home, gender inequality extends across domestic work, child care, and caregiver duties with parents and spouses.

Socialization plays an important role in subordinating women. Socialization causes people to internalize values that, in turn, lead them to enforce and act out gender roles. This socialization occurs not only in the family, but also through the media, language, schools, and religion. Images of, views of, and beliefs about gender are learned both in childhood and through adult socialization.

In Canada, women still do not hold many positions of real power in political or legal spheres. Therefore, women's issues are often ignored or receive less political attention than they deserve. In other societies, where women are more powerful politically, gender issues are dealt with more firmly and thoroughly.

QUESTIONS FOR CRITICAL THOUGHT

1. Have there been any instances in your life where you were disadvantaged because of your gender? Evaluate two competing explanations of your experience.

2. Before you read this chapter, what was your understanding of gender? Compare your previous definition with how you currently define 'gender'.

3. In your opinion, are males truly dominant in Canadian society? Explain your answer.

4. What future trends do you foresee in regard to gender and the job market?

5. Is there a glass ceiling where you work or where you worked? Try to provide examples.

6. Do males experience any disadvantages in society?

RECOMMENDED READINGS

Armstrong, Pat, and Hugh Armstrong. 1994. *The Double Ghetto: Canadian Women and Their Seg-regated Work*, 3rd edn. Toronto: McClelland & Stewart. Originally published in 1978, this book describes the demeaned condition of Canadian women in the workplace and at home, living as they were in what the authors called a female 'double ghetto'. Since then there have been two new editions and in this most recent (1994), the authors note that the condition has not changed to a large degree and that Canadian society is still organized and divided according to sex. This edition contains new sections on postmodern/anti-racist feminist theory and the gendered nature of part-time work.

Gardiner, Judith Kegan, ed. 2002. *Masculinity Studies and Feminist Theory: New Directions*. New York: Columbia University Press. Most academic research and literature on gender relations focuses on women; however, in recent years the field has embraced issues of masculinity as well as femininity, and this book reflects this flurry of interest. Here, masculinity is considered from a feminist per-spective, and, according to Michael Kimmel (who has written a foreword to the book), 'the wisdom of this collection . . . is its portrayal of feminist theory and masculinities studies as partners.' The 14 essays are written by different authors who offer divergent viewpoints, and their insights are both accessible and thought-provoking.

Kaufmann, Michael, ed. 1987. *Beyond Patriarchy: Essays by Men on Pleasure, Power, and Change*. Toronto: Oxford University Press. Although this book is not recent, it marks the beginning of an interest in sociology on the topic of masculinity. It uncovers the changing, and persisting, notions of this topic and those associated with it. The authors of the various essays are sympathetic to the feminist cause, and integrate several of its principles into their considerations of the various topics covered. The authors also discuss many of the social issues that were emerging in the 1980s that are significant to men today—fatherhood, career, homosexuality, political structure—as well as the portrayal of males in advertising, sports, and the media.

Kimmel, Michael, ed. 2007. *The Sexual Self: The Construction of Sexual Scripts*. Nashville: Vanderbilt University Press. Although sexuality was not the focus of this chapter, sexuality and gender are closely related. This book examines this interconnection with reference to 'sexual scripts', a concept developed in the 1960s by sociologists John Gagnon and William Simon. As such, the authors treat sexuality as a social phenomenon that is subject to social and cultural context.

Pinnelli, Antonella, Filomena Racioppi, and Rosella Rettaroli, eds. 2007. *Genders in the Life Course: Demographic Issues*. Dordrecht, The Netherlands: Springer. This book offers a comprehensive approach to gender and its relation to demographic behaviour through a life course perspective, including overview of topics such as intimate union formation and dissolution, fertility, migration, aging, and gender inequality. It is geared to an academic audience of social scientists and other scholars but is also useful as a taste of the field for undergraduates.

Siltanen, Janet, and Andrea Doucet. 2008. *Gender Relations in Canada: Intersectionality and Beyond*. Toronto: Oxford University Press. This book is part of a series of works on important sociological topics with specific emphasis on Canadian issues. The authors discuss the implication of gender throughout the life course, providing plenty of examples to engage the reader.

RECOMMENDED WEBSITES

Equality between Women and Men

www.acdi-cida.gc.ca/CIDAWEB/acdicida.nsf/En/JUD-31192610-JXF

This page is by the Canadian International Development Agency (CIDA), Canada's 'lead agency for development assistance', actively promoting a more equitable world. In this article CIDA overviews gender inequality as a universal phenomenon, as well as the issues associated with this problem—including the lack of human rights or access to resources for many of the women in our world. It also notes the importance of men in contributing to a modern, equitable mindset in relation to gender.

Milestones in Canadian Women's History

www.unb.ca/par-l/milestones.htm

This chronology of major events in the history of women in Canada from the 1960s to the present is provided by the Canadian Electronic Feminist Network, working with PAR-L (Policy, Action, Research List), which is a bilingual network of individuals and organizations whose focus is on women-centred policy change in Canada. Its mission is to raise awareness about women' issues and promote reform through the mobilization of support for positive change.

Gender and Work Database

wds.genderwork.ca

This database uses Statistics Canada data to create resources unavailable elsewhere. You can also use the database to adjust the data according to your own interests.

Status of Women Canada (SWC)

www.swc-cfc.gc.ca

This government website promotes gender equality in Canada. It also targets the increasing participation of women in the Canadian economy, encouraging the development of this trend. Its aim is to promote women's health and well-being, economic security, safety from abuse and violence, as well as human rights.

The Third WWWave

www.3rdwwwave.com

This is an engaging website by a group of women passionate about women's issues and dedicated to improving women's lives. They promote 'Third Wave Feminism', which began in the 1990s. The website is creative and thought-provoking, with features such as 'The Third WWWave Replies to the News' as well as others, with lots of links to more information.

Global Database of Quotas for Women

www.quotaproject.org/about.cfm

This is a website by the International Institute for Democracy and Electoral Assistance in co-operation with Stockholm University in Sweden. It targets the social, economic, and political obstacles that block women from participating in public office in over 90 countries, including Canada. Its aim is to increase women's political representation. This database is intended as a research tool.

CHAPTER 5
Sexualities

LEARNING OBJECTIVES

- To understand the terms 'homophobia', 'heterosexism', and 'transgendered'.
- To know about the history and origins of homophobia.
- To appreciate the significance of the gender binary to transgendered people.
- To become familiar with the different theories of homophobia.
- To discover the social and health consequences of homophobia.
- To learn about possible solutions to the homophobia problem.

INTRODUCTION

People with alternative sexual orientations have long suffered from ridicule, discrimination, exclusion, and even violence. Recently, however, public discussions of this topic have been strongly influenced by current thinking about human rights. Change is also visible in the ways that gays, lesbians, and others present the issue today—as constructionists would say, in terms of 'victim claiming' and 'injustice framing' (Berbrier and Pruett, 2006).

Generally, Canadians expect people to be either homosexual or heterosexual and to act accordingly. In the past, many Canadians considered homosexual behaviour to be problematic. Over the last generation, Canadian public opinion about sexual topics has changed dramatically, however. Attitudes about same-sex intimacy and marriage have become more liberal. Today, few Canadians view homosexuality as immoral or worthy of criminalization, as many did in the past. In particular, people with homosexuals as kin, friends, acquaintances, or workmates are more accepting and knowledgeable (Osterlund, 2009).

As a result, in Canada today, most people consider *anti*-homosexual behaviour—not homosexuality itself—a social problem and a potential violation of hate laws and the human rights codes. To understand how and why Canadian attitudes to sexual orientation have changed, we need first to define our key terms: sexual orientation, gender binary, homosexuality, and homophobia, among others.

SEXUAL ORIENTATION

Homosexuality is an attraction, physical and emotional, to people of the same sex. It is hard to say whether 'homosexuality' is an act (or set of acts), a preference, or an identity, and if it is something occasional, regular, or permanent. Views vary on this topic.

Sexual orientation is defined here as sexual attraction to people of a particular sex (or sexes). The word **queer**, though once thought offensive by the gay community, has now been embraced by that community as an umbrella term to describe people who identify as anything other than heterosexual (Hammers, 2009; Walcott, 2009). However, the term is still not widely accepted in the heterosexual community. So, in this chapter, we will refer to the non-heterosexual community by the inclusive term 'lesbian, gay, bisexual, and transgendered', or LGBT. In much of the literature, however, the preferred acronym is LGBTQ, where the 'Q' stands for Queer (Hoffman et al., 2009).

In early twentieth-century North America, most people held the view that sexuality is fixed and binary. 'Normal' people were supposed to be entirely heterosexual or entirely homosexual. However, the American sexologist Dr Alfred Kinsey—writing in the 1940s and 1950s, at the end of a long period of what some called 'Victorian prudery'—showed that human sexual orientation lies on a continuum, with heterosexuality at one end and homosexuality at the other. Most people are not entirely heterosexual or homosexual; sexual desires reside somewhere between the ends of the continuum. Kinsey also noted that people often do not act on their sexual desires, for fear of attracting censure or stigma (Gebhard and Reece, 2008). For these reasons, some people who think of themselves as heterosexual yet feel attracted to people of the same sex may not respond to this attraction. Likewise, people who identify themselves as homosexual yet feel an attraction to one or more people of the opposite sex

HOMOSEXUALITY Sexual attraction to people of the same sex.

SEXUAL ORIENTATION One's sexual attraction to people of a specific sex.

QUEER An umbrella term for anyone who does not identify as heterosexual.

LGBTQ Acronym for lesbian, gay, bisexual, transgendered, queer—often used to speak of the LGBTQ community.

may not respond to this attraction, in the belief that they should be consistent. Both behaviours reflect the belief that people are normally *either* heterosexual *or* homosexual.

Perhaps this very blurring of the line between homosexuality and heterosexuality leads some people to enforce the boundary with special rigour (Kim, 2007; Madureira and Amaral, 2007). This may contribute, in some cases, to homophobic behaviour, which we will discuss later. In general, how we think about sexuality is influenced by how we think about sex and gender. In both cases, we tend to fall into binary categorizations that discourage the recognition that, in reality, people are complex and varied in all these respects.

Numbering the Homosexual Population

Today, tolerance for homosexuality is widespread though the practice itself remains relatively rare. Recent surveys have established factual information about the prevalence of homosexuality in Canada. The Canadian Community Health Survey, Cycle 2.1 (2004), was the first—and most recent—Statistics Canada survey to have included a question on sexual orientation. Among Canadians aged 18–59, 1 per cent reported that they consider themselves to be homosexual and 0.7 per cent considered themselves bisexual. About 1.3 per cent of men considered themselves homosexual, about twice the proportion among women (0.7 per cent).

There is general agreement on several matters: First, it is likely that the concentration of homosexuals is greater in some communities than others: for example, in cities rather than rural areas. Second, though the homosexual population may reach as high as 10 per cent in populations where they are most concentrated, the overall proportion of homosexuals is far closer to 1–2 per cent of the national population. Third, male (gay) homosexuals are invariably found to be more numerous than female (lesbian) homosexuals; the reasons for this are unknown. Finally, debate continues to flourish about how to properly define and measure homosexuality (Ramsey and Santiago, 2004).

A recent study (McCabe et al., 2009) shows the difficulty associated with numbering the homosexual population. These researchers set out to assess past-year prevalence rates of substance use and dependency among heterosexuals and homosexuals, using a large national sample of adults in the United States—the 2004–5 (wave 2) National Epidemiologic Survey on Alcohol and Related Conditions.

The sample numbered nearly 35,000 adults aged 20 years and older, belonging to every racial and ethnic group, educational group, and social class. McCabe et al. found that roughly 2 per cent of the sample self-identified as lesbian, gay, or bisexual. However, 4 per cent reported at least one same-sex sexual partner during their lifetime. Moreover, 6 per cent reported same-sex sexual attraction. As expected, non-heterosexual orientation was generally associated with a higher-than-average risk of substance use and substance dependence (Brubaker et al., 2009; Gillespie and Blackwell, 2009). However, the more important finding, for our purpose, is that the risks of substance abuse appear to vary by a factor of three depending on how sexual orientation is defined. We must keep in mind this fact—the unclarity of our definitions and measurements (Uzzell and Horne, 2006)—in all the discussion that follows.

GENDER BINARY AND TRANSGENDERED PEOPLE

Like our society, most societies of the world code for only two sexes: male and female. Moreover, most societies consider gender a master status—one of the two most important bases of social differentiation (the other is age). Whether a person is male or female is central to that person's social identity. Since distinguishing between maleness and femaleness is so important in most societies, the idea of changing or blurring genders, or crossing gender lines, troubles many people. When someone does not fit clearly into one of the two required categories, many members of society feel uncomfortable.

However, some people fall outside the rigid gender binary: they do not fit easily into either of the socially or biologically defined roles of male and female. As a result, they also do not fit easily into the socially accepted role dichotomies (Taylor and Rupp, 2004).

The prime examples are **transgendered** people, who feel that their social identity does not match their biological sex. They do not—cannot—identify with their birth sex and socially assigned gender. For example, they may have male genitalia but identify themselves as women. 'Transgender' is a broad term that denotes anyone whose gender identity falls outside the conventional gender binaries (Cashore and Tuason, 2009). Because

TRANSAMERICA

Starring Felicity Huffman as a pre-operative transsexual, this 2005 film powerfully explores modern-day cultural and political binaries of gender.

TRANSGENDERED An umbrella term for any gender-variant person.

Transgender lawyer Micheline Montreuil poses in her office in Quebec City, November 2009. As a transgendered person, Micheline Anne Helene Montreuil, born Pierre Montreuil, became known for her legal struggles to defend her rights.

The Canadian Press/Francis Vachon

the term covers such a broad range of experience, many transsexual people—and many lesbian, gay, and **bisexual** people as well—have taken on the label of 'transgender'.

The term can include transsexual people who are pre-operative or post-operative, if they have chosen surgical means to change their sex so that it conforms to their own sense of gender. It can also include cross-dressers (who are sometimes called transvestites), inter-sexed people, and people who, regardless of their gender or sexual orientation, are viewed by others as atypical of their gender (Golden, 2005).

As mentioned, some people who identify as transgendered go through various medical procedures so they can *transition* into the sex they feel they ought to be (Hines, 2006; Winter, 2006; Okumura, 2007). The necessary treatments range from simple hormone therapy to more complicated sexual reassignment surgery. For various reasons, not all transgendered people undergo surgery. For example, some women may live with male genitalia because they lack access to surgical procedures, or simply because they do not wish to change physically.

Many view transgendered people as part of the LGBT community; yet some transgendered people feel they do not belong to that community (Concannon, 2008; McLaren, 2009). For example, they must deal with medical and discrimination issues that may be different from those experienced by lesbian and gay members of the community. As well, transgendered people must also deal with different identity issues. For example, imagine Jo—a biological male—who self-identifies as heterosexual and a woman. After surgery to become female, Jo will want to live as a woman. And if Jo still identifies as heterosexual, she may feel little attachment to the lesbian community, choosing instead to live like any other heterosexual woman.

Like other LGBT communities, transgendered communities are typically located in large urban centres (Tomassilli et al., 2009). Many transgendered people move to big cities specif-ically to find their niche. People in big cities tend to discriminate less than people in smaller cities and towns, who are generally less familiar with people outside the sexual mainstream (Hancock, 2008). However, as the account in Box 5.1 indicates, we can find new experiments in living even in small communities far away from the big city.

Coming Out

From a sociological perspective, the most important step in the sexual 'career' of an LGBT person is 'coming out'—disclosing his or her (until then secret) **sexual identity** to family, friends, co-workers, and others (Bogaert and Hafer, 2009).

This transition is sociologically important for several reasons. First, until a person comes out, he or she has difficulty fully entering into the LGBT community—a major social transi-tion from the heterosexual world to the homosexual world and, often, from old friends and activities to new ones. Second, and equally important, people's identities are linked to the social roles they play (Corrigan et al., 2009). They cannot fully enter into, or endorse, a new identity for themselves until they fully embrace the new role that it entails. So, coming out is as much a statement a person makes to oneself as it is a statement to one's partner, friends, family members, and the general community.

PERSONAL STORIES

Box 5.1 Is Society Ready for This Pregnant Husband?

To our neighbours, my wife, Nancy, and I don't appear in the least unusual. To those in the quiet Oregon community where we live, we are viewed just as we are—a happy couple deeply in love. Our desire to work hard, buy our first home, and start a family was nothing out of the ordinary. That is, until we decided that I would carry our child.

I am transgender, legally male, and legally married to Nancy. Unlike those in same-sex marriages, domestic partnerships, or civil unions, Nancy and I are afforded the more than 1,100 federal rights of marriage. Sterilization is not a requirement for sex reassignment, so I decided to have chest reconstruction and testosterone therapy but kept my reproductive rights. Wanting to have a biological child is neither a male nor female desire, but a human desire.

Our situation sparks legal, political, and social unknowns. We have only begun experiencing opposition from people who are upset by our situation. Doctors have discriminated against us, turning us away due to their religious beliefs. Health care professionals have refused to call me by a male pronoun or recognize Nancy as my wife. Receptionists have laughed at us. Friends and family have been unsupportive; most of Nancy's family doesn't even know I'm transgender.

This whole process, from trying to get pregnant to being pregnant, has been a challenge for us. The first doctor we approached was a reproductive endocrinologist. He was shocked by our situation and told me to shave my facial hair. After a $300 consultation, he reluctantly performed my initial checkups. He then required us to see the clinic's psychologist to see if we were fit to bring a child into this world and consulted with the ethics board of his hospital. A few months and a couple thousand dollars later, he told us

that he would no longer treat us, saying he and his staff felt uncomfortable working with 'someone like me'.

In total, nine different doctors have been involved. This is why it took over one year to get access to a cryogenic sperm bank to purchase anonymous donor vials, and why Nancy and I eventually resorted to home insemination.

When I finally got pregnant for the first time, I ended up having an ectopic pregnancy with triplets. It was a life-threatening event that required surgical intervention, resulting in the loss of all embryos and my right fallopian tube. When my brother found out about my loss, he said, 'It's a good thing that happened. Who knows what kind of monster it would have been.'

On successfully getting pregnant a second time, we are proud to announce that this pregnancy is free of complications and our baby girl has a clean bill of health. We are happily awaiting her birth, with an estimated due date of July 3, 2008.

How does it feel to be a pregnant man? Incredible. Despite the fact that my belly is growing with a new life inside me, I am stable and confident being the man that I am. In a technical sense I see myself as my own surrogate, though my gender identity as male is constant. To Nancy, I am her husband carrying our child—I am so lucky to have such a loving, supportive wife. I will be my daughter's father, and Nancy will be her mother. We will be a family.

Outside the local medical community, people don't know I'm five months' pregnant. But our situation ultimately will ask everyone to embrace the gamut of human possibility and to define for themselves what is normal.

Source: Beatie (2008).

Finally, disclosure is important in the organizations where individual lesbians or gay men work. People spend so much of their time and energy at work, it is important they be known for who they really are. However, many fear this may jeopardize their relations with other workers and perhaps even harm their job security (DeJordy, 2008; King et al., 2008). So, coming out at work is a big decision—a big declaration to oneself and others. Sometimes disclosure may not be the best policy. Workplaces and families vary in this respect. In some situations, secrecy is not dysfunctional—it is preferable. In a family, for example, secrecy about sexual orientation may minimize family disruption and stigma by association; and it controls the spread of information to other members of the community (Chow and Cheng, 2010).

Some LGBT people delay coming out for years (Frost and Bastone, 2008). Others, as camouflage, even marry and raise children with someone of the opposite sex, while recognizing their own deception. They may come out in middle age, after leading a life of secret wishes, desires, and activities all that time. However, coming out in mid-adulthood, after decades of secrecy and lies, disrupts relationships and leads people to fear the loss of everything they have constructed. Many grieve the loss of a 'normal' life. In short, coming out in mid-adulthood requires great courage and strength, but so does the lengthy delay of coming out (Wang et al., 2009).

Coming out affects other people, too. After their child comes out, parents have to deal with a reality that is new, incomprehensible, and perhaps even morally unacceptable to them. On top of that, they must put a good face on it for their friends and relatives (Potoczniak et al., 2009). Not all parents are able to do this—at least not very readily—and so do not immediately accept and support their children's sexual identities. Some take years to make the adjustment; others adjust quickly and some parents never do (Alpaslan et al., 2009).

ATTITUDES AND LAWS

Throughout history, sexuality has been one of the most debated and problematized of human activities. Most of us conduct our sexual activities in private and grant the same privacy to others. And, most of the time, people ignore the sexual inclinations of others unless these are brought forcefully to their attention. So, once again, we really don't know how many people identify themselves as homosexual, nor (identification aside) are we aware of how many people are having sex with someone of the same sex.

On the other hand, most people are aware of homosexuality and of prominent homosexuals; and this has always been so. For example, a great many people knew and accepted Oscar Wilde (1854–1900)—the celebrated Irish playwright—as being homosexual long before anyone thought to charge and imprison him for this then-criminal offence. It was only through the forceful efforts of John Sholto Douglas, the Ninth Marquess of Queensberry and disapproving father of Wilde's aristocratic lover, to discredit the playwright in court that Wilde's homosexuality became a public issue no one could ignore.

Contrast this sexual hypocrisy with ancient Greece, where people considered sexual relations between two men a regular and 'normal' part of life (Harris, 2009). As a citizen, a Greek man who was old enough to vote was free to have sex with whomever he wished; this included having sex with young boys. The rule, however, was that a free man must adopt the position of the 'top' or insertive partner. To 'bottom', or receive, was socially acceptable only for a non-citizen, a woman, or a young boy. For a citizen to assume this bottom position was considered dishonourable and improper. In short, homosexual activity was not only socially accepted; it had its own etiquette (Turner, 2009).

Moreover, *behaviour* that we would consider homosexual today, such as anal sex between two males, was not assumed in ancient Greece to reveal a person's sexual *identity* (see, e.g., Halperin, 1990). The Greeks felt one could not readily infer sexual identity from sexual actions. This meant that the line between homosexuality and heterosexuality was even more blurred in ancient Greece than it is today; but then, no one seemed to care.

Many cultural attitudes about homosexuality changed—indeed, homogenized—with the spread of Christianity and the Catholic Church. In Christian Europe during the early Middle Ages, the Church largely ignored or tolerated homosexual behaviour. Hostility and resentment towards homosexuals surfaced in the thirteenth century, however. The religious writings of Thomas Aquinas (1225–1274) spread the idea that homosexuality is unnatural and undesirable, obliging people who considered themselves Christians to condemn homosexual behaviour. As stigma and shame were attached to homosexuality in Christian countries, homosexual behaviour was forced underground. It didn't stop; it merely became hidden (Richlin, 2005; Findlay, 2006).

Even today, homosexual behaviour remains illegal or, at best, highly regulated in many countries. For example, in several states of the United States, sodomy remained illegal until 2003, when the US Supreme Court struck down laws prohibiting the practice. (Sodomy is defined by the *Merriam-Webster Dictionary* as anal or oral sexual intercourse with a member of the same or opposite sex, and also copulation with an animal; but enforcement of the law has normally been limited to homosexuals.) It is interesting to note that the same US states that were last to give up sodomy laws were all slave states in the nineteenth century and, for the most part, still practise capital punishment. In short, they are not progressive places.

This connection between anti-homosexual legislation and other forms of punitiveness is found in other countries of the world as well (Ferfolja, 2007). Generally, countries with restrictive morality laws (for example, Singapore and Saudi Arabia) believe that homosexual behaviour is morally wrong and threatening to society. In these jurisdictions, punishments for homosexual relations may include imprisonment, lashes, or even death. In some countries, these laws only apply to homosexual relations between two men, however (Bahreini, 2008; Whitehead, 2010). Sri Lanka's law, for example, does not even mention lesbian relations.

Despite the generally oppositional role of Christianity and Islam, not all religions have opposed homosexuality. Confucian philosophy, which regulated China and societies affected by Chinese culture, did not oppose homosexuality unless the family forbade it (Liu, 2009; Rosker, 2009). So long as sexual activity did not interfere with procreation—a familial duty—Confucianism did not forbid men from having erotic feelings for other men, nor did it forbid sexual relations between men. Still, this did not prevent the development of restrictions on homosexual behaviour in Chinese communities like Singapore. The state of Israel, by contrast, has explicitly demonstrated its support for homosexual citizens, despite the opposition of orthodox Jews in the country (Box 5.2).

There has also been an observable shift in the attitudes of social scientists towards homosexuality. The period 1975–2001 saw a significant increase in the quantity of psychological research on homosexuals, for example (Lee and Crawford, 2007). Sociologists, too, have changed their approach to homosexuality. In the past, they commonly viewed it as a learned

INTERNATIONAL COMPARISONS

Box 5.2 International Comparisons

Gunman Kills Two at a Tel Aviv Gay Youth Centre

Tens of thousands of Israelis gathered in central Tel Aviv on Saturday to express solidarity with the gay community, a week after a gunman killed two people at a gay youth centre.

President Shimon Peres led political leaders in the show of support and spoke from a podium decorated with the rainbow flag.

'The bullets that hit the gay community at the beginning of the week struck us all as people, as Jews, as Israelis . . . criminals will not set our agenda', Mr Peres said in a speech.

Last Saturday, a masked gunman burst into a community centre for gay teenagers in Tel Aviv and shot dead a 26-year-old man and a 16-year-old girl. Thirteen other people were wounded.

A crowd of tens of thousands filled Tel Aviv's Rabin Square, a focal point for major Israeli protests, for the peaceful show of solidarity, a police spokesman said.

'Israel will never reconcile itself with such a crime and will not rest until the criminal is brought to justice. . . . This terrible act of murder will not be wiped from our hearts', Mr Peres said.

Police have not revealed a motive for the shooting.

Although cosmopolitan Tel Aviv has a bustling gay scene, open homosexuality is shunned in conservative areas of Israel.

Gay pride marches in Jerusalem meet with often violent protests from ultra-Orthodox Jews, who view homosexuality as an abomination against God.

Source: Reuters (2009).

social behaviour. Today, a majority of sociologists subscribe to the essentialist school, which grants primacy to biological causes (Engle et al., 2006). That is, sociologists—like many others today—view homosexuality as the result of nature, not nurture. With this in mind, one would no more criticize, suppress, or try to change a person's sexual orientation than his age or skin colour.

HOMOSEXUAL CULTURE

The dramatic changes of the last few decades owe a lot to the efforts of gay rights activists. In fact, scholars usually trace the beginning of the modern gay rights movement to an 'enforcement' event in New York City's Greenwich Village in 1969 (Conlon, 2004).

Throughout the 1950s and 1960s, underground gay bars and clubs had begun to shape the social experience of gays and lesbians. Mainstream culture, however, still viewed homosexuality as a deviant and dangerous lifestyle. Police regularly raided known homosexual establishments (e.g., clubs and bathhouses) and arrested patrons merely for being present. In June 1969, New York City police raided the Stonewall Inn. Unlike earlier incidents, this time the gay patrons fought back. For the first time, homosexuals resisted as a group, marking the start of a long battle for the equal rights of LGBTs—a battle that continues today (Gillespie, 2008).

Like the gay and lesbian communities of New York City and San Francisco, Toronto's gay community had been routinely victimized by police raids and harassment. On 5 February 1981, during what came to be known as the Toronto bathhouse riots when Toronto police raided four bathhouses in that city and arrested nearly 300 men as found-ins in bawdy houses, the gay community again fought back. Although the LGBT rights movement had been building for a decade, this event marked a turning point in the movement's history in Canada. Protests ensued, including one in which nearly 2,000 people gathered at Queen's Park (Ontario's provincial legislature) to express their outrage. This was the largest gay demonstration in Canada up to that time. After that, many new gay organizations sprang up in Toronto and existing ones grew rapidly, with ever more access to support and resources. Eventually, the City of Toronto commissioned a report to examine and improve the relationship between police and the LGBT community. Everyone recognized it was necessary to normalize relations between the gay and straight communities (Valverde and Cirak, 2003).

Today, sizable gay and lesbian communities exist in various North American cities. Not only are these communities and their members increasingly visible, but they are increasingly outspoken. Pride celebrations and parades, occasions for the gay community to celebrate their sexuality and demand their rights, take place in almost all the major cities of Canada (Kates et al., 2001; Kuntsman, 2008).

It is no accident this protest happened when and how it did. Sexual protest in North America owed a great deal to the women's movement and to black power protest in the US. Women and urban minorities taught gays and lesbians something important about social mobilization: namely, the importance of *institutional completeness*—the creation of communities that are fully self-supporting and self-aware. They showed that through group mobilization and institutional completeness, minority *communities* survive; and through community survival, minority *identities* survive. Activists applied the same principle in building large, diverse homosexual communities in Toronto, Vancouver, and elsewhere.

LGBT and Native Communities

The Canadian Aboriginal approach to homosexuality gives us a different way of thinking about sexuality in our own culture, for it appears to have solved some problems and avoided others. In recent decades, researchers have replaced the earlier anthropological term 'berdache' with the term 'two-spirit' or 'two-spirited' to refer to North American Aboriginal thinking about Aboriginals who are gay, lesbian, transsexual, transvestite, drag queens or butches, or otherwise bend traditional and more usual gender categories (see Jacobs et al., 1997).

Often, two-spirited or the related concept of the 'third gender' in Native communities is invoked as a sort of myth to accommodate Western notions of transsexuality. However, some have argued that this attempted correspondence risks oversimplifying the 'third gender' concept. It also risks appropriating a non-Western concept for particular (Western) purposes. In this way, the popularization of the third gender concept, Towle and Morgan (2002) argue, contributes to ethnocentric ideas about other cultures.

The term 'two-spirited', devised by Native activists in 1990, has been used to reconnect with Aboriginal cultural traditions. It signals a fluid sexual identity, and in this respect it moves beyond the binary distinction between gay and straight, male and female, that is common in Western traditions (Walters et al., 2006). However, Aboriginal people who identify as two-spirited not only encounter heterosexism and sexism, but often also suffer racism from both society at large and queer identity movements (ibid.).

Still, the two-spirit concept has been a great resource for Aboriginal activists and organizers. Because it involves both sexual and gender identities, it helps to unify the Aboriginal queer movement. Eliminating the need for separate gay, lesbian, bisexual, and transsexual organizations, the two-spirit concept has successfully provided culturally sensitive and empowering support for diverse sexual issues (Meyer-Cook and Labelle, 2004).

People who identify as both Aboriginal and LGBT may face particular problems that result from the intersection of these two minority statuses. One study of men who have sex with men found that the Aboriginal subpopulation of this group was less likely to be employed, more likely to live in unstable housing, and more likely to have incomes of less than $10,000. The Aboriginal men were also found to be subject to particular risk factors for HIV infection, including sexual abuse, poverty, mental health problems, and involvement in sex work (Heath et al., 1999).

THEORETICAL PERSPECTIVES ON SEXUAL ORIENTATION

Table 5.1 Theoretical Perspectives

Theory	Main Points
Structural Functionalism	• Homosexuality threatens traditional institutions like the family, which are established largely for procreation. • Homosexual communities and movements provide social cohesion and social acceptance, in the same ways as heterosexual communities.
Conflict Theory	• Heteronormativity establishes heterosexuality as acceptable and homosexuality as unacceptable. • The gender binary forces people to accept only one gender and one sexual orientation.
Symbolic Interactionism	• People's identities reflect the roles they are permitted to play. • Stigmatization is damaging, leading to impression management and non-disclosure.
Feminist Theory	• People vary widely along a continuum of genders and sexualities. • People express their sexualities differently in different societies and cultures.
Social Constructionism	• Without claims-making and moral entrepreneurship, few would care about other people's sexuality. • Changes in the media have helped to influence a positive change in public attitudes about sexual orientation.

Structural Functionalism

The apparent decline of traditional marriage in North America—formerly comprising a dominant male household head and submissive wife—has made some people worry about the demise of the family (on this, see, e.g., Popenoe, 1993; Nell, 2005). Alongside the LGBT movement, gender politics, sexual politics, and the multiplication of sexual identities have added to a general confusion about intimate relations. From the functionalist perspective, anything that upsets clear role expectations and situational norms is socially disruptive.

So, from the functionalist perspective, the decline of heteronormativity and the blurring of gender lines pose problems for social order. On the other hand, functionalists would likely look with approval at the success homosexuals have had in organizing LGBT communities to satisfy their social needs. They have demonstrated that social pluralism works for sexual minorities, as it does for ethnic minorities.

Conflict Theory

In the past, the pressure for heteronormativity (Geller, 2009) was overt, through social preaching and restrictive laws against homosexuality. Today, the main sources of information—the media, schools, and churches, for example—still hold up a heterosexual lifestyle as the norm (DePalma and Atkinson, 2009). Government, politics, even the arts still display the power of the heterosexual majority (Stacey and Meadow, 2009). Arguably, it was not until 2005 that a major film, *Brokeback Mountain*, examined the subject of homosexuality as one possible relationship between men, rather than as a subcultural aberration (*Cabaret*), source of anguish (*The Dresser*), or 'camp' entertainment (*The Rocky Horror Picture Show*; *Priscilla, Queen of the Desert*).

In the late 1990s, a record number of Fortune 500 corporations began to extend equal benefits to all of their employees regardless of sexual orientation. Today, at least one-third of these huge organizations give their gay and lesbian employees domestic partner benefits, and likely their actions will influence the actions of smaller organizations. Because of their size and wealth, the largest and most powerful corporations act as leaders for the corporate community.

Many large corporations view domestic-partner benefit policies as 'the right thing to do'—a good business policy that helps them compete for the best employees. And a commitment to 'diversity' also attracts customers. It shows the corporate world trying to upgrade its reputation by including gay issues as part of its diversity programs and policies (Day and Greene, 2008).

Feminist Theory

Lesbianism has been connected with various forms of feminism, especially in the latter half of the twentieth century to the present. Some theorists (e.g., Denike, 2007) have even identified gender inequality and homophobia as springing from the same 'heteronormative sexual ethics'. We can see this in the ways that gay men are popularly feminized and lesbians are ascribed masculine qualities (Cohen et al., 2009; Blashill and Powlishta, 2009). Moreover, practices of discrimination around sexual orientation often have an underlying gender basis. In short, women are more tolerant of homosexuality than men.

Feminists are particularly inclined to support same-sex marriage, since doing otherwise reinforces patriarchal ideals and entrenches traditional gender roles in the family (Harding, 2007). However, feminism, too, has sometimes employed rigid, heteronormative thinking in defining certain issues like domestic violence. The feminist inclination to explain intimate partner violence (IPV) solely in terms of patriarchy has weakened its credibility, since IPV afflicts both same-sex and opposite-sex couples, and women, in some opposite-sex relationships, are physically abusive as well.

It's true that empirical studies have found a connection between 'masculinity' (as measured by 'masculine behaviors') and IPV perpetration (Próspero, 2008). However, this focus on one factor—masculine assertiveness—among many has encouraged heterosexism and limited the delivery of support services to lesbian IPV victims, for example. It has left counsellors, police, and other crisis workers insensitive to the particular dynamics of abusive lesbian relationships (Ristock, 2001; Speziale and Ring, 2006). In turn, the lack of support and protection for women in same-sex unions has made these relationships more risky.

HETEROSEXISM
Discrimination against homosexuals in favour of heterosexuals.

Symbolic Interactionism

Symbolic interactionist theories pay attention to the construction and enactment of sexual orientations. They also look at the outcomes of labelling individuals as gay, straight, lesbian, bisexual, and so on, and at how these roles are internalized.

Of course, sexual identities, like gender and other social identities, vary from one society to another, and they vary over time. Societies differ in the degree to which sexual identities are conceived to be essential or fundamental and the degree to which they are viewed as immutable and uncontrollable (versus chosen). At the same time, rapid social change in people's attitudes and identities challenges our creativity as a society, as we scurry to invent, learn about, and enact new approaches to sexuality. Some might view this lack of absolutes, of immutable Truths, as a problem, by encouraging us to embrace what is fashionable or acceptable at any given time while undermining the greater social project. However, others might suggest, as we do, that humans are almost infinitely able to change their social relationships and, for better or worse, there have been few if any immutable Truths revealed to the secular human mind so far.

The question for symbolic interactionists, then, is how do people negotiate different sexualities in different social milieux—some friendlier than others (Hequembourg and Farrell, 1999; McQueeney, 2003)? Further, how do people perceive one another as sexual partners, given different cultural traditions affecting how we view sex, seduction, intimacy, masculinity, and femininity? No sociologist has come closer to answering these questions than Stephen O. Murray (Box 5.3).

CLASSIC WORKS

Box 5.3 Stephen O. Murray's *American Gay* (1996)

Stephen Murray was born in 1950. A gay sociologist and anthropologist, he works mostly out of San Francisco. Murray attended James Madison College at Michigan State University, where he earned his undergraduate degree. He earned a Master's degree in sociology at the University of Arizona, and in 1979 received his Ph.D. in sociology from the University of Toronto. After completing his formal education, Murray did post-doctoral studies at the University of California, Berkeley. There, he studied sociolinguistics as well as the history of sociology and anthropology.

Murray has produced several provocative and controversial books and many papers about homosexuality. His better-known writings include *Latin American Male Homosexualities* (1995), *Homosexualities* (2000), and *American Gay* (1996). As a gay sociologist, Murray was especially interested in the prominently gay issue, HIV/AIDS. He worked with several California county health departments with regard to this problem. Professionally, he is on the boards of both the *Journal of Homosexuality* and the *Histories of Anthropology Annual*.

Only in recent decades have homosexuals 'come out of the closet' and felt confident expressing their sexual preferences in public. This recent change reflects dramatic shifts in popular thinking about sex and sexuality—a reflection of the sexual revolution that began in the 1950s and 1960s with improved contraception. It also reflects a long and successful process of social mobilization, by which gays and lesbians supported one another, formed communities, and influenced public opinion.

Murray's *American Gay* is especially good at discussing the formation of gay communities and cultures—at developing what sociologist Raymond Breton, in the context of ethnicity, has called 'institutional completeness'. For example, Murray discusses the role of gay bars and bathhouses in providing safe meeting places for the expression of homosexuality. He discusses the particular cultural issues that arise in this subculture, for example, the problems of 'gay promiscuity', multiple versions of sexuality (such as bisexuality, transgendering, and sado-masochism), and cross-class or cross-racial relationships within the gay community. And, most fundamentally, he is concerned with the problem of establishing stable roles and relationships— for example, couple relationships—among people who have long had to hide their relations and now have to invent norms for them.

American Gay delves deeply into the topic of homosexuality from a sociological standpoint. Being gay is often sensationalized and stereotyped in the media, which often associates it with leading a solitary life and dying alone. Murray, however, affirms that gay men care for each other just as deeply as heterosexual couples do. Murray regards gay people's efforts to be included in 'straight' institutions (such as marriage and the military) as forms of resistance, not assimilation.

At one time, sociologists who wanted to study homosexuality were doubted or even ostracized. Murray encountered considerable difficulty during the course of his Master's program in Arizona. Faculty as well as students expressed their dislike for his 'gay lifestyle'. In one instance, Murray's research proposal was rejected by his professor who ignorantly said, 'No one is interested in your lifestyle.' Overcoming this adversity, *American Gay* proved that studying homosexuality from a sociological standpoint is not only possible, but interesting and provocative as well.

HOMOPHOBIA AND HETEROSEXISM

Homophobia is the fear or hatred of homosexuals. Usually, the word 'phobia' means an irrational, uncontrollable fear or hatred. Yet, the tendency we are considering under the label of 'homophobia' comes in various forms, ranging from social distance (for example, the unwillingness to form a close friendship), to stereotyping (for example, the view that all gays

HOMOPHOBIA Fear or hatred of homosexuals, or behaviour that suggests such fear or hatred.

are the same), to religious injunctions, to bullying and harassment at school or work, to hate crimes including murder (Balkin et al., 2009; Harris, 2009; O'Higgins-Norman, 2009).

One basic feature of homophobia is 'essentialism'—the belief that all homosexuals have fundamentally the same 'basic' characteristics (Haslam and Levy, 2006; Tomsen, 2006). Psychologist Gordon Allport (1979 [1954]) proposed that any belief in group 'essences' points to a prejudiced personality. So does a rigid cognitive style that cannot accept ambiguity or changeability.

Essentialist beliefs about sexual orientation vary along two dimensions: the 'immutability' of sexual orientation and the 'fundamentality' of a classification of people as heterosexuals and homosexuals. *Immutability* refers to the belief that under no circumstances can one change a personal feature—in this case, homosexuality. *Fundamentality* refers to the belief that a certain feature—in this case, homosexuality—is central to a person's entire character. Research finds that hostile attitudes towards lesbians and gay men are correlated positively with fundamentality but negatively with immutability.

Said another way, people are more likely to hold anti-gay attitudes if they think homosexuals have a choice in their sexual orientation. They are also likely to hold anti-gay attitudes if they think of homosexuality as an essential feature or 'master' status of a person (Waldner et al., 2006).

Most gay rights activists today agree with the idea that one is born gay, and therefore it is not a choice: homosexuality is immutable and outside a person's choosing (Looy, 1995; VanderLaan and Vasey, 2008). The idea that a person is born gay is widely accepted within the gay community, and it is an idea that is gaining acceptance and support from the heterosexual public. At the same time, people are coming to realize that homosexuality is not a master status: that homosexuals vary as widely—socially and psychologically—as heterosexuals. However, they may vary in different ways, largely related to the fact that heterosexual relationships are (still) largely organized around procreation and child-rearing. This difference is important, but it need not lead to prejudice and discrimination. How *does* the perception of such a difference lead to prejudice and discrimination?

One approach, an *attribution-value* theory of prejudice, hypothesizes that people develop prejudice against groups that they feel have a negative attribute for which they are held responsible (Crandall et al., 2001). According to this theory, prejudice towards a group stems from two interrelated variables: attributions of controllability and cultural value. Thus, according to this theory, prejudice is more likely among people who hold gay men and lesbians responsible for their preferences and see a negative (cultural) value in homosexuality.

George Weinberg's (1983 [1972]) introduction of the term 'homophobia' helped focus society's attention on the problem of anti-gay prejudice and stigma. Weinberg called attention to the irrationality and harmfulness of this prejudice, which is no more acceptable than racism or sexism. However, the term 'homophobia' itself has some limitations. Its main shortcoming is the implication that anti-gay prejudice is a 'phobia'—a feeling based mainly on fear and, consequently, an irrational defence mechanism. This approach, rooted in psychoanalysis, is unable to account for historical changes in the way societies view homosexuality and heterosexuality. If we are to gain a sociological (versus psychiatric) understanding of anti-homosexual prejudice, we need a new vocabulary for discussing such behaviour.

To this end, Herek (2004) has defined three concepts that together capture the most important aspects of the notion of homophobia: (1) *sexual stigma* (the shared knowledge of society's negative regard for any non-heterosexual behaviour, identity, or community); (2) *heterosexism* (the cultural ideology that perpetuates sexual stigma); and (3) *sexual prejudice* (individuals' negative attitudes based on sexual orientation). At present, it is not clear if a shift in any of these is most responsible for the decline in anti-homosexual attitudes in the last 25 years (Figure 5.1).

MEDIA AND TECHNOLOGY

People learn a great deal about their normative sexual roles and responsibilities through the mass media. In this sense, then, the media are responsible for teaching us ways to understand sexuality.

Homosexuals, once hidden from movies, television, and other media, are now being portrayed there. Currently, many popular television shows feature at least one gay character; indeed, the token gay character has become a predictable motif just as the token black in advertising and television casting was a generation or two ago. Other television shows have dedicated episodes to gay issues. Research suggests that positive portrayals of sexual minorities in the media lead to more favourable attitudes among heterosexuals (Bonds-Raacke et al., 2007). Likewise, the daily news often includes one or more stories dealing with gay issues.

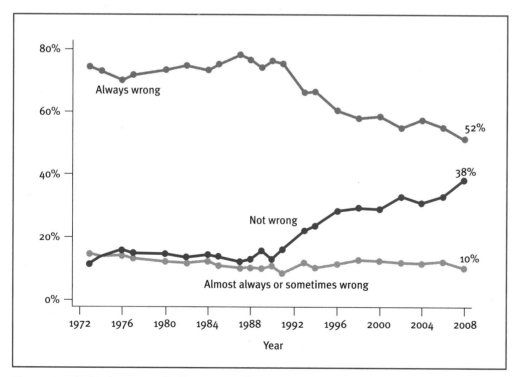

Figure 5.1 Attitudes towards Homosexuality, 1973–2008

Source: **General Social Survey, NORC/University of Chicago**

As youth see these positive changes in the media, they feel safer about coming out to their family and friends. LGBT youth now can feel there is a place for them in society.

However, many people within the gay community believe the media fail to represent them accurately. They admit that any representation at all is a step forward, but also note that television shows such as *Will and Grace* and *Queer Eye for the Straight Guy* promote an unrealistic, 'sanitized' image of gay men (Greenlee, 2005). The gay men portrayed on television are asexual, white, feminized, and well-off—qualities that make them acceptable to the heterosexual public. Moreover, few lesbian women are represented in the mainstream media at all (Oakenfull et al., 2008).

The idea of the 'good gay' makes heterosexual viewers more comfortable with homosexuality, yet it may not be accurate in its representation of homosexual life. As noted earlier, there are as many kinds of gays and lesbians as there are heterosexuals; so one might ask why the media cannot show some of this variety.

In short, there is an imperfect but gradually improved public understanding of homosexuality, thanks to the media and other opportunities for greater familiarity. Traditional homophobia has declined significantly in the last two decades as a result. Yet, homophobia has far from disappeared; it continues to pose a problem for homosexuals as a form of prejudice that promotes discrimination and even violence.

The growth of online communities has enabled LGBT people to seek support in their day-to-day interactions. Online communities have also proven useful for some transgendered people who can't access information elsewhere. In addition, these virtual communities can provide support and discussion, as one study found for female-to-male transsexuals who face the difficult task of passing the social 'test' of manhood. They need teaching, not merely medical or biological intervention (Gauthier and Chaudoir, 2004).

Reproductive technology has also had a large significance for gay, lesbian, and transgendered people who want to become parents (see, e.g., Mamo, 2007). Techniques of surrogacy and artificial insemination have been contested politically, with access to these technologies sometimes being denied to anyone other than straight couples who are unable to conceive through intercourse (Bryld, 2001). These technologies and the political contests associated with them have had important consequences in struggles over parenting and family issues.

SOCIAL CONSEQUENCES OF HOMOPHOBIA

Same-Sex Families

Parents of homosexual or bisexual children may have a hard time accepting their children's sexual orientation. They may be disappointed because they have other expectations for their child or because their child's behaviour embarrasses them. Their reactions can lead to harsh words, broken relationships, and depression. Parents often believe they want 'what is best' for their children and fear that, if gay, their child will miss valuable opportunities or suffer discrimination. Often, parents react with 'why did you do this to me?' when in fact a child's coming out has little to do with his or her parents (see Seidman, 2002).

However, this kind of attitude has been changing. Canadian sociologist Michelle Owen notes that, increasingly, same-sex families have disrupted or changed our dominant views of what 'normal' families are and what they do. Coming from a theoretical tradition known as queer theory, Owen argues that 'families headed by same-sex couples signal both a "normalization of the queer" and a "queering of the normal"' (Owen, 2001: 97).

Same-sex couples 'normalize the queer' by forming families, raising children, and gaining recognition as being just like heterosexual families in their abilities to parent, to provide stability, and to be self-sufficient. At the same time, they 'queer the normal' because their very existence force us to examine in new ways how we think of family, what we do as families, and what we want 'the family' to be.

Lesbian families, in particular, have displayed strengths that would likely benefit straight families as well (Moore, 2009; Röndahl et al., 2009). For example, Savin-Williams and Esterberg (2000) found that these families are more likely than straight families to exhibit an egalitarian decision-making structure. That said, straight parents and lesbian parents are

The Canadian Press/Nathan Denette

Lesbian couple and parents Julia Gonsalves, right, and Andrea Bruner, left, hold their child Gracie Gonsalves-Bruner as they take part in an annual Gay Pride Parade in Toronto 28 June 2009.

similar in two important ways: both practice child-centred parenting and both try to parent children according to socially produced scripts.

In their local and federal policy-making, governments should therefore focus on these similarities. However, governments have resisted becoming closely involved in the inner workings of marriage and parenthood, which they see as private family matters. This is one reason many members of the Canadian government were unwilling to debate whether gay and lesbian couples should be allowed to marry legally.

The argument to allow same-sex marriage is based on the idea that marriage benefits society by sharing resources, reducing the need for welfare and, in many ways, making them healthy and happy (Young and Boyd, 2006; Goldfarb, 2007). In short, marriage stabilizes society. Good families support their members, no matter whether they are built around same-sex or opposite-sex couples. Marriage also takes the pressure off governments to provide care, since spouses—whether heterosexual or homosexual—are assumed to do the caring.

As more countries legalize gay and lesbian unions, the number of same-sex couples wishing to adopt and raise children will naturally increase. Some have feared that children growing up in homosexual households would also be homosexual. However, there has been no evidence to support this concern. Among lesbian couples, a mother's sexual orientation neither determines the child's gender development nor increases the likelihood of any psychological problems (Mooney-Somers and Golombok, 2000). Rather, the quality of family relationships—not the sex of parents—is what influences the child's well-being. Research by Fitzgerald (1999) finds similar results for children raised by gay male-parent couples.

Some observers have wondered if children with same-sex parents would develop as well as children with opposite-sex parents. Many studies support the finding that gay and lesbian parents are just as capable in child-rearing as heterosexual parents. Children raised by homosexual parents do not have different behavioural and educational outcomes than children of heterosexual unions, nor do they feel any less loved or accepted by their parents (Mattingly and Bozick, 2001). Further, there is no more chance of children growing up gay or lesbian in a same-sex family than in a heterosexual family.

Some critics of homosexual parenting argue that lesbian unions lack a proper father figure, which could affect the growth of the child. Many gay and lesbian parents wish to dispel the notion that parenting must be synonymous with gendered assumptions about mothering and fathering, and that mothers and fathers should share a household with their children (Donovan, 2000). Many children of same-sex unions feel they gained important insights into gender relations and broader, more inclusive definitions of family by growing up with same-sex parents (Crowl et al., 2008; Biblarz and Stacey, 2010).

Until recently, most family research ignored same-sex couple families and their parenting practices. This lack of research resulted in an incomplete picture of what same-sex families are and do. Though more people are now coming to accept homosexuals, attitudes towards gay parents still remain conservative, especially among older and rural people. Only about 20 per cent of Canadians surveyed in Miall and March's (2005) study, for example, were in favour of homosexuals adopting children, compared with the 92 per cent who supported adoption by traditional married couples.

Harassment and Hate Crimes

Schools play an important part in the transmission of attitudes to homosexuality, and many studies have identified the classroom as a place where gender and sexuality are constructed. In the classroom and the schoolyard, most children first encounter the views of their peers about different sexual orientations.

Boys at school often use homophobic terms with one another. But what do they mean when they use these terms? Terms like 'faggot' tap a complex array of meanings that have precise meanings in peer cultures. Boys quickly learn to use these homophobic terms against others. Significantly, the evocative use of homophobic terms commonly occurs before puberty, before boys gain an adult sexual identity and before they know much, if anything, about homosexuality. As a result, early learning provides an entry into understanding adult sexual identities and, significantly, powerful homophobic codes are learned first (Plummer, 2001).

No wonder, then, that hate and fear persist around issues of homosexuality. To combat this, Bill C-250 was passed in 2004, making it a crime in Canada to spread hateful views about other people's sexual orientation. Under this bill, homosexuals are now among the groups protected against hate crimes under the Criminal Code, a list that includes racial, religious, and ethnic minorities.

Unfortunately, such hate crimes continue to be a problem. A study of gay and lesbian victims found that strangers in public places were the most likely to perpetrate hate crimes. However, victimization occurs in other locales, too, and perpetrators can include neighbours, schoolmates, co-workers, and even relatives. As with date-rape, not all experiences of victimization are reported. Many people have concerns about police bias and fear that public disclosure of their sexual orientation will influence how officials respond, making them reluctant to report anti-gay crimes; they also fear that perpetrators, if reported, will go unpunished and take revenge. Such concerns are typical among all victims of assault, however.

Workplace Discrimination

Many companies today claim to seek diversity in their employees. They stress that they are equal opportunity employers and that all minorities, including gays and lesbians, have an equal chance of being hired, promoted, and treated fairly once employed. These claims sound reasonable, yet many companies do not always follow through on their promises. As a result, many gays and lesbians feel a need to hide their identity while at work for fear of discrimination (O'Ryan and MacFarland, 2010).

Gay men and lesbians who experience discrimination in the workplace are sometimes unwilling to report it, however. Doing so would often mean revealing their sexual identity to even more people. Most people want to keep their personal lives quiet, and reporting discrimination can mean publicizing one's private life to the entire office. Yet gay rights groups warn that if harassment goes unreported, nothing will ever change. Homosexuals who experience discrimination clearly have an important decision to make. Moreover, the law is on their side. Provincial human rights codes and the Canadian Charter of Rights

PHILADELPHIA

Jonathan Demme's 1993 film explores a law firm's illegal dismissal of a gay employee (Tom Hanks) after the standout attorney contracts AIDS.

and Freedoms make it illegal to discriminate against a person based on his or her sexual orientation. It is also illegal, therefore, to discriminate against someone who is in a same-sex relationship.

But because employees are reluctant to invoke the law, bosses can make the workplace environment more (or less) friendly for gays and lesbians. Factors creating a more comfortable environment for homosexual workers include support from top management, policies to prevent discrimination, the presence of LGBT employee networks, and a non-heterosexist organizational climate (Ragins et al., 2003). Conversely, conditions that influence a person to stay 'in the closet' at work include a lack of racial balance and work teams that are composed mostly of men. Having a male supervisor also increases the likelihood of staying in the closet, as people report experiencing more discrimination and homophobia under male supervisors.

HEALTH CONSEQUENCES OF HOMOPHOBIA
HIV/AIDS

When the HIV/AIDS epidemic began in the early 1980s, the US government was reluctant to help communities in need (Gross and Bisson, 2009). The virus seemed to affect only injecting drug users and 'men who have sex with men'—people who were held responsible for their illness, as they were popularly believed to have complete control over their own risky behaviours. Given the belief that HIV was not affecting heterosexuals and drug abstainers, little was done to stem the growing epidemic. Most doctors at the time were uninformed about how to deal with HIV infection, and they were reluctant to learn about it, treat it, or help people who became HIV-positive.

In the early days, news reports called it a 'gay disease'. For a long time, people were unsure exactly how HIV/AIDS was passed from one person to another and, therefore, how its transmission could be prevented. Large numbers of gay men in gay communities, in New York City for example, were dying of the disease. AIDS activists tried to raise awareness about the sick and dying communities of gay men infected with the virus by calling attention to the epidemic and pointing out that government inaction was letting more and more people die.

This official indifference and lack of support outraged the gay communities. Many felt certain that if HIV were to affect heterosexual people in large numbers, the government would take immediate action. This sense of outrage led to the forming of organizations for action and support, including the AIDS Coalition to Unleash Power (ACTUP)—now one of the largest AIDS organizations fighting for awareness and research about HIV/AIDS. In New York City, posters with the slogan 'silence = death' appeared everywhere around the city.

Today, we know that HIV affects more than just homosexuals. Television commercials, posters promoting the use of condoms, and news and other forms of media have spread a public awareness of the problem. There is also more awareness of the AIDS crisis in Africa and of rising HIV rates among young North American women. Members of the gay community, through their activism, were pioneers in promoting this awareness about HIV/AIDS, by demanding more research, more access to drugs and treatment, and more protection of the rights of HIV-positive people. These actions have benefited all people infected with the virus, regardless of their sexual orientation.

Use of Health Services

The health problems facing gay, lesbian, bisexual, and transgendered people may not be caused by homophobia, but they are often worsened by the homophobia and heterosexism of some doctors and other medical professionals (Diaz et al., 2005; Rutledge et al., 2009). Sometimes, simple ignorance of LGBT issues—not hostility—leads doctors and other health professionals to treat their LGBT patients insensitively or unprofessionally. Such institutionalized homophobia frightens many homosexual people. People who fear they will be judged or misunderstood are likely to visit the doctor less often, leading to poorer health.

Many LGBT people have reported experiencing homophobia or heterosexism from healthcare professionals (e.g., Peel, 2008). The extreme cases have to do with transgendered people who are seeking sexual reassignment surgery. Some feel they should have been born the opposite sex. Feeling neither wholly male nor wholly female, they sometimes seek surgery, as well as hormone treatment, to remedy this condition. To receive such surgical intervention they must claim they feel they were born in the wrong body; but not every doctor is willing to go along with this request.

Nor is sexual reassignment surgery the only medical issue facing transgendered people. Some children are born intersexed, with ambiguous genitalia. These may include, but are not limited to, Turner syndrome, 5-alpha reductase hermaphroditism, or androgen insensitivity syndrome. In cases like these, the child may be born with both a vagina and a small penis but no testicles, for example; then, a difficult decision has to be made. Because our society works on a rigid gender binary, both doctors and parents may feel that they must choose a single gender for the child and perform the surgery accordingly. Often, repeat genital surgeries are needed as the child gets older, mainly for cosmetic purposes to make the genitals look more 'normal'.

The doctors who perform these surgeries believe that a child cannot develop properly with ambiguous sexuality, so the doctor and family must make a decision about whether the child is to 'become' male or female. These decisions, and the important actions that follow, are stressful for the doctors, parents, and the children themselves.

SOLUTIONS TO THE HOMOPHOBIA PROBLEM

One of the greatest changes in recent years has been the establishment of sexual orientation as a personal domain legally protected from discrimination.

In *Vriend v. Alberta*, a 1997 Supreme Court of Canada case, Delwin Vriend—a lab instructor at King's University College in Edmonton—argued that he was unjustly fired from his job because of his sexual orientation. This challenge was necessary because sexual orientation was not included under the Canadian Charter of Rights and Freedoms. Gay and lesbian activists in the early 1980s had sought specific inclusion in the Charter of Rights and Freedoms and in the Alberta Individual Rights Protection Act as a basis for legal protection against discrimination, but did not succeed.

Vriend successfully challenged this by arguing that sexual orientation is similar to the other grounds stated in Section 15 of the Charter, such as race, religion, and sex, and should be protected as such. As a result of this success, today no one can legally discriminate against homosexuals because of their sexual orientation, any more than they can discriminate against blacks because of their skin colour or against Jews or Muslims because of their religion.

Nonetheless, the important legal precedent achieved in *Vriend* is not quite as powerful as the explicit constitutional protection the Charter, as part of the 1982 Constitution Act, provided to women, ethnic groups, visible minorities, the disabled, and the elderly. More remains to be done to achieve equality on this score.

Canadian Research on Homophobia and Social Change

The timing of the 1982 Charter and the associated increase in court powers coincided with the beginnings of the LGBT movement. The movement was gaining ground just as Canadian courts acquired a new political importance through new constitutional decision-making.

However, legal change alone will not be enough to gain gays and lesbians full social acceptance. As with any social 'other', familiarity and visibility will continue to be important. Personal experience with LGBT people will continue to improve the relations between homosexuals and people who might otherwise disapprove of them.

Education and Policies

As we have seen repeatedly, some acts once considered sexually deviant—for example, homosexual acts—are increasingly accepted in the general population. Today, homosexuals are receiving new recognition and inclusion in the society. Increasingly, government institutions show concern about fair and equal treatment for the LGBT minority. In 1997, the Quebec Ministry of Health and Social Services proposed ways to eliminate heterosexism from health and social services, highlighting problems to which LGBT people are highly vulnerable, such as psychological distress, substance abuse, suicide, and HIV/AIDS. The Quebec government critically examined the value of public services and organizations, focusing especially on LGBT accessibility. Most important, it established a set of new interventions and outlined how these would be implemented. Then, in 1999, British Columbia's Ministry of Health and Ministry Responsible for Seniors published a similar document focusing on lesbian and gay experiences in the health system, and included a set of tips for health planners, policymakers and practitioners.

Another victory came in 2001, when the Canadian census included for the first time a question about same-sex relationships. This represented a step forward in recognizing homosexuals as a part of Canada's diverse population. The census found 34,000 same-sex common-law couples living in Canada. Likely, this number has increased since Canada's subsequent legalization of same-sex marriages. The Canadian Community Health Survey, Cycle 2.1, included a question on sexual orientation in 2004 and, as noted at the outset of this chapter, found that about 1 per cent of the population aged 18–59 considered themselves to be homosexual.

The actual numbers are important, because they influence the extent of government funding for this community. Tom Smith (1998) of the National Opinion Research Center at the University of Chicago (NORC) reports that 'few debates have been so contentious as the controversy over the sexual orientation of Americans.' The gay and lesbian communities have long adopted 10 per cent as the portion of the population that is homosexual. However, a series of recent national studies indicate that only about 2–3 per cent of sexually active men and 1–2 per cent of sexually active women are currently homosexual. These national American estimates are consistent with figures from local communities in the United States, indirect measurements, and statistics from Great Britain, France, Norway, and Denmark.

Rates of same-gender contact increase as the reference period is extended. Recent US figures indicate that 3.0 per cent of sexually active males have had a male sexual partner in the last 12 months, 3.9 per cent during the last five years, and 5.9 per cent since age 18. As the time frame is lengthened, the percentage of men with only male partners declines. Most of those who report both male and female sexual partners since age 18 report only opposite-gender partners during the last year. Lesbians follow these same patterns (Smith, 1998).

The 2001 Canadian census also revealed that 15 per cent of lesbian couples and 3 per cent of gay couples are raising children. These data, while probably underestimating the number of gay and lesbian couples, begin—finally—to number homosexual people among Canadian citizens.

Like other minority groups, homosexuals and lesbians have tried to educate the public, change the laws, and form self-protective organizations. Two kinds of organizations created by the gay community have been especially effective. The first includes formal and informal support groups. The second kind presses for political and social change by educating people outside the gay community. The latter organizations include Equality for Gays and Lesbians Everywhere (EGALE), Parents, Family, and Friends of Lesbians and Gays (PFLAG), and Gay and Lesbian Alliance Against Defamation (GLAAD), among others. Their goals are to change policies and attitudes about people who identify as homosexual (Lax and Phillips, 2009).

In recent years, there has been an increased emphasis on educating students about homosexuality. Groups such as Teens Educating and Confronting Homophobia (TEACH) have tried to teach their peers about being LGBT. Speakers present their 'coming out' stories to high school and university classes. Their goal is to get students to understand that LGBT people deserve the same respect as heterosexuals.

Some high schools include information on homosexuality in their sex education classes; and many urge their teachers to stop assuming all their students are heterosexual. These changes in education are steps in the right direction, but discrimination and harassment of gay students remains an issue (Chesir-Teran and Hughes, 2009). Many high school or elementary students use the term 'that's so *gay*' when referring to something they dislike, or use the term 'faggot' to make fun of other students. Groups like TEACH work towards making young adults aware of the harmful effects of such casual use of homophobic language.

British Columbia has led the way in trying to solve the problem of homophobia in schools. To become familiar with the problem, a Safe Schools Task Force travelled around the province, hearing about the school experiences of gay- and lesbian-identified youth. Their report noted that many LGBT students are afraid to go to school. With prodding from the homosexual community, in April 2005 the BC Ministry of Education established regulations to protect LGBT students in the public school system. It banned not only discrimination against LGBT-identified youth, but also discrimination against youth merely believed to be LGBT.

Chapter Summary

As we have seen, the LGBT community is made up of people who differ in many ways. Yet, often they are viewed and treated as just one deviant group.

Owing largely to the influence of religion, people have long stigmatized homosexuality as a sexual perversion. Some parts of Canadian society continue to do so; however, this is changing. It is hard to say whether the changing attitudes have led to changing laws, or vice versa. Religion continues to play a huge role in popular views about homosexuality, especially outside Canada. Whether in the US or Saudi Arabia, traditional religious beliefs misinform people about homosexuality and promote laws that make homosexual behaviour contemptible and even dangerous. There, the dominant belief is that homosexuality is wrong or sinful.

In Canada, liberal Christian denominations and the liberal segments within other religious faiths, such as Judaism, openly accept LGBT communities into the fold. However, even within relatively liberal denominations conflict continues. In the Anglican Church, for example, the African branch has called for the expulsion of the American Episcopalians over the issues of gay marriage, ordination of homosexual priests, and the appointment of a homosexual bishop. In short, they are calling for a return to stricter and more traditional views on homosexuality.

More moderate, secular people are much more accepting of homosexuals, as are urban people, compared to rural people, and this acceptance includes a greater willingness to protect the civil liberties of homosexuals. Urban secularists also are more willing to allow free expression to people with non-conformist political views and to support political activism. It is little wonder, then, that LGBT people continue to congregate in cities, where they form their own communities.

Changes in how the media portray homosexuality also have helped the LGBT community to become both less threatened and more open about who they are. As gays and lesbians mobilize, change is slowly taking place. With increased exposure in the media and more education, social attitudes, laws, and politics are changing to create an increasingly equal environment for LGBT people.

As we have noted, other things being equal, people who know homosexuals personally are less homophobic than people who do not. In fact, personal contact with homosexual friends and relatives has more influence on attitudes towards gay men and lesbians than any other social or demographic variable. So it is important for LGBT people to continue coming out, and for our institutions to continue encouraging, supporting, and protecting them when they do.

QUESTIONS FOR CRITICAL THOUGHT

1. In this chapter, we see how homosexuality came to be 'normalized'. Can you think of other types of sexual activity that have also been normalized in recent decades? If so, what were the processes behind the normalization of these sexual activities?

2. Think about the double standard concerning the expected sexual behaviours of males and females. Has this double standard likely affected research on the topic of homosexuality?

3. Why don't we see as many male prostitutes as female prostitutes? Discuss this from the interactionist and feminist viewpoints.

4. Identify the reasons why homosexual activity is often limited to distinct parts of cities. What purpose might this geographic segregation serve?

5. In what ways are the LGBT community similar to other stigmatized communities—for example, Aboriginals, visible minorities, homeless people, or the unemployed? In what ways are they different?

6. Can you imagine social or economic conditions under which strong homophobic sentiments might once again surface in our society (i.e., be treated as socially acceptable and even institutionalized)?

RECOMMENDED READINGS

Berlant, Lauren Gail, ed. 2000. *Intimacy*. Chicago: University of Chicago Press. This collection of 16 essays shows the ways in which intimate lives are connected with the institutions and ideologies that organize people's worlds. The book also examines the estrangement, betrayal, loneliness, and even violence that may attend the death of relationships.

Butler, Judith. 1990. *Gender Trouble: Feminism and the Subversion of Identity*. New York: Routledge. This is a classic study of gender and sexual identity, which is central to any understanding of queer theory. Butler examines traditional conceptions of identity and explains how they are themselves produced and reproduced.

Laqueur, Thomas W. 2003. *Solitary Sex: A Cultural History of Masturbation*. New York: Zone Books. The author details the changing nature of Western culture's continuing obsession with masturbation. At different periods of history, masturbation was viewed as evil, as weakness, as illness, and even as nothing important—without any shame or guilt. 'Modern masturbation' came into being around 1712 when a book published anonymously in London asserted that masturbation was a serious disease.

Laumann, Edward O., Stephen Ellingson, Jenna Mahay, Anthony Palk, and Yoosik Youm, eds. 2004. *The Sexual Organization of the City*. Chicago: University of Chicago Press. The findings in this study are based on results from the Chicago Health and Social Life Survey, which was designed to assess how people met their sexual partners. The authors propose the existence of a 'sex market', a spatial and cultural arena in which individuals search for sex partners. They identify two main types of sexual relationship: one-time meetings and longer-term dating relationships

Murray, Stephen O. 1996. *American Gay*. Chicago: University of Chicago Press. Murray examines the communities and social lives of lesbian and gay people, and regards gay people's attempts at being included in 'straight' institutions (such as marriage and the military) as a form of resistance and not assimilation. Another significant portion of the book covers the connection between World War II, the Stonewall Riots, and gay oppression.

Nelson, Claudia, and Michelle H. Martin, eds. 2004. *Sexual Pedagogies: Sex Education in Britain, Australia, and America, 1879–2000*. New York and Basingstoke: Palgrave Macmillan. This collection of seven essays shows that many kinds of texts have tried to shape their audiences' sexual understanding, from nineteenth-century erotica and twentieth-century sermons on abstinence to marriage manuals, feminine-hygiene pamphlets, Hollywood comedies about sexual coming-of-age, and picture books approving homosexuality.

RECOMMENDED WEBSITES

Human Rights Campaign: Coming Out

www.hrc.org/issues/coming_out.asp

The Coming Out Project helps LGBT as well as supportive straight people live openly and talk about their support for equality at home, at work, and in their communities. It provides resources and information pertaining to bisexuality, coming out for members of visible minorities, how straight persons can support their LGBT friends, and the transgendered.

Gay Rights—Change.org

gayrights.change.org

This site provides a guide to the progression of gay social and political rights in North America. It seeks to provide information to enhance understanding of the salience of the homosexual's fight for his or her basic rights.

Homosexuality and Mental Health

psychology.ucdavis.edu/rainbow/html/facts_mental_health.html

This website provides information regarding the unique mental health difficulties faced by the LGBT community. It provides a historical perspective and commentary regarding the American Psychological Association's stance on queer lifestyles.

Canadian Rainbow Health Coalition

www.rainbowhealth.ca

This site is designed to provide health-care news and information for and about LGBT-identified people.

The Commercial Closet

www.commercialcloset.org

This is an excellent source for tracking LGBT representation and visibility in popular culture and provides an extensive library of television commercials and ads where gay imagery has been used by marketers, Commercial Closet is a program of the Gay and Lesbian Alliance Against Defamation (GLAAD).

EGALE Canada

www.egale.ca

EGALE is a national organization that advances equality and justice for LGBT persons and their families across Canada. Articles concerning health care, education, policies, and employment can be found here.

CHAPTER 6

Age Group Relations

LEARNING OBJECTIVES

- To understand the social nature of aging.
- To look at how people's views of aging change throughout their lifetime.
- To learn basic facts about aging and the age distribution in Canada.
- To know the competing theories on aging and ageism.
- To understand how aging varies along gender, ethnic, and class lines.
- To discuss social support for aging individuals and the role of the family.
- To appreciate the social role of inheritance.
- To look at the major outcomes of aging and the causes of elder abuse.
- To learn about the social support programs launched by the government.

INTRODUCTION

This chapter is about younger people and seniors, youth, aging and ageism, retirement, and physical decline. It is also about ageism: though the average age of Canadians is rising each decade, and despite our growing awareness of older people and age variation, many Canadians openly practise ageism—direct or indirect discrimination against people based on their age (Dobbs et al., 2008; Jonson and Larsson, 2009). This includes refusing jobs to qualified and willing candidates because of stereotypic attitudes towards people—young or old— who violate the age norms and expectations of our society.

The topic of this chapter is unlike most of the other social problems or issues we discuss in this book. After all, many people will never experience sexism or racism—because many people will never be women or members of a racial minority group. However, almost everyone will get to be elderly and almost everyone who gets to be elderly will experience ageism. So, this chapter is likely about you and what will likely happen as you move from being young to being older, and then elderly.

AGEISM Prejudice or discrimination, mostly against seniors, but by implication against any member of society, based on their age.

CROSS-CULTURAL ATTITUDES TO AGING

In earlier times, advanced age usually brought respect, authority, and attention from others. In pre-industrial societies, the old enjoyed a high degree of control over their children and over young people overall (see Lasch, 1977). Today, this is no longer the case.

As Western populations industrialized, children could more readily strike out on their own as earners. They no longer had to rely on the help or good opinion of their fathers and mothers. With increased mobility, young people married, set up their own households, and made themselves less available (or willing) to provide help to aging parents (see Cullen et al., 2009). This transition, which unfolded throughout the West during the nineteenth and twentieth centuries, eventually began in the East during the second half of the twentieth century (Gottlieb, 1993).

Many cultures revere their elderly members as vessels of wisdom and authority (see Merz et al., 2007; Gans et al., 2006). By contrast, Western culture reveres youth, not advanced age. In fact, members of our culture tend to fear aging, with its concomitant physical decline towards death. Our culture tends to stereotype and exclude old people.

One common belief is that most seniors are frail and ailing and that the majority need full-time care in nursing homes or other institutional settings. However, only 1.4 per cent of men and 1.7 per cent of women aged 65 to 74 live in a special-care institution, while the vast majority live alone or with family members (Novak, 1997; Statistics Canada, 1998). Another common belief is that most elderly people are senile or rapidly headed in that direction. In fact, most seniors keep their cognitive and perceptual functions for many years. Alzheimer's disease, the most common form of neurological dementia, affects only 3 per cent of people aged 65 to 74. The prevalence rate rises to nearly 50 per cent only after people pass 80 years of age (Alzheimer's Disease Education and Referral Center, 1995).

We learn negative attitudes towards aging and older people from the mass media and from jokes and cartoons. By shaping the popular views of older people, the media create a self-fulfilling prophecy in which elderly individuals begin to think and behave as people expect, thus reinforcing and lending legitimacy to the stereotype (Angus and Reeve, 2006). Unfortunately, here, as with the other stereotypes we have examined, what people believe to be true can become true consequently.

THE IDEA OF A 'LIFE COURSE'

Our ability to think usefully about aging is helped immeasurably by the sociological idea of the 'life course'. Sociologist Glen Elder (1999), currently considered the most eminent researcher studying this topic, notes the life course approach rests on five main assumptions, and each is important to understanding age and aging.

First, Elder points out that 'human development and aging are lifelong processes' (ibid., 7). They start at birth and stop only with death. As people get older, their lives change. At each stage, certain concerns become supreme and others become trivial. Certain important life events typically are concentrated in certain periods of a person's life. Social institutions are gatekeepers in this respect. They divide and regulate life-course transitions, pushing people in and out of school, in and out of marriage, in and out of jobs, and so on (Heinz, 1996). They set up, teach, and reward the social expectations connected with a life course. We cannot understand the ideas, actions, and beliefs of people at any given age without some understanding of how they got to that age—that is, their developmental pathway. This means that longitudinal studies are the best ways of understanding all people, and especially older people.

Second, Elder (1999: 9) notes that 'the developmental antecedents and consequences of life transitions, events, and behaviour patterns vary according to their timing in a person's life.' Simply, it makes a difference at what age you make a key life transition—whether you divorce at 25 or at 55, for example, or graduate from college at 20 or at 40. The age at which people make such transitions affects how they view themselves, not least because self-image is often based on a comparison with others. However, generally, the sequence of the major changes in our lives has an important impact on the experiences we have and people we meet.

Third, 'lives are lived interdependently and socio-historical influences are expressed through this network of shared relationships' (ibid., 10). Since our lives are embedded in social relationships, we may find ourselves entering new statuses because of the actions of others, not through our own choosing. The teenage pregnancy of her daughter may make a woman a grandmother 'before her time', just as the early death of her spouse may make her a widow 'before her time'. Our degree of preparation for new roles and statuses is important for how we experience and perform our key roles and statuses.

Fourth, 'the life course of individuals is embedded in and shaped by the historical times and places they experience over their lifetime' (ibid., 13). Coming of college age means something different in wartime (as it did, for example, in the 1940s) than it does in peacetime (as in the 1970s), in prosperity (the 1950s) than in financial depression (the 1980s), in a period of gender equality (the 1990s) than in one of male dominance (the 1890s). The historical period affects our opportunities and the choices we are likely to make; and these will affect other opportunities and choices throughout our lives.

Fifth, 'individuals construct their own life courses through the choices and actions they take within the opportunities of history and social circumstances' (ibid., 15). In other words, though social forces influence our opportunities and actions, we continue to have a measure of choice in our lives. This means that within any social category or historical period, we will find variations in human lives, because people are free to choose different paths (see Wong and DeGraff, 2009). This helps us to understand why all 20-year-olds are not the same, nor are all 50- or 80-year-olds. Often, differences can be accounted for by their different choices. On the other hand, it also helps us understand why people have a fairly predictable sequence of life experiences as they move from 20 to 50 to 80, and why they feel uncomfortable when they deviate from that sequence.

In sociological thinking, the *life course* is a patterned sequence of individual experiences over time, subject to varied social, historical, and cultural influences. There is, in each society—indeed, in each social group—an expected life course, which fits (more or less) with the generally experienced life course (Handel, 1997). These life courses, ideal and actual, are not identical; the gap between the life courses we expect and those we experience may cause much distress. Living may sometimes also mean 'breaking the rules' or failing to live up to age-related expectations (Ho and Raymo, 2009).

BASIC ASPECTS OF THE SOCIOLOGY OF AGING

From birth onward, an individual's physical and mental abilities gradually improve, then decline in a biological process known as **senescence**. However, exactly at what age and in what form the decline takes place varies widely from one person to another.

Today, older people can look forward to a longer and healthier old age than in the past. Yet our culture has not fully kept up with these changes in the social definition of who is elderly and what elderly people are like, largely because with an increased interest in childhood, there had been a decreased interest in later adulthood. Paradoxically, we have lost interest in the elderly just as their numbers have been increasingly dramatically, as shown in Figures 6.1–6.5.

In 1901, only 5 per cent of the population was aged 65 or older. Over the past century, this fraction has more than doubled to 12 per cent. Canada is expected to have about 14 per cent of the population aged 65 and older by 2011 and 22 per cent in 2031 (Statistics Canada, 1994; see also Moore and Rosenberg, 2001). Though the Canadian population is aging rapidly, it is far from the oldest population. Many Northern and Central European populations have been aging for generations, with much higher proportions of elderly people than one finds in North America.

We might best describe Canada's **age pyramid** today as a diamond shape, with a small base among the youngest groups, spreading out gradually as age groups increase in size until ages 45–55, before tapering off into a high, thin peak around ages 80–90 (Statistics Canada, 2000). A diamond shape reflects a population undergoing change—a triangle that is gradually becoming a rectangle as the birth rate slows. This can be seen in the four age pyramids shown in Figure 6.1. The wide middle of the diamond in the 1999 pyramid represents the

NOBODY'S FOOL

Paul Newman earned an Oscar nomination in 1994 for his portrayal of an immature sixty-year-old construction worker who must learn to finally grow up.

SENESCENCE The biological aging of an organism as it lives beyond its maturity, usually accompanied by chemical and organic changes.

AGE PYRAMID A graphic depiction of the age composition of a population, broken down by age and sex; pyramid-shaped if the birth rate is high but otherwise more rectangular.

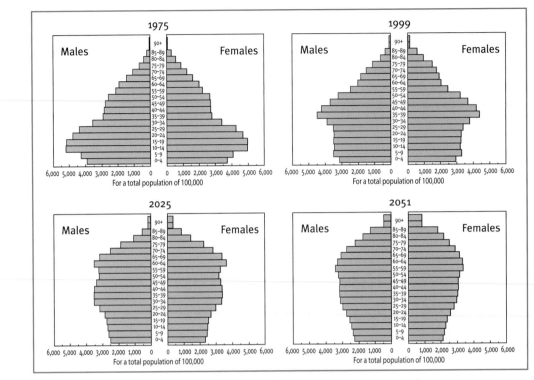

Figure 6.1 Canadian Population Age Pyramids, 1975, 1999, 2025, and 2051

Source: **Canadian Population Age Pyramids, 1975, 1999, 2020, and 2051, Figure 2.1 from *Report on the Demographic Situation in Canada, 1998–1999* found at: www.statcan.gc.ca/pub/91-209-x/91-209-x1999000-eng.pdf, page 12.**

large number of births during the baby-boom period; these baby boomers can be followed through each of the pyramids, so that, because of their sheer numbers, in the 2051 projection there are more very old people at the top of pyramid than was true in the earlier years shown. The pointed top ends represent the small number of surviving older people, while the increasingly narrower bottoms indicate the smaller number of births. The reader who wants to see Canada's age pyramids, as they existed as far back as 1901 and as they are predicted to become as far forward as 2056, is directed to the interactive Statistics Canada website at: www.statcan.gc.ca/kits-trousses/animat/edu06a_0000-eng.htm.

Age Stratification

Not all social differentiation leads to social inequality, but where aging is concerned, this does occur. Age stratification theory focuses on the way social structures affect individual aging and the stratification, or vertical segregation, of people by age. It is concerned with the segregation and mistreatment of certain age groups in the same sense that class stratification is concerned with the segregation and mistreatment of certain social classes (see, e.g., Bielby and Bielby, 2001).

Because of age stratification, aging and ageism pose various problems for society, especially as increasing percentages of the world and Canadian populations are getting older (see Figures 6.2 and 6.3). First, ageism, like discrimination based on race or gender, is repellent to a society like ours that is pledged to judging people by what they do rather than who they are. We say we believe in rewards based on achievement, not ascription. However, ageism is a sign that we do not, as a society, live up to our own proclaimed values of justice and equality. Second, ageism poses practical problems for the victims of this discrimination (Martens et al., 2004). Like all discrimination, ageism has both material and psychological effects. Materially, it limits people's opportunities to get the jobs and incomes they may need to survive. Psychologically, ageism makes people feel rejected, excluded, and degraded (Clarke and Griffin, 2008). They feel they are less than they want and need to be as human beings.

Stereotyping aside, aging poses challenges for a society. Generally, populations with a high proportion of very old or very young people—that is, low-fertility populations like our own, or high-fertility populations like, say, Iraq's—consume a high proportion of their national economy in the form of supports for dependent populations: health, education, welfare, housing, and so on. Populations with a high proportion in the workforce, aged 25–65, are able to invest more of their economy in development, savings, or war, without significantly reducing their spending on human capital.

Thus, the increased proportion of elderly people in the population means at least two important things for society: on the one hand, an increasing proportion of people who need costly care and support, and on the other hand, an increasing proportion of people who are considered useless and held in low regard.

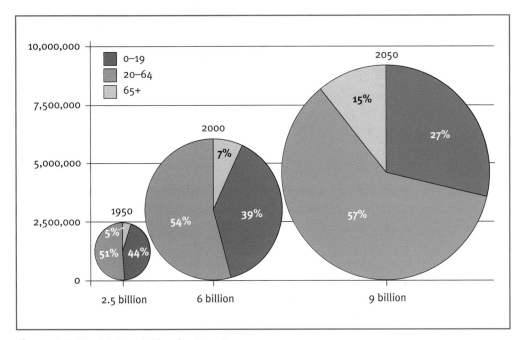

Figure 6.2 World Population by Age Group

Source: *World Population Prospects: The 2006 Revision and World Urbanization Prospects: The 2005 Revision,* http://wisdom.unu.edu/wp-content/uploads/2008/08/big-population-age-group.gif

The Canadian Press/Paul Chiasson

Rachel Pineau consults newspaper want ads in Montreal. Pineau doesn't want her age to work against her as she looks for a job after a six-month hiatus, but she believes the prejudice is there.

THEORETICAL PERSPECTIVES ON AGING

Structural Functionalism

As we have noted repeatedly, structural functionalists think that society is like a living organism, made up of interconnected parts that together work as an efficient, productive whole. This perspective, therefore, also views society as being only as strong as its weakest members. From this standpoint, society benefits least from its least active, most infirm members.

One structural-functionalist theory of aging, attributed to Elaine Cumming and William Henry (1961), is **disengagement theory**. It holds that elderly people are among the weakest members of the population and society has, therefore, devised a means of displacing them from the central positions of power and influence. As people age, they gradually decline, physically and mentally, Cummings and Henry note. Muscles weaken, bones become fragile, perceptual abilities deteriorate, and cognitive faculties become slower and weaker. Not surprisingly, elderly people are also more prone to illness and disability.

DISENGAGEMENT THEORY A theory that as people age, they voluntarily and normally remove themselves from activities and social contacts, to ease their passage into a less active lifestyle.

Table 6.1 Theoretical Perspectives

Theory	Main Points
Structural Functionalism	• All elements in society are interrelated. • Disengagement theory accounts for the relegation of older people to the sidelines of society. • Retirement serves several functions, especially the re-invigoration of social institutions.
Conflict Theory	• Conflict and change are basic features of social life. • Age-related discrimination does not benefit society. • Elderly people do not disengage, they are pushed out of the workforce. • The most powerful groups in society command resources and are the decision-makers.
Symbolic Interactionism	• Social life involves continued interaction. • Socially constructed definitions of age and aging affect one's experience of growing old. • People take on new roles as they age (they do not disengage). • Media portrayals reflect and reinforce society's stereotypes about older people.
Feminist Theory	• Aging affects men and women differently. • Women, because they live longer than men on average, are more likely to suffer the hardships associated with aging. • Generally, women provide care in aging while men receive it.
Social Constructionism	• Views of aging are shaped by moral entrepreneurship. • Popular beliefs about aging are propagated by the mass media and do not reflect reality.

This means that, at work, elderly individuals are often less efficient than their younger, stronger, and more energetic counterparts (Garber et al., 2008). For the good of society and for themselves, disengagement theory argues, elderly people should give up their positions and withdraw to the edges of society, where they can prepare for their certain death. This theory is not advocating so much as observing that this is how modern societies work: they retire their older workers on the assumption that to do so is just, necessary, and beneficial to all. If so, what function does this practice serve?

According to this theory, age-based retirement from work serves several functions for society: (1) it empties job positions, allowing younger people to move up the occupational and social hierarchy; (2) it gives the retiree a moment of celebratory recognition—for example, a retirement party—to honour his or her contribution; and (3) it ensures that society replaces outdated skills and ideas with more useful ones. Though the theory may sound cold and

ON GOLDEN POND

In this 1981 hit, a retired couple spirit away to their remote lake house, only to find themselves hosting younger family members they cannot relate to.

cynical, especially to elderly people obliged to retire from jobs they may like, structural functionalists stress that this change is both natural and crucial to society's effectiveness. Without such turnover, the economy would be less efficient and less equipped to compete globally. Thus, age-based retirement—even if discriminatory—is socially functional and, therefore, widespread.

Conflict Theory

Many, however, disagree with the assumptions of functionalism, especially with the assumption that excluding older people from financially rewarding and socially important roles is good for society. For that matter, age-related discrimination against the young is not useful to society, either. Thus, ageism does not serve society as a whole but is merely a form of inequality exercised by one group over another, to further its own interests.

Many scholars have criticized disengagement theory for being too simplistic. It seems to view humans as robots who make a 40-year contribution to society, then voluntarily jump into the social dustbin—a retirement community, perhaps—where they wait mindlessly for death to erase them (Foner, 2000). This view is wrong. Though society may need older people to disappear from the workforce, many seniors remain active, refuse to retire, and fight their obsolescence. Many refuse to withdraw from society voluntarily. Even after retirement from paid work, many stay active as long as opportunities in the family and the wider community will allow. When elderly people do disengage, it is often because of other people's wishes, not their own.

This, at least, is the perspective taken by most conflict theorists. It recognizes that people usually seek to satisfy their own goals, not the goals of 'society' as a whole. Members of different age groups hold different interests, and each group competes against the others to enlarge its share of society's resources. In this struggle, typically the very young and very old are unable to prevail since, compared to middle-aged people, they lack the organization and power needed to influence public policy. As a result, middle-aged decision-makers may ignore the interests and needs of elderly people and children. However, we should not assume that the old and young willingly consent to such treatment.

Symbolic Interactionism

Symbolic interactionists focus their attention on how we symbolize elderly people and enact aging in our society. They also study how socially constructed definitions of age and aging affect people's experience of growing old. The symbolic interactionists stress that age is a state of mind shaped by the labels society applies. To a large degree, satisfaction with aging means rejecting the definition of old age as 'inadequate' or 'depleted'.

Activity theory (Havighurst and Albrecht, 1953) argues that, contrary to disengagement theory (that people give up roles as they age), people take on new roles and identities as they age. Through such continued activity, they preserve a sense of continuity and self-worth, and gain greater life satisfaction, though by new means. People who keep up a high level of activity—whether in old activities or new ones—age more 'successfully' than people who do not (see also Steinkamp and Kelly, 1987; Schroots, 1996). This might correspond to an age-old notion that, in aging, we commonly trade passion for wisdom; so there is no loss, only change.

Feminist Theory

Feminists note that the experience of aging is different for men and women. For both men and women, aging is associated with a retirement from paid work—that is, socially enforced deprivation of authority and income. However, for women aging is associated with a culturally defined loss of youth and glamour—a less critical concern for men. Women and men also bring different resources to old age; and they are subject to different expectations in youth, middle age, and old age (Ginn and Arber, 1995). For all these reasons, women in our culture dread getting older in a way that most men do not.

Some feminist scholars suggest that this is a natural reaction to what they call the 'double jeopardy' of being female and old. According to this perspective, both 'stigmatizing' statuses combine to make older women particularly disadvantaged. Advocates of this perspective argue that more needs to be done to help older women achieve economic and social equality in later life.

One might think that, today more than ever, women and men lead increasingly similar lives, in the sense that both often aim for careers. However, their careers are likely to be in different sectors of the workforce. While in the workforce, most women earn less pay than men and accrue smaller private pensions, if any at all. Because of this, and because their spouses or partners usually die before them, women are at particular risk of finding themselves living alone on a meagre income in their later years (Hughes and Waite, 2002). As well, older women have more domestic duties and social responsibilities than older men. For example, they tend to play a more central role in kin-keeping—maintaining family contacts—through social networks and caregiving.

These social responsibilities over the lifespan have important outcomes in old age. The family caregiving roles women take on at younger ages often remove them from the labour force, limiting their pension benefits (Moody, 2000). As noted earlier, this limits their lifetime earnings and may result in poverty after retirement. At the societal level, this contributes to a 'feminization of poverty'.

SOCIAL CONSEQUENCES OF AGING

Retirement Income

After retiring from paid work, Canada's elderly support themselves in various ways: through government and private pensions, savings, and contributions by other family members. This situation promises to pose huge financial problems for Canada and other developed societies in the future. Already, the baby-boom generation has entered retirement age, and continued population aging will produce large increases in age-related government spending on public pensions and health care. More people of working age will be needed to help pay, through their taxes, for the pensions and benefits received by a growing number of elders.

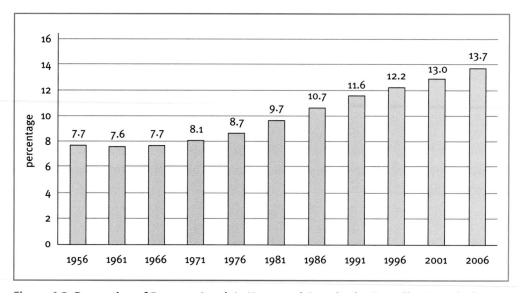

Figure 6.3 Proportion of Persons Aged 65 Years and Over in the Canadian Population, 1956–2006

Source: Proportion of Persons Aged 65 Years and Over in the Canadian Population, 1956 to 2006, at: www12.statcan.ca/census-recensement/2006/as-sa/97-551/figures/c2-eng.cfm.

In turn, efforts will be needed to increase Canadian productivity by fully integrating women, the disabled, new immigrants, and Aboriginal people into the labour market. And, despite disengagement theory, older Canadians who want to continue working for pay should not be discouraged from doing so, for economic reasons.

Recognizing the need for readiness, more and more Canadians have been saving for old age (O'Rand and Shuey, 2007). As a result, the 'feminization of poverty' has shown signs of slowing. Between 1991 and 2001, the gap in the numbers of men and women in registered pension plans narrowed significantly, from almost 1 million to less than half a million, due largely to the increase in female registration. This change is due to the growth in women's labour force participation and the drop in membership among male workers, owing largely to the recession of the early 1990s that pushed many men out of work (ibid.).

Careers and Mandatory Retirement

Throughout the twentieth century, in all industrial and post-industrial societies, most people have earned an income through paid work. Further, most paid work has been organized into careers in large organizations: government, large businesses, law firms, universities and other parts of the education system, hospitals, and so on. People have marked their professional progress through what sociologists call 'career mobility' (Bullard and Wright, 1993).

Career mobility—financial and occupational advancement over the life cycle—has largely been age-related. As people get older, they move up the occupational or organizational (or income) ladder. This rise has depended on two reliable sources of opportunity: continued economic growth and the continued elimination of old people through death or retirement.

Elderly people have been routinely pushed out of their positions to make way for younger people seeking careers.

However, this situation changed in recent years for three main reasons: lengthening of the average lifespan; a decline in economic growth; and the elimination of compulsory (or mandatory) retirement. These problems have been intensified by tightly organized labour markets that strictly control access from the outside. Consider, as an example, the profession of medicine. Many people want to enter the medical profession, yet entry is strictly limited to a few. As population size increases (through immigration and otherwise), it becomes harder and harder to get into a desirable labour market to have a career there. Meanwhile, the increasing population is more and more poorly serviced in the health field.

Careers and aging are correlated, because most career mobility is based on seniority or on the length of tenure (Brooke, 2009). Other things being equal, the longer a person works in an organization, the higher the salary and degree of authority, autonomy, and prestige that person will enjoy. However, as workplaces have become more specialized, seniority no longer guarantees advancement. Today, in an organization with many levels, people enter at different levels, according to their credentials. Some positions requiring only an undergraduate education (or less) start entrants near the bottom, while other positions, requiring a graduate degree or significant job experience, start entrants higher up the organizational ladder.

'Internal labour markets' impose a high degree of control over who enters an organization (or profession, or industry)—at what level, through what stages people will move, and at what rate. The result is that, even today, society sorts people into different types of careers. Within each of these 'internal labour markets', career progress remains largely predictable and based on seniority. However, 'achievement' has become far more important than in the past. Moreover, seniority alone will not allow a person to jump from a lower internal market into a higher one (e.g., from being a nurse to being a doctor). Thus, career mobility has been altered through industrial growth and differentiation, and through the rise of achievement as a basis for ranking (Mendenhall et al., 2008). Modern professions (such as medicine and law) are especially notable for these features, including their ability to control career entries, reward systems, and conditions of work.

Technology is another force that pushes older people out of their careers, making room for younger workers. Not surprisingly, new technology is usually built by young people for the use of other young people; it doesn't usually have the interests of seniors in mind (Pew and Van Hemel, 2004). In fact, some technologies may be harder for seniors to learn—due to arthritis and declines in fine motor skills—than for their younger counterparts. So, older people may have trouble keeping up to date, especially in fields that depend on rapid technological advancement (Magnusson et al., 2005; Blit-Cohen and Litwin, 2004).

Decisions to leave a job or career voluntarily depend on career opportunities. People stay where the opportunities are best. Seniority in the firm is much more important than age for departure decisions. Thus, a 55-year-old, low-seniority worker is more likely to leave than a 55-year-old, high-seniority worker, or even than a 65-year-old, high-seniority worker. That said, women are different from men, more often leaving the organization for personal reasons than men, and less often for career reasons.

Compulsory retirement—the legal right of an employer to forcibly retire an employee, and the accompanying eligibility of an employee to receive various private and public pensions—has been a staple arrangement of industrial societies for well over a century. In Canada, where compulsory retirement was in place until 2005, employees of most public and private organizations routinely retired at age 65, if not earlier. For most workers, salaries had peaked a decade or more earlier, in the ages 45–55; so there was little financial incentive to stay on if they were offered a satisfactory retirement package.

Self-employed professionals (for example, doctors or lawyers) or business-owners (for example, shopkeepers), however, had much more choice about when to retire. And since they would receive no organizational or union pension benefits when they retired, they had little incentive to retire at age 65 or earlier. Likely, their standard of living and quality of life would be higher if they continued to work. Also, they tended to be more engaged in their

The Canadian Press/AP Photo/Nati Harnik

Thanks to a Supreme Court decision on compulsory retirement, academics like Dr Denham Harman are able to continue their scholarly work long after age 65. In 1954, Harman developed the 'Free Radical Theory of Aging', which is now the most widely accepted theory on the aging process.

work than many wage-earning employees. For many, work was a vocation—a source of personal identity—as well as a source of income and sociability.

Before 2005, professionals working in large organizations—for example, university professors—found themselves forced to quit a job they liked and accept a much reduced income, simply because they had reached the age of 65. So, it is not surprising that academics and librarians were first to challenge the compulsory retirement laws that applied to universities and other public organizations. In 2005, the Supreme Court ruled that compulsory retirement was a form of age discrimination and, therefore, could no longer be practised (for examples of early retirement, see Kim, 2009). This had enormous financial implications. Immediately, universities and other large organizations scrambled to adjust their operations because of this change; and they continue to do so.

Issues Associated with Inheritance

'Inheritance' is what we call the downward flow of property after death, usually along kinship lines and usually from the older to the younger generation. In nearly all societies, unless other instructions are provided, it is assumed that close kin (spouses, parents, and children) will have first claim on the property of the deceased person (Payling, 2001).

Cultures differ in how they split up the resources released at death. In some societies, the dominant inheritance pattern is **primogeniture**, where the eldest son receives everything; in others, the property is split among all the surviving children. In some societies, males and females inherit equally; while in others, women are denied a portion of the inheritance except through their husbands (see, e.g., Ugiagbe et al., 2007). Historically, primogeniture has been a conservative strategy for ensuring the survival of the family by keeping the family's property intact. However, unwittingly, inheritance practices have influenced marriage patterns, the relationships between parents and children, and the relationships between siblings. That is because those who control the inheritance (usually, parents) exercise influence over those who wish to receive it (usually, children); and those siblings who receive it often exercise influence over those siblings who do not.

This influence is evident in the submissive behaviours of children, in various cultural forms and social milieux. Take **filial responsibility**—the moral responsibility of a grown child to look after his or her aging parent (Hill, 2006). Notions of filial responsibility, or filial piety, are especially marked in societies influenced by the teachings of the Chinese philosopher Confucius (that is, in China, Korea, and Japan). Recent social changes, associated with urbanization and industrialization, have weakened the traditional Confucian norms. With the nuclearization of the family, newlyweds in Asia have been setting up their own households, so daughters-in-law and mothers-in-law no longer share the same home. Thus, mothers-in-law have been deprived of a traditional source of caregiving (Kim, 1996). Similar dynamics were evident in Irish rural society, where elderly parents were able to tyrannize their adult children through the control of an inheritance (see Box 6.1).

PRIMOGENITURE A system of inheritance in which only one child, the oldest son, inherits all of the family property on the death of his parents.

FILIAL RESPONSIBILITY The sense of personal obligation or duty that adult children often feel for protecting, caring for, and supporting their aging parents; filial piety.

CLASSIC WORKS

Box 6.1 Family and Aging in a Traditional Society

A classic analysis of aging and the relationships between family generations in a traditional rural Irish community was provided in an anthropological study by Arensberg and Kimball, *Family and Community in Ireland*. A review of the third edition of this book, by Patricia Lysaght, is abridged below.

Family and Community in Ireland is a famous social anthropological study arising from an interdisciplinary research program undertaken in Ireland in the 1930s known as the 'Harvard Irish Survey' (1931–6). First published in 1940, a second enlarged edition appeared in 1968.

Ireland was considered suitable for a social anthropological study by the 'Harvard Irish Mission' as the project also was called, as it 'presented a distinctive and characteristic variant of western European civilization and a long, relatively unbroken tradition dating back to pre-Christian and pre-Roman times' (ibid., xxxi). It was also viewed by the Harvard academics as a society in transition, moving between tradition and modernity, a society with a 'distinctive culture', 'increasing in strength and autonomy' (ibid., xxxi). It was a country that had 'taken a place once again among the free nations of the world' and deserved 'to be thoroughly known' (ibid., xxvi).

The sociologist W. Lloyd Warner (1898–1970), then at Harvard and later at the University of Chicago and Michigan State University, was the director of the anthropological strand of the study. The social anthropological fieldwork in County Clare was undertaken by two doctoral students in anthropology at Harvard University, Conrad M. Arensberg (1910–97) and Solon T. Kimball (1909–82), under the direction of Professor Warner, then also at Harvard, during the two-year period 1932–4.

In the course of their fieldwork the authors became aware of the central influence of family structure and kinship on community form and life, and this became the 'principal area of investigation' (ibid., xxvi). The emphasis is on what the authors call the 'complete family', 'consisting of father and mother and sons rather than daughters alone' (ibid., 67), while the term 'incomplete' indicates those farms run by bachelors, spinsters, widowers, and widows (ibid., 66). The daily, seasonal, and annual routine of the male and female members of the farm family, centred on the 'spatial unit of land and house', is described in detail, and the authors illustrate the importance of common effort during crucial points in the annual agricultural round, when all family members, male and female, including children, contributed to the work in hand, according to their age, sex, and ability. Interfamilial co-operation ('cooring', Ir. *Comhair*) was also expected, and

expected to be reciprocated, at tasks such as turf-cutting and at harvest-time.

The farm-family children are described as 'subordinated' to their parents and remained 'boys' and 'girls' until marriage. They were trained in farm and household duties by their parents in preparation for marriage and the setting up of farm households of their own. Marriage itself is described by Arensberg and Kimball as a mechanism which united the transfer of farm ownership and economic control by the old couple to the inheriting son or daughter, and the advance to adult status for the marrying couple, in the eyes of their family and the community.

The services of a matchmaker were usually employed to negotiate the dowry to be brought in by the bride, or by the groom, if he were marrying into a farm, in order to ensure social and economic parity between the contracting parties. The introduction of the old age pension, which gave a measure of regular financial support to old farm couples, eased the relinquishing of control of the farm and household by the parents. Indeed, it might be added that an old couple in receipt of the old age pension were considered a financial asset in some households. The sibling for whom a dowry was available was in a position to marry, but the other less fortunate family members had to 'travel' and make a new life for themselves without the family farm.

A primary concern of the new family created at marriage was the birth of children, as this was necessary to preserve family unity and its identification with farm and household in the future. Indeed, the harshness of country sentiment against a barren wife, or against a young widow without issue, persisted well beyond the 1930s. Both were expected, in accordance with social custom, to accept repayment of their dowry and to return to their families. It should also be pointed out, however, that where a husband had married into land (*cliamhain isteach*) he, too, was expected to return to his people on being refunded his dowry, if no children were born of the marriage after a reasonable period of time.

While emigration was seen as contributing to the large proportion of the aged in the community, longevity was also viewed as an important factor. Arensberg and Kimball were of the opinion that the old people 'live long because they have much to live for. In their own sphere of life, they are honoured. They have power' (ibid., 162). By comparison the gatherings of the younger men, concerned mainly with recreation, and those of a third group characterized as intermediate or transitional, were of less import.

Source: Lysaght (2002).

HEALTH CONSEQUENCES OF AGING

Physical Illness

Quality of life usually declines in old age. One reason for this is senescence, the fact that physical and mental abilities naturally decline during the aging process. Muscles grow weaker, the mind less sharp; and aches and pains become routine complaints. Exactly at what age and in what form this decline takes place varies from one person to the next; but decline is inevitable (see, e.g., Johnson et al., 2009; Poon and Knight, 2009).

Health problems often arise alongside and because of changes in the life course. Widowhood and divorce are associated with health problems, for example, especially in men (Antonucci et al., 2001). Some research says that health declines accompany both retirement plans and actual retirement for women, though not for men (Midanik et al., 1990). Equally important, the loss of independence as one ages—for example, the loss of a driver's licence, or the need to rely on others for help with activities of daily living—can also cause emotional and physical distress (Lazzarini, 1990).

Home Care Issues

An aging, longer-living adult population leads to increased demands for informal (non-professional) care. Indeed, a Statistics Canada report, *Eldercare in Canada* (Keating et al., 1999), suggests the demand is already considerable. More than 20 per cent of Canadian seniors receive informal help because of long-term health problems. Compared with 30 years ago, the elderly today are more likely to live independently (see also Lau and Kirby, 2009). At the same time, more adult children in their fifties, besides being more likely than in past decades to be divorced (and therefore not having a spouse present to assist with elder care), are more likely to have a surviving parent.

One result is the so-called 'sandwich generation', middle-aged adults caring for both elderly parents and for their own young children (see Rubin and White-Means, 2009). Forty-two per cent of Canadian women aged 40–44 currently work outside the home while balancing parental care and child care. Other societal changes include a shift from institutional to community-based (in-home) care, a growing ideological commitment to elder care by the state, and (at the same time) funding cuts by the federal government for such services (Rosenthal, 1997a).

This Canadian trend to viewing elder care as a private matter rather than a public responsibility may have negative outcomes in the near future (Rosenthal, 1997b). Because of cuts to the health-care system, Canada, as well as other industrial nations with universal medical care, risks sliding back to the 'non-system' found in the US (Chappell, 1997; Hanlon and Halseth, 2005). Yet public surveys repeatedly show that Canadians value public health care, desire health and longevity, and view health as a public good, even while electing governments that impose cost reductions and ill-considered health-care reforms (Chappell and McDaniel, 1999).

AWAY FROM HER

Sarah Polley's 2006 feature is the story of an aging couple (Gordon Pinsent, Julie Christie) grappling with the effects of Alzheimer's on their relationship.

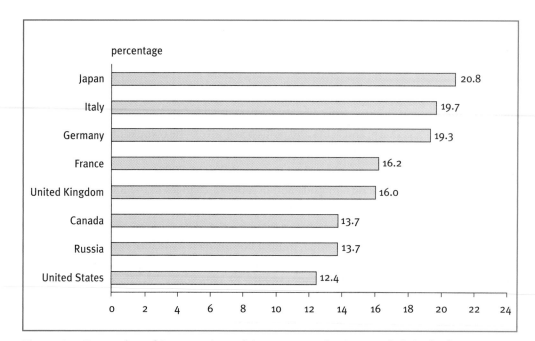

Figure 6.4 Proportion of Persons 65 and Over among the Group of Eight (G8) Countries in 2006

Sources: **Proportion of persons aged 65 years and over among the G8 countries in 2006, found at: www12.statcan.ca/census-recensement/2006/as-sa/97-551/figures/c4-eng.cfm.**

The data in Figure 6.4 show that Canada is far behind various other G8 countries (like Japan and Italy) in the current size of their aged population and, therefore, in the need to provide senior care. However, as we have seen, this is changing rapidly.

Elder Abuse

Living longer brings unprecedented opportunities but also presents serious social challenges. One of these is elder abuse. Elder abuse occurs in various settings (see, e.g., Cohen, 2006). Typically, the older person is mistreated in his or her own home by a spouse, sibling, child, friend, or trusted caregiver. Other seniors are mistreated by staff and professional caregivers in facilities for elderly people.

As the National Center on Elder Abuse (2001) has shown, elder abuse takes various forms, including physical abuse, sexual abuse, emotional or psychological abuse, neglect, abandonment, and financial or material exploitation. This last category includes improper use of an elderly person's savings, property, or assets without authorization or beyond the terms set out in a caregiver–patient contract. Such offences include stealing money or material possessions, forging signatures, and improper use of guardianship or power of attorney rights. The National Centre on Elder Abuse also notes that self-neglect can be a problem among seniors. Self-neglect shows itself in the older person's refusal or failure to give himself or herself enough food, water, clothing, shelter, hygiene, medication (when responsibly prescribed), and safety precautions.

Estimates on the prevalence of elder abuse vary, with Statistics Canada indicating that somewhere between 4 and 10 per cent of elders suffer abuse, while a survey of CARP (Canadian Association of Retired People) members suggests the number is closer to 10 per cent (www.carp.ca/advocacy/adv-article-display.cfm?documentID=3923). One study estimates that five elder abuse incidents go unreported for every incident that is reported, and elderly women are more likely to be assaulted by a family member than are elderly men. In 2003, almost 40 per cent of female victims, and 20 per cent of male victims, were assaulted by a family member (Statistics Canada, 2003).

Relatives are the most likely to report abuse, but also the most likely to perpetrate abuse and neglect (Harbison and Morrow, 1998). The typical perpetrator of domestic elder abuse is an adult child or spouse of the child; however, older family members and non-relatives may also be perpetrators. Often, the abuser depends on the victim for shelter, financial aid, or emotional support. In other words, the perpetrator may be financially dependent while the victim is physically dependent. Other common correlates of elder abuse are alcohol addiction by the abuser or prior abuse perpetrated years earlier against the present abuser by the now elderly victim.

SOLUTIONS FOR PROBLEMS OF AGING

One finds repeatedly that people who are older—also, married, healthy and religious—are the most satisfied with their lives (Wood, 1990).

Informal and Formal Social Supports

Solving the problems of aging will have to include supporting the individuals and institutions that provide social integration: caregivers, families, support networks, and community organizations (Freedman et al., 1994; Williams, 2002).

The shift from independent parent to dependent parent represents a shift in power and responsibility from parent to offspring. Depending on the quality of the relationship between parent and child throughout life, this onset of dependence may provide an occasion to repay the parent for past debts or to seek revenge for real or imagined injustices. So, this shift is not without complications.

The need for aging parents to support middle-aged children who have become unemployed or divorced is also on the rise. This can work well if the parents and children have a history of getting along well together. However, as parents age, the problems associated with supporting children multiply. Consider the older generation's own need for independence or support, the intergenerational interaction patterns set up early in the life of the family, the social class and cultural background of the family, the gender of the offspring, and the location and type of living arrangements (Connidis, 1989).

Four types of social support—informational, tangible, emotional, and integrating—all help to reduce the stress on elderly individuals. Elderly men tend to rely emotionally on their spouses, while elderly women diversify their emotional supports when possible (McDaniel and McKinnon, 1993). Even close friends can be important. Positive social contacts with friends promote well-being, so more contacts—a larger social network—lead to more well-being (Lennartsson, 1999).

Some of the support provided to seniors is instrumental, while some is emotional. Instrumental support and subjective social support protect elderly people against decline. Both types of support are needed, however; and neither can compensate for the lack of the other (Ikkink and van Tilburg, 1998). More resourceful and diversified social networks that include friends and neighbours consistently do better than narrow family-focused networks in promoting activities of daily living and self-rated health (Litwin, 1998).

Social supports—whether doctors, support groups, social networks, or assistive communication technology—help caregivers and patients. One way this occurs is by influencing sick people to comply with the treatment advice they receive from their doctors. Ensuring compliance with medication is one of the most important yet most often neglected ways of helping elderly and sick people.

Personal Efforts to Adapt

Some elderly people have a harder time than others making use of services and supports. Many elderly members of ethnic groups are now retired without a pension and, often, in poor health (e.g., Hicks and Kingston, 2009; Shugrue and Robison, 2009). Whether because of low levels of education or language problems, they may underuse social and health-care services due to a lack of knowledge about such programs or because they cannot be served in their own language. Further, they may be unwilling to enter long-term care institutions because of differences in language, customs, beliefs surrounding medical practices and death, food preferences, or the desire for privacy (e.g., Kaestner et al., 2009).

However, immigrants are not the only ones who face problems. All elderly people need to learn how to age successfully. Some role changes, such as marriage and retirement, are common and predictable; and anyone can usefully begin to think of how they will adjust to these major life events. Other changes, however, such as widowhood or becoming a father at the age of 55, may occur unexpectedly. Still others, even if expected, can be stressful and lead to loneliness or a decreased quality of life. One example is the empty-nest syndrome, which occurs when children leave home for university or marriage (e.g., Xie et al., 2010).

In short, aging *always* involves change—in friendships, health, financial status, role relationships, and more. Changes in daily routines can create stress because they force people to cope with new life situations. Anticipatory socialization can ease the stress associated with later-life role changes, however. Important aids in making these age-related changes include the social support of friends and family, the development of personal coping skills, and the presence of older peers who serve as role models (George, 1980).

Widowhood is one of the most problematic of all changes because it can occur suddenly and endure for many years; and widowhood is mainly a women's issue (see Lindström, 2009). In 2001, 45 per cent of all Canadian women over 65 years old had been widowed, compared to only about 13–14 per cent of men. What's more, widows—numbering 1.25 million in total—are four times more numerous than widowers—numbering only 300,000 (Statistics Canada, 2004).

This difference reflects the greater life expectancy of women and the fact that husbands typically are two to three years older than their wives. As well, men are more likely than women to remarry after being widowed (Dupuis, 2009). Thus, not only do more women experience this sorrowful life event, they also remain longer in the role of widow. Even a woman who becomes a widow at the age of 80 can expect an average of 9.7 more years of life as an unmarried person (Statistics Canada, n.d.).

The death of a spouse is one of the most stressful role changes in the life cycle and the most stressful one people experience in later years of life. Widowers, who are less often faced with financial burdens than widows, have more difficulty adapting to their new role, as shown by higher suicide rates, higher rates of remarriage, and higher rates of mortality soon after the death of a spouse.

The bereavement process is easier if the widow or widower has a friendship group containing other widows and widowers. In effect, they create a community-based 'widow-to-widow' program to provide emotional and social support. After a period of acute grief and mourning, the widowed person often begins to rebuild a new identity and lifestyle (see Cornwell, 2009). She or he adjusts to being alone, having no spouse to talk to, cooking for one person, losing friends who were more closely tied to the deceased spouse, and managing financial affairs alone (see, e.g., Yang and Victor, 2008). Often, the widow will also learn to live on a reduced income (Bonnet and Hourriez, 2009; Gillen and Kim, 2009).

Government Legislation

There is much disagreement about the state's duty to support retired individuals. This issue is especially significant because many older adults, especially elderly widows, live in poverty. As well, many fear that public Old Age Security funds and private pension plans may become bankrupt in the future (Brown, 1991).

Income after retirement depends on a person's pattern of lifetime employment (regular or sporadic), place of employment (whether it offers a private pension), income while in the labour force, and pattern of savings, investments, and expenses over the life course. All of these factors will affect a person's quality of life after leaving paid work.

Given this rising number of seniors (Figure 6.5), an elderly-friendly environment is needed, so we have to start planning for it now. Such an environment would include creative social policies and programs; improved private-sector products and services; changing attitudes towards health, nutrition, physical activity, and stress; political involvement and empowerment; new attitudes towards retirement and leisure; and innovative long-range financial planning during the early and middle years of adulthood. Then, with plans in hand, we have to bring about these changes.

Canadians will have to focus on creative management of private and public pension funds (see, e.g., FitzGerald, 2008). This will mean examining choices for both early and late retirement as labour surpluses and shortages occur overall or in specific regions or occupational groups. As John Myles (1988) has pointed out, 'The social character of old age is very much a product of the welfare state . . . old age became retirement.' The development of retirement as a mandated social policy, with fiscal and economic implications, is relatively recent,

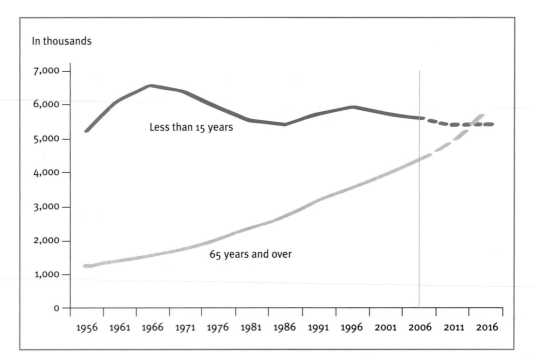

Figure 6.5 Number of Persons Aged 65 Years and Over and Number of Children Aged Less than 15 Years in the Canadian Population, 1956–2017

Sources: Number of persons aged 65 years and over and number of children aged less than 15 years in the Canadian population, 1956 to 2016, found at: www12.statcan.ca/census-recensement/2006/as-sa/97-551/figures/c1-eng.cfm

dating back only slightly over a century. Changes in the ability or willingness to pay the costs associated with retirement, therefore, will have implications even for our ideas of aging and old age.

Finally, Canadians will have to address such ethical issues as the right to die, the creation of living wills, guardianship for the dependent elderly, empowerment of the elderly population, and equity across genders, races, ethnic groups, and religions in developing policies and the delivery of services.

POLICY DEBATES

Box 6.2 Pension Reform in the Twenty-First Century

Today, pension spending accounts for roughly a tenth of GDP in most EU countries. Assuming no change in entitlement rules or benefits, population aging alone will raise this level by 30–50 per cent over the next 3–4 decades. Concomitantly, we shall witness a sharp fall in the ratio of contributors to recipients. The real challenge we face is how to ensure that we can meet this additional financial obligation.

The ongoing debate is overly dominated by actuarial concerns. This is like putting the cart before the horse. Actuarial issues only become relevant once we have decided how to allocate the additional spending burdens.

... Unless we are prepared to accept an erosion of retiree well-being, total pension outlays—be they privately or publicly financed—will inexorably rise. . . .

We need a decision rule for how to fairly allocate the additional costs of population aging. . . . The core issue of pension reform is to find an equitable formula that, at once, minimizes contribution rate growth and allocates the additional costs fairly between retirees and workers. A choice in favour of inter-generational equity must, however, also consider intra-generational fairness. . . . The idea is to fix, once and for all, a relative per capita GDP ratio between the 'old' and the 'young'. . . . Once the ratio is fixed, the tax rate is adjusted periodically to reflect both population and productivity changes. The main problem here, of course, is how to fix the ratio initially—a task that undoubtedly is easier to undertake in polities capable of forging broad social pacts. A second obstacle is that it would be difficult to apply to private and occupational pension plans that are not under government control.

The intra-generational equity problem is a question of welfare distributions within any given cohort of retirees. The necessary starting point has to do with heterogeneous life courses and 'generational luck'. . . . The pensioner cohorts of the 1950s were poor mainly because they had poor lives: Born at the close of the nineteenth century, their youth was marred by WW I; their careers straddled the difficult 20s, the depression of the 1930s, and WW II. In brief, they were unable to accumulate much during their lifetimes and this was especially the case for the weakest. Moving forward, today's retirees are broadly well-off . . . in large part because they had good lives: beginning their careers during the booming post-war decades, generally enjoying job security and rising real wages, they have accumulated substantial savings and resources. Even low-skilled males did quite well in the post-war era. . . .

Starting poorly (especially in terms of human capital) in the 'new economy' is likely to have lasting adverse consequences. Citizens with less than the equivalent of secondary education will face strong probabilities of labour market precariousness and low pay. They will in, say, 2050, look more like the retiree generation in 1950 than those now in retirement. It also is well-documented that not only is average longevity increasing (we now live 10 years more than did our grandfathers) but that longevity is positively correlated with socio-economic status: the resourceful live longer and will, therefore, end up consuming more pension benefits. Simply combining these two factors leads one to conclude that intra-generational equity must, at a minimum, require some basic, universal, and progressively financed, pension guarantee. . . .

The ultimate cause of population aging is low fertility. Yet, a return to replacement fertility now is unlikely to resolve the sustainability problem over the next decades in any event. Immigration is often cited as an alternative solution. Unfortunately, the most comprehensive simulation models show that realistic levels of immigration can help, but will not make a decisive difference. Only very unrealistic immigration scenarios, such as one exclusively based on skilled, prime age males (and without family reunification), will make a huge difference in terms of financial equilibrium. This leaves us with the two most realistic and effective policy options: raising overall employment levels among women and raising retirement age. . . . The main challenge with the 'women's-employment' strategy is that it will likely further aggravate the fertility crisis unless accompanied by adequate day-care provision.

The last—and by far most effective—solution is to raise the age of retirement. . . . Delaying retirement is a very effective tool because it cuts both ways: reducing pension years while raising contribution years simultaneously. . . . The huge educational gap that exists now between old and younger workers will disappear within the next 10 years or so (when the baby-boom generations arrive at retirement age). Additionally, the health conditions of older workers are improving rapidly.

Average expected 'disability-free' years for a 60-year-old male are now more than 10. . . .

Still, two principal problems do remain. Firstly, while older workers' productivity declines, seniority-based wage setting implies constantly rising earnings, and this affects employers' incentives to keep older workers. Secondly, given that life expectancy is correlated with socio-economic status, delaying retirement will be unfair to the lower income workers (for whom a curtailment of 'leisure years' will appear relatively more drastic). . . . The welfare inequalities within one generation swamp all differences between generations. The equity and the cost problems associated with any pension reform would be far more manageable if inequalities in earnings, careers, and life-long resource accumulation were minimal. Such inequalities spring from conditions in childhood and youth, including the impact of social origins.

In brief, the best way to think about pension reform is not to begin with the aged, but with the welfare of children. Good pensions begin at birth.

Source: Abridged from Esping-Andersen (2003).

Lobbying Efforts by Elderly People

As a varied group, elderly people have experienced widely different lives and have not voted with a common voice. Yet, through organizations like the United Senior Citizens of Ontario, One Voice, CARP, the National Academy of Older Canadians, and the Fédération de l'Âge d'Or du Québec, Canada's seniors have been making their concerns known to politicians, business, and younger voters. Such lobby groups play an invaluable role in promoting the interests of elderly people (for a European example, see Kemmerling and Neugart, 2009).

Currently, the largest lobby group for the elderly population in Canada is CARP. This set of initials once stood for the Canadian Association of Retired Persons. However, because of the changing characteristics of its membership, the group's name was changed to Canada's Association for the Fifty-Plus (though CARP remains the preferred acronym). Formed in 1984 by Murray and Lillian Morgenthau, CARP was initially no more than 10 friends who met to share their experiences of being elderly. Today, CARP is a non-profit organization with a membership of more than 400,000 Canadians and a mandate to promote the rights and quality of life of seniors.

CARP seeks to make policy-makers and the public aware of elderly people's views about social, financial, and political issues. Among other things, CARP has organized national forums on scams and frauds against seniors, on home care, and on the environment. It has also addressed health-care issues such as long-term care, hospital closures and mergers, the national health strategies, and the funding, availability, cost, and taxation of drugs. CARP has also identified and combatted incidences of ageism and elder abuse. Finally, CARP has helped to design strategies to provide safe, affordable living conditions for seniors. Its many reports, publications, and videos address various topics of interest to the elderly population (CARP, 2001).

Protecting Rights and Limiting Risks

As people get older, they often have a harder time making their wishes heard and respected by family or caregivers. When caregivers defer to the senior's choice they are showing respect to the senior and respecting values of self-determination that are central to our culture.

However, in some cases, seniors may not be the best judges of their own best interests; and where their decisions involve risk for others, collective rights must be considered. The risk of harm may be compounded by chronic diseases or mental incapacities. For example, with weakening vision and slower reaction times, elder drivers may not be the best judges of whether they should continue to drive an automobile (e.g., Gagliardi et al., 2010). It may be in the interest of the community and of the elder to withdraw the driver's licence, even though this may reduce the senior's easy mobility and independence.

The problem of respecting individual freedom versus protecting a senior from harm arises in many situations. For example, caregivers need to question whether seniors who want to continue living in their own homes should be allowed to do so at the risk of serious harm. Likewise, they need to consider whether or not to override the rights of seniors to refuse treatments that could restore or preserve their health (Newsletter of the National Advisory Council on Aging, 2006).

In these and other domains, caregivers need to balance the rights of seniors with the needs and rights of other people. Respecting a senior's right to make choices—even risky choices—does not mean withdrawing care and support. It does mean finding a balance between the wishes of the senior and the caregivers. Making a valid assessment of the senior's capabilities may call for expert testing. Competency assessments, for example, may consist of mental tests managed by health professionals to find out if an individual can reason well enough to care for himself or herself. People unfit to do so may lose the right to decide for themselves (ibid.).

This is more complicated than it sounds. For example, there is the matter of selecting the right test for the occasion, in view of possible risks to the senior and his or her caregivers. As well, a person's competency may rise and fall over time. A senior who tests as mentally competent today may not test as competent next week, and vice versa. This suggests the need for ongoing assessment, to ensure the right decision is made at the right time.

CLAIMS-MAKING AND THE SOCIAL CONSTRUCTION OF AGING

While we have discussed aging in this chapter with respect to social consequences such as poverty, the social construction of aging is extremely important as well. We should not lose sight of the fact that, as we frame and solve problems, we also are constructing ways—perhaps unnecessarily narrow ways—of thinking about these problems.

Consider the matter of male sexual potency and the role of Viagra. Does Viagra (and other drugs like it) solve a problem or create one? As one study points out, the success of this drug has contributed to the medicalization of aging masculinity (Marshall, 2007). Viagra solves a problem only after men have been persuaded that they are unmanly if their sexual performance declines—even if the decline is commonly and normally associated with aging. In effect, this represents a wholesale redefinition of beliefs about aging and sexuality, not hard scientific evidence about men's health in later life (Vares, 2009).

A constructionist perspective takes 'old age' as a culturally arbitrary category. After all, the boundaries between middle age and old age are often based on loose, poorly defined criteria (Kehl Wiebel and Fernandez Fernandez, 2001). In a capitalist society, people falling into the category of 'old' may be seen as problematic because they are failing to participate in the labour force (Ben-Moshe, 2004; Vincent, 1996). Equally, in a consumerist society, people who are failing to consume their time and money in youthful ways may be viewed as problematic. It is important, then, that we try to get around discourses that treat the 'elderly' as an easily distinguished group of people or that view age as necessarily disabling.

Some have even challenged well-established ideas about universal stages of development. One comparative study, for example, found that the concept of adolescence (normally associated with ages 12–18) is differently constructed in communities around the world. That is, different social expectations are associated with this particular age category in different societies. At the other end of the age distribution, the 'very old' stage (ages >75) does not even exist in some places (Chatterjee et al., 2002). As well, the idea of a universal progression has been challenged along gender lines, with some authors arguing that such false universals deny women's unique life experiences (Smith, 2001).

The reality of aging, like many other issues, is complicated; and few today would hold to a totally constructionist or totally essentialist view of aging. Biology, culture, and physical and social environments all interact to some degree in determining life experiences—as we acknowledged in an earlier discussion of the life course. This is true even of 'health' in later life, however we define the term 'health'.

Thus, constructionist perspectives help us better to understand aging—its main features and its many variations. They remind us that the definitions and meanings a society attributes to age are as important from a sociological view as the biological process of aging.

CHAPTER SUMMARY

Medicine, disease control, and biotechnology have brought us large increases in life expectancy in the past century or so. As scientists continue to improve their knowledge of how the human body ages, they will be ever more likely to design treatments and drugs that can compensate for or delay the processes of deterioration.

Perhaps in future, people will not only live longer, they will also experience a better quality of life in the later stages (see, e.g., McMunn, 2009; Saini and Jasal, 2009; Windsor, 2009). We are unlikely to discover a magical fountain of youth any time soon. However, medical technology may be able to reduce the significant differences in physical and mental functioning between young adults, middle-aged people, and the elderly population.

Still, we must not lose sight of the social construction of aging. In important ways, we are taught 'suitable' ways to behave at each age, and these age rules can act like straitjackets. The mass media, in both their programming and advertisements, are the main vehicles of socialization about the meaning of age. In part, the media give back to viewers what they already want and believe. What we see on television, in movies, and in print largely reflects what many already value and deride. However, the media also shape how we view the world. Largely, the media promote images of elderly people that are outdated, disrespectful, and ridiculous.

These images support ageism, which in turn supports discrimination in the workplace and elsewhere. As a result, seniors may not receive the opportunities, payments, or legislation they need, because ageism discourages those with political power from developing programs to help the elderly population.

From the functionalist perspective, aging is a social problem because the institutions of modern society fail to meet the needs of the dependent aged. Conflict theorists, on the other hand, view problems of the elderly population as stemming from their lack of power to shape social institutions in ways that meet their needs. Symbolic interactionists show us that elderly people are stigmatized because they do not conform to the images, ideals, and norms of a youth-oriented culture. Feminist theorists note that the most disadvantaged seniors are women and other social minorities.

Governments, voluntary associations, and informal and formal social networks all help to promote successful aging. However, elderly people also need to play a role in securing their own well-being. Research has confirmed that regular social contact with friends and relatives improves well-being among elderly people. Social integration is good in its own right, because we are social beings: we need and value the company of other people. As well, social integration markedly improves quality of life by reducing stress and increasing positive health practices. Isolated people, lacking social and community ties, are at the greatest risk of illness and premature death, other things being equal. The media can play a valuable role in promoting health and social integration among elderly people, and in this way will help to solve age-related problems.

Aging is unavoidable and every society takes note of this in its own culturally meaningful way. Increasingly, however, every society in its own way has to deal with the public responsibility for increased longevity and reduced family care. This will be one of the leading social problems of the twenty-first century.

QUESTIONS FOR CRITICAL THOUGHT

1. What is the main factor that has contributed to a significant rise in the proportion of older people worldwide?

2. Under conditions of an economic recession, how do you think the large population of old people will impact your life in Canadian society?

3. How are the experiences of aging different for women and men, and how would you explain these differences?

4. A Statistics Canada survey found in 2003 that poorer and less educated seniors were no more likely to seek health-care services than their wealthier, more educated counterparts. Do you find this surprising; and if so, how do you explain it?

5. How are the concepts of 'childhood' and 'adolescence' socially constructed? What is their social role or value?

RECOMMENDED READINGS

Ariès, Philippe. 1962 [1960]. *Centuries of Childhood: A Social History of Family Life*, trans. Robert Baldick. New York: Knopf. This classic work about the social construction of childhood, remains interesting. Although some modern researchers question the validity of Aries's analysis, this book was highly influential during the 1960s. It examines the history of Western society's invention of the concept of childhood with the advent of education and other social changes.

Bengston, V.L., N.M. Putney, and D. Gans, eds. 2009. *Handbook of Theories of Aging*, 2nd edn. New York: Springer. This highly useful book for students covers differences among aging theories. The authors promote a cross-disciplinary theorizing in the field of gerontology, with an aim to inform public policy and contribute to positive social changes for older adults.

Carmel, Sara, Carol A. Morse, and Fernando M. Torres-Gil, eds. 2007. *Lessons on Aging from Three Nations*. Amityville, NY: Baywood. A book on the 'art of aging well', the authors examine aging populations in three countries—Australia, Israel, and the United States—and compare the societal issues older adults face in these three contexts. Among the topics examined are how people cope with aging and especially how they deal with health problems in their respective countries.

Chappell, Neema, Lynn McDonald, and Michael Stones. 2008. *Aging in Contemporary Canada*, 2nd edn. Toronto: Pearson Prentice-Hall. This useful introduction to social gerontology in Canada provides comprehensive and up-to-date demographic, theoretical, and research information on aging in relation to women, ethnic groups, health and well-being, health care, families, retirement, and so on.

Cole, Jennifer, and Deborah Durham, eds. 2007. *Generations and Globalization: Youth, Age, and Family in the New World Economy*. Bloomington: Indiana University Press. This collection of studies argues that societal conceptions of childhood, youth, adulthood, and old age will shift as the world continues to globalize, transitioning to a global economy and an international flow of information. Relationships between generations will alter, and new social scripts and hierarchies will be introduced.

Connidis, Ingrid Arnet. 2001. *Family Ties and Aging*. Thousand Oaks, CA: Sage. This book examines issues of intergenerational family ties from a microsociological focus. From specific examples, the author draws out the significance of macrosociological implications of these relationships in reference to aging.

RECOMMENDED WEBSITES

Canadian Association on Gerontology (CAG/ACG)

www.cagacg.ca/whoweare/200_e.php

This is a 'national, multidisciplinary, scientific, and educational association established to provide leadership in matters related to the aging population'. A charity founded in 1971, CAG strives to become the national authority on both individual and population aging in Canada and seeks to improve the lives of older Canadians. CAG is currently a member of the International Association of Gerontology and Geriatrics and also publishes the *Canadian Journal on Aging*.

International Association of Gerontology and Geriatrics (IAGG)

www.iagg.com.br/webforms/index.aspx

An organization of national societies on gerontology and geriatrics, the mission of the IAGG is to promote research and training in these fields, and to promote health care and other social services to the aging population worldwide.

The Gerontological Society of America (GSA)

www.geron.org

The oldest (founded in 1945) and largest (5,000 plus members) organization concerned with research and practice in the field of aging, the GSA is devoted to promoting interaction and collaboration among its members and lobbies policy-makers and other leaders to improve the lives older people. It produces the *Gerontologist* and *Journals of Gerontology*, among the top journals in the field.

World Health Organization (WHO) Ageing and Life Course Programme

www.who.int/ageing/en

WHO co-ordinates with other organizations such as the United Nations to promote discussion of global issues, such as raising awareness about the many barriers older people face with health-care services and the impact such barriers have on their well-being.

Zoomer Magazine Canada

www.zoomermag.com

Launched in October 2008, *Zoomer* targets Canadian 45+ and is a lifestyle publication providing information on such topics as home, travel, health, sex, money, and so on to the largest demographic in Canada.

Canadian Association for Adolescent Health (CAAH)

www.youngandhealthy.ca/caah

A not-for-profit organization founded in 1993, CAAH joins Canadian professionals in different research fields to contribute to educate youth about physical, mental, and sexual health, as well as other important topics. It strives to get adolescents thinking about their later health, to ensure a long and prosperous lifespan.

CHAPTER 7
Crime and Violence

iStockphoto.com/Rade Lukovic

LEARNING OBJECTIVES

- To know the definitions of 'crime', 'laws', and 'social order'.
- To be able to distinguish among different types of crime.
- To appreciate the demography of crime.
- To learn about theories explaining crimes.
- To understand the economic, social, and psychological outcomes of crime.
- To discover the impact of crime on health.
- To know about possible solutions to the crime problem.

INTRODUCTION

Crime is a social problem for several reasons. First, as we will see, crime has real effects on people's health, safety, and sense of well-being. Victimization can be traumatic. It can cause people to withdraw from normal social life (Turner et al., 2010). Consequently, victimization on a large scale can reduce people's trust in social institutions and their willingness to take part in community life (Pottinger and Stair, 2009). Thus, the fear of crime can reduce a community's vitality and cohesion. Third, crime and its aftermath can damage the central institutions of civil society—families, workplaces, and schools, for example (Palmer et al., 2005)—and in this way hinder our ability to carry out the most basic social activities of learning, earning, and raising children (Kitchen and Williams, 2010; McKee and Milner, 2000).

As we will also see, crime is a social activity, with social causes and effects (Lovell, 2009). Men are more likely than women to be involved in violent crimes, both as victims and as offenders. Men are more likely than women to commit acts of murder, forcible rape, armed robbery, aggravated assault, and arson, for example. Many researchers believe that differential socialization provides the best explanation for this pattern (Lauritsen and Heimer, 2008).

Researchers from different theoretical backgrounds differ in their views about criminal causation and responsibility. Some argue that criminal behaviour, especially where property crimes are concerned, is a result of rational calculation that takes into account the profitability and risk of a crime. Others argue that crime will result whenever groups have unequal amounts of power and influence. As a result, crime will increase whenever social inequality increases (Farrell, 2010). Some argue that strict law enforcement and harsh sentencing will solve the 'crime problem'. Others argue that prisons cause as many problems as they solve—that, in fact, they teach crime and harden criminals (Clear, 1996).

We will also learn in this chapter that, where crimes are concerned, moral panic tends to run rampant, especially in cases involving sex, violence, or children. Griffin and Miller (2008) have called this phenomenon 'crime-control theatre'. Consider the intense public interest in child abductions. The mass media, public safety organizations, and the public together have constructed a social mythology and recurrent moral panic about the supposed pervasiveness of this threat to children. The result has often been harsh 'memorial' legislation enacted in response to sensational cases. One outcome in the US, where such panics have been most common, is America's Missing Broadcast Emergency Response (AMBER) alert system, designed to interrupt serious child kidnappings in progress by soliciting citizen tips to help officials quickly rescue victims. Research suggests that AMBER Alert has not achieved and probably cannot achieve the ambitious goals that inspired its creation (ibid.). AMBER is an imaginary 'solution' to a socially constructed problem, one that encourages public officials to symbolically address fear of a threat that will never go away. Such crime-control theatre creates unintended problems, such as public backlash when the theatrical policy fails—and a distorted public debate about the nature and extent of crime in our society.

DEFINING CRIME, LAWS, AND SOCIAL ORDER

All societies have rules about good and bad behaviour, and they all punish bad behaviour. Economically developed societies like Canada's proliferate and codify these rules—that is, make formal rules called 'laws'—about what their members can and cannot do; and they use large, specialized agencies—the police and courts—to enforce these rules.

We know these formal rules as **laws**; and when someone breaks a law, we say that he or she has committed a **crime**. Such laws are important tools for promoting good behaviour—if people know the police and courts will enforce these laws. The regularity of enforcement and harshness of punishment, in turn, reflects how seriously a society takes the offending behaviour.

Social order exists only when people obey rules. Though most of us don't like following rules we didn't make ourselves, social order is better than **social disorder**, for with social order, life is more predictable and 'safe' (Aradau and Van Munster, 2009). The rules in place not only serve to show which behaviours are acceptable, they also allow people to predict the behaviour of others. But social order does not emerge routinely out of kind impulses and spontaneous co-operation; there are simply too many people and too many competing interests for this to happen. Order must be manufactured and protected. Under the best circumstances, a social order emerges that is fair and widely accepted (Jackson and Bradford, 2009).

LAWS Rules of conduct that may provide for the punishment of violators. In other words, the formal rules about what a society's members can and cannot do.

CRIME Any behaviour that, in a given time and place, is prohibited by applicable statutory law. When a law is violated, a crime is said to have been committed.

SOCIAL ORDER The prevalence of generally harmonious relationships; used synonymously with social organization. This condition exists when rules are obeyed and social situations are controlled and predictable. Rules serve not only to indicate which behaviours are acceptable, but also to allow participants to anticipate the behaviour of others.

SOCIAL DISORDER The uncertain and unpredictable condition in which rules are not obeyed. The environment is generally unsafe, and the boundaries of acceptable behaviour have broken down.

CRIME IN CANADA AND ELSEWHERE

A few crimes that are common, easily investigated, and cheaply prosecuted account for most of our criminal statistics at any given time. Chiefly, these are simple assaults and property crimes, what criminologists call 'street crimes'. So, changes in a society's crime rate likewise reflect changes in the reporting and prosecution of a few particular crimes. Changes in the crime rate also reflect changes in victims' willingness to report crimes and the ability of police to investigate them.

The most important thing to understand about criminal statistics is that the most familiar of them—statistics for conviction and or imprisonment—offer the palest reflection of the total amount of crime in Canadian society. By contrast, a stronger but—for obvious reasons—not always reliable picture is provided by victimization statistics. The reason is that criminal justice operates like a funnel: of the many criminal incidents, only a few are reported, and of these even fewer result in arrests and convictions, let alone imprisonment. This is nicely depicted in Figure 7.1 below. Though the data are from a decade ago, the process, and resulting funnel shape, has not changed for decades.

For this reason, when criminal statistics change, we often have trouble knowing if this reflects a change in the incidence of crime or in the enforcement of laws against crime. As the data in Figure 7.2 show, in the past decade, the Canadian crime rate has been falling—indeed, has continued to fall—and so has the severity of the average crimes committed.

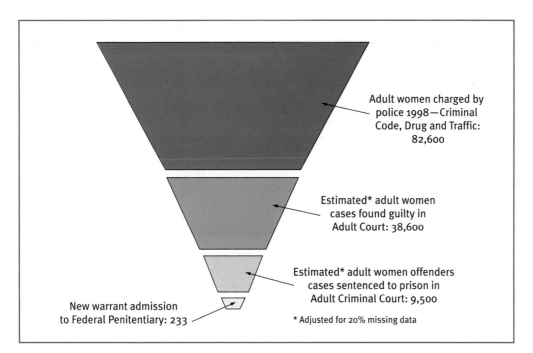

Figure 7.1 Women's Crime Funnel, 1998–9

Source: Adapted from *Federal Imprisonment Trends for Women 1994–95 to 1998–99* by Roger Boe, Cindy Lee Olah, and Colette Cousineau. Research Branch, Correctional Service of Canada, December, 2000.

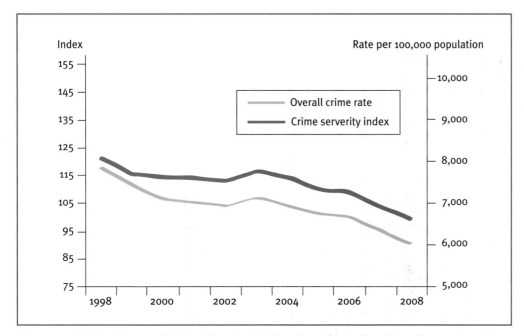

Figure 7.2 Police-Reported Crime Rate and Crime Severity Index, Canada, 1998–2008

Source: Police reported crime statistics, at: www.statcan.gc.ca/daily-quotidien/090721/dq090721a-eng.htm

SELF-REPORTING
The victim reports to authorities that a crime has occurred. This is the most direct method of measuring crime rates. However, it is not the most accurate, as changes in the crime rate reflect changes in victims' willingness to report.

VICTIMIZATION SURVEYS Samples of people are asked how many times within a given time period they have been the victim of particular crimes.

Measuring the total rate of crime is difficult since both police reporting and **self-reporting** typically are incomplete. Victimization surveys may yield a more precise account, because victims have a closer connection to the crimes committed; they have directly suffered the effects. In **victimization surveys**, samples of people report how often, within a given period, they have been the victims of particular crimes (Vollaard and Koning, 2009). However, these surveys, too, are subject to distortion. Thus, all of the sources on which we rely for our information—including official statistics on arrest, conviction, and imprisonment, self-reports, and victimization statistics—are incomplete and possibly biased.

As the data in Figure 7.2 suggest, it is useful to consider the seriousness of the crimes committed, if we are to have a good idea of the 'seriousness' of the crime 'problem' in Canada. According to a Statistics Canada report in 2008, a decrease in the number of break-ins made a key contribution to the drop in the severity of overall crime in a 10-year period. Over the same period, the seriousness of (less frequent) violent crimes remained stable. The crime index that tracks changes in the severity of police-reported crime assigns each offence a weight, with more serious crimes like break-ins and robberies assigned higher weights and others, like shoplifting, lower weights. According to the index, overall crime severity fell by 20 per cent from 1998 to 2008, driven by a 40 per cent drop in break-ins.

Crimes of Violence

CONVENTIONAL CRIMES
The traditionally illegal behaviours that most people think of as 'crime'. For example, homicide and sexual assault are given the most media coverage but account for only 12 per cent of all crimes.

HOMICIDE The killing of a human being by another, directly or indirectly, by any means; includes murder, i.e., the unlawful killing of another human being with malicious intent, and manslaughter, the unlawful killing of another person without sufficient intent to constitute murder.

Contrary to the impression presented on the nightly news, violent crimes account for only about 10–12 percent of total crimes reported in Canada (Gotlieb, 2002). Yet, criminologists refer to these types of offences as **conventional crimes** because they are the illegal behaviours that most people think of as crime. Also, they are crimes that most people agree are serious and deserve harsh punishment. They are conventional in every sense except their relative rarity (Ruback and Thompson, 2001).

The most headline-grabbing violent crime is **homicide**, the killing of one person by another. Homicide can be subdivided into two categories, murder and manslaughter, depending on whether the homicide involves malicious intent (Cole and Gramajo, 2009). Typically, men are more likely to be involved in homicides than women, both as victims (67 per cent of all victims are men) and as offenders (88 per cent of those charged with homicide are men). Contrary to what the media suggest, we tend to kill and to be killed by people close at hand. Victims of homicide are more likely to be killed by a family member or acquaintance, for example, than by a stranger. Still, homicides are rare in Canada. Homicide and attempted homicide accounted for only 0.4 per cent of all crimes of violence in 2004, for example.

By contrast, *assaults* are common, accounting for nearly 90 per cent of all violent crimes reported (Statistics Canada, 2005a). Assaults can be differentiated depending on whether a weapon was involved or if major bodily harm was inflicted. *Sexual assault*, most seriously rape but also sexual harassment, is another form of violent crime. Social science and law enforcement experts agree that most sexual assault victims probably do not report their experience to the police (Betts et al., 2003).

The Canadian Press/Toronto Star-David Cooper

Acting on information from Toronto homicide detectives, Toronto Marine Unit divers located a steel barrel in the harbour with what they believe to contain a body incased in cement, just off of the new Sugar Beach east of Redpath's Sugar on Queen's Quay in Toronto, 23 May 2010.

Stalking has recently emerged as a new social problem. This crime has gained much notice in recent years because it has become common and is associated with gendered harassment, abuse, and violence. Surveys have found that repeated stalking is reported by up to 62 per cent of young adults, although results vary depending on the sample and on the precise definition of 'stalking' used (Davis and Frieze, 2000). Most stalkers are former, rather than current, intimates, and they are more likely to be men than women. Typically, stalking includes efforts to re-establish a former relationship. It is a worrisome type of relationship abuse that may evolve into other physical, psychological, and sexual forms, including violence against women. Stalking has various determinants—socio-cultural, interpersonal, dyadic, situational, and intrapersonal (White et al., 2000), often with deep roots in the history of the stalker.

Violence between intimates is common, with men especially likely to carry out the most extreme types of violence, up to intimate-partner homicide (Browne et al., 1999). The combination of violence with stalking frequently is lethal. Compared to battered women (who are only occasionally stalked), women who are relentlessly stalked report more severe physical violence, sexual assault, and emotional abuse after separation. They also suffer higher rates of depression and post-traumatic stress disorder (Mechanic et al., 2000).

Non-Violent Crimes

Most crimes committed in Canada, as already suggested, are non-violent crimes. The major non-violent crimes include theft, mischief, and property damage; drug production and trafficking; and breaking and entering.

In this category we also find vice crimes, including the use of illegal drugs, illegal gambling, communication for prostitution, and the possession, distribution, or sale of child pornography. These crimes provide the greatest opportunities for organized crime, since most societies bar legal access to these goods and services, yet many people are willing to pay for them nevertheless.

White-collar crimes can be defined as crimes 'committed by a person of respectability and high social status in the course of his occupation' (Sutherland, 1949). These include fraud, bribery, insider trading, embezzlement, computer crime, and forgery, and they can amount to anywhere from hundreds to millions of dollars. Often, white-collar criminals take advantage of gaps in the social structure—for example, loopholes or confusions about new laws or economic conditions—to profit from their crimes (Tillman and Indergaard, 1999). They prosper wherever governments decline to supervise the economic marketplace, as has happened increasingly in capitalist societies over the past 30 years. Typically, governments give white-collar crime a lower priority than conventional crime, despite evidence that white-collar crime does economic, physical, and psychological harm to a much larger number of people than does street crime (Friedrichs, 1995).

Organized Crime: A Window on Our Culture?

North Americans are fascinated by the glamour and excitement of organized crime, as depicted in numerous films and television programs. However, organized crime is far from glamorous—it is vicious, harmful big business with transnational networks that reach across the globe. Organized crime rings that currently exist in Canada include the Sicilian Mafia, Chinese Triads, the Big Circle Boys (Chinese), the Colombian Mafia, the Russian Mafia, and motorcycle gangs like the Hell's Angels and Outlaws (Cheloukhine, 2008; Dawson, 2009). These groups have been variously involved in vice crimes—drug trafficking, prostitution, extortion, bribery, money laundering, and pornography—as well as in assaults, homicides and contract killing, kidnapping, human trafficking, counterfeiting, insurance fraud, auto theft, truck hijacking, and the illegal arms trade. Worldwide, the gross value of organized crime activities has been estimated at between $600 billion and $1.5 trillion (Knight and Keating, 2010: 277).

Early sociologists believed that crime results from poverty and crime in poor neighbourhoods results from social disorganization: the more disorganization, the more crime. After around 1940, however, with the publication of William Whyte's classic *Street Corner Society*

VICE CRIMES Deviant behaviour that may be defined as immoral (for example, gambling, prostitution, drug trafficking). These crimes provide the greatest opportunity for organized crime.

WHITE-COLLAR CRIMES The crimes committed by white-collar workers and management in the course of their occupations. They always are distinguished from conventional criminal offences such as robbery or murder. White-collar crimes are performed in the course of normal work and usually occur in reputable organizations.

ORGANIZED CRIME A group or system of professional criminals who practise illegal activities as a way of life and whose criminal activities are co-ordinated and controlled through a hierarchical system of bosses.

The conflict approach focuses on crimes committed by privileged people such as financial advisor Earl Jones. Joey Davis, with the Earl Jones Victims Organizing Committee, a group representing victims of Earl Jones, speaks to reporters at a news conference to re-introduce anti-white collar crime legislation on 3 May 2010 in Montreal.

(1981 [1943]), sociologists changed their views. They came to recognize that crime—especially crime in poor neighbourhoods—was often highly organized and, indeed, often connected to 'organized crime'. It was also closely connected with the social, political, and economic life of the people in the community. Crime, then, was a basic part of city life—and, indeed, of national corporate and political life.

Modern organized crime today operates at the crossroads of legitimate and illegitimate business, family, and formal organization. It has as strong connections to white-collar crime as it does to vice crimes (such as drug trafficking, pornography, and prostitution). Organized crime draws on the talents of professionals and amateurs, older and younger criminals. What organized crime shows us is that crime is a learned, organized social activity with historical and cultural roots—not disorganized irrationality. It is often grounded in traditional notions of kinship and friendship, honour and duty, for example. Organized crime is by nature a social phenomenon, not a departure from normal social life. It is fully a part of our society, and plays a crucial role in the world's economic and political activities (Dawson, 2009).

Organized crime in urban North America prospers under four key conditions. First, organized crime flourishes under conditions of scarcity and inequality. It is most common in poor communities with a wide range of economic inequality and, often, strong family traditions. Second, it is common where poverty and prejudice keep people from moving easily to find work elsewhere. Third, organized crime provides protection in communities that lack good access to welfare, health care, good-quality education, and police protection. Finally, organized crime flourishes among people who lack human capital and cultural capital. North American capitalism is one type of economic and social system that produces these conditions, though it is not the only one. In these respects, South American neo-feudalism and Russian neo-capitalism produce these conditions just as well (ibid.), and failing and failed states, and those societies undergoing rapid change, provide a breeding ground for organized crime: for example, post-Communist Russia; Iraq; Afghanistan; Albania.

THE DEMOGRAPHY OF CRIME

Members of the Canadian population are unequally likely to commit crimes, and unequally likely to be victimized by criminals. In some instances, these two go together: for example, young, less-educated men are more likely to be both perpetrators and victims of crime than the Canadian adult average, especially for crimes like assault.

However, Figure 7.3, which indicates the relative risks of victimization for disadvantaged groups, suggests that some Canadians are disproportionately likely to be victimized. We will

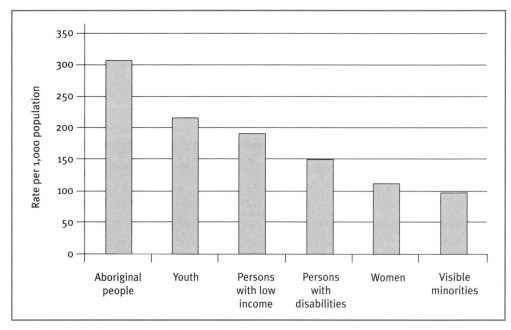

Figure 7.3 Criminal Victimization in Canada
Source: **Department of Justice, at: www.justice.gc.ca/eng/pi/rs/rep-rap/jr/jr13/p6b.html.**

briefly discuss some of the inequalities here, and return to them throughout the chapter—for the relationship between crimes and victims provides an entrée into Canadian crime as a whole.

Gender: Offenders

Women commit far fewer crimes than men; and the gender gap in crime—whether organized, professional, or amateur crime—is nearly universal (Steffensmeier and Allan, 1996). There are a few exceptions to this rule, however. One exception is the rate of females killing intimate partners, which is *nearly* as high as that of men killing intimate partners (0.75:1), at least in North America (Wilson and Daly, 1992). As well, women are twice as likely as men to be arrested for prostitution (Wrangham and Peterson, 1997).

Otherwise, the statistics for crimes are mainly about men. Of the more than 566,000 Canadians adults charged with a Criminal Code offence in 2004, only 18 per cent were female. Among youths, the female percentage is slightly higher, at 23 per cent.

This gender gap is especially pronounced with respect to violent crimes. In Canada, for example, the ratio of males to females charged with violent crimes in 2004 was more than 4.5:1. Research shows that men are 7 times more likely than women to commit arson, 9 times more likely to commit murder, 10 times more likely to commit armed robbery, 35 times more likely to discharge a firearm with the intent to harm, 54 times more likely to commit sexual assault, and 78 times more likely to commit forcible rape (ibid.).

Men are more than twice as likely as women to commit fraud, 7 times more likely to engage in illegal gambling, 8 times more likely to vandalize, 8.5 times more likely to be arrested for drunkenness, 9 times more likely to steal a car, and 11 times more likely to commit a break-and-enter offence (Statistics Canada, 2005a; Wrangham and Peterson, 1997). So the generalization is: men commit more crimes than women, though the gender gap varies according to the type of crime.

As well, there are signs the gender gap is starting to close (Statistics Canada, 2005a; Canadian Centre for Justice Statistics, 2005). This is true especially among youths. In 1984, for instance, females 17 and under accounted for 19 per cent of all violent offence charges laid; by 2004, that figure had increased to 26 per cent (Statistics Canada, 2005a).

Explanations of these gender differences vary. Some researchers say that biology is the answer, that higher levels of testosterone incline men towards aggressive and hostile actions. Others say that **differential socialization** is the cause: the male subculture is more violent and young males are encouraged to use aggressive and violent behaviours to solve problems. Of these two, the hormonal theory of gender differences is clearly less able than the socialization theory to account for observed declines in the gender gap in recent decades, so it is probably the weaker theory.

Gender: Victims

Just as criminal offenders are mainly male, so are the victims of crime. This is true for most criminal offence categories, including homicide, robbery, and assault. There are, however,

MONSTER

Based on the life and crimes of Aileen Wuornos, this 2003 film explores the importance of gender in the depiction and prosecution of a female serial killer.

DIFFERENTIAL SOCIALIZATION The processes whereby individuals learn to behave in accordance with prevailing standards of culture or gender. For example, boys and men learn to be less inhibited in using aggressive and violent actions, and this may account for the disproportionate number of males involved in criminal activity.

several exceptions. For example, men are disproportionately the perpetrators of domestic and sex-based crimes, and women are disproportionately their victims.

Domestic abuse—violence against women and children—is a serious social problem throughout the world, and it is especially problematic in cultures that subscribe to a patriarchal world view in which wives and daughters are inferior to husbands and sons (Alaggia et al., 2009). Canada, like other nations populated largely by immigrants of scores of ethnicities, is caught in a dilemma. On the one hand, Canada wants to provide its citizens with free religious, cultural, and ethnic expression. On the other hand, it wants to protect the rights and safety of its more vulnerable members, including women and children. This may mean depriving men in some households of the right to use patriarchal (cultural) norms to justify their criminal abuse of women.

Victims of sex-based crimes, including sexual assault and rape, are also mainly female (Doepke and Tertilt, 2009). One social explanation for this is the continued ambivalence that North American society holds towards sex and, in particular, female sexuality. On the one hand, the female body is endlessly displayed on television, in films, and in marketing campaigns as a sexual object for male consumption. At the same time, women who take control of their sexuality are often accused of being too aggressive and characterized as 'tramps' or 'sluts'.

On the whole, women are safer and freer today than they were in the past. Increased gender equality may, in the long run, reduce rates of sexual abuse. Whaley and Messner (2002) have referred to this as the 'ameliorative hypothesis'. On the other hand, there are often great risks to women in the short run: as gender equality increases, so do rates of sexual assault against women. This 'backlash hypothesis' is popular among radical feminist theorists. Both theories are compatible, and both receive support from research on this topic by Rosemary Gartner (1997).

Age

Stated simply, young people are more likely to commit crimes than old people. This is above all true for property crimes, where we see a lot of juvenile crime, then a large drop in the number of people accused after the age of 18. For this reason, as the Canadian population has aged, the crime rate has dropped (Kong, 1999).

An older society is a more law-abiding society. One explanation is that young people are more likely than people aged 20–60 to be unemployed or to work in low-wage jobs. As sociologist Robert K. Merton (1938) has argued, they are more likely to use criminal 'innovations' to achieve their culturally desired goals (that is, money and material goods). They have less investment in the old, conventional ways of doing things.

In addition, aggressiveness is a cultural norm for many young men. This means that wherever social occasions bring together large numbers of young men—especially unemployed or underemployed young men—there will be high risks of crime. This is especially true of cities with high unemployment rates and high rates of recent immigration from less developed countries.

Sociologists know, however, that crime rates reflect at least three realities and only one of these is the commission of crimes. First, there are the actions of the criminals: they commit the crimes that are measurable and measured. Second, there are the activities of victims: they may choose to report or not report information about crimes to which they have been subjected. Third, there are the actions of police: they investigate and document the 'facts' of the crime and may or may not lay charges.

VICTIMIZATION FROM CRIME

Demographic and Community Correlates of Criminal Victimization

As individuals, some people are at higher risk of victimization than others. These risk factors include demographic variables, such as being male, young, unmarried, or unemployed (Arnold et al., 2005). As well, some neighbourhoods are riskier than others. Many factors determine the safety of a neighbourhood or community: socio-economic vitality, social cohesion and trust, community resources and infrastructure, and mechanisms of informal social control. In general, crime rates go up when neighbourhoods decline—for example, with drops in average household income and home ownership. As crime increases, a vicious cycle is established, driving community cohesion down and crime up.

Suitable Targets

Suitable targets are people who are routinely exposed to crime or who, for other reasons, have heightened vulnerability. For example, taxi drivers have a greater than average risk of victimization because of their repeated interaction with strangers at night (Elzinga, 1996). Gay men and lesbians have a higher than average risk of assault because of hostile public attitudes towards them in some quarters (Tiby, 2001). Tourists are more likely than natives of the same class background to experience victimization while on holiday in a strange place (Mawby et al., 1999).

Three characteristics put people at particular risk of victimization. They are the target's (that is, victim's) vulnerability (for example, a physical weakness or psychological distress), gratifiability (for example, female gender for the crime of sexual assault), and antagonism (for example, an ethnic or group identity that may spark hostility or resentment) (Finkelhor and Asdigian, 1996). With some exceptions, poor and powerless people are more vulnerable than rich and powerful people, with one exception: people with more and better property—larger homes, newer cars—are more likely to have their property stolen (Mesch, 1997).

As we have noted several times, women run a higher risk of certain kinds of victimization than men do. For some crimes, such as assault, men are more likely to be victimized by strangers or acquaintances, while women are more likely to be victimized by intimates. Female homicide victims, for example, tend to be killed by a spouse, another family member, or an intimate partner during domestic violence. Men, by contrast, are more likely to be killed by a stranger in a public place (Pratt and Deosaransingh, 1997).

CLASSIC WORKS

Box 7.1 Richard Ericson's *Reproducing Order* (1982)

Richard Ericson (1948–2007) was a leading Canadian sociologist in the field of criminology, especially police research. He received a BA from the University of Guelph, an MA in sociology from the University of Toronto, and a Ph.D. in Criminology from Cambridge University. Besides holding a position as Principal of Green College at the University of British Columbia, Ericson was a Professor of Law at that university (1993–2003) and a Professor of Criminology at the University of Toronto (2004–7).

Ericson was known by his colleagues for his dedication and rigorous research in various topics such as youth and offenders, crime reports in the media, and the role of coroners in death investigation and public safety. As well as many journal articles, he published 12 books that include *Making Crime: A Study of Detective Work* (1981), *Reproducing Order: A Study of Police Patrol Work* (1982), *Visualizing Deviance* (1987), *Policing the Risk Society* (1997), and, most recently, *Crime in an Insecure World* (2006).

As its subtitle suggests, *Reproducing Order* examined how the patrol police preserve, reinforce, and restore social order. It approached this topic by asking: How do the police spend their time? What do they concentrate on and what do they ignore? How do they deal with the public? Whose interests are served by those outcomes? What wider functions of the police can be theorized from this? Ericson argued that the police job is not primarily 'fighting crime' but merely reproducing—that is, reinforcing—social order.

To do this study, Ericson and a team of five researchers employed a mixture of field observation and qualitative measures to study patrol officers in an 'urban area of Eastern Canada'. First, using field observation, they studied the police force for five months in 1976. During the 348 shifts observed on ride-alongs, the team recorded a variety of activities, noting general shift activities, how contact in police–citizen encounters was initiated and by whom, which violations were recorded and which were ignored. This structured observation was supplemented by unstructured interviews with police, supervisors, and other officials. Additionally, the team studied the way negotiations were conducted between police and citizens.

Ericson found patrol officers have little work to fill their time during shifts. Police work is often boring. Officers spend little time directly combatting criminal behaviour, instead dealing with only one or two altercations and two or three minor incidents (e.g., traffic violations) in any eight-hour shift. Ericson comments that 'the bulk of the patrol officer's time was spent doing nothing other than consuming the petrochemical energy required to run an automobile and the psychic energy required to deal with the boredom of it all.'

When the police did interact with citizens, almost half the interactions were launched by officers because of real or perceived affronts to the public order, in the view of patrol officers. These incidents usually did not involve crime, but displayed an offensive demeanour and lifestyle. Specifically, Ericson notes that many interactions were initiated with 'pukers'—young men of low socio-economic status—and/or minorities. The police were able to apply wide discretion in choosing when, how, and against whom to apply law and force. They did so in ways that not only preserved social order but also preserved the status quo. They showed respect to middle-class people but less respect to poor people and minorities. In this way, they reproduced the value system of the existing class structure.

While some have criticized his research method, others note that Ericson was professionally rigorous and provided more information than previous works about policing. The significance of this study lies mainly in the theoretical framework it brings to the study of police work. It also encourages readers to question the effectiveness of official institutions in upholding social control, and leads the reader to wonder how police resources can be used more effectively and justly.

Elderly people run higher risks of victimization than middle-aged people, especially for crimes of robbery, intimidation, vandalism, and forgery or fraud. Robbery is the most serious offence committed against elderly victims, and men and women are equally likely to experience it (Bachman et al., 1998). Their risk of theft-related homicide is also relatively high because seniors are more likely than younger people to be seen as suitable targets and lack capable guardians. This risk is particularly high among seniors who are socially isolated.

At the other end of the age distribution, juveniles aged 12–17 are more likely than adults to be victims of violent crimes and suffer from crime-related injuries. Juvenile victims are more likely to know the people who victimize them (Hashima and Finkelhor, 1999). A Canadian study of high school students in Calgary found that, except for sexual victimization, males report higher victimization rates, in and out of school, than females. As well, younger students report higher rates of victimization at school than older students. Finally, students who report moderate to high levels of victimization are more likely to report moderate to high levels of delinquency (Paetsch and Bertrand, 1999), confirming the link between crime and criminal victimization.

Immigrants and ethnic minorities are at higher than average risk of victimization, especially for crimes against persons. In some instances, these may be 'hate crimes'. Gay men and lesbian women are also victims of hate crimes. Recent debates about the cultural and legal status of sexual-orientation minorities have increased the awareness of violence against gays and lesbians (Tewksbury et al., 1999). It is not clear whether anti-gay violence has increased, however. Our information about the extent of hate crimes against these groups is hindered by a reluctance of gays and lesbians to report victimization because of additional concerns about police abuse (Peel, 1999).

Inmates of 'total institutions' also suffer high risks of victimization. Common offences against prisoners include assault, robbery, threats of violence, theft of property from cells, verbal abuse, and exclusion (O'Donnell and Edgar, 1998; Wooldredge, 1998). The main perpetrators are other prisoners; though much has been said and written about the abusiveness of guards, such abuse is harder to document.

Secondary Victimization

Being the victim of a crime is painful and stressful. Often, however, the trauma does not stop with the crime itself. The victim may suffer additionally as she navigates the complex and often frustrating justice system in hopes of seeing justice done.

Secondary victimization refers to 'the victimization which occurs, not as a direct result of the crime, but through the response of institutions and individuals to the victim' (Canadian Resource Centre for Victims of Crime, 2005). Examples of secondary victimization include the refusal by law enforcement officers to recognize an individual's experience as a victim of crime and intrusive or inappropriate conduct by police or judicial officers. Psychological stress associated with the criminal investigation and trial process, and criminal justice processes and procedures that ignore, marginalize, or discount the role and input of the victim are other problems victims often face. They all serve to discourage victims from seeking official assistance after victimization.

SECONDARY VICTIMIZATION
Victimization that occurs through the response of institutions (e.g., police) and individuals (e.g., family members) to the victim's experience.

THEORETICAL PERSPECTIVES ON CRIME

Table 7.1   Theoretical Perspectives

Theory	Main Points
Varieties of Structural Functionalism	
Social Disorganization Theory	• Crime results from a breakdown in social norms and social integration following rapid social change. • Social disorganization leads to a loss of social cohesion, which in turn increases the likelihood of criminal behaviours such as robbery and assault. • Exposure to chronic random violence produces individuals who are more likely to act violently themselves. • Increased cohesion reduces crime.
Social Bond Theory	• Travis Hirschi's social bond theory (1969) argues that developing a strong social bond, established in childhood, can prevent people from giving in to the temptation to commit criminal acts. • Four elements are involved in a strong social bond: an attachment to other people, a commitment to conventional goals, an involvement in conventional activities, and a belief in the legitimacy of conventional values, norms, and moral standards encouraged by society. • Criminal activities increase where bonds are weak and individuals are exposed to anti-social values and activities.
Anomie Theory	• Merton (1938) theorizes that anomie and strain arise whenever unequal social opportunities prevent some people from achieving the culturally defined goals (such as money) by using legitimate means (such as a job). • One way to circumvent the gap between culturally approved ends and the culturally approved means to achieve them is through innovation (e.g., theft, robbery, tax fraud, embezzlement, and organized crime). • This theory assumes that criminals hold the same values and goals as everyone else.
Subculture Theory	• Violent subcultures, such as gangs, provide minority youth with an alternative community for achieving social status, friendship, and economic mobility. • Using violence to right a wrong or defend one's honour may be considered justifiable under the value and belief system of delinquents and criminals.

Continued

Table 7.1 Theoretical Perspectives—*Continued*

Theory	Main Points
Conflict Theory	• Conflict theories of crime and violence point to inequalities in society as the cause of such deviant behaviour. • Criminal activity increases as inequality increases. • Dominant ideology and formal laws protect the privileged status of the ruling class and mask white-collar crimes that benefit the social elite.
Varieties of Symbolic Interactionism	
Social Constructionism	• Constructionists look at how deviant behaviours come to be defined as 'deviant'. • Behaviours are not innately right or wrong; they only become wrong, deviant, or criminal when someone in power ascribes a moral value to them.
Labelling Theory	• Deviance is not a quality of the act a person commits, but rather a consequence of the application by others of rules and sanctions to an 'offender'. • Being labelled as deviant or criminal may promote further deviancy because the labelled person is unable to escape stigmatization and internalizes the 'deviant' identity.

Structural Functionalism

The functionalist approach to deviance includes a variety of theories that unite around a few central views, namely, that crime is normal, universal, and unavoidable—in short, that it is to be expected in any society. Here, we review one theory about the link between crime and social disorganization and one competing interpretation of the 'functions' served by crime: strain (anomie) theory. Other structural functionalist approaches—social bond theory and subculture theory—are outlined in Table 7.1.

Social Disorganization Theory

Durkheim's early work in *Suicide* (1951 [1897]) provides the basis for a theory that crime and other social pathologies (including suicide) result from a breakdown in social norms and social integration.

This breakdown, in turn, typically results from rapid social change and organizational problems associated with rapid change—for example, rapid increases in population, cultural diversity, and social (or geographic) mobility associated with the rise of urban industrial society. As the theory would predict, international data show that people in developing and transitional countries have higher victimization rates, express less satisfaction with law enforcement, and support a more punitive approach to controlling crime than people in fully industrialized societies (Zvekic, 1996).

STRAIN (ANOMIE) THEORY Merton holds that strain is produced when social structure prevents people from achieving culturally defined goals through legitimate means, and, according to Durkheim, anomie is a condition characterized by a breakdown of norms and personal disorganization, which may lead to crime. Merton outlines various adaptive strategies: conformity, ritualism, retreatism, rebellion, and innovation. Innovation is most commonly associated with criminal activities, which include theft, robbery, tax fraud, embezzlement, and organized crime.

SOCIAL BOND THEORY A type of control theory. A strong social bond prevents most people from succumbing to the temptation to engage in criminal activities.

SUBCULTURE THEORY This approach to the study of deviance investigates the norms that set a group apart from mainstream society. Specifically, it gives special insight into the subculture of the criminal, looking into the values and belief systems that may be conducive to delinquent and criminal action.

Social disorganization leads to the loss of social cohesion—a central concern of functionalist theory. Other things being equal, a loss of social cohesion increases the risk of robbery and assault near home and of robbery and assault by strangers, for example (Lee, 2000). Areas with high crime rates also have higher mortality rates from all causes, suggesting that crime rates mirror the quality of the social environment (Kawachi et al., 1999). Also, random violence and exposure to the continual use of guns and knives in the community produces children who are more likely to act violently themselves (Scott, 1999). In short, according to this theory, we can reduce crime mainly by increasing community cohesion.

Strain Theory

By contrast, strain theory focuses on inequality: the gap between what people want and what they can get by legitimate means. Implicit in strain theory—pictured schematically in Figure 7.4—is the idea that criminals hold the same values and goals as everyone else; they just use alternative means to pursue those goals and values. If everyone wants a nice house in the suburbs, a shiny new car, and a comfortable income, people with less education or fewer job opportunities may find crime the best way to get these things.

This approach would predict that people who are economically disadvantaged will react to inequality by getting money through unlawful means, such as robbery or embezzlement. For similar reasons, it would predict that declining wages will lead to increased rates of 'quick cash' crimes, especially in societies lacking a safety net of unemployment benefits, universal health insurance, and income security (Gaylord and Lang, 1997).

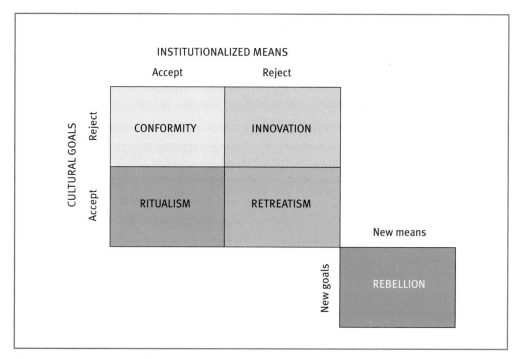

Figure 7.4 Merton's Deviance Typology
Source: **Robert Merton**

This approach, however, does not work as well to explain crimes against persons (such as assault, rape, or murder of an intimate) or crimes against property that yield no gain (such as vandalism). For this, we must turn to conflict theories.

Conflict Theory

Conflict theories of crime and violence point to inequalities in society as the cause of such deviant behaviour. Obviously, they would predict that, as inequality increases in a society, crime also will increase; and that people most subject to inequality would be the most likely to commit crimes.

For less obvious reasons, people who are disadvantaged are also more likely to embrace violent subcultures of violence, leading to higher rates of crimes against other people. These are subcultures preoccupied with amassing and protecting honour and respect, and they typically are found where cults of masculinity (machismo) are present. These tend to be found in less-prosperous, less-educated, and more traditional (often, rural) communities, though they may also be found in urban ghettos marked by a culture of poverty. As a result, homicide rates are the highest in poor communities marked by a high percentage of female-headed families, a high dropout rate from schools, and low welfare payment levels (Rosenfeld, 2009).

This last variable may seem counterintuitive at first glance, but research finds that welfare payments serve as an 'investment in youth', buffering them against the temptations of crime (Hannon, 1997). These offences against persons, not property, support the idea that social inequality produces 'hidden injuries of social class', which in turn promote anti-social behavior (Sennett and Cobb, 1972).

The conflict perspective notes that people in privileged positions work to preserve their status. In other words, the conflict approach also focuses on white-collar crime and the crimes committed by privileged people. Both the dominant ideology and formal laws—social constructs shaped and upheld by the ruling class—help the powerful to stay on top. They ensure, for example, that most people in society will view street crimes, such as public drug use and vagrancy, which are more common among the disadvantaged, as deviant and undesirable. At the same time, corporate crimes that profit the wealthy but harm far larger numbers of people continue to be hidden from the mass media, the public, and policy-makers.

Conflict theory also focuses on power differences between men and women in male-dominated societies. One example of such inequality is the perpetuation of 'rape myths', which depict women as responsible for their own victimization. The beliefs ingrained in some cultures and subcultures that 'no' means 'yes', that a revealing style of dress is like 'asking for' sex, and that 'good girls' do not get raped are examples of sexist myths that occasionally help acquit men of wrongdoing. They illustrate the conflict theorist's contention that people in power benefit from the criminal laws, while people without power do not. So, for example, as the material in Box 7.2 reminds us, women who make a living from prostitution are likely to be arrested and prosecuted, while the men who solicit and use their services are not.

Currently, despite higher rates of female arrests and convictions than in the past, there is little evidence that women are committing higher numbers of crimes today, only that they

PERSONAL STORIES

Box 7.2 Academic Arrested in Prostitution Sting

Brandy M. Britton has worked for years to build up her résumé—doctorate from the University of California at San Francisco, sociology professor at the University of Maryland in Baltimore County, director of the Institute for Women and Girls Health Research Inc.

But Howard County vice officers say she was also developing a résumé of a much different sort: The 41-year-old mother of two is accused of running a prostitution service from her Ellicott City home under the alias Alexis. According to charging documents, Britton advertised her services and rates on a website. . . .

Police began investigating Britton 10 months ago after receiving complaints about her website, which was shut down yesterday. This week, a police officer working undercover made an appointment with her. According to charging documents, Britton opened the door and led the officer to an upstairs bedroom. She told him to undress and place $400 on a table by the door. After leaving the marked police bills, the officer went to the front door and let other officers inside to arrest Britton, according to documents.

Police found 150 condoms and other pieces of evidence, the documents said. Officers also removed several business records that they say tie her to the website and prostitution, the documents said. . . .

Police charged Britton with 'engaging in prostitution, maintaining a building for the purpose of prostitution, allowing a building to be used for prostitution and allowing a person into a building for the purpose of prostitution'. Each charge carries a penalty of up to one year in jail or a fine of $500 or both sanctions.

The website that police say Britton ran included pictures of a blonde woman in erotic poses and in various states of undress. The woman's face was concealed by pixilation. The site advertised massages and included a disclaimer that any fees were for modelling and companionship, not sex.

Most of Britton's neighbours declined to talk about her yesterday, saying only that she was a nice woman whose daughter visited from college occasionally. They also said she had two pet pigs. Neighbour Bonnie Sorak said that she often saw 'nice' cars in Britton's driveway and that most of the visitors she saw were men. . . .

Source: **Abridged from Trejos (2006).**

are more likely today to be treated as criminals. This suggests an equalization of treatment of males and females by the police and courts, or even a disproportionate tendency to criminalize women for certain crimes.

Social Constructionism

As we noted in the first chapter, social constructionism looks at how deviant behaviours come to be defined as 'deviant'. This perspective stresses that no behaviours are inherently right or wrong: they become wrong, deviant, or criminal only when someone in power attaches a moral label to them.

As a result, we can view hate-motivated violence, or hate crime, as a social construct. Some deny that hate crimes are different from, or need different treatment from, equally severe crimes of violence. The specification of 'hate crime' was originally developed to combat expressions of racial, ethnic, and religious prejudice. In recent years, gays, lesbians, children, and women have been seen as potential victims of hate crimes, too. The enlargement of this umbrella to protect more types of victims has resulted from claims-making by special interest groups documenting such crimes and calling for legal remedies (Jenness, 1995; Lyons, 2008).

Constructionist theories illuminate the ways in which the notions of crime, violence, and criminality are built up and sustained. However, there is currently no agreement on how best to depict crime and violence, if our goal is to prevent or deter such acts. For example, stories about violence against women that depict incidents as somehow routine or inevitable may lead to a 'culture of resignation', which is as dangerous in its own way as a moral panic. In short, while few researchers would deny that violent crime—domestic and otherwise—is problematic in society, the extent to which there is a 'crime problem' is always open to debate.

Differential Association Theory

This theory can be most easily viewed as a functionalist theory, because it is about the ways people, through simple association, are socialized into their criminal environment and reproduce the prevailing order. There are two distinguishing features of differential association theory. First, it is a sociological rather than psychological theory: it proposes that people are social and imitate one another, to gain acceptance and approval. Second, it is a theory that assumes social organization, not social disorganization; crime is a result of too much of the 'wrong kind' of organization, not too little of the 'right kind' of organization (Kissner and Pyrooz, 2009).

Living in a high-crime neighbourhood and merely seeing others benefit from a criminal lifestyle are enough to raise the likelihood of someone engaging in similar illegitimate activities. Seeing criminals act illegally, without seeing them condemned or punished, is likely to teach people not only the techniques of crime, but also the motives for, rationalizations of, and attitudes of such a lifestyle. In this respect, jails are graduate schools for crime. Time spent in jail or prison is time spent fostering friendships, dependencies, and interests that lead to continued anti-social behaviours on release from prison (Church et al., 2009).

SOCIAL CONSEQUENCES OF CRIME AND VIOLENCE

Poverty and Inequality

The crimes most often featured in the media are violent street crimes. And, of all the people arrested for violent street crimes, most are under-educated, poor, unemployed, or working in low-wage, low-status jobs. Other kinds of crimes and criminals receive less attention, both from the media and the police.

Conflict theories have a lot to say about this tendency of police and courts and politicians to target lower-income criminals and overlook upper-income criminals. They suggest that if police explored corporate, occupational, and political crimes nearly as energetically, they would find equally high rates of crime among the wealthy. As a result, 'the wealthy might even be convicted and punished more than the poor' (Pepinsky and Jesilow, 1984: 81).

ENRON: THE SMARTEST GUYS IN THE ROOM

This 2004 documentary explores the peculiarities of white-collar crime by probing the case of Enron founder Kenneth Lay.

However, the arrest and conviction of poor people is not merely a result of bias in the police and courts (Bush, 2010). The existing social order generally treats poor people worse than it treats the rich and well-educated. John Braithwaite (1993) provides a useful distinction between what he calls 'crimes of poverty' and 'crimes of wealth'. The former are motivated largely by a need to get goods for personal use, and the latter by a greedy desire to obtain goods for exchange—that is, goods beyond those needed for personal use. Social inequality and economic inequality promote both kinds of crime. A system of wide inequality and extreme competitiveness results in a class of needy poor and a class of greedy rich. A large middle class, meanwhile, strives endlessly to avoid falling into the former and succeed in rising into the latter category.

The Racial Dimension

Class, gender, and age are not the only social characteristics that predict criminality and conviction. Over the last few decades, Canadian researchers have paid more attention to the unduly large number of Aboriginal people arrested and convicted of law violations. Aboriginal adults make up only 2 per cent of the Canadian population according to the 1996 census, yet they made up 19 per cent of those people sentenced to provincial custody and 17 per cent of those sent to federal penitentiaries in 2000–1 (Reed and Roberts, 1999: 10). In other words, they were about eight or nine times more likely to end in jail than their numbers in the population would lead one to expect.

This over-representation of Aboriginals in the criminal justice system is especially striking in Manitoba and Saskatchewan. In Manitoba, for example, Aboriginal people make up only 9 per cent of the population but 69 per cent of the prison population. As well, compared to non-Aboriginal inmates, Aboriginal inmates are younger, more likely to come from dysfunctional backgrounds, and likely to have had more run-ins with the criminal justice system, that is, more previous arrests (LaPrairie et al., 1996; Roberts and Doob, 1997).

One common explanation is that, like some other ethnic groups, Aboriginal people are mostly poor, and poverty drives them to crime. Other explanations include a racially prejudiced law enforcement and correctional system; a conflict between the values of Aboriginal culture and mainstream Canadian culture; social and economic consequences of colonization and oppression by European settlers; and a breakdown in the traditional social fabric of Aboriginal communities. These explanations are not mutually exclusive. In fact, these factors support and interact with one another.

It is likely that any solution to this problem will require more cultural sensitivity on the part of non-Aboriginal policy-makers than in the past. Indeed, many of the more promising initiatives—healing and sentencing circles, First Nation police forces, elders' courts, and so on—are being developed by Aboriginal communities themselves.

However, because Canadian authorities do not tabulate crime statistics by the race of the offender, the connection between race and crime is hard to flesh out quantitatively. In general, we know little about the racial characteristics of people convicted of committing different crimes, and many people would say that is a good thing. Many police forces oppose collecting statistics based on race. They fear that doing so might encourage the racial pro-filing of suspects that is a constant issue in law enforcement. It might also attract negative attention from the public and the media. Others believe that collecting and publishing race-based crime data would serve to reinforce existing racial stereotypes.

POLICY DEBATES

Box 7.3 The Issue of Racial Profiling

Racial profiling is usually defined in a law enforcement context. One study published in the *Canadian Review of Policing Research* defined it as 'a racial disparity in police stop and search practices, customs searches at airports and border-crossings, in police patrols in minority neighbourhoods and in undercover activities or sting operations which target particular ethnic groups.'

The Ontario Human Rights Commission took a broader approach, defining it as 'any action undertaken for reasons of safety, security or public protection that relies on stereotypes about race, colour, ethnicity, ancestry, religion, or place of origin rather than on reasonable suspicion, to single out an individual for greater scrutiny or different treatment.' Accusations of differential treatment arise in areas where authorities can exercise their discretion . . . . when that discretion is exercised, members of many minority groups feel that they come out on the short end of the baton—that they somehow always have to prove their innocence. . . .

Police chiefs say their forces try to weed out racists and can often point to disciplinary action or firings related to racist behaviour. But critics say racial profiling is often more subtle and, therefore, difficult to monitor. Formal stats are often hard to come by and can be open to alternate interpretations. And some people worry that the collection and publication of any race-based data will simply reinforce racial prejudices.

Most police forces in North America don't collect race-based data on such things as traffic stops. That's why a series of articles published in 2002 in the *Toronto Star* caused such a sensation. The articles were based on stats collected by the police. Analysis of those figures by *Star* reporters suggested that blacks in Toronto were over-represented in certain offence categories like drug possession and in what were called 'out-of-sight' traffic violations, such as driving without a licence. The analysis also suggested that black suspects were more likely to be held in custody for a bail hearing, while white suspects facing similar charges were more likely to be released at the scene.

A study of police statistics in Kingston, Ont., released in May 2005 [also] found that young black and Aboriginal men were more likely to be stopped than other groups. The data showed that police in the predominantly white city were 3.7 times more likely to stop a black as a Caucasian, and 1.4 times more likely to stop an Aboriginal person than a white.

Several field studies in Canada have also uncovered evidence that some minority groups, especially black youth, are far more likely to report 'involuntary police contact', as one researcher called it, than either whites or Asians.

Some argue that all the debate over whether racial profiling exists is missing the point. They say if a huge portion of an ethnic group believes it exists, then that by definition amounts to a serious problem that must be addressed. University of Toronto criminologist Scot Wortley wrote that 'being stopped and searched by the police . . . seems to be experienced by black people as evidence that race still matters in Canadian society. That no matter how well you behave, how hard you try, being black means that you will always be considered one of the "usual suspects".'

Wortley argues for more research and more data collection by police forces, saying the refusal to deal with it will 'ensure that the issue of racial discrimination continues to haunt law enforcement agencies for decades to come.'

Source: **Abridged from CBC News (2005).**

There is reason to believe that racial profiling is already a conventional practice among Canadian police. A study of possible racial bias by the police of Kingston, Ontario—described as the first study of its kind in Canada—showed that between October 2003 and September 2004, blacks were much more likely to be stopped and questioned by police than members of any other racial group. Young black males aged 15–24 were the demographic group most likely to be pulled over by officers (Wortley and Marshall, 2005). Although, as the researchers note, these results do not conclusively prove the existence of racial profiling, they suggest that at least some 'routine' police stops are racially motivated.

ECONOMIC CONSEQUENCES OF CRIME

Crime costs a society a lot of money. The financial costs result from losses of property through identity theft, bank robberies, auto theft, breaking and entering, embezzlement, and copyright violations. Other costs result from criminal violence; they include the loss of productivity by injured workers and the medical costs of treating crime victims. And even 'crimes without victims' carry financial costs. Just consider the unrecorded or illegal spending on drugs, prostitution, gambling, and other underground activities; it all diverts cash away from legitimate businesses and goes untaxed.

Increasingly, criminal activity is shifting to cyberspace. And increasingly, new computer-based technologies are being used to commit new types of crimes, or to commit old crimes more effectively. A rapidly growing concern is the rise of 'identity thefts', which come in a variety of forms, as depicted in Figure 7.5.

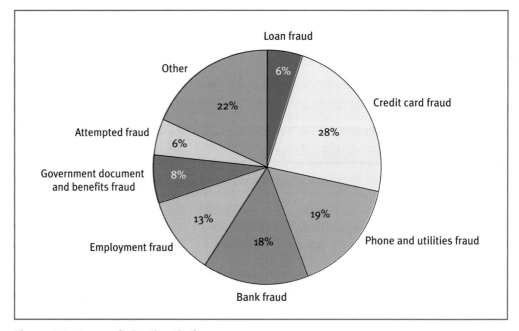

Figure 7.5 Types of Identity Theft
Source: http://cybercrimeonline.com/crimes/identity%20theft/idtheft.htm.

Besides victims' financial losses, crime also imposes an economic burden on the broader public through government spending on law enforcement, the criminal court system, and correctional services. According to *Police Resources in Canada, 2008* (Statistics Canada, 2008), the number of police has risen steadily over the past 10 years, resulting in a total of 65,000 active police officers. This has also meant a steady increase in police expenditures for 11 consecutive years. In 2007, the amount spent on policing in Canada was $10.5 billion, or $320 per Canadian. This level of spending was 43 per cent higher than a decade earlier. This has occurred despite a continuing decline in the recorded crime rate. 'The 2007 crime rate was at its lowest point in over 30 years. At the same time, the proportion of crime solved by the police reached a 30-year high' (ibid., 5).

On average, it costs taxpayers $240.18 per day to house one inmate in a federal penitentiary (though only $141.75 per inmate in a provincial/territorial prison) (Statistics Canada, 2005b). For $240 per day—$87,665 a year—two or three readers of this book could pay their entire year's costs of tuition, room, board, books, clothing, and recreation at a college or university. Some might consider that a better way to spend the money—if only we could find ways to prevent the crimes that jailed offenders are committing.

HEALTH CONSEQUENCES OF CRIME AND VIOLENCE

Not surprisingly, crime carries costs for its victims. Victims of crime usually report lowered levels of well-being after their victimization, and victims of *violent* crime are especially likely to suffer psychological distress (Denkers and Winkel, 1998). They also report lower levels of health and physical well-being, with younger victims of violent crime reporting the largest decreases in their health.

Victims of property crime also report lowered levels of health and physical well-being, but older victims suffer the most negative effects of these crimes (Britt, 2001). Violent crimes result in physical pain and suffering because of the injuries inflicted. However, violent victimization also results in lowered self-esteem. As a result, the victims of violent crimes report more distress and more stressful life events than non-victims and victims of non-violent crimes (Johnson, 1997).

In particular, rape (sexual assault) especially exacts a heavy psychological and social toll. Because of the trauma associated with rape, fear of retaliation by the rapist, and fear of stigmatization, victims of rape are often unwilling to report their victimization to the police. Many victims also have trouble trusting men again and establishing or resuming intimate relations.

The emotional outcomes of criminal victimization can be serious. Victims of crimes are more likely than non-victims to suffer from post-traumatic stress disorder (PTSD), major depressive episodes, and various phobias. A victim's reaction depends largely on the type of crime. Completed rape, for example, is likely to cause deep and long-lasting emotional disturbance, while robbery and burglary are not (Boudreaux et al., 1998).

TRAFFIC

Steven Soderbergh's 2000 hit explores the labyrinthine geo-political and economic issues endemic to the global drug trade.

The Health of Criminals

Crime is also hard on criminals, and for most offenders, a life of crime is stressful. Always looking over one's shoulder, on guard against the authorities, leads to an unhealthy level of stress that eventually harms a person's health.

Prisons are especially harmful to one's health. The criminal justice system, with its reliance on punishment and coercive social control, increases the risk of drug abuse and HIV/ AIDS infection, among other things (Welch, 1999). Violent assaults, rapes, unsanitary and overcrowded conditions, and staff brutality also harm the prisoners' health. Prisons, lacking the facilities to do otherwise, often ignore all but the most severe mental illnesses, such as schizophrenia or other psychotic disorders. As a result, in prison, post-traumatic stress disorder, often from rape and violent assaults, can go undiagnosed or untreated because of inadequate treatment resources, fears of stigmatizing the inmates, and lack of anonymity and safety (Kupers, 1996).

At the same time, some aspects of prison life are *intended* to pose health risks to inmates. These mechanisms are part of a strategic ceremonial degradation of prisoners, to break their will and increase their submission. Michael Vaughn and Linda Smith (1999) list six forms of intentional ill-treatment in prison facilities: (1) the use of medical care to humiliate prisoners (e.g., invasive procedures that may not be necessary); (2) the withholding of medical care from prisoners with HIV and AIDS; (3) the withholding of medical care from other prisoners; (4) the subjection of inmates to sleep deprivation and extreme temperature changes; (5) the use of dental care as a means of torture; and (6) the falsification of prisoners' medical records.

While these health risks are common in all prisons, they may not be as common in some prisons as in others, and they may not be as consciously intended in all cases. However, it seems safe to say that prisons are not designed to ensure the well-being of prisoners. Since prisons are run with efficiency, not prisoners' health, in mind, at least some penal health-care providers may violate their professional ethics from time to time.

Psychological Effects

Not all crimes are violent, but the violent crimes are most likely to make news and remain in our minds. Violent crimes can shatter people's lives. As well, such crimes may create '(a) diminished faith in a free economy and in business leaders, (b) loss of confidence in political institutions, processes and leaders, and (c) erosion of public morality' (Moore and Mills, 2001: 54).

At the societal level, violent crimes breed fear and wear down neighbourhood cohesion. People grow suspicious of one another; in turn, increased isolation and social distance reinforce prejudicial stereotypes based on race, gender, and age. As the US National Research Council (1994: 5–6) concluded, 'If frightened citizens remain locked in their homes instead of enjoying public spaces, there is a loss of public and community life, as well as a loss of "social capital"—the family and neighbourhood channels that transmit positive social values from one generation to the next.'

There are harmful outcomes for the criminal, too, especially the psychological and social issues that must be dealt with after being labelled a 'criminal'. Sometimes, these harmful outcomes increase the likelihood a criminal, after labelling, will become a repeat offender.

Not all criminals become repeat offenders after their release from court, probation, jail, or prison. However, a criminal record often takes away many opportunities. Convicts returning to the community from prison are sometimes greeted with unease and fear. Many cannot find jobs, or the jobs they can find are often degrading and menial. At the least, an ex-convict carries the social stigma of having once been a criminal. Some find a return to the criminal lifestyle is the only available means of survival. This produces a vicious circle: a first act of (primary) deviance results in labelling. In turn, labelling leads people to expect further acts of (secondary) deviance, so they close their doors to the ex-convict. The closing of doors, in turn, fulfills these expectations, forcing some criminals to return to illegal ways of earning a living.

SOLUTIONS TO THE CRIME AND VIOLENCE PROBLEM

Reducing Crime

Communities are better off preventing crime than punishing it. Investments in crime prevention can include improving education, creating jobs, supplying daycare, upgrading low-income housing, increasing access to health care, and otherwise supporting poor families. All of these front-end strategies to prevent crime are likely to work better, in the long run, than trying to cure crime through imprisonment.

Other useful strategies of crime reduction may include more use of probation, better gun control, and expanded treatment for drug addicts (Anderson, 1994). Reducing crime means addressing the social factors that are directly related to producing crime. This means reducing teenage pregnancies, high school dropout rates, youth unemployment, drug abuse, and the lack of job opportunities.

The Criminal Justice System

Part of the crime problem in many societies is that people feel dissatisfied with and distrustful of public officials and institutions—especially politicians, police, lawyers, and courts. Though they dislike crime and criminals, they also dislike and distrust people in authority.

Though the crime rates have been declining for over a decade, there is still much public frustration about crime and victimization in Canada, not all of it the result of media manipulation. Some of it reflects the inadequacy of the justice system to prevent or deter crime. The Canadian criminal justice system is largely based on the principle of deterrence. This principle assumes that most crimes are rational acts in which the offender weighs the imagined benefits of committing the crime against the chance of being caught and the severity of the punishment. This assumption may be unwarranted. The implication is that the

DETERRENCE A justice system based on deterrence assumes that crimes are rational acts in which the offender weighs the perceived benefits of committing the crime against the probability of being caught and the severity of the punishment. It assumes that the probability of being punished is high and that the law enforcement agencies are competent and efficient in apprehending offenders.

threat of punishment will keep most people from breaking the law, or from breaking it a second time.

However, a criminal justice system based on deterrence assumes that the likelihood of being punished is high—that is, that law enforcement agencies are efficient in catching offenders. This assumption also may be unwarranted. The deterrence approach ignores the subcultural (criminal) socialization that takes place in jails and prisons. And, worst of all, a deterrence-based approach to criminal justice fails to address the societal, economic, and political factors that encourage crime: unemployment, racial inequality, poverty, and the unequal distribution of resources and opportunities.

The Victims' Rights Movement

In the past few decades, a victims' rights movement has emerged that seeks to expand the rights of crime victims (Carrington and Nicholson, 1984). This grew out of the feminist movement, in particular, in response to domestic violence and sexual abuse. All of Canada's 13 provinces and territories have now set up a victim's Bill of Rights that is similar to statutes enacted by other jurisdictions worldwide. Though the precise rights vary from one jurisdiction to another, they all include access to information throughout the trial; the right to file a victim impact statement at sentencing; compensatory damages for victimization; offender restitution; notification of parole hearings; and the right to submit a victim impact statement at parole hearings (Smith et al., 1990).

Though not binding 'rights', they serve as guidelines for judicial officers to keep in mind as they conduct their cases. Only in Manitoba are victims' rights rigorously enforced in the legislation, and a procedure for filing complaints is in place should those rights be violated (Canadian Resource Centre for Victims of Crime, 2006).

Some critics have argued that, by giving the injured party an equal voice in the criminal justice process, the movement has mainly resulted in demands for harsher and more punitive verdicts. So, while pretending to speak for crime victims, some groups—mainly a subset of the conservative 'get tough on crime' proponents—are more concerned about lobbying for more severe penalties (Sanborn, 2001; Smith and Huff, 1992).

CHAPTER SUMMARY

Crime has been among Canadians' top five concerns for most of the last 20 years. Considered the most serious form of deviance, a crime is any act formally banned by law, specifically by the Criminal Code of Canada. Defining certain acts as 'crimes' gives the state the authority to seek, arrest, try, convict, and punish offenders, and the Criminal Code specifies an allowable range of punishments for each crime.

Within the Criminal Code, many different kinds of crime are specified. Some are crimes considered harmful by most people, such as murder, armed robbery, extortion, arson, sexual assault, and kidnapping. In general, there is widespread agreement in Canadian society—and in most other societies—that these behaviours are wrong and should be harshly punished. In contrast, there are also crimes, like the possession of marijuana, over which people disagree so much that the law has, in effect, lost control.

Then there are the more standard or common crimes. Most people consider them wrong but do not wish to debate or increase the severity of punishment. These include offences against property, like breaking and entering, automobile theft, and shoplifting; minor assaults; drunk driving; and 'white-collar' offences such as embezzlement and fraud. All of these offences have a victim or (as with drunk driving) run a serious risk of harming someone.

Despite biases and errors in reporting, the data on crime are credible enough to permit several inferences. First, crimes against property have increased over the last 20 years, but the rates of homicide and other 'serious' crimes have declined. Contrary to what we might hear in the media, there is no wave of violent crime sweeping our towns and cities. Second, crimes of violence are rarely committed for gain; they often result from fights between spouses or friends. This is especially true when women are the victims. Men, more than women, are likely to be attacked by mere acquaintances or even strangers. Third, crimes committed for gain—for example, drug peddling, solicitation for prostitution, illegal gambling, and extortion—are often tied (however indirectly) to organized crime.

Common or street criminals, as we have seen, tend to be young, poor men. The complex connection between these demographic variables and criminal behaviour is a result of the interaction of economic, social, and cultural variables. And, paradoxically, criminals are more likely to be victimized than non-criminals, largely because of the factors discussed in differential association theory.

QUESTIONS FOR CRITICAL THOUGHT

1. Referring to their causes and effects, in what respects are non-violent crimes likely to be different from violent crimes?

2. What is the process by which a person becomes a criminal? Compare the ways theorists from different theoretical backgrounds might answer this question.

3. What role does poverty play in producing crime? Discuss different methods that a society might use to counter the effects of poverty on crime.

4. What differences can you find in the likely motives of people who commit opportunistic crimes and those who commit white-collar crimes?

5. How would you rate the effectiveness of the penal system? Recommend changes that would make the system more 'effective' in achieving its stated goals.

6. Canada has lower rates of violent crime but higher rates of property crime than the United States. What, if anything, does this tell us about the social organization of both nations?

RECOMMENDED READINGS

Haggerty, Kevin D., and Richard V. Ericson, eds. 2005. *The New Politics of Surveillance and Visibility*. Toronto: University of Toronto Press. This collection of 15 articles focuses on the theory of surveillance and visibility; the role of police and military surveillance; and the interplay between surveillance, electronic media, and consumer culture.

Longrigg, Clare. 2004. *No Questions Asked: The Secret Life of Women in the Mob*. New York: Hyperion. The author interviewed daughters and wives of mobsters, and they reveal the complex, chancy reality of life among the wise guys. In this book, she moves beyond popular stereotypes to present many portraits drawn from America's Cosa Nostra. Some are familiar figures, but some of the more obscure women are even more interesting.

Peterson, Ruth D., Lauren J. Krivo, and John Hagan. 2006. *The Many Colors of Crime: Inequalities of Race, Ethnicity, and Crime in America*. New York: New York University Press. This wide-ranging treatment of the link between race, ethnicity, and crime views the relevant data through a socio-historical lens and comparative perspective. Race and ethnicity are considered central organizing principles in why, how, where, and by whom crimes are committed and enforced.

Rapping, Elayne. 2003. *Law and Justice as Seen on TV*. New York: New York University Press. Law-related television shapes the way the North American public perceives justice, criminals, courts, and the law in general. However, since the late 1940s, the author detects a gradual shift from generally liberal viewpoint towards a more conservative perspective, focusing on those who protect the middle class against all sorts of crimes and criminals. This reflects a change in social consciousness—especially, a growing sympathy for the law enforcement officers and prosecutors who chase and imprison them.

Reynolds, Marylee. 1995. *From Gangs to Gangsters: How American Sociology Organized Crime, 1918–1994*. New York: Harrow and Heston. The author provides information that explains how sociologists of the Chicago School in the 1920s could describe lower-class crime and deviance in their city as social disorganization, when hindsight shows clearly that it was highly organized; and how over the next decades they came to recognize and study organized crime.

Simon, David R., and Frank E. Hagan. 1999. *White-Collar Deviance*. Boston: Allyn & Bacon. This book discusses a new conceptualization of the terms 'elite deviance', 'white-collar crime', and 'economic crime'. It includes both criminal and non-criminal deviance by individuals and organizations, as well as the conduct of the elite and non-elite.

RECOMMENDED WEBSITES

Facts about Organized Crime in Canada, Public Safety Canada

www.ps-sp.gc.ca/policing/organized_crime/FactSheets/org_crime_e.asp
This brief summary of the issues surrounding organized crime in Canada is from the archives of Public Safety Canada. Providing basic information on government policy regarding policing and prevention, this is a suitable introduction to the topic of Canadian organized crime.

Organized Crime, It's in Your Neighbourhood

crimeorganise.ca
This website, run by the government of Canada, is devoted to raising community awareness to neighbourhood-based organized crime. Though not a serious academic resource, this website still provides basic information on a myriad of issues related to organized crime and provides links to relevant government agencies.

Nathanson Centre for the Study of Organized Crime and Corruption

www.yorku.ca/nathanson/default.htm

Run from York University, the Nathanson Centre is an excellent resource for those seriously studying organized crime and corruption, providing a wealth of free academic publications on the subject. The website also provides many links, a list of databases, and a full bibliography.

RCMP, Commercial Crime

www.rcmp-grc.gc.ca/fio/commercial_crime_e.htm

The RCMP's policies regarding commercial crime are outlined on this site. Links are provided for further information on various aspects of organized crime and corruption, including fraud, scams, insolvency, and counterfeiting.

Criminal Intelligence Service Canada

www.cisc.gc.ca

This website contains comprehensive information regarding organized crime in Canada. The agency releases an Annual Report on Organized Crime in Canada. The report highlights how organized crime affects our daily lives and what actions are taken to reduce organized crime.

National Crime Prevention Strategy

www.prevention.gc.ca

The purpose of the website is part of a greater government initiative to curb reactive responses to crime in favour of early intervention to prevent crime and victimization. Included is a comprehensive list of documents and research data available in the research and evaluation section.

International Association for the Study of Organized Crime

www.iasoc.net

This website provides a rather comprehensive bibliography of sources to begin any research about organized crime. It also offers quarterly trend reports, Internet links, and organized crime news.

Institute for Intergovernmental Research

www.iir.com/nwccc.htm

The IIR provides links to various websites for American data on white-collar crime and other types of non-violent crime. There are also several links to the National White Collar Crime Center.

CHAPTER 8
Addictions

iStockphoto.com/andrew bedinger

LEARNING OBJECTIVES

- To understand the health risks and effects of addiction.
- To learn about the changing attitudes towards drug use.
- To know what is meant by 'drug abuse'.
- To examine arguments about whether 'abuse' is a social problem.
- To appreciate the difference between legal and illegal drugs.
- To identify possible solutions to the abuse of drugs and alcohol.

INTRODUCTION

We are used to hearing, and even using, the word 'addiction' to refer to behaviour that is uncontrollable, repeated or frequent, socially disapproved, and possibly harmful. So, for example, people talk about alcohol addiction and alcoholics or drug addiction and drug addicts as people who cannot stay away from alcohol or drugs, even though these substances are harming their bodies and their social relationships.

More recently, we have started to hear about other addictions that describe socially disapproved behaviours, such as sex, shopping, Internet, or eating addictions. So far, there has been too little research on any of these topics to discuss them here, and it is unclear whether they should even be included in a chapter on 'addictions'.

Perhaps they are not addictions—but habits, hobbies, minor sins, or what people used to call 'personal weaknesses'. By calling them 'addictions', we give them a medical label and imply that they are as important as other behaviours labelled addictive, and perhaps also that they should be dealt with medically. Besides, even if we think these are symptoms that can be 'treated', we wonder if they should be called 'addictions' or 'obsessions', which terms imply a different set of symptoms and treatments.

These questions are especially pressing in respect to gambling addiction, or problem gambling, which has come closest to proving itself as a new important form of addiction (Griffiths, 2009). Therefore, we begin this chapter with a brief discussion of 'addiction', then consider problem gambling (or compulsive gambling, or gambling addiction), and then spend the rest of the chapter discussing alcohol and drug abuse.

ADDICTION

The medical definition of addiction, based on criteria used by the American Psychiatric Association (DSM-IV) and the World Health Organization (ICD-10), has seven criteria. Deciding whether a person has an alcohol or drug addiction, therefore, requires asking and answering questions in only seven categories (Table 8.1).

A person answering 'yes' to questions in three or more of the categories shown in Table 8.1 meets the medical definition of addiction. As we will see, researchers use a very similar instrument to detect gambling addiction, or problem gambling.

Note that, in the definition outlined in Table 8.1, there is nothing about how often a person uses the drug or alcohol: whether once a month or once an hour. The issue is whether you have trouble controlling your use, and whether there are negative effects, whenever you do use the substance.

Why is addiction a social problem? Alternatively, what turns this personal trouble into a public issue? In part, the answer is that the *social effects of addiction*—whether by drugs, alcohol, or (as we will see) gambling—are huge, in broken families, health consequences for addicts and their loved ones, lost days at work, and the cost of treating and 'fixing' the addicts. In addition, there are crime and safety issues at stake (Lozgacheva, 2008).

If we turn aside from a purely medical, psychiatric, or psychological understanding of addiction, we can take a sociological or public health approach. Moreover, doing this

ADDICTION Socially disapproved behaviour that is uncontrollable, repetitious, and possibly harmful.

Table 8.1 Addictive Behaviour

- **Tolerance**
  Has your use of drugs or alcohol increased over time?

- **Desire to cut down**
  Have you sometimes thought about cutting down or controlling your use? Have you ever made unsuccessful attempts to cut down or control your use?

- **Withdrawal**
  When you stop using, have you ever experienced physical or emotional withdrawal? Have you had any of the following symptoms: irritability, anxiety, shakes, sweats, nausea, or vomiting?

- **Difficulty controlling your use**
  Do you sometimes use more or for a longer time than you would like? Do you sometimes drink to get drunk? Do you usually stop after a few drinks, or does one drink lead to more drinks?

- **Negative consequences**
  Have you continued to use even though there have been negative effects to your mood, self-esteem, health, job, or family?

- **Putting off or neglecting activities**
  Have you ever put off or reduced social, recreational, work, or household activities because of your use?

- **Spending significant time or emotional energy**
  Have you spent a significant amount of time getting, using, hiding, planning, or recovering from your use? Have you spent a lot of time thinking about using? Have you ever hidden or minimized your use? Have you ever thought of schemes to avoid getting caught?

---

allows us to see that the other factor that turns this personal trouble into a public issue is recognition of the *social causes of addiction*. Whereas the medical approach focuses attention on the addicted individual and his or her personal pathology, the sociological and public health approaches focus on the social forces that increase the risks that certain people, or groups, will develop addictions (Hammersley and Reid, 2002). This point of view argues that we need to understand what it is about our society, and our social policies, that promote harmful, addictive behaviour, and how we can change society to reduce these risks.

ADDICTIVE GAMBLING

There are factors in our society, our communities, and our families that predispose people to a gambling problem or gambling addiction. However, before we look at these factors, let us define and measure problem gambling.

OWNING MAHOWNY

This 2003 film portrays the gambling addiction that threatens to destroy the life of Toronto banker Dan Mahowny (Philip Seymour Hoffman).

Gambling is a behaviour on a continuum, ranging from non-gamblers to recreational gamblers to problem gamblers (Hodgins et al., 2008; Dervensky and Gupta, 2004). In any population, a fraction will progress across this continuum.

How widespread is this problem and why should we care? A 2001 Ontario population survey using the Canadian Problem Gambling Index (CPGI)—which we will discuss in detail shortly—reported a prevalence of 3.1 per cent of the population for moderate and 0.7 per cent for severe gambling problems (Wiebe et al., 2001). A follow-up survey conducted in 2005 found rates of 2.6 per cent and 0.8 per cent, respectively (Wiebe et al., 2006). The 2002 Canadian Community Health Survey found the likely problem gambling prevalence in Ontario is 2.0 per cent (with a 95 per cent chance the true value lies between 1.6 per cent and 2.4 per cent). This rate reportedly is identical with recent national estimates (Rush et al., 2007).

While the estimates vary slightly, they suggest that roughly one Canadian adult in 50 has a serious gambling problem. This means that, in a population of roughly 32 million Canadians, of whom 75 per cent are over age 20, there are roughly 480,000 Canadians with a gambling problem.

Table 8.2 Elements of the Canadian Problem Gambling Index

Behaviours

- *Bet more than you could afford:* How often have you bet more than you could really afford to lose?

- *Increased wagers:* How often have you needed to gamble with larger amounts of money to get the same feeling of excitement?

- *Returned to win back losses:* How often have you gone back another day to try to win back the money you lost?

- *Borrowed money or sold anything to gamble:* How often have you borrowed money or sold anything to get money to gamble?

Adverse Effects

- *Felt gambling problem:* How often have you felt that you might have a problem with gambling?

- *Suffered criticism:* How often have people criticized your betting or told you that you had a gambling problem?

- *Feelings of guilt:* How often have you felt guilty about the way you gamble or what happens when you gamble?

- *Financial problems:* How often has your gambling caused any financial problems for you or your household?

- *Negative health effects:* How often has your gambling caused you any health problems, including stress or anxiety?

The CPGI is a scale developed to measure problem or addictive gambling. To give some idea about the nature of the problem created by problem gambling, consider the items that make up this index (Table 8.2).

Note the similarities between this measure of problem gambling and the more general measure of addiction we examined earlier. The chief differences are that we can detect physiological effects in drug or alcohol addiction that we can't detect in gambling addiction. Conceivably, with brain imaging research, we will eventually find similar effects within the brain pleasure centres. At present, the problem gambling measure (CPGI) focuses more on financial and social outcomes.

Gambling has become a major global industry in the last 20 years, and it continues to grow rapidly (Moodie and Hastings, 2009). Gambling is advertised everywhere as a source of fun and recreation. What's more, national, provincial and state, and local governments help to promote gambling to raise their own revenues. Governments appear to reason that people are going to gamble anyway, so they should take a percentage in taxes. Like alcohol and drugs, gambling historically has been a major source of revenue for organized crime. In the second

The Canadian Press/Corner Brook Western Star/Gary Kean

It's not the sort of issue most families would want made public, but the Pierceys say sharing the story behind their 31-year-old daughter Susan's suicide could help others dealing with the scourge of compulsive gambling. They say her 10-year obsession with video lottery terminals—an addiction that cost her and her family more than $100,000—played a significant role in her recent suicide.

half of the twentieth century, many governments decided to legalize gambling and take a share of the profits, then promoted gambling for even greater economic returns. Some of this money is reinvested in 'public goods' that even include research on problem gambling.

Gambling has become a *public* health issue, in the usual sense: it has social causes and health outcomes (Afifi et al., 2010). Gambling is not merely the expression of a personal taste, individual psychopathology, or genetic inclination. It is a behaviour learned socially in the usual ways—through observation, experimentation, reward, and emulation, or through the modelling and example of social role models. Often, people learn to gamble in families during childhood (McComb et al., 2009).

Features in society and the gambling environment contribute to gambling problems. These include game features—for example, features in the design of slot machines or video lottery terminals (VLTs)—that get us to bet more than we planned to, by using speed, noise, flashing lights, and slanted information. They include advertising and other mass media messages that shape our views about gambling and normalize it, making gambling seem cool, fun, and desirable (Valentine, 2009). They include the widespread and growing availability of gambling—increasingly available, in casinos and online, 24 hours a day, seven days a week. And they include casino promotions and incentives—free buses to the casino, free meals and drinks, and even free hotel accommodations and other perquisites for high rollers who play (and lose) often.

> **LABELLING** The process of defining and treating others as deviant. Labelling theory explores the effects of negative labels on individuals' self-conceptions and is interested in the development of a 'deviant identity'. Social reactions of condemnation and criminalization can lead actors to alter their individual characteristics and to adopt the values of their labelled identity.

CLASSIC WORKS

Box 8.1 Howard Becker's *Outsiders* (1963)

Born, raised, and trained in Chicago, sociologist Howard Becker spent most of his professional life in the Chicago area. There, he learned the characteristic Chicago style of ethnographic sociology from Everett Hughes and other masters of the practice. Moreover, as a professional jazz musician, Becker gained insights into the 'outsiders'—jazz musicians and marijuana smokers—he described in *Outsiders*, the book that made him famous.

In *Outsiders*, Howard Becker set the groundwork for **labelling** theory, as it is known today. Becker notes, '*Social groups create deviance by making rules whose infraction constitutes deviance*, and by applying these rules to particular people and labeling them as outsiders' (Becker, 1963: 9). Deviance is thus the result of a dominant group—insiders—devising and applying moral rules to less powerful groups of 'outsiders'. These groups often respond by further entrenching themselves in 'secondary deviation', including deviant careers and deviant subcultures.

This is not a book about the reasons people smoke marijuana or commit any other deviant act. The causes of deviance may be unknowable or unimportant, compared to their consequences. Moreover, Becker wants us to focus attention, instead, on the social context that labels people deviant.

A key point in *Outsiders* is that we must pay as much attention to the rule *enforcer* as we do to the rule *violator*. Instead of asking, 'Why are they deviant?' we should ask, 'Why do we label such behaviour as deviant, and with what consequences?' Doing so removes the assumption of fault, blame, dysfunction, or illness. The pleasures of smoking marijuana or playing jazz or stealing cars may remain unclear to people who forewear these activities. However, sociologists have to assume the actors' motives 'make sense', though we cannot necessarily understand them or identify with them.

Most social science work on gambling takes a psychological approach: it focuses on the thinking and behaviour of individuals without considering their social environment. For example, it views addictive gambling as the result of cognitive distortion—bad thinking—about the odds of winning and the value of chasing losses (Kuo et al., 2009). The goal of psychological counselling is to get gamblers to think differently about what they are doing and act differently, whatever their personal inclinations.

This is not to deny the importance of psychological factors in gambling behaviour. A large body of research has identified links between gambling and mood disorders, including depression, anxiety, and bipolar disorder (Di Nicola et al., 2010). This suggests there are genetic bases to problem gambling, as there are to these mood disorders. Equally, research has found that problem gambling, more often than by chance, is linked to people who are impulsive or display anti-social behaviour, who drink too much, who are lonely or socially isolated, or who display excessive or inappropriate anger—leading us to wonder if poker promotes or capitalizes on the display of violence.

However, the psychological model of behaviour change places the burden of 'responsible gambling' squarely on the shoulders of the individual gambler, citing personality weaknesses or cognitive distortion as the cause of gambling problems (Westphal, 2007). Policy-makers, industry representatives, and the public all share this viewpoint. It is reflected in everything from government gaming policies to gambling treatment and intervention programs.

ARE DRUGS AND ALCOHOL SOCIAL PROBLEMS?

DRUG Any substance that causes a biochemical reaction in the body.

We can define a **drug** as any substance that causes a biochemical reaction in the body. However, it is against the law to induce some biochemical reactions inside your body (Moreno and Janda, 2009). What people define as a legal drug or an illegal drug usually depends less on its chemical properties—less on the reactions in your body—and more on surrounding economic, social, and political factors (Hogan, 2009). Thus, as Figure 8.1 shows, cannabis use increased dramatically between 1994 and 2002.

In Canada, the use of legal drugs, such as alcohol, tobacco, and prescription medicine, is much more common than the use of illegal drugs, such as heroin, cocaine, and marijuana. Many members of society treat the use of illegal drugs as a major problem while ignoring the harm done by legal drugs. Society's response to drug use is, therefore, largely irrational. Some substances that harm public health, such as alcohol and tobacco, are welcomed or tolerated almost everywhere in society. Yet, others that may not be as dangerous, such as marijuana, are often condemned and banned.

Our attitudes towards specific drugs vary over time and from one society to another (Figure 8.2). When social and cultural sensibilities shift, people start rejecting what they once accepted. Therefore, we cannot understand drug attitudes and drug laws without a historical account that explains how and why the attitudes have evolved (McBride et al., 1998).

Examples of such attitude changes abound. Consider opium, from which morphine and heroin are derived. Opium was a commonly used painkiller until the early 1900s (Witters et al., 1992). Opium and cocaine were thought dangerous and subjected to strict control, if not an outright ban. The reason is sociological, not pharmacological. That is, the chemical

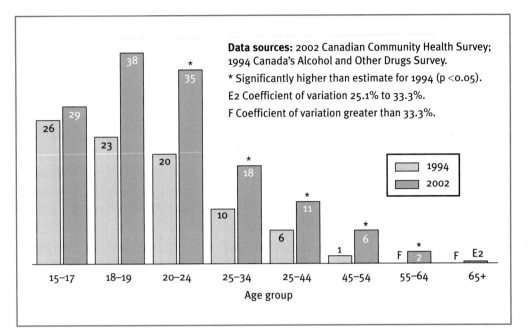

Figure 8.1 Percentage of Population Aged 15 or Older Who Used Cannabis in Past Year, by Age Group, 1994 and 2002

Source: Figure 8.1—Health Reports, Vol. 15, No. 4, July 2004, page 43, at www.statcan.gc.ca/ads-annonces/82-003-x/pdf/4194124-eng.pdf.

Table 8.3 Selected Addiction Statistics

Prevalence and incidence

- 1 in 10 Canadians 15 years of age and over report symptoms consistent with alcohol or illicit drug dependence.

- 3.8 per cent of adults in Ontario are classified as having moderate or severe gambling problems.

Who is affected?

- Young people age 15–24 are more likely to report mental illness and/or substance use disorders than other age groups.

- Overall, men are 2.6 times more likely than women to meet the criteria for substance dependence; 25 per cent of male drinkers are high-risk drinkers compared to 9 per cent of female drinkers.

Cost to society of addictions

- Tobacco is responsible for one-quarter of cancer deaths in Ontario.

- $34 billion is the cost of mental illness and addictions to the Ontario economy.

Source: Centre for Addiction and Mental Health, Mental Health and Addiction Statistics, at: www.camh.net/News_events/Key_CAMH_facts_for_media/addictionmentalhealthstatistics.html.

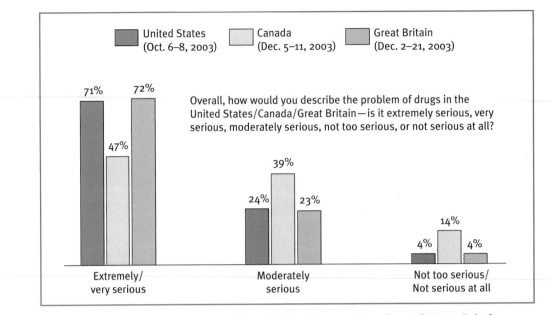

Figure 8.2 **Severity of the Drug Problem: United States, Canada, and Great Britain**
Source: **Gallup, http://media.gallup.com/GPTB/healthcare/20040210_1.gif**

properties of the drugs did not change; only the public's opinion of their effects and those who used them changed.

In this and other instances, a commonly used drug was restricted or criminalized when prevailing attitudes changed. The changes were rarely because of new medical research findings or even new discoveries that the drugs caused social problems. Often, as with cocaine and marijuana, the changes were because of new attitudes towards immigrants or racial minorities who were somehow associated with the drug (Herzog et al., 2009). These changes, in turn, often reflected new economic and social concerns. Typically, these changes penalized the least powerful members of society.

In the same vein, what makes up **drug abuse** depends largely on what people define as an 'acceptable' drug at a particular time and place. Overall, trends in alcohol, cigarette, and cannabis (marijuana) use are similar in the United States and Canada. Adolescent alcohol use in Ontario and throughout the US—perhaps throughout Canada—has steadily decreased since the late 1970s. Both cigarette and cannabis use peaked in the late 1970s, decreased throughout the 1980s, and then began to increase dramatically in the early 1990s. The same study shows that cocaine use was consistently higher in the United States and LSD use consistently higher in Ontario over the period 1975–95. The similar trends in use of alcohol and cigarettes in the United States and Ontario suggest similar shifts in basic attitudes over time. Different trends in the use of less common drugs—cocaine and LSD—may reflect deeper cultural differences or national differences in drug policy or availability (Ivis and Adlaf, 1999).

As we have seen, the ideas of alcohol 'abuse' and drug 'abuse' begin with a notion of extreme or unsuitable use that results in social, psychological, and physiological harm. There

DRUG ABUSE This concept begins with the notion of excessive or inappropriate drug use resulting in social, psychological, and/ or physiological impairments. It stems from a chronic physical and psychological compulsion to continue taking a drug in order to avoid unpleasant withdrawal symptoms.

are two aspects to this idea of abuse: objective and subjective. The objective aspect relies on physical, mental, or social evidence that the use of a drug harms the individual and society. For example, drug abuse may lead to **drug dependency**, that is, the routine need for a drug for physical reasons (for example, to avoid withdrawal symptoms) or for psychological reasons (for example, to keep a sense of well-being) (Hathaway et al., 2009).

Related to drug dependency is the notion of tolerance. **Tolerance** refers to the decreased effectiveness of any given drug because of repeated use. People dependent on drugs and alcohol experience increases in tolerance to the substance over time, meaning they need larger and larger doses of it to get the same effects. Typically, people who do not drink on a regular basis have low levels of tolerance to alcohol, and often feel the effect of intoxication after just one or two drinks. Often, occasional drinkers are labelled as being unable to 'hold their liquor'. However, individuals who are able to withstand large amounts of liquor are not immune to its effects. They have simply had more experience drinking heavily.

MEDICALIZATION AND THE TRANSFORMATION OF A PROBLEM

Increasingly, over the past century we have seen a tendency to 'medicalize' addictions to drugs, alcohol, and even gambling. **Medicalization** is the process through which behaviours—especially those formerly defined as deviant, sinful, or immoral—are reconceived as instances of illness, that is, they are deemed no longer sinful since they are outside personal control (Murphy, 2009; Suissa, 2007).

This process of medicalization, which we discuss further in the chapter on health, has become increasingly important in defining social problems with the triumph of science over religion in the past century and a half. Where alcohol abusers were once thought sinners or moral weaklings and subjected to scorn or criticism, with medicalization they became sick people in need of treatment (Warden et al., 2004). This was a new way of controlling the same deviant behaviour, but it put control in the hands of doctors rather than clergy. In the end, medicalization is a means by which the medical profession extends its turf and influence in society, to the point where medical doctors are deemed the ones who are able to declare people fit for society. Medicalization temporarily excuses the 'affliction'—a perceived benefit to the drug abuser—and raises the power of doctors in society (Valverde, 1998).

The redefinition of alcohol abuse as a disease is not merely a process of medicalization. The temperance and prohibition movements of the last two centuries also reflected deeper cultural themes—for example, the importance of purity, hygiene, and health. The specific targets of historical temperance movements have varied over time and have included alcohol, drugs, smoking, prostitution, and homosexuality (Wagner, 1995). The common element was an obsession with cleanliness (also purity, virtue, and hygiene) versus dirt (also sin, wickedness, and filth). Below the surface of this cultural dichotomy raged classic struggles between clean and dirty classes (middle and upper classes versus the working classes), clean and dirty communities (native-born versus immigrant), clean and dirty subcultures (rural versus urban),

DRUG DEPENDENCY The routine need for a drug for physiological and/or psychological reasons.

TOLERANCE A symptom of repeated and frequent drug use. It refers to the decreased effectiveness of any given drug.

MEDICALIZATION The process through which behaviours are reconceived as instances of illness and are deemed no longer sinful since they are outside personal control.

clean and dirty sexes (female versus male). These struggles provide excellent examples of the processes of exclusion and decoupling that we discussed in the introductory chapter.

A century later, groups and professions still fight over the right to define drug use and abuse. Currently, those who use alcohol in moderation are considered 'clean' but those who use illicit street drugs are considered 'dirty' and part of a **drug subculture**. An example can be seen in current views about crack cocaine, spread mainly by the police and religious-moral leaders in their 'war on drugs'. Three prevailing views are that crack is instantly addictive, that it leads people to binge on drugs, and that it inevitably ruins their lives (Reinarman et al., 1997). Poor people are said to be more likely than others to use crack cocaine, while middle- and upper-class people are more likely to use powder cocaine (Alden and Maggard, 2000). Because of its class connotation, the label 'crack head' is intensely stigmatizing (Furst et al., 1999).

DRUG SUBCULTURE A group of people who share common attitudes, beliefs, and behaviours surrounding drug use. These attitudes and beliefs differ significantly from those of most people in the wider society.

Social and Physical Characteristics of Addictions

Alcohol

Like most other drugs, alcohol is relatively harmless when used moderately and responsibly. However, it is one of the most destructive substances when abused (Murray et al., 2010). People drink alcohol to achieve its chemical effects: to relax, smooth social events, reduce tension, and slow down perceptual, cognitive, and motor functioning (Vaughan at al., 2009). The goal of drinking, then, is to escape from the speed, boredom, stress, or frustration of everyday life and, often, to do so in the company of others, as part of a shared, sociable haze. Impaired judgement often accompanies these chemical changes (Kuntsche et al., 2010).

Many people drink responsibly, remaining below their tolerance limit, practising restraint around minors, and giving up their driving duties to a designated driver. Other drinkers are not so responsible. Men are much more likely than women to drink heavily and suffer the physical outcomes (for example, injury or death). Women drink much more responsibly than men (Carey and DeMartini, 2010); however, as Box 8.2 shows, they are likely to use other chemical substances to cope with stress.

Higher education also exercises a moderating influence on drinking. 'Canadians with university degrees are the least likely of all education groups to report regular heavy drinking. One-fifth (21 per cent) of Canadians with less than a high school education regularly drank heavily, compared with just 12 per cent of current drinkers with a university education' (Health Canada, 1999: 177).

Aside from sex and education, age is the most important determinant of alcohol use. According to data from the recent Canadian Addiction Survey, 'past year use' peaks between the ages of 18 and 24, with about 90 per cent of those in this age range consuming alcohol within the past year (Adlaf et al., 2005). The 2004 Canadian Campus Survey reveals that

BACK IN HISTORY

Box 8.2 Why Did Women Turn to Pills So Often?

When *Desperate Housewives*' Lynette Scavo (Felicity Huff-man) raided her kids' Ritalin to get through her day, you had to wonder how June Cleaver and Margaret Anderson managed their pearls- and picket fence-perfect lives. Maybe Mom didn't leave it to Beaver. Maybe she left it to Miltown. Or Tuinal. Or Nembutal. Or one of the other tran-quillizers the mostly male doctors of the time would pre-scribe for millions of middle-class and upper middle-class women who were unhappy with their lot in the baby-manu-facturing boom.

After all, during the war years, they had paycheques, independence, and identity.

Afterward, as Betty Friedan would note in her land-mark 1963 bestseller *The Feminine Mystique*, they had Betty Crocker, Swanson dinners and the Fuller Brush Man. Which might explain a curious event last month in Tulsa, Oklahoma. Citizens there excitedly turned out to watch the unearthing of a 50-year-old time capsule—a 1957 Ply-mouth Belvedere loaded with artifacts of its era. Among them, a 'typical' woman's purse which contained bobby pins, gum, loose change, a compact, cigarettes, an unpaid parking ticket . . . and a bottle of tranquillizers.

The fact that the town officials considered a purse con-taining tranquillizers—as well as a photo of a 20-year-old bride—as representative of womanhood in 1957 reveals much about the tenor of the times.

'What was that culture saying about women?' says Toronto therapist Barbara Everett, speaking on behalf of the Canadian Mental Health Association (Ontario). 'That this was as common as lipstick, that they needed to be drugged.' In his 2003 book *Prozac on the Couch: Prescrib-ing Gender in the Era of Wonder Drugs*, Dr Jonathan Michel Metzl reviews the history of women and psychotropic drugs from a socio-cultural perspective. He notes that, in the 1950s, 'the anxiety caused by women's discontent . . . threaten(ed) to rupture civilization's progress narra-tive.' Women and tranquillizers has long been a common motif—from Judy Garland to Marilyn Monroe to Jacque-line Susann's *Valley of the Dolls*. Hysteria, after all, was a descriptor used exclusively for women. According to Metzl, in the 1950s, Miltown was the 'happy pill', the 'restorative cure' that would 'bind' the unhappy pre-women's liberation housewife to her restrictive life.

According to statistics prepared for the *Star* by IMS Health Canada, a private health information firm, nearly twice as many prescriptions for psychotropic drugs such as tranquillizers and anti-depressants are filled for women than for men.

Source: **Zerbisias (2007).**

roughly one-third of undergraduate students engage in harmful drinking practices, such as binge drinking, and exhibit signs of alcohol dependency. Students who do not live with their families, students from the Atlantic region, and students who value recreational activities such as parties and athletics are more likely than average to join in risky levels of consump-tion. As well, 10 per cent report incidents of alcohol-related assault, 9.8 per cent report alco-hol-related sexual harassment, and 14.1 per cent report having unplanned sexual encounters while under the influence of alcohol (ibid.).

These demographic variables provide a snapshot of drinking patterns in Canada and sug-gest that social factors affect drinking habits. Specifically, social factors shape alcohol use and abuse in at least two ways: by influencing the odds that a person will learn to use alcohol to cope with stress, and by influencing the opportunities a person has to use alcohol for any reason.

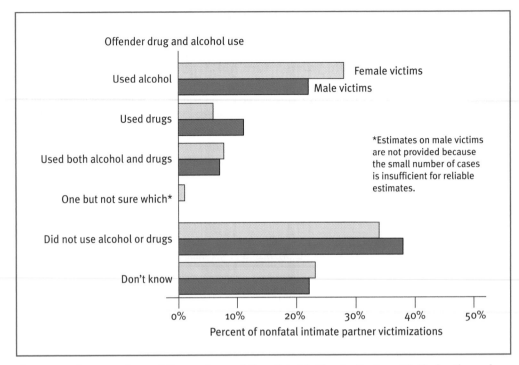

Figure 8.3 Average Annual Percentage of Non-fatal Intimate Partner Victimizations, by Offender Alcohol and Drug Use and Victim Gender, 2001–5

Source: US Bureau of Justice Statistics, at: http://bjs.ojp.usdoj.gov/content/intimate/circumstances.cfm.

Tobacco

Tobacco is Canada's other major legal drug. Like alcohol, nicotine—the psychoactive substance in tobacco—is highly addictive; a drug to blame for many health problems, and a costly habit, both for the individual and for society.

Tobacco remains hugely popular, though a concerted public health movement has led to steadily declining tobacco use in recent years. In 2005, for example, roughly five million Canadians—20 per cent of the population 15 years and over—reported smoking daily or occasionally, a drop from nearly seven million Canadians in 1996–7 (Statistics Canada, 2005; Health Canada, 1999: 164).

Most adult smokers develop their habit of smoking before the age of 20. As with alcohol, men are more likely than women to use tobacco, although the gender gap has been narrowing for the past quarter-century. Health Canada has found that girls are more likely to smoke than boys until age 18, when boys begin to outpace girls. Unlike alcohol use, there is a simple linear relationship between education and cigarette smoking: 'People with less than a high school education are almost three times more likely than university graduates to be current smokers' (Health Canada, 1999: 165).

And like alcohol, tobacco smoking is influenced by social factors. A study of more than 22,000 Ontario high school students found that teenagers are at increased risk for smoking if they (a) have smoking friends, (b) have smoking family members, and/or (c) attend a school with a relatively high senior-student smoking rate (Leatherdale et al., 2005). European data also suggest that smoking is more common among teenagers in single-parent households and blended-family households than among those in intact families. The researchers suggest that these trends may be due to lower levels of attachment, a tendency towards rebellion, and less parental supervision in stepfamily and lone-parent homes (Griesbach et al., 2003).

Among adolescents who experiment with smoking, the development of a smoking habit is positively correlated with poor academic performance, parental smoking, and having more than half of one's friends smoking. It is negatively correlated with attending a school with a clear anti-smoking policy and having confidence in one's ability to succeed academically (Karp et al., 2005).

Illicit Drug Abuse

Much of what we have said about alcohol abuse applies equally to drug abuse. In general, factors that reduce the likelihood of drug use and abuse include strong family bonds, which reduce the use of all illegal drugs except marijuana (Ellickson et al., 1999), a strong religious commitment (Yarnold, 1999), and normative boundaries that separate adolescents who occasionally use drugs socially from those who use them often or in isolation (Warner, Room, and Adlaf, 1999).

Marriage and parenthood are also important influences (Liu and Kaplan, 1999). Married people and parents who adhere to conventional values may use illegal drugs when they come under stress, for the control of stress so they can continue to conform to dominant values. The drugs reduce stress in a private and non-disruptive fashion (ibid.).

Factors that increase the likelihood of drug use include friends who are users and parents who use tobacco or alcohol (Colson, 2000), early initiation into drug use (Dishion et al., 1999), and a history of parental abuse (Bensley et al., 1999). Working conditions also make a difference. Workers with low cognitive ability make more use of cigarettes, alcohol, and marijuana the more complex their jobs are; workers with high cognitive ability, on the other hand, make less use of these substances the more complex their jobs are (Oldham and Gordon, 1999).

Even more than alcohol use, drug use is a learned behaviour that depends on social opportunities and on inclusion in social occasions where drugs are being used. Opportunities to use drugs are more common as youths get older. The likelihood of trying drugs, given the opportunity, also increases with age. Ethnic and gender differences in adolescent drug use correspond to differences in opportunities to try drugs with acquaintances, dating partners, and even parents (Moon et al., 1999).

Males tend to have more opportunities than females to use marijuana, crack cocaine, and other forms of cocaine, and at a younger age. However, they are no more likely than females to begin using drugs once an opportunity has arisen (Delva et al., 1999; Van Etten et al., 1999). Normative boundaries restricting girls' access to and use of drugs are largely due to traditional gender roles that limit girls' access to certain types of leisure and sociability. Male

DRUGSTORE COWBOY

A group of drug addicts, led by charismatic Bob (Matt Dillon) travel the country, robbing drug stores in hopes of feeding their addictions.

peers enforce these norms as drug dealers and distributors (Warner, Weber, and Albanes, 1999). While males are more likely to receive offers of drugs from other males and even parents, often in public settings, drug offers to females are more likely to come from other females or dating partners, often in private settings (Moon et al., 1999).

In Canada, the rates of overall illicit drug use are low. However, drug use is prominent among certain populations, including people who are economically disadvantaged, live in jail or communities with other social problems, or suffer from mental problems.

Substance Abuse among the Aboriginal Population

For thousands of years after arriving in North America, Aboriginal peoples lived in many small communities or bands that varied widely but had certain features in common. A strong sense of community and communal cohesion, with cultural custodians who stood guard over the group's traditions, promoted the sharing and defence of group values.

Selective use of psychoactive substances has long been a part of the customs and rituals of the Aboriginal population in North America (French, 2008). However, the contact of Natives with explorers and settlers of Western Europe severely affected Aboriginal culture and its practices. The European assimilation has contributed to social, health, and economic problems that currently are widespread on First Nation reserves and in northern Aboriginal communities, as well as among Aboriginal people living in urban areas (Johnston et al., 2008).

Because of poor living conditions, illicit substances provide an escape for Aboriginal people today. They are no longer an intricate part of a cultural tradition. Besides experiencing a difficult life, many Aboriginal people suffer from trauma related to sexual abuse and family violence, and have parents who abuse substances. These factors, as well as others, increase the likelihood of these individuals abusing substances themselves.

Alcoholism has been part of the negative Native American image for many years (French, 2008). Does this image hold truth today? A recent survey by Kovas et al. found that in the United States, 'alcohol related arrests, morbidity, and mortality' are still high among American Indians (Kovas et al., 2008: 183). In addition, according to Kunitz, the age of first alcohol use has become younger in the Native population over the past 50 years (Kunitz, 2008). Thus, this issue is still very prominent in Canada today.

Drug use is a significant problem among the Aboriginal population. As mentioned by Ehlers et al. (2007: 291), several studies show that 'the use of marijuana is disproportionately higher among Native than non-Native American adolescents.' Various psychosocial factors contribute to this finding, including poor academic performance, stress, and delinquent behaviour. Mehrabadi et al. (2008) found that female Aboriginal survivors of sexual abuse in Canada are especially prone to using illicit drugs. They are vulnerable, also, to serious emotional and physical health problems (ibid).

One study found that Aboriginal people benefit from treatment programs, decreasing their alcohol intake, arrests, and suicide rate (Evans et al., 2006). However, in order to improve a patient must be willing to get better and make the necessary behavioural changes to ensure continued improvement. The method of treatment that has worked best is addiction counselling by other Native people, sharing Aboriginal experiences, relearning the traditional culture, and practising Aboriginal rituals. Using this approach, the Shuswap people on the Alkali Lake Reserve in British Columbia went from 100 per cent addiction to 95 per cent sobriety in 15 years (Hodgson, 1987).

THEORETICAL PERSPECTIVES ON ADDICTION

Table 8.4 Theoretical Perspectives

Theory	Main Points
Structural Functionalism	• Alcohol and drug abuse results from the social structure's influence on the individual. • Drug and alcohol use is common because it serves social functions.
Social Disorganization Theory	• Institutions that traditionally discourage deviant behaviour are rendered less effective by rapid social change. • Breakdown in community norms and traditions deprives individuals of a sense of meaning and moral guidance. • Relearning or re-establishing traditional institutions can reduce substance abuse.
Merton's (1957) Strain (Anomie) Theory	• Drug and alcohol abuse is the result of the incongruence between culturally defined goals and the socially approved means for attaining these goals (i.e., anomie). • One adaptation to this gap is to retreat (abandon efforts to achieve goals, escape reality via substance abuse).
Conflict Theory	• Alcohol and drug use affect different socio-economic groups differently. • Powerful capitalist members of society are in a position to define whether a substance is legal or illegal. • The poor tend to suffer harmful outcomes of substance abuse more than the rich, due to labelling and the criminalization process.
Symbolic Interactionism	• The social meanings and values associated with drug and alcohol use and with the labels attached to people when they use these substances are the focus for understanding. • The term 'alcoholic' is laden with negative characterizations, judgements, and stereotypes in a way that 'social drinker' is not.

Structural Functionalism

Structural functionalists hold that alcohol and drug abuse, like all social problems, result from the way social structure influences the individual.

Some argue that recreational drug and alcohol use are common because these substances serve an important social function. For example, alcohol use, for many people, is almost compulsory on certain occasions—for example, Mardi Gras in New Orleans or Carnival in Rio de Janeiro, or New Year's Eve almost anywhere—where it breaks down personal inhibitions and fosters conviviality. Structural functionalism also seeks to explain substance abuse. Two of the more influential camps within this perspective are social disorganization theory and anomie theory.

Social Disorganization Theory

Social disorganization theory argues that institutions that have traditionally acted to discourage deviant behaviours become less effective during times of rapid social change. Rapid changes cause norms and values to become unclear. Without traditional sources of moral guidance to restrain behaviour, deviancy—including drug and alcohol use—becomes more common.

We can usefully apply this perspective to Canada's Aboriginal population and its problem with addictive substances, especially alcohol. Forced off their traditional hunting lands and onto reserves by the arrival of whites, Aboriginal community norms and traditions broke down, speeded by the imposition of residential schooling. Alcohol abuse and suicide spread among Aboriginal peoples throughout the nineteenth and twentieth centuries. Few methods worked to stem this problem because they did not address the issue of social disorganization: the loss of traditional controls and values passed on by family, community, and religion. With the reversal of social disorganization through treatment, alcohol abuse has begun to subside.

Merton's Strain Theory

According to Merton (1957), the cause of excessive drinking and other substance abuse lies not in an absence of values and institutions but in the conflict between them. According to this theory, excessive drinking is driven by a basic conflict or paradox—a gap between culturally defined goals and socially approved means for reaching those goals.

Merton, using American society as his example, argues that one of the primary goals of that society is success, especially in getting money, material goods, and 'the good life'. Most people have been taught to value success. Yet social inequality ensures that most people will not succeed because they will not have access to the socially approved (that is, legal) means and resources that allow them to attain success—for example, higher education and good jobs. Merton has called this gap between goals and means 'anomie'. This state of anomie allows for various solutions, which Merton called possible adaptations. They include what he called ritualism, retreatism, rebellion, and innovation. Substance abuse results from adopting one such adaptation—retreatism.

However, the use of drugs and alcohol is not merely an individual adaptation; it is socially organized. Groups of individuals with higher levels of social capital, especially social network connections that offer them access to valued jobs, have less need for the numbing escapism that drugs and alcohol offer. Those exposed to adverse community-level conditions—poverty, unemployment, and other measures of social breakdown—are more likely to retreat from their harsh realities.

Conflict Theory

Conflict theorists focus largely on the labelling and criminalization processes. They note that in a capitalist economy, the powerful members of society are able to define whether a substance is legal or illegal. The powerful are also able to criminalize drug use by the powerless through their control of the law and police activities.

Besides, they are able to benefit from widespread drug use even while they publicly reject it. Alcohol and tobacco, for example, are produced and sold by the powerful. Both of these billion-dollar industries are regulated but not considered illegal. Both also heavily brand and market their addictive products, reaping huge profits for wealthy stockholders while harming the heavy users, who tend to be poor. Conflict theories also note that banned substances are often forbidden not only because of their harmful pharmacological properties, but also for social and political reasons.

Symbolic Interactionism

Symbolic interactionists focus on the social meanings and values associated with alcohol and drug use and on the labels people attach to others when they use drugs.

What do you think of when you hear the term 'alcoholic'? Does it bring to mind a person who cannot control the harmful effects of alcohol use? A person who is less educated, unemployed, and trapped in the lower socio-economic strata of society? Contrast that image with the 'social drinker'. Friendly 'social drinking' is the drinking code of middle-class people in a modern, capitalist society. Some individuals not only drink in their free time, but often do so to have a good time (Carruthers, 1992). Yet only 'alcoholics' and heavy drinkers are stigmatized and stereotyped in our society.

SOCIAL CONSEQUENCES OF ADDICTIONS

Crime and Violence

According to the Criminal Intelligence Service Canada (2006: 8), 'the illicit drug trade . . . is the most prominent criminal market for organized crime groups.' For example, Vietnamese criminal organizations and the Hell's Angels motorcycle gang play major roles in the Canadian domestic marijuana trade, while Southwest Asian crime groups are especially active in heroin trafficking.

Drug use has a strong link to other forms of deviant and even criminal activity, though the chain of cause and effect is often unclear. In a study of young men in prison, respondents who reported using drugs during their last year of freedom before imprisonment—especially those who used a combination of drugs, alcohol, and tobacco—were likely to have engaged in violent crimes in the past and, even, in that same year (Brownstein et al., 1999). Another study found that chronic drug users are significantly more likely than non-drug users to have assaulted, shot, stabbed, or robbed someone. They are also significantly more likely to have been both victims and observers of all violent acts (McCoy et al., 2000).

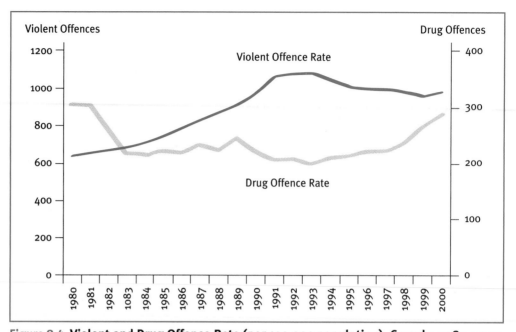

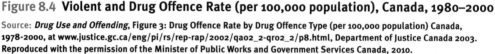

Figure 8.4 Violent and Drug Offence Rate (per 100,000 population), Canada, 1980–2000

Source: *Drug Use and Offending*, Figure 3: Drug Offence Rate by Drug Offence Type (per 100,000 population) Canada, 1978-2000, at www.justice.gc.ca/eng/pi/rs/rep-rap/2002/qa02_2-qr02_2/p8.html, Department of Justice Canada 2003. Reproduced with the permission of the Minister of Public Works and Government Services Canada, 2010.

As the data in Figure 8.4 show, however, from 1980–2000 no correlation appears to exist between rates of drug use (as measured by drug offences) and rates of violence. Perhaps this is because most drug offences involve marijuana, a drug that is not typically associated with violence.

Alcohol use is more strongly and more consistently associated with both violent and non-violent offences than is marijuana and heroin use (Dawkins, 1997). Alcohol use and abuse are often involved in incidents of physical assault, both among the perpetrators and the victims (Scott et al., 1999). The research literature suggests that alcohol use causes biochemical changes and behaviours that would not have occurred otherwise; it also provides a convenient excuse to engage in violent behaviours (Patton and Baird, 2000). A review of the literature reveals that 50 per cent of all homicide offenders and victims are intoxicated from drugs or alcohol at the time of the crime (Auerhahn and Parker, 1999). Further, alcohol consumption is strongly linked to domestic abuse. Drunkenness, not drinking per se, is the main predictor for threatening behaviour and wife-battering by husbands (Hutchison, 1999).

Poverty and Income

Although alcohol use rates are higher among well-educated, high-income people than among poorly educated, low-income people, alcohol abuse and problem drinking are reported more often among the latter group (Spillane, 2008). Whether poverty causes drug abuse or drug abuse causes poverty is hard to distinguish. This may reflect the operation of a vicious circle, with poverty leading to substance abuse and abuse, in turn, reinforcing joblessness and poverty (Mulia et al., 2008).

Racism

The 'war on drugs', especially in the US but also to a degree in Canada, served to increase racial and class injustice by targeting the poor and racial minorities unduly. It has focused on drug users and street traffickers, not others (such as money launderers) in the drug economy, and has credited their drug abuse and criminality to moral weakness rather than to a loss of manufacturing jobs (Duster, 1997).

African Americans were four times more likely to be arrested for drug abuse violations and as much as 10 times more likely to be arrested in some major cities (Meddis, 1993). Even though the majority of crack cocaine users were white, about 96 per cent of the crack defendants in federal court were non-white. Equivalent race-based drug arrest data are not available for Canada. However, given recent concerns about racial profiling practices among Canadian law enforcement agencies, there is reason to believe that similar trends may exist here as well.

In short, the enforcement of laws against substance abuse reflects an undue bias against racial minorities that, in turn, reflects a biased focus on poor and working-class people or racism, or both (Coker, 2003).

HEALTH CONSEQUENCES OF ADDICTIONS

Alcohol and Drug Abuse

Generally, substance abuse is bad for health, though different kinds of drugs have different effects on different parts of the body. Further, they are likely to affect people somewhat differently, for example, according to their size, sex, age, and physical fitness.

Some evidence suggests the volume of alcohol consumption per occasion has more harmful effects than the overall drinking volume; that is, binge drinking is more harmful in its social effects than drinking or drunkenness per se (Rehm and Gmel, 1999). Overall, chronic drug users show greater health-care needs than non-users and are less likely to receive suitable health-care services (McCoy et al., 2000). Poor eating habits and malnutrition are positively related to heavy drinking, as are social and family disorganization (Santolaria et al., 2000).

Health effects are not limited to the alcohol user, however. Pregnant women who drink may also be placing their unborn children at risk. Fetal alcohol syndrome (FAS) occurs as a result of prenatal exposure to alcohol, and can result in facial abnormalities and stunted growth after birth. In addition, damage to the central nervous system can lead to attention deficits and to intellectual, memory, and learning disabilities. FAS occurs in roughly one to three live births per 1,000, which is unfortunate as it is considered one of the most preventable forms of birth defect in Canada (see Williams and Gloster, 1999).

Health outcomes faced by users of illegal drugs include shortened lifespans, dietary irregularities, severe weight loss, vomiting, mucous membrane damage, and brain lesions. Among injection drug users, the risk of contracting HIV/AIDS from sharing contaminated needles is very high. A conservative estimate by the Canadian Centre on Substance Abuse and the

LEAVING LAS VEGAS

Nicholas Cage won an Oscar for his turn as Ben, an alcoholic Hollywood screenwriter in this 1995 film.

Centre for Addiction and Mental Health (Schechter et al., 1999) shows that one in every five AIDS cases in Canada was related to intravenous drug use. Drug users run a higher-than-average risk of HIV infection, partly from sharing needles and partly from unprotected sex with multiple partners (Inciardi et al., 1999). These practices are common in prisons, as well as outside. Even women drug offenders are found to engage in many high-risk drug and sexual behaviours while in prison; on release, they are a major public health risk. Criminal justice policies, grounded in deterrence and based on imprisonment, may be contributing to the spread of HIV infection in the wider society.

Drug abuse can also lead to mental health problems. White and Labouvie (1994), for example, have shown that drug users are more likely to develop anxiety disorders, phobias, depression, and anti-social personalities. Suicide is also more common among drug users, especially adolescents. Marijuana, the illicit drug of choice among teenagers, has been associated with short-term memory loss, impaired learning, amotivational syndrome, and emotional deficits. Further, of all students in Ontario who reported alcohol problems in 1998, 40 per cent reported damaged mental health as a direct result.

Tobacco

Tobacco smoking, despite decades of public health warnings, remains the primary cause of lung cancer, which is the leading cause of cancer death. In 2006, over 19,000 Canadians were expected to die from lung cancer and nearly 23,000 were expected to develop the disease.

Another 12,000 were expected to die of cancer to the mouth, larynx, esophagus, stomach, bladder, kidney, and pancreas, all of which have been linked to cigarette and cigar smoking (Canadian Cancer Society/National Cancer Institute of Canada, 2006). Further, smoking can lead to elevated risk of asthma, pulmonary disease, emphysema, heart disease, stroke and other cardiovascular diseases, spontaneous abortions, and premature births. (For detailed information on these and other smoking-related health problems, see the Action on Smoking and Health website at ash.org/.)

Smoking near infants and children can also increase the child's susceptibility to sudden infant death syndrome (SIDS), asthma, respiratory infection, and mental retardation. Every year, smoking kills more people than alcohol, AIDS, car collisions, illegal drugs, murders, and suicides combined. In the United States, the yearly number of tobacco-related deaths is equivalent to three 747 jumbo jets crashing every day for an entire year, with no survivors. Not surprisingly, then, smoking is the leading cause of preventable disease and death in Canada and elsewhere.

CLAIMS-MAKING AND CONSTRUCTION OF ADDICTION

Few would challenge the notion that many drugs have harmful effects, and that high doses of many drugs can be fatal. However, some have challenged the idea that 'drugs kill', arguing that such a logic is based on unfalsifiable theorizing about an imaginary world without drugs. Thus, the construction of 'drug deaths' is not a neutral statistic, but one that is shaped by political ideas and designed to justify the war on drugs.

Mariana Valverde (1998), in a study on the historical construction of alcoholism, notes that alcoholics and their families have resisted the medicalization of drinking and the associated treatment. We can see this resistance to labelling in other populations as well, yet drug users may be relatively powerless compared to those voices calling for punitive or medical responses to what they present as drug problems. Social construction analyses draw our attention to the battles fought for the right to define drug use and abuse in a particular way—as individual failing, uncontrollable disease, or social problem.

As well, constructionists cast doubt on the veracity of the disease model of addiction, which they claim did not arise out of scientific discoveries but from a widening of the addiction concept to include more and more activities. In calling the disease model into question, the sociologist's intent is not to diminish the weight that addictions carry for those afflicted. Rather, it is to remind us of the ways in which the view of addiction as disease justifies both humane health services and repressive drug policies (Reinarman, 2005).

POLICY DEBATES

Box 8.3 Exam Cheating Alert over Brain Drugs

Schools and universities could soon be facing a different kind of drug problem: a rise in students taking brain-enhancing pills to boost their exam results.

Government advisers warned yesterday that new drugs to treat conditions as varied as Alzheimer's disease, attention deficit disorder, and narcolepsy are in danger of being misused by students eager to bump up their grades.

The use of brain-boosting drugs, many of which are designed to improve memory and attention span in people with serious degenerative brain diseases, could become as big a problem for the education system as performance-enhancing drugs are in sport, the experts said.

The warning comes in a report from the Academy of Medical Sciences, which was commissioned by the [British] government in 2006 to survey the implications of expected progress in brain sciences and drug research. The report urges the government to be alert to the misuse of 'cognitive-enhancers' and to prepare the ground for regulations and even urine tests to control their use in schools, universities and workplaces.

'Students using cognitive-enhancers raises exactly the same issues as athletes using drugs to improve their performance. The risk is they could give people an unfair advantage in exams—and examination results stand for a lot in this country', said Professor Les Iversen, a pharmacologist at Oxford University and co-author of the report.

Since the drugs are designed to be taken by people with dementia and other serious disorders, there is scant data on how safe or effective they are if taken by healthy people, the report warns.

The group of scientists behind the report identified six categories of drugs, already available on prescription, which claim to boost brain function. These include modafinil, which is used to treat narcolepsy, ritalin and related amphetamines for attention deficit disorder, and donepazil for Alzheimer's disease.

Prof. Iversen said that while most of the drugs are officially available only on prescription, the number of websites beginning to sell brain-enhancing drugs was increasing. 'The situation right now is very haphazard. There's a big business in smarter drugs but no one to regulate it. This is a very active area and we'd better be prepared for a number of new drugs becoming available in the near future', he said.

Source: **Sample (2008).**

SOLUTIONS TO ADDICTION

Legalizing Drugs

By framing substance abuse as an enforcement issue rather than a health issue, countries that take this punitive approach continue to rely on fines and imprisonment to discourage addictive behaviours. Other governments, including Canada's, have recognized the flaws of this strategy, and have experimented with progressive, practical policies that focus on minimizing harm rather than punishing offenders. The Insite safe-injection experiment in Vancouver is one such experiment in harm reduction (Bailey, 2010; DeBeck et al., 2009).

The alternative is much worse: just like alcohol prohibition in the 1920s, drug prohibition in North America has produced a large, profitable criminal industry. Research shows that decriminalization of the possession of marijuana elsewhere since the early 1970s has resulted in decreased costs of enforcement and prosecution of marijuana-related offences (for a detailed account of this, see Haans, n.d.). However, so long as drug use is illegal, we can do little to oversee the quality of drugs available to users or the conditions under which people use these drugs.

The Canadian Press/Jonathan Hayward

Locked containers for used needles can be seen hung on the walls of the injection booths at Insite in Vancouver, 6 May 2008. Insite is the first legal supervised injection site in North America and is located in Vancouver's east side.

Why not regulate all the drugs we take? Where alcohol, caffeine, and prescription medicines are concerned, food and drug laws seek to ensure that we do not consume dangerous or poor-quality substances. (The same cannot be said of cigarettes, which contain known carcinogens as well as nicotine.) Similarly, health protection rules would apply to recreational drugs if they were legalized.

One reason for repealing Prohibition in the US was the realization that when quality-controlled alcoholic drinks are not available, people will drink just about anything. In the 1920s and 1930s, people died or went blind from drinking beverages that contained dangerous impurities or the wrong alcohol (that is, methanol instead of ethanol). Similarly, some drug users have died of drug overdoses because they had no way of knowing the strength of the drug. Legalization could prevent this by regulating strength and quality so the user would be always aware of how much is a safe amount to use.

When drugs are illegal, users also take fewer health precautions. Needle-sharing among intravenous drug users, for example, is a primary factor in the spread of HIV/AIDS in many developing nations (DeBeck et al., 2009). By driving the drug culture underground, punitive drug laws work against safety, good hygiene, and disease prevention. Programs in other countries—for example, Switzerland—have reduced the sharing of contaminated equipment without increasing drug use.

Media and Technology on Addiction

People around the world are spending increased amounts of time in front of the television, listening to music, playing video games, and using the Internet and other electronic media. Some researchers suggest that the extent of this technological involvement has contributed to various unhealthy behaviours that have a significant impact on society (Escobar-Chaves and Anderson, 2008).

These behaviours include 'physical inactivity, poor eating habits, smoking, alcohol use, sexual behaviors, and violence' (ibid, 147), which are at the root of some of modern society's pressing social problems. Advertisers and television corporations are aware that youth, owing to their inexperience, are particularly vulnerable to media messages. For instance, many studies provide evidence that youth are likely to view smoking favourably and become smokers themselves 'as a result of exposure to smoking in the media' (ibid, 157).

In the same way, alcohol advertising on television, at sporting events, and in popular movies contributes to adolescent drinking (ibid.; McClure et al., 2006). Alcohol use and brand appearance are widespread in Hollywood movies (which are distributed internationally). So, youth 'are exposed to hours of alcohol use depictions . . . and most of this exposure is from movies rated for this segment of the population' (McClure et al., 2006).

Today, many youth—especially as college students—conclude from media depictions (e.g., beer advertisements) that heavy drinking is a social norm. They are inclined to drink heavily because they think it is normal and socially attractive to do so. However, many are unaware of the long-term health effects of this behaviour.

It will be hard to control the mass media advertising that promotes such views. However, we can find examples of successful efforts. For instance, a project tested in Montana in 2005 portrayed drug users unfavourably on television (as unhygienic, dangerous, and bad-tempered). This promoted a negative attitude towards substance abuse among those who watched the specified programs (Erceg-Hurn, 2008). The project is a model of using the most popular and effective means to spread a health-conscious message. It is being tried out in various parts of the United States.

Canada would benefit from such a project, given that many channels broadcast in Canada are American. However, for now, Canada has different policies for handling substance abuse issues.

Canada's Drug Strategy

Survey evidence shows that many Canadians still oppose the use and sale of illegal drugs and some oppose their legalization. However, many others are indifferent to legalizing recreational drugs: they just do not care. They oppose efforts to mount a 'war on drugs', which they consider unnecessary. Some strongly favour legalization, for the reasons noted above.

Canada's current federal drug strategy was first conceived in 1987 and was most recently renewed in 2003. In its present form, the strategy is built on four pillars:

- *prevention* to teach about the dangers of harmful substance use and to provide information on how to adopt healthy behaviours;
- *treatment* for those with an unhealthy dependency on substances;
- *harm reduction* to limit the secondary effects of substance use, such as the spread of infectious diseases like HIV/AIDS and hepatitis C;
- *enforcement* to prevent the unlawful import, export, production, distribution, and possession of illegal drugs (Health Canada, 2005).

The first three pillars—prevention, treatment, and harm reduction—recognize that drug abuse is a public, medical, and social health issue, and that it should be averted and discouraged where possible and treated where necessary. The last pillar—enforcement—recognizes that the supply of illicit drugs must be controlled and limited if the other pillars are to achieve their targeted goals. The government of Canada in May 2003 announced an investment of $245 million over five years to support various programs implemented under this federal initiative.

The Canadian effort towards prevention, treatment, and reduction of harm has gone through important changes in recent years. It builds on public health lessons learned from various infectious diseases and pushes for an integrated approach to both legal and illegal drugs (Erickson, 1998). Methadone maintenance programs are good examples of harm-reduction efforts; heroin addicts stabilized on methadone can reduce illicit drug use and criminality and improve their life conditions even though they have not achieved abstinence (Cheung and Ch'ien, 1999).

Together, prevention, treatment, and harm reduction, with minimal reliance on criminal law, may be the most effective public health policy on drugs. The government can license the production and sale of soft drugs to regulate their quality, explore the potential of access mechanisms for drugs (free market versus government monopoly versus medical control), and tax the profits on legalized drug sales, then use the taxes for drug education. Equally, governments can reduce the penalties for using hard drugs, treat unlicensed drug-selling as a regulatory or tax offence punishable by huge fines, develop a public health approach to addressing drug problems, and educate the public against drug overuse and the use of harmful drugs.

The federal government has heard renewed calls from influential groups, including the Canadian Medical Association and a Senate Special Committee on Illegal Drugs (2002), to amend the Controlled Substances and Drugs Act to decriminalize the possession of small amounts (roughly 15 grams) of marijuana. Decriminalization is not the same as full legalization. While it still would be illegal to have the drug for personal use, this would be considered a non-criminal offence similar to a parking violation, and also punishable by a ticketed fine.

In other words, marijuana's legal status would not change, only the manner of the law's enforcement. However, decriminalization is opposed by other groups, including many municipal police, who worry about increased drug trafficking; and by the US government, which is concerned that easier access to drugs in Canada will trickle drugs south across the border.

CHAPTER SUMMARY

To some extent, we all have 'addictions'—to television shows, video games, or favourite pastimes. However, these so-called 'addictions' are unlike those to harmful substances such as drugs and alcohol. Such substances alter the mind and behaviour, and therefore interfere with every aspect of the abuser's life.

Substances we consider 'drugs' are not always defined as good and bad by any absolute criteria. Instead, their definition depends on politics and culture. In this sense, drugs—our perceptions of them and responses to their use—are social constructions. Likewise, laws that specify which drugs are legal and which are not are socially constructed and influenced largely by politics. Laws are not consistently based on a drug's potential for harm. As we have noted, many legal drugs, including nicotine and alcohol, may be more harmful to health than illegal drugs such as marijuana or even heroin.

Criminalizing drugs may be causing more harm than good. Criminalization creates a black market, encourages organized crime, prevents quality control, and puts heroin drug users at higher risk of HIV/AIDS. People with a high socio-economic status are most likely to be heavy drinkers, yet they are safe from the law. How we view a drug, use it, and regulate it can have a large effect on how the person experiences and uses the drug. Our peers and social milieux influence these views.

Substance abuse, as we have seen, has many negative outcomes for users and for individuals around them. These outcomes involve other social problems and, often, severe health problems for users and their associates. For these reasons, we must view, and handle, substance abuse as a social problem.

QUESTIONS FOR CRITICAL THOUGHT

1. Evaluate the view that 'Since human beings are chemistry sets with an obvious desire to perform experiments on themselves, we spend far too much time and money trying to control a few of these experiments.'

2. Given the long, historic connection between drug use and sacred ritual, how do we account for the continued popularity of drug use in increasingly secular societies?

3. Discuss why some drugs are legal and others are illegal. In connection with this, explain what factors play a role in defining some drug use as a 'drug problem'.

4. Howard Becker explains that one must learn how to use marijuana. Is there any evidence that people also need to learn to use and enjoy other drugs—for example, alcohol, nicotine, ecstasy, or cocaine?

5. Do you support the decriminalization of marijuana? Use sociological theories you have learned in this chapter to support your views on the issue.

6. 'Widespread drug use—of whatever kind—is symptomatic of a society in crisis.' Evaluate this statement in respect to several different societies, communities, or groups for which you have information.

RECOMMENDED READINGS

Frey, James. 2003. *A Million Little Pieces*. New York: Anchor Books. This national bestseller nicely illustrates the process by which a drug user can overcome circumstances to become a non-user. As an abuser of alcohol and drugs, Frey checks into a treatment facility and battles with AA's 12 steps.

Herlihy, Patricia. 2002. *The Alcoholic Empire: Vodka and Politics in Late Imperial Russia*. New York: Oxford University Press. This book explores various attempts launched by both civil and official groups, with greatest focus on temperance societies, to curb the worst abuses of alcohol. A historical work, it examines the prevalence of alcohol in Russian social, economic, religious, and political life across a vast period.

McAllister, Patrick A. 2005. *Xhosa Beer Drinking Rituals: Power, Practice and Performance in the South African Rural Periphery*. Durham, NC: Carolina Academic Press. Among the rural Xhosa-speaking people of South Africa's Eastern Cape Province, beer rituals became a crucial mechanism through which to develop and maintain rural social and economic relations, to instill the values that supported these, and to provide a viable view of the world that countered the disillusionment and suffering in black urban areas.

McKnight, David. 2002. *From Hunting to Drinking: The Devastating Effects of Alcohol on an Australian Aboriginal Community*. London and New York: Routledge. This study reveals the devastating effects that alcohol has had over a period of 30 years on Mornington Island, off the North Queensland Coast, Australia. Drinking has become the main social activity and it now affects all reaches of community life. The amount of alcohol consumed per year has reached a disturbing level, suicide and homicide rates are alarmingly high, and people are drinking so much that alcohol-related illness is rife.

Salinger, Sharon S. 2002. *Taverns and Drinking in Early America*. Baltimore: Johns Hopkins University Press. This overview of the role of taverns in the American colonies draws our attention to a paradox. Colonial public houses were both open public spaces and exclusive quasi-private clubs.

Since the tavern was overwhelmingly the preserve of adult white males in unhindered possession of their labour, tavern-going fostered particular racial and gender identities and also contributed to an emergent class-consciousness.

Valentine, Douglas. 2004. *The Strength of the Wolf: The Secret History of America's War on Drugs*. New York: Verso. Douglas outlines the war on drugs and the various federal agencies that have been put in charge of monitoring various controlled substances. Though a dense work, it is a detailed examination of the American war on drugs.

Wilkins, John, and Shaun Hill. 2005. *Food in the Ancient World*. Oxford: Blackwell. Focusing on the Egyptians, Greeks, Celts, and Romans, the book shows that in each of these civilizations, people in power viewed bars, taverns, hotels, and other public eating places with suspicion because of the rebellious political discussions and competitive drinking that often accompanied people's visits to these establishments.

RECOMMENDED WEBSITES

Health Canada—Alcohol and Drug Prevention Publications

www.hc-sc.gc.ca/hl-vs/pubs/adp-apd/index-eng.php

Health Canada provides free, government-funded reports on alcohol and drug abuse in Canadian society. While some of the reports are myopic in focus, most relate to a specific aspect of alcohol or drug abuse, such as the effect of substance abuse on youths, Aboriginals, or seniors.

Leave the Pack Behind

www.leavethepackbehind.org

Leave the Pack Behind is a peer-to-peer initiative designed to reduce smoking rates among various groups of students. The website provides quitting information as well as research on smoking and its effects.

MADD: Mothers Against Drunk Driving

www.madd.org

This activist organization provides education information for students. As one of the largest crime victim organizations in the world, MADD is able to generate quite a bit of attention towards research on alcohol use and abuse.

National Institute on Alcohol Abuse and Alcoholism

www.niaaa.nih.gov

Run by the US Department of Health and Human Services, the website of the NIAAA is dedicated to creating awareness regarding the social effects of alcohol abuse and alcoholism. The site provides free publications, research links, news, and other resources for investigating the effects of alcoholism on society.

Substance Abuse Issues and Public Policy in Canada: Parliamentary Action (1987-2005), Library of Parliament

www.parl.gc.ca/information/library/PRBpubs/prb0605-e.html

The brief report on substance abuse issues and public policy is made available by Canada's parliamentary library. While the article itself only briefly addresses ways in which policy could be used to combat substance abuse issues, many links to additional Canadian legislation on the issue are provided.

CHAPTER 9
Health Issues

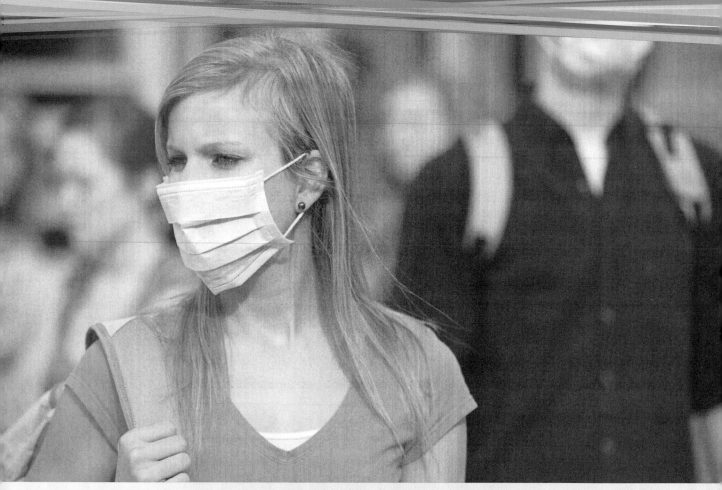

iStockphoto.com/Sean Locke

LEARNING OBJECTIVES

- To know the biomedical and biopsychosocial definitions of health.
- To understand different ways to measure population health.
- To recognize the basic facts of Canadian and global health threats.
- To know how globalization and air travel affect the nature of disease.
- To identify the social determinants of health and illness.
- To understand how public health interventions improve population health.
- To discover the problems in Canada's health-care system.

INTRODUCTION

We usually like to think of health and disease as 'objective' facts about us or other people. However, this chapter will argue that much social construction and labelling also go into perceiving and dealing with illness and disease. Robert Aronowitz (2008), for example, calls our attention to the process of 'framing disease', which he considers 'an underappreciated mechanism for the social patterning of health'. Epidemiologists have focused on material and psychosocial causes of illness, especially the ways income inequality causes health disparities. Aronowitz, however, argues for the need to note the ways we generally recognize, define, name, and classify disease states and assign them to a cause or set of causes.

These framing effects influence beliefs about health and illness; patterns of consumption and other behaviours; perceptions of what interventions and policies work; class, ethnic, and other social dynamics; and clinical and public health practices. Important characteristics of such 'framing phenomena' are their capacity to be self-perpetuating and affect people's behaviours. As always in social life, the 'Thomas Dictum' proves correct about sick as well as healthy behaviour: what we believe to be true is true in its consequences.

In one sense, illnesses are *personal problems* that we face. As sufferers, we alone feel the physical and neurological pains of an illness. Although family and friends may sympathize, in the end we bear the experience of sickness and internalize the identity of being 'sick' as individuals.

However, health and illness are also *social problems* for several reasons. First, many diseases and illnesses are common, affecting millions of people. Second, as we will see, health and health-care resources are unequally divided throughout society. One of the main areas of research in **medical sociology** involves the social factors that promote illness and contribute to health inequalities. Other areas focus on the practice of medicine and explore the social construction of 'illness' and 'health', the economics and politics of health-care delivery, and the features of physician–patient interaction. Finally, inequalities in health and health care are social problems because, as we see at the end of this chapter, improving the health of whole populations will need the efforts of governments and other large institutions (Raphael, 2009).

> **MEDICAL SOCIOLOGY**
> The field of sociology that examines the social context of health, illness, and health care.

DEFINING AND MEASURING HEALTH

Definitions of Health and Illness

According to the **biomedical view of medicine**, which has dominated industrial societies since early in the twentieth century, health is the absence of illness. By this standard, health is a 'passive', default state of normalcy, illness, an 'active' problem in need of treatment (Engel, 1977).

This emphasis on illness is partly due to the Western medical profession's focus on curing the sick rather than preventing sickness from occurring first. In the biomedical model, the doctor is like a mechanic and the human body is like a machine to be fixed. Only when something goes wrong—a broken spark plug, a failing kidney—are the professionals called in to mend or replace the faulty part and get 'the machine' working again.

> **BIOMEDICAL VIEW OF MEDICINE** A medical perspective that emphasizes Western scientific principles, defines health as the absence of illness, views the human body as a machine that sometimes requires repair, and promotes the use of therapeutic intervention (e.g., drugs, surgery) to 'cure' disease and injury.

Defining health in strictly somatic terms is inadequate in several ways. There is a growing recognition that the symptoms of biologically identical illnesses vary with differences in personal history, socio-economic condition, and cultural background (Ritsatakis, 2009), leading doctors to 'treat the patient rather than simply the disease'.

More ideas about health have therefore moved away from a solely physiological model towards a more holistic understanding. Here, health is viewed almost synonymously with **well-being**—that is, as a state of existence characterized by happiness, prosperity, and the satisfaction of basic human needs. The World Health Organization (WHO), for example, defines **health** as 'a state of complete physical, mental, and social well-being', a definition that has gone unchanged since the organization's formation after World War II (WHO, 1946). Health Canada takes an equally broad stand on the meaning of 'health', viewing it as a state of social, mental, emotional, and physical well-being that is influenced by a broad range of factors, including biology and genetics, personal health practices and coping skills, the social and physical environments, gender, socio-economic factors such as income and education, and cultural practices and norms (Joint Working Group on the Voluntary Sector, 1999).

These various definitions represent the **biopsychosocial view of health and illness** (White, 2005). As the name implies, this perspective recognizes that health and disease are products of the interaction of body, mind, and environment, and not just of biology alone. As well, it reminds us that health is not an all-or-nothing condition. The relative contributions of each factor—mind, body, and social environment—vary from condition to condition and from case to case. The challenge is to find out the role of each factor and tailor interventions—medical as well social—accordingly.

Measuring Health and Illness

Epidemiology is an applied science that examines the causes, distribution, and control of disease in a population. Epidemiologists use various techniques to study the patterns of health and illness in society, drawing on the knowledge of many disciplines, including medicine, public health, sociology, psychology, and economics, among others (Vetter, 2004).

Rather than trying directly to assess vague ideas like 'well-being', most epidemiologists measure health with standard quantitative indicators. One of the most common is **life expectancy**, the average number of years remaining to a person at a particular age, given current age-specific mortality rates.

Global life expectancy has increased dramatically because of advances in medicine, public health, and technology. Fifty years ago, worldwide life expectancy was 47 years; by 2005, it had increased to 65 years (UN, Population Division, 2005). However, important disparities in life expectancy still exist between rich and poor nations. Japan, for instance, continues to lead, with an average life expectancy in 2005 of 82 years, while Botswana has the lowest, at barely 37 years (ibid.). Canadian life expectancies increased dramatically from roughly 60 years in 1920 to 80 years in 2002—with women's expectancy several years higher than men's in every instance. However, as data in Figure 9.1 show, the gender gap is slowly diminishing, as men gradually catch up with women.

WELL-BEING A positive state of existence characterized by happiness, prosperity, and the satisfaction of basic human needs, and not simply the absence of negative conditions, such as illness or injury.

HEALTH 'A state of complete physical, mental, and social well-being' (WHO).

BIOPSYCHOSOCIAL VIEW OF HEALTH AND ILLNESS A medical perspective that considers health and disease as products of the interaction between body, mind, and environment.

EPIDEMIOLOGY An applied science that examines the causes, distribution, and control of disease in a population.

LIFE EXPECTANCY The average number of years remaining to a person at a particular age, given current age-specific mortality rates.

Figure 9.1 Canadian Life Expectancy at Birth, by Gender, 1979–2005
Sources: Statistics Canada, CANSIM Table 102–0511.

As well as life expectancy, epidemiologists examine mortality rates (typically measured as deaths per year per thousand people in a population). The maternal mortality rate refers to the number of deaths of women because of complications during pregnancy, childbirth, or abortion.

In Canada, abortions are mainly carried out under safe medical conditions. As a result of the wide availability of contraceptive technology, the number of abortions continues to fall. They are, clearly, a last resort for preventing unwanted births, at least in Canada. However, the same cannot be said for many countries of the world, where uncontrolled pregnancy often leads to unwanted births and dangerous abortions. As might be expected, a large majority of induced abortions in Canada are for women under 30 years of age (Figure 9.2).

The maternal mortality rate is a problem clearly linked to global poverty, with 99 per cent of all pregnancy- and childbirth-related deaths worldwide occurring in developing countries (WHO, 2005a). Thus, in the developing world maternal mortality is the leading cause of death and disability among women of reproductive age (15–49 years), with an estimated 533,000 women dying yearly.

The infant mortality rate (number of deaths of children under one year of age per 1,000 live births) and the under-five mortality rate (U5MR) are two other statistical indicators of population health, focusing on society's youngest and most vulnerable members. Globally, the infant mortality rate was estimated at 54 deaths per 1,000 live births in 2004, while the U5MR was roughly 79 deaths per 1,000 live births; again, both indicators are highest in the developing world. At the national level, war-ravaged Sierra Leone had the world's highest U5MR in 2004, at 283 deaths per 1,000 live births. By contrast, Canada's U5MR rate during the same year was six deaths per 1,000 live births (UNICEF, 2005).

MORTALITY RATE The death rate of a given disease or population, typically measured as deaths per year per 1,000 people.

MATERNAL MORTALITY RATE The number of deaths of women due to complications during pregnancy, childbirth, or abortion, typically measured as deaths per year per 1,000 live births.

INFANT MORTALITY RATE Number of deaths of children under one year of age per 1,000 live births.

UNDER-FIVE MORTALITY RATE (U5MR) Number of deaths of children under five years of age per 1,000 live births.

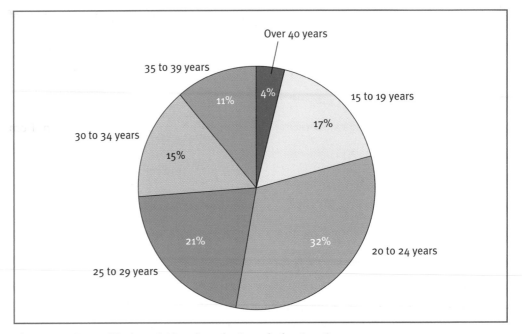

Figure 9.2 Rate of Induced Abortions in Canada by Age Group, 2002
Source: **Statistics Canada and novanewsnet.ukings.ca/nova_news_3588_7656.html.**

MORBIDITY RATE The extent of disease in a population, reported by incidence (the number of new cases in a given population during a given period) and/or its prevalence (the total number of cases of a disease in the population at a particular point in time).

The **morbidity rate** shows the extent of disease in a population. Morbidity can be reported according to its *incidence*, the number of new cases in a given population during a given period of time, or its *prevalence*, the total number of cases of a disease in the population at a particular time. Diseases also can be classified as *endemic*, or constantly present within a population; *epidemic*, being a local or national outbreak; or *pandemic*, an epidemic of international or global proportions. Like mortality rates, morbidity rates vary according to social variables such as sex/gender, racial grouping, and social class.

THREATS TO CANADIAN AND GLOBAL HEALTH

The AIDS Pandemic

'Rare cancer seen in 41 homosexuals'—so read the headline from the 3 July 1981 edition of *The New York Times*, among the first mainstream media reports about what would become known as acquired immune deficiency syndrome (AIDS).

Yet despite exponentially rising infection rates throughout the 1980s, AIDS was too often labelled—and thereby dismissed—in those early days as a disease for 'them' rather than 'us', an affliction limited to three socially marginalized populations: homosexuals, injection drug users, and Haitians. According to a US Centers for Disease Control (CDC) spokesperson interviewed in *The New York Times* article, 'the best evidence against contagion is that no cases have been reported to date outside the homosexual community or in women' (Altman, 1981).

Today, we know better. By the end of 2005, an estimated 40.3 million people worldwide, including 17.5 million women and 2.3 million children under 15 years old, were living with

AND THE BAND PLAYED ON

Based on Randy Shilts' book, this 1993 film traces the research and discussion of the AIDS pandemic, beginning with its 1981 discovery.

the human immunodeficiency virus (HIV), the pathogen commonly viewed as the cause of AIDS. Nearly five million people were infected in 2005 alone. The number of global AIDS-related deaths is equally staggering—25 million since 1981, with 3.1 million in 2005 alone (UNAIDS, 2005). Globally, AIDS is the leading cause of death among adults ages 15–59, and the fourth leading cause of death overall (WHO, 2005a).

HIV is transmitted via the exchange of bodily fluids. Infection occurs mainly through unprotected sexual intercourse, sharing of intravenous needles, perinatal transmission (from an infected mother to a fetus or newborn), infusion of tainted blood products, and, rarely, through the breast milk of an infected mother. Worldwide, heterosexual intercourse is the primary mode of HIV transmission (Gayle, 2000), while in Canada, homosexual intercourse between two men carries the highest risk (Public Health Agency of Canada, 2006).

SARS, Pandemic Influenza, and the 'Globalization' of Infectious Disease

The AIDS pandemic is a stark reminder that infectious disease remains a major health problem throughout the world. Malaria, a disease almost exclusive to the world's poorest nations, claims over one million lives each year and is estimated to have slowed annual economic growth in Africa by 1.3 per cent. Tuberculosis, once thought to be wiped out, has made a comeback in recent years (UN, 2005).

The World Health Organization also estimates that, every year, somewhere in the world a new infectious disease emerges that is previously unknown in humans and for which we have no natural immunity (WHO, 2003b). Infectious illnesses with more opportunistic transmission and incubation profiles than AIDS, however, create extra risks in our increasingly interconnected world.

A striking example of how present-day globalization has increased the risks posed by emergent communicable viruses is the 2003 outbreak of severe acute respiratory syndrome (SARS). The epidemic has been called 'a product of globalization' because its rapid spread from Guangzhou, China, to Singapore, Hanoi, Toronto, and elsewhere was promoted by the movement of people along international air travel and trade routes (So and Pun, 2004: 5).

By the end of the outbreak in July 2003, 8,422 cases of SARS and 916 SARS-related deaths had been officially reported in 30 countries, including places as far from southern China as Kuwait, South Africa, Canada, and Brazil (WHO, 2003a). Global economic costs due to lost trade and declining tourism were estimated in the tens of billions of dollars, including a $1.5 billion loss for Canadian businesses (Conference Board of Canada, 2003). The volume and speed of global commerce and international air travel—as many as 700 million tourist arrivals per year, according to one estimate (Gössling, 2002)—have increased the risk of major infectious pandemics, as at least was feared with the appearance of the H1N1 (swine flu) virus in Mexico in 2009 (Box 9.1).

As it turned out, the H1N1 epidemic fizzled—which is certainly for the best, given the trouble displayed by governments at every level in making enough vaccine available to large numbers in easily accessible places. This governmental reaction, both excessive and inadequate, has led some to wonder what role pharmaceutical companies may have played in orchestrating this flu panic.

The Canadian Press/Ryan Remiorz

Evan Tordorf, 4, cries as he gets his flu shot as his mother Karen Joly looks on at an H1N1 vaccination centre Friday, 6 November 2009, in Montreal.

MENTAL HEALTH The capacity for individuals to feel, think, and act in ways that enhance the quality of daily functioning, the range and depth of social relationships, and the ability to adapt to both positive and negative life changes.

MENTAL DISORDER A condition 'characterized by alterations in thinking, mood, or behaviour (or some combination thereof) associated with significant distress and impaired functioning over an extended period of time' (Health Canada).

Scientists have since expressed concerns that SARS was merely the forerunner to an even larger global pandemic, one that is likely to involve a new strain of virulent influenza. Major influenza outbreaks occur in human populations about three or four times per century, the most recent being the 1918 Spanish flu, the 1957 Asian flu, and the 1968 Hong Kong flu. The deadliest of these, the 1918 Spanish flu outbreak, killed an estimated 30,000 to 50,000 people in Canada and 20–50 million people worldwide, more than the number of combined military and civilian deaths during World War I.

Mental Health and Mental Illness

Mental health refers to the ability of individuals to feel, think, and act in ways that improve the quality of daily functioning, the range and depth of social relations, and the ability to adapt to life changes.

Conversely, a mental disorder, according to one definition by Health Canada, is a condition 'characterized by alterations in thinking, mood, or behavior (or some combination thereof) associated with significant distress and impaired functioning over an extended period of time' (Health Canada, 2002:16). Although *mental disorder* and *mental illness* are often used

INTERNATIONAL COMPARISONS

Box 9.1 Swine Flu Vaccine: Competition or Co-operation?

Governments are scrambling to buy up hundreds of millions of doses of swine flu vaccine but health experts warn the poor may lose out as wealthy countries corner strictly limited supplies.

The World Health Organization has unofficially estimated that the world's labs may only be able to produce around 900 million doses for the H1N1 strain per year, for a planet that is home to 6.8 billion people.

Global pharmaceutical companies are more optimistic about how much of the drug they can produce but, since each potential victim needs two doses, most of the world's population will inevitably miss out.

And there are already signs that the wealthiest countries will snap up more than their fair share in the rush to halt the outbreak, while Africa, Asia, and Latin American will struggle to secure adequate amounts of vaccine.

'The lion's share of these limited supplies will go to wealthy countries. Again we see the advantage of affluence. Again we see access denied by an inability to pay', WHO director Margaret Chan said last week.

France, for example, placed a firm order for 94 million doses of vaccine doses and an option for 36 million more. Starting in October [of 2009], it hopes to be able to protect . . . every member of its population of 64 million.

The United States has set aside at least a billion dollars to buy vaccine, and Britain hopes to protect at least half of its 60 million population by the start of next year [2010] and the other half as soon as possible afterwards.

Australia has also ordered enough vaccine for its 21 million people, and as more countries follow suit the world's potential stock of the drug will soon run out, while prices are set to rise. . . .

Pharmaceutical firms are racing to increase their capacity to produce an H1N1 vaccine, once tests confirm that one has been developed, and hope to begin releasing stocks in late September or early October.

But even if they manage to make double the expected 900 million doses per year, this would still fall far short of the amount that would be needed to protect every man, woman, and child on the planet from the pandemic.

In these circumstances, some countries and independent experts think the best way forward is for authorities to focus on immunizing health workers and the most vulnerable patients in order to conserve stocks.

The WHO is negotiating with vaccine producers to secure donations or sales at lower prices for developing countries, while richer nations are being asked to donate some of their vaccine stocks. . . .

The swine flu virus has spread to almost every country in the world since it was discovered at the end of March [2009]. It was declared a global pandemic in June and is thought to have caused at least 800 deaths.

Source: Abridged and adapted from Trauth (2009).

---

interchangeably, some reserve the term **mental illness** for clinical diagnoses requiring medical and psychotherapeutic treatment. Mental illnesses and disorders should not be confused with the momentary feelings of loneliness, sadness, or emotional agitation that we all experience.

Mental disorders and illnesses are social problems because they often interrupt the normal functioning of families, groups, and other social institutions (Fenwick and Tausig, 2007). At the same time, their causes are still poorly understood, which contributes to a general sense of unease and stigmatization by the public (Phelan et al., 2000).

The most widely accepted classification for mental illness is the American Psychiatric Association's (APA) *Diagnostic and Statistical Manual of Mental Disorders* (DSM-IV) (American Psychiatric Association, 1994). The most common categories of mental illnesses are anxiety disorders; mood disorders, including depression and bipolar disorder; schizophrenia and other forms of psychosis; dementias, including Alzheimer's disease; eating disorders, including anorexia nervosa and bulimia; and personality disorders, such as obsessive compulsive disorder (OCD).

MENTAL ILLNESS
Clinical diagnosis of mental disorder requiring medical and/or psychotherapeutic treatment.

Most experts now agree that most mental illnesses arise from a complex interaction of genetic/biological, psychological, and social/environmental factors (Plakun, 2009). Major social disruptions, such as wars or natural disasters, can also promote the development of mental illness through stress and the breakdown of social order. Other experts contend the individualistic nature and speeded up pace of life in modern industrialized societies erode traditional sources of social stability, such as family and religion.

Occurrence and Impact of Mental Illnesses in Canada and Worldwide

In industrialized nations, major depression, bipolar disorder, schizophrenia, and OCD account for four of the 10 leading causes of mental illness.

Globally, mental illness, with alcohol and drug addiction, comprises the leading cause of disability, accounting for one-third of total years lived with a disability among adults 15 years and older. Unipolar depressive disorders make up the single largest category of non-fatal disabling conditions and are the third-leading cause of lost years of productivity (WHO, 2004). Depression alone is expected to become the world's second-leading cause of disability by 2020 (Statistics Canada, 2003).

As a consequence, large numbers of people around the world rely on anti-depressants to get through the day. As the data in Figure 9.3 show, the numbers consumed vary widely, with Central Europe (Slovak Republic, Hungary, and Czech Republic) at the low end and Scandinavia (Iceland, Sweden, and Denmark) plus Australia at the high end. Conceivably, these figures reflect pharmaceutical availability as much as (or more than) the sheer incidence of

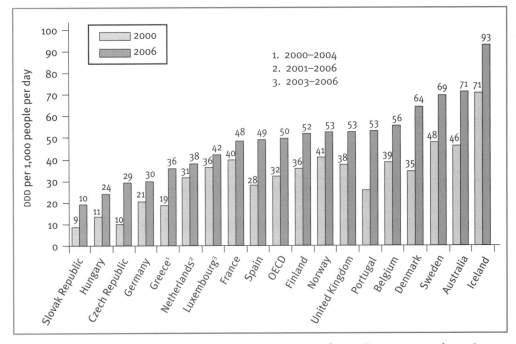

Figure 9.3 Anti-Depressant Consumption per 1,000 People per Day, 2000 and 2006

Note: DDD = defined daily doses.

Source: OECD, at: www.oecd.org/dataoecd/6/48/41686440-pdf.

depression. Note, further, that the rates are increasing over time, across the board. Regrettably, no comparable statistics are available for Canada.

However, mental illnesses are far from unknown in Canada. Here, mental disorders have a combined lifetime prevalence rate of roughly 20 per cent, meaning one person in five—or roughly 6 million Canadians. Among young adults aged 15–24, the age group at which most mental illnesses first appear, the risk is about one in four.

Often, the presence of one mental illness predisposes an individual to other mental health problems, for example, depression and anxiety. This condition is known as co-morbidity. According to a major US study of mental illness involving nearly 10,000 adults, 45 per cent of those who experienced mental illness within the past 12 months had suffered from more than one disorder during that time (Kessler et al., 2005). Stephens and Joubert (2001) estimate the economic costs of mental health problems in Canada—the direct costs of treatment (including psychological and social work services not covered by public health care) and the indirect costs due to lost productivity—at $14.4 billion. This analysis does not include the great psychic and social costs to family members who care for sick relatives.

Overall rates of most mental illness are higher among women than among men, while substance dependence is higher among men (see Statistics Canada, 2003; Mathers et al., 2003; Health Canada, 2002). When one-year prevalence rates for both mental health disorder and alcohol and drug addiction are pooled, a roughly equal number of men and women are affected—1.2 million or 10 per cent of the male population versus 1.4 million or 11 per cent of the female population (Statistics Canada, 2003).

Mental health is also poorer among marginalized ethnic and cultural groups, in particular among Canada's Aboriginal populations. Shah (2004) reports that Aboriginal communities have much higher suicide rates than those for the general population. Suicide in turn is highly correlated with depressive and mood disorders. One study of suicide in the Northwest Territories and Nunavut found that 50 per cent of suicide victims between 1981 and 1996 had a history of depression or emotional distress, 46 per cent had a history of alcohol abuse, and 28 per cent had sought help for social or mental health problems (Isaacs et al., 1998).

Some think the link between mental disorders and social class can be explained by social selection and various 'downward drift' hypotheses. These propose that mental illnesses prevent some people from functioning effectively, resulting in poorer educational outcomes, higher rates of unemployment, increased downward social mobility, and consequent over-representation among the lower classes (e.g., Goldberg and Morrison, 1963). Others have proposed social causation theories. These argue that stresses associated with life in the lower social classes—featuring poverty, unemployment, discrimination, family fragmentation, and the absence of social supports—promote frustration and despair while eroding coping abilities. They also contribute to the onset of mental health problems among vulnerable individuals and groups (Hudson, 2005; Clarke, 2001).

Obesity

Throughout the world, obesity and excess weight are increasing at an alarming rate (WHO, 2006). The primary causes are energy-dense, nutrient-poor diets high in saturated fats and

CO-MORBIDITY The predisposition of an individual with an illness to additional health conditions.

SOCIAL SELECTION A correlation suggesting but not proving causation, because a third, unmeasured factor is involved; also known as adverse selectivity.

SOCIAL CAUSATION Common social factors that produce widespread health problems. Prime examples might include the effects of epidemics and other infectious diseases, and the effects of poverty, access to health care, and work-related health problems; related to social determinants of health.

sugars, and sedentary lifestyles with little physical activity or exercise. Also to blame are larger portion sizes, increased television viewing, and an urban environment that encourages driving over walking (Frank et al., 2004; Cameron et al., 2003; Caballero, 2001).

BODY MASS INDEX (BMI) Weight in kilograms divided by the square of height in metres (kg/m²); 'overweight' is defined as 25 kg/m² and 'obesity' as 30 kg/m².

The most common measure of 'obesity' is the body mass index (BMI), defined as weight in kilograms divided by the square of height in metres (kg/m²). 'Overweight' is defined as a BMI measurement over 25 kg/m², while 'obesity' is defined as a BMI measurement over 30 kg/m². Using these definitions, researchers estimate that, globally, at least 700 million people are overweight, including 17.6 million children under the age of five; and at least 300 million more are clinically obese (WHO, 2005b). Surveys have found rising rates of obesity in almost all developed regions, including Canada (see Rennie and Jebb, 2005; CIHI, 2004b; Matsushita et al., 2004; Cameron et al., 2003; Flegel, 1999). Figure 9.4 shows how the BMI works, and how you can calculate BMI, overweight, and obesity.

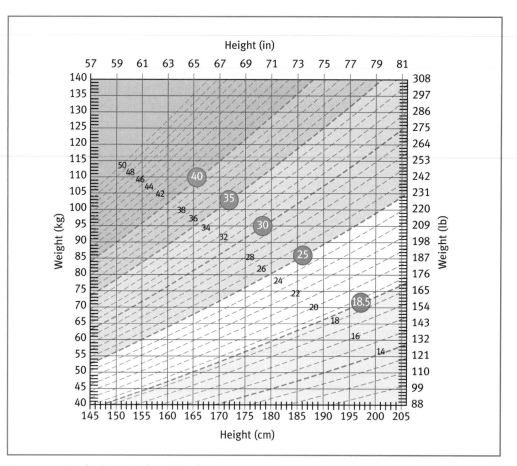

Figure 9.4 Body Mass Index Calculator

To estimate BMI, locate the point on the chart where height and weight intersect. Read the number on the dashed line closest to this point. For example, if you weigh 69 kg and are 173 cm tall, you have a BMI of roughly 23, which is in Zone B. You can also calculate your BMI using this formula: BMI = weight(kg)/height(m²).

Source: **Health Canada. *Canadian Guidelines for Body Weight Classification in Adults*. Ottawa: Minister of Public Works and Government Services Canada, 2003.**

Obesity is a Canada-wide problem, with rates increasing especially in Atlantic Canada and the Prairie provinces (CIHI, 2004a). However, province and region per se have not been identified as a separate risk factor for obesity, once we control for factors like education and socio-economic status (Le Petit and Berthelot, 2005). The direct costs (related to health-care expenditures) and indirect costs (associated with economic output lost because of illness, injury-related work disability, and premature death) of obesity to the Canadian economy are estimated to total $4.3 billion per year (Katzmarzyk and Janssen, 2004).

THEORETICAL PERSPECTIVES ON HEALTH, ILLNESS, AND HEALTH CARE

Table 9.1 Theoretical Perspectives

Theory	Main Points
Structural Functionalism	• Health is normative, and is maintained by social institutions and structural relationships. • Health care is a social institution responsible for maintaining the well-being of all members in society. • Illness is a form of deviance that threatens the ability of society to function. • The ill adopt a 'sick role', allowing them to temporarily *withdraw from society while they recuperate.*
Conflict Theory	• Problems in the delivery of health care result from the capitalist economy, which sees medicine as a commodity that can be produced and sold. • People struggle over scarce resources (medical treatments). • Health, health care, and research are affected by wealth, status, and power or the lack thereof.
Symbolic Interactionism	• Unique meanings and experiences are associated with specific diseases and with being labelled as 'sick'. • What constitutes 'health' or 'sickness' varies from culture to culture. • Crises in health care are socially constructed notions and can be used to promote certain political objectives.
Feminist Theory	• Gender is an important social determinant of health. • Women's health often has been defined and understood on the basis of a male model and male norms.

Structural Functionalism

For structural functionalists, good health is considered the normal, desirable state of an individual; it allows a person to be active and productive, which benefits society. Sickness, on the other hand, is a deviant state of being that threatens the ability of society to work effectively.

Widespread illness—during an epidemic, for instance—can undermine a society and damage its social, economic, and political infrastructure. Structural functionalists therefore stress the role of social institutions and relationships in preserving the health of society's members.

The earliest contribution to a sociology of health was, undoubtedly, Émile Durkheim's book *Suicide* (1951 [1897]), which showed that we can—in fact, must—explain personal health issues like suicide in social-structural terms. This insight is not only the basis of all sociological research; it is the basis of all public health research.

The social institution mainly responsible for a population's health is the health-care industry, which includes doctors, nurses, pharmacists, allied health professionals, and health administrators, and material structures such as hospitals, clinics, laboratories, and dispensaries (Raphael, 2009). As well, societies devise procedures for isolating the ill and reintegrating them into society when they are 'well'. Talcott Parsons's idea of the 'sick role' is the classic statement of this perspective. In Parsons's view, people who are 'sick' take on a specific role and must fulfill this role to be accorded sympathy, assistance, and exemption from their normal daily roles. The assumptions of this role are that the sick person is without blame or fault for her or his condition, that she or he will try to get well, and that, in trying to get well, the sick person should seek competent medical help and co-operate with medical practitioners.

Conflict Theory

Conflict theorists see health and medical services as 'goods' that are unequally distributed among different social groups. According to this view, health inequalities are largely the result of income, economic, and social inequalities that expose vulnerable populations to harm and hinder access to medical services and health-affirming lifestyles.

In *The Condition of the Working Class in England* (1844), political philosopher Friedrich Engels showed how the deplorable conditions of disadvantage in Manchester—substandard housing, lack of sanitation, inadequate diet and clothing, and harsh work environments—affected the city's death rate. Four years later, the German physician Rudolf Virchow, often credited as the 'father of modern pathology', completed a state-commissioned investigation of a typhus epidemic in the Prussian province of Upper Silesia, finding the root causes of the outbreak were regional poverty, poor education, and inept government policy-making. He famously remarked that 'medicine is a social science and politics is nothing else but medicine on a large scale' and asked, 'Do we not always find the diseases of the populace traceable to defects in society?' (Rather, 1985).

There is now ample evidence confirming Virchow's statements that people who are socially, economically, and politically disadvantaged—including women, the elderly, visible and ethnic minorities, the homeless, and others—experience poor health relative to their counterparts who are better off (e.g., Marmot, 2005; Mackenbach and Bakker, 2003).

Symbolic Interactionism

Researchers who adopt the symbolic interactionist perspective remind us that the ideas of 'health' and 'illness' vary from one society to another and are constructed by groups that reflect their needs, values, and beliefs.

Mainly, symbolic interactionists examine microsociological issues connected with health. For example, they might look at the ways medical and nursing schools teach students their new 'professional' identities, or the ways doctors and patients talk during medical visits, following a predictable script that reflects the power difference within these relationships.

Feminist Theory

Perhaps the single most important social factor affecting health, aside from social inequality (or poverty), is gender. Gender and its social construction are important social determinants

PERSONAL STORIES

Box 9.2 Kept from a Dying Partner's Bedside

When a loved one is in the hospital, you naturally want to be at the bedside. But what if the staff won't allow it?

That's what Janice Langbehn, a social worker in Lacey, Wash., says she experienced when her partner of 18 years, Lisa Pond, collapsed with an aneurysm during a Florida vacation and was taken to a Miami trauma centre. She died there, at age 39, as Ms. Langbehn tried in vain to persuade hospital officials to let her visit, along with the couple's adopted children. . . .

The case, now the subject of a federal lawsuit in Florida, is being watched by gay rights groups, which say same-sex partners often report being excluded from a patient's room because they aren't 'real' family members.

And lawyers say the case could affect the way hospitals treat all patients with non-marital relationships, including older people who choose not to marry, unmarried heterosexual couples, and single people who rely on the support of close friends rather than relatives.

One point of contention in the lawsuit is whether a hospital has a legal duty to its patients to always give visiting rights to their designated family members and surrogates. . . .

As recounted by Ms. Langbehn, the details of the Miami episode are harrowing. It began in February 2007, when the family—including three children, then ages 9, 11, and 13—travelled there for a cruise. After boarding the ship, Ms. Pond collapsed while taking pictures of the children playing basketball. . . .

Ms. Langbehn says that a hospital social worker informed her that she was in an 'antigay city and state' and that she would need a health-care proxy to get information. (The worker denies having made the statement, Mr. Alonso, a hospital spokesman, said.) . . .

Despite repeated requests to see her partner, Ms. Langbehn says she was given just one five-minute visit, when a priest administered last rites. She says she continued to plead with a hospital worker that the children be allowed to see their mother, even showing the children's birth certificates.

'I said to the receptionist, "Look, they're her kids"', Ms. Langbehn said. (Mr. Alonso says that except in special circumstances, children under 14 are not allowed to visit in the trauma unit.)

Ms. Langbehn says she was repeatedly told to keep waiting. Then, at 11:30 p.m., Ms. Pond's sister arrived at the unit. According to the lawsuit, the hospital workers immediately told her that Ms. Pond had been moved an hour earlier to the intensive care unit and provided her room number.

At midnight, Ms. Langbehn says, her exhausted children were finally able to visit their unconscious mother. Ms. Pond was declared brain-dead at 10:45 that morning . . . .

In her lawsuit, Ms. Langbehn is being represented by Lambda Legal, a gay rights group. 'We want to send a message to hospitals', said Beth Littrell, a lawyer for the group. 'If they don't treat families as such, if they don't let patients define their own circle of intimacy and give them the dignity and care to be with their loved ones in this sort of crisis, then they will be held accountable.'

Source: **Abridged from Parker-Pope (2009).**

of health. However, because gender interacts with each of the other determinants in complex ways, its connections to health are often addressed within these other discussions.

Historically, men have controlled women's bodies—as fathers, husbands, and even employers. They have also controlled women's bodies as physicians, by defining how women's symptoms and experiences might be interpreted medically. It is easy to find, in such assumptions, 'scientific' legitimacy for the sexual objectification of women, for women's secondary social status and low self-esteem, and for the tendency to dismiss women's health complaints as unfounded. Depression, for instance, was viewed as a women's mental health disability and a form of 'gendered incompetence' (Eckes and Trautner, 2000).

Even today, 'women's' illnesses and health conditions are often considered more trivial or shameful than men's. Consider menopause. Women going through menopause often view their physical symptoms as embarrassing or disruptive. They struggle to hide and control the changes, to keep up appearances (Kittell et al., 1998). Canadian research has shown that some doctors view the conditions associated with menopause as psychiatric problems, owing to a multiplicity of losses and the lack of a meaningful occupation (Lock and Kaufert, 1998).

THE SOCIAL DETERMINANTS OF HEALTH

Research shows that major improvements in population health over the past century have mainly been the result of improved socio-economic conditions rather than improved individual behaviours (Raphael, 2002, 2009). Others, pointing to flaws in the health-care system, argue that poor health is the result of not enough access or funding (Raphael, 2008). However, health inequalities still exist where universal, publicly funded health care is provided, so access alone is not the problem.

SOCIAL DETERMINANTS OF HEALTH The complex causal relationships between various social, economic, and political factors and population health outcomes.

Social scientists have turned towards examining the effects of various social, economic, and political factors—together commonly referred to as the **social determinants of health**—on population health outcomes (Raphael, 2009). Some researchers have adopted a *materialist* approach, arguing that disadvantaged populations suffer from higher levels of total exposure to negative conditions over their lifetimes, resulting in poorer health outcomes than more advantaged groups (Fox and Meier, 2009). *Neo-materialists* agree that material conditions are important, but also point to important social structural contributors (including income inequalities, systemic racial and gender discrimination, and cuts to government social spending) as playing a key role in health disparities.

Finally, *social comparison* theories have been developed to explain the noted health inequalities that exist even among well-off people. The best example of this is found in the Whitehall studies of British civil servants. Since the groups in question were all white-collar and at least middle-class, differences in health status cannot be attributed to material deprivation. These workers experienced subtly different opportunities and varying degrees of control over their life decisions; both affected health through accumulated psychological stress.

A mountain of research has followed the Whitehall studies (for example, Marmot, 2005; Wilkinson and Marmot, 2003). Europe in general and the United Kingdom in particular have been especially open to the notion that health status is closely and subtly related to the social environment and that health policies must harmonize with social policies. Canada, too, has been active in theorizing about the social determinants of health but has been less successful in translating academic research into government policies.

A York University conference of experts in 2002 identified key social determinants of health in Canadian society, and the following list captures the most important elements recurring in the public health literature.

1. *Early life*. The benefits of healthy development begin at the earliest stages of life. Programs that provide parenting education and enough nutrition for young mothers and their infants help to ensure the best start to life (Wilkinson and Marmot, 2003). Governments are also beginning to realize that healthy child development is a national interest; therefore, more countries are funding early childhood education and care.

2. *Education*. Educational attainment in adolescence and early adulthood is also linked to health outcomes later in life. A solid education helps build the skills, resourcefulness, and sense of mastery that prove useful when dealing with problems later in life. In fact, worldwide, literacy is a more sensitive predictor of health status than is education level, income, ethnic background, or any other single socio-demographic variable (Ronson and Rootman, 2004).

3. *Food security*. Nationwide, food bank use has increased 118 per cent since 1989 (Canadian Association of Food Banks, 2005). However, food insecurity is more than simply lacking enough food to eat; it is also 'the inability to acquire or consume an adequate diet quality . . . or the uncertainty that one will be able to do so' (MacIntyre, 2004: 174).

4. *Housing*. Renters have lower average incomes than homeowners, yet face a national shortage of affordable rental housing. This shortage means a difficult choice for the poor: either live in substandard housing conditions—for example, in illegally converted basement apartments or decaying apartment complexes—or rent costly apartments that leave little after-rent income for necessities.

5. *Employment security and work conditions*. Many factors besides pay level distinguish good jobs from bad ones, including: job security; high control and low demand in work responsibilities; opportunities for growth and personal challenge; work–life balance; safe conditions; and suitable managerial acknowledgement of workers' efforts. At the bottom of the job hierarchy, women and ethnic minorities disproportionately fill unskilled manual labour and service industry positions.

6. *Income inequality*. Income and economic inequality, discussed in Chapter 2, are key determinants of health disparity. Research has consistently shown that as one moves up the income hierarchy, health status improves. Researchers have shown that health inequalities exist along the entire income spectrum, even among the richest members of society (e.g., Marmot, 2004).

7. *Social exclusion*. Social exclusion refers to the marginalization of some groups in society from the economic, social, cultural, and political resources that affect quality of life. As Galabuzi (2004) points out, social exclusion is both a process and an outcome. Research finds a clear link between exclusion and health. Exclusion reduces access to education and work opportunities, health-care services, and technological and social innovations.

8. *Aboriginal status*. Aboriginal communities have higher-than-average rates of mortality, infant mortality, suicide, potential years of life lost, infectious disease, and many chronic

illnesses. Aboriginal people are also more likely to smoke, abuse alcohol and drugs, gamble to excess, suffer from food insecurity, be overweight, and have unprotected sex, and they are less likely to be immunized or get physical exercise (Shah, 2004).

9. *Social safety net.* The social safety net includes unemployment insurance benefits, welfare payments, publicly managed pension plans, universal health-care access, job training, and other community programs and services provided by the state as a system of supports for those who for various reasons are unable to cope on their own. The existence of this net reduces the negative health effects of unemployment, poverty, racial and social exclusion, and other social problems.

10. *Health-care services.* Health-care services are obviously related to health outcomes. Unequal access to health care, which research has shown to be especially prevalent among poor and marginalized people, contributes to society's health disparities. Unless the problems currently affecting Canada's universal health system are solved, differential health outcomes will become more pronounced.

CLAIMS-MAKING AND THE SOCIAL CONSTRUCTION OF HEALTH ISSUES

Our approach throughout this book has been one of population health, showing in many cases the demonstrable health effects of a particular social problem. Indeed, in our view, the negative health effects of a particular social condition lend credibility to calling the condition a social problem. Health and health care have been researched using a social construction perspective to reveal the ways in which health messages are delivered to us (McPherson and Armstrong, 2009; Bern-Klug, 2009).

One Swedish study found that such messages were selectively delivered and stressed individual blame for health while discounting the impact of social determinants of health (Sachs, 1996). As we have seen, such determinants are quite important, so any messages playing down their influence should raise flags.

The construction of medical issues in the public mind is of great interest to many researchers. Studies have looked at the successful and unsuccessful claims made by many actors about the risks posed by particular phenomena, such as sleep disorders (Kroll-Smith, 2000), adolescent aggressive behaviour (Potter, 2003), and physical inactivity (Bercovitz, 2000). As we noted earlier, some authors see the medical and pharmaceutical industries as being complicit in these processes of **medicalization**. After all, they stand to profit from the 'discovery' of new diseases to research, combat, and treat.

MEDICALIZATION The process whereby the medical profession comes to be viewed as being relevant to an ever-widening range of traditionally non-medical aspects of life.

However, the medical industries are not alone in their claims-making activity. The media, as well, play a large role in the construction of health problems. One study, which examined media reports on second-hand smoke, found that the actual science involved featured less heavily than a moral narrative of the battle between individual liberty and public health (Malone et al., 2000).

So, many actors can be involved in constructing health problems. Social constructionist ideas about health point to the need to trace back claims to the actors making them. Of course, many claims-makers and lobbyists are attempting to gain public support or at least public awareness of truly destructive illnesses or conditions. However, we should be aware that many supposed health problems—such as the construction of 'fat' or obesity as a health issue—have more to do with social and cultural issues than with actual health risks (Pieterman, 2007).

SOLUTIONS TO PROBLEMS IN HEALTH OUTCOMES AND HEALTH-CARE DELIVERY

Public Health Promotion

Most of the improvements in global population health and well-being over the past century and a half are due not to advances in medicine, pharmaceutical agents, or lifestyle changes, but to socio-economic development and public health programs that focused on preventive medicine rather than treatment or cure (e.g., Marmot, 2004). The **population health perspective**, a framework for understanding health and illness in society, highlights the importance and benefits of preventive health care. It recognizes that preventive actions are not only the most effective way to improve societal health indicators, but they are also the most economically cost-effective.

Primary prevention refers to steps people take to prevent a disease from occurring. Louria (2000) identifies four aspects to the primary prevention of infectious diseases: (1) immunization; (2) a well-functioning public health infrastructure; (3) prudent use of antimicrobial medicines; and (4) 'the amelioration of the societal variables that provide the milieu in which emerging and re-emerging infections arise and flourish'—that is, improving the social determinants of health.

The need for better health promotion is especially urgent in the developing world. Spreading information about causes, effects, and prevention is vital to controlling outbreaks of communicable diseases. For example, AIDS education among commercial sex workers in India has resulted in promising declines in HIV infection rates in some areas. A concentrated effort to educate prostitutes in Kolkata's Sonagachi red-light district about ways to prevent sexually transmitted diseases (STDs) has resulted in condom use rates as high as 85 per cent and a resulting decline in HIV prevalence among sex workers from 11 per cent in 2001 to 4 per cent in 2004 (NACO, 2004).

Effective public health delivery means adapting to local circumstances and recognizing that the target individuals are whole human beings. Consider the differing approaches taken by two Southeast Asian countries in dealing with the HIV/AIDS epidemic. In Myanmar, women found having a condom face imprisonment, as the contraceptive is considered evidence of prostitution. Not only does this severe policy fail to stem the transmission of HIV between sex workers and clients, it further intensifies the problem by discouraging non-prostitutes from practising safe sex.

By contrast, in Laos, efforts to contain the spread of HIV/AIDS among sex workers are practical and creative. Careful attention to the social hierarchy led researchers to recognize the influential, almost maternal role that *mamasans* (female brothel-owners) played within

POPULATION HEALTH PERSPECTIVE An approach to health that focuses on social determinants of health, and societal, preventive strategies and societal responses to health problems.

PRIMARY PREVENTION Proactive steps taken to prevent a disease from occurring.

SICKO

Michael Moore's 2007 investigation of public health in America seeks to bring international attitudes toward health care access to American audiences.

the industry. By giving *mamasans* incentives to provide condoms and sex education to their 'staffs', higher rates of condom use soon resulted.

Finally, research points to the importance of information-sharing between governments and international bodies. For example, China has been criticized for trying to cover up the extent of the SARS epidemic in its southernmost regions during the early stages of the 2002–3 outbreak. Most epidemiologists would agree that early detection and response are crucial to the effective control of communicable diseases, so it is likely that this delay cost lives. How many lives were lost this way cannot be estimated.

Improving Health in the Developing World: Honouring Global Commitments

Improving global health will require co-ordinated reforms that address underlying social inequalities that complicate efforts to deliver health prevention, screening, and treatment programs (Hecht et al., 2009).

In 2000, the United Nations adopted the Millennium Development Goals, an unprecedented agreement between all 191 member nations and participating international agencies to co-ordinate efforts to wipe out poverty and improve global health by 2015. Three of the eight goals plainly address population health needs; the others address issues like poverty, development, and vulnerability to disease that affect population health. Together, they form the central objectives of the UN development agenda, for the first time addressing jointly the related issues of peace, security, fundamental freedoms, and human rights.

In the years since the Millennium Development Goals were stated, some targets have been met while others have been delayed. Achievements in some areas—better access to safe drinking water, lower child mortality rates, and global increases in girls' primary school enrolment—have been tempered by such setbacks as the continuing HIV/AIDS pandemic and higher rates of hunger in Southeast Asia and sub-Saharan Africa. More must be done to meet these goals. For example, five diseases—pneumonia, diarrhea, malaria, measles, and AIDS—account for over half of all deaths globally among children under five years old.

Many of these deaths can be prevented through inexpensive interventions, such as encouraging the breast-feeding of infants and increasing the availability of antibiotics, vaccines, and oral rehydration salts (UN, 2005). According to UNICEF's *State of the World's Children 2006* report, at the current rate of progress, meeting the target of reducing child mortality by two-thirds will not happen until 2045, 30 years beyond the agreed-on date for this goal's achievement. Because of the delay, 50 million children will not gain access to the food they need; 70 million, to cleaner water; and 170 million, to improved sanitation (UNICEF, 2005).

Meeting the Millennium Development Goals is slowed by a lack of funds. In 1970, the developed nations of the UN agreed to give 0.7 per cent of their respective gross domestic products (GDP) to development aid, a target set up by an international commission led by former Canadian Prime Minister Lester B. Pearson. Commitment to achieving this target was reaffirmed at UN summits in 1992 and 2002. By 2005, total development aid in dollars had reached an all-time high, but remained at a historic low as a percentage of the donor countries' combined GDP.

Only five nations—Denmark, Luxembourg, the Netherlands, Norway, and Sweden—have met or exceeded the 0.7 per cent mark; however, at least eight others have committed to doing so by 2015 (UN, 2005). The Canadian government, which currently gives about 0.26 per cent of its GDP to foreign aid, has pledged to increase this amount. So far, however, it has yet to commit to the goal of 0.7 per cent by 2015, arguing that doing so would be fiscally irresponsible.

Health research funding must also overcome biases. This is especially true of the so-called '90/10' research gap. This refers to the estimate that 90 per cent of global spending on medical and pharmaceutical research is aimed at finding treatments for diseases that affect only 10 per cent of the world's (wealthiest) population. As a result, much of the research on diseases in developing nations—malaria, tuberculosis, typhoid fever, etc.—is severely underfunded. Various humanitarian aid programs, many supported by private donors and corporations, have tried to correct this imbalance (ibid.).

Health-Care Reform in Canada

The debate over health-care reform in Canada is complex and often divisive. Its focus mainly is on access and the role for-profit health services can or should play in Canada's supposedly universal system (Contandriopoulos and Bilodeau, 2009).

Health-care access in underserviced areas, especially in northern Canada, is one critical area in need of improvement. Among the 47 recommendations in the final report of the 2002 Royal Commission on the Future of Health Care in Canada was a call for targeted funding to improve care for Canadians living in smaller communities in rural and remote areas (Romanow, 2002).

International medical graduates, who traditionally have provided health-care services in areas that have had trouble recruiting domestically trained medical school graduates, are one potential source of well-trained doctors. Efforts are underway to reduce the bureaucratic hurdles that immigrants face in getting a licence to practise medicine in Canada. Medical school initiatives, such as BC's Northern Medical Program (a partnership between the University of British Columbia and the University of Northern British Columbia) and the Northern Ontario School of Medicine, are another possible source.

Programs such as these are designed specifically to produce young doctors who are trained to deliver health-care services in northern, remote, and Aboriginal communities and in francophone communities in English-speaking Canada. According to Figure 9.5, high rates of pregnancy and childbirth are found in many remote, relatively poor communities of the North, and such high rates, as we learned earlier in this chapter, are often associated with maternal injury and death in the developing world. It is difficult to say whether the same holds true of Canada. According to experts Bartholomew and Liston (2006), 'in Canada this information is not well captured. This leads to under-ascertainment of maternal deaths due to unintentional injury, violence and mental illness.'

Telehealth—the use of computer and communication technologies to aid health-care delivery—is a growing industry that may revolutionize the medical profession's ability to service its patients. Specialists hundreds of kilometres away now routinely send out diagnostic

TELEHEALTH The use of computer and communication technologies to facilitate health-care delivery across geographic space.

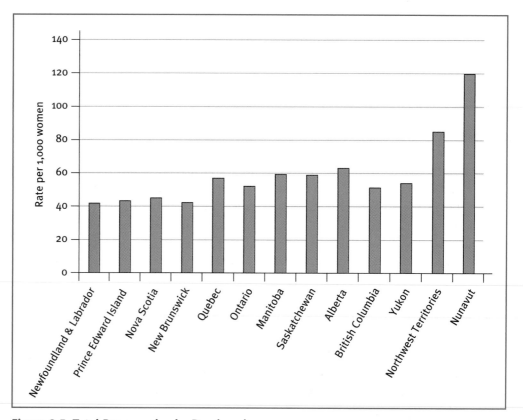

Figure 9.5 Total Pregnancies by Province in 2005

Source: **Based on Statistics Canada data at: www40.statcan.ca/l01/cst01/hlth64a-eng.htm.**

images, such as X-rays and MRI scans, and pathology images, such as diseased tissue and blood samples, electronically from rural or remote locations for review. Similarly, video-conferencing technology now allows medical consultations, mental health assessments, and observation of surgical procedures for educational purposes to take place over vast geographic distances (Sevean et al., 2009).

Further, automated voice response systems, electronic health records, emergency response monitoring devices, the Internet, telemedicine and telehomecare, and video-conferencing make it more convenient and more efficient to do anything from booking an appointment to researching a drug or illness. They have the potential to reduce doctor and hospital visits and to ensure that emergencies are dealt with quickly and accurately.

Waiting Times: How Long Is Too Long?

A major concern among health-care providers is 'waiting time'—especially since a federal court has determined the state is responsible to pay for treatment in another jurisdiction if doctors cannot provide timely treatment in the home province. This judgement, some say, may start the historic movement towards two-tiered health care in Canada (Siciliani and Verzulli, 2009).

The fact is, our society cannot afford to provide immediate, high-quality care to everyone who needs it. This fact of economic life, in a society preoccupied with efficiency and speed, irritates many of us and, in the end, will frustrate practically everyone at some time. We spend much of our lives waiting. To adjust, we have created social arrangements like waiting rooms, queue etiquette, and call waiting (Finamore and Turris, 2009).

The waiting issue has at least two parts, both worth exploring. First, what causes long waiting times? And second, what causes people to be upset about long waiting times? To answer the first question, long waiting times are caused by too many customers and too few servers, too slow service, or too slow allocation of customers to servers. This we would call the 'demography of waiting'. Viewed from another angle, we could call this the 'economics of waiting', and if we consider the issue of power and social inequality—the possibility that some people push to the front of the line—it becomes the 'politics of waiting'.

If we start from the assumption that there will never be enough money to erase waiting, we need to consider why people react to waiting as negatively as they do, and we need to devise ways to make the inevitable waiting more tolerable. Here, social science offers various suggestions. Research shows that people waiting for significant medical care are upset by pain, danger, fear of death, interrupted daily life, a sense of unfair treatment, confusion about outcomes, and so on. As well, many things shape people's willingness and capacity to 'be patient' while waiting. Of course, there is also a 'psychology of waiting'. Some people, given their personality, cannot endure waiting. Others are calmer, more docile, and more patient. As well, social comparison makes a difference: people feel better about waiting when they compare themselves to people who are worse off.

Typically, sick people become frightened if their condition worsens or their pains increase while they are waiting for treatment (Fitzsimons et al., 2003). The longer patients remain on a waiting list, compared to how long they expected to wait, the more anxiety and depression they experience (Vermeulen et al., 2005; Conner-Spady et al., 2005). That said, men and women react to waiting differently (Parry, 2004). Among patients waiting for coronary bypass surgery, for example, despite similar heart rates and blood pressure levels, men suffer much less anxiety during the wait than women do. And one interesting and counterintuitive finding is that waiting patients who are accompanied by someone else find the wait to be much *longer* than patients who come on their own (Barlow, 2002).

Most important, patients' reaction to waiting depends on the time they *expect* to wait. Among patients waiting for cataract surgery, for example, those who wait less than their maximum acceptable waiting time are retrospectively more satisfied with their wait than patients who waited more than their maximum acceptable waiting time (Conner-Spady et al., 2004). Patients are least satisfied when waiting times are longer than expected. Other things being equal, they are most satisfied when waiting times are shorter than expected.

Research finds repeatedly that the *perceived* waiting time has more impact than the actual waiting time on views of the wait and the assessed service quality Patients who receive information about the reasons for delay are significantly more satisfied with their wait because they feel better served (De Man et al., 2005).

Also, patients like to see a doctor early in the waiting. They want to make contact and receive some coping advice (Westbrook, 1995). Patients waiting for surgery respond best if

JOHN Q

In this 2002 picture, Denzel Washington plays a hysterical father who holds a hospital hostage in hopes of moving up his son's heart transplant.

they also have periodic follow-up appointments with their doctor and are continually told the length of the waiting line. This makes the waiting easier (Sarmento et al., 2005).

Cross-national research suggests that differences in *actual* waiting time may not matter much at all because *expectations* are what matter. After a heart attack, waiting times for coronary surgery or angioplasty are much longer and rates of surgical intervention much lower in Canada than the US. Yet, there is little difference in patients' satisfaction with the service received in these two countries (Mark et al., 1994).

Simple interventions can play an important part in easing the common anxieties people feel while waiting. Doctors can lessen the negative effects of long waiting times by spending more time with their patients, for example (Feddock et al., 2005). As well, patients who are kept busy in the waiting room are less likely to be dissatisfied (Dansky and Miles, 1997). Patients who are given instructional materials while they wait to see the doctor are more satisfied with their clinic experience than patients who receive nothing to occupy their minds (Oermann, 2003).

To repeat, what the research shows us, time and again, is that for most people, it is not the *actual* waiting time that matters; it is the *perceived* waiting time. And the perceived waiting time—whether the wait feels long or short—results from a comparison between the *actual* waiting time and the *expected* waiting time. It is at this point that rewards, distractions, and explanations become very important.

This suggests that health-care providers need to work on improving people's expectations as much as on their speedy treatment. This may mean developing a better social organization of waiting. Here, sociologists need to study ways to organize the process of waiting more effectively, to provide supportive 'waiting communities'. Clearly, waiting is easier when people are aware of their position in the queue, know how fast the queue is moving, and understand the reasons for delays. However, we do not know if communication with other people who are waiting or with past people in similar queues might be helpful.

Case management of waiting may solve the problem, for example, by giving every person in a queue a case manager to sympathetically answer questions, provide information, and connect with the relevant medical personnel. Court systems increasingly use such case managers to ensure that cases move smoothly from one stage to the next. These caseworkers may not supply personal counselling, but they do provide an ongoing review of the client.

Perhaps such a social arrangement would solve the waiting problem for people with prolonged or chronic medical problems as well. This would not speed up the illness or the cure, but for many—even most—it would speed up the perception of a cure. It would provide a sense of forward movement and a feeling that people are working to remove the barriers to health recovery. Humans would be there to rationalize, explain, and excuse the unavoidable obstacles, delays, and waiting periods. For most health conditions, such waiting would have no adverse effect on the patient's health.

Managing Costs: Is For-Profit Health Care the Answer?

Cutting across the various challenges facing Canada's health-care system is the debate over privatization. The typically heated and divisive nature of the debate is not surprising, since in survey after survey most Canadians cite universal health care as our most cherished social program and a source of national pride.

Note, however, that much of Canada's health-care system is already 'privatized'. Thirty per cent of health-care spending in Canada comes from private sources, through either out-of-pocket expenses or health insurance. Already, most physicians practising in Canada operate as private entrepreneurs, billing their provincial governments for services provided to the public. In addition, most hospitals in Canada are private institutions, although they are managed on a not-for-profit basis. In essence, the universal public health system is a health insurance program that uses public money to pay for privately delivered care (Currie and Stabile, 2003).

The Canada Health Act does not plainly ban private health insurance; it limits private health-care insurance to services not covered by the public insurance plan. By stating that all 'medically necessary' treatments by doctors and in hospitals must be delivered through the public system, Canadian health policy exercises a monopoly over health care in the country. Canada is the only OECD country that so staunchly divides health-care services into public and private spheres.

The debate over 'privatization' is therefore a debate over whether health care is a private commodity or a public good. The champions of privatization argue the various 'crises' of

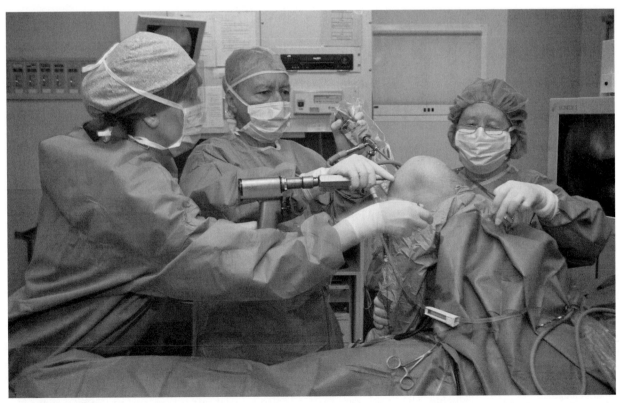

The Canadian Press/Bayne Stanley

A surgical team led by Dr Brian Day (centre) performs arthroscopic knee surgery at the Cambie Surgery Centre in Vancouver, BC. The Cambie Surgery Centre is a for-profit, private hospital that has often been discussed in the debate over privatization of health care in Canada.

cost and access plaguing the system can be eased by ending the state monopoly on health care in Canada. A for-profit health-care system governed by free-market principles, it is claimed, will inspire more efficient delivery models, provide more access and choices for treatment, and produce economic benefits through job creation. Supporters also argue that people who can afford more care choices should have the right to exercise them. Finally, proponents note that many industrialized countries, including Australia, France, and the Netherlands, run publicly funded health-care systems while allowing their citizens to upgrade their services through a privatized health insurance scheme.

On the other side, opponents of privatization argue that allowing for-profit medicine into the health-care regime would result in a two-tier system. The for-profit tier would provide better-quality services to the rich and the not-for-profit tier would suffer from decreased funding, burned-out health-care professionals, and poorer service overall. The quality of public health care in Canada would suffer from the gradual loss of health professionals and funding dollars to the private for-profit tier.

The international body of literature on for-profit versus not-for-profit medicine is plentiful, with each side of the debate able to cite empirical evidence to support its own arguments. The arguments for and against health-care privatization are too complex to be addressed in detail here. Interested students are encouraged to consult the vast literature (as a starting point, see the recommended readings at the end of this chapter).

CHAPTER SUMMARY

Throughout this text, we have stressed a population health approach to the study of social problems. One recurring theme has been: 'Does a given social condition negatively affect population health, and if so, does that make the social condition a *social problem*?'

The current chapter directly adopts a population health perspective that focuses on how social structural variables influence the physical, psychological, and social well-being of large groups of people.

We learned first that different groups view the ideas of health and illness differently, and that we must begin any evaluation of population health issues with a consideration of cultural values and beliefs. We also learned that some groups are more vulnerable to health threats than others, and these different levels of risk are usually stratified by economic and social inequalities.

At the same time, the health-care system, the purpose of which is to improve societal well-being, is troubled by serious defects that further threaten population health. Again, not all social groups feel the effects of these health-care inadequacies, if they even recognize that such inadequacies exist. Some problems—for example, the nationwide shortage of specialist doctors and nurses—will likely have effects for everyone; other structural inequalities—such as increasing opportunities to bypass hospital waiting lists or the ability to travel to the US or elsewhere for immediate treatment—ensure that the impact will be least disturbing for the social elite. The health-care system is also a social institution, and so it contains socializing processes, such as medicalization and **professionalization**. Finally, we explored some possible solutions to current health problems, both globally and locally.

PROFESSIONALIZATION
When used to refer to the medical industry, the gradual process whereby physicians established autonomous control over the institution of health care and elevated their collective status in society to become authoritative judges of disease definitions and gatekeepers of medical services.

QUESTIONS FOR CRITICAL THOUGHT

1. Do you think that modern medicine should incorporate varying cultural beliefs and traditional practices, associated with different socio-cultural groups, into the diagnosis and treatment process?

2. What are some of the factors that can cause mental illness? Describe the individualistic view of mental illness. What is the link between social class and mental illness? Describe the two theory types that have been used to describe this link.

3. According to Parsons, what are the rights and obligations of the sick role? Give a critique of the sick role concept.

4. Educational attainment has been found to have a positive impact on health. Discuss the factors that may contribute to the beneficial impact of education on health. Are there instances where higher education has a negative impact on health?

RECOMMENDED READINGS

Aneshensel, Carol S., and Clea A. Sucoff. 1996. 'The Neighborhood Context of Adolescent Mental Health', *Journal of Health and Social Behavior* 37: 293–310. This study investigates the effects of neighbourhood socio-economic status and segregation on the mental health of adolescents.

Bourgeault, Ivy. 2005. *Push! The Struggle for Midwifery in Ontario*. Montreal and Kingston: McGill-Queen's University Press. This book explains the history behind the integration of midwifery into the medical system in Ontario, and offers an account of current trends in education and provision of midwifery.

Durkheim, Émile. 1951 [1897]. *Suicide: A Study in Sociology*. New York: Free Press. This classic book offers a comprehensive case study of suicide by looking at the relationship between various sociological factors and rates of suicide.

Gillett, James. 2004. 'Gender Differences in Health: A Canadian Study of the Psychosocial, Structural and Behavioural Determinants of Health', *Social Sciences and Medicine* 58: 2585–2600. This article examines the causes of gender differences in health, considering both differential exposure and differential vulnerability factors in order to explain gender differences in health.

Hwang, Stephen W. 2001. 'Homelessness and Health', *Canadian Medical Association Journal* 164: 229–33. Homelessness is associated with a wide range of negative health consequences. This study sets out to describe some of the common health problems faced by homeless people, including issues related to the provision of health care.

Mirowsky, John, and Catherine E. Ross. 2003. *Social Causes of Psychological Distress*. New York: Aldine de Gruyter. This book describes the relationship between social problems and psychological distress. It explains how patterns of social inequality influence various health outcomes.

Noh, Samuel, and William R. Avison. 1996. 'Asian Immigrants and the Stress Process: A Study of Koreans in Canada', *Journal of Health and Social Behaviour* 37: 192–206. Using the stress process paradigm, this article examines the interplay between stress-inducing factors in the environment, social and psychological resources that affect the impact of environmental stressors, and psychological distress among a sample of Korean immigrants in Toronto.

Wilkinson, Richard G. 1994. 'The Epidemiological Transition: From Material Scarcity to Social Disadvantage?', *Daedalus* 123: 61–77. Wilkinson analyzes the relationship between the economic inequality and health.

RECOMMENDED WEBSITES

Public Health Agency of Canada

www.phac-aspc.gc.ca

The Public Health Agency of Canada provides information about health promotion, food safety, travel health, immunization, and emergency preparedness.

National Aboriginal Health Organization

www.naho.ca

NAHO is 'an Aboriginal-designed and -controlled body committed to influencing and advancing the health and well-being of Aboriginal Peoples by carrying out knowledge-based strategies.' The website contains statistical information, job postings, and other Aboriginal health information.

Health Canada

www.hc-sc.gc.ca

The Health Canada website contains links to health concerns currently in the news and offers a variety of ways for those interested to contribute to the promotion of health in Canada.

Ontario AIDS Network

www.ontarioaidsnetwork.on.ca

The Ontario AIDS Network offers services and information to those who need it. The website contains information about events and gives visitors the chance to help by offering a donation or signing up for volunteer opportunities.

CHAPTER 10

War and Terrorism

US Air Force photo by Tech. Sgt. Cohen A. Young/Released

LEARNING OBJECTIVES

- To define war.
- To be able to identify and understand various causes of war.
- To describe the potential social, economic, and health consequences of war.
- To briefly describe the evolution of warfare throughout history.
- To discuss the spread, and potential, of nuclear warfare.
- To describe the nature of war and terrorism in the twenty-first century.
- To describe how gender roles have shifted during times of war.
- To identify common strategies of war and to discuss common war crimes.
- To compare different theoretical approaches to war and terrorism.
- To discuss ways of reducing the frequency of war in the future.

INTRODUCTION

This chapter is about war and terrorism, conflict and combat, soldiers and civilians. At no point in recorded history has there been a complete absence of conflict between human groups. It seems as though when societies form, wars inevitably occur. Thus, warfare and violent conflict appear to be a human universal, at least to some degree.

Yet, Canada is an especially un-warlike nation. Compared with the US military, the Canadian Forces are few, little funded, and equipped with old aircraft, ships, vehicles, and weapons (Robinson and Ibbott, 2003). As most Canadians seem to lack the desire for war, it follows that the above assumption—the claim that the wish to wage war is a human universal—is fundamentally unreasonable. Canadians go to war only when they are pushed into it, usually by loyalty to a close ally like Britain, as occurred during both world wars.

We cannot understand warfare without understanding politics and statecraft since, as the early nineteenth-century Prussian military thinker Karl von Clausewitz (1993 [1833]) wrote, 'war is not merely a political act, but also a real political instrument, a continuation of political commerce, a carrying out the same by other means.' Just as some groups are more warlike than others, some periods of history have been more warlike than others. It is likely that sociological variables can be used to explain this variation. Though we may never find ways to erase war, we can hope to find ways to reduce war's frequency by using sociological analyses.

In this chapter, we will see that wars—including how they are explained and how they are fought—are largely the result of social construction. They often begin with the social construction of a sense of threat: the depiction of dangers and enemies waiting to overwhelm us. Depictions of the enemy follow, and are often intended to confuse us and dehumanize the enemy, making it easier for us to hate those in question (Meyer, 2009).

Changes in warfare have been examined by various sociological approaches, and different conclusions have been reached. War continues to have important social and health outcomes (Miller and Rasmussen, 2010). Though often good for the economy, war is bad for living things; with the pursuit of nuclear, chemical, and bacterial weapons, it is likely to get worse (Moore and Moore, 2009). Though social problems related to poverty and conflict may be improved by warfare in the short run, in the long run everyone suffers. To understand its resurgence, we need to understand war's roots in politics, ideology, and religion. Only then will we start to understand why people let their children go off by the hundreds of thousands to be killed in battle.

POLITICS, THE STATE, AND WARFARE

The Role of the State

The state is a set of public organizations that makes and enforces decisions binding every member of a society (Weber, 1946). It includes an elected government, civil service, courts, police, and military. At one extreme of political life, we find the authoritarian state—one that tries to fully dominate civil society and penetrate everyday life.

In Canada, the military has rarely played an important role in state decision-making. A society like Canada's, in which power is shared among competing political, bureaucratic, and economic elites, is likely to have difficulty mobilizing the will and the assets to wage war. We can see, then, that decentralized leadership is likely to be less warlike than centralized or, especially, dictatorial leadership. This political organization helps to explain why Canada engages in war less often than, say, the US, with its highly developed military–industrial complex.

Ideology and Religion

Another factor influencing politics and war is ideology. An **ideology** is a system of beliefs about how society is or should be organized. Ideologies are important for social change because they motivate and control people.

In the last few decades, organized religions and religious leaders have gained more power than they had in much of the twentieth century. This rebirth of religion as a political force testifies largely to the downfall of Communism, an ideology and political system that had tried to destroy organized religion, which Karl Marx had viewed as 'the opiate of the masses' (see Tucker, 1978). In many parts of the world today, fundamentalist religions are gaining power—Christian fundamentalism is politically important in the United States, Jewish fundamentalism in Israel, and Islamic fundamentalism in Pakistan, Iran and other Islamic states.

Here, too, Canada has been distinctive: there is no state religion and no official dedication to preserving religion or religiosity. Canada's formal commitment to multiculturalism makes a strong, unified religious or ideological belief almost impossible, although some observers today see the federal Conservative government as leaning dangerously towards a narrow Christian ideology (see McDonald, 2010).

World System Theory

Politics occurs between states as well as within them. One theory that examines the relations between states in a global system is **world system theory** (see Wallerstein, 1976, 2004). We cannot understand Canada's role in the world's 'war system' unless we understand Canada's role in the world economic system.

In this world system, industrial core states like the US and the UK—and, increasingly, China and India—take much of the raw materials and cheap labour they need from less developed peripheral states. Because they are financially and politically dominant, core states have the power to extract an economic surplus from the periphery. Investors from the core states effectively control the economies of peripheral states. As a result, profits made in the periphery drain out of the local economy and flow back to the core.

Core states frequently are accused of engaging in **imperialism**, the exercise of political and economic control by one state over the territory of another (Moore, 2009). Historically, imperialism has been carried out most often through military means. However, domination does not always require military conquest and colonization. In fact, under the right conditions, economic imperialism is far safer, less costly, and usually more stable than military or political imperialism (Petrosian and Fatkina, 2009).

IDEOLOGY A system of beliefs that explains how society is, or should be; any system of ideas underlying and informing political action. In a Marxist sense, ideological ideas justify and legitimate subordination of one group to another.

WORLD SYSTEM THEORY A conception of the modern social world that views it as comprising one interlinked entity with an international division of labour unregulated by any one political structure. Developed by Immanuel Wallerstein (e.g., 1976), this theory seeks to explain the uneven pace of development in the world by looking at the unequal relations between different countries.

IMPERIALISM The exercise of political and economic control by one state over the territory of another, often by military means. Developing countries are often the focus of imperialistic and exploitive activities that stifle their own development and concentrate their resources and labour for the profits of advanced capitalist countries.

With the increased imbalance in political affairs since 1989, military imperialism has once again resurfaced in Iraq and elsewhere. David Harvey (2005), in his book *The New Imperialism*, notes the diversity of different forms of imperialism and argues that the move towards a militarized neo-conservative imperialism in the United States, as demonstrated, for example, in the one-sided determination to invade Iraq, suggests weakness rather than strength in the US's quest to preserve its dominant position in the world.

Globalization Processes

Economic **globalization** as it exists today is a form of world social organization with six defining features. To understand the current state of global politics and war, we must recognize the following characteristics:

1. There is *global economic interdependence*. This means that most societies trade goods and services with one another. All people are buyers and sellers in a single world market.
2. A driving force for change is *scientific and technological innovation*. New methods for producing goods and services are continuously being developed.
3. The key actors in a global economy are *'built' or corporate entities*, especially multi-national corporations (like General Motors, IBM, Toyota, and Exxon). Individuals, small local firms, and even nationwide businesses lose in the competition for international markets.
4. *Cultures and polities are polycentric*—that is, they are found in and influenced by activities in many nations. More cultures today are dispersed, with centres of activity throughout the world.
5. A changing 'world culture' *homogenizes human ambitions*, narrowing the variety of aspirations and lifestyles. More people everywhere act like Americans; meanwhile, Europeans think and act more like the French, English, and Germans—the dominant actors in the European Union. Homogenization results from large numbers of people of different cultures being influenced by the world's most dominant cultures.
6. Most relevant to this discussion, *economic globalization forces nation-states to change*. With less influence over the culture and economy, governments have less influence over the people they rule. With these changes come political stresses and upheavals and the formation of new **social movements** and ideologies.

THE NATURE OF WAR AND TERRORISM
Definitions of War

Most people consider **war** to be an armed conflict between two countries or between groups within a country. However, many would expand the definition of war to include undeclared battles, guerrilla wars, covert operations, and even terrorism (Wright, 1964). Most countries have a war system in which units of their social institutions, such as economies and governments, and their cultural practices promote warfare as a normal aspect of life—even if no war is being waged at that particular moment (Cancian and Gibson, 1990).

GLOBALIZATION The integration on a world scale of economic activities and peoples by units of private capital and improved communications technology and transportation. In other words, globalization is the trend of increasing interdependence between the economies and societies of the world.

SOCIAL MOVEMENTS Broad social alliances of people who seek to effect or block an aspect of social change within a society. While they may be informally organized, they may in time form formal organizations such as political parties and labour unions. Examples of social movements include political movements, labour movements, the women's movement, environmental movements, and peace movements.

WAR Violent, usually armed conflict between states or people. This includes armed conflict, undeclared battles, civil conflicts, guerrilla wars, covert operations, and even terrorism. It is often argued that warfare is a culturally influenced phenomenon rather than simply biologically determined (instinctual aggressiveness). This would explain why some countries and cultures are more prone to warfare.

War is an institution of **collective violence**—organized group violence used to promote an agenda or to resist another violent group. Unlike **interpersonal violence**, which is episodic, unorganized, and impulsive, modern warfare relies on impersonal killing and advanced technology. Because of advances in military technology, modern weaponry used in combat is exponentially more deadly than ever before. A single precision-guided missile released by a B-52 bomber thousands of feet above a war zone can kill hundreds of enemy soldiers. The nuclear bombs dropped on Hiroshima and Nagasaki in the last days of World War II are estimated to have killed close to 200,000 people instantly. Total deaths for that war exceeded 62 million of which an estimated 50 per cent were civilians. No wonder, then, that the twentieth century was the bloodiest hundred years in the history of humanity.

Terrorism: The Common Man's War

Terrorism can be defined as:

> the calculated use of unexpected, shocking, and unlawful violence against non-combatants (including, besides civilians, off-duty military and security personnel in peaceful situations) and other symbolic targets perpetrated by a clandestine member(s) of a subnational group or a clandestine agent(s) for the psychological purpose of publicizing a political or religious cause and/or intimidating or coercing a government(s) or civilian population into accepting demands on behalf of the cause. (Hudson and Den Boer, 2002)

A dispassionate formal definition of the term is difficult because terrorism is an ideological and value-laden term, as well as a description of events. An even broader, simpler definition characterizes terrorism as any act by an individual or by a group that is intended to undermine the lawful authority of a government or state.

The roots of terrorism can be found in the religious, ethnic nationalist, political, economic, and social differences that prevent people from living together in peace. There is no evidence to suggest a single motive behind the use of terrorism, but the most accepted theory is that participants feel that, all things considered, violence is the best course of action. A rational cost-benefit analysis—not reckless impulse—leads them to this conclusion, often because of various frustrating or limiting social, political, and economic conditions.

Many of the suicide bombers in the Middle East have come from both oppressed and impoverished circumstances, and one factor in accepting suicide is the promise of large cash 'compensations' to their families by states, wealthy sympathizers, and various organizations. Hudson and Den Boer (2002) report that terrorists, and especially their leaders, are mainly men from middle- to upper-class backgrounds, typically with a higher than average education. They have specific skills and strong political motivation afforded to them by prestige that accompanies their educational background and social class position. Increasingly, terrorist organizations in the developing world recruit younger members. Often, the only role models these young people have to identify with are terrorists and guerrillas.

COLLECTIVE VIOLENCE Often organized by a group of individuals or a social movement, this type of violence is used to promote an agenda or to resist an oppressive other.

INTERPERSONAL VIOLENCE Violent interactions occurring between individuals, such as murder, rape, and domestic and child abuse.

CLASSIC WORKS

Box 10.1   Franz Fanon's *The Wretched of the Earth* (1961)

The book's title comes from the first line of 'The Interna-tionale', the official anthem of the international Commun-ist movement. In his introduction to the book, philosopher Jean-Paul Sartre asserts the book is a call to revolutionary violence. It is also a social-psychological analysis of the pathologies caused by colonial suffering. Fanon argues that by internalizing the views of the colonizers, the colonized develop a lack of self-respect and a sense of perpetual inferiority, ensuring their continued economic and political subordination. Promoting self-respect and creating a sense of identity, Fanon believes, is a crucial step towards freeing colonized people. Moreover, violence is a key ingredient in achieving this freedom.

To overcome the injustices of the past, and to equalize all races, a revolution is considered necessary to redress the colonial damage. Only by expelling colonial rulers and addressing the harm they did will the colonized be able to break free of their pathological ties to the colonizer. Vio-lence is important because it proves the oppressed are just as able to take action as the oppressors. Peaceful solutions fail to bring the self-respect necessary to 'cure' the natives and convince them of their own power and sovereignty. Vio-lence binds together the oppressed and engraves in them a national identity—a sense of common cause and collective history.

State-sponsored terrorism is the state-sanctioned use of terrorist groups to achieve for-eign policy objectives. In the eyes of the current US government, there are four countries on the 'terrorism list': Cuba, Iran, Sudan, and Syria (US Department of State, 2010). Notably, three of these are Middle Eastern or North African with mainly Muslim populations. Other governments and groups might compile different lists. In the eyes of some, the United States might also be viewed as a state that sponsors terrorism, with the aim of destabilizing foreign governments and undermining particular political movements.

The irony of state-sponsored terrorism is that while it can be a powerful form of clandes-tine warfare, it also can be vulnerable to shifts in the international political arena. On various occasions, developing world rebel groups, like various governments, have found themselves suddenly deprived of support from the foreign sponsors they had relied on. For example, Iraq's Saddam Hussein was enlisted by the United States as an ally against Iran, only to be villainized later (Ehud, 1991). Religious fundamentalists such as the Taliban and even Osama bin Laden received support from the United States and its allies to undermine the Russians after the Soviet Union invaded Afghanistan at the end of 1979, but they would be dropped and defamed later.

Violent Political Protest

As societies industrialize and become democratic, movements of political protest tend to become less violent. Political protest continues in many forms, varying in terms of dur-ation, reasons for initiation, scope of activities, degree of engagement in collective violence, motivations of the participants, and means for mobilization for action.

The Canadian Press/Peter Bregg/1970

A newsboy holds up a newspaper with a banner headline reporting the invoking of the War Measures Act on 16 October 1970, the first time Canada had invoked the act in peacetime. The act was put into effect following the kidnapping of British diplomat James Cross and Quebec Labour Minister Pierre Laporte by the terrorist FLQ.

In stable democracies, political protest is normally peaceful. Some protests become violent, but in countries like Canada, violent political protests are less common than in the past. In that respect, the violence of the Front de libération du Québec (FLQ)—most widely remembered in connection with the October Crisis of 1970—was uncharacteristic.

The FLQ was a national terrorist group that wanted to see Quebec separate completely from Canada and establish itself as an independent nation. The group's actions first became violent during the 1960s, when they began bombing national symbols, such as mailboxes, resulting in injuries to police officers. Throughout the decade, as the frustration of radical Québécois nationalists seemed to grow, the bombings became more violent and sophisticated. In October 1970, members of the FLQ kidnapped visiting British trade official James Cross and provincial labour minister Pierre Laporte. Those responsible for the kidnapping threatened to murder both Cross and Laporte unless their demands were met by the federal government, then under the leadership of Prime Minister Pierre Trudeau. These demands included a public broadcasting of an FLQ communiqué expressing their political belief that English-Canadian culture and American imperialism were overtaking Quebec culture. Trudeau and the federal government responded by imposing the War Measures Act, which allowed for the indefinite suspension of civil liberties. Laporte's body was eventually found in the trunk of a car, and shortly thereafter the crisis was resolved through having Cross safely released in exchange for allowing a safe exile to Cuba for his kidnappers. Those implicated in the killing of Laporte were tried and convicted for their crimes (*Maclean's*, 1990).

Where protests arise, many worry that lines between criminal activities and political protest will be blurred by efforts to maintain order. In industrialized societies, non-violent tactics have been used to reduce the likelihood of protests. Even urban planning plays a part in this process, by replacing public space (such as a sidewalk or a public square) with 'carceral' spaces—architecture that is more secure and easier to defend against attack.

Though some movements of protest are spontaneous, brief, and disorganized, most are planned, continuing, and rooted in both formal and informal networks of social contact. The most developed form of social protest is exemplified by a revolution.

Revolution

CHE

Steven Soderbergh's 2008 two-part biopic about Che Guevera shows the development of Che from anonymous Argentine doctor to revolutionary icon.

Zimmermann (1983: 298) defined revolution as 'the successful overthrow of the prevailing elite by a new elite who, after having taken over power, fundamentally change the social structure and therewith also the structure of authority.'

Revolutions are important events for individual countries and for the politics of the world as a whole. Although they are events of immense political and moral contradiction and occasions for celebrating the heroic and the idealistic, revolutions rarely achieve their original goals. Whatever their goals and ideals, revolutions usually substitute one form of restrictive power for another. They rarely replace despotism with a secure democracy, and often they replace one form of despotism with another. Nevertheless, revolutions—even if they do not achieve their intended goals—affect other countries and the world as a whole, as can be seen from considering the French Revolution, the Russian Revolution, the Chinese Revolution, the Cuban Revolution, and many other smaller-scale revolutions.

In analyzing the revolutions in France, Russia, and China, Skocpol (1979) notes that revolutionary crises developed in those countries when the old aristocratic regimes failed to meet emerging challenges. Skocpol defines pre-revolutionary France, Russia, and China as 'fully established imperial states'. Since these states were not fully bureaucratic or parliamentary, however, they could not offer representatives from the dominant class an opportunity to take part in political decision-making.

As a result, the landed class developed a capacity for 'self-conscious collective organization'. It was in a position to 'obstruct monarchical undertakings that ran counter to their economic interests' (ibid.). Their obstructions had the unintended consequence of destroying the military and administrative integrity of the imperial state. In effect, the landed aristocracy undermined its own traditional position in the society.

Historical research by Barrington Moore (1967) shows that the outcome of a revolution depends, largely, on which social classes attack the ruler. When the attackers are primarily peasants, as in China, Vietnam, and Cuba, the result is a Communist regime that introduces land reform and social equality. When the revolutionaries are independent farmers, craftsmen, and other 'middle-class people' the result is likely to be parliamentary democracy, as in England, France, and the United States. However, when the attackers are primarily military—supported by a coalition of the landed aristocracy, Church, and large business interests—the result is Fascism, as in Germany, Italy, and Spain.

Rebellion

Rebellion is armed opposition by a portion of the citizenry to an established government or other authority. The difference between a *rebellion* and a *revolution* lies in the outcome. If the rebellion succeeds in overthrowing the government and making significant social and political changes, then it is considered a revolution.

The rebellions of 1837 in Upper and Lower Canada did not overthrow the government and few changes were the result. Everyone who engages in rebellion against a government is liable to the criminal penalties of treason established by that government. If a rebellion becomes widespread, involving a considerable proportion of the country, and the rebels receive the recognition of foreign nations, the government in charge treats captured rebels merely as belligerents. If the rebellion succeeds and the rebels form a new government, the rebels are no longer criminals: they are considered heroes and rulers (Coates, 1997).

Revolutions and rebellions are crimes against the government of the day and whether history views the rebels as heroes or villains usually depends on whether they succeed. Winners typically rewrite the history books to show themselves as heroes conforming to a higher standard of moral conduct. Where rebellion is attached to a group that persists in the society, as was the case with the 1869–70 and 1885 Métis rebellions in western Canada led by Louis Riel, opinion may be divided: Riel was condemned and executed as a traitor by Canada following the 1885 rebellion and today is little known by most Canadians, yet the first rebellion was instrumental in the creation of the province of Manitoba and he continues to be celebrated by Native people and by francophones as a hero and martyr. William Lyon Mackenzie, leader of the unsuccessful 1837 rebellion in Upper Canada, is not forgotten because his rebellion paved the way for responsible government in Canada and, eventually, independence.

War Crimes

Having atrocities committed during war defined as 'war crimes' may seem strange, considering that the fundamental ambition of combat is to kill your enemies, and the barbarous way warriors typically carry out much of the killing. However, many nations hold the view that slaughtering soldiers is an acceptable cost of war while the intentional slaughter of civilians is an indefensible horror. These distinctions are socially and politically, if not morally, meaningful.

Acts of political violence—including war crimes—differ from other kinds of violence in that representatives of one political or national group inflict such violence to perpetuate or change the relative political status of another political or national group or to prevent that group from achieving the changes its members want (Kanaaneh and Netland, 1992). Rationalizations are commonly devised to 'explain away' the extent of violence, its effects, or its lack of fairness.

These rationalizations begin by distinguishing between 'us' and 'them'. A group defined as outsiders or strangers is more easily defamed and attacked—more easily viewed as a means to an end, or fully expendable. The most horrific manifestation of this is **genocide**, the systematic execution of an entire national, ethnic, racial, or political group. The most notorious case of genocide was the attempted extermination of the Jews and Roma (gypsies) by Nazi Germany during World War II. Many others—including Slavs, homosexuals, and mentally impaired people—were also murdered. In all, six million Jews were killed, many in concentration camps like Auschwitz, where an estimated one million died.

Though many vowed after 1945 that such an atrocity should never be allowed to happen again, genocides continue to occur—in the former Yugoslavia and in Rwanda, to name the most notorious recent cases. However, the world now has procedures for dealing with genocidal war criminals.

Issues involving the prosecution of war crimes fall into at least four categories: (1) assigning responsibility for criminal acts; (2) trying and punishing the criminals; (3) bringing about national reconciliation; and (4) ensuring that a nation remembers its criminal past and learns from it. The International Criminal Court (ICC), which Canada was instrumental in establishing and which opened on 1 July 2002, set up a permanent, international court to prosecute war crimes and crimes against humanity. Some countries, however, most notably the United States, have refused to be participants in this international forum for justice because they do not want to cede any of their own jurisdictional control and because they claim their own soldiers (or leaders) might be apprehended and tried unfairly.

On the whole, the calls for international war crime tribunals, which are established on an ad hoc basis in contrast to the permanency of the ICC, are sporadic because of tensions between selfishness and idealism within liberal states. Also, the war crimes tribunals are physically unable to process thousands of trials. Nevertheless, these tribunals represent a superior alternative to acts of vengeance by aggrieved parties. Right actions following wrongdoing, such as changing institutions, reparations, or giving apologies, may help to bring about healing and peace (Bass, 2002).

Reparations and apologies are grand principles. On the ground, it may be more difficult to reorganize people's lives after a genocidal episode. Babic (2002) studied 180 war migrants, including returnee Croats, returnee Serbs, and refugee-immigrants in one county in Croatia. He found the coexistence of the hostile Croats and Serbs remains a problem, both for groups of war migrants in local communities and for the state of Croatia. The returnees are burdened with memories of the conflict, human and material losses, and issues of unforgiveness and compromise. Ironically, all three groups confirm that, *before* the war, they each valued peaceful coexistence. The groups today differ in who they think is responsible for the war.

GENOCIDE The deliberate, systematic, and planned killing of an entire national, ethnic, racial, or political group.

Rape as a Weapon of War

Despite prohibitions outlined in the Geneva Conventions, rape, assault, and enforced prostitution of women have all continued during armed conflicts. For example, in the years of World War II, the Japanese military forced up to 200,000 young women into prostitution as 'comfort women' for military personnel, with many eventually dying of sexually transmitted diseases and from torture. During the conflicts in Bosnia-Herzegovina and Rwanda, and in most other hostile actions as well, roving bands of soldiers raped, beat, and killed women (Amnesty International, 1995).

Buchanan (2002) specifically notes the problem of 'gendercide'—genocidal acts committed against women as women and men as men—as human rights violations. Gendercide against women typically involves rape, which has come to be recognized as a war crime. Against men, such crimes involve the selective separation of young civilian men 'of military age' (that is, 18–45 years) from old men, children, and women of all ages for punishment, torture, and execution.

The Canadian Press/Sean Kilpatrick

Honorine Kabuo, left, bids farewell to Governor General Michaelle Jean following her visit to Goma, Democratic Republic of the Congo, Africa, on 20 April 2010. Kabuo was raped in 2001 by a gang of militant rebels. She was slashed in the neck and had her pregnant stomach cut open and lives to tell of her now eight-year-old daughter she named Victory for her survival.

Formerly, many believed that rape was an unintended consequence of invasion by foreign soldiers—as occurred in Berlin in 1945, when Soviet soldiers overran the defeated city. For centuries, warriors have considered captive women to be part of the booty of warfare. However, today many believe that a systematic campaign of rape against civilian women is designed to humiliate and break the resolve of an enemy nation, and in some African conflicts it has been used intentionally to spread HIV. It also destroys families by turning husbands, fathers, and brothers against the young women—wives and daughters—who have been victimized.

Finally, when rape results in pregnancy, it changes the ethnic composition of a conquered society—a further source of humiliation and conflict that will continue for at least a generation. In some countries, such as Korea, which over the years has been occupied by Mongolian, Chinese, Japanese, and American troops, mixed-ethnic children have been shunned and socially isolated (Greenfeld, 2006).

International feminist activists and women's organizations have played an important role in prosecutions of war crimes committed against women, especially rapes and sexual enslavement (Cooper, 2002). Feminists successfully pressured the UN to label crimes against women as prosecutable human rights abuses and to include female prosecutors and judges in tribunals. Indeed, Louise Arbour, who became a Supreme Court of Canada justice and later served as the UN High Commissioner for Human Rights, was Chief Prosecutor of War Crimes at the International Criminal Tribunal for Rwanda and the former Yugoslavia in The Hague from 1996 to 1999 and indicted Slobodan Milosevic, the former Yugoslavian president, among others, for war crimes. In 2001, the ICTY convicted three Bosnian Serb men for their role in the mass rape of Muslim women in the city of Focal during the conflict in Bosnia-Herzegovina.

Environmental Destruction

The wilful destruction of the environment as a strategy of war, as practice for war, or as punishment for the defeated occurred at least as early as Roman times and persists in modern-day society. Roman armies routinely destroyed crops and salted the earth to ruin the land's fertility. A millennium later, the Russians burned their own crops and homes not once but twice, to prevent the invading armies of Napoleon and, later, Hitler from making use of them. In a different but no less destructive behaviour, Allied navies during World War II routinely used the whales of the North Atlantic for target practice (Mowat, 1984).

When the Allied forces pushed the Iraqi forces out of Kuwait in 1991, the Iraqis set fire to 732 of the country's roughly 900 oil wells, producing one of the worst environmental disasters in history. Black smoke from the fires blocked out the sun and produced record low temperatures along a 950-kilometre tract of land. Rescue efforts recovered over 22 million barrels of oil, but more is thought to have leaked from the destroyed oil fields into the local environment, contaminating soil and water supplies. Saddam Hussein also ordered the release of an estimated 11 million barrels of oil into the Arabian Gulf, damaging local marine life.

Military operations also harm the environment during peacetime. According to Martin Calhoun, the US military is the largest producer of dangerous materials in the country, and 'decades of improper and unsafe handling, storage and disposal of hazardous materials while building and maintaining the world's most powerful fighting force have severely polluted America's air, water and soil' (Calhoun, 1996: 60). Disposal is a major problem, and the drafters of disarmament treaties often have trouble suggesting a safe place for disposal of missiles, mines, bombs, and nuclear warheads.

Modern warfare and the innovative war technologies of the twenty-first century have given rise to nanopollution. The impact and health risks of nanopollutants, such as dust at the nanoscale, have become a concern for researchers. These microscopic particles can enter the bloodstream of humans and disseminate throughout the body, developing new diseases with unusual symptoms and other yet-to-be-studied health problems (Gatti and Montanari, 2008).

THEORETICAL PERSPECTIVES ON WAR AND TERRORISM

Table 10.1 Theoretical Perspectives

Theory	Main Points
Structural Functionalism	• All elements in society are interrelated. • War and terrorism reinforce group identity and increase social cohesion as well as conformity. • Increased employment and production of weapons lead to economic benefit.
Conflict Theory	• Conflict and change are basic features of social life. • War and terrorism reflect struggles between opposite groups over power, limited resources, or ideological domination. • Only some groups benefit, namely corporations, politicians, intermediaries, and black marketers.
Symbolic Interactionism	• Socialization and labelling shape attitudes and the roles people adopt towards war efforts and conflicts. • In times of war, leaders use propaganda and euphemistic language to legitimize combat and to reduce the rational and emotional impact of *death*.
Feminist Theory	• In Western culture, primarily men have fought in wars. • War is seen as misguided protective chivalry or paternalistic sexism toward the 'lesser' sex. • Consequences of war: women are raped, forced into prostitution.
Social Constructionism	• Propaganda legitimizes war and reduces the rational and emotional impact of death. • Political parties deflect criticism by focusing national attention on real or imagined enemies, on the valour of the nation's fighting forces, and on the 'good' they are doing the country that has been invaded. • People mobilize to form social movements and to influence public policy.

Structural Functionalism

As we have said repeatedly, structural functionalists believe that most elements in society exist to serve some purpose. Conflict and violence are the results of a system malfunctioning—for example, some system needs for integration and consensus not being met. From this standpoint, wars may occur because groups or societies do not know how to resolve their conflicts peacefully. They lack shared values or institutions for lawfully resolving disagreement. They lack the leadership and assets to bring peace. By this reckoning, war results from the breakdown of peace. Wars may even arise because military institutions and activities hold great importance within the society and culture.

A large-scale conflict increases social cohesion and group identity. Internal squabbles between political parties, ethnic communities, special interest groups, and so on are put aside, at least temporarily, as the entire nation bands together in a show of patriotism to defeat a common enemy (Thomas et al., 2009). Only when this common enemy is no longer a threat to national well-being do the internal conflicts resume. Sometimes the solidarity between allies created through the defence of shared interests lasts for a while even after the war is over.

Conflict Theory

Conflict theorists state that wars are struggles between opposing groups over power, limited assets, or ideological domination taken to their logical, violent conclusions. Just as social classes may battle one another for economic positions within a society, so nation-states and interest groups within the society may go to war with one another. The difference is that they routinely use weapons and kill one another.

Conflict theory stresses the ways in which war benefits some groups—most notably, corporations, politicians, and the military—but not others. The 'military–industrial complex', a term first introduced in warning by US President Dwight D. Eisenhower in 1961 as he left office, refers to the close relationship between the military and the private defence industry and their combined control of the political agenda. The sociological and structural underpinnings of this combination of power were earlier analyzed by C. Wright Mills in his classic work, *The Power Elite* (1956). In Canada, for example, the former Conservative Minister of National Defence, Gordon O'Connor, was a career officer in the Canadian military, retiring as brigadier general, and then worked as a defence industry lobbyist for several major military suppliers until he entered politics in 2004.

In the US, several leading figures in the Bush administration, notably former Vice-President Dick Cheney and Defence Secretary Donald Rumsfeld, had previously been involved with companies that profit from war. Corporations contracted by the Pentagon to design, develop, and make weapons are guaranteed profits even if they overrun their budgets. It is sensible, therefore, for these companies to ensure that global conflicts and threats to national security continue so they can run the profitable war machine. Industrialists, politicians, brokers, and black-marketers, among others, make enormous fortunes from war and weapons of war. This has an important effect on the class structure of society.

According to one estimate, governments throughout the world were collectively spending $1 trillion per year, or roughly $2 million (US) per minute, to finance various military efforts by the end of the 1980s (Brown et al., 1992). These costs included the salaries of military personnel, research into and development of weapons and combat technology, the purchase and manufacture of artillery and wartime machinery, and veterans' benefits. Of course, this also means that $1 trillion was *not* being spent globally on health care, education, infrastructure, or social services.

Figure 10.1 maps the global distribution of spending on military troops and technologies. Almost half of the total spending is by the US government. However, remarkable sums are spent even by impoverished African and Central and South American states.

One might expect indicators of peacemaking to vary inversely with indicators of war-making, such that countries that spent a lot of money on the military would rank low on a peace index. However, this is only partly true. For example, African countries rank relatively low on military spending, in comparison with other countries (though they may rank much higher in their per capita spending as a fraction of GNP); and they also rank very low on the Global Peace Index. And, at the other end, the US ranks very high on military spending but also ranks medium high on the Global Peace Index (Figure 10.2). The Global Peace Index—developed by the Institute for Economics and Peace— measures the relative position of a nation's 'peacefulness'. The Peace Index is composed of 23 separate indicators, including perceived criminality in society, jailed population, political instability, and weapons exports,

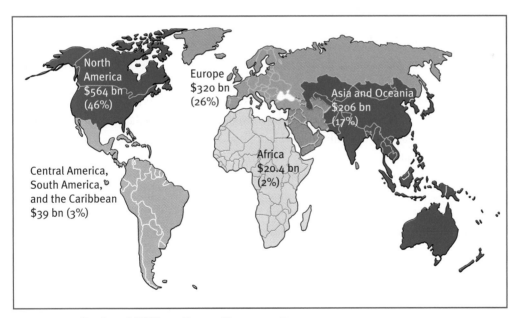

Figure 10.1 Regional Military Expenditure, 2008

Though more countries have increased their military spending, it is generally concentrated in North America, Europe, and, increasingly, Asia, as shown in the above representation of military spending by continent.

Source: Global Issues, © Copyright 1998–2009, under a Creative Commons License & SIPRI.

Figure 10.2 The Global Peace Index, 2009

The Global Peace Index attempts to rank nations on various indicators of peace. The top-ranking nations on the Global Peace Index in 2009 were New Zealand, Denmark, Norway, Iceland, Austria, Sweden, Japan, Canada, Finland, and Slovenia.

Source: **The Global Peace Index, 2009, Courtesy Vision of Humanity.**

to name a few. Countries are given a score based on these indicators that range from 1 being the most peaceful to 5 being the least peaceful (Vision of Humanity, 2009).

Note also that the countries that rank highest on the Peace Index—among them, New Zealand, Denmark, Norway, Iceland, Austria, Sweden, Japan, Canada, and Finland—spend very little (per capita) on the military and score highly on other measures of social development and quality of life.

Among NATO countries—and bearing in mind that this is a military alliance—Canada spent only 1.2 per cent of its GDP on military expenditures in 2005, compared to the US at 3.9 per cent, France at 2.6 per cent, and the UK at 2.3 per cent (Table 10.2). A fuller table would show comparably low spending figures for the other nations rated high on the Peace Index.

Symbolic Interactionism

Symbolic interactionists examine the ways in which cultures socialize people to adopt certain attitudes towards war and conflict. Adult members of society encourage aggression and the resolution of conflicts through physical force as early as childhood, mostly in boys.

Symbolic interactionists also study the language and labels of war. Thus, propaganda techniques are employed by the government, businesses (for example, munitions manufacturers),

Table 10.2	Defence Expenditures of Selected NATO Countries, 2005, Based on Current Prices and Exchange Rates (US$ millions)		
Ranking	NATO Member Country	Expenditures ($ millions)	% GDP
1.	United States	462,099	3.9
2,	France	51,877	2.6
3.	United Kingdom	48,918	2.3
4.	Germany	37,920	1.4
5.	Italy	30,642	1.8
6.	Spain	12,632	1.3
7.	Canada	11,601	1.2
8.	Turkey	10,207	3.5
9.	Netherlands	9,640	1.7
10.	Greece	5,887	2.9

Source: **NATO–Russia Compendium of Financial and Economic Data Relating to Defence (2005), at: www.ipb.org/ Canada's%20Alarming%20Rise%20in%20Military%20Spending.pdf.**

the military, and 'patriotic organizations' (such as veterans' groups) to describe the current global 'war on terror' as a 'justified war' against 'evil' terrorism.

In particular, the media play an important role in the spin-doctoring of this message. In times of war, leaders use a special language to legitimize combat and reduce the rational and emotional impact of the deaths that will follow. Soldiers on both sides are not 'murder victims', they are 'casualties'. A missile does not blow up an enemy barracks, it 'services the target'. The unplanned but 'unavoidable' killing of innocent civilians is reported in official documents as 'collateral damage'. Nuclear missiles are not weapons of mass destruction, they are 'peacekeepers'.

Feminist Theory

Masculinity and militarism have had a close relationship over time and across cultures, and the 'meanings attached to masculinity are so firmly linked to compliance with military roles that it is often impossible to disentangle the two' (Enloe, 1987: 531). The association between masculinity and militarism begins in childhood socialization. For instance, in Western culture, boys wage make-believe wars with GI Joe figurines, while girls are much more likely to play with dolls and act out domestic routines such as baking and child-rearing. Children whose parents deliberately raise them in pacifist traditions may have difficulty enacting those values among their schoolmates.

With only a few exceptions through the history of Western culture, it has been mainly men who have fought wars. This is due in part to women's smaller physical stature, to the nature of warfare (which traditionally has involved much face-to-face, close range, physical combat), and to men's greater tendency towards aggression and violence. Some say that a protective chivalry or paternalistic sexism towards the 'lesser sex' is involved in men's largely exclusive role in warfare; men try to protect women, they argue.

Some authors argue that the perception of the role of women in war is limited, extending only to women's strategies of survival, resistance, and efforts to protest war and counter its effects. Feminist studies contest the claim for a natural link between women and peace (Blanchard, 2003) and argue that the participation and support of women in war-making, as well as their involvement in shaping the agenda of war, simply have been neglected. Understanding the gender dynamics of war requires a focus on women's contributions in reshaping the discourse of the war and using it for political gains.

Major wars have also allowed women greater entry into the workforce, both as soldiers and as civilians, to replace the men recruited for war. During World War II, this meant opening new job opportunities for women, who until then had been limited to a narrow range of traditionally female jobs. They later found opportunities working in 'essential' industries such as engineering, metals, chemicals, vehicles, transport, energy, and shipbuilding (Summerfield, 2000).

Today, women—a large fraction of the paid workforce—are still only a small minority of all military personnel. The data in Table 10.3 show that women represent about 2 per cent of Canada's regular military forces, though they are much more numerous in the reserves. Compare this with Israel, which has made a conscious effort to treat men and women equally in this respect:

Table 10.3   Canadian Forces Personnel Serving in Combat Arms, 31 March 2006

Category	Total	Male	Female	% Female
Regular Force combat arms	12,054	11,829	225	1.9
Regular Force officers	2,640	2,541	99	3.75
Regular Force non-commissioned members	9,414	9,288	126	1.34
Primary Reserve combat arms	13,897	12,972	925	6.7
Primary Reserve officers	1,909	1,832	77	4.0
Primary Reserve non-commissioned members	11,988	11,140	848	7.1

Source: **CBC News (2006).**

Most Israeli citizens are required to serve in the Israel Defense Forces (IDF) for a period of between two and three years. Israel is unique in that military service is compulsory for both males and females. It is the only country in the world that maintains obligatory military service for women. But the IDF grants general exemptions from compulsory service to various segments of the population, including Israeli Arabs, students engaged in religious studies in an accredited Jewish Law institution, women who are married, are pregnant or who have children, and women who declare that they lead a religiously observant life and who choose to pursue 'national service'—community work. All eligible men and women are drafted at age 18. Men serve for three years, women for 21 months. (GlobalSecurity.org, n.d.)

Social Constructionism

This approach stresses the role of moral entrepreneurs in mobilizing support for social causes—for waging wars, for example.

To illustrate, false propaganda and misinformation produced by the US administration were used to gain support from American citizens for the 2003 invasion of Iraq. The so-called facts used to justify this unilateral pre-emptive war—such as the presence of weapons of mass destruction and the claimed co-operation between Osama bin Laden and Saddam Hussein—have since been exposed as deceptions and red herrings. Remarkably, however, once such a war has begun, public awareness of politically motivated lies—to the extent the public is even aware of the deception or believes it to be true—changes nothing when the propaganda machine continues to proclaim the necessity of war to secure the 'homeland' against 'evildoers'.

Propaganda also supports the vilification of certain groups during wartime. Consider the effects of Canada's War Measures Act on Canadian race relations (and vice versa). The War Measures Act was originally legislated in 1914 as a response to anxieties connected with World War I. This legislation was used during both world wars and, in particular, was further used to justify the unjust treatment of Japanese Canadians during and after World War II. Using this Act, the Canadian government uprooted Japanese Canadians from their homes, placed them in internment camps, and had their properties confiscated; some were even deported (Kage, 2002). The war and the War Measures Act helped to justify derogatory and racially hostile views that already existed. In short, it made racism acceptable in Canada (Dhamoon and Abu-Laban, 2009). Also, it blamed the Japanese Canadians for racially hostile sentiments that they had played no part in creating (Clement, 2008).

The social constructionist paradigm also considers the role of the media in the vilifying and victimizing war participants. Take, for instance, the coverage of the Israeli–Palestinian conflict by the Israeli press. Despite human losses on both sides—indeed, much greater losses of both life and the means of living for Palestinians—claims-making in the media has resulted in one-sided victimization of the Israelis in the Israeli press. Reporters engage in the dramatization of injury by stressing the severity of the Palestinian terrorist attacks and

THE FOG OF WAR

Documentarian Errol Morris's 2003 film explores the use of rhetoric and propaganda in America's military forays into Communist Vietnam.

in the dramatization of innocence by focusing on the undeserved fate of the Israeli victims (Cromer, 2005).

SOCIAL CONSEQUENCES OF WAR

The two most socially consequential facts about war are: (1) it kills many people, and (2) it is expensive. The rise in both casualty rates and military expenditures in modern warfare is partly due to the larger scale of conflict and partly due to the advanced technology used in waging war. Additionally, warfare shatters morale and the fabric of civic society and has lasting negative impacts on the health of populations.

Effects on the Economy

Wars sometimes bring economic benefits. For example, Canadian participation in World War II led to increased employment and production, helping to end the financial downturn of the Great Depression. After the war, North America, which did not experience the degree of devastation of many European and some Asian countries, rode the financial momentum throughout the next several decades, experiencing prosperity and growth in all parts of society.

Canadians, the strongest trading partner of the United States, also enjoyed a financial boom during and after the war: the gross national product (GNP) doubled, industry developed exponentially, and consumer spending rose with the baby boom generation (Girvan, 2000). The defeated, including Germany and Japan, suffered significant setbacks to their economies for many years after the conflict ended.

Wars lead to scientific and technological innovations that may benefit society in peacetime. Military research on laser-based defence made it easier to develop laser surgery; experimentation with nuclear weaponry allowed for the widespread development of nuclear power stations; the airline industry's technological innovations were made possible largely through the work of military defence departments; and the Internet grew out of research sponsored by the US military as a possible emergency communications network in case of nuclear war.

In this sense, innovations in weaponry are social innovations as well as engineering feats. At the same time, many technological advances have what may be called a dual-use status, that is, any technological advance has both benefits and risks associated with it. Though the Internet emerged from research sponsored by the US military, it has become a threat with the rise of cyberterrorism.

According to Weimann (2005), there is a rise in anxiety about cyberterrorism in American society due to the combination of two modern fears: the fear of arbitrary, violent targeting and the distrust of computer technology that could lead to catastrophic attacks against computer networks. Further examples relate to new advances in applications meant for hazard detection, prevention, and response to terrorist attacks.

On top of their intended benefits, these same advances can have unintended consequences and contribute to terrorist motives. For instance, differential access to these technologies could work to increase stresses in already divisive societies by, for example, widening a digital divide (LePoire and Glenn, 2007).

Effects on Children

Increasingly, wars are being waged with the help of child soldiers. Though the United Nations Convention on the Rights of the Child states that children under the age of 15 are not to be used as soldiers, children are still being used as soldiers. The *Child Soldiers Global Report*

PERSONAL STORIES

Box 10.2 Memoirs of a Boy Soldier

We must have been walking for days, I do not really remember, when suddenly two men put us at gunpoint and motioned, with their guns, for us to come closer. We walked in between two rows of men carrying machine guns, AK-47s, G3s, and RPGs. Their faces were dark, as if they had bathed them in charcoal, and they stared intensely at us with their extremely red eyes. When we got to the back of the line, there were four men lying on the ground, their uniforms soaked with blood. One of them lay on his stomach, and his eyes were wide open and still; his insides were spilling onto the ground. I turned away, and my eyes caught the bashed head of another man. Something inside his brain was still pulsating and he was breathing. I felt nauseated. . . . One of the soldiers was looking at me, chewing something and smiling . . . 'You will get used to it, everybody does eventually', he said. . . .

After the late breakfast, we lined up facing the corporal, who handed us AK-47s. When it was my turn, he looked at me intensely, as if he was trying to tell me that he was giving me something worth cherishing. . . . Still looking straight at me, he reached into a wooden crate and pulled out the gun. He took out the magazine and handed me the AK with two hands. I hesitated for a bit, but he pushed the gun against my chest. With trembling hands I took the gun, saluted him, and ran to the back of the line, still holding the gun but afraid to look at it. I had never held a gun that long before and it frightened me. . . .

We continued the training exercises we had been doing earlier in the morning, but this time we carried with us AK-47s that didn't contain any ammunition. We crawled with the guns on our backs, in our hands, and ran around the building with them. . . . We broke for a minute lunch and began a different drill. We were taken to a nearby banana farm, where we practiced stabbing the banana trees with bayonets. 'Visualize the banana tree as the enemy, the rebels who killed your parents, your family, and those who are responsible for everything that has happened to you', the corporal screamed. 'This is how I would do it.' He took out his bayonet and started shouting and stabbing the banana tree. 'I first stab him in the stomach, then the neck, then his heart, and I will cut it out, show it to him, and then pluck his eyes out. Remember, he probably killed your parents worse. Continue' . . . . When he said this, we all got angry and drove our knives in and out of the banana trees until they fell to the ground. 'Good', he said, nodding and pondering something that made him smile longer than usual. Over and over in our training he would say that same sentence: 'Visualize the banana tree as the enemy, the rebels who killed your parents, your family, and those who are responsible for everything that has happened to you.'

That night . . . I couldn't sleep. My ears rang with the gun sounds, my body ached, and my index finger was sore. There had been no time to think all day, but now I could. I could become angry, yes, begin to visualize scenarios of shooting or stabbing a rebel. 'The rebels are responsible for everything that has happened to you.' I imagined capturing several rebels at once, locking them inside a house, sprinkling gasoline on it, and tossing a match. We watch it burn and I laugh.

Source: **Abridged from Beah (2007: 100–13).**

(Coalition to Stop the Use of Child Soldiers, 2009: 389) estimates that roughly 300,000 child soldiers are currently fighting in more than 40 countries around the world. This is not counting the large numbers of children who have enlisted themselves in civil wars as part of liberation armies in Ireland, Palestine, and elsewhere.

This use of children in warfare has been promoted, unwittingly, by technological innovation—specifically, by the development and manufacture of lightweight automatic weapons. These weapons are light enough for a young child to carry and are easy to use (Human Rights Watch, n.d.: 91). The story in Box 10.2 illustrates the harrowing experiences of one child soldier in Africa. No doubt, there are hundreds of thousands of such stories; we have yet to learn the long-term physical and psychological effects of such military service by children.

HEALTH CONSEQUENCES OF WAR

One estimate is that military conflicts in the twentieth century have led to the deaths of over 100 million soldiers and civilians—more than the total number of casualties in all previous wars in human history combined (Porter, 1994).

If these numbers seem appalling, they pale in comparison to the possible death tolls humanity would achieve were a full-scale nuclear war to break out. Currently, the nuclear weapons in major military arsenals are more than 4,000 times as powerful as the atomic bombs dropped on Japan. George Friedman and Meredith Friedman (1996) estimate that a nuclear war today would kill 160 million people instantly. Another billion would perish in the first few hours because of radiation poisoning, environmental devastation, and massive social chaos, while hundreds of millions more would die slowly over the following years.

Just as death is an unavoidable outcome of war, so, too, are physical and psychological injuries. The number of military personnel and civilians who are injured or maimed during a war usually exceeds the number of deaths. Indeed, one common military strategy is to maim rather than kill the enemy since it takes more resources to care for the wounded than to discard their bodies. Anti-personnel landmines are especially suited to this vicious task, since they are largely undetectable by civilians or enemy troops without proper equipment and do not need a soldier present to 'pull the trigger'.

Surviving a war physically unscathed does not guarantee complete well-being. Many veterans of war suffer the slow torture of psychological disorders. Much of the mental health literature on the effects of war focuses on **post-traumatic stress disorder** (PTSD), which researchers had previously studied under labels such as 'shell shock', 'concentration-camp syndrome', 'survivor syndrome', and 'war neurosis' (Summerfield, 2000).

SOLUTIONS TO WAR AND GLOBAL CONFLICT

Arms Reduction

As we have already noted, with the coming of the twentieth century the scope of battle increased; more combatants and more civilians were killed by more potent weapons. Thus, a chief concern has been to find ways to reduce the number and types of weapons in

BROTHERS

In this 2009 film, Sam (Tobey Maguire) returns from serving the military in Afghanistan, only to find himself experiencing severe post-combat mental distress.

POST-TRAUMATIC STRESS DISORDER (PTSD) A form of psychological distress produced by a traumatic experience such as crime victimization, sexual assault, or military combat. Symptoms include nervousness, sleep disturbances, disruption of concentration, anxiety, depression, irrational fear, and flashbacks triggered by loud noises such as thunder or a car's backfiring.

people's hands, and especially to find ways of protecting civilians against weapons and their misuse.

A prime example of this effort has been the Landmines Convention that Canada and its Foreign Minister, Lloyd Axworthy, were instrumental in achieving. Landmines have been widely and indiscriminately used around the world as a means of killing foot soldiers and spreading fear among enemy combatants and civilian populations. Often, they have remained in place after wars have ended—or have been moved by flooding and slope processes to new locations—and have maimed and killed many unsuspecting civilians, including children. The Convention on the Prohibition of the Use, Stockpiling, Production and Transfer of Anti-Personnel Mines and on their Destruction, known as the Ottawa Convention, opened for signature on 3 December 1997. By the end of 1998, fully 133 countries had signed the Convention, and 55 of those had ratified it a year later. The Convention came into legal force in March 1999.

Many countries contributed funds to making this Convention work: Canada alone contributed $2.8 million for mine-action projects in seven countries in Central Europe, Africa, and the Middle East. An example of the work done with this money includes demining activities in Cambodia, where over 32,000 mines were removed and 10,000 people, as a result, were able to return to fields where they could then safely grow rice. (For more on this topic, see Cameron et al., 1998.)

Other efforts have been made to limit the production and sale of small arms. As the United Nations has noted, 'small arms and light weapons destabilize regions; spark, fuel, and prolong conflicts; obstruct relief programs; undermine peace initiatives; worsen human rights abuses; hamper development; and foster a "culture of violence"' (disarmament.un.org/cab/salw.html).

International co-operation on this matter took a giant step forward when the United Nations held a Conference on the Illicit Traffic in Small Arms and Light Weapons in All Its Aspects in July 2001. On that occasion, the participating states agreed to adopt a Program of Action to Prevent, Combat, and Eradicate the Illicit Trade in Small Arms and Light Weapons, in All Its Aspects. This agreed-on program includes a number of measures to legislate, destroy weapons, and co-operate in tracing illicit arms. In the 2005 World Summit Outcome Document (A/60/L.1) the General Assembly reiterated its support for the implementation of this Program.

Arms are big business. According to the Stockholm International Peace Research Institute (SIPRI, 2008), in 2008 the top 10 arms exporters in the world were, in descending order, the United States, Russia, Germany, France, the United Kingdom, Spain, the Netherlands, Italy, China, and Israel. That year the United States exported $6.16 billion worth of weapons, down from $18.5 billion in 2004—then four times as much as its nearest competitors, Russia and France (at roughly $4.5 billion each) and 20 times as much as sixth-place Canada in 2008 (which shipped a 'mere' $900 million worth).

Though the total value of exports has decreased dramatically, arms exports in the US still amounted to close to 29 times as much as Canada (which ranked as the fifteenth largest arms exporter in 2008). Military sales—most of it by private contractors to the US government—usually account for a full 20 per cent of the US national budget and in 2008 the US accounted for 41.5 per cent of the world's collective military spending—by far the highest proportion of any nation in the world—which helps to explain the claim that, in the US, there is a military-industrial complex with huge political as well as economic power.

An illegal trade in small arms is common in many countries and regions of the world—particularly those affected by political instability. Often, the legal arms trade feeds an illegal arms trade, with legally purchased weaponry being resold for illegal purposes. In this way, the arms industry poses global problems due to its (often secret) business practices (en. wikipedia.org/wiki/Arms_trade).

The Control Arms Campaign, founded by Amnesty International, Oxfam, and the International Network on Small Arms, estimates that over 600 million small arms are in circulation in the world, with over 1,135 companies based in more than 98 different countries occupied in manufacturing them. The result is an average of over 500,000 deaths every year, roughly one death per minute. Many people see the supplying of weapons for conflict as immoral and dangerous behaviour that carries little personal, national, or corporate risk. In this way, the global arms industry enables a few to profit from war and death by prolonging wars that might otherwise dwindle to an end if the arms supply dried up (ibid.).

Redistributing Economic Assets

Some believe that terrorism and warfare will be reduced, and peace ensured, only by redistributing economic assets more equally among nations and among people within nations. We know that disparities in wealth and assets have been and are causes of many wars, past and present. Thus, we can probably reduce conflict through a more equal distribution of assets. However, it is unlikely that prosperous nations will readily agree to lower their standards of living at home to benefit less wealthy societies.

Redistributing economic wealth from core nations to peripheral nations does not guarantee that poorer nations will have a better standard of living. There must be proper rules to ensure that citizens will benefit from aid funds. Otherwise, politicians and state elites may appropriate the funds to further their own interests at the expense of their citizens.

In addition, aid funds must be targeted for social development, not for military spending—much of US foreign aid, for example, has been targeted for arms to client states such as Saudi Arabia and Israel, just as it was in the past to Saddam Hussein in Iraq, to Osama bin Laden and freedom fighters against the Soviet invasion of Afghanistan, to the Shah of Iran, and to numerous dictatorial regimes in Latin America.

The Role of International Peacekeeping Bodies

Another harm-reduction and risk-reduction strategy has been to form an international body dedicated to peacekeeping and preventing global conflict. The most prominent organization trying to carry out this task has been the United Nations. UN peacekeepers have been patrolling war-torn regions since 1948, when the UN Truce Supervision Organization was created to oversee the ceasefire agreed to by Israel and its Middle East neighbours.

Canadians have been active peacekeepers in the world since 1956, when then Secretary of State for External Affairs (and eventual Prime Minister) Lester B. Pearson sent Canadian forces to Egypt. Seeing a chance to ease tensions around the Suez Canal conflict, Pearson suggested creating a worldwide peacekeeping force to oversee the withdrawal of armed forces from the area and serve as a long-term barrier between Egypt and Israel. This was the first UN peacekeeping mission to be lightly armed and to have more than simple observer status (Knight and Keating, 2010: 176). The United Nations mission, led by Canadians, was a success, and resulted in Pearson's winning the Nobel Peace Prize in 1957.

Since the use of peacekeeping troops in Suez, there have been 60 UN peace operations involving more than 750,000 military, police, and civilian personnel. Missions have served all over the world, creating buffer zones in Cyprus and the former Yugoslavia, bringing aid to Haiti and Rwanda, and providing observers to conflicts in Angola and El Salvador.

Peacekeepers assume that their neutrality will allow them to insert themselves between combatants, to act as a safeguard. In theory, their presence provides a physical and psychological barrier against shots being fired. In practice—for example, in Rwanda during the mid-1990s—the peacekeeping force had no such effect and could not prevent bloodshed. Peacekeeping also assumes that fighters on all sides are sincere in their wish for peace. When this is not the case, violence can break out, as occurred in the former Yugoslavia, where broken ceasefires led to general fighting in 1995 and the first withdrawal of UN troops.

Interventions by UN peacekeeping forces have undoubtedly prevented wars and saved lives. However, UN actions have not been enough to eliminate war, as many outbreaks of war have occurred under 'the watch' of the United Nations. To this list we can add the 2001 and 2003 invasions of Afghanistan and Iraq by the United States, Britain, and others, which were launched in spite of extensive efforts by the UN to preserve diplomacy and peace.

CHAPTER SUMMARY

Some have thought of war as the natural outcome of innate aggression. The opposing view is that people are not born to be violent or aggressive, but that we learn to act so. According to this latter explanation, war is a result of social organization and cultural tradition and a response to cultural symbols.

We could think of the arms race as a symbolic show of power and as a means of securing peace through mutual deterrence. However, the negative outcomes include the obvious potential for mass destruction and the enormous monetary cost. The assets spent to produce and preserve armaments could instead be assigned to relieving other social problems, both at home among the big military spenders and abroad in countries of the developing and less developed world, where the need for these assets and for foreign aid is most prominent.

Terrorism can exist for different reasons. Common forms are revolutionary terrorism, in which rebels wage war on the state, and repressive terrorism, in which the state wages war in an attempt to repress its citizens. Other forms include transnational terrorism or terrorism by autonomous agents.

Massive economic inequalities exist between nations. **Relative deprivation** breeds resentment, and resentment can foment aggression. War will pose a problem for humanity as long

RELATIVE DEPRIVATION
The feelings and judgements of an individual or members of a group when they compare themselves to others who are better-off materially. People make judgements relative to standards or frames of reference. The feelings generated contribute to the formation of social movements.

as widespread inequalities in wealth and power between nations and extensive differences in beliefs and interests persist along with prevailing weaknesses in bodies—such as the United Nations—that are charged with keeping the world's peace.

QUESTIONS FOR CRITICAL THOUGHT

1. Is war justifiable? If not, what can people justifiably do to fight injustice and break free of oppression?

2. Fighting for peace and paying for war: our tax dollars support and contribute to military spending. What are your thoughts about Canada's military role in the world? Should it be expanded?

3. Will concerns about the spread of nuclear weapons blind us to the value of older, more conventional strategies of war?

4. What important similarities or differences exist between these forms of violence: war, capital punishment, terrorism, and personal violence for revenge?

5. When and how should we intervene on humanitarian grounds in conflicts in other parts of the world—for example, against the abuses of women and children in many parts of Africa and the Middle East?

RECOMMENDED READINGS

Beah, Ishmael. 2007. *A Long Way Gone: Memoirs of a Boy Soldier*. Vancouver: Douglas & McIntyre. In his memoir, former child soldier Ishmael Beah tells the story of how the civil strife in Sierra Leone destroyed his childhood innocence when rebel forces forced him to leave his home and village and travel the deserts of Africa. Beah's tale is a riveting snapshot of childhoods stolen from many, not just in Sierra Leone but also in Somalia, Iraq, Palestine, Afghanistan, and other places ravaged by civil wars.

Bertell, Rosalie. 2000. *Planet Earth: The Latest Weapon of War*. London: Women's Press. Dr Bertell offers an assessment of environmental damage caused by military activity, stating that 'the military is testing radically new weapons which imperil the earth and all life on it.' Her work demonstrates how the space program, 'Star Wars' research, and electromagnetic weapons have destabilized the natural balance of the Earth's ecosystem, causing widespread devastation.

Einholf, Christopher J. 2007. 'The Fall and Rise of Torture', *Sociological Theory* 25, 2: 101–21. In this paper, Einholf argues that the use of torture follows the same patterns in contemporary times as it has in earlier historical periods. He analyzes two historical trends of the twentieth century that have caused torture, as well as changes in the nature of national sovereignty. This comparative and historical analysis uses past precedents to provide a look into the potential for and current use of torture in society.

Farkhar, Hannah Beech. 2001. 'The Child Soldiers: War and Revenge Is All the Young Recruits of the Northern Alliance and Taliban Know', *Time* [online], 16 Nov. 2001, at: <www.time.com/time/

world/article/0,8599,182805,00.html>. In many countries, children are singled out for recruitment by both armed forces and armed opposition groups, and exploited as combatants. Most of these children are 15–18 years old. However, significant recruitment starts at the age of 10 and the use of even younger children has been recorded. This article draws attention to the issue of child recruitment and training in Afghanistan, a country that has been and continues to be in the midst of heavy political turmoil since the turn of the century.

Ferguson, C., and W. Potter. 2005. *The Four Faces of Nuclear Terrorism.* Monterey, CA: Center for Nonproliferation Studies. This comprehensive and thoughtful guide to nuclear warfare moves beyond the description of how terrorists may acquire or produce nuclear arms by also offering in-depth analyses of terrorist threats to nuclear plants as well as the potential for using radiological weapons. As a more comprehensive approach than one focused just on the bomb, this book provides analyses and recommendations concerning priority issues and potential solutions to the possible impact of nuclear warfare.

Fry, Douglas P. 2009. *Beyond War: The Human Potential for Peace.* New York and Oxford: Oxford University Press. In a broad look at our species, social anthropologist Douglas P. Fry documents groups of people that have lived entirely without war for decades or longer. War, thus, is not inevitable. Fry refutes the common notion that human nature is essentially warlike and claims that war does not have evolutionary roots and, therefore, can be stopped.

Jones, David H. 2005. 'On the Prevention of Genocide: The Gap between Research and Education', *War Crimes, Genocide, and Crimes against Humanity* 1, 1: 5–46. A comparison of the recommendations for prevention of genocide commonly proposed by historians, social scientists, and other scholars contrasted with the preventive measures supported by a majority of genocide educators.

Moore, Barrington, Jr. 1967. *Social Origins of Dictatorship and Democracy: Lord and Peasant in the Making of the Modern World.* Boston: Beacon Press. The author outlines the divergent paths different societies and countries take towards modernity, and how these paths influence them. He analyzes modern political systems with reference to the backdrop of their development.

Pearse, Meic. 2007. *The Gods of War: Is Religion the Primary Cause of Violent Conflict?* Nottingham, UK: Inter-Varsity Press. In his provocative and timely book, Pearse claims that the principal causes of human warfare are culture and greed, with religion playing a lesser role. Pearse offers keen analyses of global history and current events, discusses theological aspects of 'just war', and points beyond cultural and secular explanations for alternative solutions.

Waltz, Kenneth N. 2001. *Man, the State, and War: A Theoretical Analysis.* New York: Columbia University Press. Originally written as a doctoral thesis more than 50 years ago, Kenneth Waltz's book continues to be a staple in the field of international relations theory. His groundbreaking theory is a thorough analysis of the difficulties associated with the war–peace continuum. Waltz emphasizes the need to look beyond the individual and state causes of war towards the system for answers.

Recommended Websites

The Coalition to Oppose the Arms Trade

coat.ncf.ca

The Coalition to Oppose the Arms Trade (COAT) was formed in late 1988 to expose and oppose armx, which was, at the time, Canada's largest weapons bazaar. COAT's campaign resulted in a City of Ottawa motion banning all future military trade shows from municipal property. The website provides information about COAT's *Press for Conversion! Magazine* and about upcoming peace rallies, vigils, conferences, and campaigns against the arms trade.

rabble.ca/News for the rest of us

www.rabble.ca

This registered not-for-profit organization publishes original news stories, in-depth features, and commentaries. The site presently draws over 100,000 visitors each month looking for an alternative viewpoint on politics, entertainment, society, world issues, community, and life in general.

Reach All Women in War

www.rawinwar.org

Reach All Women in War is a new international human rights NGO supporting women human rights defenders and women and girl victims of war. Civilians, and especially women, have become the primary targets of armed groups and rape is increasingly being used as a weapon of war.

The Sierra Club of Canada

www.sierraclub.ca

Sierra Club Canada is a member-based organization that empowers people to protect, restore, and enjoy a healthy and safe planet. Although ecological disturbances brought on by war have been occurring for thousands of years, modern warfare has increasingly severe impacts.

War Child International

www.warchild.org

War Child International is a worldwide network of independent organizations co-operating to help children affected by war and to advance the cause of peace.

CHAPTER 11

Families

LEARNING OBJECTIVES

- To understand the historical evolution of the family and its structure.
- To distinguish between the myths and the realities of the family.
- To be familiar with the various definitions of 'family'.
- To learn about the disparities between Aboriginal and non-Aboriginal families.
- To understand the current patterns of marital unions and parenthood.
- To be alert to the effects of marital disharmony on children.
- To appreciate the different feminist theories on family life.
- To recognize the stressful elements of family life and their health impacts.
- To explore possible solutions for various family issues.

INTRODUCTION

For most Canadians, family life is about three main social relationships: between spouses or partners, between parents and children, and between siblings. An important feature of family life is that members interact with each other on a micro level. At the same time, the macro level of society plays a large part in framing the circumstances—economic, political, legal, religious, and otherwise—that shape these interactions. Some even believe that sociology promotes certain illusions or beliefs about families that are polemical—unjustified by scientific evidence, yet aimed at bringing about important social changes. Thus, the image and functioning of families is also a result of social construction (King, 2007; Brabant, 2006). Consider current debates about the rights and agency of children within the framework of traditional family relations. What are the rights of children and the responsibilities of parents, given certain assumptions we make about the agency of children?

Family life is central to our society. The family produces and socializes the next generation of citizens. Families provide the emotional support and economic security that people and societies need (Paradise and Rogoff, 2009). Because families are so important, problems in family living become important social problems for society as a whole.

DIFFERENT KINDS OF FAMILIES

Families vary from one society to another, just as they vary within our own society. In most societies, families exist within larger social networks—within kinship groups and clans. The members of a household—the husband and wife, parent and child, brother and sister—are thoroughly integrated into a larger web of kin, and their lives cannot be understood without reference to this larger web and the entire community.

A *kinship group* is a group of people who share a relationship through blood or marriage and have positions in a hierarchy of rights over the property (Skoda, 2007). Kin relationships may also control where the members must live, whom they can marry, and even their life opportunities. The definition of a kin relationship varies between societies, but kin relationships are important everywhere (Dixon, 2007).

Some societies trace kin relationships through the male line, so any individual's relationships are determined by his or her father's relationships; we call such kinship systems *patrilineal*. Others trace relationships through the female line; these are *matrilineal* systems (Rao, 2005). Still others count relationships through both lines; they are *bilateral* kinship systems (Aguilar, 2009).

If the kinship system is patrilineal, a person gains a position in the community just by being the child of his or her father. In a matrilineal kinship system, a person has certain property rights as the child of his or her mother. However, that kinship *system* is independent of which sex holds more *authority* in society; men can be the dominant sex even in a matrilineal society. In matrilineal societies, the person whose kinship link is most authoritative and important to a child is not the biological father but the mother's brother, as is the case among the Ashanti in West Africa and within several North American Aboriginal societies (Mikell, 1990).

Generally, in Canada, our family system follows the Western pattern, in which property typically is inherited along the male line. Where families settle down is traditionally determined by the husband's job, not the wife's, although this, too, is changing. However, our society also has certain *matrifocal* characteristics. Because women have been accepted as the primary kin-keepers—the people who preserve family contacts—children usually have stronger ties with their mother's kin (Rosenthal, 1985; Thomson and Li, 1992: 15).

Our society is neither matrilineal nor patrilineal—it is bilateral. This means that relatives of both of our parents are thought of as kin. We have maternal and paternal aunts, uncles, grandparents, cousins, and so on. Bilateral descent fits well with an equalitarian authority structure where father and mother have a roughly equal say in family matters.

In many societies, including our own, a household usually consists of parents and their unmarried children. In others, what we consider the **family** is embedded in a much broader web of kinship relations, and a household will include many kin. These two main forms of family household are referred to, respectively, as the nuclear family and the extended family.

The **nuclear family** is the most common family household in our society. It consists of one or two generations living together—typically, one or two parents and their children (Phillips, 2009). The nuclear family is a *conjugal* family, in which priority is given to marital ties over blood ties. Western families are *neolocal*, i.e., marriage brings with it the expectation that each of the partners will leave the parental home and set up a new residence, forming another independent nuclear family (Loveless and Holman, 2007).

An **extended family** is one in which two or more generations of relatives live together. It may include grandparents or grandchildren, and uncles, aunts, and cousins. The extended family is a *consanguine* family, since preference is given to blood ties over marital ties. Consanguine families stress relationships between parents and their children, and with other 'blood-related' members of the kin group.

As shown in Table 11.1, a great many families today have no children at home, and many common-law couples do have children. These are relatively new developments.

Sociologists have adopted some new approaches to studying family life in a diverse and fluid society. The life course approach follows the variety of social and interpersonal dynamics of close relations and examines how they change throughout our lifetimes. It notes how families change to meet new needs, such as those created by the arrival, care, or departure of children (Petts, 2009).

Another new approach is to look at family relations from the perspectives of different family members. This recognizes that different family members have different interests and experiences as members of any given family. Because different family members often have different interests, it is often inappropriate to speak of 'the family' as though it has a single interest and acts in a unified way.

Still another approach is to collect data in new ways so that family diversity can be studied. One example is Statistics Canada's Longitudinal Survey of Children and Youth (Willms, 2002: 71–102, 359–77). This survey follows individual children as they grow up, interviewing them and their families every two years. Data are collected on family changes, schooling, health, and a range of variables that affect children's lives. Findings suggest the negative effects on a child's mental or physical health, or school readiness and achievement, of living

FAMILY A group of people related by kinship or similar close ties in which the adults assume responsibility for the care and upbringing of their natural or adopted children. Members of a family support one another financially, materially, and emotionally.

NUCLEAR FAMILY A family unit comprising one or two parents and any dependent children who live together in one household separate from relatives.

EXTENDED FAMILY More than two generations of relatives living together in a household. The arrangement often includes grandparents, aunts, uncles, and dependent nephews and nieces.

Table 11.1 Census Families by Number of Children at Home, Canada, 2006

Family Structure	Couple Families	Married Couples	Common-law Couples
All families	8,896,840	7,482,775	6,105,910	1,376,870
Families without children at home	3,420,850	3,420,850	2,662,135	758,715
Families with children at home	5,475,990	4,061,930	3,443,775	618,150
1 child at home	2,429,695	1,558,880	1,267,625	291,255
2 children at home	2,132,830	1,732,505	1,497,755	234,755
3 or more children at home	913,465	770,540	678,405	92,140
Total children at home	9,733,770	7,586,250	6,517,600	1,068,650
Average number of children at home per family	1.1	1.0	1.1	0.8

	Lone-parent Families	Female Parent	Male Parent
All families	1,414,060	1,132,290	281,775
Families without children at home	0	0	0
Families with children at home	1,414,060	1,132,290	281,775
1 child at home	870,815	682,025	188,790
2 children at home	400,325	327,660	72,665
3 or more children at home	142,920	122,605	20,320
Total children at home	2,147,520	1,746,475	401,045
Average number of children at home per family	1.5	1.5	1.4

Source: **Census families by number of children at home, by province and territory (2006 Canadian Census), at www40. statcan.gc.ca/l01/cst01/famil50a-eng.htm (September 2010).**

with a single parent, are due to more than simply the effect of the low incomes such families often have. The good news from this longitudinal research is that good parenting can largely overcome these harmful effects.

Studying families in a context of change reminds us to stay away from any simple definitions or theories about family life that assume all families are the same, and stay the same, regardless of historical context. Consider, for example, how family members may be differently affected by changes in the economy. Young adult children may stay in school longer because they cannot find jobs, or cannot find jobs that pay enough for them to live independently. Similarly, children may be differently parented because of changing policies on parental leave, enabling younger ones to have full-time parents for a period in their early lives, compared to older siblings where the parents returned to work soon after birth (Nguyen et al., 2009).

MYTHS OF THE FAMILY

In North American culture today, most people still think the 'ideal' family is based on a formal marriage between two people of different sexes who have come together freely to build a monogamous and enduring relationship that includes reproduction and the rearing of children (Grutzmacher, 2007). Many members of the public still view alternatives to this as 'departures from the ideal', if not as unusual as they were in the past. Single parenting, stepfamilies, common-law relationships, and same-sex couples may be patterns of families growing in familiarity (and therefore acceptance), but they remain departures from the cultural ideal.

Patriarchy and Family Values

By **patriarchy**, we mean male dominance that is justified in a society's values and, therefore, tied to the ideology of gender.

MR. MOM

This 1983 film plays with conventional concepts of parental responsibility, as an unemployed father (Michael Keaton) switches roles with his now-employed wife.

PATRIARCHY Male dominance that is justified in a society's system of values. This dominance is tied to the ideology of gender and can be found in practically every society.

The Canadian Press/Aaron Harris

Single mother Lianne Thompson and daughter Bryanna, 3, make dinner at home in Toronto. 'Traditional' no longer describes the universal ideal for family in Canada, as 2001 census numbers from Statistics Canada suggest.

In Canada today, many of the dominant beliefs include a woman's right to choose contraception, to divorce, and to have a legal abortion; the increasing need for women of all cultures to work outside the home; and an increasing acceptance of gay relationships and marriage. However, the patriarchal nuclear family remains a powerful ideological image in our society and serves to control and socialize race, class, gender, and sexual orientation (Chambers, 2000). In North America, an influential source of mythology about family life in recent decades has come from fundamentalist Christians and social conservatives. The term *family values* was first used in the United States in the mid-1960s to describe a set of moral guidelines for defining the structure and role of a family and its members, supported by appeals to tradition.

BASIC ASPECTS OF CANADIAN FAMILIES

Sociologists use different definitions of 'family' for particular purposes. For purposes of the census, the Canadian government defines the economic family as 'a now-married couple (with or without never-married sons or daughters of either or both spouses), a couple living common-law (again with or without never-married sons and/or daughters of either or both partners), or a lone parent of any marital status, with at least one never-married son or daughter living in the same dwelling' (Statistics Canada, 2001).

A broader sociological definition of the family, one that sociologists generally support, is 'a group of individuals, related by blood, marriage, or adoption, who support one another financially, materially, and emotionally' (see, e.g., Murdock, 1949). This definition does not consider same-sex partnerships between people who are not related by blood, legal marriage, or legal adoption. To include these relationships, sociologists recast the term 'family' to focus on social processes that typify marriage, such as financial, material, and emotional support.

Most Canadian families—70 per cent in 2001—are classifiable as a 'married-couple union'. However, this group has declined in size since 1981, when 83 per cent of all families were based in legal marriage (Statistics Canada, 2002). Alongside the decreased rate of marriage, we see a matching increase in common-law unions. Statistics Canada defines a common-law couple as 'two persons of opposite sex who are not legally married to each other, but live together as husband and wife in the same dwelling' (ibid.). The common-law union is the fastest-growing family category today: the proportion of common-law families increased from 5.6 per cent to 14 per cent between 1981 and 2001.

The social groups we think of as families typically share many features. These commonalities can help us begin to understand the nature of families. Because families are extraordinarily diverse, it is difficult to generalize about them. However, it is possible to focus our attention on their common processes.

First, all families have in common attachment and some kind of dependency or interdependency. Compared to other types of intimate relations (at work, or school), family relations are special in that they tend to include long-term commitments, both to each other and to the shared family per se. They are, by tradition and law, organized to regulate dependency (economic and otherwise).

Second, adult partners within families typically have, or are expected to have, a long-term, exclusive sexual relationship, whereas among co-workers and among friends, sexual relations are either absent or of short duration. In families, sexual relations are permitted and expected between certain members (e.g., between spouses) but prohibited between other members (e.g., between parents and children). Nevertheless, sexual abuse of children and of elders sometimes occurs within families.

Third, parents and relatives are supposed to keep children safe from accidents and household dangers, and away from drugs, alcohol, predators, and other forms of harm. As well, spouses are supposed to protect one another, and adult children are supposed to protect and help their parents. In reality, family members often fail to protect each other sufficiently, and worse, some people neglect, exploit, or abuse family members. However, those who break the cultural rules tend to face criticism and disapproval.

Fourth, families have distinctive structures for making decisions and assigning resources. Often, the family is controlled by a dominant male (typically, the father), and, in much of family law and policy, such patriarchal domination was seen as a right. In recent years, family decision-making has become much more egalitarian (between spouses) and many households are controlled by women.

If we think about families in ways that are defined by process, rather than by structure, it is easier to see the similarities among families having different forms, and easier to understand the problems families have faced in adapting to modern economic life.

Families in Aboriginal Communities

Aboriginal families have, in some respects, had the hardest time adapting to modern economic life, and their family lives have suffered as a result. However, their families have suffered for other reasons as well. Aboriginal communities were once the victims of a systematic campaign to assimilate them forcibly into mainstream Canadian society. This was done, in part, by isolating Aboriginal youth from their families and placing them in residential schools (Petten, 2007). The effects were disastrous.

Years of marginalization, failed assimilation, and abuse have made Aboriginal people sensitive to outside threats against their culture and community. Although Aboriginal cultures in Canada are diverse in terms of language, norms, practices, and beliefs, there have been historical commonalities among these groups regarding child-rearing processes. Aboriginal mothers and families traditionally place high regard on the maintenance of Aboriginal cultural, religious traditions, and socio-cultural values within the family (Cheah and Chirkov, 2008). Historically, Aboriginal societies have been largely egalitarian. That is, every member of the family is regarded as important, sharing responsibility for collective wellness. Further, the role of the extended family was traditionally very important in Aboriginal communities. For example, daily responsibilities of grandparents, such as parenting and teaching cultural and moral values to children, have been extensively documented (ibid.).

Unfortunately, harsh conditions have had an intense effect on nurturing and parental skills within Aboriginal families. Aboriginal child-rearing patterns—including the transmission

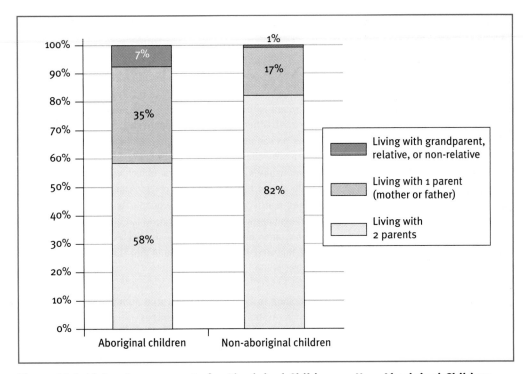

Figure 11.1 Living Arrangements for Aboriginal Children vs Non-Aboriginal Children Ages 14 and under, 2006

Source: Based on Statistics Canada data, at: www12.statcan.ca/census-recensement/2006/as-sa/97-558/table/t4-eng.cfm.

of cultural and parental knowledge—have weakened among many Aboriginal groups. These alterations are thought to be a result of residential schools and the resulting breakdown of traditional cultural values, as well as an increase in alcohol abuse, drug dependency, and suicide rates (ibid.).

Same-Sex Couples

In most industrialized countries, gays and lesbians are unable to marry legally since marriage continues to be defined as a union between a man and a woman. In some places this has changed. Indeed, the legal treatment of lesbian and gay families in the United States and Canada has been changing since the late 1970s, as is obvious in child custody, access, and adoption cases in which sexual orientation was a factor (Arnup, 1999).

By challenging the definition of 'spouse' and applying to the courts to formalize their relationships with their children by adoption, lesbian parents have challenged the normative content of spousal relations and have changed the law itself as a gendering strategy (Gavigan, 1999). Such a challenge, of course, was instrumental in the former federal Liberal government passing Bill C-38, the Civil Marriages Act, on 20 July 2005. This Act validates the legality of marriage between same-sex couples.

INTERNATIONAL COMPARISONS

Box 11.1 Bride Kidnapping and Arranged Marriages

In some cultures—in regions of Caucasus and in areas in the Middle East, Southeast Asia, and Africa—bride kidnapping is a traditional practice that exists to this day. In recent years, this practice has become especially prevalent in Kyrgyzstan, a country in Central Asia formerly part of the Soviet Union, following the fall of the Communist government. Lori Handrahan (2004: 207–8) has written about the evolution of bride kidnapping in Kyrgyzstan:

Like many revised traditions, tracing the origins is a difficult task. Many Kyrgyz have little idea how or why bride kidnapping was originally practised. The severe climate and lifestyle of mountain nomads mandated capable and equal male–female partnerships. Thus, initially bride kidnapping was perhaps devised, unconsciously, as a means to ensure marriages that could improve survival rates. In the old tradition a man asked the father's permission for a horserace with the daughter in question. The woman received a fifteen-second start and a thick leather whip to beat off the man. If the man could catch the woman and kiss her on horseback, then he won the right to ask for the woman's hand in marriage. The resulting tradition is known as *Kyskuumay*, or kiss the girl, and is now played as a game at festivals representing Kyrgyz traditions.

Bride kidnapping today is radically different. Although some kidnappings are mutually agreed to, more often the new version involves three or four men, a car, and lots of vodka. The men go in search of either a girl/woman that they know or any woman they deem attractive. Sometimes kidnapping is done in daylight with the woman captured as she is walking down the street. Other times, the kidnapping is planned at night and she is tricked out of her house or yurt. The man may already have a full wedding feast waiting at home. Once the kidnapped woman crosses the threshold, the oldest woman in the man's family places the *jooluk* scarf, on her head and she is considered married, although some people assert that marriage happens later with consummation, which often involves rape. If the woman decides to escape she likely faces rejection by her family and village on the ground that she has dishonoured Kyrgyz tradition.

In addition to bride kidnapping, other forms of violence against women in Asian and African countries include rampant sexual assault, wife-battering, bride burning, kidnapping for sale into prostitution, 'honour killings', and trafficking of brides (Shah, 2005; Plambech, 2005; Blanchet, 2005).

In Bangladesh, India, and Pakistan, arranged marriage remains the most common form of marriage. In some cases, a child's future marriage is arranged with another child's parents. The children are then betrothed to each other and wed when they reach an appropriate age (Buunk et al., 2010). Sometimes girl children are betrothed to much older men.

In Western cultures, factors such as physical attractiveness and passionate love are valued characteristics in partners. In Eastern cultures, family values and wishes have more significant influence on mate selection (Kline and Zhang, 2009).

FERTILITY TRENDS

The World Pattern

The most interesting and revealing fact about families today, in Canada and around the world, is that they have fewer children. A classic study on this topic, by sociologist William J. Goode (1963), has revealed that this decline in child-bearing has been part of a larger change in the size, structure, and functioning of modern families around the world. We discuss this further in Chapter 14, on population trends.

For the time being, note the declines in fertility shown for all the regions of the world in Figure 11.2. Declines are obvious everywhere. They are most marked in regions of the world that only began fertility reduction in the mid-twentieth century—for example, in Asia; and

PERSONAL STORIES

Box 11.2 One Big Gay Family

Alex Vamos and Jen Woodill, who are just one of the 3,785 same-sex couples who are raising children in Canada. What makes this family unique is their arrangement to keep the sperm donors of their son, Morgan, in his life. Many lesbian couples choose sperm banks over people they know to avoid the emotional and legal disputes that could potentially arise. Instead, Vamos and Woodill decided that they wanted 'a donor who would be willing to have a relationship with the child'.

They met Neil Semer after months of searching. He was a gay man 20 years older, who longed to be a father. The relationship between the three of them progressed cautiously. According to co-parenting expert, Rachel Epstein, many prospective parents get so caught up in the excitement of finally having a child that they neglect to clearly and honestly express their demands. After the child is born, the possibility of conflict heightens as expectations are unfulfilled. Moreover, in Ontario, donor contracts and co-parenting agreements are not held legally binding as they are not included in the Family Law Act. The fear of messy legal battles kept Vamos and Woodill mindful of what they were getting into.

As time progressed, and after eating in all the Greek restaurants in Toronto, Semer's long-time partner was introduced to the picture. Jim Luisi was first apprehensive to the idea. Semer and he were old enough to be a child's grandparents after all. Nevertheless, he left the United States and arrived in Toronto with an open mind. There must have been good chemistry between the four of them. Luisi was sold on the idea in just a few hours. Even though doubts persisted, and Semer and Luisi were scrutinized by the women's friends and families—they were determined to put their plan into action.

So it began. It was decided that Vamos would carry the baby, while either Semer or Luisi would fly-in to donate their sperms (according to whoever had more free time). It was a long and painstaking process. Canadian reproductive technology laws require special permission from Health Canada before accepting the sperm of gay men, as they are considered as a high-risk group for HIV. Even after permission is granted, the semen must be frozen for six months and regularly tested for HIV. To avoid the hassle, they decided to conceive at home using a large syringe; it was called the turkey baster method. The process started in September of 2003. Vamos visited the fertility clinic every day at 7a.m. to monitor her cycle, while either of the men arrived weekly, rain or shine, or snowstorm. Vamos successfully became pregnant with Morgan at the end of the summer of 2005, and he was born in March 2006.

A month after Morgan was born, the four parents signed a co-parenting contract before a notary. The detailed and well-thought out contract gave Vamos and Woodill full custody, and visitation rights of five days a month for Semer and Luisi. Contingency plans are laid out in case of separation on either side, and in case of the women's deaths. So far, their lives together have been satisfactory. There is a strong affection and friendship between the four parents. Most importantly, there is mutual respect: they reach decisions after long debates and the needs of the child always come first. Currently, they are looking forward to adding another child to their clan.

Source: Adapted from Balkissoon (2009).

---

they are least marked where fertility decline began much earlier (in Europe and North America) or has yet to begin significantly (in West Africa).

The Canadian Pattern

Historical records show a strong decline in the Canadian birth rate from the mid-nineteenth to the mid-twentieth centuries in average numbers of births (Gee, 1986). Women born between 1817 and 1831 had about 6.6 children, compared with 1.7 children for women born between 1947 and 1961.

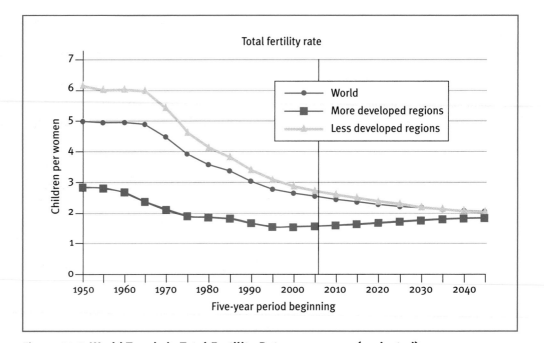

Figure 11.2 World Trends in Total Fertility Rate, 1950–2040 (projected)

Source: **United Nations,** *World Population Prospects: The 2004 Revision.* **© United Nations 2005.**

Today, we spend less of our lives occupied with parenting. This happens because we live longer and because our patterns of entering parenthood have changed. For instance, Gee (ibid.) found that Canadian women born between 1831 and 1840 spaced their first and last births an average of 14 years apart (often, with many births between). This compares with an average of only 1.8 years between first and last births for women born between 1951 and 1960.

This century-long downward trend in child-bearing continued with only a brief interruption—the baby boom between 1947 and 1967. Today, the average number of births per woman is roughly 1.5, an all-time low. On this, Statistics Canada (2005a) reports, 'Nearly one half of the women who gave birth in Canada were age 30 and older . . . . In fact, in Ontario and British Columbia, mothers age 30 and older were already in the majority. This reinforces the long-term trend among Canadian women: they have been waiting longer and longer to start families.'

In these respects, Canadian fertility is similar to what one finds in Northern and Central Europe, Russia, China, and Australia (Figure 11.3): stable, below replacement child-bearing that will erase the national population in foreseeable centuries unless immigrants and their children continue to arrive.

China's One-Child Policy

Until about a decade ago, the strictest policies on fertility control were exercised in the People's Republic of China, where a one-child policy was in effect. Then, China represented

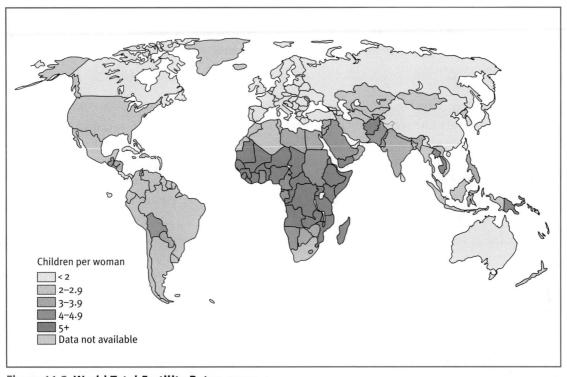

Figure 11.3 World Total Fertility Rates, 2000–4

what we might call a 'coercive (or involuntary) model' of fertility decline. Before the People's Revolution in the 1940s, China had a huge population with a high fertility rate. The government formed in 1948 saw a need to modernize and industrialize China as quickly as possible. This included laws fixing the equal rights of women and changing women's conditions of work and marriage.

As part of this policy, the Chinese government addressed child-bearing directly with compulsory permits for marriage and pregnancy. In 1971, it began its 'wan, xi, shao' (or 'later, longer, fewer') campaign, which asked people to marry later, leave a longer space between births, and bear fewer children in total. Then, in 1980, it legislated the one-child-per-couple policy. Today, there is no explicit law in China preventing couples from having more than one child. However, the government used coercive strategies to increase compliance—for example, fines for couples who break the rule.

A survey carried out in 1983 showed that these policies had achieved rapid and dramatic success. In 1965, the average Chinese woman had been bearing an estimated 6.1 children in her lifetime—the same rate we see in Central Africa today. By 2005, 40 years later, total fertility was down to 1.7 children—less than the population replacement (or zero growth) level (CIA, 2005).

Therefore, within two generations, Chinese marriage and fertility patterns had changed rapidly from those of a developing country to those of a Western industrial country.

Combined with other policies, this coercive fertility policy changed Chinese women's lives. Those born in the 1920s (for example) had received little or no education, married young, produced many children, and worked in the fields when not bearing children. Today, many Chinese women are afforded many more options, in terms of family structure, careers, and life in general.

Such coercive family planning can be viewed as one of many preventive health programs. Fertility decline reduced the health risks and costs associated with pregnancy and childbirth. In addition, by reducing the number of children, it reduced the number of parenthood experiences (or years spent in parenthood) and the attendant joys and stresses. The one-child program tacitly endorsed Thomas Malthus's concern with overpopulation and the need for abstinence; and in so doing, tacitly repudiated the century-old Marxist position on population control.

BACK IN HISTORY

Box 11.3 Rethinking the Notion of Family

Sarah Elton (2007), in *Canadian Family*, explores the new phenomenon that has been observed in our generation: the redefinition of parental roles that are shaping new parenting practices.

In the past, getting married and having children was expected by society. Now, it is a conscious choice. According to Statistics Canada, in the 1960s women were getting married for the first time at an average age of 22.6, while men were approximately 25. In the 1980s women were getting married at 23.5, while men were getting married at an average of 25.7. Today the average age for brides is 31.7 years, while grooms are 34.3. The women having the most babies are between 30 and 34.

Psychology professor Jeffrey Jensen Arnett claims that the experience of 'emerging adulthood' (a term he coined to describe the period of life between the ages of 18 and 29) is shaping us into new kinds of adults. This new period of independence has a profound impact on our lives. It makes us want to be adults who are different from our parents and grandparents. We want to be adults that not only parent our children, but also have fun with them as well.

Elton describes the modern manner of raising children as being visible in the luxury goods market. High-end maternity clothing, baby strollers, and organic baby foods are some of the products that were never seen before, but are now widely popular. Parents today want to remain as 'cool' and 'hip' as they were in their bachelor/bachelorette days. They refuse to compromise their previous jet-setting lifestyles for the suburban minivans, preferring to take their toddlers in tow while exploring the terrains of, say, Guatemala.

This new reality is also evident in our vocabulary. There are new expressions such as *yummy mummy*, 'a slang term for an attractive or glamorous mother', and *alterna-dad*, i.e., a 'hip dad'. There are WAHMs (working-at-home mothers) and WAHDs (dads), and *mompreneurs* who start their own kid-focused businesses after having kids of their own. For many career-driven women, they also approach parenting in a professional manner. They read numerous books on child-rearing and attend classes on baby signing and storytelling, among others. There is the same desire to excel at the home front, as they have at work.

Professor of sociology Anne-Marie Ambert asserts that marriage at an older age ensures financial and emotional readiness to care for a child. She claims that these are also the conditions creating an involved father. Men are comparatively more ready to participate in the inglorious side of parenting such as diaper changes, shampoo time, and visits to the doctor. For Jeff Loucks, 'Instead of reading the newspaper and having a scotch, I'd rather give my son a bath, get him ready for bed and just be there to witness it all.'

Source: Elton (2007).

At the same time, China's coercive one-child policy carries obvious costs. First, the Chinese traditionally shun daughters because China has historically been a patrilocal society. Many Chinese women who become pregnant suffer pressure to abort their child: first, if they are not married or not allowed to be married; second, if they are married but not permitted to have a child; and third, if they are allowed to have a child but don't want to have a daughter. (In China, as elsewhere, ultrasound technology makes it possible for women to know the sex of their unborn child.)

By contrast, a voluntary program of family limitation, such as those of Brazil or India (for example, the sterilization program started by Indira Gandhi), works more slowly but is more humane. The key to this strategy is to lower the infant mortality rate, reduce the economic value of children, and make available an improved lifestyle to people who consume less of their income raising children.

THEORETICAL PERSPECTIVES ON THE FAMILY

Table 11.2 Theoretical Perspectives

Theory	Main Points
Structural Functionalism	• Elements in society are all interrelated. • Families provide nurture and socialization. • A gendered division of domestic labour is functional. • The family is a central institution in society. • The family is a microcosm of society—individual family members come together in a unified and productive whole (Lehmann, 1994). • The familial division of labour is the key to a family's success (Parsons and Bales, 1955). • The regulation of sexual behaviour and reproduction, the provision of physical and psychological needs of members, and the socialization of children are important family functions. • Modern functionalism argues that certain family forms are natural or inevitable.
Conflict Theory	• Social reproduction in families supports capitalism. • Families maintain the workforce without pay. • It should not be assumed that families operate as units, perform functions, or accomplish tasks for the good of society. • Families must be understood historically and placed in the context of political and economic changes. • Families are no longer self-sustaining economic units, but are consumption units dependent on outside sources of income for survival.

Continued

Table 11.2 Theoretical Perspectives—*Continued*

Theory	Main Points
	• Working-class men had to sell their labour power to the bourgeoisie in exchange for an income, while women gained exclusive control over the home with responsibility for child-rearing, food preparation, and emotional support. All this work by women was without financial remuneration, despite the importance of the tasks, which amounted to exploitation of women that benefited their husbands' employers. Thus, sexual inequality increased under industrial capitalism. • Gender inequality arises out of economic exploitation, not the need of 'society' or even of a given family for task differentiation based on gender.
Feminist Theory	• The domestic division of labour is arbitrary. • Just as factory workers depend on capitalists for a living wage, wives depend on their husbands; the dependence is easily turned into subordination. • Women have historically endured not only economic reliance on men in the household, but also political and social inferiority. • The capitalist economy affirmed old patriarchal tendencies by providing men differential access to the labour market.
Symbolic Interactionism	• Families involve continued interaction. • They are maintained by shared myths and beliefs. • Their main role is to socialize the next generation. • A married couple builds a shared definition of their family—its goals, identity, and values.
Social Constructionism	• Family life is shaped by moral entrepreneurship. • Popular beliefs about families are media myths. • The development and use of family ideologies need to be studied and understood. • Moral entrepreneurs appeal to people's interest in and concern about their family lives, and so channel popular anxieties into hostility against minority groups—single mothers, gays and lesbians, and divorced people, to name a few.

Structural Functionalism

Functionalists view the family as a central institution in society. They see the family as a microcosm of society, with individual family members coming together in a unified and productive whole (Lehmann, 1994).

In Talcott Parsons and Robert Bales's functionalist analysis (1955), the family's division of labour is the key to its success. In a traditional family, the husband of the household performs an instrumental role as the breadwinner, decision-maker, and source of authority and leadership, while the wife fulfills an expressive role as homemaker, nurturer, and emotional centre of the family. Though these roles of the husband and wife have changed since the 1950s, functionalists still view the family institution as accomplishing several important functions, including the regulation of sexual behaviour and reproduction, the provision of physical (food, shelter) and psychological (nurturance, learning) needs of its members, and the socialization of children.

Functionalism today surfaces in arguments about the naturalness or inevitability of certain family forms. For example, psychiatrists Ronald Immerman and Wade Mackey (1999) argue that almost all marriage systems across the world support monogamy. In communities where people have multiple partners, sexually transmitted diseases increase. So do various societal dysfunctions, such as out-of-wedlock births, infant morbidity, violent crime, and lower educational attainment. These outcomes reduce the ability of the community to compete with other societies that have maintained pair bonding. This, in turn, reduces the survival capacity of the community.

Others make structural arguments to show that cohabitation is inferior to traditional (legal) marriage. Linda Waite (2000) argues that cohabiting relationships are often less permanent, fail to provide the many benefits that marriage offers to both participants, are less likely to involve extended families, and provide less support for the cohabiting partners during a crisis.

Conflict and Feminist Theories

Unlike functionalists, conflict theorists do not assume that families operate as units. Rather, they take a historical approach and focus on political and economic changes.

They note that with industrialization, families moved from being self-sustaining economic units (e.g., a farming household) to consumption units (e.g., a dual-income household that purchases shelter, food, clothing, services, and luxuries). In doing so, they became dependent on outside sources of income to meet their survival needs. This meant that working-class men had to sell their labour power to the bourgeoisie in exchange for an income. In this process, women gained exclusive control over (or, more accurately, were relegated to) the home, becoming responsible for child rearing, food preparation, and the provision of emotional support.

However, as both conflict and feminist theorists emphasize, women did this work without financial remuneration. In short, gender inequality arises out of economic exploitation, not the need of 'society' or even of a given family for task differentiation based on gender.

There are historical reasons for this development, and for its association with the rise of industrial capitalism. Feminist theorists argue that, just as factory workers depend on capitalists for a living wage, wives depend on their husbands. This dependence easily turned into subordination. Women have historically endured not only economic reliance on men in the household, but also political and social inferiority. Though these patriarchal tendencies are very old, the capitalist economy affirmed them by providing men with preferential access and treatment within the labour market.

Feminists argue that these patriarchal tendencies are most common in traditionalist religions. An orthodox Jewish religious community in Belgium demands that women get married and start a family 'while young', as their dictated role in life is solely that of a house worker. This traditional mentality prevents girls from pursuing higher education and, subsequently, meaningful employment (Longman, 2008). At the same time, feminists are alarmed by the seeming trend in liberal societies where educated, highly paid women are voluntarily leaving their careers to focus on motherhood (Aune, 2008). However, evangelical Christian (i.e., faith-centred) feminists claim that evangelicalism is 'a strategic form of women's collective action', empowering them while also calling men to take responsibility for their families. Yet, in their call to unite women through a religious definition of family, other women, such as single mothers, working mothers, and lesbian couples, are excluded (ibid).

Symbolic Interactionism

As we have seen, interactionists focus on the micro level of sociological phenomena. Symbolic interactionists study the ways members of a family interact with one another and resolve conflicts within the boundaries of their roles in the family. An important part of this process is the creation and revision of myths about family.

Social constructionists focus on the development and use of family ideologies such as the 'family values' promoted by right-wing religious leaders and social conservatives in the United States and Canada. By appealing to people's interest in and concern about their family lives, these moral and political entrepreneurs channel popular anxieties into hostility against such groups as single mothers, gays and lesbians, and divorced people.

These antipathies produce support for political initiatives that reduce social welfare spending and coerce the behaviour of other minorities—for example, urban blacks in the United States or Aboriginals in Canada. By implication, these groups become a focus for part of the outcry against those who are accused of failing to lead moral family lives or to instill family values in their children (McMullin, 2004).

SOCIAL CONSEQUENCES OF FAMILY LIFE

Stressful elements in family life such as abuse, employment and unemployment, and divorce all have serious social and health outcomes that can affect the individual, his or her family, and society as a whole (Raphael, 2009). Every family has problems to deal with, and some do a better job of it than others.

In recent decades, the cost of living has substantially increased. As a result, this prevents most families from surviving comfortably on a single income. The desire of families after World War II for more and more of the products of industrialization and technology, coupled with the wartime acceptance of women working outside of the home, established a cycle of demand and affluence that encouraged suppliers to keep raising prices higher and higher. Eventually, the second income no longer provided luxuries but became vital to providing the revised norm of 'minimal' comfort. In brief, over the course of a generation or two, 'luxuries' became 'necessities'. As a result, today, usually both parents have to work to make enough money to cover the necessities, pay for the occasional luxury, and perhaps save enough for their children's post-secondary education and their own retirement (Marshall, 2009). As well, the demands of employers for workers' time are often in direct conflict with the needs of the family.

Managing a career is difficult for women, especially if they are mothers of young children. As a result, many educated women delay marriage, preferring to go to school, work, and achieve financial independence. Others avoid marriage altogether, opting instead to have a career and aim for only those personal relationships that do not hinder their professional lives. The higher we look in the occupational hierarchy, in professional or managerial jobs, the more likely we are to find women who never married, who married and divorced, who married early but did not have children, or who married late and had few if any children (Houseknecht et al., 1987; Heathcote et al., 1997).

Women today wait longer to get married than they did in the past. Balestrino and Ciardi (2008) argue that this is due to a change in the costs and benefits of marriage. With the rise of the welfare state, young men and women are less dependent on marriage for social and economic care, and thus are more free to choose who and when they marry. Other changes, such as women's greater participation in the labour force, have made women less dependent on marriage for income. In the past, having children was seen as necessary for survival in old age.

However, with the introduction of adult care institutions, older adults are less dependent on their children for survival during later stages of life. This means that intangible qualities, such as love and companionship, are emerging as primary incentives in deciding to get married and form a family.

Whatever their education and career goals, women who marry and bear children usually face a double shift: modern women's dual roles as both breadwinners and homemakers (Medeiros et al., 2007). Several factors put particular pressure on the boundary between work and home life: (1) a spouse who often works overtime; (2) a bad work schedule; (3) a heavy workload; and (4) a troubled relationship with the boss. These work–home conflicts produce emotional exhaustion, psychosomatic health complaints, and sleep deprivation (Geurts et al., 1999). Parenthood and employment are not separate categories, but are woven together throughout life.

DOUBLE SHIFT Modern women's dual roles as breadwinner and homemaker.

While more and more women have been joining the workforce, women still bear an unequal share of the domestic work at home. For example, mothers make up 96 per cent of the caregivers for disabled Canadian children (Roeher Institute, 1999). This creates a dilemma in work–family relations, because the changes in women's labour force participation have not been accompanied by a change in men's caregiving patterns. Thus, women have the disadvantage of having to manage work-related responsibilities, while at the same time shouldering most of the child-rearing and household duties at home.

Divorce

At the beginning of the twentieth century, divorce was rare in Canada. In 1900, a mere 11 divorces were registered (Snell, 1983, cited in Eichler, 1997: 10). People widely disapproved

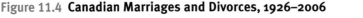

of divorce, as expressed both in religion and popular opinion and in the law that restricted it. Until 1968, adultery was the only ground for divorce.

The Divorce Act in 1968 brought about a massive change in family behaviours. This law allowed judges to grant divorces on the grounds of 'marriage breakdown' after a couple had been separated for at least three years. Between 1968 and 1970, the number of divorces nearly doubled (Oderkirk, 1994). An amendment to the Divorce Act in 1985 reduced the minimum period of separation to one year. In 1968, before the reforms, marriages that finally ended in divorce lasted an average of 15 years.

The liberalization of divorce laws shortened the process. At the beginning of the twenty-first century, the average was 12.7 years. In 2005, 71,269 Canadian couples divorced, up only slightly from 2001 (when 71,110 couples divorced), and in step with the growth of population (Statistics Canada, 2005b). Canadian divorce rates are higher than one finds in many other Western nations: 2.6 divorces per 1,000 people, compared, for example, with 2.2 in Sweden and 2.0 in Germany, based on 1996 data (Ambert, 2002). In a recent report, sociologist Anne-Marie Ambert notes that 'The latest estimates by Statistics Canada (2008) put the risk of divorce by the thirtieth wedding anniversary for recently married couples at 38 per cent for the country as a whole—ranging from 21.6 per cent in Newfoundland and Labrador to 48.4 per cent in Quebec.' By comparison, the divorce rate for the US is estimated at 44 per cent (Baklinski, 2009). Figure 11.4 shows Canadian divorce and marriage trends for the period 1926–2006.

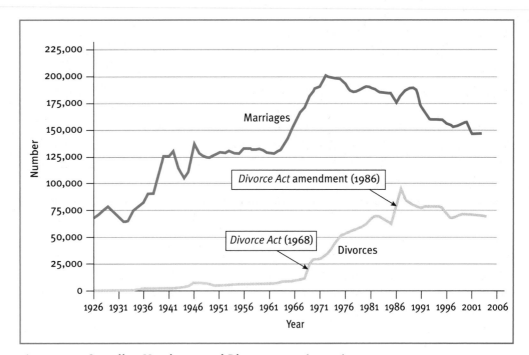

Figure 11.4 Canadian Marriages and Divorces, 1926–2006

Source: **Statistics Canada, at: www.statcan.gc.ca/pub/91-209-x/2004000/part1/figures/figure6-3-eng.htm.**

Consequences of Divorce

Divorce affects men and women differently because of gender inequalities in the wider society. Economically, divorce affects women much more negatively than men (Bould et al., 2008). A formal separation lowers women's standards of living by 73 per cent on average, but raises men's by 42 per cent (Mahoney, 1995). Forty per cent of ex-wives lose half their family income following the separation compared to less than 17 per cent of ex-husbands (Arendell, 1995). Custody of children is usually granted to mothers, compounding the economic burden on women. So, for women, not only is income reduced after the divorce, but that smaller income often must go towards caring for one or more dependants as well.

Taking on the role of primary caregiver also consumes a lot of time. Lone working mothers often report severe time stress and a feeling of being overwhelmed by responsibilities. Combining work, child-rearing, and household maintenance leaves little time to develop a social life (Trias, 2000).

Maria Franks, executive director of the Legal Info Society of Nova Scotia, stands near the Property Guys booth at the Divorce Fair she helped organize in Halifax on 15 January 2010. The fair helps those going through a divorce connect with the services they might need.

The Canadian Press/Jeff Harper

Following a separation or divorce, men are usually better off financially than are women because they were the dominant income earners during the marriage and they continue to have larger salaries or wages after the divorce. As well, men experience more freedom following a divorce, since children of a marriage usually live with the mother. Thus, men have more opportunities to work, travel, return to school, and explore other relationships (McManus and DiPrete, 2001).

The negative impact of divorce on children has also been well-documented. Much of the effect of divorce on children can be predicted by conditions that existed before the separation occurred, and 'at least as much attention needs to be paid to the processes that occur in troubled, intact families as to the trauma that children suffer after their parents separate' (Cherlin et al., 1991). Family and personal distress caused by conflict, poverty, or unemployment leads to less effective parenting—a complex notion that involves inadequate time and resources for fun, inadequate resources to make substantial plans for the future, perceived lack of achievements to celebrate, difficulty with surveillance, lack of respect from the children who want parents to succeed, loss of control over the child's behaviour, lack of warmth and support, inconsistency, and displays of aggression or hostility by parents or older siblings.

Depression is common among children of divorce, as are declines in academic performance, higher rates of emotional problems, and increased chance of anxious or anti-social behaviour (Roizblatt et al., 1997). These problems can continue into adulthood. Amato and Keith (1991), for instance, report that adult children of divorced parents register poorer psychological well-being (in the form of depression and low self-reported life satisfaction); lower educational attainment, income, and occupational prestige; an increased risk of undergoing a divorce themselves; and poorer physical health.

The debate over divorce and children's well-being has been especially fierce. Extreme positions on whether it causes harm have not given a clear picture of the results of growing up in a single-parent family or stepfamily (Cherlin, 1999).

Caring for the Elderly

Canada's population is aging as the result of lowered fertility and general increases in life expectancy for both men and women. 'Data from the 2006 Census showed that the number of seniors aged 65 years and over surpassed the 4 million mark for the first time. As a result, the proportion of senior citizens has increased from 13.0 per cent in 2001 to 13.7 per cent in 2006' (Statistics Canada, 2007). With continued declines in fertility, this percentage will continue to rise.

Elder care can drastically affect personal time for other family relationships, as well as for work and leisure. According to one study from the 1990s, 42 per cent of Canadian women aged 40–44 cared for elderly parents while raising their own children and working outside the home (Rosenthal, 1997). In fact, however, until parents reach the age of 75, the flow of support favours the children: they receive more help from parents than they give to them (Spitze and Logan, 1992). Using data from Canada, the United States, the United Kingdom, West Germany, and Japan, Harald Kunemund and Martin Rein (1999) found that the giving of services by older people to their adult children increases the chance they will receive help from them. In this way, generous welfare systems that give resources to elderly people help to increase rather than to undermine family solidarity.

Most Canadian seniors continue to live on their own well into advanced age, and most of the care they receive comes not from their children, but from other members of the same generation, usually a spouse (Martin-Matthews, 2000). Friends and neighbours may also provide essential help when seniors live alone (Martel and Legare, 2000).

The Boomerang Effect

In her book *The Boomerang Age* (2005), Canadian sociologist Barbara Mitchell notes that important domestic changes are taking place in the lives of young adults in Western industrialized societies. Today's young people often move through a larger variety of family-related roles, statuses, and living arrangements.

Among the most prominent changes is the rise of 'boomerang kids'—young adults returning to the parental home after their first entrance into the adult world. According to the General Social Survey in 2001, 33 per cent of men and 28 per cent of women between the ages of 20 and 29 have returned home at least once after previously moving away. The number of young adults returning home has been increasing year by year, reaching 41 per cent in 2001, the last year for which data were available. Twenty years earlier, the proportion was only 27 per cent. Statistics Canada analysts offer several explanations: adult children returning home after failed marriages, delayed marriage, more people in their twenties still in school, and the difficulty for those young adults of finding jobs (*Globe and Mail*, 2002).

Based on recent Canadian census data about young adults living at home, Clark (2007) reports that young adults are taking longer to make the typical transitions into adulthood: from school to work, from singlehood to marriage, and from the parental home into their own home:

> The transitions of today's young adults are both delayed and elongated: delayed, because young adults take more time to complete their first major transition (leaving school), thus postponing all subsequent transitions; and elongated, because each subsequent transition takes longer to complete and stretches the process from their late teens to their early thirties. In contrast, the 1971 cohort pack[ed] more transitions into the years from their late teens to their mid-twenties and fewer into their early thirties.

At the same time, this report also shows that the delayed process has been strongly gendered. Women are making the transitions about as quickly as they did in past years, 'although they are more likely to include full-year full-time work and less likely to include marriage and childbearing'. Men, on the other hand, 'at age 34 have made fewer transitions than 30 years ago' and 'are less likely to have full-year full-time work than their fathers did 30 years earlier' (ibid.).

Boyd and Pryor (1989) report that couples who thought that their children had grown up and 'flown away' are now discovering the family home (nest) being refilled with adult children who are returning to school (or have never left school), having trouble finding or keeping jobs, getting separated or divorced, or even having children of their own.

The return of grown children to their parental home, usually for financial reasons, is an especially vivid example of the generational transfer of wealth from older to younger adults. A significant shift in occupational opportunities or marital status may be enough of a jolt to the young person's finances to send him/her back into the family nest (Mitchell et al., 2000). Parental satisfaction with the arrangement is greater when children provide support in return, are more autonomous, and are closer to completing adult roles (Mitchell, 1998).

The future may reproduce the past: some families already live in refilled nests only out of need and do not see themselves as creating anything new, merely pooling housing and resources to survive. Others, however, may see huge creative possibilities in refilled nests, such as for child care by grandparents while parents work; for sharing housework among more family members; for reducing environmental problems by having fewer accommodations; for developing new ways of intergenerational caring for elders.

Domestic Violence

Family or domestic violence includes domestic and intimate-partner abuse, child and adolescent physical and sexual abuse, and elder abuse (discussed in Chapter 6). Such violence is responsible for a significant portion of intentional injury recorded in Canada. As such, it is a major social and health problem (Kaplan, 2000).

Child abuse can take the form of physical or mental harm, sexual abuse, neglect, or maltreatment (Ungar et al, 2009). Of these, neglect is the most common form of reported child abuse. Children also run the risk of sexual abuse, more commonly by a stepfather or a boyfriend of the mother than by their biological father.

Abused children often display anti-social behaviour, aggression, low self-esteem, depression, and poor school performance. In adulthood, self-destructive behaviours often continue, including depression, low self-esteem, anxiety, and an increased risk of alcohol or drug abuse and suicide. Children who witnessed or were victims of physical abuse have an increased risk of becoming abusers themselves when they enter adulthood (Gelles and Conte, 1991).

Even after controlling for other socio-demographic variables, poverty, substance abuse, and (young) maternal age are strong predictors of confirmed reports of all types of child maltreatment. Young mothers and impoverished mothers are at particular risk of abusing their children (Malo et al., 2004). This suggests that we need a comprehensive approach to the problem of child abuse, one that lessens the economic stress on young mothers while improving their parenting skills (Lee and George, 1999).

Other variables likely to distinguish men who batter their wives are alcohol and drug abuse, low education, and low levels of self-control that lead to frequent arguments with the spouse. Abusing husbands typically also have a (childhood) background of family violence and marital arguments (Coleman et al., 1980). Many women have trouble leaving an abusive relationship or even seeking help when they are in the abusive relationship. Should they divorce, they are often left with the care of children and a lack of financial child support

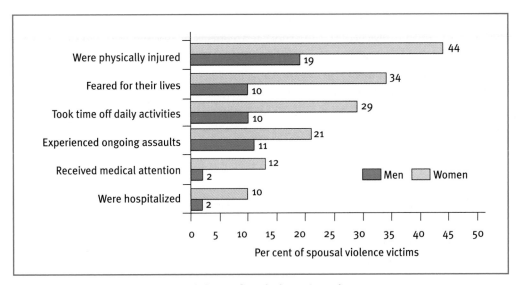

Figure 11.5 Impact of Spousal Violence for Victims: Canada, 2004

Note: **Figures may not add up to 100 per cent due to multiple responses.**

Sources: **Statistics Canada, General Social Survey, 2004, and Statistics Canada, Measuring Violence Against Women, Statistical Trends 2006, at: www.victimsweek.gc.ca/2008/res/r52.html.**

from the children's father. Thus, the co-dependency of abused people is as often a financial problem as it is a psychological or emotional one.

Same-sex relationships also are subject to partner abuse (Blosnich and Bossarte, 2009). Lesbians and transsexual people are not always comfortable in women's shelters, as they may experience homophobic violence from heterosexual women. Gay men have no shelters they can use other than homeless shelters, which offer little security from abusive partners and no long-term housing.

HEALTH CONSEQUENCES OF FAMILY LIFE

Research shows that marriage usually adds to people's health and happiness, especially for men and when contrasted with divorce and separation. However, what matters is the stability and quality of the relationship, not its legal status. Some common aspects of family life are not healthy at all.

One study (Choi, 2006) found that being married, as compared to being single, was associated with lower odds of mortality. However, this effect was mainly indirect, in the sense that marriage buffers the harmful effects of poverty and other disadvantage. When the moderating effect of marriage on the association between socio-economic status (SES) and health was tested, being married compared to being single was found to protect against the negative effects of lower income on survival and worsened functioning, particularly for men. Even being in a high-disagreement marriage (compared to being single) was found to buffer the income-mortality gradient for men. However, among the married, both men and women who experienced an increase in marital disagreement were more vulnerable to the negative effects of education and income stratification on their health.

A Canadian study (Strohschein et al., 2005) likewise confirmed the mental health advantage of marriage and revealed that the short-term effects of moving into and out of marriage on psychological distress are similar for men and women. Again, the quality of the marriage matters a great deal. There is also some evidence that staying unhappily married is more detrimental than divorcing. Such couples also have lower levels of life satisfaction, self-esteem, and overall health than individuals who divorce and remain unmarried (Hawkins and Booth, 2005).

Divorce and Remarriage

Divorce is an emotionally draining and stressful experience. This is not surprising because divorce results in the loss of a sexual partner and companion, potential decrease in contact with children, lower financial standing, single parenthood, and so on. Children of divorced parents have more substance-abusing friends and fewer coping and social skills than children whose parents are married (Neher and Short, 1998).

One contentious issue concerns the circumstances under which it is in the child's best interest for parents to separate rather than to stay together. An investigation by Jaap Dronkers (1996) examined whether serious conflicts between non-divorced parents have a stronger negative effect on the well-being of their children (in terms of use of drugs, illness, violence and crime, mental health, etc.) than living in a single-mother family caused by divorce. Three of Dronkers's findings are relevant to the current discussion. First, the well-being of children living in single-mother families was higher than that of children living in two-parent homes marked by a great deal of parental conflict. Second, the well-being of children living in single-mother families with a low level of parental conflict and with a high degree of contact with the non-residential father was still lower than that of children living in two-parent families with an equally low level of parent conflict.

Finally, the degree of parental conflict after divorce was more important for the well-being of the children than was contact with the departed father. These results suggest that, as measured by well-being outcomes, divorce may the best alternative for children, depending on the parental conflict in the marriage. Conflict is bad for children—worse than divorce, it seems.

SOLUTIONS TO FAMILY PROBLEMS

Work–Family Solutions

Many families suffer from the conflict between work life and family life. Even within family-friendly companies that offer their workers various programs designed to increase the time available to spend with family, few employees took advantage of the programs. Although many workers state a wish to cut back on their 'workaholism' and spend more time with spouses and children, 'programs that allowed parents to work undistracted by family concerns were endlessly in demand, while policies offering shorter hours that allowed workers more free or family time languished. . . . Only flextime, which rearranged but did not cut back on hours of work, had any significant impact on the workplace' (Hochschild, 1997).

Three explanations have been offered to account for these worker preferences. One is that workers cannot afford to cut back on work hours, despite their wishes to the contrary. This is most obviously true among lower-tier workers whose combined household incomes bar either partner from scaling back. However, this theory does not explain why top-level executives, whose salaries are large enough to allow the adoption of a shorter workweek, also choose against such policies as job-sharing and part-time work.

A second explanation is that workers choose not to use family-friendly programs because they are afraid of being laid off. Although company policies often encourage employees to spend more time with their families, workers doubt the sincerity of such offers. This argument implies that family-friendly programs are often mere ornaments designed to soothe external critics but not to solve workers' problems.

A third explanation is that despite what workers say about wanting to spend more time with their families, they find the time spent at work is often more pleasant and rewarding than time spent at home. In her three-year study of a top US company, Hochschild (ibid.) found that the duties of home life—caring for the children, sharing household duties, trying to preserve intimacy and love with one's spouse, and so on—were often very stressful. As a result, one's family becomes in many ways like work—in fact, a 'second shift'.

For these reasons, work-based solutions to the family–work issue are helpful, but they must be fine-tuned, made more widely available, and accepted more widely by workers and management. At the same time, families need to seek new answers through reorganizing domestic work.

Caregiving Solutions

Caregiving is a fundamentally social activity, and increasingly, it is a family activity. Social support networks are important for caregivers and care recipients alike. Clear and continuing communication between informal and formal caregivers, on the one hand, and health-care and social service providers, on the other, is a necessity. Family and community organization is central to good caregiving.

Rosalie Kane and colleagues (1999) followed the experiences of family caregivers of older people hospitalized for stroke or hip fracture in three US cities. The researchers studied the families for one year after the hospitalization, tracking the demands that providing care placed on the families and how families responded to those demands. They found the primary caregiver—often aged 65 or older—regularly spent 20 hours or more every week caring for the spouse or relative. What surprised the researchers was the variety of ways that families reorganized to meet these new demands.

Perhaps the most striking information to come from this study was that the difficulties that caregivers reported facing were related less to specific task performances than they were to dealing with feelings, managing time, and adjusting to changing relationships and life plans. This tells us that understanding how caregiving affects a family and its organization

ONE TRUE THING

Anna (Renee Zellwegger) must leave her job at New York Magazine to take care of her ill mother (Meryl Streep) in this 1998 family drama.

might significantly contribute to efforts to help families deal with the many problems associated with long-term care (ibid.).

Solutions to Family Violence

We can learn a great deal from research about the best ways to intervene to solve problems of family stress and violence. First, violence is a major factor causing women to leave their marriages and children to leave their parents' home. Second, programs that attempt to address abuse directly—such as civil restraining orders, treatment programs for batterers, and policies requiring mandatory arrest and no dropped charges—are usually not effective in solving the problem of domestic violence (Davis and Smith, 1995), but they are a necessary first step in protecting the woman and any children in the family. By contrast, treatments aimed at reducing alcohol and drug abuse may make a long-term difference to the likelihood of future violence (O'Farrell and Murphy, 1995; Brannen and Rubin, 1996).

Third, problems like stress and violence require active problem-solving. If we want to reduce family stresses, we must create a society that is family-friendly, with increased social support and practical assistance to working parents with small children. Fourth, research shows us that the health and social service provisions are inadequate. Fifth, research shows us that personal lives, and families, are increasingly diverse. Recently arrived immigrant and refugee women, for example, have needs that differ markedly from battered women in the general population by involving language, cultural, and immigration issues (Huisman, 1996).

In the end, however, we must recognize there will be no major decline in violence against family members until societies reduce stresses on family members, place greater personal value on all people, and treat all people with respect and dignity—especially children, women, elderly people, and sexual and visible minorities. Societies must also reject the cultural justifications for domestic violence and deprive violent people of opportunities to hide or to repeat their behaviour. Ending domestic violence is a societal project no less complex than dealing with unemployment, illiteracy, AIDS, or any other recognized social problem.

CHAPTER SUMMARY

There can be little doubt that many people have turned their backs on the traditional, idealized family of 50 years ago. Today, people are getting married later in life and having fewer children. The fraction of childless couples also has increased. Closely related to this trend has been an increase in the number of couples who cohabit. The divorce rate has increased dramatically in the last few decades. Yet, most young people continue to come together in long-term relationships and make them survive.

Although more women have been entering the workforce, women still do more housework than men in dual-income households. This so-called double shift has harmful health outcomes, and places stress on the relationships between spouses and between parents and children.

As we have seen, families often have to deal with serious problems. The negative consequences of divorce, both emotional and financial, tend to be greatest for women and children. One-seventh of all Canadian families are single-parent households. Women head about 90 per cent of these single-parent families, which are more prone to financial and emotional strain. However, most families, single-parent or not, are experiencing financial and emotional strain these days. Family violence is more common than many people recognize. Although women and men are just as likely to take part in violence, women are the ones most often hurt.

QUESTIONS FOR CRITICAL THOUGHT

1. Why is the nuclear family the norm in our society, while in others the extended family is the norm? What social demands do nuclear families fulfill? And how is societal change bringing about new family structures?

2. What are 'traditional family values' and why have they been changing? Which social movements helped to alter these attitudes?

3. In a community composed of families from different cultural backgrounds, opinions about parenting may clash. What kinds of conflicts might arise? Suggest some probable solutions.

4. In what ways can technology be used to improve the quality of family life? Conversely, how can technology negatively affect family life?

5. Aboriginal families experience many social problems that lead to poor health. What are the various causes of these problems, and how are they related? What can be done to solve the more important of these problems?

RECOMMENDED READINGS

Alaggia, Ramona, and Cathy Vine, eds. 2006. *Cruel but Not Unusual: Violence in Canadian Families*. Waterloo, ON: Wilfrid Laurier University Press. This book provides the latest research on domestic violence in Canadian families. While it uses feminist theory as a framework, it also employs other approaches to examine and respond to critical aspects of domestic violence. It focuses on the particularly vulnerable, including Aboriginal communities, the young, the elderly, and same-sex couples.

Albanese, Patrizia. 2009. *Children in Canada Today*. Toronto: Oxford University Press. This book provides insights into the experiences of childhood in Canada, with a focus on the role of the family as an agent of socialization and its resulting influence on children as they become socially 'functioning' adults.

Cheal, David, ed. 2007. *Canadian Families Today: New Perspectives*. Toronto: Oxford University Press. This collection of original essays, written by prominent Canadian scholars, presents an overview of the historical structure of the family and its many current variations, and explores key social issues experienced by Canadian families, such as parenthood, religious and ethnic diversity, caregiving, intimacy, domestic violence, work, the state, etc. Finally, it attempts to predict the practices of tomorrow's families.

Fox, Bonnie, ed. 2008. *Family Patterns, Gender Relations*, 3rd edn. Toronto: Oxford University Press. In this revised edition, Professor Fox explores the complex dynamics and patterns of family life. She uses a wide range of materials from Canada, the US, and the UK to provide readers with a comprehensive and comparative perspective.

Garner, Abigail. 2004. *Families Like Mine: Children of Gay Parents Tell It Like It Is*. Toronto: HarperCollins. After having grown up in an LGBT household, the author interviews five dozen others who had grown up in the same environment. She provides an insider account of the experiences, emotions, and challenges of being raised by gay parents.

Higham, John. 2009. 360 *Longitude: One Family's Journey around the World—A Memoir*. Boston: Alyson Books. Humorous and insightful, this book provides a glimpse of what it is like to be a global citizen. More importantly, it depicts the new ideas and practices held by modern families, breaking the mould of the former generation's suburban parenthood.

McKenna, Katherine, and June Larkin, eds. 2002. *Violence against Women: New Canadian Perspectives*. Toronto: Inanna. This collection of articles focuses on the issue of male violence against women. The articles are grouped into three sections: the prevalence and nature of violence against women; violence and women's health; and structural forms of violence against health.

Peterson, Gary W., Linda Haas, and Steven K. Wisensale. 2006. *Families and Social Policy: National and International Perspectives*. London: Routledge. This book explores the latest research on the impact of government policy—or lack of policy—on family life in various developed and developing nations. Authors use empirical data to highlight the comparisons between countries and their common family problems.

Recommended Websites

World Family Organization

www.worldfamilyorganization.org

Adhering to the principles of the United Nations, this organization aims to protect and support families in all cultural, political, and social systems. Their archives include documents from international projects and forums, offering global and up-to-date news on families around the world.

Centre for Family Research—University of Cambridge

www.ppsis.cam.ac.uk/CFR

This prestigious institution for family research aims to increase understanding of children, parents, and family relationships with a focus on topics that are central to public policy, health care, and people's lives. Their major research areas include: Early Social Development and the Family; Non-Traditional Families; Genetics, Health and Families; and Bioethics and the Family.

Hot Peach Pages—International Directory of Domestic Violence Agencies

www.hotpeachpages.net

In conjunction with a multitude of UN organizations and international non-governmental organizations, Hot Peach aims to provide people all over the world with the resources and information on their local domestic violence agencies. It also provides an array of studies, statistics, and reports on domestic violence worldwide.

Family Service Toronto

www.fsatoronto.com

This local agency provides family support services to families, individuals, and communities in Toronto. Special emphasis is made to care for the marginalized and the disadvantaged. Organizational policies enforce a commitment to assist people of all ethnicities, languages, races, ages, abilities, genders, sexual orientations, and political or religious affiliations. The website includes up-to-date local, regional, and national news and events affecting the Canadian family.

CHAPTER 12
Workplaces

iStockphoto.com/Dmitry Vasilyev

LEARNING OBJECTIVES

- To know some basic facts about work and unemployment.
- To see how work and employment can be considered as social problems.
- To understand the role of multinationals in the global economy.
- To make the connection between bureaucratization and unemployment.
- To know the major sociological theories about work and unemployment.
- To be able to explain the role technology plays in unemployment and work.
- To be aware of health outcomes of work and unemployment.

INTRODUCTION

This chapter is about employment and unemployment, workers and workplaces, productivity, labour, industry, profits, manufacturing, and health. In particular, it is about work in Canada. But what constitutes 'work' and what are the boundaries of this definition? For example, does it include 'sex work'? Sandy (2009) applies this question to her study of sex workers in Cambodia. She notes that, in global discourses about sex work, the image of the 'sex slave' has been influential in constructing the view of women working in the sex industry in developing countries as 'victims'. Such discourses have been perpetuated through powerful lobbying groups and socially conservative governments. This framework situates women working in the Cambodian sex industry as 'victims', but such an approach may be inadequate. Based on ethnographic research and interviews with sex workers in the port city of Sihanoukville, Cambodia, Sandy's paper questions prevailing stereotypes of 'trafficking victims' and the image of 'defiled' or 'duped' women and girls central to such frameworks. It finds that, in the transition to a market economy, women's choices are constrained by hierarchical structures such as gender, class, socio-cultural obligations, and poor employment opportunities. This is the case whether women take up sex work or not—in all instances, they are both victims and agents.

Compare this with Besen-Cassino's (2008) analysis of teenagers in precarious and undesirable jobs in North America. She notes that some scholars characterize typical teenage jobs as 'exploitive': highly routinized service-sector jobs with low pay, no benefits, minimum skill requirements, and little time off. To understand the lived experience associated with these jobs, Besen-Cassino focuses on the lived work experience of particularly affluent suburban teenagers who work in these jobs and explores the meaning they create during their everyday work experience.

Based on a large ethnographic study conducted with the teenage workers at a national coffee franchise, she finds that outsider views of these 'bad jobs' differ from the everyday experience of the actors. From the perspective of the teenagers, these 'exploitive jobs' are often seen as fun, social, and empowering; they provide free spaces where the teens can express their creativity and individuality. This finding shows the importance of using a constructionist view to understand teenage employment and inequality. It also argues that the nature and quality of work—whether experienced as opportunity or victimization—is subjective, largely in the eyes of the beholder. Of course, the point of view might differ with subjects who are not affluent suburbanite teenagers but lone-parent young women, immigrant children who work at McJobs to help support their families, or school dropouts for whom such jobs can represent a dead end. Table 12.1 outlines the reasons why people of different age groups work part-time.

In short, our perceptions of work are shaped by our understanding of opportunity and inequality, as well as by claims made about choice and constraint. In this respect, work has not changed much since the days when Marx wrote about the 'alienation' of labour under capitalism. He, too, was concerned about the deprivation of choice and its effects on one's identity, social position, and social perception.

Table 12.1 Reasons for Part-time Work by Age Group (both sexes), 2009

Reason	Total	15–24	25–44	45 and over
		%		
Own illness	3.5	0.6	3.6	6.5
Caring for children	9.4	0.9	26.6	4.2
Other personal/family responsibilities	2.9	0.6	3.7	4.7
Going to school	28.9	72.4	10.5	0.8
Personal preference	26.8	5.4	17.5	55.4
Other voluntary	0.8	0.4	1.1	0.8
Other[1]	27.6	19.7	37.1	27.7
Total employed part-time (thousands)	3,220.5	1,138.6	920.8	1,161.1
% employed part-time[2]	19.1	46.9	12.4	16.7

1. Includes business conditions and unable to find full-time work.
2. Expressed as a percentage of total employed.

Source: **Reasons for Part-time Work by Sex and Age Group (both sexes), at www40.statcan.gc.ca/l01/cst01/labor63a-eng.htm (September 2010).**

COMPARATIVE ECONOMIC SYSTEMS

Capitalism and Socialism

CAPITALISM The economic system in which private individuals or corporate groups own the means of production and distribution. Capitalists invest capital to produce goods and services, which they sell for profit in a competitive free market.

SOCIALISM An alternative economic and political ideology that flourished in the nineteenth and twentieth centuries. It favours the public ownership of the means of production and distribution, and the investment of public capital in producing goods and services.

Capitalism refers to the economic system in which private individuals or corporate groups own the means of production and distribution and invest private capital to produce goods and services to be sold for profit in a competitive market. Socialism is an alternative economic and political ideology that flourished in the nineteenth and twentieth centuries. It favours public ownership of the means of production and distribution and investing public capital in producing goods and services (Cullen, 2009).

For those who defend socialism—generally Marxists—the capitalist system is just one step in humanity's historic development. They argue that from the early days of human civilization social inequalities were established based on an individual's relationship to material wealth (Wood, 1998). As societies became more industrialized and capitalistic, imbalances in the relations of production between social classes—that is, between those who had the wealth to purchase and control the engines of production, and those who did not—became entrenched in social structures, institutions, and economic organizations. As well, according to this viewpoint, capitalism itself contains certain internal contradictions based on the market structure and the way in which the bourgeoisie exploits the labour of the working class while keeping economic surpluses for itself (Hanke, 1996).

Marxists believe in the eventual inevitability that the proletariats will seize the means of production and redistribute wealth according to a more equitable scheme, for the well-being of the society as a whole.

Those who oppose socialism, on the other hand, consider capitalism to be 'the end of history' (Fukuyama, 1992). They argue that socialist societies are inefficient because the common will never drives people to work as hard as their own individual interests and benefits. In the view of capitalists, the market system ensures maximum efficiency because it maximizes the competition between firms, corporations, and individuals. This competition also guarantees that resources are assigned in the best way, because production for profit always follows the consumers' demand. Most importantly, supporters of capitalism state that the contradictions pointed out by Marxists will be solved as the system develops. This optimistic view has been challenged by Marxists and others. After all, what drives capitalism is the need for ever-more resources, the need for ever-increasing profits, and the assumption of endless economic growth—and therefore consumption—with some ups and downs along the way. Almost 40 years ago the Club of Rome pointed out the limits to such growth (Meadows et al., 1972), as have many others since that time.

Industrialism and the Industrial Revolution

Since the late eighteenth century, industrialism has transformed the way we work. In pre-industrial societies, people worked collectively in mainly agricultural settings. Because of the small, localized scale of rural communities and the interconnectedness of people's experiences, work was largely inseparable from family and personal life. People led similar lives and held similar moral, religious, and political beliefs (Crisman, 2009).

Two major economic developments changed this: an agricultural revolution and the Industrial Revolution. By the early eighteenth century, an agricultural revolution that began thousands of years earlier with plant and animal domestication had reached a point where farmers could produce a large surplus of food, thus enabling many people to work at enterprises outside of food production (Aiken, 2009).

This great number of non-farm workers and technological developments, such as the steam engine, drove the Industrial Revolution. The new system of production introduced innovations in agricultural practices, further increasing efficiency. The new factory system created a large surplus in the manufacturing areas, beginning with the textile and steel industries. Such surpluses in most economic activities, along with the influx from the countryside of large numbers of workers paid with wages, increased dramatically the complexity of the market and laid the foundations for the emerging capitalist system (Abrams et al., 2009) and the modern city.

During the Industrial Revolution, machines replaced human hands and tools in the production of particular products, while steam (and later, electrical) power replaced much human exertion as the source of energy. As the manufacturing process became more complex, jobs became more specialized (Rosenberg and Trajenberg, 2004). Early in the twentieth century, Henry Ford invented the assembly line (Schildt, 2006). Cities grew rapidly as people came together in factory towns to seek work in return for wages. Prior to industrialization, family life and work life had been carried out in the same place—often on a farm.

Now, the two realms of activity became distinct and exclusive, the one still located at home, the other in a factory or office. This marked a new separation of men and women, men's work and women's work, adult work and children's work, and formal education.

The Global Economy and Post-Industrialism

In the late twentieth century, industrialism evolved into post-industrialism. Post-industrialism is characterized by the shift from a manufacturing-intensive economy to an economy based on services and information (Chen et al., 2003).

With post-industrialism, geography, distance, and national borders have lost much of their meaning as barriers in communication. Technology and other factors have increased the flow of information, products, and people (Yoon, 2001). They include multinational trade agreements, such as the North American Free Trade Agreement (NAFTA), the European Union, MERCOSUR, which includes several countries in South America, and the proposed Free Trade Area of the Americas (FTAA), and international economic organizations, such as the World Trade Organization (WTO), the World Bank, and the International Monetary Fund (IMF). These agreements and organizations, while benefiting relations between countries, have been laced with political agendas.

Trade agreements are aimed at removing tariffs for import and export. International organizations pressure less developed countries to open their borders to global trade, dangling the promise of foreign investments and economic prosperity. When this happens, corporate multinationals find it easier to gain access to raw materials in foreign countries, to employ cheap labour overseas, and to avoid government controls over workers' rights and environmental pollution. Many believe this process benefits rich nations at the expense of poor ones, and large multinational organizations at the expense of smaller organizations and nation-states.

Global capitalism has supported the growth of huge multinational corporations with revenues larger than the GDPs of most nation-states. They are the dominant political and economic force in the post-industrial world. Sometimes, they produce jobs and new wealth (Langman, 2008). In other instances, they destroy jobs—leading to unemployment—and put more wealth in the pockets of the already wealthy (Heinrich, 2008).

Some people leave their birth countries to seek employment—in search of better work conditions or to gain international experience and some adventure along the way. Many Canadians have also gone abroad to live and work, and most of them in the prime of their working lives (see Figure 12.1).

Technological Dualism

The explosion of telecommunications and computer technology has resulted in unemployment and in the growth of jobs that demand skilled workers. Fast-paced development has caused skills to become outdated faster than ever. Constant upgrading is needed now for

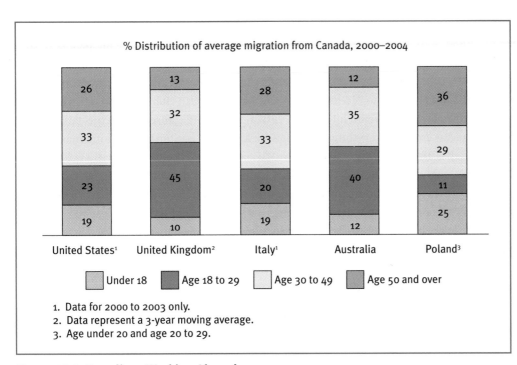

Figure 12.1 **Canadians Working Abroad**

Source: **Canadians Working Abroad at: www.statcan.gc.ca/pub/11-008-x/2008001/c-g/10517/5004369-eng.htm.**

workers (and economies) to remain competitive in a continuously changing job market (James, 2003).

However, not everyone can achieve this. Such spirited self-improvement is largely limited to those with the financial and educational means to do so and those who work in a sector of the economy that wants and promotes such changes. For workers mired in low-wage, dead-end positions—in the retail industry, for example—the market may not force rapid adaptation to technical change, but neither does it offer many opportunities for greater self-improvement and wealth (James, 2002).

Workers in the manufacturing industry increasingly are being threatened with job cuts made possible by the automation of production. Computer-controlled machinery benefits corporate managers for several reasons. First, it removes human error in jobs that are boring and repetitive. Second, high-tech machines can manufacture products with greater uniformity and precision than can human workers. Third, computerization replaces humans with machines that can run continuously, resulting in significant cost-effectiveness.

Fourth, computerization and mechanization reduce human conflict between workers and bosses by reducing the number of humans involved. Computing devices do not demand an income, never go on strike (although they do break down), never become tired of or bored by their work, and can work around the clock. As technology continues to transform the workplace, more efficient and less costly machines take over tasks once done by human labour. Only a few well-trained employees are needed to program, supervise, and maintain the otherwise robotic manufacturing process (Fernandez, 1995).

Technology has also affected social interaction and social bonds. The benefit of telephones, fax machines, e-mail, and Internet chat rooms is the convenience of allowing people separated by great physical distances to remain in real-time contact with one another, either over a wire or in cyberspace. On the downside, these and other technological inventions have reduced the need for face-to-face contact (Torney et al., 2009). Often, we have replaced activities that once involved human interaction with a machine. Because of the expectations that technology has created, everything must now be accessible and instant. Among many other things, this has changed the way we work.

An increasingly prevalent effect of modern technology in the workplace is the emergence of virtual work—that is, the completion and performance of work duties away from the traditional office through the use of computer technology (Golden and Veiga, 2005). Modern technology enables work to transcend its traditionally designated setting. Virtual work has become commonplace throughout North America. Nearly 28 million workers in the United States regularly work from home—or from various other remote locations—in addition to spending time at the office.

THE BUREAUCRATIZATION OF WORK

Besides factories and cities, bureaucracies are a defining feature of modern work life. Bureaucracies are large, complex organizations employing specialized workers who work within the context of what Max Weber (1947) called a *legal-rational authority* structure. This form of authority is distinguished by thorough written rules governing how people are to perform their jobs.

A facet of modern bureaucracy is the legal idea of 'limited liability', which allows a corporation to manage investment and profits impersonally. In principle, bureaucracies distinguish between the rights and duties attached to a position and the characteristics of the person who (temporarily) holds a position of authority. The impersonal connection between office-holders and the organization also makes bureaucracy different from patronage and other personalized systems, such as organized crime.

Industrialization and capitalism favoured the rise of bureaucracies. Bureaucracies are good at controlling large workforces—even highly educated and differentiated workforces. As organizations grow, their differentiation usually increases. Problems of co-ordination and control—formalization, decentralization, and supervision—are bound to arise. Often, reorganization is needed, especially if the number of personnel is large and growing rapidly. As industrial enterprises grow with the mechanization of work, control structures (that is, for management and administration) usually grow as well.

Structurally, every member of a bureaucratic organization is enmeshed in a network of **reporting relationships** (Brumback, 2007). The ideal **bureaucracy** is a spruce-tree-shaped structure that branches out, with the hierarchy narrowing towards the top (Henshaw, 1988). At the bottom of the hierarchy, many people have to (1) carry out orders from above, (2) report work-related information to their superiors, and (3) uphold linkages between the organization and its client or customer base. At the top of the hierarchy, only a few people

REPORTING RELATIONSHIPS An official hierarchical relationship established within a bureaucracy. This relationship is characterized by a power dynamic in which subordinate members adhere to a set of predetermined roles, processes, and functions.

BUREAUCRACY A large, complex organization employing highly specialized workers who work within the context of what Max Weber called a legal-rational authority structure.

get to (1) issue orders to their subordinates, (2) process information received from below, and (3) preserve linkages between the organization and other organizations—political, economic, and social. In addition, those at the top of this organization are to share information between the heads of planning, manufacturing, shipping, public relations, and other sectors of the organization.

Below the surface of the ideal or formal structure, which prescribes how a bureaucracy ought to work, there inevitably exists an informal structure (Taylor, 2000). This informal organization is developed through communication based on trust. Trust is formed through friendship, acquaintance, and gossip about third parties that strengthen existing ties. People have stronger attachments to other workers than they do to 'the organization', an abstract entity.

THEORETICAL PERSPECTIVES ON WORK AND UNEMPLOYMENT

Table 12.2 Theoretical Perspectives

Theory	Main Points
Structural Functionalism	• Work is a basic human need. • Everyone profits when everyone works. • Work is the most basic of social institutions. • Everyone needs love, work, and hope. • Work provides a basis for social interaction, social solidarity, and cohesion.
Conflict Theory	• Capitalists benefit from the current organization of work. • Globalization produces jobs. • Work promotes social inequality. • Work is a place of repression and mistreatment. • Power elites, to boost profits, use unemployment. • Unemployed people depress wages and provide a reserve army of labour.
Symbolic Interactionism	• Work can be organized in a variety of ways. • Socialization and labelling shape the content and perception of different jobs. • Meanings are found in work and unemployment. • Work provides a major part of our identity. • People treat work as a status symbol, and jobs are used as a method of making judgements. • Chronic unemployment is a learned trait—a culture of poverty that perpetuates a sense of learned helplessness.

Continued

Table 12.2 Theoretical Perspectives—*Continued*	
Theory	**Main Points**
Feminist Theory	• Women continue to be disadvantaged at work. • Patriarchy operates in the workforce. • Women are paid less than men for the same jobs and work in lower-paying sectors. • Capitalists benefit from the hard unpaid work of women.
Social Constructionism	• The organization of work is an evolving social process. • It reflects changes in technology and worker–management conflict. • The structure of work evolves based on relations between workers and employers. • Technology is a new force in the evolution of work organization.

Structural Functionalism

The structural-functionalist perspective asks, as always, *what function* does work perform? This perspective stresses that, along with the family, work is the most basic of social institutions. Functionalists believe that everyone needs love, work, and hope. Work is especially important because it lets people acquire the material necessities of life—food, water, shelter, and clothing—for themselves and their families.

Not only does paid work give workers an opportunity to satisfy their physical needs, it also allows them to satisfy their emotional needs. These include the wishes to be a productive and valued member of society, to gain recognition and praise, and to interact and co-operate with others. Thus, work has social purposes. It provides a basis for social interaction, social solidarity and cohesion, and the sharing of lifestyles and meanings. The workplace, ideally, lets people exercise all of their social and creative impulses while earning a living.

Conflict and Feminist Theories

Conflict theorists, by contrast, ask: *Who gains the advantage* from the current system of work? The competing interests of different classes lead inevitably to conflict. Karl Marx (e.g., 1936 [1887]) claimed that class relations under capitalism cause all the conflict within and between societies.

To his mind, the members of a capitalist society can be divided into two factions. The ruling class, or bourgeoisie, comprises the wealthy owners of the means of production, and the working class, or proletariat, comprises the labourers who work for the bourgeoisie. One group wants to hire labour for the lowest possible price; the other wants to sell its labour for the highest possible price.

Given their opposed interests, the two classes are locked in a conflict that plays out largely in the workplace. In this 'contested terrain' (to use economist Richard Edwards's term), there can never be peace and co-operation, or a universally accepted definition of efficiency, because the interests of workers and capitalists are opposed. From this point of view, the workplace is not a place for sociability and creativity; it is a place for repression and mistreatment, in which some groups of workers are even more vulnerable than others. In this system, low-end workers—the most vulnerable workers, those most in need of a stable income—are often the first to lose their jobs when the economy goes into a slump.

Feminist theorists also ask: *Why don't women benefit* from the capitalist organization of work? They note that Canadian women still are disproportionately engaged in work that has little or no pay—that is, in social reproduction. As a result, capitalists profit from the hard work of women even more than they profit from the hard work of working men; and men, who usually occupy higher-paid jobs than women, often profit at the expense of women. The

CLASSIC WORKS

Box 12.1 Rosabeth Kanter's *Men and Women of the Corporation* (1977)

Rosabeth Kanter's classic work, *Men and Women of the Corporation* (1977), challenges assumptions about the traditional system of merit and reward within organizations. Contrary to the common belief that women's opportunities are limited because women act differently from men (for example, that they are too 'feminine'), Kanter's study shows that women have less opportunity for promotion so they are forced to act 'like women': subservient, devious, yet seemingly unambitious. When men and women have the same opportunities, both act in the same way. People—male or female—who suffer from blocked opportunity, powerlessness, and tokenism display less ambition and low productivity, a result of holding weak positions.

All women connected with large organizations—whether executives, secretaries, or even wives—are in a similar bind. Secretaries, however ambitious and talented, are tied to the fortunes of their male bosses. Their earnings rise and fall directly with those of the boss, regardless of the women's own efforts. Similarly, the wives of organizational executives, also often ambitious and talented, are tied to their spouses' fortunes. Both secretaries and wives are powerless, yet heavily dependent on men; their fates rise and fall with those of the men to whom they are linked. Moreover, because of this powerlessness, they behave in 'typical' female fashion. These seemingly typical female performances support the male view that women, by nature, are not good executive material.

Kanter hypothesizes that people who are in a numerical minority will feel restricted in what they can do. The more outnumbered they are, the more stress they will experience. As their numbers increase, however, social distance between the minority and majority groups will lessen, and interaction and communication across group boundaries will increase. However, adding a few 'token women' to an organization will not result in a significant increase in choices for women, nor allow women to flourish. Kanter's tokenism theory can be applied to any organizational setting that contains different 'kinds' of people, whether men and women, racialized workers and whites, anglophones and francophones, immigrants and native-born, and so on. We can apply the general principle—that tokenism prevents us from seeing how people could potentially adapt and grow into their roles—in a wide variety of situations. That makes Kanter's work fertile and valuable, even beyond the study of gender.

It is in an organization's interest to make the best possible use of its human capital—for example, its talented women. However, external relations with clients and other firms in the industry may hinder an organization's ability to change. More often than not, organizations copy one another and remain locked into patterns set up elsewhere. As well, large organizations have an internal environment that resists change, despite the best wishes of one or more bosses. They contain islands of vested interest—small domains with their own culture and power structure. Those in control will resist change.

result is job dissatisfaction, a lack of job control, and a rising prevalence of depression and other psychosomatic illnesses among women (Renzetti and Curran, 2003).

Symbolic Interactionism

Symbolic interactionists, as always, ask the question, *how* are jobs and job differences *symbolized*, negotiated, and communicated? They focus on the meanings of work and unemployment for the individual.

Work, especially in a modern, individualistic culture, provides a major part of our identity. Because a person's line of work is so central to his or her identity, others often use it as a source of information. 'So what do you do for a living?' is the second-most popular question asked whenever two strangers strike up a conversation.

Whether true or not, it is commonly believed that knowing one's occupation can provide clues to that person's character, personality, and interests. Many people also treat occupational titles as status symbols, basing their assessments of an individual largely on the prestige and income associated with the work that he or she does.

Social Constructionism

Finally, related to this approach, social constructionists always ask, *how* did the arrangement *emerge*?

An example of this would be the work by Richard Edwards (1979) on the historical evolution of management practices, from simple (or direct) control to technological control to what he calls bureaucratic control. This evolution of management strategies and ideologies reflected changes in the work done and technology used in the workplace. Even more, it reflected changing worker strategies to thwart managerial practices of control. As one means of control no longer worked, another would be invented and taught to new generations of managers.

In addition, social constructionists would be interested in the evolution of popular thinking about work. In the 1950s and 1960s, the dominant concern was with alienating work—how work in large organizations makes people robotic. In the 1970s and 1980s, the dominant concern was the exploitation of workers here and abroad, the possibility of computers replacing humans in the workplace, and with securing more leisure. Since then, alongside the rise of globalism, the principal concern has been job insecurity, job loss (that is, the export of jobs to low-wage countries), and the spillover effects of bad work lives into people's health and family lives.

SOCIAL CONSEQUENCES OF WORK

Gender Discrimination

The 'glass ceiling' that results in earning differences between women and men, and other gender-related workplace concerns, such as harassment, are discussed at length in Chapter 4 (Eze, 2009).

The problem of gender inequality in the workplace is important because the income earned at work affects a person's access to the necessities of life, education of children, and leisure. Women are over-represented in the lower end of the occupational marketplace, where dead-end and/or part-time work dominates. Low wages and job instability often mean that even full-time workers must live in poverty (Yap and Konrad, 2009).

Stereotypes persist of women as nurturing and emotional and of men as more dominant and rational. As a result, female workers are expected to be the primary caregivers. This expectation has carried over into the world of work, often resulting in women being excluded from occupations that require higher education and skill development. Consider advancements within the information technology industry in Canada. While this has led to mass employment opportunities, women seem to be largely under-represented within this sector of work in Canada (Kelan, 2007). For these and other reasons, women are still under-represented in leadership positions.

Women's unpaid household labour may account for as much as one-third of the world's economic production. When unpaid agricultural work and housework are considered with wage labour in developing countries, women's work hours are estimated to exceed men's by 30 per cent (UN Population Fund, 2000: 38).

Racial and Ethnic Discrimination

Workers who belong to ethnic and racial minorities are especially disadvantaged in their search for jobs, in the incomes they receive once hired, and in opportunities to advance based on merit (Li, 2003). In part, these problems reside in stereotypes—employers are unwilling or unable to imagine that certain types of people can do good work. Equally important, these problems are due to weak social networks. People with more social capital are in a better position to hear about good jobs, and employers are more likely to hear about them (Ooka and Wellman, 2006).

Many organizations have made a conscious effort to overcome these barriers by reaching out to minority communities, and by welcoming minority people who come to work in their midst.

SOCIAL CAPITAL
Sociologists call having larger, more varied, and more powerful interpersonal networks 'having greater social capital'.

Worker Dissatisfaction and Alienation

In an ideal world, work is invigorating, satisfying, and socially useful. It fulfills the individual's need for meaningful labour and society's need to get work done. In reality, however, many jobs are not stimulating and challenging. They are repetitive, boring, and often not even socially useful.

As mentioned earlier, at least as far back as Marx, social analysts have noted that industrialization and the resulting division of labour have separated the worker from the work process, from the object he or she produces, and from his or her co-workers. This experience of alienation involves feelings of powerlessness, meaninglessness, normlessness (anomie), estrangement, and social isolation in the workplace. Specialized work roles mean that each individual worker is given few responsibilities, performing narrowly defined tasks lacking in

ALIENATION
This experience involves feelings of powerlessness, meaninglessness, normlessness, estrangement, and social isolation in the workplace.

PERSONAL STORIES

Box 12.2 Toronto Police Proud to Show Their Increasingly Multicultural Face

When Deputy Chief Keith Forde joined the Toronto police in 1972 as an immigrant from Barbados, he was only the second visible minority ever to serve in his division. In the whole force, there were perhaps 30 or 40 non-white officers. 'You could drive the city and not see a visible minority in uniform for a day or two', he recalls.

Nearly four decades later, he is finally beginning to realize his dream of a force that reflects the multicultural reality on the streets. Today's service has more than 1,000 non-white officers. When the latest batch of 138 graduated from Police College last week, 38 per cent were visible minorities. In the total organization, 18.6 per cent are non-white, up 9.5 per cent from as recently as 2000.

Two of the force's four deputy chiefs are black: Deputy Chief Forde and Jamaican-born Peter Sloly, who is to take office next week. One of the six staff superintendents and six of the 43 inspectors are non-white.

There are more women, too. The number of female officers in uniform recently passed 1,000 for the first time, or 17.5 per cent. The new head of the homicide squad is a woman. The fraud and sex crimes units are led by women.

It's a far cry from the days when Toronto police were almost exclusively white, male, and tall (thanks to a ridiculous height rule). Now they come in both sexes and all sizes and colours.

That matters in a city where about half the residents are non-white. As a purely practical matter, it helps to have more police who are familiar with the city's many ethnic communities. Fifty-nine per cent of last week's police college grads speak a language other than English.

Symbolically, it means even more. 'Police control the power of the state', as Deputy Chief Forde puts it. To have that power mainly in white hands in a city increasingly populated by others set up a nasty dynamic. It wasn't many years ago that a series of shootings—white cops killing black men—strained race relations to the breaking point. Deputy Chief Forde remembers being called downtown to police angry black demonstrators, who called him a traitor to his race.

Out of those traumatic days—would Toronto become another Detroit?—came a determination to change the face of policing in the city. Police Chief Bill Blair has made officer diversity a big part of his drive to reach out to troubled neighbourhoods and communities.

Existing visible minority cops are made 'ambassadors' to their communities, spreading the word that it's okay to be a cop. Once hired, minority cops are welcomed into support groups for, say, Aboriginal or South Asian officers, to help each other along. The Toronto force was named one of Canada's best diversity employers in a competition, joining 35 other organizations and companies. Courtney Betty, a black lawyer who has been active in community issues, says that, 'For the police force to be the one to actually be leading the way is I think just great.'

Source: **Gee (2009).**

variety and challenge, often below his or her full intellectual, physical, and emotional potential, as demanded by the employer. Sociologists have disagreed about the origins of these problems: Marx attributed them to capitalism, Durkheim (1964 [1893]) to specialization, and Weber to rationalization.

Employees become just another cog in the wheel, mindlessly churning out the products wanted by their employers as part of a factory line, clerical office, filing department, or retail shop. In extreme cases, this narrow range of tasks is repeated daily for years, even decades. The result is a decline in worker loyalty and production, since employees are no longer dedicated to doing an especially good job. Many studies have shown that low levels of work satisfaction result from these work circumstances (Langfred and Moye, 2004; Stanton et al., 2002; Sikora, 2002).

Surveys show that several factors consistently are related to job satisfaction. The list includes safe working conditions, job security, challenging and stimulating work content, pleasant and like-minded colleagues, respect and consideration from superiors, and opportunities for creativity, initiative, and advancement. In addition, it is important that the worker's expectations of the job match the work experience. When the two diverge, resentment, job dissatisfaction, and alienation arise. Perhaps most importantly, people crave some measure of autonomy and control over their work (Lambert et al., 2009).

VULNERABLE POPULATIONS

Sex Workers

Whatever the power of personal experiences that incline a person towards sex work, such work is possible only under specific cultural conditions. Sex work is built on a sexual double standard, widespread poverty, and a gendered labour market. Poor women and children, especially in societies without a social welfare net, are most likely to be engaged in sex work.

In India, for example, women suffer from the double standard of morality that governs a profitable sex trade. Despite the financial vulnerability that leads them to enter sex work and

Indian sex workers participate in a rally to mark International Women's Day, and demand that they be given the same rights as workers and be brought under the protection of the Labour Act, in New Delhi, India, 8 March 2006.

The Canadian Press/AP Photo/Saurabh Das

the health hazards they suffer, Indian sex workers endure stigmatization because they must sell their bodies to live. In particular, 'floating' sex workers who return to their families after work suffer from the sense of leading a discreditable double life.

In Canada, sex work itself is legal. However, one can be arrested for related offences such as communicating (solicitation) offences, bawdyhouse offences, or procuring (pimping) offences. Even in jurisdictions where sex work is illegal, places to find sex are well known. There, sex workers gather in so-called 'red-light districts'. These districts may come and go: the unstable location of sex work in a city results from the interplay between the ordering strategies of the police and community protestors and the resistive tactics adopted by sex workers. These strategies depend on whether the society believes in the legalization or criminalization of sex work. With decriminalized sex work, distinctive red light or brothel districts are created to isolate sex work from more socially approved activities and people and to keep women from walking the streets, propositioning potential clients (Hubbard and Sanders, 2003).

Sex work entails relations between a sex worker, her client, and her pimp. Street-level sex work includes both pimp-controlled and independent entrepreneurial sex work. Pimp-related violence is common towards women involved in pimp-controlled sex work (Williamson and Cluse-Tolar, 2002). Even so, the social bonds between pimps and sex workers follow certain rules. As with other forms of vice and crime, public violence is bad for business, so efforts are made to control sex work activities without much violence, or at least to reserve violent methods of control for when it can be delivered in private.

In many countries, female sex workers must switch daily between the roles of mother and sex worker. As a result, they are constantly subjected to society's double standard for women (Castaneda et al., 1996). Sex workers divide their lives between the mother/saint and traitor/sex-worker roles. Rationalizations of those who wish to legalize sex work include justifying it as a better-paying employment opportunity for women and as a type of social service.

These practical considerations, however, are often drowned by moral outcries. Because of these difficulties, sex workers have had difficulty mobilizing for their own protection and advancement. Some sex workers have tried to improve their health and social standing by forming social movements. For the first time, sex workers are politically organizing and expressing their claims and grievances in the public debate about sex work—a debate from which they are usually excluded (Mathieu, 2003).

Usually, people enter the sex trade because they can see no other choice. To confirm this, Nixon and colleagues (2002) studied data from three western Canadian provinces and found that young women tend to enter sex work out of financial necessity. Once there, many experienced violence with such consistency that it almost seemed 'normal'. Many sex workers, here and elsewhere, grew up in harsh and even abusive families. Often, they have limited educational backgrounds or have not completed high school, thus making their exit from sex work into other types of work even more difficult.

Survey results (Kramer and Berg, 2003) show that both white and minority women engaging in sex work experienced high rates of physical and sexual abuse in childhood, as well as parental substance abuse. The result is a spread of sex work among adolescents with its attendant problems (Bamgbose, 2002). Gaudette et al. (1996) state that the average age in which a sex worker enters the sex trade is 14. As is the case throughout the industry, adolescent sex workers vary: some are in brothels while others are streetwalkers, call girls, and casual, part-time, or floating sex workers. Among sex workers in many countries, parental substance abuse, neglect, and emotional, physical, and sexual abuse are common in the girls' lives. They run away from turbulent home lives and are trapped by the illegal world of underground sex work.

Thus, it may be easy in some places and circumstances to drift into sex work; often, it is far more difficult to leave. Manopaiboon et al. (2003) studied Thai women's ability to leave sex work and the factors influencing their lives after leaving. All but one of the 42 current and former female sex workers surveyed had quit sex work at least once before. Women's ability and decisions to leave sex work are determined mainly by four factors: financial situation, link with a steady partner, attitudes towards sex work, and HIV/AIDS experience. Most women assume their risk for HIV infection to be lower after leaving sex work, yet three of the 17 HIV-infected women were infected after having left, presumably from their steady partners.

Everywhere in the prosperous West, sex workers are being imported from Eastern European, Asian, and Latin American countries. The rapid expansion and diversification of the international sex trade can be credited to several factors. Among them are the simultaneous rise in service occupations, temporary work, and corporate-fuelled consumption; an increase in labour migrations, tourism, and business travel; the connection between the information economy and the privatization of commercial consumption; and new forms of gender, sexuality, and kinship (Bernstein, 2002).

Young women suffer the assaults of war, and in addition face the intensifying levels of sexual and domestic violence, poverty, and social dislocation that war brings. As well, they may be preyed on by international criminal rackets exploiting the invisibility of poor young women in war zones for illegal sexual, domestic, and industrial labour—part of the tragic underbelly of development that yields billions of dollars annually.

Child Labour

Child labour is especially common in rural areas where the capacity to enforce minimum age rules for schooling and work is lacking. Most children in rural areas work in agriculture or as domestics, while urban children tend to work in trade and services, with fewer in manufacturing and construction. Though children are poorly paid in these jobs, they still serve as major contributors to family income in developing countries. The lack of good schools also encourages parents to send their children to work rather than to school. Rigid cultural and social views about children and childhood may also limit educational goals and increase child labour.

Working children are the objects of extreme exploitation, toiling for long hours at low pay. Furthermore, three-quarters (171 million) work under risky conditions in mines, with chemicals, or with dangerous machinery. Not surprisingly, this exposure leads to lasting physical and psychological harm. Working at rug looms, for example, may leave children disabled with eye damage, lung disease, stunted growth, and a vulnerability to arthritis as they grow older. Many children work in order to attend school, so abolishing all child labour may only hinder their education. However, in general, improving the financial condition of struggling families would free children from full-time labour. Sometimes, a child's work can be helpful to him or her and to the family. Working and earning can be a positive experience in a child's growing up, not least by teaching important lessons in responsibility, independence, and the value of a dollar. This depends largely on the child's age, the conditions in which the child works, and whether work prevents the child from going to school. Invariably, exploitative child labour hampers the child's development and preparation for adult life in a post-industrial world.

Without an education and a normal childhood, some children are reduced almost to slavery. Some are kidnapped and forced to work. Many are beaten or subjected to other severe physical abuse. An extreme form of child labour, bonded labour, takes place when a family receives a small advance payment (sometimes as little as $20) to give a boy or girl over to an employer. Usually the child cannot work off the debt, nor can the family raise enough money to buy the child back. Bonded child labour is widespread in countries around the world; millions of such children work in India alone.

The Canadian Press/Kelowna Courier-Gary Nylander

Child rights activist Craig Kielburger makes a speech in Kelowna, BC, on 4 May 2002. Kielburger is asking governments to do more to improve life for young people.

Currently, there is no international agreement defining child labour, making it hard to isolate cases of abuse, let alone abolish them. However, eliminating child labour is one of the four fundamental principles of the ILO's Declaration on Fundamental Principles and Rights at Work. ILO Convention 182 calls for the prohibition and immediate action to expel the 'worst forms of child labour'.

It defines a child as a person under 18 years old, and 'worst forms of child labour' as all forms of slavery or practices similar to slavery such as the sale and trafficking of children, debt bondage and serfdom, forced or compulsory labour, including forced or compulsory recruitment of children for use in armed conflict; the use, procuring, or sale of a child for prostitution, pornographic performances, or illicit activities—especially, for the production and trafficking of drugs. In short, the Declaration calls for an end to all work that is likely to harm the health, safety, or morals of children (International Labour Organization, at: www.ilo.org/public/english/standards/ipec/about/factsheet/faq.htm).

By contrast, work by children in Canada is regulated and the worst forms of child labour are banned. Free primary and secondary schooling are universally available, and school attendance is compulsory until at least age 16. In addition, the federal, provincial, and territorial governments have adopted many laws banning or restricting the employment of children to ensure that their participation in work does not affect their health and development or interfere with their schooling.

At the national level, the Federal Committee Against the Commercial Sexual Exploitation of Children was created specifically to examine programs underway across Canada to fight the exploitation of children and youth in the sex trade (for more on this, see Canadian Strategy Against Commercial Sexual Exploitation of Children and Youth, at: sen.parl.gc.ca/lpearson/htmfiles/hill/17_htm_files/Committee-e/Exploit_EN.htm).

UNEMPLOYMENT AND ITS EFFECTS

Types of Unemployment and Their Measurement

Researchers distinguish between discriminatory and structural unemployment. **Discriminatory unemployment** is unemployment resulting from discrimination against particular groups, such as ethnic minorities and women (Reitz and Breton, 1998). **Structural unemployment** results from social and economic factors that affect workers equally across all groups (Heaton and Oslington, 2010). These factors include corporate layoffs, capital flight (caused by corporate mergers and the move of operations to another geographic region—so-called 'runaway plants'), and automation (replacing human labour with machinery).

Researchers base their measures of unemployment on the percentage of the workforce currently without jobs, actively seeking employment, and available to work. This definition excludes women who work as homemakers without pay and **discouraged workers**, i.e., those who have turned their backs on the traditional work system and abandoned efforts to work for pay (Maich, 2008). These discouraged workers consist disproportionately of women and racial minorities. Other people do not take part in the labour force because they are in school, retired, injured, sick, or otherwise unable to work.

DISCRIMINATORY UNEMPLOYMENT Unemployment resulting from discrimination against particular groups, such as ethnic minorities and women.

STRUCTURAL UNEMPLOYMENT Unemployment caused by social and economic factors that affect workers equally across all groups, such as corporate downsizing, capital flight (caused by corporate mergers and the move of operations to another geographic region—'runaway plants'), and the automation of work processes.

DISCOURAGED WORKERS Those people who are not actively seeking employment. Specifically, they are thought to have turned their backs on the traditional work system and to have abandoned any desire to be gainfully employed.

Table 12.3	Seasonally Adjusted Employment (ooos) by Age, Sex, Type of Work, and Class of Worker				
	August 2008	July 2009	August 2009	July 2009 to August 2009 (% change)	August 2008 to August 2009 (% change)
Canada, all ages	17,100.2	16,780.3	16,807.4	0.2	−1.7
15–24 years	2,598.2	2,395.9	2,391.0	−0.2	−8.0
25 years and over	14,502.0	14,384.4	14,416.4	0.2	−0.6
Men	9,018.3	8,752.4	8,753.8	0.0	−2.9
Women	8,081.8	8,027.8	8,053.5	0.3	−0.4
Full-time	13,958.7	13,521.5	13,518.0	0.0	−3.2
Part-time	3,141.4	3,258.8	3,289.4	0.9	4.7
Employees	14,476.8	14,053.5	14,091.2	0.3	−2.7
Public sector[1]	3,416.7	3,408.1	3,396.6	−0.3	−0.6
Private sector[2]	11,060.1	10,645.4	10,694.6	0.5	−3.3
Self-employed	2,623.4	2,726.8	2,716.2	−0.4	3.5

1. Those who work for a local, provincial, or federal government, for a government service or agency, a Crown corporation, or a government-funded establishment such as a school (including universities) or hospital.
2. Those who work as employees of a private firm or business.

Sources: **Employment by age, sex, type of work, class of worker and province (monthly, Canada), at www40.statcan.gc.ca/l01/cst01/labr66a-eng.htm (September 2010).**

As the data in Table 12.3 show, rates of employment vary quite widely from one part of Canada to another, and also from one age group to another. Young workers and private-sector workers have been affected the most by the recent recession.

Because of these exclusions, most official unemployment rates understate the true percent-age of the unemployed (Blendon and Benson, 2009). This in turn underestimates the size of the unemployment problem. Official employment rates also do not distinguish between full-time and part-time work, nor do they recognize odd jobs, temporary work, and other forms of underemployment as different from full-time work. A person who reports working as little as one hour per week is formally considered 'gainfully employed'. This definition less-ens the visible problem of unemployment. So, in the end, our estimates of unemployment provide too rosy a picture of the actual reality in the work world.

Predictors of Unemployment

Some explanations of unemployment focus on the social and financial environment in which jobs are lost; others focus on the individuals who lose their jobs. In the former category, research has been done on the causes and effects of downsizing. For example, researchers found that downsizing cut out about 60 per cent of the workforce and one-quarter of the job titles in the British Columbia sawmill industry, largely in response to an economic recession in the early 1980s. Job loss tended to affect the youngest workers most severely (Ostry et al., 2000).

Other researchers focus on the characteristics of people who lose their jobs or who are at particular risk of losing their jobs in a recession. Often, they focus on human capital characteristics, such as educational attainment or particular job-related skills. Age is a predictor of unemployment. Older workers (over age 40) who have been laid off find it harder than younger workers to get a job, especially in work, like construction, that demands physical strength. Family characteristics play a part, too. For example, single marital status predicts unemployment after a layoff among construction and forest workers (Liira and Leino, 1999). Parental divorce, low parental emotional involvement, and parental unemployment (for males only) predict the unemployment of youth (de Goede et al., 2000).

Some have argued that health problems often predate and cause unemployment. To some degree, the effects of illness on working life depend on the duration of a disability. In one study, over half of the workers who became limited in activities of daily living as adults had unemployment spells lasting less than two years. Few disabled people who remained outside the workforce for four years re-entered it (Burchardt, 2000). More than half of the non-working disabled reported that economic, social, and job-based barriers contributed to their inability to work, and one-fourth of working disabled people reported having been discriminated against in the last five years (Druss et al., 2000). Mental as well as physical health is linked to transitions to early retirement or other unemployment (Wray, 2000). Above-average mental health plays a protective role in keeping workers in the workforce rather than laid off, on sick leave, or unemployed.

However, health problems do not always lead to long-term unemployment. Specific health conditions, such as asthma or visual impairment, may be associated with work limitation, yet they are not among the main determinants of continuous unemployment (McCarty et al., 1999; Yelin et al., 1999). The risk of unemployment for chronically ill people largely depends on active labour market policies—specific efforts made by government to stimulate employment, job training, and worker mobility. Employment protections also play a role, as shown by lower rates of unemployment and inactivity in Sweden than in Britain (Burstrom et al., 2000).

UP IN THE AIR

George Clooney stars in the 2009 comedy-drama about a man whose profession is to execute company layoffs.

SOCIAL CONSEQUENCES OF UNEMPLOYMENT

As unpleasant as work can be, the alternative is often even worse. Unemployment does not only deprive most people of the basis for material survival, it also takes a toll on society. With people out of the workforce, the economy cannot reach its utmost potential for production. Another reason unemployment affects the overall economy is the cost of preserving a social support network to help those who are between jobs (Slebarska et al., 2009).

From a social-psychological perspective, unemployed people are often marked with the stigma of being lazy and unwilling to work. Some think that unemployment insurance and welfare undermine the work ethic that has motivated so many others to succeed in life. People who see themselves as masters of their own fate hold those who are unemployed responsible for their own condition and do not think that they deserve public aid. On the other hand, people who have experienced forces beyond their control are able to believe that those others who are unemployed due to ill health, discrimination, recession, or corporate downsizing deserve help.

HEALTH CONSEQUENCES OF WORK

Workplace Safety Issues

Health and safety hazards in the workplace are an obvious social problem. For example, in 1998, 798 Canadian workers died because of an occupational injury and another 793,666 were injured on the job. In 2004, the number of workplace deaths in Canada had risen to 928: 'the Canadian Centre for the Study of Living Standards investigated safety at workplaces in rich nations around the world. Canada's rate of workplace fatalities—seven deaths per 100,000 workers—tied for top spot as the worst. Canada's record for reducing workplace fatalities over the previous 20 years stood alone as the worst' (CBC News, 2007). This dismal record is explainable, in part at least, by the extent to which Canada, relative to other wealthy countries, is still reliant on the dangerous work of resource extraction—logging, fishing, oil drilling, mining—and on heavy manufacturing.

A report on industries under federal jurisdiction showed that, in 2002, 1,020,699 employees suffered occupational injuries in Canada. Though many of these injuries were minor, roughly one-third were classed as disabling, resulting in significant losses in hours worked (www.sdc.gc.ca/en/lp/lo/ohs/statistics/images19982002/oicc9802.pdf).

Some industries are more dangerous than others. The manufacturing sector, in particular, is a dangerous place to work, accounting for nearly 30 per cent of the total occupational injuries reported in Canada in 1998. Incidence rates were highest among the logging and forestry, construction, and manufacturing industries, and lowest within the finance and insurance sector. In general, the occupations with the highest risk of occupational injury or death are those that involve semi-skilled manual labour, such as equipment operator and installer, manufacturer, and machine assembler. The occupations with the lowest risk of work-related injury or death are senior management executive, business, and finance professions (HRDC, 2000).

Work Stress

Another health-related feature of employment that is increasingly being studied is work-related stress. This can lead to the neurological condition called 'burnout' as well as other significant physical and mental health outcomes. When the demands of the job exceed the abilities, resources, or needs of the worker, job stress occurs (Ariganello, 2009).

Statistics on hours spent at work cannot capture either the full amount of time spent working or the stress associated with work. It is possible to be 'at work' without working. One could be at home, yet preoccupied with job issues. It is possible to work 10 hours a day in a leisurely fashion yet do less work and feel less stressed than someone who works seven intense hours a day. Increasingly, for example, professional and managerial workers are expected to take their work home with them and to be on call as needed. Overwork is a big problem in Canada today, as illustrated by the continuing conflict between work life and family home life. Perhaps nowhere is this problem bigger than in Japan, as the story in Box 12.3 shows.

Substance Abuse

Unemployment increases the risk of consumption of alcohol, tobacco, and other drugs, especially in young men (Fillmore et al., 1998; MacDonald and Pudney, 2000; Montgomery et al., 1998). Alcohol abuse, associated with unemployment, is correlated with a heightened risk of death by suicide, violence, and driving accidents (see, e.g., Stefansson, 1991).

Increased alcohol consumption is one of the mechanisms connecting unemployment and suicide (Hintikka et al., 1999). Unemployment increases the risk of alcohol abuse, and

INTERNATIONAL COMPARISONS

Box 12.3 Overwork a Silent Killer in Japan

Pushed to their limits, thousands of Japanese are literally working themselves to death each year, a scourge the Asian power has started to address but which could get worse in the global economic crisis. . . .

The Japanese call the problem 'karoshi', or death by overwork. And with the global downturn sapping demand for Japanese exports and leading companies to slash jobs, the stress on workers is becoming even more severe.

A survey carried out in October by Japan's main labour union federation Rengo found that 53 per cent of workers say they have recently been suffering more stress.

While for some the overwork is simply annoying, for others it causes everything from poor blood circulation to arteriosclerosis to strokes.

'Neither the government nor businesses offer figures that completely take stock of the problem', said Hiroshi Kawahito, a lawyer who represents relatives of karoshi victims.

Police say that more than 2,200 Japanese committed suicide due to work conditions in 2007.

But Kawahito said that figure represented only a fraction of the problem. He estimated some 10,000 workers in the same year suffered heart attacks or strokes, which were sometimes fatal, due to stress.

He said that fewer than 10 percent of the incidents were reported to authorities or companies because of the long time it takes to certify cases and the fair chance the effort will be in vain.

In 2007, 58 per cent of people who sought compensation for a loved one's karoshi had their application refused. However, this was still a big improvement on 20 years ago when 95 per cent of cases were rejected.

'There is growing public pressure for this scourge to be better recognized', Kawahito said.

In May 2007, the head of a construction site in the Tochigi region north of Tokyo committed suicide after putting in 65 to 70 hours every week for six months, plunging him into ill physical health and depression.

Authorities reporting to the labour ministry agreed to certify the suicide as a work accident and offered his widow three million yen (32,000 dollars) a year in compensation.

But even if the government is addressing the problem, few families of karoshi victims dare to go to former employers.

'The topic remains taboo in Japan with businesses thinking that their employees' mental state is their private problem', said Hajime Urushihara, the pointman on working conditions at Rengo, the union federation.

Nearly half of all businesses have no measures at all in place to prevent workplace stress, according to an investigation by the union.

The vast majority of overworked employees are men, many in their thirties who are working their way up the corporate ladder. . . .

Source: Abridged from AFP (2009).

re-employment reduces the prevalence of alcohol abuse (Claussen, 1999a, 1999b). In turn, alcohol abuse increases the risk of violence, especially family violence (Rodriguez et al., 1997). If we control for alcohol use, unemployment has no effect on family violence. Alcohol abuse also increases the likelihood of fatal car crashes at night; insofar as unemployment reduces the frequency of car accidents, it is because those without jobs no longer spend time on the road commuting to and from work (Gonzalez and Rodriguez, 2000).

Psychological Consequences: Depression and Anxiety

More than anything else, unemployment affects health by increasing anxiety and depression (Comino et al., 2000; Montgomery et al., 1999; Viinamaki et al., 1993, 1996; Ytterdahl, 1999).

Job loss typically arouses defensive feelings, lowers self-esteem, and creates doubt about the future. It often causes people to become passive and to withdraw from social life, further harming their mental health (Underlid, 1996). Unemployed people report more stress, boredom, doubt, and dissatisfaction with themselves and their lives than do the gainfully employed (Gien, 2000). Typically, unemployment causes people's resources to dwindle, having a negative impact on their views of themselves, their aging, and the possibility of leading a productive life (Schmitt, 2001).

Researchers disagree about whether unemployment has the same effects on women and men. Some researchers find that men feel more threatened by job loss than women, explaining a higher frequency of depression among unemployed men (Lahelma, 1992; Ytterdahl and Fugelli, 2000). Women, it is argued, have less of their self-identity defined by paid work and can usually invest themselves in housework, if necessary, though unemployment for women also involves a loss of personal identity (Desmarais, 1991). Others note that women can suffer great distress from unemployment, even after giving birth when they are much involved in their maternal role (Saurel Cubizolles et al., 2000). Thus, some have concluded that, in responding to unemployment, women and men are more similar than they are different (Nordenmark, 1999), though they may show their distress in slightly different ways. Job loss results in anxiety disorders in women, while unemployed men often fall victim to substance abuse, depression, and anxiety. When a spouse loses a job, women more often than men suffer both from the financial outcomes and from increased marital conflict (Avison, 1996).

Unemployment produces distress, fatalistic attitudes, feelings of a lack of control over one's life, and feelings of personal inefficacy. Poor mental health, in turn, reduces the likelihood of finding a job. Depression caused by unemployment may lead to continued unemployment. Conversely, success in finding a job is predicted by a positive attitude and an active way of dealing with unemployment (Schaufeli, 1997).

SOLUTIONS TO UNEMPLOYMENT

Unemployment Interventions

Interventions for the problem of unemployment might take the form of reducing the number of people who experience unemployment, reducing the stresses of unemployment, strengthening individuals' life skills and psychosocial resources, and providing counselling and clinical interventions (Avison, 2001).

Job-creation programs can reduce some unemployment. Here, it is important that job creation occurs mainly in full-time, stable, and skill-intensive fields. Such 'good' positions are less likely to result in a return to unemployment further down the road. Jobs that are temporary and fail to build new skills and contacts are a waste of effort (Rose, 2009).

As well, since education is the best weapon against unemployment, governments should ensure that schooling is made available to as many people as possible. Schooling opportunities are especially needed by those whose financial condition might otherwise prevent them from getting higher education, including poor people, rural people, disabled people, and Aboriginal people. This initiative should include adult education programs, which can be another effective tool for increasing the chance of re-employment and career advancement.

Labour unions, which historically have been effective tools in pressuring employers to provide better wages and working conditions for employees (Blanchflower and Bryson, 2010), have experienced a decline in recent decades (Godard, 2009). Initiatives that support unions and political parties that promote working-class interests, such as the New Democratic Party in Canada and equivalent parties abroad (for example, the traditional Labour Party in Britain), are key to ensuring that wages and working conditions remain on the legislative agenda.

MATEWAN

John Sayles' 1987 film vividly documents the battles between labour and management through the 1920s in the small mining town of Matewan, West Virginia.

Workplace Health and Safety

To reduce the number of annual occupational injuries and deaths, governments will have to obligate employers to respond to the health and safety concerns of their workers more effectively. It will likely cost more to do business this way, which is why the government will have to take the initiative and impose penalties for non-compliance (Tombs and Whyte, 2010).

Already, there is strong evidence of support for such changes. Closer public and media scrutiny, combined with constant pestering by anti-corporate and human rights groups, has forced some companies to improve their workplace conditions, especially in the overseas factories of transnational organizations. More of the same pressure, with resulting changes to the workplace, is needed at home as well as abroad (Bello et al., 2009).

Increasingly, workers and lobby groups want more than a minimally hazard-free workspace. They want a higher standard of quality of life at work. In response, progressive employers, aware of the link between employee well-being and corporate profitability, are offering workers on-site health education and medical care. Some have begun to outfit their workplaces with gyms, swimming pools, and other recreational facilities, as well as provide their workers with lunchtime yoga classes and healthy food options in the cafeteria. These attempts to improve employee health and fitness, whether sincere or self-serving, can help ensure that work itself does not become a health risk.

Job Satisfaction

If we accept the view that a happy worker is a productive worker, then it is in the employer's best interest to ensure that job satisfaction levels remain high. This means designing jobs, careers, and workplaces that provide meaning and stimulation, and opportunities that allow workers to apply the full scope of their abilities (Burke and Fiksenbaum, 2009).

The most satisfying work allows workers to take part in consequential decision-making. It also allows room for workers' needs and commitments outside the workplace. Communication among workers should also be encouraged, as should harmonious employee–employer relations. Regardless of the particular strategy or incentive chosen by the employer, any attempt to improve job satisfaction will necessarily involve an awareness of what people wish to gain from working (Turcotte and Schellenberg, 2005).

Extrinsic rewards are important, so income, recognition, promotions, and benefit packages all need to be shared in a way that mirrors both personal performance and company prosperity. Equally or more important are the **intrinsic rewards** or benefits of work, which vary from job to job and from worker to worker. Indeed, job satisfaction is an intricate, subjective, and inseparable mix of intrinsic and extrinsic rewards (see Figure 12.2). Some people, for instance, crave a high degree of independence and lack of structure (for example, freelance writers or entrepreneurs), while others find themselves most comfortable and

EXTRINSIC REWARDS
When work rewards the worker with money, prestige, respect, and social recognition.

INTRINSIC REWARDS
When work rewards the worker with the feeling of a 'job well done'.

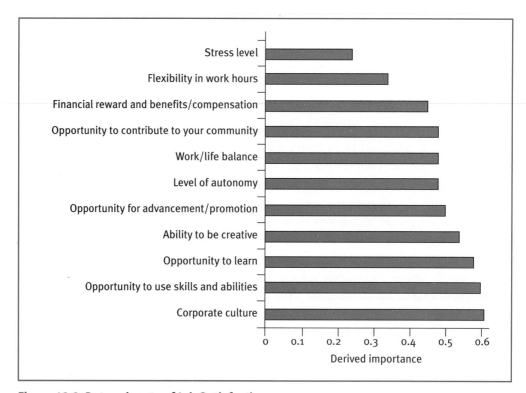

Figure 12.2 Determinants of Job Satisfaction

Note: Derived importance was calculated using Correlation Analysis. Respondents were asked to rate their jobs on 11 attributes on a scale of 1–10. They were then asked to rate their overall job satisfaction on a scale of 1–10. The correlation between each of the 11 attributes and overall job satisfaction revealed the underlying derived importance of each attribute. We were then able to use the derived importance scores to rank the attributes in terms of overall importance. To determine the top 20 jobs, we combined each job's score on the 11 attributes so that the overall job ranking was based on the relative performance of each job on all of the 11 drivers of job satisfaction.

Source: Adapted from Workopolis study of 8,750 working Canadians on the top 20 jobs as indicated by the respondents. NorthStar Research Partners for Workopolis, at: sssubaiei.kau.edu.sa/Files/0005441/Subjects/Top20JobsWhitepaper.pdf.

happiest in a job that is rule-bound and rigidly defined (for example, chartered accountants) (Wallace and Kay, 2009).

CHAPTER SUMMARY

As we have seen, workplace problems include racial and gender discrimination, difficulties juggling work and family, technological advances, and worker exploitation. Some lines of work, such as sex work, can be extremely taxing and dangerous and attach stigma to the workers. Workplaces can also be hazardous and extremely stressful. Such problems can lead to worker dissatisfaction, stress, and health problems. Even so, the alternatives associated with unemployment can be worse.

Unemployment can cause health problems, depressive disorders, and consequently a higher mortality rate. Solutions to unemployment can come from either the community or the individual. Accessible education, financial support for the unemployed, and a positive attitude towards re-employment possibilities are paramount. Companies also need to be more sensitive to workers' needs to ensure their health and job satisfaction.

QUESTIONS FOR CRITICAL THOUGHT

1. Often, your server at a restaurant is a woman. However, most celebrity chefs are male. Does this prove the existence of discrimination against women in the most prestigious, best-paid ranks of restaurant work?

2. The benefits of a unionized workplace outweigh the costs. Do you agree?

3. Proving one's worth at work has taken on a new meaning, especially in the current economy. Is it still realistic to dream of career advancement or is it merely a matter of surviving the next layoff? Relate this to Marx's concept of alienation.

4. Compare the types of barriers faced by Aboriginal people and immigrants in terms of job application. To what extent are both groups similar and how do they differ? Draw up possible policy recommendations to help these vulnerable populations.

5. The growth of ethnic businesses can be observed throughout Canada. Examine how this will contribute towards the transformation of the Canadian labour market.

RECOMMENDED READINGS

Chaulk, Kimberly, and Trevor C. Brown. 2008. 'An Assessment of Worker Reaction to Their Union and Employer Post-Strike: A Canadian Experience', *Relations industrielles/Industrial Relations* 63: 223–45. The article examines the consequences of a five-month strike on workers and union members. Results imply working off the job may not be worthwhile after all.

Dean, JenniferAsanin, and Kathi Wilson. 2009. '"Education? It is irrelevant to my job now. It makes me very depressed . . .": Exploring the Health Impacts of Under/Unemployment among Highly Skilled Immigrants in Canada', *Ethnicity & Health* 14: 185–204. In-depth interviews with highly skilled immigrants to Canada reveal that under/unemployment leads to mental health problems.

Doyle-Bedwell, P. 2008. '"With the Appropriate Qualifications": Aboriginal People and Employment Equity', *Canadian Women Studies* 26, 77–9. In this deeply stirring article, the author, an Aboriginal female who succeeded as a lawyer, describes the existing flaws and realities of Canadian employment equity as it related to Aboriginal peoples; also includes suggestions for future directions.

Johnson, Laura C., Jean Andrey, and Susan M. Shaw. 2007. 'Mr. Dithers Comes to Dinner: Telework and the Merging of Women's Work and Home Domains in Canada', *Gender, Place and Culture* 14: 141–61. This article examines the advantages and disadvantages of female teleworkers who were told to work from home.

Roscigno, Vincent J. 2007. *The Face of Discrimination: How Race and Gender Impact Work and Home Lives*. Lanham, MD: Rowman & Littlefield. This work focuses on the prevalence, character, and consequences of racial and sexual discrimination in the workforce and its impact on other aspects of society, such as home life.

Sennett, Richard, and Jonathan Cobb. 1977 [1972]. *The Hidden Injuries of Social Class*. Cambridge: Cambridge University Press. This book introduced new theories about the effects of social class on those at the bottom of it, including its effect on personal feelings and interactions experienced by those who cannot find a way of improving their situation

Recommended Websites

Human Resources and Skills Development Canada

www.hrsdc.gc.ca/eng/labour/index.shtml

This government website provides a comprehensive overview of the Canadian labour market, including workplace safety, equality, and labour law and relations.

Service Canada

www.servicecanada.gc.ca/eng/home.shtml

Service Canada provides specific populations in Canada (e.g., seniors, Aboriginal peoples, newcomers) with valuable resources such as online applications/updates for employment insurance (EI), job placements for veterans, and a national job bank for all Canadians.

Travel and Work Abroad

www.international.gc.ca/iyp-pij/iyp_introduction_page.aspx

This website is especially relevant for Canadians who wish either to travel abroad for some international work experience or who seek long-term employment in partner countries. Navigating the site may give one a better understanding of what it actually means to be a permit worker in other foreign countries—and what it must be like for foreign workers in Canada.

Working Temporarily in Canada

www.cic.gc.ca/english/work/index.asp

This website is extremely useful for foreign workers who wish to seek employment in Canada. It offers detailed information on how to determine one's eligibility, as well as application guides and forms to help ease the transition to the Canadian workplace.

Aboriginal Workers

www.canadianlabour.ca/human-rights-equality/aboriginal-workers

The Canadian Labour Congress has a unique outreach program to help Aboriginal people, with a focus on advocating the rights of Aboriginal workers and conducting policy work relating to their communities.

CHAPTER 13
Schools

iStockphoto.com/Ryan Balderas

LEARNING OBJECTIVES

- To understand the links between schooling and society.
- To compare major sociological theories on education and schooling.
- To understand the manifest and latent functions of the education system.
- To understand how inequality is perpetuated in the education system.
- To recognize how trends in inequality differ by class, gender, and race.
- To understand credentialism and over-education, and their related effects.
- To understand the impact of education on social inequality.
- To recognize the gender reversal in educational attainment.
- To examine changes in Aboriginal education over time and see their outcomes.
- To appreciate the impact of media and technology related to education today.

INTRODUCTION

This chapter is about students, teachers, school administration, and school curriculum. It is about the successes and failures of schooling in Canadian society. Social inequality pervades the schooling experience. We deal with issues of educational opportunity, as well as the various social and cultural hindrances that influence educational outcomes.

How much education a person has influences her or his everyday life. This chapter examines the impact of educational credentials and socio-economic conditions, as well as individual and group ethnic backgrounds as determinants of educational success or failure.

DEFINING EDUCATION AND ITS SOCIAL PROBLEMS

Ascribed Statuses, Stratification, and Inequality

Ascribed statuses are social statuses assigned to people or groups beyond their control and without regard for achieved merit; they significantly affect individuals' educational outcomes (Sasaki, 2000). Examples of ascribed statuses include family structure, socio-economic status, sex, and race or ethnic background. Each of these characteristics alters future economic advantages later in life. The pursuit of higher education can produce greater social and economic advantage (Holley et al., 2006).

Education is a means of gaining upward **social mobility**—a process by which individuals and families move up an economic or status hierarchy. Traditionally, educational achievements have been viewed as means by which *talented* and *motivated* individuals advance socially or economically. McMullin (2004) argues, 'Canadians would prefer not to believe the educational system is also a place where societal inequalities are reproduced and where privileged groups solidify and maintain their advantages.'

The first thing to understand about higher education—indeed, about education in general—is that social factors (age, sex, and social class) all affect how much education a person gets. This is clearly shown in Figure 13.1.

Careers: Linking School and Work

Why is schooling important in our society, and what factors interfere with the 'ideal' functioning of education, leading to social problems associated with schools and schooling? We can begin to answer these questions most effectively if we take a step back and get the big picture by focusing on the linkage between schools, work, and social class. Let's do so by considering the idea of 'career'—one of many versions of work in our society, but one that will plunge us immediately into debates about education, work, and class.

The word 'career' originates in words that mean 'racecourse' and 'road for cars'. To say that a person has a 'career' implies he or she is rapidly moving towards a goal alongside, or in competition with, others. Every career, like every horse or auto race, has a starting point. Starting from there, competitors move forward past road markers. Ideally, no one starts ahead of anyone else, and no one fails to pass a marker. Some competitors progress faster than others; a few competitors might be said to have 'won' the race, while others 'place' or 'show'. Over an

ASCRIBED STATUSES
Statuses assigned to individuals because of certain traits beyond their control.

SOCIAL MOBILITY
The process by which individuals and families move up an economic or status hierarchy.

CHEATERS

In this 2000 film, a teacher (Jeff Daniels), angered by educational inequities, encourages his inner-city students to cheat at the citywide academic decathalon.

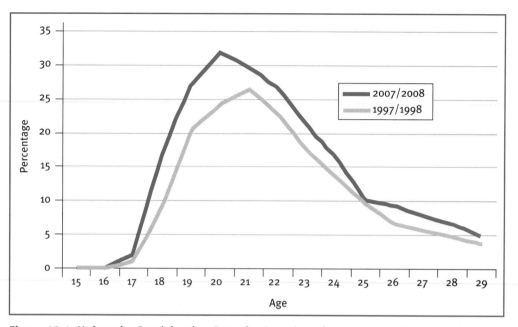

Figure 13.1 University Participation Rate, by Age, Canada, 1997–8 and 2007–8

Source: University Participation Rate, by age, Canada, 1997/1998 and 2007/2008, at: www.statcan.gc.ca/pub/81-582-x/2009001/c-g/c-ge1.1-eng.htm and www.statcan.gc.ca/pub/81-582-x/2009001/tbl/e1.1-eng.htm.

extended period, many competitors get to the finish line (i.e., complete their careers) before leaving the track or steer off the track, though we do not consider them winners.

Although simplified, this depiction captures the essence of many careers, traditional and modern. However, as the world of work grows larger and more complex, people with different educational credentials enter at different job and income levels (McMullin, 2004). Typically, post-secondary graduates enter above less-educated candidates. As well, competitors may not pass all the usual road markers in the same order.

For example, more highly motivated 'high achievers' may move about more within an organization or occupation, gaining wider experience and exposure. And, with the development of widely accepted credentials (such as valued post-secondary educational degrees), high achievers can often move from one organization to another, gaining additional experience and exposure within an industry while continually increasing their status and rewards (Halperin, 1990).

Thus, career mobility increases both through industrial differentiation and through the rise of educational achievement as a basis for ranking. Modern professions (such as medicine and law) are particularly notable for the importance of higher education and educational credentials, with a remarkable ability to control career entries, reward systems, and conditions of work (Donnelly, 2009).

Of course, ambition and education are not everything. Ascribed characteristics—characteristics people are unable to change—have never fully lost their importance as ordering and selection principles. Today, many careers remain gendered, with many ambitious women bumping into 'glass ceilings' (Harkness, 2001). As well, many employers continue to prefer candidates from particular ethnic or racial groups or from certain elite backgrounds (Reitz, 2001). However, all employers, increasingly, favour highly educated candidates over less educated ones (Watt and Bloom, 2001).

Formal education plays an important part in this career-making process. People enter a given career—for example, teaching, or medicine, or engineering—at roughly the same age and advance at similar (though not identical) rates. Over the ages 18–30, their chances are structured, first, by differences in credentials, skills, and ambitions. These shape people's educational hopes and achievements and their occupational ambitions. This process of movement through the world of work starts with movement through the world of schooling, however.

Four major theories help us to understand the young adult's transition from school into the labour force. *Segmented labour market theory* notes the labour market is stratified, and entry and upward mobility are difficult for people with only a high school education (Meerkerk, 2006). *Human capital theory* attributes the problems of new labour force entrants to deficiencies in their training that lessen their value to the hiring organization (Reitz, 2001). *Signalling theory* refers to the employer's use of signs or signals to judge the potential worth and trainability of a young employee (Greening and Turban, 2000). Finally, *network theory* describes the importance of social networks and social capital in gaining employment based on the 'word' of a friend or relative, who vouches for the quality of the potential employee (Rosenbaum, 2001).

In college and university, the sorting of students into different programs with different curricula also influences later opportunities by sending prospective employers different messages about the abilities of job candidates. Thus, a BA in philosophy sends a different message from a BA in physics or in political science. In organizations, the sorting of workers into different authority levels amplifies the effects of college attainment on earnings. Graduates of preferred colleges continually receive ever-greater earnings, though these colleges have no further direct effects on earnings.

Such institutional linkages are valuable to societies, employers, and employees. Though economic theory warns about the inefficiencies of institutional linkages, school–employer linkages can enhance incentives, the flow of information, and employment outcomes. The student's school-to-work transition is improved if schools make academic instruction vocationally relevant, employers base hiring on applicants' achievement in school, and we have properly designed and set up school–employer linkages (Brinton, 1998).

We build institutional linkages on three expectations about the flow of labour: dependable supply, dependable skills, and dependable quality. Ideally, the school–workplace linkage can efficiently supply needed workers with the needed skills and verify their quality. In this way, they support a reward system at work that is based on merit. What we need, first, is that high school counsellors play a more active role as gatekeepers. They must act more vigorously to discourage students whose college plans are inappropriate—in effect, helping them to address unpleasant realities. Only in this way will employers come to trust available school information (for example, grades) when hiring youth, and rely less on social networks or impressions gained during interviews. Doing so may also lead employers to respond to skill shortages by hiring skilled young workers rather than merely retraining the present work staff or lowering their expectations.

Thus, careers are job-related pathways over the life course. On the individual level, careers reflect differences (and similarities) in opportunities and human capital. On the corporate level, they reflect linkages within firms, across firms, and across institutions. Just as careers tie together life events, so they also tie together institutional activities.

Careers take place within submarkets or economic sectors, in which a segmentation of jobs and careers has occurred. Primary and secondary labour markets coexist within every region, province, and size of community. The **primary labour market** consists of jobs that offer good wages, chances to get ahead, and job security: it includes jobs like lawyer, plumber, and teacher (Furlong, 2008). The **secondary (marginal) labour market** consists of jobs that pay low wages, offer little chance to get ahead, and promise little job security: jobs like taxi driver, secretary, or bank teller (Jaarsveld et al., 2009).

People with different social traits, backgrounds, and skills often locate in different markets. For example, far more women and visible minorities have moved to the secondary labour market, and far more white men are in the primary labour market than could have occurred by chance. Within markets, we find submarkets that also contain different kinds of jobs and different kinds of people. The big difference between primary and secondary markets tends to blur important differences among jobs in the *same* market. For example, though both are in the primary labour market, few teachers feel they have the sort of benefits and opportunities that doctors do. Though both are in the secondary labour market, few bank tellers consider their work to be the same as that of taxi drivers.

PRIMARY LABOUR MARKET High wage-paying jobs that provide chances to 'get ahead' and that offer job security.

SECONDARY (MARGINAL) LABOUR MARKET High-turnover, lower-paying, and generally unstable employment. These jobs offer very little chance to get ahead and little job security.

Class: Social Mobility and Educational Inequality

However, all of this 'racing for rewards' takes place against a backdrop of social inequality. The social class you are born into will affect your educational ambitions and educational pursuits. That is why family origin and socio-economic status, for example, tend to be reproduced across generations. Among others, Canadian sociologists Guppy and Davies (1998) show the effect of class on educational attainment is an especially enduring feature of inequality. Researchers repeatedly find interrelations between social class and educational attainment, and, more generally, among class structure, class mobility, and class formation. With the expansion of higher education in economically developed societies, more and more young people have stayed in school for longer periods. As a result, the educational attainment of average citizens has risen significantly. Yet, the class structure—the shape or extent of social inequality—has not changed markedly.

Canada is one of the countries in which this has happened. We should not be surprised, since in Canada, all citizens, regardless of race/ethnicity or class, have the same right to take part in community activities and social institutions. However, for people lower down the economic ladder, higher education may still seem like more of a privilege than a right. As a result, in Canada as elsewhere, 'class differentials in educational attainment have changed little . . . from those in early decades of the century onwards' (Goldthorpe, 1985). Children in less advantaged class positions are still less likely than children of more prosperous origins to pursue and earn higher educational degrees.

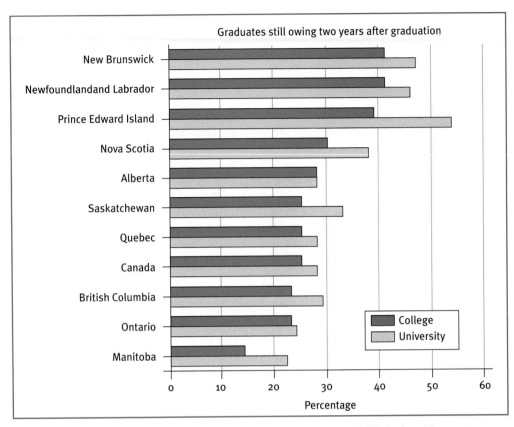

Figure 13.2 **Percentage of College and University Graduates Still Owing Money to Government Student Loan Programs Two Years after Graduation, Class of 2005, Canada and Provinces**

Source: **Percentage of College and University Graduates Still Owing Money to Government Student Loan Programs Two Years After Graduation, Class of 2005, Canada and Provinces at: www.statcan.gc.ca/pub/81-582-x/2009001/c-g/c-ge1.1-eng.htm.**

The reason is that children from less affluent families are less able to incur the financial debts needed to complete a post-secondary education, and these debts can be burdensome upon completion of a degree (see Figure 13.2). Further, for reasons not fully understood, the extent of people's indebtedness varies from one province to another—likely reflecting differences in the cost of living, the cost of education, and the availability of loans and bursaries in different provinces.

EDUCATION AND GENDER

Until recently, literature on educational gender inequality focused on the women's disadvantages. Today, however, formal education—especially university and college education—has opened many social and economic opportunities for females in Canada.

Before Confederation, young girls went to school with the boys, but often family duties kept many of them from getting as much primary education as they wanted. Until 1862, young women had no chance to gain a higher education in Canada. Then, Mount Allison

CLASSIC WORKS

Box 13.1 *Crestwood Heights* (1956)

Crestwood Heights began as a project to learn about the mental health of children in Canada, part of the National Mental Health Project, with the aim to promote positive mental health and increase the understanding of life in the suburb of a large Canadian city, in this case the affluent Forest Hill area in Toronto, which the researchers called 'Crestwood Heights'. The specific goal of the study by John Seeley, Alexander Sim, and Elizabeth Loosley was to learn about 'the culture of the child under pressures for conformity'. In other words, it was a study of education, but also a study of childhood and children aimed at understanding the culture of children, their values, goals in life, and problems. Seeley and his colleagues wanted to uncover the main guiding principles and pressures for conformity during childhood. To do so, they focused on significant institutions and on the strains and conflicts in the family and the community.

To parents in this community, the child was seen as a problem to be solved, like other problems in the managerial world. The parents themselves were a mixture of 'new money' and 'old money'—successful and upwardly mobile people in business or the professions. Many were the children of immigrants, with high hopes for themselves and their children. They were mainly white Anglo-Saxon Protestants (WASPs), though a disproportionate number of people in this area of Toronto were Jewish. For them, careers were the priority and career success was important. As well, they wanted their homes, appearances, and activities to look like Hollywood movies or haute couture magazines. Therefore, they trained their children to be 'perfect': competitive and successful in all their pursuits.

Even at a young age, children were taught to seek success in Scout groups, music lessons, hockey teams, and summer camps. And school, rather than religion, was the most important institution. The school was viewed as the authority on child-raising and as the main place where children could prove their perfection. Parents turned their children over to the school (and associated institutions), hoping to get them back more mature. Concern with schooling, according to the researchers, also made the Parent–Teacher Association the most significant voluntary association. At the high school, the PTA mediated between the school and the home. It retrained parents in the 'newer' ideas and techniques of child-rearing. Teachers and administrators were increasingly important as sources of authority, and were viewed as experts, or at least as specialists.

This was complicated by stresses within the school itself. Some of these had to do with school organization, and some with the conflicting goals of education. On the one hand, the school was charged with training the children for 'bureaucratic crawl'. With the increasing bureaucratization in industrial society, child-rearing values shift from a stress on individual achievement, independence, and competition to a stress on co-operation, other-direction, and a submergence of the individual in the group. Therefore, school, as Seeley et al. determined, trained the middle-class suburban child for 'bureaucratic crawl' as it taught the 'new' techniques of co-operation and group orientation.

At the same time, school tried to teach traditional values of competition and individual effort. This caused tension for the students, parents, and teachers. The tension was worsened by the effects of bureaucratization on the jobs of teachers. Parents also pressed teachers for higher grades (more successes for their children)—the beginnings of grade inflation. No wonder many students experience a troubled transition from high school to university, and much personal stress in both locations.

In your estimation, in what ways has schooling changed and in what ways has education remained the same in the more than half-century since the *Crestwood Heights* study was done? Also, to what extent do you think the findings from one affluent community are applicable in the wider society?

University in New Brunswick enrolled its first female students. Shortly after, other Canadian universities and colleges opened their doors to female students.

In earlier years, many college women—regardless of their interests and aptitudes—were urged to take general arts degrees or domestic science courses. Though women were allowed to become nurses, they were prevented from studying medicine. At the end of the nineteenth century, hospitals in Montreal refused to accept any female doctors. As a result, by 1893 all Canadian universities had closed their doors to women medical students. Most Canadian universities would not reopen their medical programs to women for another 50 years.

Elsie McGill, the first Canadian woman to get a degree in electrical engineering, graduated from the University of Toronto in 1927. However, it was not until much later that women were entering male-dominated fields of study such as business, engineering, medicine, and law in noticeable numbers. By 1981, though women remained in the minority, census figures had recorded a dramatic increase in female enrolments in these fields (www.swc-cfc.gc.ca/dates/whn/2003/facts_3.pdf).

Increasingly, government and other bodies began to encourage young women to continue schooling and careers in non-traditional fields such as science and engineering. According to 1999–2000 data on the status of women in universities, in Canada women received 59 per cent of all post-secondary degrees, including 59.9 per cent of all bachelor and first professional degrees, 52.3 per cent of all master's degrees, and 40.7 per cent of all Ph.D.s. Women were a clear majority of degree recipients in health professions (73.1 per cent), humanities (63.7 per cent), and social sciences (58.3 per cent).

Nonetheless, even though women continue to achieve doctoral degrees in non-traditional areas in increasing numbers, they are largely under-represented in engineering, applied sciences, and in mathematics. According to Gomme (2004), even though women seem to be making gains, they continue to suffer disadvantages. Women continue, far more than men, to enter social sciences, fine arts, and humanities, but these fields are less directly marketable than others like engineering and applied sciences, where men outnumber women. Further, education in these areas (for example, engineering and computer science) usually leads to jobs with higher levels of pay.

However, it is not merely that women seek out lower-paying careers. Research also shows that careers tend to lose both prestige and pay as larger numbers of women enter them. In effect, these formerly male-dominant jobs become proletarianized as they become feminized, for example, in pharmacy and law. It remains to be seen whether other feminizing professions such as medicine and dentistry follow suit. In part, this reflects the increased supply of job candidates. Increased competition in any job domain usually depresses wages. However, the connections to female participation are hard to miss. No satisfactory explanation of this phenomenon has yet been provided.

The social benefits of education are dramatic for both men and women, but especially for women. Evidence collected in Canada and other industrial countries shows those women who gain the highest levels of education come closest to job and income equality with men. As it is for racial minority groups and poor people, for women higher education is an important way towards social equality. Though it does not solve all the problems women face, education solves many.

A large part of the continuing problem of gender inequality in less developed parts of the world is educational. Families, governments, and economies do not give young women high priority in education and jobs in many parts of the world. Women are especially likely to be illiterate in sub-Saharan Africa, the Arab states, and South Asia (the Indian subcontinent).

EDUCATION AND RACE

Many of the educational disadvantages faced by ethnic minority groups in Canada stem from long-standing economic exploitation and disadvantage. Issues of class and race are closely bound. In this section, we will examine the issues of race/ethnicity and its multifaceted impact on education.

The most prominent Canadian example is that of Aboriginal Canadians. First, we will show issues of disadvantage and inequality from a historical perspective—the European dominance over North American Aboriginals that resulted in forced residential schooling of Aboriginal youth. The results of these actions are still observable today, in the form of economic hardship, residential segregation, and various social, family, and individual pathologies. Second, we will analyze more recent trends—especially, the impact of visible minority status on higher educational attainment.

Aboriginal Issues and Education

In 1867, through the terms of the British North America Act, the federal government of Canada declared responsibility for managing 'Indians and lands reserved for Indians' (Stonefish, 2007).

With governments and the Euro-Canadian majority dismissive of their heritage and overall autonomy, Aboriginal people were defined legally as 'non-citizens and wards of the state' (Furniss, 1992). In 1876, the Indian Act further perpetuated coercive legislation aimed at assimilation, providing government with 'sweeping powers' to control and regulate almost all aspects of Aboriginals' lives across Canada. Part of this included regulating education.

The Canadian government's effort to assimilate the Aboriginal population through the development of the residential schools system is one of the most blatant examples of Canadian *racialization*—a term for how social institutions impose racial identities on minorities. The residential school system shows how 'educational programs' can be directed by racist and class-based ideology (Nicholas, 2001). The Canadian government, through the Roman Catholic, Anglican, Methodist, United, and Presbyterian churches, which were responsible for running the residential schools, tried to mould Native identities.

Aboriginal youth were separated from their families and communities. Residential schooling was compulsory for most of the Aboriginal youth population. The intent was to produce a young generation of 'modern Indians' (Davies and Guppy, 2006), by forcing young people to abandon their cultural heritage and to replace their 'nomadic hunting and fishing lifestyle' with the ways of the 'civilized' Europeans (Furniss, 1992: 13). Many of the subjects of this 'grand' social experiment were left hanging between two worlds: a white society that rejected them and a Native culture they had been deprived of knowing.

Forty-five residential schools were fully funded by 1894. These schools were modelled on the first two 'successful' schools in southern Ontario, the Mohawk Institute founded in 1829

BACK IN HISTORY

Box 13.2 Timeline of Residential Schools, 1620–2009

1620–80 Boarding schools are established for Indian youth by the Récollets, a French Roman Catholic order in New France, and later by the Jesuits and the Ursulines, a female order. This form of schooling lasts until the 1680s.

1820s Early church schools are run by Protestants, Catholics, Anglicans, and Methodists.

1847 Egerton Ryerson produces a study of Native education at the request of the assistant superintendent general of Indian affairs. His findings become the model for future Indian residential schools. Ryerson recommends that domestic education and religious instruction comprise the best model for the Indian population. The recommended focus is on agricultural training, and government funding will be awarded through inspections and reports.

1860 Indian Affairs is transferred from the imperial government to the Province of Canada, following the Britain's shift in policy from fostering the autonomy of Native populations through industry to assimilating them through education.

1974 The government gives control of the Indian education program to band councils and Indian education committees. Aboriginal education systems see an increase in the number of Native employees in the school system. Over 34 per cent of staff members have Indian status.

1975 An Ontario Task Force on the Educational Needs of Native Peoples hears recommendations from Native representatives to increase language and cultural programs and improve funding for Native control of education. Also, a Department of Indian Affairs and Northern Development publication reports that 174 federal and 34 provincial schools offer language programs in 23 Native languages.

1979 Only 15 residential schools are still running in Canada. The Department of Indian Affairs evaluates the schools and creates a series of initiatives. Among them is a plan to make the school administrations more culturally aware of the needs of Aboriginal students.

1986 The United Church of Canada formally apologizes to Canada's First Nations people.

1989 Non-Aboriginal orphans at Mount Cashel Orphanage in Newfoundland make allegations of sexual abuse by Christian Brothers at the school. The case paves the way for litigation for residential school victims.

1990 Phil Fontaine, leader of the Association of Manitoba Chiefs, meets with representatives of the Catholic Church. He demands that the Church acknowledge the physical and sexual abuse suffered by students at residential schools.

1991 The Missionary Oblates of Mary Immaculate offers an apology to Canada's First Nations people.

1993 The Anglican Church offers an apology to Canada's First Nations people.

1994 The Presbyterian Church offers a confession to Canada's First Nations people.

2001 The Canadian government begins negotiations with the Anglican, Catholic, United, and Presbyterian churches to design a compensation plan. By October, the government agrees to pay 70 per cent of settlement to former students with validated claims. By December, the Anglican Diocese of Cariboo in British Columbia declares bankruptcy, saying it can no longer pay claims related to residential school lawsuits.

19 Sept. 2007 A landmark compensation deal for former residential school students comes into effect, ending what Assembly of First Nations Chief Phil Fontaine called a 150-year 'journey of tears, hardship and pain—but also of struggle and accomplishment'. The approved agreement will provide nearly $2 billion to the former students who had attended 130 schools. Indian Affairs Minister Chuck Strahl said he hoped the money would 'close this sad chapter of history in Canada'.

11 June 2008 Prime Minister Stephen Harper apologizes to former students of Native residential schools, marking the first formal apology by a prime minister for the federally financed program. 'The treatment of children in Indian residential schools is a sad chapter in our history', he says in a speech in the House of Commons.

10 June 2009 Indian Affairs Minister Chuck Strahl announces the appointment of Judge Murray Sinclair, an Aboriginal justice from Manitoba, as chief commissioner of the Truth and Reconciliation Commission for residential schools.

Source: **Adapted from CBC News (2009).**

Sun Media/St Catharines Standard-Julie Jocsak

Aboriginal Achievement Award recipient John Henhawk spent part of his childhood living in a trailer, often without heat, scrambling to get food. This fall, the 24-year-old St Catharine's resident will be the first in his family to graduate from university.

and the Mount Elgin Industrial School that began in 1848. Officially, residential schools operated in Canada between 1892 and 1969. After 1969, the Canadian government was no longer officially involved in running residential schools. Several schools, however, did continue to run until the mid-1990s; and Akaitcho Hall in Yellowknife, the last residential school in Canada, closed only in 1996. The abusive and humiliating experience of residential schooling is still being felt by generations of Aboriginals across Canada.

Native children were taught that their heritage was brutish, unacceptable, and shameful. They were stripped of their culture, language, and distinct world view. The goal of creating new identities for the Canadian Natives was explicit—the 'Indian problem' would no longer exist if the Native population assimilated into the dominant culture. This meant wearing European clothing, speaking the dominant language, and working as labourers within the colonial economy. In essence, the goal was to produce a subordinate working class that would not be disruptive towards the Euro-Canadian majority (Ng, 1993).

To be sure, the experiences of Aboriginal peoples varied across the country and changed significantly over the course of Canadian history; indeed, some would say it improved dramatically. Box 13.2 provides a historical understanding of the changes in residential school policies from the beginnings of Canadian history up to the present.

Aboriginal Educational Attainment Today

Today, the schooling of Aboriginal youth is still the responsibility of the federal government. Present-day efforts to educate Aboriginal students remain ineffective. The levels of education that Aboriginal students earn are drastically lower than the levels for non-Aboriginal students (Statistics Canada and CMEC, 2000). In 1996, 42 per cent of Aboriginal youth did not complete high school compared to 22 per cent of the non-Aboriginal population. Rates of higher education are still low, with only approximately 7 per cent of Aboriginal people achieving a post-secondary certificate or degree.

Andrew Siggner and Rosalinda Costa (2005), using the 2001 census, show that 'there is some cautious good news.' Between 1981 and 2001, the rate at which Aboriginal youth received higher levels of education notably increased. This increase, however, was observable only among Aboriginal populations living in urban areas, and was much more dramatic for females compared to males.

Between 1981 and 2001, major census metropolitan areas (CMAs) saw more Aboriginal youth earning high school diplomas. In several CMAs, such as Toronto, Sudbury, and Calgary, many more Aboriginal males completed high school. In these CMAs Aboriginal male youth who had *not* completed high school notably declined. In that same period, most of the CMAs saw a rise in Aboriginal youth out of high school going on to post-secondary education, often earning a degree or diploma.

Overall, the proportion of Aboriginal males ages 25–34 who have completed post-secondary education has increased to approximately 25 per cent. School attendance, too, has increased. In 1981, school attendance was from 30 to 46 per cent for Aboriginal youth aged 15–24, this rate ranged from 50 to 66 per cent in 2001 (Figure 13.3).

Immigrants and Visible Minorities: Contemporary Canadian Trends

Historically, Canada has upheld one of the highest rates of immigration across all nations worldwide. Recent census data suggest that visible minority groups will constitute half of Toronto's population by 2017 (Statistics Canada, 2005). Over the past several decades, immigration patterns have produced a diverse multicultural student population. How have these changes affected schooling and educational attainment in Canada?

In Canada today, visible minorities and recent immigrants are more educated than the general Canadian population. This is largely a result of Canada's immigration policy. Recruiting strategies have changed over the past 50 years from a 'former bias of seeking both manual and skilled labour from Europe to a policy of seeking more educated labour from around the world' (Davies and Guppy, 2006: 42).

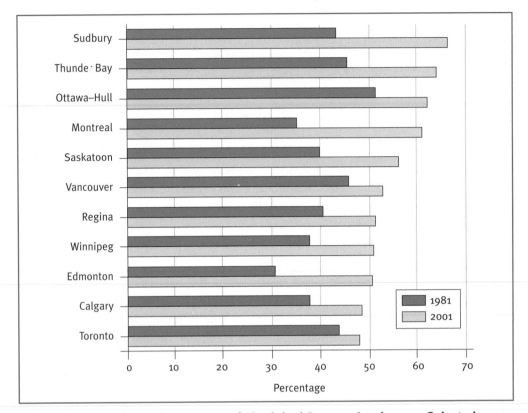

Figure 13.3 School Attendance Rates of Aboriginal Persons Aged 15–24, Selected Cities, 1981 and 2001

Source: School Attendance Rates of Aboriginal Persons Aged 15–24, in Selected Cities, 1981 and 2001, at www.statcan.gc.ca/pub/81-004-x/2005003/8612-eng.htm#Footnote1.

As a result, immigration policies have produced a highly educated group of immigrant workers. However, analyses of employment and income indicators show that access to higher social status and economic positions in Canada is unequal. Some research points out that racial discrimination is still prevalent in Canadian society.

The question remains, how should schools be (further) reformed and improved to provide the best possible education for Canada's many diverse communities? One approach recently taken in Toronto has been the creation of an Africentric school (Box 13.3), in the belief that African Canadians might be better served by schools focused heavily on their culture and history, rather than on conventional topics of Canadian schooling.

Work Discrimination and Unemployment

Foreign-born visible minorities experience larger gaps between their education attainment and their occupation than do other groups. For example, fewer than half of foreign-born visible minorities with a university degree work in jobs with a high skill level, especially during difficult economic times.

Many recent immigrants find that their educational and work credentials are not recognized in the Canadian employment system. They are forced into jobs below their training and

PUBLIC ISSUES

Box 13.3 Africentric School Makes History

Drummed into school to a standing ovation and a rocking West African beat, 115 children made Canadian history yesterday in vivid vests of African cloth.

Less than two years after fierce public debate over the idea of a school focused on African culture, one of the most controversial educational experiments in the country began with a surprise 30 per cent surge in enrolment.

From the opening assembly, the Africentric Alternative School began weaving African culture into Ontario school culture.

Students sang 'O Canada', followed by a black national anthem written a century ago by a Florida poet, then said a pledge—'The Best Possible Me'—popular in Africentric schools in the US. It includes a promise to take school seriously.

'Let me hear you say "best!"', called principal Thando Hyman-Aman, a part-time jazz singer and the parent of a student at the school. She will lead a bid to lower the 40 per cent dropout rate among black students by stretching the curriculum beyond its European roots.

'You will always be the . . . what?' she called, holding the microphone out to the children, some of whom have come from Scarborough and Mississauga to attend the program, housed in Sheppard Public School, near Sheppard Ave. and Keele St.

'Best!' they responded.

When dignitaries at the assembly cried 'ashe', the Yoruba word for 'amen', the audience called it back.

If enrolment continues to grow—there is room for 150 students—the school may add another teacher, and will try to find a male to join the currently all-female staff, said school trustee James Pasternak, who represents the ward.

'We hire on the basis of ability, but we do need a male role model, so we are going to be actively recruiting male talent', said Pasternak.

'I like the fact they say that pledge', said community worker Rebeckah Price, whose son Jahbril is in Grade 5. 'They'll say it every day and one day they'll believe it.'

Jahbril said last night he enjoyed the first day at school: 'We learned the seven principles of Kwanza, which is an African holiday that's almost a version of Christmas.' The 9-year-old, who went out last Hallowe'en as Barack Obama (this year as Michael Jackson), said he can't wait to learn about 'my heritage—Jamaica, but also Africa, where my ancestors came from.' . . .

Long-time supporters of the project were emotional at seeing the school finally open its doors.

'Victory is won!' said Angela Wilson, one of two mothers who pushed for the school, first proposed in 1994 by Ontario's Royal Commission on Learning, as a way to make education more relevant for black students.

Mother Hazel Bridgeman said, 'The issue affecting most young black kids is self-esteem, and this school is going to try to address that.'

Source: Brown (2009).

---

expertise. A longitudinal survey of this problem by Statistics Canada found that six out of 10 immigrants to Canada did not work in the same field after their arrival. Four main factors affect the entry-level job status of immigrants: (1) the specificity of skills required by the nation's immigration policy; (2) the educational competition experienced between immigrants and the native-born; (3) the labour market structure; and (4) the welfare state (Reitz, 2001).

THE EFFECTIVENESS OF SCHOOLING

Contemporary efforts to reform schools, or to measure school effectiveness, in Canada and the United States have been continuing for several decades. The Coleman report was the first empirical study to evaluate educational programs, addressing issues of unequal academic opportunities and outcomes. Published on 4 July 1966, largely in response to the racial seg-regation of black and white students in the US, this study concluded that overall, schools contributed little to reducing inequalities. Specifically, Coleman argued that variables such as spending per pupil, teacher experience, and the number of books in libraries, for example, contributed very little in terms of achievement. These conclusions led to the belief that stu-dents' socio-economic status (measured by parental education, job status, and income) sig-nificantly influences student outcomes.

Various researchers subsequently challenged this position. These challenges included George Weber's *Inner-City Children Can Be Taught to Read* (1971); Good, Biddle, and Brophy's *Teachers Make a Difference* (1975); and Neville Bennete's *Teaching Styles and Pupil Progress* (1976). These researchers suggested that, contrary to Coleman's views, curriculum development, school organization, and teaching methods *significantly* affect schools, educa-tional quality, and students' achievements.

In reality, both of the above perspectives are valid. While it is true that poverty has substan-tial effects on achievement, economic indicators are not solely responsible for student success. Although research consistently shows a link between a person's school success and socio-eco-nomic factors, non-economic factors are also relevant. Although parental education, income, and occupational prestige are relevant to children's school success, the lack of these variables in this relationship may not be as inauspicious as various studies have suggested.

In fact, David Johnson's (2009) study of Ontario schools suggests that economic inequality may not be as decisive for schools and students as previously thought. In association with the C.D. Howe Institute, Johnson shows how non-economic factors account for students' school performance on standardized Grade 3 and Grade 6 tests. To control for economic fac-tors, Johnson examined data from the Ontario public school testing authority that outlines various socio-economic demographics associated with different school zones, including the percentage of university graduates, recent immigrants, single mothers, Aboriginals, and so on. Using census data, as well as information about students' socio-economic background, Johnson predicted how various schools across Ontario would be expected to do on Grade 3 and Grade 6 standardized tests, based solely on these demographic factors. He found that the fit was far from perfect, indicating that organizational factors also make a difference.

His results show that 'good' schools in Ontario have 'principals, teachers and other staff who are making a positive difference in student performance regardless of their students' socio-economic backgrounds' (Johnson, 2009). Johnson was able to show how a school's students perform on standardized tests, which simplified a comparison of schools that per-form better or worse than other schools with students from similar backgrounds. This shows how the quality of principal and staff has contributed to student performance in schools with students of a similar economic background.

Consider the example of Cornell Junior Public School located in Scarborough, Ontario. The average annual household income in the surrounding area is under $50,000, and only 21.5 per cent of the residents have earned a university degree. Yet, 80 per cent of the Grade 3 students passed the standardized tests in reading, writing, and mathematics. Given the socio-economic makeup of Cornell Junior Public School, students should have had a pass rate of 7.9 per cent below the provincial average, yet their overall score was 15.1 per cent above.

These findings suggest that 'good' schools are not only to be found in 'good' neighbour-hoods, and vice versa. No matter what neighbourhood students are from, the schools they attend have the potential to provide a quality education. Overall, significant differences exist in the quality of instruction across schools that are located in neighbourhoods whose students come from similar economic backgrounds. This means that student success should not be taken for granted if the students live in rich neighbourhoods or come from rich families; nor should their failure be taken for granted if they come from poorer families and live in poorer neighbourhoods.

According to these results, good teachers can make a difference, and so can bad teachers. Sub-standard teachers fail to foster the belief that children can learn, and they may not have the necessary skills to promote student success. So, as one of the most significant educational resources, teachers are fundamental to school improvement efforts. This means it is necessary to ensure that competent and talented people are working as teachers, that their teaching quality is high, and that *all* students have access to high-quality teachers. However, successful teaching is not possible unless the school atmosphere is organized, peaceful, and controlled. Clear rules for student behaviour must be consistently enforced and regulated by school officials.

THEORETICAL PERSPECTIVES ON EDUCATION

Table 13.1 Theoretical Perspectives

Theory	Main Points
Structural Functionalism	• The function of schooling is to give people the human capital society needs for economic growth. • Additionally, schools socialize people for the work world and for citizenship.
Conflict Theory	• Schooling is a means by which people are trained to endure the boredom and subordination of alienating work. • The myth of upward mobility through merit at school is used by the ruling class to justify social inequality.
Symbolic Interactionism	• Schools help people develop identities that are appropriate to the social roles they will play as adults. • Schools are as important for discouraging disadvantaged people as they are for encouraging advantaged people. • This was particularly true of residential schooling for Aboriginal students.
Feminist Theory	• Schools have historically treated boys and girls differently, subtly reinforcing sexism. • Today, girls are doing better at every level of schooling and boys are more likely to drop out prematurely.
Social Constructionism	• Public issues around schooling are connected to a variety of concerns about class, race, and income inequality. • Claims about school quality—quality of education generally—are back in the news, and hard to verify.

Structural Functionalism

From the functionalist perspective, the school as a social institution performs the imperative function of socialization—the processes surrounding the internalization and learning of culture, most of which occurs during childhood. In this way schools 'help prepare new adults for generational succession—they are the major means by which one generation prepares its own replacement' (Davies and Guppy, 2006: 23). Accordingly, then, the education system is one of the most important social institutions. It contributes to the maintenance of social order and provides opportunities for people to become socially mobile.

Functionalists see schools as 'great equalizers', and as neutral social organizations that are designed to both socialize and educate. Under these circumstances, success, then, can be largely attributed to a student's merit or ability. If you succeed in school, you earned it; but if you do not succeed, this is because of a personal flaw or weakness. Schools, if they are fair, create equal opportunity, social mobility, and even meritocracy—the holding of power or authority by certain people based on their ability. However, what happens when a society becomes over-educated in relation to the occupational positions available to its citizens? If this occurs, then some people will be forced to take jobs *below* their acquired educational credentials. Functionalism today emerges in such arguments—the notion of *over-education* and *credentialism*. We will discuss this further.

From the functionalist perspective, social problems related to education occur when schools fail to perform their *manifest functions*—the visible and intended goals, consequences, or effects of social structures and institutions. Examples of the intended functions of schools include *socialization*, *assimilation*, *transmission of knowledge*, and *social control*, as well as *change* and *innovation*. With this in mind, many of the social problems discussed in this book, such as poverty and unemployment (Chapter 2) or crime and delinquency (Chapter 7), can be linked to the failure of educational systems to accomplish their basic functions. As we have stressed throughout this text, many social problems are *interconnected* or *intertwined* with one another. Often, social and economic disadvantage permeates many aspects of people's lives, and educational attainment (or the lack thereof) is one mechanism by which disadvantage leads to problems.

Conflict Theory

Conflict theory exposes disequilibrium in the education system, arguing that certain groups are favoured over others while inequalities are perpetuated based on class, race, and gender. While it might seem as though the official goal of education is to provide a universal and equal mechanism for success and achievement, educational opportunity and the quality of education available are far from equally distributed across Canadian society.

To illustrate the conflict perspective, consider the issue of student dropouts. Students who drop out of high school, according to Bowlby and McMullen (2002: 143), 'were much less likely to have a parent with a university degree (11 per cent) than students who graduated from high school (30.6 per cent)'. Thus, our social class position directs our educational pursuits. Further, in terms of obtaining a post-secondary education, children of disadvantaged class origins are more likely to experience lower educational outcome. Educational systems,

SOCIALIZATION The process by which people internalize and learn their culture, much of which occurs during childhood.

MERITOCRACY The holding of power or authority by people selected because of their ability.

thus, have the tendency to support and perpetuate prevailing schemes of stratification in society.

Symbolic Interactionism

The symbolic interactionist is concerned with *individuals* and the ways they interact in *small groups*. From this perspective, social interaction is usefully viewed as 'dramaturgical performance where one infers meanings and impressions from the verbal and non-verbal expressions given off by others' (Murphy, 1979). If we apply this perspective to micro-level processes in the education system, we learn things about classrooms and peer group relations that we might otherwise miss.

Feminist Theory

From a historical perspective, the experience of education has been vastly different for men and women. These differences were not only manifest in educational outcomes, but also in terms of normative societal and cultural expectations adopted by mainstream society during particular times.

Influenced by the Enlightenment, Mary Wollstonecraft contested popular attitudes towards women and education in *The Vindication of the Rights of Women* (1997 [1792]). Wollstonecraft argued that women deserve social equality and should be given the necessary education in order to obtain it (Zeitlin, 2001). Accordingly, Wollstonecraft asserted that 'the virtue of *knowledge* of the two sexes should be the same in nature, if not in degree, and that women, considered not only as moral but rational creatures, ought to endeavor to acquire human virtues (or perfections) by the *same* means as men, instead of being educated like a fanciful kind of *half* being' (1997 [1792]). Overall, she expressed that men and women, by sharing the same virtues, should be treated the same and given the same opportunities.

Feminist theorists and researchers who study education have focused on the extent to which disparities occur within the school system that produce and perpetuate social and economic disadvantages for girls and women. Historically, in terms of educational opportunity and outcome, young boys obtained greater long- and short-run advantages over young girls. According to Dillabough and Arnot (2002: 34), 'the long-term goal of feminism here was to empower women to take up their rightful place throughout the development of female autonomy.' A central issue for the freedom of choice and greater autonomy was the removal of barriers towards occupational choice, subject preference, and decisions surrounding sex roles. Equal opportunities were seen as crucial in producing an adaptive, flexible, and undifferentiated workforce.

SOCIAL CONSEQUENCES OF EDUCATION

Over-education and Credentialism

Theories of **credentialism**, embodied in theories of school legitimacy, argue that formal school systems have increasingly become institutions that provide credentials but not

CREDENTIALISM A process of social selection that gives class advantage and social status to people who possess academic advantage.

necessarily educations. This allegation has led theorists to wonder what, exactly, an educational certificate represents. Does it truly improve job skills and prepare students for the workforce? Alternatively, does it provide graduates with a piece of paper that serves as an occupational ticket?

In *The Credential Society* (1979), Randall Collins argues that contemporary schools are over-educating students. Collins states that the economy cannot support the number of educationally qualified people who are graduating from high school, college, and university. Accordingly, Collins alleges that the contemporary school system is amplifying credential inflation—the process by which labour-market competition encourages people to acquire schooling and employers raise required credential levels for reasons that are not connected to their needs for skilled employees. Stated differently, modern education devalues educational credentials in the same way that monetary inflation devalues money.

If so, what use do employers make of educational credentials—the supposed proof that job candidates have particular skills and aptitudes? Collins argues that most employers rarely look at student grades when hiring. That happens because, according to Collins, the school curriculum develops on its own terms, not with the goal of meeting the needs of employers or the demand for particular skills in the labour force. If credentials were, in fact, closely tied to the specific needs of employers, then employers would hire on the basis of school grades. Yet, most of the time, a college diploma is all that is required. Specific grades are irrelevant.

That said, more years of schooling—and more distinguished sets of diplomas—bring higher returns in the labour market. Entry into select professional or managerial jobs is limited and closely guarded. In particular, 'professionals' such as doctors and lawyers strictly control entry into their numbers, by limiting the numbers who are permitted to get the desired credentials. This they do successfully by claiming to play an important, almost irreplaceable role in society and, consequently, by gaining from governments the ability to be self-regulating professions, on the assumption that their professional expertise is such that only they have the knowledge to evaluate and adjudicate issues involving the profession. In this way, too, they justify their high-paying positions.

The demand for more credentials in turn creates occupations that seek to limit the number of entrants. In effect, what we mean by professionalization is the process by which an occupation raises its standing by limiting the number of entrants (Anleu and Mack, 2008). Through such an exertion of power, many occupations have turned into 'classic' professions (such as law or medicine). This was accomplished by creating multiple layers of specialization and professional training—even though, as Collins has stated, much schooling is highly theoretical and has little to do with on-the-job experience or training.

Canada has one of the highest rates of post-secondary attainment in the world and, in general, this is viewed positively. However, there is growing evidence that the skills of the Canadian workforce are not being used to their full potential. Over-education means having more education than is needed to carry out a particular job or fulfill a particular role. Immigrants arriving in Canada, for example, often discover that the education they have acquired becomes underutilized in the Canadian labour market (Chiswick and Miller, 2008). Similarly, Livingstone, Hart, and Davie (2003) indicate, in a survey of Ontario residents from 1994 to 2002, that rates of over-qualification were reported to have risen from 16 per cent to

CREDENTIAL INFLATION
The tendency of schools to provide and employers to demand ever-more schooling and ever-higher credentials for work that is no more demanding or complex.

PROFESSIONALIZATION
The process by which an occupation raises its standing by limiting the number of entrants and regulating their behaviour.

OVER-EDUCATION
Having more education than is actually needed to successfully perform employment roles and functions.

21 per cent. While university graduates increased by nearly 150 per cent from the 1970s until the early 1990s, the number of jobs requiring a university education increased by only 40 per cent (Expert Panel on Skills, 2000).

The projected increase surrounding the underutilization of educational credentials has led researchers to consider various social consequences. Some have suggested that increases in job dissatisfaction, worker discontent, and greater political alienation, as well as weakened loyalty to dominant achievement ideology, may result. However, these outcomes show different results depending on the extent of over-education.

School Dropouts

Dorn, Bowen, and Blau (2006) separate student dropouts into three main categories: *dropout*, *pullout*, and *pushout*. By this reckoning, *dropout theories* focus on students who find themselves unable to cope intellectually (or cognitively) with school materials. *Pullout theories* are class-based theories and focus on students who withdraw from schooling because of financial troubles. Finally, *pushout theories* focus on the school and community as contextual factors that influence rates of high school dropouts. So, for example, communities in which the schools offer little encouragement to their students—where, for example, guidance counsellors urge their students to aim low, to avoid disappointment—would fall into this pushout category, as would communities in which there are few role models exemplifying the possibilities and benefits of higher education.

As we have seen, people in Canada with post-secondary education benefit from various social and economic advantages compared to people who have less formal education. Some of these benefits include higher incomes, increased job security, and greater occupational prestige. These higher levels of education are correlated with greater levels of economic return over one's lifetime. A growing body of evidence also shows that higher levels of education allow for easier transitions into the workforce. Obtaining a high school diploma becomes exceedingly important in a credential society. In part, that is because more education gives people more skills and resources for work-related tasks; also, higher credentials open doors to more select job opportunities.

At the very least, a high school diploma is a strong signal for prospective employers that a person can stick to a task to its completion, an indication of a certain degree of self-discipline. It also gives people the opportunity to enter post-secondary education, whether college or university. Recent data from Statistics Canada illustrates the impact a high school diploma has on rates of unemployment. Unemployment rates, for example, are nearly double for people aged 25–44 who do not have a high school diploma (Bowlby, 2005).

Most teens in Canada both attend high school and complete a high school education. In terms of attendance, for example, in recent years school attendance rates for 15–19-year-olds was 82 per cent to 84 per cent. According to a Statistics Canada report, this is markedly higher than attendance 25 years ago when just about two-thirds of all teens attended high school. Not surprisingly, dropout rates have also significantly declined. During the 2004–5 school year, dropout rates decreased 37.2 per cent from the 1990–1 school year (Figure 13.4).

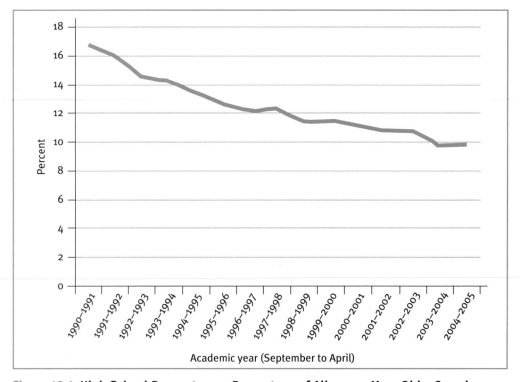

Figure 13.4 High School Dropouts as a Percentage of All 20–24-Year-Olds, Canada, 1990–1 to 2004–5

Source: High School Drop-outs as a Percentage of All 20–24-year-olds, Canada, 1990–1991 to 2004–2005, at www.statcan. gc.ca/pub/81-004-x/2005004/8984-eng.htm#a.

If dropping out is becoming less common in all parts of Canada, why are social scientists so concerned? Although the decline is pervasive across Canada, the same cannot be said about all regions equally.

The Increasing Prevalence of Male Dropouts—Reversals in Attainment

Analysis of the school success rates of males and females indicates that a substantial change has occurred in terms of gendered attainment over the past several decades. The previous gender imbalance in attainment—depicting a favourable outcome for males—began to change during the 1950s. Today, females surpass males on most measures of attainment. In fact, in terms of dropout rates, females drop out of high school 'in fewer numbers, graduate more often, enter universities in greater numbers, and score higher on many standardized tests' (Davies and Guppy, 2006: 111).

The majority of dropouts have been male students—of the 212,000 students who dropped out in 2004–5 almost 135,000 were male. In other words, the dropout rate for males was almost double that for females: 12.2 per cent compared with 7.2 per cent. For both genders—overall—the rate has declined since 1990–1 from 19.2 per cent to 14.0 per cent in 2004–5.

For some time, males have dropped out of school disproportionately compared to females. What is new, however, is the overall rate of men leaving compared to women. A study from

Statistics Canada suggests that in '1990–1991, a sizable majority of drop-outs were men (58.3 per cent), but by 2004–2005, that proportion had increased to 63.7 per cent' (Bowlby, 2005). In other words, the trend is not due to more men dropping out per se (because there has been an overall decrease in the number of male dropouts), but this increased affect has been caused by a substantial decrease in the rate of young women dropping out. This is true for all provinces across Canada. In particular, these rates are strongest in Quebec where, in 2004–5, seven out of 10 dropouts were males (Figure 13.5).

What accounts for this trend? The Youth in Transition Survey indicated several reasons behind the decision to drop out of high school. Differentiating between males and females, the survey showed that young men were less likely to have an intellectual, social, or emotional investment in school endeavours. They were anxious to work and earn money, so they dropped out of high school more quickly.

Teenage pregnancy, however, plays a more crucial role in the rate of female dropouts. The Youth in Transition Survey showed that 15.9 per cent of female dropouts occurred due to a pregnancy or the need to take care of a child. The trend for young female dropouts is further influenced by the fact that almost four out of 10 have children or were the primary caretakers of a household.

Consistently, the primary reason for females dropping out of high school has been due to their role as caretaker or mother. Since the beginning of the 1990s, however, the overall rate

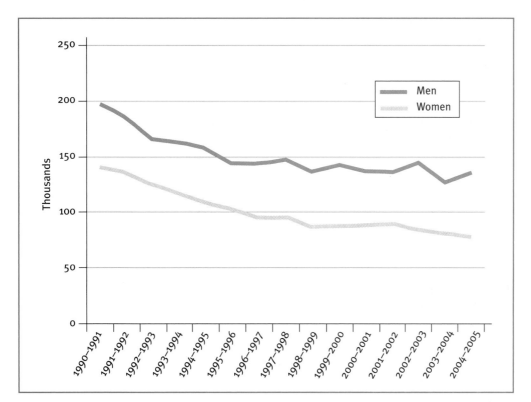

Figure 13.5 **Thousands of High School Dropouts, by Gender, Canada, 1990–1 to 2004–5**

Source: Thousand of High School Drop-outs, by Gender, Canada, 1990–1991 to 2004–2005, at www.statcan.gc.ca/pub/81-004-x/2005004/8984-eng.htm#c.

of female dropouts has decreased. The number of female dropout mothers heading house-holds in Canada has fallen remarkably, by half (Bowlby, 2005).

HEALTH CONSEQUENCES OF EDUCATION

As we have previously suggested, educational attainment in adolescence and early child-hood is linked to health outcomes later in life. People with more advantaged socio-economic status are healthier. For example, Cockerham (1995) notes, 'the fact remains that people at the bottom of the society have the worst health of all, regardless of what country they live in . . . and the level of health care they receive.'

People with higher levels of education adopt better health habits and lifestyles compared to those with lower levels of education and lower socio-economic statuses. Education helps to build useful life skills and the sense of mastery that are needed when dealing with prob-lems later in life. For instance, engaging in positive health behaviours—such as exercising, drinking in moderation, avoiding obesity, refraining from smoking, and regularly visiting the doctor—greatly prolong one's life. It is not surprising that these types of behaviours are strongly associated with individuals who have high educational achievements (Ross and Wu, 1995).

Barbara Ronson and Irving Rootman (2004) provide an additional perspective regarding the effects of education on health. In *Literacy: One of the Most Important Determinants of Health Today*, they argue that literacy predicts health status more accurately than educa-tion level, income, or ethnic background. Various research studies suggest that literacy is directly related to people's overall health status, mental health status, co-morbidity burden, and life expectancy (Ronson and Rootman, 2004; Guerra et al., 2005). Other dangers of illit-eracy include difficulty reading medications, baby formula instructions, and other written medical- or nutrition-related material (Kalichman et al., 1999).

To summarize, higher education enables people to engage in healthy lifestyles and to learn healthy habits. Even a basic education can provide the means for living in a safe neighbour-hood, having a steady job, or developing the ability to understand health information.

Bullying

Bullying is formally defined as any form of repeated aggression in which an observable power differential occurs between individuals (Juvonen and Graham, 2001). However, we usually think of bullying as a kind of childhood terror-tactic. There are two important ele-ments of bullying that capture its complexity. First, bullying is characterized as aggressive or assertive behaviour that is imposed from a position of dominance or power. This power can either be physical—strength or size—or social/hierarchical—belonging to a higher social status peer group, strength in numbers, or systemic power. Second, acts of bullying must be repetitive to be influential.

As Shariff (2005) suggests, bullying is typically expressed in either of two forms—*overt bullying* and *covert bullying*. The former involves 'physical aggression, such as beating, kick-ing, shoving, and sexual touching'. The latter, however, is typified by exclusionary practices

BULLYING Any form of repeated aggression marked by an observable power differential between individuals.

MEAN CREEK

This powerful 2003 movie, set in small-town Oregon, tells the story of a disastrous attempt by a group of teenagers to play a cruel prank on the town bully.

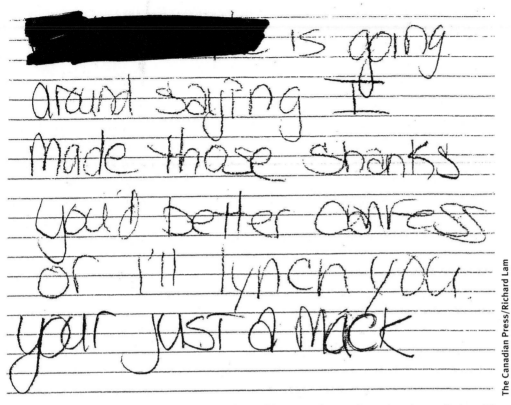

Drawings and a note by Kelly Ellard are part of an evidence package released to the media by a BC Supreme Court Judge, 2 June 2005, which the Crown used in the sentencing of Ellard in early July. Ellard was convicted of second-degree murder for the killing of Victoria teen Reena Virk.

from peer groups. These include being gossiped about, verbally threatened, or harassed. Interestingly, while boys in secondary school are more likely to become victims of bullying, studies show that girls are more likely to fear being bullied at school (Pitts and Smith, 1995; Arnot et al., 1999).

How common is bullying in Canada? Children are far more likely to *be* bullied and *become* bullies themselves compared to children in many other countries. According to the Health Behaviours in School-aged Children Survey conducted by the World Health Organization, 'Canada ranked a dismal 26th and 27th out of 35 countries on measures of bullying and victimization' (Pepler, 2007). This suggests that bullying in Canada has become a pervasive and prevalent social problem.

Cyber-bullying: Media and Technology

In 2004, nearly 75 per cent of Canadians were Internet users (Ekos, 2004). These rates were even higher among Canadian youth—93 per cent of people under 25 and 86 per cent of those between 25 and 44 were regular Internet users (Lenhart et al, 2005).

It is clear that an overwhelming majority of Canadians have access to, and use, the Internet—in particular, young Canadians. Recent data suggest that in terms of time spent, the average Canadian spends far more hours using the Internet now than was the case five and 10 years ago (Quan-Haase and Wellman, 2002; Wellman and Hogan, 2004). The increased use of the Internet, coupled with other forms of technology, has changed the nature of social interaction, perhaps especially among young people.

One example of the effects of technology on Canadian youth is **cyber-bullying**, a technological extension of physical bullying. It occurs when a person uses information technology (IT) to embarrass, harass, intimidate, or threaten others. Sometimes called 'Internet aggression', 'digital harassment', or 'Internet bullying', cyber-bullying is becoming increasingly prevalent as the use of new technologies increases. This emerging form of bullying involves using computers or other IT devices, such as personal digital assistants (PDAs), cell phones, and portable gaming consoles to cause harm to targeted individuals. Colt, Meyer, and McQuade (2009) further caution that cyber-bullying seems to have become so prominent or 'technologically insidious', that classical 'physical' forms of bullying may be increasing as a result.

A large body of research has emerged relating to the impact of cyber-bullying on student safety and learning, which has prompted researchers to consider various legal implications associated with cyber-bullying—ultimately, in an effort to reduce the prevalence of this emerging problem. As Shariff (2005) notes from a Canadian context, however, 'there has been less attention paid to understanding the role of law as it relates to cyber-bullying in the Canadian education system.' This may explain, in part, the stable bullying trends in Canada throughout recent years. According to Shariff, 'one in every seventeen children is threatened on the Internet . . . and one in four youth aged 11–19 is threatened via computer or cell phone' (ibid.). In addition, Li (2005) found in a study of 177 middle school students in Calgary that 41 per cent were bullied by cellphone text messaging, 35 per cent in chat rooms, 32 per cent by schoolmates, 23 per cent of respondents were bullied by e-mail, 16 per cent by multiple sources (including schoolmates), and 11 per cent by people outside of their school. This study raises an important challenge for the supervision and monitoring of cyber-bullying: most cases are *anonymous*. In fact, 41 per cent of the students surveyed by Li reported not knowing the identity of their cyber-bullies.

The anonymity of cyber-bullying, as Shariff (2005) argues, 'distracts *all* students (victims, bystanders, and perpetrators) from schoolwork. It creates a hostile physical environment where students feel unwelcome and unsafe.' Ultimately, in this type of atmosphere, it becomes difficult for students to contribute to class discussion and learn successfully (Harmon, 2004; Shariff, 2005).

SOLUTIONS TO EDUCATIONAL SOCIAL PROBLEMS

Improving Student Learning and Performance

Student achievement and school performance are widely variable—even among schools and students with similar (at times low) socio-economic backgrounds. As we have discussed, student learning is influenced by many factors, including family resources, school organization, effective school curriculum, and teacher skills, attitudes, and practices.

CYBER-BULLYING
A technological extension of physical bullying occurring when an individual uses information technology (IT) to embarrass, harass, intimidate, or threaten others.

In the short run, factors such as family and community background are difficult for policy-makers to influence. What can be improved, however, are teacher quality and teaching practices. In fact, there seems to be a wide-ranging consensus that improving 'teacher quality' is the most influential factor in terms of student achievement (Santiago, 2004; Schacter and Thum, 2004). If instruction and teaching quality are improved, student learning and achievement will also improve.

Improving teaching—especially in low-performing schools—is challenging. Schools must be diligent to ensure that students get on track, stay on track, and receive quality instruction (Quint et al., 2008). The Organization for Economic Co-Operation and Development (2005: 26) claims 'that moving from being taught by an average teacher to one at the 85th percentile of teacher quality would lead to students improving by more than 4 percentiles.' Sanders and Rivers (1996) have estimated that teacher effects are large and cumulative over time. A string of successful teachers narrows the average attainment gap between students from low to high socio-economic status families. In this way, low-performing students benefit more from teachers that are more effective.

Solutions to Dropping Out

It has become common to blame students themselves for dropping out of school. In 1987, Chester Finn—the assistant secretary of education in the United States—argued that school-oriented strategies would be ineffective in reducing rates of student dropouts. His reasoning was that dropouts are disproportionately from lower socio-economic backgrounds in society. Nearly all studies conducted during this time period suggested that dropping out is highly correlated with low SES, minority status, low-test scores and grades, and school dissatisfaction (Wehlage et al., 1989). Today, it is still much more common for students from low socio-economic backgrounds to drop out of school. However, many have come to question whether dropping out is primarily caused by social factors beyond school influence.

As Dupuy and Schweitzer (1995) point out, nearly one-third of school dropouts failed one or more grades in elementary school prior to dropping out. As such, particular attention must be given to students especially in the early years of their education. Such remedial or preventative actions support students' motivation and overall self-confidence, and decrease the risk of dropping out. All of this must occur, according to Dupuy and Schweitzer, through a clear curriculum that is supported by both teachers and parents. Active participation by both sides is a crucial component.

Multicultural Education

Schools also have the potential to *reduce* other social problems. The education system, for example, is one way to overcome racial discrimination. Schools are important sources of formal socialization and are effective in providing their students with socially approved belief, value, and ideological systems. Moreover, informal means of socialization also occur during the school years, since they represent for most students the first opportunity for substantial interaction with other people of similar ages and interests.

The mixing of Canada's diverse young people at school—a source of informal socialization—leads to more interracial friendships and relationships, increases exposure to and acceptance of other cultural practices, and lessens the significance of skin colour. However, the educational curriculum remains Eurocentric, putting an undue emphasis on Western ideas, events, and ideas. As this may not be significant to Canada's diverse population, introducing more multicultural content may broaden all students' cultural knowledge and better engage those students who, because of their heritage, feel disconnected from the education institution.

CHAPTER SUMMARY

Historically, people have argued that schooling outcomes reflect differences in personal abilities. This perspective has fuelled the view that students who are low achievers will ultimately underperform. Underperforming schools have often been labelled as a 'lost cause'. However, the evidence we have presented suggests differently. Teachers, for example, *can* make a difference. While social and economic disadvantage greatly affect student performance, schools, too, can make a measurable impact on the life chances of all students. David Johnson's evaluation of schools in Ontario shows how exceptional schools, in disadvantaged areas, can succeed against unequal odds. Schools like Cornell Junior Public School in Scarborough should not be treated as outliers or out of the ordinary. When schools and teaching practices become successful, it is important to understand *how* and *why* this has occurred. In doing so, educational success can be felt throughout society, not just among dominant and affluent groups.

QUESTIONS FOR CRITICAL THOUGHT

1. Why and how, both historically and today, has the process of obtaining an education in Canada been unequal among various social and cultural groups?

2. John Porter states: 'Educational systems and industrialization have grown together.' Explain and evaluate this statement, using what you know (now) about education and credentialism in present-day society.

3. Over the last three decades there has been a shift in gendered educational attainment. How do you think this will affect educational and occupational pursuits in Canada in years to come?

4. What impact have modern media and technology had on bullying in Canada? How does Canada compare to other nations in terms of these bullying trends? Explain the differences you find.

5. Can students and schools overcome the unfair and damaging effects of poverty and socio-economic inequality? If so, how?

6. If you were a paid consultant, how would you suggest schools should reorganize themselves to become more successful at their main line of work, i.e., education?

RECOMMENDED READINGS

Bowles, Samuel, and Herbert Gintis. 1976. *Schooling in Capitalist America: Educational Reform and the Contradictions of Economic Life.* New York: Basic Books. This classic work is one of the best-known Marxist analyses of education. The authors argue that American schooling systems inhibit social mobility. They explain that schooling systems promote capitalist ideology in the workforce because children are 'groomed' for the capitalist economy throughout their schooling career.

Coleman, James. 1961. *Adolescent Society.* New York: Free Press. This classic sociological work from a credentialist perspective grapples with the interesting fact that youth culture is deeply dysfunctional to a modern, post-industrial (or information) society, and concludes that, in many respects, youth culture largely mirrors the worst aspects of adult culture.

Collins, Randall. 1979. *The Credential Society.* New York: Academic Press. Collins argues that contemporary schools are over-educating students and points out that the economy cannot support the number of educationally qualified people who are graduating from high school, college, or university. Accordingly, Collins alleges that the contemporary school system is amplifying credential inflation.

Davies, Scott, and Neil Guppy. 2006. *The Schooled Society: An Introduction to the Sociology of Education.* Toronto: Oxford University Press. In this up-to-date and well-written textbook, Davies and Guppy outline contemporary debates surrounding the sociology of education today. Particularly interesting are their discussions of alternatives to public education.

Murphy, Raymond. 1979. *Sociological Theories of Education.* Toronto: McGraw-Hill Ryerson. This work outlines and compares the dominant sociological perspectives surrounding education and its related social outcomes.

RECOMMENDED WEBSITES

Truth and Reconciliation Commission of Canada

www.trc.ca/websites/trcinstitution/index.php?p=3

The Truth and Reconciliation Commission of Canada strives to 'learn truth' of the residential schools system and to inform Canadians of these events. Documenting these events is done by accounts of the experiences of survivors and the families and communities that were affected by the residential school experience.

Bullying.org

www.bullying.org

Bullying.org is dedicated to increasing the awareness of bullying and to preventing, resolving, and eliminating school violence and abuse. To accomplish this, they provide educational programs and workshops to various organizations and educational institutions. Further, this organization provides on-line mentoring support programs to educate individuals on how to deal effectively with bullies and bullying.

PREVNet

www.PREVNet.ca

PREVNet is a nationwide network of Canadian researchers, NGOs, and governments who are committed to stopping bullying and violence in schools. The group's website offers a wide range of resources and literature aimed at achieving this goal. As well, conferences and events are organized and advertised through this organization.

CHAPTER 14

Populations, Cities, and Neighbourhoods

iStockphoto.com/Nikada

LEARNING OBJECTIVES

- To find out about the history of the world's population.
- To learn what is meant by the demographic transition.
- To understand competing perspectives of population growth.
- To know the historical founding theories of urban sociology.
- To know about the historical and social significance of suburbanization.
- To discover the social significance of neighbours and neighbourhoods.
- To understand urban issues such as heavy traffic, sprawl, and gentrification.
- To learn of possible solutions to urban problems.

INTRODUCTION

This chapter is about population, cities, and neighbourhoods. It examines the interactions between human society and the built environment, and problems that emerge from these interactions. In doing so, it brings together two central topics of modern sociology—population studies and urban sociology.

Two common threads run through these fields of study. The first is that each topic directly addresses the physical and material backdrops of social life; the second is that human ingenuity (or more concretely, technology) is both at the root of various social problems and is the source of potential solutions to these problems.

Some worry that we face insuperable population problems. Others are not given to worry at all. Economic theorist Julian Simon (1996), for example, believed that human beings are 'the ultimate resource'. Simon's work—a direct rebuff to the Malthusian perspective—remains controversial. Some of Simon's theories about the infinite productiveness of the planet have been disproved as too simplistic. Still, one element of Simon's central thesis is hard to refute: namely, the human species, throughout its short history, has proven hugely creative when confronting difficulty.

Simon would argue that, to solve the problems associated with population growth, we may not need *fewer* people but, instead, better-equipped and better-educated people; and not a *suspicion* of technology, but instead a commitment to using technology for the good of humanity. The problems we discuss in this chapter are not population and cities per se, but the human failure to manage these facets of human design more creatively and effectively. Humanity is the problem we are discussing, and a better-organized humanity is likely the solution.

Still, we must recognize that humanity faces important population-related problems. One central problem relates to the imperfections in how societies are organized; in the twenty-first century, this mainly means how cities are organized. The continued growth of the world's population only worsens our urban problems by making them larger and more complex. Another problem is the rapidity of population growth and urbanization—processes that sped up dramatically in the last few centuries (see, e.g., Xu and Zhu, 2009; Gajdos, 2009).

WORLD POPULATION IN CONTEXT

The history of the world's population unfolded in two general stages: an extended period of slow growth from the time when the first humans appeared to around the mid-eighteenth century; and a brief period of explosive growth after 1750.

According to one estimate, human population growth before the modern era was barely a hundredth of a per cent per year. Since then, the world's population has increased rapidly—sometimes exponentially—with especially rapid growth since the beginning of the Industrial Revolution in the late 1700s.

Consider this in terms of the earth's population doubling. Between the year 1 AD and 1750, it is estimated that population size doubled only once, from 300 million to 750 million. In the last 250 years, the world's population has doubled three times, surpassing 6 billion before 2000. As estimated by the United Nations, the world's population reached 6.5 billion in 2005.

Even though the global population continues to increase today, worldwide growth rates peaked in the 1970s and have been in decline for several years now. Currently, the growth is around 1.3 per cent per year and is expected to decline to 0.5 per cent by 2050 (Attane, 2006). Population growth occurs unevenly around the world, with most developed nations, including Canada, experiencing zero or even negative growth. Italian demographer Massimo Livi-Bacci (1992: 202) predicts that 'developing countries will account for approximately 95 per cent of world population increase in the period 1990–2025 . . . . [As a result] between 1950 and 2025 the developed country share of world population will decline from 33.1 per cent to 15.9; Europe's share will decline still faster, from 15.6 per cent to 6.1.'

It seems that excessive population growth will soon become a social problem of the past. However, other population-related problems will replace it: problems having to do with location, immigration, internal migration, crowding, and depopulation. But first, how has this problem of population growth (nearly) resolved itself? As we will see, it was partly through population planning—through the application of official coercion and incentives—but mainly through the so-called 'demographic transition'.

THE DEMOGRAPHIC TRANSITION

DEMOGRAPHIC TRANSITION Shift in a population or society through a series of stages from high birth and death rates to low birth and death rates.

The **demographic transition** refers to a shift in demographic patterns from high birth and death rates to low birth and death rates (see Johanson-Hanks, 2008; Lehr, 2009). Typically, this demographic transition occurs in parallel with a society's socio-economic development.

During the first stage of the demographic transition, when a society is still in its premodern phase, the number of births and deaths are both high but equal, resulting in a steady population size with only minimal growth. Stage 2 usually arrives as the population enters the early stages of urbanization and industrialization, when socio-economic advances result in declining death rates. During this period, birth rates remain high, resulting in explosive population growth and a young population profile.

However, in stage 3, this changes dramatically. Birth rates begin to fall, slowly reaching levels comparable to the death rate. As a result, the population continues to grow but the rate of increase slows down. By stage 4, when a society has reached a post-industrial phase of development, population is once again stable, with rates of births and deaths equal again and at historic lows. At this point, with low birth rates, the overall population begins to age. Most important, there is no population growth due to excess births over deaths. Canada is currently at this stage—apparently, past this stage, since Canada has a declining natural growth rate. Were it not for immigration, Canada's population would shrink each year.

Numerous thinkers have attempted to explain this remarkable, worldwide decline in child-bearing over the past century. The seminal work of William Goode is discussed in Box 14.1.

CLASSIC WORKS

Box 14.1   William Goode's *World Revolution and Family Patterns* (1963)

In *World Revolution and Family Patterns*, William Goode reviews changes to family organization around the world in the first half of the twentieth century. Notably, Goode examines the relationship between changing family patterns and industrialization. He draws attention to several major cross-cultural trends. First, family patterns are moving towards the conjugal (nuclear) model. The family unit is smaller today, a self-sustaining unit of production and consumption, separate from the kinship group. In addition, with an increase in the use of contraceptives and decrease in birth rate, family size has begun to shrink. Role relations within the family have also changed. Individual members have more freedom; for example, parental authority over children has declined. With an increase in women's rights, husband's patriarchal control over wives has also dwindled. Gradually, dowries and payment for brides have disappeared. A final example of the transformation is an increasing acceptance of changes in social 'morals' and virtues, including the increased acceptance of divorce, the use of contraception, abortion, cohabitation, and premarital sexual relations.

The family does not change directly because of a modern industrial system; rather, this family model better fits industrial demands. Smaller family units have more freedom and flexibility to meet the changes in industry, for example. The influences of industry on family life are not one-sided, however; family demands, such as housework and child care, act as 'barriers' to a complete industrial takeover of family life. Moreover, according to Goode, the family was subject to economic progress and political developments even before industrialization.

Therefore, Goode notes that family systems often resist change, but changes do occur in family life over time. While the global trend is towards the nuclear family, this change has not occurred uniformly (at the same rate) throughout the industrial world. The change towards a conjugal family is not a direct result of industrialization, as it is mediated by cultural influences that predate the industrial revolution. And, finally, changing social conditions of various kinds shape the development of ideas about what makes up the 'ideal' family.

CONTRASTING PERSPECTIVES ON POPULATION CHANGE

The Malthusian Position

This natural decline in population growth was not foreseen. In fact, the opposite—a continued population explosion—was feared throughout much of the nineteenth and twentieth centuries (Clark and Cummins, 2009; Weil and Wilde, 2009).

Modern scientific theories about population growth and its effect on societies began with the ideas of Thomas Malthus (1959 [1798]). Malthus is famously remembered for his theory of population, which can be stated briefly as follows:

> Population when unchecked increases in a geometrical ratio. Subsistence only increases in an arithmetical ratio. . . . [Therefore] the power of population is indefinitely greater than the power in the earth to produce subsistence for man.

Malthus reasoned that a population growing exponentially (that is, through a series such as 1, 2, 4, 8, 16, etc.) at a constant rate adds more people every year than the year before. Consider, for example, a population of 1,000 women and 1,000 men. Each woman marries and has four children. If all survive, in the next generation there are roughly 2,000 women and 2,000 men. If all of those women have four children each, then in the next generation there are roughly 4,000 women and 4,000 men. With a constant pattern of four births per woman, the population doubles every generation (roughly 30 years). In only 300 years, the original population of 2,000 has grown to a million people! (As you can verify, this is because of 10 doublings.)

On the other hand, Malthus said that increases in the food supply are only additive, or arithmetic (that is, in a series such as 1, 2, 3, 4, 5, etc.). Limits on available land, soil quality, and technology all constrain the growth in food supplies. Malthus believed there is a real risk of populations outgrowing the food supply. Therefore, the chance of running out of food poses a real threat to humanity. For that reason, checks (or limits) are needed to keep population growth in line with growth in the food supply. Welfare schemes to help the poor by redistributing wealth are futile, said Malthus. If we feed the hungry, they will reproduce until they run out of food and are hungry again (Crafts and Mills, 2009).

POSITIVE CHECKS Part of Malthusian theory, these prevent overpopulation by increasing the death rate. They include war, famine, pestilence, and disease.

PREVENTIVE CHECKS In Malthusian theory, these prevent overpopulation by limiting the number or survivals of live births. They include abortion, infanticide, sexual abstinence, delayed marriage, and contraceptive technologies.

The only sure solutions are positive checks and preventive checks. **Positive checks** prevent overpopulation by increasing the death rate. They include war, famine, pestilence, and disease. **Preventive checks** prevent overpopulation by limiting the number or survival of live births. They include abortion, infanticide, sexual abstinence, delayed marriage, and contraceptive use. Among these preventive options, the Reverend Malthus approved only of delayed marriage and of sexual abstinence (Simkins, 2001; Nicolini, 2007).

Today, people who believe there is still a 'population problem' make some of the same arguments as Malthus did two centuries ago. Neo-Malthusians believe the world is becoming overpopulated, that population growth will outstrip agricultural growth, and that this population burden will permanently harm the environment (see e.g., Shandra et al., 2003; Hoffmann, 2004). World population is still growing. Even allowing for slower growth, experts predict that in 30 years the current population of 6.5 billion people will be nearly three billion larger.

With population growth come new challenges, including increased competition for nonrenewable resources, the need to feed, nurture, and educate a larger proportion of young people, increased pressures on the health and welfare systems, and the need for governments to prevent and deal with economic and natural disasters.

Criticisms of the Malthusian Perspective

It is far from certain that the planet's carrying capacity will be fatally strained by population increases; for that matter, is it not clear that population pressures will cause wars. Others blame the recurring conflicts over space and resources on capitalism, imperialism, fascism, tribalism, or a variety of other political motivations. And, evidently, some governments are both less warlike and more inclined to handle the population issue in a peaceful, progressive way. Therefore, Malthus and the Malthusians who followed were wrong in some of their fears and predictions (Clark and Cummins, 2009).

Some note that Malthus was wrong in supposing that food supplies can increase only arithmetically. Long-term food production trends reveal that in technologically advanced societies, food production has increased at a faster rate than the human population owing to better seeds, fertilizers, and growth techniques. Past warnings of an impending global food shortage by the end of the twentieth century have been proven unwarranted.

Writing in 1949, the eminent demographer Alfred Sauvy described potential overpopulation as a 'false problem' and argued against efforts to control global population (Sauvy and Demeny, 1990). He suggested examining countries case by case to see whether they lack the raw materials and natural resources that can support a larger population. Otherwise, we run the risk of underpopulating a country (such as Canada) that could support a much larger population. A larger population is not necessarily good, but if unavoidable, we need to find its benefits. And this we can do only if we confront the issues of social and political organization.

Demographer Joel Cohen (1995) notes that a fundamental problem may lie in the notion of a single 'carrying capacity' for the planet. This concept, he argues, does not translate well from the plant or animal models on which it was based to human societies. Most animals and plants are stuck with the environment they inhabit. However, humanity—because of its ingenuity, resourcefulness, inventiveness, ability to adapt, awareness of the future, and stubborn free will—can modify its environment through technology.

Therefore, humanity is constantly defying standard ecological models of population behaviour. As well, population sustainability is tied not only to reproductive trends, but also to countless economic, political, and social processes.

POPULATION DENSITY

Some believe that the biggest problems facing humanity result from too much **population density**. Population density is the number of people who live within a geographic area, usually expressed as people per square mile or square kilometre (Millward, 2008). It is a measure of the concentration of people in space or, as some might say, a measure of crowding—of how many people have crowded into a house, neighbourhood, community, city, or country (Millward and Bunting, 2008).

All of human history—but especially in the past 300 years—has tended towards increased population density. Since the earth's surface is finite and fixed in size, the growth of human population has inevitably meant an increased population density on the earth's surface.

A potent factor in this growth has been the urbanization of the world—the movement of people from sparse rural settings to concentrated urban settings. In cities, population is more dense than in rural villages, for example. This density is sometimes accomplished by packing more people into households. More often, it is carried out by reducing the distance between houses, so each household has less property. Often it is accomplished by stacking people vertically in high-rise high-density apartment buildings, tenements, or condominiums.

However, the historic transition from hunting to agriculture, and from nomadism to settlement, meant a once-and-for-all movement towards growing population density on

POPULATION DENSITY
The number of people who live within a geographic area, usually expressed as people per square mile or square kilometre.

earth. Population density arises in two main ways: through high fertility combined with low mortality, and through a migration of people to places of perceived greater opportunity. Moreover, these two elements are linked: reproduction has been shown to be density-dependent for a wide variety of species, including humans. Indeed, population density has also been linked to the historic transition from high fertility rates to low ones. Lutz et al. (2001) find a consistently negative connection between human fertility and population density in a variety of societies. Even individual fertility preferences decline with population density. In short, as density increases, fertility (eventually) declines.

At the same time, with growing population density the impetus to develop technology increases: there is a pressure towards innovation. Even today in horticultural villages, population density promotes innovation. Researchers find two different effects of population pressure on rural economies in south-central Ethiopia from 1950 to 2004. One is a pressure on existing households to feed and house a growing number of children. The other is an increased demand on the economy for more jobs. When both demand levels are low, people extend agricultural production, taking advantage of the availability of land. When both demand levels are increasing, people intensify and diversify their agricultural practices, often leading to innovation (Malmberg and Tegenu, 2007). No wonder, then, that in rural communities, major agricultural growth and rural development occur in districts with high population density, less constrained environments, and better access to markets, irrigation canals, and capital loans (Ali, 2007).

These changes in response to population density—for example, reduced fertility and increased innovation—are largely a result of the changed *perception* of available resources and the sense something can be done. A perceived lack of resources tends to reduce family size and brings about changes in all demographic variables. As Bandy (2005) points out, the historic transition from hunting and gathering to agricultural village life was associated with a two-stage demographic transition—first, to high population growth rates when nomads first settled the land, then finally much lower growth rates when they started to experience population pressures.

In general, the growth of population density is associated historically with economic growth, the growth of cities, the development of urban lifestyles, and the buildup of creativity. Most people—including sociologists and historians—view this as an advance in human civilization. Cities—owing in large part to their density and large numbers—make possible certain social and cultural experiences that are not possible in smaller, sparser human settlements.

In short, the population density in cities allows for what economists call 'economies of scale'. These are efficiencies—low per-unit costs—made possible by a large volume of production (and consumption) (see Huiban, 2009; Kasman and Turgutlu, 2009). Certain activities are only profitable if they are large enough and only large enough if they can draw on a large enough market or demand. Cities are large markets, so they make possible human experiences—for example, going to the opera, dining in fine restaurants, and browsing in mystery bookstores—that are economically impossible in smaller, less dense places.

Cities make it easier for humans to interact, and one of the great benefits of dense urban areas is that they promote social interactions. Likely, the resurgence of big cities in the 1990s was due, in part, to the increased demand for these interactions and due to the reduction in big-city crime, which had made it difficult for many urban residents to enjoy these social amenities (Glaeser and Gottlieb, 2006).

However, not everyone benefits from the urban density, because different urban opportunities are spatially segregated. MacIntyre et al. (2008), who examined the location of urban resources in Glasgow (Scotland), found that poorer, more deprived neighbourhoods are 'rich' in certain kinds of resources—public nurseries, public primary schools, police stations, pharmacies, credit unions, post offices, bus stops, bingo halls, public sports centres, and outdoor play areas, but also in vacant and derelict land and buildings. More prosperous areas are rich in other kinds of resources: private schools, banks, museums/art galleries, subway stations, tennis courts, bowling greens, private health clubs, private swimming pools, colleges, hospitals, parks, and tourist attractions. On the face of it, both benefit from density; however, the more prosperous areas contain more desirable, private, or elite locales.

The growth of population density associated with urbanization has brought many benefits to humanity, and we are still enjoying these benefits today. The human race advanced socially and culturally when it 'came together' in dense settlements and we are still benefiting from this development today. It is because of these benefits that most of the Canadian population lives in or near a large metropolitan area, or at least a city.

URBAN SOCIOLOGY: A PRIMER

Cities, as Max Weber (1958 [1921], 1981 [1924]) pointed out, are among humanity's great social inventions. Most important, cities make possible a range of experiences that are unavailable in smaller rural areas or small towns. The sheer size and diversity of city populations allow for specialization and diversity in the goods and services on offer.

Yet, for all that, city life has been surrounded by controversy since the beginning. Some have hailed cities as affording liberty, especially the freedom to think and act as one wishes. Others have viewed cities as lacking in neighbourliness and community spirit. They have depicted city-dwellers as lonely atoms, deprived of purpose and control. Much of twentieth-century American sociology examined these competing views of cities. At first, research on cities was skewed by the dominance of research on the city of Chicago, owing to the overwhelming presence of the Department of Sociology at the University of Chicago. When this department was at its peak, roughly 1900–40, Chicago was a living laboratory for the study of city populations, especially the poor, the marginalized, and the stigmatized. In the last half of the twentieth century, the main goals of urban sociologists broadened to understand a wider variety of cities, and especially suburbanization, urban renewal, and the development of enormous cities in the Third World.

According to a United Nations Development Program international survey of mayors, the number-one urban problem in the world today is unemployment. The second-most serious problem is insufficient solid waste disposal; the third—which may be related to unemployment—is poverty. Many of the high-profile social problems people associate with urban centres—crime, poverty, and racial segregation, for instance—are found in rural areas as well, though these problems are especially pronounced in cities.

MY WINNIPEG

In this acclaimed 2007 documentary, director Guy Maddin explores the peculiarities of the history, development, and character of his hometown of Winnipeg.

Contrasting Images of Urban Life

The earliest sociological theories about cities and city life—by Ferdinand Tönnies, Louis Wirth, and Georg Simmel, and others—were first developed more than a century ago. For example, Tönnies (1957 [1887]) asked, 'What social bonds tie together people in small, stable communities, compared with large, fluid communities?' For Tönnies, the movement from rural to city life meant a loss of *Gemeinschaft*—the characteristics typical of rural and small-town life, including a stable, homogeneous group of residents with a strong attachment to one particular place (Brint, 2001). Socially, *Gemeinschaft* is characterized by dense networks, centralized and controlling elites, multiple social ties, intimacy, and emotional meaning. With everyone constantly viewing each other's behaviour, someone deviating from the prevailing social norms would feel social pressures to conform.

In contrast, Tönnies notes, the ties among people in a city take the form of *Gesellschaft*. In urban settings, residents have different personal histories and impersonal, brief relationships. They interact around similar interests, not similar characteristics, moralities, or histories. Social networks in cities are less connected, less centralized, less cliquish, and less redundant.

Following Tönnies's lead, early American sociology considered cities to be anonymous and stressful. In his article 'Urbanism as a Way of Life', Louis Wirth (1996 [1938]) explained that cities unavoidably foster less social integration or cohesion than smaller communities because of their huge population size, variety, and fluidity (Vortkampt, 1998; Otte and Baur, 2008). A large population ensures that most people will not know one another, nor feel tied to one another in ways that control deviance and support co-operation. A high degree of variety—in values, norms, and interests—can create confusion if not outright conflict, when irresolvable differences collide. Fluidity means people are forced into many interactions with strangers.

To partially offset the confusion of these interactions, they develop means of control—informally, by social norms of behaviour such as distancing and civil inattention and, formally, through such institutions as the police—to deal with socially unacceptable behaviour or to tame strangers in public places.

The German sociologist Georg Simmel (1950 [1917]) was among the first to sense how life in a large city affects people psychologically and emotionally. City life is too stimulating, Simmel wrote. Strangers surround us on all sides. We experience countless strange noises, smells, sights, dangers, and opportunities. Walking a city street, we must pay constant attention to our environment. In the end, sensation overload takes its toll on our nervous systems (Bodemann, 1998).

Research supports at least some of these suppositions. The tempo of life is faster in a large city—more costly, arousing, and engaging than in a small town. People walk faster, talk faster, and even eat faster, mostly because more people must crowd into the same spaces every hour. City people also make more noise: the larger the city, the more car horns there are for irritated people to honk and the more ambulance and police sirens are heard day and night. In these various ways—through isolation and stresses on mental health—the city enslaves people who may have expected to gain freedom through city life.

GEMEINSCHAFT Social situations in which those involved treat one another as ends rather than as means; primary relationships based on sentiment, found most often in rural life.

GESELLSCHAFT Social situations in which those involved treat one another as means rather than as ends; secondary relations based primarily on calculation and individual interest, found most often in city life.

The History of Urbanization

Contrary to what some people might first imagine, cities existed thousands of years ago. Babylon, Jerusalem, Byzantium, Alexandria, Athens, and Rome were large and important cities in the premodern era. The Maya and Inca, in Central and South America, developed large city-states, and nearly 1,000 years ago, Cahokia, in present-day Illinois, 'had a population estimated at 30,000 to 40,000' and 'was bigger [in extent] than contemporaneous London, England' (Dickason, 2002: 29). Paris, London, Venice, and Florence were established as world cities long before massive economic developments in the late eighteenth century kick-started rapid **urbanization**, the process by which a large portion of the human population came to shift from rural to urban homes.

However, modern cities are new in human history, only a few centuries old. With the rise of the urban mode of life came a focus on efficiency, high standards of living, liberty, diversity, and innovative ideas and lifestyles. Modern cities are a prime example of a social organizational strategy, an organic solution to the problem of how to co-ordinate a growing human population. Simply, modern cities are creative efforts by humans to deal with large numbers of varied, mobile people concentrated in a small space. So far, however, a great many of the organizational strategies devised by city governments have been flawed. These flaws have resulted in problems such as overcrowding, epidemics and sanitation issues, inner-city poverty, housing shortages and homelessness, traffic and noise problems, and a tension-filled pace of life.

Statistics Canada defines an 'urban area' as one with a population of at least 1,000 and no fewer than 400 persons per square kilometre. All territory outside an urban area is considered rural. The term used for cities in Canada is 'census metropolitan area (CMA)', defined as a region with an urban core population of at least 100,000.

While these definitions suffice for Canada, they do not apply as well to other nations. For example, in populated countries such as India, virtually all areas have a density of more than 400 persons per square kilometre, yet many do not display any other characteristics associated with 'urban' life. For these countries, the criteria for 'urban' versus 'rural' may require a higher density, or may include other factors such as economic output (that is, agricultural or non-agricultural). When comparing across countries or reporting on regional or global trends, the United Nations simply allows that 'urban' is however each nation defines it. In Japan, for example, an urban area has at least 50,000 people, but in Norway a centre with 200 inhabitants is considered urban (Norton, 2010: 439).

One of the central concerns voiced about urbanization is its association with population growth rates: with how quickly the population is increasing from one year to the next. This issue is troubling because large, rapid growth rates demand flexibility and ingenuity by our political leaders, who need to respond creatively with new housing, jobs, schools, and services. As the data in Figure 14.1 show, of all the large, major industrial nations Canada currently faces the largest problem of this kind.

What is most remarkable is how very quickly the world's population has urbanized. Canada, for example, has gone from a mere 20 per cent urban-dwellers in 1871 to just over 80 per cent today (Figure 14.2).

URBANIZATION The growth in the proportion of the population living in urbanized areas. There is also an increasing appearance in rural and small-town areas of behaviour patterns and cultural values associated with big-city life.

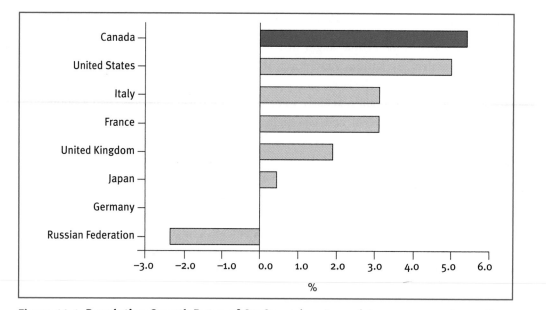

Figure 14.1 Population Growth Rates of G8 Countries, Annual Average, 2001 to 2006

Note: **Population as of July 1.**

Source: **Population Growth Rates of G8 Countries, Annual Average, 2001 to 2006, at: www41.statcan.gc.ca/2008/3867/ grafx/htm/ceb3867_000_1-eng.htm.**

Many consider the twenty-first century humanity's first 'urban century', a consequence mainly of the pace of urbanization in the developing world (United Nations Population Division, 2006). Historically, the emergence of cities has reflected an increasing complexity

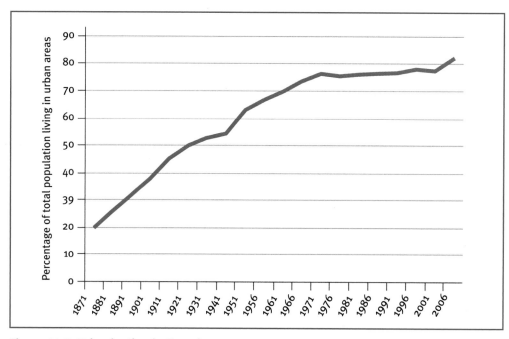

Figure 14.2 Urbanization in Canada

Source : *The Sustainability Report*, at www.sustreport.org/signals/canpop_urb.html.

in regional development. Cities, as we have learned, are economic engines. They foster new businesses and attract foreign investments and tourists. The development of cities in the world's poorer regions, then, is a promising sign of economic growth.

The pace of urban growth in the developing world is outstripping the ability of many local and state governments to provide the infrastructure (for example, the roads and communication networks) needed to house, employ, and support the influx of people into their cities (see Jung et al., 2009; Sahoo and Dash, 2009). Many cities are experiencing the serious social and health hazards associated with overcrowding, poor sanitation, slum developments, and a lack of clean water—the same urban problems that plagued Western industrial nations in the eighteenth and nineteenth centuries. In addition, many megacities are expanding chaotically, without any co-ordinated urban planning or management.

A lack of overall vision will likely increase urban problems in the future. Already, seven of the 10 largest cities in the world are located in developing countries. By 2050, it is estimated that Tokyo will be the only urban centre on that list from the developed world; India alone will have three cities in the top 10.

Suburbanization

In North America, the period of prosperity following World War II changed the urban landscape dramatically. During the post-war economic boom, spending and birth rates were high, unemployment was low, and families prospered. The affordability of the automobile led to the purchase of homes outside the urban core in the 1940s and 1950s, causing land developers to extend residential housing into outlying regions. In this way, the modern suburb was born.

Suburbanization is the process by which lower-density housing spreads into once-rural regions surrounding the city core. This process greatly expanded the geographic size of cities. For instance, Chicago's population has increased only 4 per cent in the past 20 years, yet its spatial geography increased by 46 per cent between 1980 and 2000.

The first people to move to the suburbs were mainly wealthy middle- to upper-class whites (see Fortin et al., 2008; Poulton, 2007). This movement intensified the racial and ethnic segregation of minorities in urban centres. Further, as wealthier residents migrated to the outskirts of the city, their property taxes went with them, leaving the city's centre with less revenue for schools, roads, and other services. Then, as now, suburbanites who work in the city use the city's services, such as road, water, and sewer systems, but do not pay for them. As a result, while the suburbs flourished amid a surplus of property tax income, downtown areas stagnated and dried up.

THE IMPORTANCE OF NEIGHBOURS AND NEIGHBOURHOODS

Tönnies was wrong to suppose that cities lack communities or community sentiments, or that city-dwellers would not care about such sentiments. As sociologist Claude Fischer showed, cities are collections of communities each with its own subculture.

SUBURBANIZATION The process by which housing spreads almost unhindered into once rural regions surrounding the city core. This greatly expands the geographic size of cities and takes out of production valuable agricultural land, and there is a noticed shift of the affluent out of the urban centre to these surrounding areas.

People want to live alongside others whom they consider to be similar to themselves in important ways. Largely as a result of that tendency, residential segregation by race, ethnicity, and social class is a common feature of life in North American cities (Emerson et al., 2001; Westaway, 2007) and has an enormous impact on people's social relations and social identities. This voluntary sorting of people into urban communities based on culture, language, ethnicity, and income, and on resulting distinct identities, is a major source of Canada's continuing multiculturalism. It is also an antidote to the randomizing, anonymizing effects of large cities.

Despite the tendencies of mass education and the mass media to make everyone similar, neighbours and neighbourhoods are still important today as sources of personal identity and difference. The importance that people attach to their neighbourhoods can be seen in reactions of NIMBYism ('not in my backyard') under certain circumstances—for example, to the placement in their neighbourhood of public housing, halfway houses, or treatment facilities for recovering drug addicts (Oakley, 1999). Largely, it is because cities are *not* agglomerations of undifferentiated strangers, and because people feel so strongly about keeping strangers and people unlike themselves at a distance, that cities have trouble solving typical problems such as homelessness and fear of victimization.

In many cities of the world, and certainly in Canada's largest cities, homelessness is a large and growing problem. It is, often, a problem we prefer to ignore; but it is hard to ignore when—as in Box 14.2—we put faces and names to the people who experience this condition of homelessness.

For people who live in houses, neighbours and neighbourhoods continue to be important. Some problems associated with neighbours and neighbourhoods—such as traffic, crowding, and turnover—we discuss later in this chapter. They are characteristic of cities as a whole, and of all cities—large and small, whether in the West or in less developed countries.

What does require discussion is the connection between neighbourhood and social inequality—and the geography of what sociologists call 'social capital'. Put simply, most people lead most of their lives within neighbourhoods. This is particularly true of school-children, homemakers, retired people, unemployed people, and chronically ill people (or shut-ins). This means that their life experience will be shaped dramatically by the quality of the neighbourhood in which they live: on whether it has good schools, good shopping facilities, well-kept homes and parks, safe roads, good sewage facilities, easy proximity to transportation, hospitals, and social services, and so on.

People whose neighbourhoods lack these advantages are effectively disadvantaged; their lives are diminished in quality. This is made even worse if their neighbourhood is dangerous, with high rates of criminal victimization and poor policing (Platt, 2009). People who live in such neighbourhoods are less likely to feel safe in, or make use of, public space. This diminishes their social life and their range of social contacts. It will diminish their confidence in government and their trust in neighbours. People who live in socially and economically unequal neighbourhoods will have different life experiences, regardless of their own social and economic characteristics. This fact is amply clear among racial minorities who live together in segregated neighbourhoods, regardless of education or social class.

PERSONAL STORIES

Box 14.2 Homeless in the City: Bruce Lived Here

When the police and bylaw officers arrive Bruce has some of his goods spread out and a jar of peanut butter open beneath the canopy of a cherry tree at Old Riverside Park. His cart nearby is precariously loaded with an assortment of black plastic bags containing his collectables. When approached by Abbotsford Police officers Sgt. Doug Sage and Const. Shaun Nagel, his reaction is muted. He's gone through the process before. He has been living in the green space adjacent to Chief Dan George Middle School and a nearby church for some time.

The city has received complaints, and Const. Nagel has already had a conversation with him a week or so ago about moving his camp to a less conspicuous location.

Bruce is given 48 hours to move all his goods or city workers will. The bylaw officer staples a red removal warning poster to the tree trunk. The police officers offer to contact the Salvation Army, and ask Bruce if he has somewhere he can stay. He had a room last summer but he had to leave because he had too much stuff. This time he's going to take his belongings to a storage locker. He does not take the offer of shelter.

As they leave the park, both officers say they have dealt with Bruce before. The 62-year-old former civil servant has been living rough for close to a decade.

He poses the obvious question: Just what neighbourhood should [homeless people] be moved to? 'It's not against the law to be a drug addict.' The city has a standard protocol when it comes to camp removal. Homeless camps are usually reported to bylaw officers by the parks department or citizens. If they are inhabited, the Salvation Army is contacted and its outreach workers connect with the individuals before any enforcement action. If the camp is still not evacuated, the bylaw officers post a warning. When the camp is cleaned up, workers are accompanied by police and outreach workers who advocate for the occupants.

Nicole Giguere, with the Salvation Army, says if someone doesn't opt to take shelter, they are encouraged to at least come back for a shower and a meal.

There are a variety of reasons people don't want to move into the shelter, says Giguere. They don't want to leave their belongings, they don't feel safe in a room of strangers, or they have mental health or addictions issues. People often stay in camp because they can't use drugs while at a shelter. Giguere would like to see more mental health workers, especially those who do outreach work on the streets, funding to allow single room shelter beds, and more low-barrier housing.

In trying to deal with homelessness and establish affordable housing, the city is tackling problems it doesn't necessarily have the resources for.

'Property taxes were never intended to deliver social services. Homelessness is really a problem of the provincial or federal governments. The city is doing what it can by donating valuable land to supported housing projects, but the demand is so high it's really difficult to meet the needs. We're stretched . . . but it doesn't mean we'll quit trying.'

Source: **Baker (2009).**

Neighbourhood Effects

Do neighbourhood features affect people's lives and, if so, how? This question is the subject of heated international debate among sociologists, geographers, and policy-makers.

The first problem, of course, is to define what we mean by a 'neighbourhood'. French sociologist Jean-Yves Authier (2008) asserts the contemporary city neighbourhood is 'neither dying, nor the only place of living, nor a "village within the city" unifying its inhabitants in multiple social networks, nor the place of all disadvantages'. A neighbourhood is, however, the 'geographic unit that produces socially and spatially differentiated experiences of city living'. Therefore, it is very important in people's lives.

Four broad questions relate to the 'neighbourhood effect' issue. (1) Is there a strong relation between housing mix and social mix? (2) How does the social composition of neighbourhoods affect residents' social interaction and behaviour? (3) Do neighbourhoods structure the social opportunities of individual residents? And if so, (4) to what extent is this produced through neighbourhood social interaction? Most researchers hypothesize that neighbourhood effects are less pronounced in countries like Sweden, for example, where planning practices, social class differences, segregation patterns, and welfare state regulations differ significantly from those in such a country as the US. However, empirical studies confirm the existence of neighbourhood effects even in Sweden (Andersson, 2008; Urban, 2009).

Measurement problems hinder research on this topic, however. Six major challenges confront statistical researchers trying to measure the independent effect of neighbourhood context on individuals: (1) defining the scale of 'neighbourhood'; (2) identifying mechanisms of neighbourhood effect; (3) measuring appropriate neighbourhood characteristics; (4) measuring exposure to neighbourhood; (5) measuring appropriate individual characteristics; and (6) endogeneity (that is, the entanglement of causal variables). Increasingly, to surmount these challenges, sociologists are turning to datasets with multi-domain measures of neighbourhood characteristics and statistical models for testing non-linear neighbourhood effects that consider residential group, density of local social interactions, and duration of residency (Galster, 2008).

Geographers, too, are discussing these problems of measurement. There has been considerable discussion in health geography of neighbourhood effects on health: the idea that people's health in one geographical area may be influenced not only by the composition of that area's population, but also by the area's geographical context. For example, Burdette and Hill claim that as neighbourhood disorder and disorganization increase, so do rates of obesity within the community. This claim supports past research suggesting that residents of neighbourhoods characterized by socio-economic disadvantage, social disorganization, and disorder often exhibit increased rates of obesity, relative to the wider population (Burdette and Hill, 2008).

However, although neighbourhoods and their boundaries are sometimes obvious to local residents, researchers often disagree on the size and contents of a neighbourhood. As well, findings may differ substantially according to how the data are combined. For this reason, some believe the effect of neighbourhood conditions should be looked at using several different ways to define neighbourhoods, for the size and composition of these neighbourhoods may be different in different parts of a study area (Flowerdew et al., 2008).

Individual Effects versus Neighbourhood Effects

Some supposed 'neighbourhood effects' might be due to the kinds of people who collect in certain neighbourhoods. If so, 'neighbourhood problems' are due to the characteristics of the inhabitants, not the neighbourhood per se (Schieman, 2009). This may be especially important if, through migration, some neighbourhoods attract disadvantaged people and lose advantaged ones. Therefore, we must examine the role of individual- versus neighbourhood-level variables and the role of migration in shaping neighbourhood characteristics.

Consider childhood accidents: are they a result of neighbourhood influences, family influences, or the characteristics of individual children? Reading et al. (2008), using data from the Avon (UK) Longitudinal Study of Parents and Children, examined information about accidents, as well as extensive social, health, and developmental data throughout the first five years of life. This information was combined with census and geographical data to identify neighbourhood influences on accident risks. The data analysis found a small but statistically significant amount of between-neighbourhood variance in accident risk, especially for accidents resulting in injury that needed medical attention. However, this variation between neighbourhoods was accounted for by various individual, parental, and household factors. Conclusion: apparent differences in accident risk between neighbourhoods are explained by the geographical clustering of similar types of (accident-prone) children, families, and households.

Alternatively, consider health behaviours: are they a result of neighbourhood influences, family influences, or individual characteristics? Duke-Williams and Shelton (2008), using data from the London (UK) boroughs of Camden and Islington, studied obesity, alcohol intake, smoking, walking, and self-rated health. Irrespective of the boundary definition, between-area inequalities were small compared with inequalities between individuals. Further, alternative definitions of the neighbourhood boundaries had little effect on the estimates of these neighbourhood inequalities.

Neighbourhood composition is mainly shaped by migration, and different people are more or less likely to migrate. People who can move when and where they wish tend to seek out others like themselves. As a result, they are usually happy with where they live. Such moves are often—perhaps usually—the result of hopes and plans. On the other hand, people who are unable to move usually adapt themselves to where they must live: they take satisfaction where they find it.

Evidence of Neighbourhood Effects

Despite the dangers of overestimating them, researchers continue to find evidence of **neighbourhood effects**. This should not surprise us: many people develop important relationships with their neighbours, and these relationships can be fulfilling. Considerable evidence in the psychology and sociology literature shows that social relationships promote happiness for the individual. But how big and important are these effects?

To measure them, Powdthavee (2008) used 'shadow pricing' to estimate the monetary value of the life satisfaction gained by an increase in the frequency of interaction with friends, relatives, and neighbours. Using the British Household Panel Survey, he estimated that an increase in social involvements could be worth as much as £85, 000 a year in greater life satisfaction. Actual rises in income, by contrast, buy very little satisfaction.

If neighbours make a difference, then, the quality of neighbourhood should make a difference. Take a simple case of neighbourhood effect: that of freshmen students in colleges. Ehrmann and Massey (2008), using data from the National Longitudinal Survey of Freshmen, found that male students residing on campus are exposed to higher levels of violence and disorder than females during their first year of college. The harmful neighbourhood effects on academic performance appear to be stronger for females than males. However, relatively

NEIGHBOURHOOD EFFECTS Influences on people's lives that result from living in one type of neighbourhood (for example, rich versus poor, or dangerous versus safe) rather than another.

few females experience high exposure to violence and social disorder, and, as a result, male grades are more influenced by this campus neighbourhood effect.

Other aspects of health and well-being are also reportedly affected by neighbourhood. Wright and Muhajarine (2008), noting that respiratory illness is a significant cause of infant mortality, examined the relationship between neighbourhood level variables and rates of respiratory illness for children less than two years old born in Saskatoon between 1992 and 1994. They found that rates of respiratory illness, as measured by proportion of children hospitalized and frequency of hospitalization and ambulatory visits to doctors, are higher among infants who live in socially disadvantaged neighbourhoods.

Is life in a largely same-race neighbourhood good for emotional well-being? Yuan (2008) explored question using a random sample of Illinois residents. He found that living in a largely same-race neighbourhood does indeed improve the emotional well-being of blacks and Hispanics. Mainly, this is because of greater social support provided by others of the same race (especially among blacks). Thus, neighbourhoods confer not only economic resources to their residents, but social and emotional resources as well. These benefits or resources are sometimes called 'social capital'.

Consider how neighbourhood social capital affects the health of adult female caregivers. Carpiano (2008), using data from the Los Angeles Family and Neighborhood Survey, showed that specific types of social capital are directly associated with positive and negative health outcomes. For example, a female caregiver's social network can promote good health or damage it, depending on whether social contacts provide support or, by demanding support, deplete personal resources.

Alternatively, consider how neighbourhood disadvantage—as measured by levels of concentrated poverty, residential instability, and immigrant concentration—affects the likelihood of early adolescent sexual activity. Using a sample of youth, ages 11–16, from the Project on Human Development in Chicago, Browning et al. (2008) find evidence that neighbourhood disadvantage increases the likelihood of adolescent higher-risk sexual activity—for example, having two or more sexual partners versus one sexual partner (risky because it increases the chance of sexually transmitted diseases).

Neighbourhood influences are not only strong, they are also persistent. Because of persistent neighbourhood stratification, the racial inequality in America's neighbourhoods that existed a generation ago has been transmitted, almost unchanged, to the present day.

Combinations of Individual, Familial, and Neighbourhood Effects

In social science, most outcomes are a result of multiple influences—individual, familial, and institutional; and this is just as true of neighbourhood influences. They combine or interact with social variables working at different micro- and macro-sociological levels.

So, for example, Button (2008) reports that approval of family violence is both an individual-level and neighbourhood-level phenomenon. Neighbourhood features such as social disorganization, crime, and collective efficacy, in addition to the individual factors of gender, race, and a history of child maltreatment, all influence the acceptability of using violence within the family.

Not only do neighbourhood influences combine with other factors to produce victimization and misbehaviour, they also combine to produce arrests. Different neighbourhood contexts in which different racial and ethnic groups live lead to variations in criminal outcomes. To show this, Kirk (2008) combined individual-level data with contextual data from the Project on Human Development in Chicago Neighborhoods (PHDCN). Findings reveal that black youths face multiple layers of disadvantage relative to other racial and ethnic groups, and these layers work to create differences in arrest.

At the family level, unstable families explain much of the disparity in arrests across race and ethnicity. At the neighbourhood level, significantly higher levels of concentrated poverty and lower levels of collective efficacy disadvantage black youth compared to white youth. That said, even after accounting for relevant demographic, family, and neighbourhood-level predictors, large residual arrest differences remain between black youths and youths of other racial and ethnic groups, perhaps pointing to discrimination.

Neighbourhood influences also combine with other factors to produce poor health. Drawing on four waves of the Americans' Changing Lives Study, Yao and Robert (2008) examined the contributions of individual and neighbourhood socio-economic status to explain racial disparities in self-rated health trajectories among black and white older adults. The results show that black older adults have greater declines in self-rated health over time than white older adults, and these disparities are explained by individual and neighbourhood socioeconomic status (SES). That said, there is another cost to blackness not captured otherwise: black disadvantage in mortality exists at older ages, and persists net of individual and neighbourhood SES. These results suggest that racial and socio-economic disparities in self-rated health and mortality persist throughout old age, and that individual and neighbourhood socio-economic context—as well as race—contribute to perpetuating these disparities.

As always, perceptions are important—as important as 'objective reality' in their effects on people's well-being. Individuals' views of where they live may provide some clues to better understanding the influence of place on outcomes. Muhajarine et al. (2008) present findings from an analysis that incorporates the subjective responses of individuals, living in three socially contrasting neighbourhoods, to their local environment. They find that both perceived neighbourhood characteristics and individual socio-demographic factors are significant correlates of self-rated health and quality of life. Besides, the type of perceived neighbourhood characteristics and the extent of their influence on self-rated health and quality of life vary depending on whether the respondents live in high- versus low-SES neighbourhoods.

Findings on the effects of neighbourhoods are different in Canada in some respects from the US. Such research findings may vary from one society to another. In Saskatoon, Oreopoulos (2008) finds that household exposure to concentrated poverty is substantially less than in the United States. However, the available evidence suggests that, within nations, neighbourhood effects may work the same way as discussed above.

Policy Implications

What, then, are the policy implications of this research into the effects of neighbourhood on well-being? Ambitious work is being done on this issue in Saskatoon by a multidisciplinary group of social scientists funded by the Social Sciences and Humanities Research Council of Canada.

According to Williams et al. (2008), the University of Saskatchewan's Community-University Institute for Social Research is taking a multi-stakeholder approach to the ongoing sustainability of Saskatoon as a healthy city with an improving and a more equitably distributed quality of life. Using quantitative and qualitative analysis, this research is examining the quality of life in three Saskatoon neighbourhoods, representing low, middle, and high socio-economic status in both 2001 and 2004. The project is committed to publishing its findings far beyond the usual academic channels: (1) by engaging local media on a consistent basis; (2) by holding community forums to ensure community co-operation; (3) by helping the work of a steering committee; and (4) by employing an action researcher as a policy entrepreneur.

A part of this process is the City of Saskatoon's Local Area Planning (LAP) Program, a community-based approach to developing comprehensive neighbourhood plans (Kellett et al., 2008). So far, eight LAPs have been adopted by City Council and 212 recommendations have been approved. Resources have been earmarked to co-ordinate implementation, work with communities, and carry out the various recommendations. In addition, over 1,000 people representing various interests have engaged in one or more LAP committee or implementation meetings. In these ways, partnerships have been formed, program and service delivery has been improved, and, most importantly, communities have taken ownership of their plans.

The LAP communities, City Council, and city planners have committed themselves to measuring changes and progress in the LAP communities. In recognition of this, the Saskatoon's City Planning Branch will be working with LAP communities, the Community-University Institute for Social Research (CUISR), and other stakeholders to develop a framework for statistically measuring changes in LAP communities and to monitor 'Neighbourhood Success Factors'. The Neighbourhood Success Factors will work to detect negative socio-economic conditions before they reach a point of crisis.

THEORETICAL PERSPECTIVES ON URBAN LIFE

Structural Functionalism

Some structural functionalists would view social problems in the city as resulting naturally from growth and specialization. For example, more wealth in cities typically means more theft and robbery; higher density equals more intense competition for resources; and more privacy translates into more private vice, such as drug use.

Other structural functionalists focus on those tendencies of the city—its size, variety, and fluidity in particular—that promote social disorganization, weak social controls, and consequent deviance and distress. From this perspective, social problems such as crime, addiction, and mental illness are foreseeable consequences of urbanization. They are functional in the

Table 14.1 Theoretical Perspectives

Theory	Main Points
Structural Functionalism	• Malthus argued that excess population would lead to human disasters (e.g., war, plague, and starvation) that would reduce the excess. • Demographic transition theory argues that high fertility rates decline to establish a new level of population equilibrium. • Too-rapid urban growth produces disorganization, crowding, and stress.
Conflict Theory	• 'Overpopulation' is a myth, and the problem is an unequal distribution of wealth. • High rates of population growth produce conflicts over scarce territory and resources. • Cities contain neighbourhoods of greater and lesser comfort, as well as homeless people.
Symbolic Interactionism	• Cities are not undifferentiated masses of people but neighbourhoods containing distinctive subcultures. • We all have to learn how to live effectively in cities, using urban etiquette (e.g., civil inattention).
Social Constructionism	• The manufacture of concerns about crowding and population pressure reflect antagonism to poor and racial minorities.

sense that they are the normal price to be paid for the positive aspects of city life; they contribute to the survival of the city by promoting integrative reactions.

Pre-industrial societies were mainly small, rural settlements in which members shared the same experiences and developed similar values, norms, and identity. Émile Durkheim (1964 [1893]) called this *common (or collective) conscience*. Besides, the lives of these people were often interconnected in a tight, homogeneous social order, which Durkheim called **mechanical solidarity**. The new social order was based on interdependent, though not necessarily intimate, relationships. Under this **organic solidarity**, no member of society was self-sufficient; all people were dependent on others for survival and prosperity.

Conflict Theory

Unlike functionalists, conflict theorists always ask whose interests are served by the actions of dominant groups in society and by their ideology. These theorists attribute urban problems such as homelessness and poverty not to the effects of size, variety, and fluidity, but to the workings of capitalism. By their reckoning, cities suffer problems because it is in no powerful group's interest to prevent this from happening.

MECHANICAL SOLIDARITY Durkheim's term for the kind of tight, homogeneous social order typical of a pre-industrial, primarily rural society.

ORGANIC SOLIDARITY Durkheim's term for the new social order of industrial society, which was based on interdependent, though not necessarily intimate, relationships.

Unlike functionalists, conflict theorists also believe that solving urban problems will require more than simply addressing economic stagnation. Unequal power, competing class interests, capital investment decisions, and government subsidy programs mediate the growth of cities. The distribution of urban wealth—not merely its creation—determines whether the majority of city-dwellers will live or die, stay or leave. The flight of well-off residents from the inner city to distant suburbs suggests a lack of interest in solving these problems among those who have the power to do so.

Symbolic Interactionism

Symbolic interactionists study the ways people experience city life on an everyday basis. One of the earliest writers to take this approach was Simmel (1950 [1917]). Others, such as Herbert Gans (1982), have focused on how the meaning of city life varies among groups and subcultures.

SLACKER

Richard Linklater's 1991 Generation-X drama explores a hip, sophisticated subculture of unemployed "slackers" in Austin, Texas.

A subculture is a group of people who share some cultural traits of the larger society but who, as a group, also have their own distinctive values, beliefs, norms, style of dress, and behaviour. Subculture membership allows individuals who are otherwise isolated within an impersonal city to form connections with their neighbours. An ethnic community is an example of a subculture, as are skinheads and youth gangs. The corporate elites, who have determined the future of urban areas, are also, by this view, a subculture.

Social Constructionism

Social constructionists, as we have seen, study the ways social issues are brought to public attention or are submerged from it. Issues are brought to attention or hidden through various techniques we have discussed throughout the book, most notably, agenda-setting, creating moral panics, and using scientific 'evidence' selectively to highlight certain parts of a story.

These techniques of social construction are evident in at least two of the topics we discuss in this chapter. First, they have been widely used to excite or tranquilize public opinion over issues around population growth and overpopulation. In the 1950s and 1960s, concerns about overpopulation were widespread, culminating in the famous Club of Rome study, *Limits to Growth* (discussed later in this book). Today, concerns about overpopulation have largely dropped out of sight, only partly because birth rates have continued to fall throughout the world. The public has wearied of this topic and focuses on other topics, for example, issues around environmental pollution and the economy.

In the area of urban life, we see continued jockeying for power between the major core cities, their suburban peripheries, and the provincial and federal governments. These issues concern taxation, planning, and responsibility for delivering services to urban residents. They are expressed in battles over transportation (for example, who should pay for the road system that allows commuters to come downtown to work every day) and education (for example, who should fund inner-city schools that bear the greatest costs of large-scale immigration). On all of these issues, certain themes are highlighted where others are ignored or distorted, to gain political advantage.

SOCIAL CONSEQUENCES OF POPULATION GROWTH AND URBANIZATION

Sprawl

Some social scientists have attacked urban sprawl as an inefficient and ineffective urban form that contributes to many of the social problems we discuss in this book, and **gentrification**—the revitalization of inner-city neighbourhoods—has been touted as one solution to the outward spreading of cities (see Box 14.3). Others have accepted sprawl as a new paradigm in today's urban life.

Urban sprawl is most often characterized as haphazard or unplanned growth, resulting in undesirable land-use patterns. It includes such patterns as scattered development, 'leapfrog' development, strip or ribbon development, and continuous low-density development. In Canadian cities, large low-density, low-rise bedroom suburbs dotted by strip malls, shopping centres, and industrial parks epitomize suburban sprawl, and much of the nation's best agricultural land has been and continues to be lost under urban sprawl (Alasia et al., 2009; Ghitter and Smart, 2009).

GENTRIFICATION The restoration and upgrading of deteriorated urban property by middle-class or affluent people, often resulting in displacement of lower-income people.

The Canadian Press/Jeff McIntosh

Urban sprawl on the outer limits of Calgary on 6 September 2008.

PUBLIC ISSUES

Box 14.3 The Two Sides of Neighbourhood Gentrification

Gentrification is the process whereby established working-class neighbourhoods, usually in the inner city, are converted into middle- and upper-class neighbourhoods. This is typically accomplished through the renovation of existing buildings and landscapes and the introduction of businesses and services catering to higher-income residents. The process results in higher property values and taxes and the gradual displacement of the poor.

For some, gentrification is an essentially positive force, an economic, social, and aesthetic 'rehabilitation' of a once run-down, stagnant neighbourhood. Although the dislocation of the relatively poor is usually acknowledged by the defenders of gentrification, this social cost is justified by the salvation of valuable real estate, the injection of private investments, and resuscitation of the local tax base. For others, the process is tinged with class discrimination, a type of economic genocide in which the vibrant and diverse working-class collectives of artists, labourers, and ethnic minorities are pushed out of their communities, replaced by banal middle-class interests (Atkinson, 2003). Often, the poor are forced to relocate in less desirable neighbourhoods, resulting in the further segregation and concentration of poverty (Fong and Shibuya, 2000). Ironically, as the urban boom continues to reverse the residential trends of the past half-century, the suburban pockets surrounding the revitalized central core are becoming the new 'undesirable' neighbourhoods.

More than any other single factor, the spread of the automobile allowed suburbanization to take place by allowing residents to commute long distances every day between where they lived and where they worked. The vast highway programs of the 1950s and 1960s fostered massive migration to the suburbs and a corresponding deterioration of urban centres, though more so in the United States than in Canada (Wassmer, 2008; Johnson and Schmidt, 2009).

The prevalence of auto-centred transport systems largely determines a nation's pattern of transportation and urban sprawl (Squires, 2008). Today, many developing nations are adopting Western standards of 'automobility' but face unique problems such as unequal access, inadequate roads, and the cost of importing oil. These nations represent an emerging market for automobiles as well as an environmental threat. China, for example, faces a shortage of arable land that will be further compromised by auto-centred transport systems. Similar problems beset South Africa, Mexico, India, and other countries.

Los Angeles is a particularly vivid and well-known example of the sprawl problem. The history of California has been characterized by spectacular growth in all aspects: population, economic output, housing construction, and the global impact of its cultural values (Wrobel, 2008). Yet, this growth has come at the price of sprawl and traffic congestion, distressed older neighbourhoods, air pollution, inadequate urban services, and a decline in quality of life (Pastor et al., 2004).

Not everyone criticizes this outcome or sees it as a failure to achieve another kind of order. Some view the evolution of economics, politics, and culture in Los Angeles—historically depicted as outside the mainstream of US urban culture—as having successfully created a new style of urban life. In contrast to the Chicago School, this emerging Los Angeles School of urban sociology regards LA as a model for many of the emerging urban centres in North America and around the world, all of them characterized by dispersed patterns of low-density growth, multicultural and ethnic enclaves, and an array of urban centres in a single region (Dear, 2003; Gilbert and Wehr, 2003).

Traffic

Another major problem mainly affecting urban centres in both the developed and developing world is vehicular traffic (Fazal, 2006). At present, many car users choose the car over alternative modes of transport because it is more convenient and saves time, and because public transport, even when it is a feasible alternative, is deemed bothersome. In most North American cities, cars are given more priority than pedestrians or bicycles, as reflected, for instance, in the parking space devoted to cars.

In Paris and Amsterdam, two cities famous for their metropolitan charm and pedestrian-friendly streetscapes, there is only one parking space for every three people living in the central area. By contrast, Houston, with its sprawling web of highways slicing through the urban core, allots 30 spaces per resident. This reflects consumption patterns as well: for the same reason, the parking lots of major suburban shopping centres are larger than the malls themselves.

The problems related to traffic are many. Hundreds of thousands of people worldwide suffer death or injury in traffic-related accidents each year. Generally, traffic accidents are caused by our increased dependence on autos and the supremacy of the automobile over social space. When auto traffic is dense, as in cities, accidents are bound to occur. However, human behaviour is also to blame.

For instance, the use of cell phones by drivers unnecessarily increases the risk of a collision 4–16 times (Kalkhoff et al., 2009). Analysis of 699 drivers who were involved in motor vehicle collisions that caused substantial property damage but no personal injury found that 24 per cent had used a cellular telephone during the 10-minute period before the collision.

Congestion is another problem caused by traffic. Canadians are travelling farther and farther to get to their workplaces—for example, a median distance of 9.6 kilometres in 2001 for workers in census metropolitan areas. Not surprisingly, as commuting distances increase, more workers choose to drive rather than to take public transit or other modes of transportation (e.g., bicycles, walking). However, even when the distance to work is less than five kilometres, the car remains favoured over any other single mode of transportation. Moreover, as the rate of growth of new work opportunities in suburban areas outpaces the growth in downtown business districts, more and more workers are travelling across town to get to work, a journey they usually make by car. In most large metropolitan areas, as many as 90 per cent of workers commute by car, either as a driver or passenger, when their job is located 20 or more kilometres outside of the city centre.

Traffic also interferes with people's enjoyment of their neighbourhoods. The high-speed, multi-lane roads that cut through residential areas are often too dangerous for children to cross alone, resulting in their dependence on parents to drive them everywhere: to and from school, to sporting and recreational events, to visit friends' homes, and more. In a study comparing 10-year-olds in a traditional, light-traffic, small Vermont neighbourhood with their counterparts in a new Orange County, California, suburban development, those in Vermont enjoyed three times more mobility than their California peers (cited in Calthorpe, 1993: 9). In short, traffic has a negative effect on neighbourhood cohesion and community integration.

HEALTH CONSEQUENCES OF POPULATION GROWTH AND URBANIZATION

Health problems are most concentrated in urban areas. In part, this is a result of large numbers of people gathering in small, densely populated areas. Under conditions of poor housing and sanitation and crowding, rates of illness and disease inevitably rise with increases in population size (see McKenzie, 2008; Ng et al., 2009).

At the same time, city life is stressful, and this, too, poses health problems. The rush of traffic, the pace of change, the cost of living, jostling with strangers, the fear of victimization, economic competition, the noise—all of these characteristics are common in the city, and all are stress-inducing. Though people can manage the occasional experience of acute stress, chronic exposure to high stress levels can lead to serious health problems, including heart disease and a weakened immune system.

The homeless and the mentally ill (Yu, 2008), two populations who suffer especially high levels of poor health, also are concentrated in urban inner cities. For instance, in a 2002 Toronto Daily Bread Food Bank survey of their clients' self-reported health, over 40 per cent rated their health as fair or poor compared with others of their age. By comparison, when middle-income earners were asked the same question, only 12 per cent rated their health as fair or poor (Daily Bread Food Bank, 2002).

Another urban health concern is the massive amount of sewage, litter, and solid waste produced by the millions of people crowded into a small area. For example, of the 162 sites in Chicago considered highly polluted, 98 (60 per cent) are in the mainly African-American South Side neighbourhood. As well, all 10 of the city's communities with the highest levels of lead poisoning (caused by toxic levels of lead in the paint used in residential buildings) are made up of at least 70 per cent minorities (Cohen, 1992).

ENVIRONMENTAL RACISM A type of discrimination that results in the concentration of poor racial minorities in densely packed, poorly served urban neighbourhoods, often with greater levels of pollution and located near waste dumps and heavy industry.

Some researchers have labelled this correlation between social class, neighbourhood racial composition, and pollution level, replicated in surveys of cities around the world, as a form of environmental racism. It is the result of several factors, including fewer public services—sanitation workers, garbage disposal units, road maintenance crews, and so on—being devoted by local governments to the undesirable areas; and a perception among corporate polluters that the local residents lack the political clout to prevent the dumping of industrial trash in their communities. Another contributor is the shared sense of general demoralization by the economically deprived residents that reduces the likelihood of any concerted effort to preserve and improve the neighbourhood.

The Canadian Press/Frank Gunn

Striking City of Toronto worker Elliott Davis assists residents by piling garbage they have dropped off at Commissioner's Road transfer station in Toronto on Wednesday 24 June 2009.

SOLUTIONS TO POPULATION PROBLEMS

Perhaps in no other area have so many efforts been voiced, and so many ideas floated, to solve the problems discussed here.

In respect to population issues, countries have continued with varying success to promote contraception and family planning. Generally, these measures have been successful almost everywhere, although fertility has declined at varying rates. The solution to this population problem, then, would seem to be a continued effort to educate people about the value of family planning and make contraceptive devices available to them. However, as we have seen, a new problem—population aging—has arisen as a result of this fertility decline. Much more effort will be needed to solve this problem, which previously was seen as a matter of private (family) concern, but now, increasingly, it has become a matter of public (state) concern.

Alongside the continued declines in mortality and rises in life expectancy throughout most of the world, other new problems have arisen: specifically, how to improve the quality of life for hundreds of millions who would, in past years, have died at a younger age. This means increasing the access to, and quality of, education and health care; equally important, it means providing employment for those who are employable and long-term care, as well as income, for those who are not. As with fertility decline, mortality decline calls for more effort to solve the new problems. The goal will be to not merely increase the duration of life, but to improve the quality of longer living.

Cities continue to grapple with a wide variety of problems as we have seen; and different cities, in Canada and around the world, have looked for solutions in various ways. They have attempted to deal with increased inner-city density by creating and maintaining green space and by regulating traffic. Cities have devised mixed-income housing projects to reduce some of the toxic social problems associated with the geographic and social segregation of poor and minority populations. They have improved public transit to move people more quickly and safely, while reducing traffic congestion on the roads and cutting down on auto-related pollution. They have devised new social housing strategies and policies to help with troubled populations, such as the homeless. Some have applied, or considered applying, a surcharge or luxury tax on motor vehicle use in inner cities, to discourage automobile use and promote walking, bicycling, and public transit. And other jurisdictions, such as British Columbia, have devised legislation to limit urban sprawl by seeking to protect agricultural land around the perimeter of urban areas.

None of these solutions has been fully tested. Ideally, in coming years, sociologists and planners will explore the outcomes of these varied solutions and promote the best of them for widespread use in Canada and abroad.

CHAPTER SUMMARY

As mentioned at the beginning of this chapter, issues surrounding population growth and urbanization are complex, and each could justify its own textbook, let alone chapters within a book. In addition, both of these issues impinge on the problem of environmental degradation, the subject of the next chapter. These topics are related in several important ways.

First, issues of population size feed naturally into discussions of urban problems, since the latter are fuelled in part by the former. Second, transecting all three subjects is the notion of human ingenuity (and its manifestation, technology), which has been both the cause and often the solution to the urban troubles facing the world today. Third, each represents a separate component of the material backdrop of social life. To borrow Shakespeare's metaphor of human life as a play, the human population represents the world's actors; our cities, the set; and the natural environment, the stage upon which everything plays out.

Finally, the topics discussed in this chapter are unique in that they will outlive any one individual and, therefore, serve as legacies to later generations in a way that other social problems (for example, drugs or crime) do not. Eventually, our collective choices will control the outcome of these population-related problems—that is, whether the urban centres of the future are energizing and beautiful or stagnant and bland. Just as we must take collective responsibility for these present problems, so, too, must we draw upon collective efforts to find their solutions.

QUESTIONS FOR CRITICAL THOUGHT

1. China is famous for its so-called 'one-child policy', aimed at reducing the birth rate of one of the most populous countries in the world. Research this policy and its effects, noting the drawbacks to such a policy and whether you believe the advantages outweigh the possible disadvantages.

2. It seems as though in a big city there is something for everyone. Pick a certain subculture, such as the gay and lesbian community or ethnic enclaves, and explore its presence in your city. Are certain services, facilities, restaurants, bars, and shops concentrated in a certain area? Do they share similar characteristics? Where are they found, and why there?

3. Everything around us, from banking to movie-ticket sales, is becoming automated. Machines are replacing people's jobs, and human interaction seems to be a nostalgic idea of the past. What might sociologists have to say about this apparent shift away from personalized and intimate relationships?

4. There is no doubt that suburbanization is a major force permeating the modern urban landscape. What effect has this had on your own life? Does living near the city centre offer a different lifestyle than suburban living? Discuss using specific examples and figures.

5. Do you agree that while population density is considered (by some) a social problem, it may also be a solution to other social problems? Is there a way to reap the benefits of population size and density while addressing the problems it has been linked to?

RECOMMENDED READINGS

Bennett, John W. 1993. Human Ecology as *Human Behavior: Essays in Environmental and Development Anthropology*. New Brunswick, NJ: Transaction. Bennett proposes solutions to the problem of relations between humans and the natural environment. Taking a macro perspective, the author advocates an analysis of the historical, cultural, and economic contexts in which humans create problems.

Dobkowski, Michael N., and Isidor Wallmann, eds. 2002. *On the Edge of Scarcity: Environment, Resources, Population, Sustainability, and Conflict*. Syracuse, NY: Syracuse University Press. This collection of essays deals with the problem of vital resource shortage—a topic that is unsettling yet realistic, as the growing world population continues to devour the natural environment. Problems of rising population and resource depletion are considered with reference to the social conflicts they will cause.

Dunlap, Riley, Frederick Buttel, Peter Dickens, and August Gijswijt, eds. 2002. *Sociological Theory and the Environment: Classical Foundations, Contemporary Insights*. Lanham, MD: Rowman & Littlefield. An overview of sociological theories of the environment, both classic and modern, the book discusses the major themes that include globalization, urbanization, the rising world population, resource consumption, and more.

Dyson, Tim, Robert Cassen, and Leela Visaria, eds. 2004. *Twenty-first Century India: Population, Economy, Human Development and the Environment*. Oxford: Oxford University Press. India's population is growing at an unprecedented rate, and the authors undertake the complicated task of analyzing data to determine how the large increase in people will impact India's urbanization, education, health care, employment, poverty, economy, and relation to the environment.

Goodwin, Stefan. 2006. *Africa's Legacies of Urbanization: Unfolding Saga of a Continent*. Lanham, MD: Lexington Books. A modern consideration of rapid urbanization in Africa, this book rejects Eurocentric assumptions about urban development and examines the complex history, ecology, anthropology, and geography of this diverse area.

Ness, Gayl D., and Michael M. Low, eds. 2002. *Five Cities: Modelling Asian Urban Population: Environment Dynamics*. Singapore: Oxford University Press. This book, on the dynamic relationship between population growth and urban change, focuses on five smaller cities in Asia: Faisalbad in Pakistan, Khon Kaen in Thailand, Cebu in the Philippines, Pusan in South Korea, and Kobe in Japan. The focus on smaller cities is useful, since most of the future population will live in such cities where most urban development will take place.

Polèse, Mario, and Richard Stren, eds. 2000. *The Social Sustainability of Cities: Diversity and the Management of Change*. Toronto: University of Toronto Press. This book uses 10 case studies of cities across Canada, the US, Europe, South America, and Africa to explore how urban centres can make policies that promote higher levels of cohesion, inclusiveness, and social sustainability among their inhabitants.

RECOMMENDED WEBSITES

Canadian Technology Network

www.rcti-ticn.ca/en

The Canadian Technology Network links federal and provincial government labs and agencies, universities, community colleges, industry associations, technology centres, and economic development agencies. Together, these organizations provide innovative Canadian companies with quick and personal access to expertise, advice, and information about how to meet technology and related business challenges.

Neptis Foundation

www.neptis.org

The Neptis Foundation conducts and publishes non-partisan research on the past, present, and future of urban regions. An independent, privately capitalized, charitable foundation, Neptis contributes timely, reliable knowledge and analysis on regional urban development to support intelligent public decisions and foster understanding of regional issues.

Population Reference Bureau

www.prb.org

The Population Reference Bureau is dedicated to informing people around the world about populations, health, and the environment. Its purpose is to empower people to better their lives and the lives of others.

CHAPTER 15

The Natural Environment

iStockphoto.com/MattStauss

LEARNING OBJECTIVES

- To appreciate the impact of technology on the environment.
- To understand the history of environmentalism.
- To find out about the environmental issues of metropolitan areas.
- To understand issues such as climate change, desertification, and ozone depletion.
- To distinguish sociological perspectives on urban life and environmental issues.
- To understand the social and health effects of continued environmental degradation.
- To learn of possible solutions to urban and environmental problems.
- To know the history of environmental social movements.

INTRODUCTION

Today, compared to a generation or two ago, we are much more aware of the natural environment in which our society is situated (Mesic, 1998; Rucht, 1996). This is due in large part to the rise of the environmental movement as expressed in the important work of environmental and climate scientists, as well as campaigning scientists, from Rachel Carson in the 1950s and 1960s to our contemporaries David Suzuki and Ulrich Beck. Equally, organizations like Greenpeace have raised our awareness of deeply problematic issues, from Alberta's tar sands extraction projects to the accumulation of plastic in our oceans. Former US Vice President Al Gore's prize-winning film *An Inconvenient Truth* drew international attention to climate change.

By natural environment, we mean all of those natural processes that affect us as animals with survival needs similar to those of other animals. For example, processes that affect the fertility of the land—the availability of soil nutrients, water, sun, and other fundamentals. All humans need food and water: so concerns about the food supply and clean water are essential. This is why Thomas Malthus was interested in the relation of the food supply to population growth (Bandarage, 2008). For his part, Karl Marx was interested in the plight of the wage worker, who needed to sell his or her labour to purchase food and shelter. And this is why sociologists study agribusinesses—giant corporations that, today, control our access to reliable, good-quality food.

Humans compete with other species for survival. We developed tools and strategies that provide advantages over these species: we invented weapons to hunt some animals for food and keep predators at bay. We learned how to domesticate and harvest animals that provide food—chickens, cows, pigs—and are constantly improving our efficiency at doing so. We are struggling to keep up with the rapid mutation of sometimes fatal viruses and bacteria.

We understand and control many biochemical interactions, creating pesticides, herbicides, fungicides, and antibiotics and other medicines. We are increasingly able to manage our relationships with problematic species—from bacteria to protozoa, mosquitoes to cockroaches, invasive plants to cereal rusts. Currently, it looks like this war is at a standstill: the possibility that we could ever fully destroy our smaller competitors seems unlikely, not to mention, given the complexity of the biosphere, markedly unwise. But we do usually keep them under control. Now and then, however, an epidemic like SARS, swine or avian flu, or HIV/AIDS reminds us that we have much to learn (Lamal, 2009).

Currently, water is an especially valuable resource, and its rapid depletion by (mainly) developed nations will increasingly make water conservation even more important. As we know, humans are greatly dependent on water for drinking, washing, and cleaning, but also for economic survival. Water is used in manufacturing, mining, agriculture, and energy production, as well as for other purposes (PRB, 2008). According to a 2008 report by the Population Reference Bureau, 'modern society's demands on water grew rapidly during the last century [and] . . . global water consumption grew six-fold—twice the rate of population growth in the same period' (ibid).

This consumption has been made possible by the building of dams and reservoirs, which affect over 50 per cent of the river basins in the world. However, the water available to humanity is not equally distributed. Currently, 2.3 billion people live in areas that lack an adequate water supply, and by 2050, 3.5 billion people will be in this condition (ibid).

Like water, most of the natural resources we need are non-renewable: there is only so much petroleum, aluminum, and iron to be had. Once we have used it all . . . well, no one knows how to finish this sentence. One preventative strategy is recycling. Another is to invent alternatives (for example, nuclear energy) or find natural alternatives (for example, wind or solar power). A third strategy is to find another planet to inhabit, or perhaps to look for new resources in currently inaccessible places (for instance, under the sea or deep in the earth). A fourth is to reduce the rate at which we use these resources. However, the latter is only a short-term answer. It only slows down the inevitable disappearance of these vital finite resources.

THE ENVIRONMENT AND SOCIAL CONSTRUCTION

There is no denying that social construction plays a large role in our understanding and response to the so-called 'environment problems' we are facing (Hannigan, 2008). Environmental sociology has been divided by a debate between realists and constructionists centring on the knowledge claims of ecological science—for example, about climate change and global warming (Martell, 2008).

Some believe the problem results, in large part, from the persistent failure of social scientists to bring into environmental impact assessments socially constructed environmental concerns held by potentially affected communities. Others might see the problem in the opposite light: as a failure and even refusal of citizens to learn about environmental dangers, in hopes they will be able to avoid taking costly and uncertain precautions.

Sociologist Raymond Murphy (2004) notes that there is much theoretical debate, including claims that nature is being socially constructed or even abolished. Some authors celebrate this development and others lament it. Still others bracket nature's dynamics out of the analysis.

Expanding society into wilderness areas has brought these new disturbances of nature into society and under sociological analysis. Pristine nature has been replaced by a socially engineered nature. Engineered nature *remains* embedded in technology; its potential to escape technological control also implies further applications of technology. For example, if a mining town (socially engineered from natural materials) has lost its purpose with the closing of the mine (socially engineered pristine nature), the town might also be abandoned. Restoring something of the state of pristine nature to the mine and to the town site would require further technological expense. Hybrids of nature and technology (such as all human settlements; all resource extraction projects; all engineering projects such as dams and bridges and tunnels) constructed by humans and non-humans recombine processes and materials of nature. Now that this recombinant nature has been integrated into society and new primal dynamics of nature have been internalized (i.e., have come to be taken for granted by people), there is increasing reason to incorporate the forces of nature into sociological analysis.

The term 'environment' originates from the French word *viron*—meaning a circle, a round, or the country around. The environment can be understood as various external conditions and influences that affect all life, organisms, and human societies on earth. Human societies are embedded in the natural environment, consisting of the physical and material bases of all life on earth— including land, air, water, and mineral resources (Humphrey et al., 2002).

Severe damage to the environment began about two centuries ago, with industrialization in the West. Various social practices that organize our development and use of products and technologies began to affect ecological and human communities. Since then, governments have often ignored environmentally harmful practices because the industries responsible for much of the pollution in our skies, land, and water also power the economy. In less developed countries, environmental damage has occurred mainly because governments are trying to attain the wealth that older industrial countries enjoy.

Harmful practices within Canada can affect the daily lives of individuals everywhere— especially, among vulnerable and disadvantaged populations in less developed nations. For example, many empirical studies have suggested that there is a relationship between environmental degradation and economic development. Popularly known as the environmental Kuznets curve (EKC), it is argued that an inverse-U-shaped relationship exists between a country's per-capita income and its environmental quality. That is, increased incomes are associated with an increase of pollution in poor countries, but a decline in pollution in rich countries (Copeland and Taylor, 2004).

This theory, however, has been met with some concern. Critics have argued that EKC results are 'not robust to various changes in the specification of the econometric model', and that while theoretic models confirm the U-shaped curve, there are 'differing explanations for why the curve occurs' (Bartz and Kelly, 2006). Nonetheless, EKC literature has made lasting and significant contributions. It has raised central empirical questions about how economic growth and trade affect our natural environment (Copeland and Taylor, 2004).

As for effects within our nation, there are many environmental dilemmas to overcome. For example, traffic congestion—in lost time, wasted fuel, and higher insurance rates—is considerable and mounting fast (Greenberg, 2009). Related to the growth of congestion is the increase in air pollution, noise, and lack of green space in and around cities. Automobile and truck exhaust releases a huge amount of carbon monoxide into the air, contributing to global warming. The other greenhouse gases produced by cars (and other machines) all help to create the thick, dirty cloud of smog that can be seen hanging over many car-heavy cities (Scheelhaase et al., 2010).

Environmental problems often result from human inefficiency and waste. For example, industrial pollution reflects inefficiencies in manufacturing, the result of by-products created when the raw materials used in production are not fully converted into usable products. The causes and consequences of these problems involve entire populations, not only those organized into cities. Therefore, we turn now to problems arising from humanity's impact on the natural world.

THEORETICAL PERSPECTIVES ON ENVIRONMENTAL PROBLEMS

Table 15.1 Theoretical Perspectives

Theory	Main Points
Structural Functionalism	• Environmental problems result naturally from population growth, density, and specialization. • Cultural ideologies support ecologically harmful practices (e.g., materialism and the growth ethic emphasize the triumph of progress and ingenuity, and encourage the discarding of the old in favour of innovations).
Conflict Theory	• Environmental problems negatively affect the poor more often and more severely than the rich. • The solution to environmental problems is through redistribution of wealth. • Collective action by underclass is needed to gain political attention to their needs.
Symbolic Interactionism	• How are environmental issues imbued with meaning? • The focus is on the lived experience of humans. • How are environmental issues constructed as 'problems'? • Environmental polluters manipulate symbols to protect themselves from criticism.
Feminist Theory	• Ecofeminism links destruction of the environment and male-centredness in the political and corporate worlds. • The domination over women and nature ultimately leads to gender inequality and environmental degradation. • Humans' relationship with nature should be more nurturing and co-operative.

Structural Functionalism

Functionalists are not surprised that modern people's values and activities have contributed to the pollution of our natural surroundings and the overharvesting of resources. Several types of cultural ideologies help support these ecologically harmful practices.

One example is the **cornucopian view of nature**. In this way of thinking, nature is viewed as a storehouse of resources that exists only for the use of humans—especially, currently living humans. Another environmentally unfriendly belief is the **growth ethic**, especially popular in North America. This view, linked closely with *materialism*, celebrates the (imagined) ability of technology to easily solve all the problems in the world, including those that technology itself has caused. This promotes the belief that things will always get better and therefore encourages us to discard just about everything in favour of the production and consumption of new items.

CORNUCOPIAN VIEW OF NATURE Nature is seen as an almost endless storehouse of resources that exist only for use by humans, especially by those currently living.

GROWTH ETHIC A cultural or subcultural commitment to the idea that economic growth is good in itself, whatever its social effects.

Finally, the Western notion of **individualism**, which recommends personal goals and desires over collective interests, is the driving force behind the **tragedy of the commons**, which refers to what happened when English lords opened their uncultivated pastures to allow commoners to freely graze their livestock. These open fields became known as the commons, and they created a dilemma. The commoner could seek short-term personal gain by increasing his herd, thus putting more pressure on the common land, or he could forgo greater personal gain on the assumption that others would take a similar wise course of action. Of course, many people in such a situation fail to look beyond immediate personal gain to the greater good and sustainability of the resource. Soon cattle and sheep were so numerous that the commons were exhausted and could no longer sustain any them.

Conflict Theory

A conflict theorist will emphasize that when environmental problems arise, they hurt the poor more often and more severely than the rich. Over 90 per cent of disaster-related deaths, for instance, occur among the poor populations of developing countries, while developed nations experience 75 per cent of disaster-related economic damage since there is more of value to lose in materialist, developed societies. This will mean that an agricultural drought in Canada's prairie region, for example, may result in reduced crops but almost no deaths. In Pakistan or Indonesia or Ethiopia, by contrast, a drought can lead to catastrophic famine and many deaths. Of the 25 per cent of the world's population currently living in regions prone to natural disaster, most live in less developed countries (Smith, 2001).

Sociological research shows that disasters result more often from 'the spread of capitalism and the marginalization of the poor than from the effects of geophysical events' and offers possible solutions that involve 'the redistribution of wealth and power in society to provide access to resources than . . . the application of science and technology to control nature' (ibid.). The scale of destruction caused by the South Asian tsunami of December 2004, for example, would have been lessened had the region's protective coastal mangrove forests not been significantly destroyed earlier to make room for aquaculture farms and upscale tourist resorts, and had the coral reefs not been slowly decimated by years of unsustainable fishing methods.

The rich alone possess the economic means to protect themselves from the health consequences of locally occurring disasters, such as floods and hurricanes. The wealthy are also more often able to physically remove themselves from an area once disaster occurs, permanently or temporarily moving to where they can weather the storm. But the progressive destruction of the planet eventually will leave the rich with nowhere to flee to, either.

Symbolic Interactionism

The symbolic interactionist perspective studies how the meanings and labels learned through social interaction affect environmental problems, with a particular focus on how they alter people's perception of these problems.

Here, the social constructionist framework is particularly relevant. Sociologists who approach environmental problems from this perspective ask why and how certain environmental problems enter the public consciousness: they ask what kinds of 'claims' make the greatest impact, and under what circumstances. For instance, sociologists Clay Schoenfeld, Robert Meier, and Robert Griffin (1979) have looked at how environmental issues have become a 'problem' in the public's eye. How and why, for example, does the greenhouse effect become a widespread public concern one year, and AIDS or women's rights or child labour in India become a concern another year?

PUBLIC ISSUES

Box 15.1 Eco-Friendly Labelling?

Of the more than 2,000 self-described environmentally friendly products in North America examined by the environmental marketing firm TerraChoice, only 25 were found to be indisputably 'sin free'. The rest were 'greenwashing', a term environmentalists coined to refer to misleading environmental ads or claims.

'There are dramatically more green products this year than the last', said Scott McDougall, president of TerraChoice, the private company contracted by Environment Canada to oversee its EcoLogo certification program. 'But greenwashing is unfortunately more rampant, and it's changing.'

A new trend involves companies suggesting they have obtained third-party certification, by marking a product with an official-looking stamp that includes language such as 'eco-safe'.

Greenwashing is especially prevalent in the promotion of cleaning products, cosmetics, and children's toys and products, McDougall said.

Of particular concern to parents of young children will be this: All products the group found claiming to be 'bisphenol-A free' also appear to be greenwashing. That is because there is no international certification program verifying company claims that their plastic products don't contain the chemical, which in the human body can act like the hormone estrogen and has been linked to cancer and infertility.

BPA has been found in hard plastic materials, including baby bottles. The federal government introduced legislation to ban baby bottles containing it last year.

But, of the companies producing self-proclaimed 'BPA-free' products found in 12 large Ottawa stores, TerraChoice couldn't find any indication they had verified their claims with an independent lab, McDougall said.

'We don't have information to know if it's true. It asks a lot of parents to trust their claim', said McDougall. . . .

The Competition Bureau of Canada set out new guidelines for environmental claims last year, but gave industry a year to bring advertisements and labels in line.

The guidelines state that environmental claims 'shall be accurate and not misleading' and 'shall be substantiated and verified'.

But that verification doesn't need to come from a third party, said Dominy McClellan, a senior investigator with the bureau. 'They need to provide adequate and proper testing under the act. You can't assume third-party certification is more adequate or proper.'

McDougall's firm condensed the guidelines into a 'six sins of greenwashing' checklist for consumers. [These include: hidden trade-offs; no proof; vagueness; irrelevance; fibbing; and lesser of two evils.] A seventh, 'worshipping false labels', refers to the fact some marketers are mimicking third-party environmental certifications on their products to draw consumers.

In Canada, most transgressions fell into three categories: lack of proof, vague language, or 'hidden trade-offs'—the practice of emphasizing a product's green aspects while concealing others that are environmentally damaging. . . .

'It's like a magician drawing attention to the left hand so you can't see what the right hand is doing.'

Source: Abridged from Porter (2009).

The symbolic interactionist perspective also offers insights into how environmental polluters manipulate symbols to protect themselves from criticism. Many companies and businesses, increasingly sensitive to greater public awareness over their impact on the environment, have attempted to boost their image and profits by using a public relations strategy known as **greenwashing** (see Box 15.1). This technique involves redesigning and repackaging their products as 'environmentally friendly' or 'green', playing to (some) consumers' wish to help solve the environmental problem by purchasing ecologically friendly items or by purchasing from environmentally conscious companies. Of course, such greenwashing can backfire if words are not backed by actions, as British Petroleum (BP) recently discovered when its Deepwater Horizon oil drilling rig exploded in the Gulf of Mexico off the Louisiana coast in April 2010, causing an uncontainable blowout from the wellhead at the ocean floor. This unprecedented human-caused environmental disaster was preceded by BP's ad campaign re-branding the company as 'Beyond Petroleum', which trumpeted the firm's research and technological innovations in eco-friendly energy sources.

GREENWASHING The process of promoting false ideas about the environmental friendliness of certain commercial products.

Feminist Theory

The feminist perspective questions the prevailing capitalist celebration of increasing growth, unlimited resources, and unregulated commerce. Ecofeminism emerged as a social movement that linked the exploitation of marginalized groups within society and the degradation of nature in Western cultural values.

Ecofeminists unite in a central belief in the convergence between women and nature. Francoise d'Eaudonne coined the term 'ecofeminism' 'to identify theoretical work on the potential for women to bring about an ecological revolution and to ensure the survival of the planet' (Humphrey et al., 2002). Accordingly, then, ecofeminism is a value system, a social movement, and a practice. It encourages political analysis, exploring the links between androcentrism and environmental destruction (Rynbrandt and Deegan, 2002). Ecofeminists adopt a 'feminine' way of engaging with environmental social problems, one that is more nurturing, co-operative, and communal.

A central argument for ecofeminists is that the mutual domination of women and nature finally leads to environmental destruction and gender inequality. Some ecofeminists identify a link between the exploitation of women and the 'rape of the wild' (Plant, 1990; Rynbrant and Deegan, 2002). According to Greta Gaard, the environment as a social problem 'is a feminist issue'. As Gaard (1993: 5) argues:

> The way in which women and nature have been conceptualized historically in the Western intellectual tradition has resulted in devaluing whatever is associated with women, emotion, animals, nature, and the body, while simultaneously elevating in value those things associated with men, reason, humans, culture, and the mind. One task of ecofeminists has been to expose these dualisms and the ways in which feminizing nature and naturalizing or animalizing women has served as justification for the domination of women, animals and the earth.

These arguments are validated when we consider the connection between women, politics, and the environment. In nations where women are more highly involved in political activities, ranging from voting to policy-making, progressive environmental behaviour is more prominent. Furthermore, nations with a greater proportion of women in parliament demonstrate higher rates of environmental treaty ratification.

SOCIAL CONSEQUENCES OF ENVIRONMENTAL PROBLEMS

Canadian and Global Environmental Problems

Unlike most other social problems, environmental issues are global in their effects. They affect us all in ways that many social problems, such as alcohol and drug abuse or race and ethnic relations, may not.

Still, as with other social problems, there are important connections between social problems of the natural environment and the economic organization of society. Often, the people in power cause the greatest environmental damage, through harmful industrial practices and wasteful personal lifestyles. Meanwhile, people lacking an economic or political voice pay an unequal toll in their personal health and social well-being (Comim et al., 2009). Again, the problem is not humankind's consumption of natural resources, but the reckless exploitation of these resources for short-term and self-interested gains.

Air Pollution

In large cities around the world—whether Los Angeles, Paris, Budapest, or Beijing—smog has become a major problem. The air is thick and the sky yellowish-grey near major thoroughfares.

Emissions from cars and trucks, mixed with other chemicals released by manufacturing and other forms of fuel combustion, create high levels of pollution by releasing carbon monoxide, sulphur dioxide, and lead into the atmosphere. In Taipei, Tokyo, and other large Asian cities, one often sees people walking on the street—or, ironically, driving motor scooters—with their faces covered by masks to strain out the air pollutants. This daily exposure to air pollution has become a universal urban sensation, part of humanity's sensory experience of the world.

In principle, nature can repair itself. Through the process of photosynthesis, trees and other vegetation cleanse the air of the carbon dioxide that humans and other organisms produce, replacing it with breathable oxygen. However, the available amount of greenery—trees and other vegetation—limits these natural processes and their ability to clean the air. Trees and bushes can remove only so much pollution per day. When the pollutants exceed what trees can remove, these pollutants build up in the atmosphere, making the air potentially dangerous to breathe.

Ozone Depletion

The ozone layer is a thin veil in the stratosphere that shields the earth against the sun's harmful ultraviolet (UV) radiation. Without this protective layer, UV rays would seriously damage most of the life on the earth's surface. Unfortunately, certain industrial chemicals—including chlorine chemicals, halons, and the chlorofluorocarbons (CFCs) used in most refrigerators, aerosol cans, and solvents—have weakened the ozone layer, allowing UV rays to go through it. This is the ozone depletion problem.

Ozone declines of varying severity have been detected at several middle latitude locations and over the Arctic Circle. The damage has been most severe, however, in the Antarctic region. There, by 2003, an area of extreme thinning within the ozone layer (the ozone 'hole') had grown to a record size of 29 million square kilometres (larger than the land mass of Canada, the United States, and Mexico combined). It had begun to stretch into densely populated areas of South America.

However, some researchers argue the combined global effort to reduce industrial chemical pollutants over the past decade may be having an effect. The National Institute of Water and Atmospheric Research in New Zealand reported in late 2004 the Antarctic ozone hole had shrunk 20 per cent from the previous year. This in turn prompted some experts to predict guardedly that the ozone layer, at least in that region of the world, is beginning to recover.

Others are less optimistic. According to the United Nations Environment Program (UNEP), the size of the ozone hole has fluctuated throughout decades, and is thus

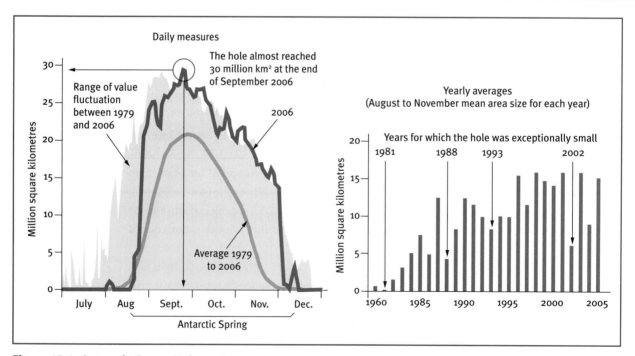

Figure 15.1 Antarctic Ozone Hole, 1980–2006
Source: UNEP/GRID-Arendal.

unpredictable (see Figure 15.1). Most alarmingly, the size of the hole reached unprecedented growth in 2006. This suggests that while there may be some hope for recovery, ozone depletion remains an important environmental problem with potentially fatal effects on future generations.

Global Warming

Climate change, as caused by global warming, is possibly the single biggest environmental threat that humanity faces today because people can do little to reverse the process. All we can do is slow down the change. Certain greenhouse gases, such as CFCs, carbon dioxide, and methane, accumulate in the atmosphere, trapping the heat reflected off the earth's surface. This causes global temperatures to rise. The process is known as the greenhouse effect.

As students of global warming might have predicted, 2005 was the world's warmest year on record, surpassing the previous mark set in 1998. The five warmest years in human history all occurred in the past eight years (NASA, 2006). The 1990s were estimated to be the warmest decade in the past millennium. As well, experts have noted that the high temperatures in 1998 were driven by an unusually strong El Niño effect, making its record at the time a meteorological abnormality. However, the 2005 El Niño episode was weak and had little effect on overall global temperatures. Therefore, the record temperatures of 2005 cannot be blamed on the El Niño weather phenomenon.

These patterns of climate change have been attributed to the greenhouse effect (WMO, 2000). Even a small increase in global temperatures can lead to elevated sea levels and devastating changes in precipitation rates. Such climate changes, in turn, harm the natural vegetation and wildlife of local ecosystems, alter the crop yields of agricultural regions, and allow deserts to take over fertile regions. As a striking example of the effects of global warming, Greenpeace reported that small islands in Kiribati in the Pacific Ocean have entirely disappeared because of rising sea levels (Greenpeace, 2001).

There are also economic costs because of rising sea levels. For example, 0.06 billion US dollars are expected to be lost because of 50 centimetres of sea level rise. In Japan, estimates reach US$3.4 billion. These estimates take into account 'costs multiplying a quantity loss (land or capital) of "displaced" (people), by the unitary "price" of the item lost or of the displacement' (Bigano et al., 2008).

As of July 2006, 164 of 168 participant countries have both signed and ratified the Kyoto Protocol (the four holdouts are Australia, Croatia, Kazakhstan, and the United States). Canada did not ratify until December 2002. Even then, it did so in the face of vocal opposition. The United States, for its part, has called the Kyoto Protocol irresponsible because the reduced use of fossil fuels required by the accord would hinder the American oil industry and economic growth. Moreover, few signatory countries are currently on track to meet the emissions reduction targets set out within the accord.

In late 2005, the US, Australia, China, India, Japan, and South Korea—which together account for approximately half of the world's greenhouse gas emissions—agreed to sign an alternative international agreement known as the Asia-Pacific Partnership on Clean

CLIMATE CHANGE
A departure from expected patterns of temperature and other climatic properties resulting mainly from an accumulation of greenhouse gases in the atmosphere, trapping the heat reflected off the earth's surface.

Development and Climate (AP6). This agreement allows member nations to set targets for reducing emissions individually, without a mandatory enforcement scheme. In 2006, Canada's federal Conservative government announced cuts to environmental funding intended to move Canada towards the Kyoto Protocol goals and indicated a desire to adopt the AP6 agreement instead. At present, the Kyoto Protocol may be dying by a thousand small cuts.

Further, as Box 15.2 indicates, the federal government's decision to downplay and ignore this issue is not being treated lightly. Environmentalists and their supporters have already begun a struggle to push Canada towards a more active role.

However, this turned out to be too little, too late. At the international talks on climate change in Copenhagen in 2009, Canada's Conservative government—like the US—refused to make significant changes. Many throughout the world heralded the Copenhagen talks as a dismal failure for environmentalism, though some believed that US President Barack

POLICY DEBATES

Box 15.2 Activists Sue Federal Government over Kyoto

Environment groups are suing the federal government for failing to comply with a law that requires it to meet Canada's international commitment to cut greenhouse gas emissions.

The Kyoto Protocol Implementation Act, which came into force last June after being passed by the House of Commons and Senate, gave the government 60 days to come up with a plan 'to ensure' Canada meets its target — a 6 per cent cut in emissions below 1990 levels by 2012. The groups argue the government's response, right at the deadline on 21 August, fell far short of what's required. The government is ignoring the rule of law by failing to comply with an act passed by Parliament, says an application filed yesterday in the Federal Court of Canada by EcoJustice, a non-profit environmental law firm, on behalf of Friends of the Earth Canada.

MPs and senators from the minority Conservative government voted against the legislation, introduced last year by Montreal Liberal backbencher Pablo Rodriguez. Nevertheless, the opposition parties pushed it through both chambers and it received royal assent on 22 June. The 21 August plan would not hit the Kyoto target until 2025. Trying to achieve the cuts by 2012 would be disastrous for Canada's economy, Environment Minister John Baird said. His August

document basically restated the Conservatives' official climate change plan, 'Turning the Corner', released last April.

Because of Canada's resource-based economy, growing population, and 'vast northern geography', attempting to follow the Kyoto timetable would cut Canada's gross domestic product by more than 6.5 per cent, reduce personal incomes, lead to higher unemployment and energy prices, and kick the economy into a deep recession, the August plan states. Environmentalists reject the gloomy forecast and argue, instead, that pursuing efficiency and innovation would boost the economy.

In any case, they say, the law is the law and the government must obey it. They want the court to rule Baird has not complied with the act and, then, to order him to come up with a plan that does comply. 'We are asking the court to declare that the government is bound by the act's requirements and to require the government to comply with it', said Chris Paliare, a lawyer representing the groups.

The case 'goes right to the heart of the matter—we have a law and the government must comply with the law', said Bea Olivastri, Friends of the Earth's CEO. A spokesperson for Baird defended the government's record on climate change but would not comment on a case before the court.
Source: **Gorrie (2007).**

Obama had signalled a willingness to begin dealing with important environmental issues. In the end, the following goals were stated:

- to hold the increase in global temperature to below two degrees C (over 100 nations had wanted a lower maximum of 1.5 degrees C);
- to co-operate in achieving a turnaround of global and national emissions as soon as possible, recognizing that developing countries will take longer to do this;
- to start work immediately on achieving national emissions reductions pledged in 2005 for 2020;
- to commit funds to prevent deforestation and to further technology development and capacity-building;
- to provide new and additional resources amounting to $30 billion for 2010–12 with developed countries together aiming to mobilize $100 billion a year by 2020 to address the needs of developing countries.

Water Pollution and Scarcity

Water pollution is another environmental problem, and it is largely caused by technological and industrial practices. Fertilizers, waste from industrial plants, oil spills, and acid rain have polluted much of the world's drinking water.

For example, the Great Lakes, a major source of fresh water in North America, have experienced much pollution (Gilbertson and Watterson, 2007). Pollutants from the surrounding regions—heavily farmed rural areas and densely populated urban areas—have found their way into the lakes, poisoning the water, promoting the extreme growth of algae, and killing the aquatic life (Phillips, 2006). Today, most of the beaches along the shores of the Great Lakes are too polluted for authorities to allow swimming. Similar conditions have been reported at points all along the North American seacoasts.

Global water use—especially for agricultural purposes, as well as for explosive population growth in arid regions such as the US Southwest that cannot naturally support high population densities—has increased greatly in the past 50 years. Such use further strains the supply of clean, drinkable water, and Canada has been among the worst of water abusers. Among the 29 members of the Organization for Economic Co-operation and Development (OECD), the most developed industrial nations, 'only Americans use more water than Canadians'. As Boyd (2001) notes, 'Canada uses 1,600 cubic metres of water per person per year. This is more than twice as much water as the average person from France [uses], three times as much as the average German, almost four times as much as the average Swede, and more than eight times as much as the average Dane. Canada's per capita water consumption is 65 per cent above the OECD average.'

More and more countries are experiencing 'water stress', a level of supply that is so low that each person has available an average of only 1,000 to 2,000 cubic metres of water per year. Other countries are at the level of 'water scarcity', defined as a level of supply that is less than 1,000 cubic metres of water per person per year. By contrast, Canada's per capita per year water availability is 120,000 cubic metres (IFPRI, 1997).

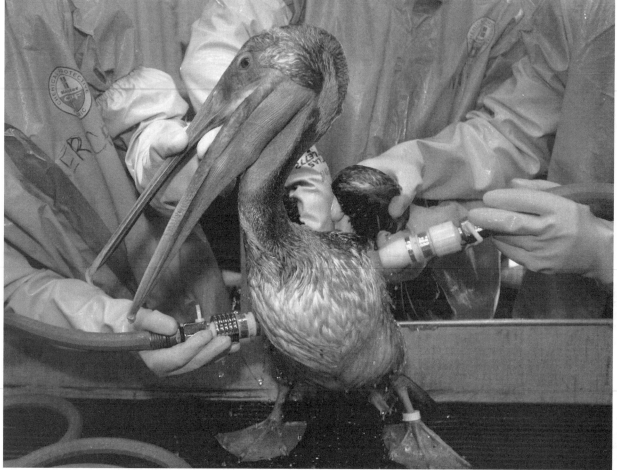

A Brown Pelican is cleaned at the Fort Jackson Wildlife Rehabilitation Center in Buras, Louisiana. The bird was rescued after being exposed in an oil spill in the Gulf of Mexico, now known as the worst oil spill in US history.

Water resources have always been of major importance to the welfare of Canadians. However, resource exploitation and project development, according to O'Riordan and O'Riordan (1993), have been traditionally 'dominated by powerful agencies, backed by political patronage'. Various water projects in Canada often have been set into motion before community consultation procedures were conducted.

Water resources have been viewed within a supply-management framework. Canadian waters have been exploited through the construction of 'megaprojects', such as dams, diversions, canals, and resource extraction—from the Klondike gold rush at the end of the nineteenth century to Alberta's tar sands today. Often, there is very little concern for environmental degradation, downstream consequences of alterations in water flow regimes, or social and community disruptions (Windsor and McVey, 2004).

Alcan's Kemano water diversion project, involving the Nechako River in northwestern British Columbia, is an example of negative social and community impacts because of water megaprojects (Wood, 1994). On 8 April 1952, the gates of the dam were closed and the waters of the reservoir began to rise. Alcan's Kenney dam flooded several square kilometres of Crown and private land, including various Native reserves and graveyards. The flooding forced the Cheslatta T'en Indian band, a once self-sufficient and prosperous hunter/gatherer society, to leave their ancestral lands and move to new reserves. This forced migration destroyed their close-knit communities and former lifestyle. Now, the Cheslatta are not only displaced from their homes, but from their traditional lands and way of life.

However, water scarcity issues in Canada pale by comparison with the problems many nations face in Africa, where massive deforestation and desertification have marked a chronic lack of water (see Figure 15.2).

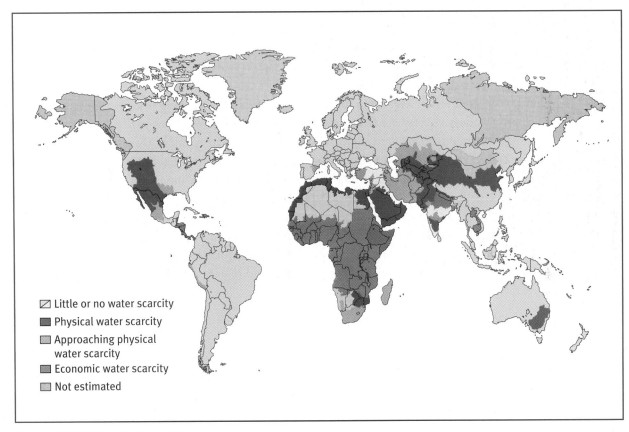

Figure 15.2 Where Water Is Scarce

Notes:

Little or no water scarcity: Abundant water resources relative to use. Less than 25 per cent of water from rivers is withdrawn for human purposes.

Physical water scarcity: More than 75 per cent of river flows are allocated to agriculture, industries, or domestic purposes (accounting for recycling of return flows). This definition of scarcity—relating water availability to water demand—implies that dry areas are not necessarily water-scarce, e.g., Mauritania.

Economic water scarcity: Water resources are abundant relative to water use, with less than 25 per cent of water from rivers withdrawn for human purposes, but malnutrition exists as a result of underdeveloped agriculture. These areas could benefit by development of additional blue water (aquifers, lakes, rivers, dams) and green water (soil moisture), but human and financial capacity are limiting.

Approaching physical water scarcity: More than 60 per cent of river flows are allocated. These basins will experience physical water scarcity in the near future.

Source: © International Water Management Institute, www.iwmi.org.

Deforestation

In principle, nature is a self-cleaning system. In various ways, trees remove carbon dioxide from the air and convert it to oxygen. However, as forests have been continuously harvested, mainly by commercial logging operations, the rate of carbon dioxide removal from the atmosphere has markedly decreased. Up to 30 per cent of the atmospheric accumulation of the carbon dioxide directly responsible for global warming is due to deforestation, according to an estimate by the World Resources Institute (1998).

Forests are also vital to the health of a region because they help to protect the thin layer of fertile topsoil from wind erosion. Widespread clear-cutting—whether for harvesting or to make room for expanding farmland and ranching—often results in the expansion of deserts (Anonymous, 2008). When this happens, the topsoil may be worn out too quickly or carried away by wind. Deforestation of the world's rain forests also results in the dislocation of indigenous peoples and the loss of many animal and plant species. In extreme cases, as in parts of the Amazon rain forest, distinct peoples themselves are at risk of extinction because of deforestation.

Sometimes, it helps us to think about the future by running history backwards. At one time, the barren Sahara Desert in Africa was woodland. All of the parched and sandy beach land around the Mediterranean Sea was covered with trees. Today, there are few trees and the land cannot be farmed; it can be used only for grazing, fishing, or tourism. Similar transitions likely will take place eventually on BC's Vancouver Island, in the vast wooded interior of New Brunswick, and in northern Ontario, although different environmental and climatological regions, with widely differing population densities, respond to long-term stresses and change in various ways. Nonetheless, damage done to the environment is not necessarily irreparable and permanent. The future health of Canada's vast forests can be retained, but to do so requires a program of sustainability and rejuvenation that must be started today.

Waste Disposal and Pollution

WALL•E

Ostensibly a family film, Pixar's 2008 animated hit provides a trenchant commentary on issues of waste disposal and terrestrial pollution.

The mass production process also creates useless by-products that need disposal. People produce a great deal of leftover paper, clothing, food, metals, plastics, and other synthetics. These materials are used and then thrown away. Canadian governments and businesses alone generate millions of tonnes of garbage each year.

There are two main methods of waste disposal: landfills and incinerators. Many products produced by today's industries that end up in these sites consist of plastics and other synthetic materials. Organic materials decompose naturally in a short period if suitably disposed of. By contrast, plastics can survive in one piece almost indefinitely when left in a landfill site. Another option is to burn the plastics, along with other forms of waste, using incinerators. However, this process converts many synthetics into hazardous chemicals that are then released into the air as pollutants (Hoag, 2006).

Compared to citizens of the developed world, citizens of developing countries use few resources and recycle the resources they do use. This is more out of necessity than out of environmental consciousness. Unfortunately, city authorities in the developing world seem set on duplicating the solid waste management systems of developed countries without considering the people who make their living from picking waste (Pacione, 2001). It is possible that when these cities begin to develop economically, they will be less environmentally friendly than the average North American city is today.

Non-Renewable Resources

All industrial societies use massive amounts of energy because energy—petroleum, coal, natural gas, nuclear, hydroelectricity—powers technology. The first three of these cannot be renewed once we have exhausted the planet's supplies.

Nuclear energy produces radioactive waste as a primary by-product, posing serious disposal problems, security concerns, and long-term health uncertainties. As well, hydroelectric power, in the form of massive dams and flooding, alters ecosystems, destroys species, and displaces humans who happen to be in the way. The US Energy Information Administration (2001) has estimated that the world's energy consumption will increase from 382 quadrillion British thermal units (382×10^{15} BTUs) in 1999 to 607 quintillion (607×10^{18}) BTUs in 2020. As US President George W. Bush noted in his State of the Union address in early 2006, 'America is addicted to oil.' The same could be said of most Western industrial nations, including Canada.

Already we are beginning to suffer the economic consequences of the world's declining fossil fuel reserves, with gas prices in Canada and elsewhere increasing significantly since the early 1980s. The exchange of Western money for Middle Eastern oil results in a huge transfer of funds from the West to Arab and other developing countries. The issue of peak oil has emerged as a major topic of concern within the global geopolitical debate (Balaban and Tsatskin, 2010). Crude oil reserves are limited—once oil is taken from the ground, it cannot be replenished. In addition, what remains in the ground is deeper down and more difficult and expensive to remove (Curtis, 2009).

Moreover, as supplies slowly dwindle, control over the remaining petroleum reserves—mainly located in the Middle East, with the Alberta oil sands accounting for a significant secondary source—will become increasingly entangled with political, military, and economic interests. The term 'peak oil' refers to the theoretical point at which world oil production reaches its maximum level and then begins to decline (Eriksson, 2009). From that time on, oil will become an ever-scarcer resource. According to most expert projections, the global peak period has either already occurred or will occur within the next decade (Klare, 2004).

Current reliance on non-renewable energy sources is also devastating the environment. Coal (when burned) contributes substantially to the carbon dioxide and sulphur dioxide production that increases global warming and acid rain. However, since first becoming aware of the potential energy crisis, some people have given thought to renewable energy sources, such as hydroelectric, solar, wind, and geothermal energy (Elena and Velazquez, 2010; Verbruggen et al., 2010). Of these alternative options, the least expensive and therefore most widely used is hydroelectric power. Even so, hydroelectricity is not without its drawbacks, mainly in the form of environmental damage caused to the local wildlife, waterways, and ecosystems by the massive dams constructed to harness the water's energy (Cizek, 2004).

PEAK OIL The peak in global oil production, when the maximum rate of global petroleum extraction is reached, after which the rate of production goes into permanent decline.

Table 15.2	Top 19 Oil-Consuming Countries, 2008 (barrels/day)	
	World	80,290,000
1	United States	20,800,000
2	European Union	14,570,000
3	China	7,000,000
4	Japan	5,353,000
5	Russia	2,916,000
6	Germany	2,618,000
7	India	2,438,000
8	Canada	2,290,000
9	Korea, South	2,130,000
10	Brazil	2,100,000
11	Mexico	2,078,000
12	Saudi Arabia	2,000,000
13	France	1,999,000
14	United Kingdom	1,820,000
15	Italy	1,732,000
16	Iran	1,630,000
17	Spain	1,600,000
18	Indonesia	1,100,000
19	Netherlands	1,024,000

Source: Adapted from *CIA World Factbook 2008*.

HEALTH CONSEQUENCES OF ENVIRONMENTAL PROBLEMS

Environmental problems have harmful health consequences. This is particularly striking in the poorer regions of the developing world. The World Health Organization (1999) estimates, for instance, that 'poor environmental quality is directly responsible for 25 per cent of all preventable ill-health in the world today, with diarrheal diseases and respiratory infections heading the list.'

Health consequences are also socially constricted: a majority of all the preventable ill health that results from environmental conditions affects children. Further, children and adults living in rural and semi-urban areas are more affected than people in urban areas (WHO, 1997; see also Aronowitz and Cutler, 1998; Helfgott, 1988). Even in developed nations, pollutants, chemicals, and other environmental hazards constantly bombard people. A major Canadian example occurred during the summer of 2000, when an outbreak of E. coli bacteria in the water supply of Walkerton, Ontario, killed seven people and infected thousands more. Although a board of inquiry looking into the deaths eventually blamed insufficient government regulation and human error, this event proved that water supplies in even the most technologically advanced regions are not safe from environmental contamination. Likewise, the Native community of Fort Chipewyan on the shores of Lake Athabasca in northern Alberta—in a circumstance perhaps more akin to problems in developing countries—has experienced unusually high cancer rates, among other health issues, and Lake Athabasca is downstream from Alberta's huge oil sands projects as well as close to the radioactive tailings from uranium mining in northern Saskatchewan.

The list of health consequences is too long to present here, but consider just a few examples. The number of asthma cases treated in hospital emergency departments increases after a period of severe air pollution (Li et al., 2010; Yogev-Baggio et al., 2010). Noise pollution, most apparent in dense urban environments and a result of our industrialized lifestyle, has been shown to contribute to hearing loss (Neitzel et al., 2009). The thinning of the ozone layer has meant an increase in the amount of harmful UV rays that penetrate the atmosphere (Debrovner, 2002). This has resulted in a parallel increase in the number of skin cancer cases, particularly melanomas, which have increased 15 times in prevalence in the past 60 years. This upsurge in UV-caused cancer accounts for eight out of every 10 skin cancer deaths.

The use and haphazard dumping of ecologically harmful chemicals into the local environment have allowed persistent organic pollutants (POPs), such as pesticides, to accumulate in the food chain and, eventually, in human food supplies. Chronic exposure to POPs in our food and air has resulted in an alarming buildup of harmful synthetic chemicals and heavy metals in our bodies, a phenomenon that has been termed **body burden** (Coming Clean, 2006). On a global scale, climate change resulting from global warming has led to a rise in the occurrence of droughts and famines, particularly in Africa and in regions along the equator, and to increases in the number of floods.

BODY BURDEN A buildup of harmful synthetic chemicals and heavy metals in our bodies.

Not everyone is affected to the same degree. For example, age makes a difference. Children in both developed and developing nations are especially vulnerable to chemical, physical, and biological pollutants in the environment since their immune systems are only partly developed. Indoor air pollution caused by fossil-fuel combustion (for cooking and heating) is responsible for respiratory infections that cause 20 per cent of the deaths among children under five years of age. Diarrheal diseases claim another 2 million children a year, mainly because of unclean drinking water and lack of hygiene. Ailing and elderly members of society are also at a higher than average risk because of their declining health status.

Environmental contamination events continue to raise public concern about health. The public has become much less tolerant of unintended environmental consequences associated with technology and industrial development. Many Canadians are aware of infamous global environmental catastrophes, including the events in Chernobyl and Bhopal. These incidents have raised public awareness regarding individuals' health and safety worldwide.

Populations in Canada, too, have suffered health consequences because of environmental contamination. In Cape Breton, Nova Scotia, the Sydney Tar Ponds have been referred to as 'the most contaminated industrial site in the country' and arguably the worst in North America (Burra et al., 2006). Over 100 years of improper waste disposal practices—associated with steel production and coke oven operations—have severely contaminated soil and surface groundwater. This site contains over 700,000 tonnes of contaminated sediments, including PAHs, hydrocarbon (HC) compounds, coal tar, PCBs, coal dust, and municipal sewage (Haalboom et al., 2006).

Numerous health studies have been conducted because of community concerns, specifically regarding cancer and reproductive outcomes. According to Burra et al., '[r]esidents of Sydney have been shown to experience higher mortality rates as well as a higher incidence of particular cancers than elsewhere in the province' (2006). In fact, stomach, breast, and lung cancers occur at a rate more than double the national averages—19 per cent of men and 14 per cent for women (ibid.).

The Sydney case—discussed in Box 15.3—represents what Beck (1992) and Giddens (1990) have called a **risk society**—a society that frames technological risks embedded within a technologically and scientifically driven culture to encompass the 'dark side of progress'. Contemporary risks, in this view, are chronic disease, environmental destruction, pollution, etc., which are pervasive, non-class-specific problems that span nations, populations, and cultures, without pinpointing the industrial sources of those risks.

RISK SOCIETY A society in which risk is increased by technological and economic developments, raising the need for more cautious awareness but, also, active risk-taking is considered a core element of economic and social progress.

The technologies people have devised to improve our material conditions and advance our collective quality of life can also have adverse health implications. These technologies include nuclear power plants, automobiles, X-rays, food preservatives, breast implants, and pesticides. As we suggested above, industrialized societies are experiencing more and more technological emergencies, including accidents involving hazardous materials or nuclear power and mass transportation (for example, airplanes, buses, and trains).

Another, more controversial, example of technology having potential adverse health consequences is agricultural biotechnology, the union of molecular biology research, applied engineering, and farming (Madeley, 2009). For millennia, farmers have experimented with natural cross-pollination and selective breeding techniques to improve the genetic stock of crops and livestock. However, the long-term health effects of this new technology, which involves the introduction of genetic material from other species to create fast-growing, disease-resistant 'super' plants and livestock, may lead to the creation of new allergies and other, more serious forms of technology-induced disease (Wolfenbarger, 2002).

Others have raised environmental concerns, noting that the agribusiness industry's practice of monoculture—where entire fields are planted over multiple growth cycles with a single genetically modified (GM) crop—destroys diversity and soil health, contaminates the genetic pool of non-GM crops, and may create harmful complications in the developmental cycle of other species. Already, for example, studies have shown that populations of monarch butterfly larvae have been harmed by eating genetically modified corn (WHO, 1999).

Concerns over the unknown medium- and long-term consequences of GM foods on human and environmental health led the European Union (EU) to impose in 1998 a six-year moratorium on new GM crops. When the ban was lifted, the EU implemented a series of strict regulations requiring food-packaging labels to identify the presence of GM ingredients and for these GM ingredients to be carefully traced through the production process. Powerful agribusiness lobbyists in the US, as well as in Canada and Brazil, who claim that EU labelling regulations violate international free trade agreements, oppose these regulations. Whether

BACK IN HISTORY

Box 15.3 Tracking the Tar Ponds

. . . It wasn't until the end of the nineteenth century that Sydney, and much of the area around it, was thrust into the industrial age.

The consolidation of several coal mines in nearby Glace Bay and New Waterford and the construction of a steel plant near Muggah Creek spelled prosperity for the area and gradually the people there grew to depend on steel, coal, and fishing for their livelihood.

At the centre of that prosperity was the Sydney Steel Co., or Sysco as it is known. For almost a century, the smoke that belched from its tall stacks spelled jobs for residents of the city. Few of them could have known that it also spelled serious health problems and environmental disaster.

What prosperity had existed soon faded. The three industries that supported Sydney, and most of Cape Breton, began to collapse. In 1967, the Nova Scotia government bought the Sydney Steel Co. after its previous owner shut it down. For the next few decades it limped along supported by government handouts.

Little money was spent to reduce the large volumes of water and air pollution that the plant's old furnaces and coke-ovens produced. It was this pollution that eventually created the area's infamous tar ponds.

At the heart of the tar ponds disaster was the coke-oven. A coke-oven is a large chamber where coal is heated. At a certain temperature undesired tar and gases are separated off from the desired coke.

These toxic wastes, which included benzene, kerosene, and naphthalene, were being poured off into a nearby brook and slowly collecting into an estuary that flows into Sydney Harbour; this area is known as Muggah Creek.

More than 80 years of this type of coke-oven operation left the groundwater and surface water in the area seriously contaminated with arsenic, lead, and other toxins. It also led to the accumulation of some 700,000 tonnes of chemical waste and raw sewage, 40,000 tonnes of which are PCBs (polychlorinated biphenyls).

The locals have come to refer to the area—the size of three city blocks—as the Tar Ponds.

Many of the side effects caused by the tar ponds are still unknown. Residents of Sydney have reported an orange goo seeping into their cellars and basements.

Others have said that when it rains, puddles in the area turn fluorescent green. Those who live near the ponds, especially those in Whitney Pier, adjacent to the site, have complained of massive headaches, nosebleeds, and serious breathing problems.

It's also believed that the wastes which make up the tar ponds contain 15 varieties of cancer-related chemicals. Today, Sydney has one of the highest rates of cancer, birth defects, and miscarriages in Canada.

The effects on animal and plant life in the area have also been severe. In 1980 chemical by-products from the coke-oven process were discovered in lobsters.

In May 2010, once the multi-million dollar cleanup had begun under the aegis of the Sydney Tar Ponds Agency, residents in the area complained of the foul smells resulting from heavy equipment beginning the task of excavating the many thousands of tonnes of contaminated sludge. As one resident noted, 'it smells like an open sewer.' Some days, the smell was of mothballs, 'from the naphthalene that comes from coal tar'.

Sources: Abridged and adapted from CBC News (2004, 2010).

the artificial manipulation of other species will, in future, introduce new health problems in humans—or cause irreversible harm to ecosystems—remains to be seen.

Most important of all, in a highly technological society like ours, technological problems—even disasters—are predictable and almost inevitable. In that sense, we are sure to experience what sociologist Charles Perrow (1999) has called **normal accidents**. To prove this point, Perrow examined a variety of technological disasters—including the nuclear accidents at Three Mile Island in Pennsylvania and at Chernobyl in Ukraine—and considered nuclear power as a high-risk system for producing energy. He also examined detailed records

NORMAL ACCIDENTS
Likely accidents in complex systems of people and machines, resulting from the unanticipated interaction of multiple failures.

on aircraft accidents, marine accidents, and accidents at dams, mines, petrochemical plants, and elsewhere. For Perrow, the 'villains' in all these cases of catastrophe are system complexity, on the one hand, and subsystem coupling, on the other. Conventional engineering tries to ensure safety by building in extra warnings and safeguards. However, this approach fails because it increases system complexity. Adding to complexity not only makes system failure more likely, it creates unexpected new kinds of accidents. In other words, highly complex systems have more chances of failing and more ways to fail. The more tightly connected (or coupled) a system's parts are, the more inevitable it becomes that one part's failure will trigger another failure. Thus, simplicity and loose coupling are preferable from a safety standpoint, but complexity and tight coupling are increasingly the norm. Technological catastrophes are often blamed on human error, but invariably such error is simply the social side of a built-in technological risk.

There is perhaps no clearer example of Perrow's 'normal accidents' than what occurred with the Gulf of Mexico blowout of April 2010. This accident could have been prevented, but a combination of faulty regulation, haste, greed, and indifference led British Petroleum and the other companies involved (for example, the builders and contractors) to ignore taking simple precautions like installing an emergency shut-off valve and drilling a relief well.

Social Responses and Solutions to Environmental Problems

The ways we think, work, create, and purchase have significantly changed because of increased concern for our natural environment. As we have suggested, however, this does not mean that all of our problems with environmental degradation are by any means solved. At the very least, these concerns and emerging changes represent an important step in the right direction.

Today, concern for the environment has become embedded within popular culture (Curran, 2006). Many would argue that there is now widespread agreement that we face pervasive environmental challenges, and that social, economic, and political change must occur. In other words, unless human beings change their behaviours on a meaningful and widespread scale, the quality of life on earth—or life itself—will be threatened. For example, the past 20 years have witnessed growing scientific and public consensus that global warming is a genuine social and environmental problem (Norgaard, 2002). It is now widely regarded that if climate change continues to occur, then we will be faced with extremely negative consequences. In the following section, we outline several initiatives and changes that have emerged as a result.

Environmental Social Movements

Various environmental movements and pressure groups gained momentum during the 1970s. At that time, environmental problems emerged as significant areas of discussion within national political arenas.

Environmental social movements have emerged as the most 'vibrant, diverse, and powerful social movements occurring today, across all corners of the globe' (Doyle, 2005). At the beginning of this century, for example, the United States 'boast[ed] at least 150 national environmental organizations, 12,000 grassroots groups, and an estimated 14 million members' (Carter, 2001). Considering the size and scale of the environmental movement, it has become a significant force in many industrialized nations, as well as in the less developed world.

Most pressure group activity involves conventional political activities, such as lobbying and educational initiatives. During the 1980s, the rapid growth of this movement provided a wealth of resources for groups to 'become highly professional organizations and to win regular access to policy elites' (ibid.). Undoubtedly, these groups have become largely responsible for the progressive environmental change that has occurred in Canada and the United States.

Two notable waves of pressure-group mobilization can be identified. First, emerging during the late nineteenth century was the *conservationist* movement. This focused on wildlife protection as well as on the preservation of natural resources. Some prominent groups still exist today, such as the Sierra Club and the Audubon Society in the US and the National Trust and the Royal Society for the Protection of Birds (RSPB) in the United Kingdom. During the 1960s the second wave of pressure group mobilization occurred—resulting in increased group size and intensity of involvement.

As Carter explains, '[r]eflecting the international nature of modern environmentalism, new groups such as Friends of the Earth and Greenpeace rapidly became international organizations with national affiliates in many countries' (ibid.). Concern for industrial pollution, nuclear power, and the increased magnitude of global problems became prominent issues within these groups during this time.

Environmental pressure groups (EPGs) are varied. As a result, some observers argue that we should not identify the environmental movement as a single movement 'because the differences between the groups are more significant than the similarities' (ibid.). However, Dalton (1994) proposes the 'green rainbow' as an all-inclusive term: 'Differences between groups reflect tendencies along a continuum between a conservative orientation and an ecological orientation' (Carter, 2001). This approach, as Roots (1999) proposes, illustrates a 'broad network of people and organizations engaged in collective action in the pursuit of environmental benefits'. Still, regardless of how we classify or conceptualize EPGs as a social movement, it is clear that a considerable amount of environmental change has occurred as a result.

Population Control

As discussed in the previous chapter, a growing global population size is not in itself a social problem. However, overpopulation in the developing world and under-population in the developed world are problems because they reveal flaws in the organization and migration of human populations.

Industrialization, urbanization, education, mass literacy, and the emancipation of women were all key parts of the voluntary reduction in child-bearing over the past century and a half.

Invariably, birth rates have fallen wherever women have received more education, delayed marriage, and enjoyed more social, economic, and political equality with men (Couchman, 1986).

Several developing societies—among them Costa Rica, Sri Lanka, and Kerala state in India—have had notable success in lowering birth rates. There, low mortality and fertility rates are the result of a long process that began with fairer income distribution, better nutrition, more education and autonomy (especially for women), higher rates of political awareness and participation for all, and universal access to health services. In addition, income and land redistribution gave people more sense of involvement in their own lives—hence, more to gain from changing their fertility decisions. This is particularly true of women, who with more education and autonomy are no longer as reliant on children for the maintenance of social roles in the large social fabric and for income security.

In Canada today, by any standard, there are not too many people for the land to support. Nor is the population growing too quickly through high rates of fertility. Yet some people view high rates of immigration as a population problem and a social problem. Immigration has become an explosive political issue. Many people who have immigrated want the chance to bring their relatives to Canada. Many outside the country want a chance to get in. However, whenever the economy weakens, many Canadians resist the push for more immigrants. Some even want the immigration rate cut back.

Because population per se is not the cause of urban problems or environmental damage, population control alone cannot solve these problems. However, social organization is harder to improve and social problems are harder to solve when a population is large and growing rapidly. So much effort and money are diverted to dealing with population issues—for example, the care and education of the young, and the creation and maintenance of housing and roads—that money is unavailable for new initiatives like job creation or research and development.

Science as an Environmental Claims-Making Activity

Think for a moment about a pressing environmental problem—global warming, ozone depletion, or water and air pollution, to name a few. All of these are examples of problems that have been uncovered through scientific observation. In fact, it is rare to find an environmental problem that is not strongly rooted to a body of scientific research. Scientific researchers act as 'gatekeepers', screening potential claims for credibility (Hannigan, 1995). The support and focus of the scientific community lifts environmental problems into the mainstream, often above most other social problems and inequalities that are dependent on moral claims alone (ibid.).

At the same time, this is the crux of the science/technology problem in regard to the environment. Far too often, the self-appointed, government-appointed, and industry-appointed and -refereed gatekeepers simply don't know enough and pretend to know more than they do. The collapse of the North Atlantic cod fishery might have been averted if federal Fisheries and Oceans scientists, who set quotas and estimate stock biomass, had listened to inshore fishers and their local ecological knowledge in the years and decades preceding the collapse in the early 1990s rather than only to their own models and the biased observations of the fish processors and their trawlermen, who urged for ever-higher quotas (see, e.g., Coward et al., 2000). What has happened recently with the massive oil spill in the Gulf of Mexico would have been averted if economics, greed, and science had not trumped the essential tenet of the environment and development issue—the **precautionary principle**. Economics and science can create an unholy alliance where cost/benefit analysis determines what can or might be done—and most people would be appalled and alarmed to know what, in these scientific models, is considered as bearable 'cost' (even in a 'polluter pays' scenario) in terms of human and other life and in terms of environmental degradation.

However, science has become the focus of environmental claims-making. Consider, for example, debate surrounding genetic engineering and its harmful effects over the natural environment. In this case, claims-makers reject science for traditional, cultural rationality—ultimately, arguing that science is interfering with the natural order of our environment.

Environmental Policies

Environmental problems, because of their broad, snowballing nature, are difficult and expensive to solve. Still, all levels of society must plan remedies because of the seriousness of the problems and their costs for humanity and the planet.

At the highest levels, national and international policies need to be formulated to ensure that we follow a common, co-operative path. Under this approach, governments should try to establish policies that will make it profitable for industries to clean up the environment and exercise ecologically friendly practices. We must also demand greater readiness of emergency response organizations, including local government, fire, and police departments and special response teams, to respond to crises caused by insufficiently regulated industries.

Government policy should encourage individuals to reduce their impact on the environment. Borek and Bohon (2008) examined the effect of national environmental policies of EU countries on individuals' decisions to drive an automobile. They determined that individuals living in nations that adopt strong pro-environmental policies report a greater likelihood of driving less for environmental reasons. Ultimately, this suggests that national policies that focus on environmental sustainability are associated with pro-environmental behaviour and attitudes among individuals. While this research looked specifically at member countries of the EU, it logically aligns with evidence from North America. In short, the United States (Vogel, 2003; Zito, 2005) and Canadian (CBC, 2007) refusal to meet Kyoto Protocol requirements is mirrored by Americans and Canadians being among the very highest global consumers of energy and water, and the producers of some of the highest rates of pollution in the world.

Despite actions to reduce greenhouse gases in Canada, businesses, voluntary groups, and various political leaderships have demonstrated very weak efforts. Greater international co-operation and strengthened domestic policy on environmental issues is necessary to improve individual behaviours.

PRECAUTIONARY PRINCIPLE A tenet of environmentalism as it interfaces with economic development, which insists that when serious or irreversible damage could result from development, the wise and necessary decision is to not go ahead with that course of action, regardless of assumptions that technology could or will resolve any future problems or damage.

DARWIN'S NIGHTMARE

This important 2004 film shows how poverty and the remnants of colonialism cause horrible environmental damage in modern-day Tanzania.

Post-Materialist Values

A theory proposed by Ronald Inglehart, a political scientist at the University of Michigan, argues that there is wide public support for solving the problems of technology and environment we have discussed here. He attributes this new environmental activism to a culture shift that originates in a generation accustomed to prosperity. Inglehart (1990; see also Tepperman, 2001) argues that people who grow up in prosperous and secure conditions develop high personal and social goals. These include the goals of belonging, self-esteem, and self-actualization. Throughout the Western world, the post-war generation grew up with these goals.

Over time, this generation replaced earlier generations as voters and in elite positions of influence. In the West, according to Inglehart, the result is a new political culture. The new generation's goals have increasingly come to define the political agenda of Western democracies. The new political culture links a variety of political, social, and economic views. As a result, it represents a new outlook on life. It is post-materialist in the sense that it places less importance on personal wealth, economic development, and economic determinants of social life. In this respect, the new outlook is also post-Marxist. The new **post-materialist culture** contains political attitudes and potentials for action. It encourages more political involvement, and more protest, than the materialist culture did. However, much of this activity occurs outside the framework of elections and traditional political parties.

Inglehart's research examines anti-establishment, grassroots politics and skepticism about material progress. One major part of this post-materialist shift is the growing support for environmentalism and for movements that seek solutions to these problems. Linked as they are to preferences for specific political issues and parties, these 'new' needs produce 'new' political behaviours, including shifts in goals and partisanship. Post-materialists, who also report higher levels of material satisfaction, are said to be more politically active than materialists (Inglehart, 1977).

If Inglehart's theory is valid, the problems we have discussed in this chapter are already on the way to being solved. New environmentalist movements and political parties will gain ever more support, form governments, and ban environmentally unsound practices. Human life will become healthier and happier. However, evidence does not support the theory's predictions (see Tepperman, 2001). Some say that Inglehart's approach is surprisingly simple or naive—a one-dimensional view of political culture that pits materialism against post-materialism. Some say that we cannot assume that a shift in cultural values towards environmentalism will translate into political action. We need only to look at the negative North American political response to the Kyoto agreement to know that strong feelings about the environment do not necessarily equate with committed political action when elected officials must also contend with competing economic and political interests in a highly complex world.

We may not be able to rely on a new political culture of post-materialism to bring about environmental or technological change, to improve our health and well-being. People will have to mobilize to consider, discuss, protest, and enact new policies. Furthermore, several factors, including global capitalism, stand in the way. So long as 'the commons' is not

POST-MATERIALIST CULTURE A new cultural orientation that puts less emphasis on material consumption and class issues, and more on non-material (quality of collective life) benefits, such as environmental improvement.

understood to include the entire planet, 'the tragedy' will continue to play itself out as those with power and influence seek personal short-term gain over longer-term equity.

Resource Management

Part of the social nature of environmental problems comes in the form of resource management. More specifically, the social process of deciding who should get what amount of some resource can lead to intergroup strife, political tension, and, at times, violence. As resources dwindle, competition for what remains will become increasingly fierce (Homer-Dixon, 1994).

However, conflict over resources does not need to be seen as inevitable, as evidenced by a case from northern British Columbia involving the formation of an alliance between the Cheslatta T'en, a First Nations tribe, and non-Native local residents (Larsen, 2003). Beginning in the 1980s, the Cheslatta leaders sought to expand their social networks to increase their political power and mobilize efforts to control the land they saw as rightfully theirs. Through grassroots efforts, a coalition was formed that empowered all locals, Native and non-Native, and legally bypassed the (often lengthy) treaty settlement process. In addition to bringing together disparate groups, this inter-ethnic alliance fought effectively to protect the environment. According to Larsen (ibid., 74), 'Cheslatta leaders used cultural exchanges and social networks generated by the alliance to fashion territorial initiatives that, when taken together, channel popular environmentalism, provincial forestry policies, and ancestral ethnoecology into collective identity, action, and authority. As a result, the band has attained political influence over its traditional lands without participating in the province's treaty settlement process.' In short, it is an important example in simultaneously improving our social and natural worlds.

Effective resource management is not only the result of grassroots activists. Consumers and business owners can help combat negative environmental trends as well. For example, the Pacific coast of British Columbia contains some of the last areas of temperate rain forest in the world (Suzuki and Dressel, 2002). During the 1990s, logging companies successfully lobbied for the permission to cut down a portion of this forest. Despite the loggers' having consent from the government, a boycott of wood taken from the BC forests has forced all parties involved to agree to a moratorium on logging in the most vulnerable areas of temperate rain forest ecosystem (ibid.). Further discussion of individual strategies will highlight how you can hope to make a difference.

Voluntary Simplicity

The term 'voluntary simplicity' refers to individuals choosing to reduce spending on goods and services, replacing these behaviours with non-materialistic sources of satisfaction and meaning (Etzioni, 2004). Voluntary simplicity movements have emerged as a criticism of consumerism, as well as in overall discomfort for the overarching goal of the capitalist economy.

The Canadian Press/Toronto Star/Michael Stuparyk

Sarah Susanka, architect and author, is regarded as a simplicity pacesetter and perhaps even a prophet. In 1998, she published 'The Not So Big House: A Blueprint for the Way We Really Live'. It quickly became a bestseller and more 'Not So Big' titles followed.

Originally, support for this movement was slight, occurring mainly among the followers of various countercultures. However, in recent years a significant number of individuals in Western societies have embraced these values. As Inglehart (1977: 3) suggests, 'the values of Western publics have been shifting from an overwhelming emphasis on material well-being and physical security toward greater emphasis on the quality of life.' As individuals have increasingly come to adopt post-materialist values, they place less emphasis on material comforts and unnecessary luxuries. Therefore, when people engage in voluntary simplicity, they autonomously decide to reduce—if not erase—conspicuous consumption and pursue activities and experiences that have greater intangible rewards.

Levels of voluntary simplicity are wide-ranging, and occur along a scale of least to most consumption reduction: (1) *downshifters*—consumption is only moderately reduced; (2) *strong simplification*—a significant reduction in consumerism occurs; and (3) *holistic simplification*. Downshifters are typically affluent, well-off members of society who reduce consumption while maintaining a rich and consumption-oriented lifestyle. For example, they may decide to 'dress down', 'wearing jeans and inexpensive loafers, t-shirts, and driving beat-up cars' (Etzioni, 2004), taking pride in their moderate tastes and modest lifestyles.

Strong simplifiers take this process one step further, by giving up high-paying and prestigious jobs to work fewer hours and earn less income. This group chooses less income and lower pension payouts for a more leisurely, family-oriented lifestyle. The final group, the *holistic simplifiers*, adjusts their entire life patterns according to voluntary simplicity ideologies. According to Etzioni, '[t]hey often move from affluent suburbs or gentrified parts of major cities to smaller towns, the countryside, farms and less affluent or less urbanized parts of the country with the explicit goal of leading a "simpler" life' (ibid., 409). As a result, a social movement sometimes called *the simple living movement* has emerged, with a plainly anti-consumerist philosophy.

Although voluntary simplicity mainly affects the individual (see Box 15.4), it has significant consequences for society as a whole. Consider, for example, the social and environmental benefits that would emerge if increasing members of society chose to embrace the voluntary simplicity movement.

CHAPTER SUMMARY

In this chapter we have discussed the causes and consequences of environmental problems and environmental degradation. Ironically, both the causes and solutions rest within the unique impact of human ingenuity, and environmental social movements have been

PERSONAL STORIES

Box 15.4 Extreme Green Living

Mornings at the Beavan household look pretty ordinary. The Beavans have breakfast, brush their teeth, and get 2-year-old Isabella ready for day care. But look a little closer: There's no morning paper, no morning television, and no coffee. Coffee isn't grown locally, so it's off-limits.

Colin Beavan and his family are midway through a year-long experiment to see if they can live their lives without creating any waste, and therefore, have no negative impact on the environment. Colin has dubbed himself the 'No Impact Man', and he is writing a book about the family's experience. The experiment has just entered its next stage: turning off the electricity.

'The first night we turned off the electricity I said, "What the hell are we doing?" I wanted to read', said Colin. 'Slowly you adapt and then you start to see the good things about it. . . . It's the transition that I found hard at times.' The family gets power from a solar panel on the roof and also uses candles and solar lamps, and Colin says that the family

is spending more time outside since they turned off the electricity.

Colin said that overall, the experiment has helped his family and friends become closer. 'For entertainment, we don't watch TV. We play charades or something. . . . It's building community', he said.

For most of us, the Beavans's rules seem extreme. The family buys nothing new, nothing that comes in any packaging, no food that isn't grown or made within 250 miles and they don't use transportation—even public transportation, including elevators.

Colin and Michelle share a scooter to get around New York, and they walk up and down some 50 flights of stairs a day. He shaves with a straight razor, makes bread for the family, and shops at a local farmer's market.

'The average piece of food Americans have on their plate has travelled 1,500 miles', Colin said. 'That produces a lot of carbon dioxide.'

Source: **ABC News (2007)**.

important, both historically and today, in seeking solutions. The problems discussed in this chapter include some of the greatest challenges faced today because many of the problems hold wide-ranging and potentially irreversible effects. For this reason, the actions that we take today—either 'problem-solving' or 'problem-creating'—will be long-lasting.

Environmental destruction is a problem that occurs on a global level. This destruction will increase as a function of population growth, urban concentration, and technologies associated with industrial production. Disposing of solid and toxic waste is a major problem as it demands new landfills and can cause disruption of the ecosystem. Depleting non-renewable resources is also a serious problem. Developed countries are most to blame here as they are far more wasteful than developing countries. Since industry is profit-oriented, it is not likely to take responsibility for pollution; more government regulation will be needed.

We have shown that environmental problems have harmful health outcomes. Those affected most are the poor living in rural areas. Environmental harm accounts for 3 million premature deaths from exposed air pollution alone, and 90 per cent of these deaths occur in developing countries. Climate change resulting from global warming has led to a rise in droughts and famines, particularly in Africa and in other regions along the equator, and to an increasing the number of natural disasters, such as floods and violent storms.

As we have seen, the reckless use of technology is an increasing concern. Focusing on short-term gain and practising wilful ignorance about environmental consequences has been devastating. Even today, many are still prepared to sacrifice the environment for short-term gains in comfort and wealth. This will not change without large-scale change in attitudes and legislation to protect the environment.

QUESTIONS FOR CRITICAL THOUGHT

1. What is the relationship between human beings and the natural environment? Why are sociologists interested in studying the environment? How do the two camps of environmental sociologists—realists and constructionists—interpret environmental issues differently?

2. In your view, does technology lead human beings to destruction or to progress? Give examples and explain. Also, do you agree with the 'normal accidents' theory of Charles Perrow that technological problems are predictable and almost unavoidable?

3. With deforestation comes the displacement of indigenous peoples and many animal species from their natural habitats. In addition, peoples and species may be at risk of extinction because of such activities. Chart out the advantages and disadvantages of deforestation. Do you feel it is an ethical practice? Should governments set limits? Research specific examples to back up your claims.

RECOMMENDED READINGS

Brunsma, David L., David Overfelt, and J. Steven Picou, eds. 2007. *The Sociology of Katrina: Perspectives on a Modern Catastrophe*. Lanham, MD: Rowman & Littlefield. This collection of articles explores Hurricane Katrina and its aftermath from a sociological perspective. By analyzing the early post-storm data and literature, the book clarifies how race, class, and capital have affected the residents in New Orleans during the disaster and afterwards.

Coward, Harold, and Andrew J. Weaver, eds. 2004. *Hard Choices: Climate Change in Canada*. Waterloo, ON: Wilfrid Laurier University Press. Composed of articles from different disciplines, this book offers an outline and assessment of climate change and its impacts on Canada from physical, social, technological, economic, political, and ethical/religious perspectives. Special attention is given to Canada's response to the Kyoto Protocol, as well as an assessment of the overall adequacy of Kyoto as a response to the global challenge of climate change.

Dale, Stephen. 1996. *McLuhan's Children: The Greenpeace Message and the Media*. Toronto: Between the Lines. This book is an important resource for those interested in the symbolic interactionist perspective, which is concerned with constructing an environmental problem. Dale also addresses the political implications of constructing a claim of environmental damage.

Flannery, Tim. 2006. *The Weather Makers: How Man Is Changing the Climate and What It Means for Life on Earth*. New York: Atlantic Monthly Press. This popular work considers the current status of global climate change, energy consumption, and the geopolitical implications of our looming environmental problems.

Gould, Kenneth A., and Tammy L. Lewis, eds. 2008. *Twenty Lessons in Environmental Sociology*. New York: Oxford University Press. Comprising 20 lectures on environmental sociology by various scholars, this text examines the key topics in the field, from the social construction of nature to the growing influence of global media on our understanding of the environment, which in turn provides a comprehensive introduction to the subject.

Pellow, David Naguib. 2007. *Resisting Global Toxics: Transnational Movements for Environmental Justice*. Cambridge, MA: MIT Press. Every year, nations and corporations in the 'global North' produce millions of tons of toxic waste. Too often this dangerous material—linked to high rates of illness and death and widespread ecosystem damage—is exported to poor communities of colour around the world. In this book, Pellow examines this practice and charts the emergence of transnational environmental justice movements to challenge and reverse it.

Perrow, Charles. 1999. *Normal Accidents: Living with High Risk Technologies*. Princeton, NJ: Princeton University Press. This book analyzes the social side of technological risk. Perrow argues that the conventional engineering approach to ensuring safety—building in more warnings and safe-guards—fails because system complexity makes failures unavoidable. He asserts that typical pre-cautions, by adding to complexity, may help create new categories of accidents. By recognizing two dimensions of risk—complex versus linear interactions, and tight versus loose coupling—this book provides a powerful framework for analyzing risks and the organizations and economic system that insist we live in a risk society.

Timmons, Robert J., and Bradley C. Park. 2006. *A Climate of Injustice*. Cambridge, MA: MIT Press. In this book, the authors analyze the role that inequality between rich and poor nations plays in the negotiation of global climate agreements. They argue that until people recognize that reach-ing a North–South global climate pact requires addressing larger issues of inequality and strik-ing a global bargain on environment and development, the current policy gridlock will remain unresolved.

RECOMMENDED WEBSITES

World Wildlife Fund

www.worldwildlife.org

The World Wildlife Fund is dedicated to protecting the world's wildlife and wildlands. Its conservation efforts are directed towards three global goals: protecting endangered spaces, saving endangered species, and addressing global threats.

Environment Canada

www.ec.gc.ca/envhome.html

Environment Canada's mandate is to preserve and improve the quality of the natural environment, including water, air, and soil quality; to conserve Canada's renewable resources; to conserve and protect Canada's water resources; to oversee weather systems (meteorology); to enforce the rules made by the Canada–US International Joint Commission relating to boundary waters; and to co-ordinate environmental policies and programs for the federal government.

The UN Environment Program (UNEP)

www.unep.org

The UN Environment Program is the appointed authority of the United Nations system in environmental issues at the global and regional levels. Its website provides information on international environmental projects and development, news of environmental issues around the world, as well as research and publications.

Environmental Health News

www.environmentalhealthnews.org

Environmental Health News is a website published daily by Environmental Health Sciences. Its mission is to advance the public's understanding of environmental health issues by publishing its own journalism and providing access to worldwide news about a variety of subjects related to the health of humans, wildlife, and ecosystems.

Intergovernmental Panel on Climate Change (IPCC)

www.ipcc.ch

Intergovernmental Panel on Climate Change is the leading body for assessing climate change, and was established by the United Nations Environment Program and the World Meteorological Organization (another UN agency) to provide the world with a clear scientific view on the current state of climate change and its potential environmental and socio-economic effects. Its website provides a wide range of scientific reports on climate change.

Pembina Institute

www.pembina.org

The Pembina Institute, based in Alberta, supports innovative environmental research and education initiatives that help people understand the way we produce and consume energy, the impact of energy generation and use on the environment and human communities, and options for more sustainable use of natural resources.

Canadian Institute for Environmental Law and Policy (CIELAP)

www.cielap.org

CIELAP is an independent, not-for-profit research and education organization whose mission is to provide leadership in the research and development of environmental law and policy that promotes the public interest and sustainability.

PART 5
The Future

CHAPTER 16

What Problems Are on the Way?

iStockphoto.com/OlgaLIS

LEARNING OBJECTIVES

- To learn what 'futures studies' are.
- To discover what past theorists have predicted for our future.
- To appreciate the changing definition of social problems.
- To discuss trends in social problems that may continue.
- To understand controversies surrounding genetic manipulation.
- To learn about implications for the future of cyberspace.

INTRODUCTION

Unlike the other topics we have discussed in this book—poverty, crime, addiction, and so on—which are only partly socially constructed, 'the future' is entirely constructed (Fuller and Loogma, 2009). It doesn't exist yet; we have to imagine it, based on current trends, hopes, wishes, fears, and calculations of chance.

THINKING ABOUT THE FUTURE

A recurring theme in this book is the interconnectedness of social problems. None of the social problems we have discussed stands alone—each is related to other social problems. Such complexity suggests that a change in one area of social life will affect other areas. Another important aspect of the social problems we have discussed is their historical basis. Most problems today are the result of long-standing neglect and simmering conflict.

At the same time, social problems change. For example, as we saw in the chapter on alcohol and drug abuse, what is considered an unlawful substance and, therefore, a social problem when used or abused can shift markedly over time (Herzog et al., 2009).

Cocaine and opiates were considered proper medicinal and recreational drugs at one time, but now are strictly banned by the criminal justice system (Katz and Mazer, 2009). Public

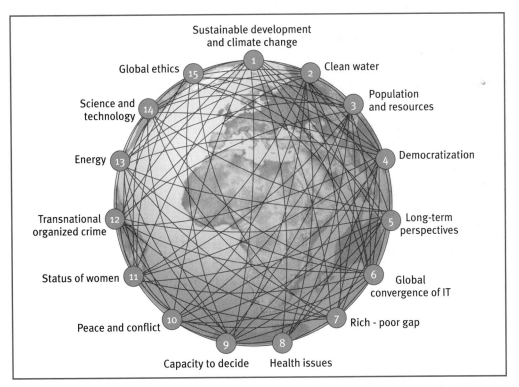

Figure 16.1 A Projection of the Fifteen Most Pressing Global Challenges Facing Humanity during the Twenty-First Century

Source: **2010 State of the Future** by Jerome C. Glenn, Theodore J. Gordon, and Elizabeth Florescu, The Millennium Project. © **2009 The Millennium Project**

officials considered marijuana use legal, then illegal; today we have tightly limited legal access to marijuana for strictly therapeutic purposes, and the prospect of the effective decriminalization of marijuana use (Hyshka, 2009). Not all social problems have long histories, and clearly people and societies, for various reasons, will continue to create and influence new problems within society.

The dynamic nature of social problems poses difficulties not only for people actively working to improve social conditions, but also for researchers trying to foresee the social problems of the future. The organization of sociological research makes precise forecasting difficult, though improvements can be made (Aligica, 2009). Our goal as sociologists in thinking about the future is to formulate possible solutions to the social problems that we predict are likely to occur or recur.

WHAT IS FUTURES STUDIES?

People have been discussing the possibilities and problems of predicting and studying the future for centuries. Writing about 'Utopias'—places where everything works in perfect harmony—started with ancient peoples imagining the origins of humanity and imagining the afterlife. At least since Sir Thomas More (influenced by Plato), who wrote the book *Utopia* 500 years ago, authors repeatedly have invented societies to illustrate important principles of social organization. Some of these inventions have been called 'dystopias' because they picture important negative principles of social organization—things to avoid. Of these books, one of the most famous is George Orwell's book *1984*, written in 1948 to show the dangers of Soviet totalitarian government.

If Utopian thinking has a long history, so does debate about its value. In an essay written over 50 years ago, American social theorist Andrew Hacker (1955) decided that critics of Utopian thinking fall into three categories: Democrats, Dialecticians, and Devil-Hunters. The Democrats think that Utopia may invoke dictatorial tendencies. Historically, many idealized societies, starting with Plato's *Republic*, have indeed imagined unequal and unfree, although humane, societies. The Dialecticians believe in the value of discovering historical laws. They see Utopian thought as idle speculation or dreaming. The Devil-Hunters are concerned with the importance of overcoming original sin or, at least, the notion that humans are *unable* to change their ways significantly.

FUTURES STUDIES
The area of research concerned with forecasting possible scenarios—technological, economic, political, social, environmental—in order to prepare for and shape what may come.

Utopian thinking has value, if it is rooted in empirical knowledge about human beings and their behaviour. This means that **futures studies** seek to make use of our understanding of the past and present. Humans will not inevitably repeat the past, but neither are they likely to depart completely from past behaviour. Humans are unlikely—suddenly and en masse—to become saints or devils. What some people like to call 'human nature' is not going to change, for the most part. Our single best guess about the future is that people will continue to respond positively to new opportunities, and that these new opportunities will continue to be provided by new technology, among other things (Byrne et al., 1981).

Therefore, 'technology might offer some opportunity for predicting the future—as science moves through networks of implication, and each discovery suggests a set of later steps. From these data, scenarios of possible alternative futures are created, which are then used as choices within strategic planning initiatives' (University of Houston–Clear Lake, 2001). This is the reason most futurology and futures research focuses on technological change. Almost as often—for example, in market and political research—it focuses on demographic change. In the following discussion, we will consider both of these foci. What they have in common is an attempt to predict or 'forecast' the future from the past (Pourezzat et al., 2008).

Alternative Forecasting Methods

Forecasting methods fall into several main categories, many of which were identified by David Walonick (1993). So-called *genius forecasting* is a method that relies mainly on intuition and insight; a prime example would be the forecasts provided by H.G. Wells (1902), some of which are discussed below. Many genius forecasts turn out to be wrong, but others turn out to be right. As Malcolm Gladwell (2009) has argued, individuals make very rapid intuitive judgements, decisions, and predictions, and many of them turn out to be correct. Some individuals produce consistently accurate forecasts by this method, and their forecasts are useful because they are reliably accurate, even if we do not understand how they achieve their accuracy. Likely, the reason genius forecasting works as well as it does is because it builds on our own experiences. In this respect, it is a personal form of 'trend extrapolation'.

Trend extrapolation examines trends and cycles in historical data; it uses mathematical techniques to predict the future from the past—for example, to predict the birth rate in Canada in 2050 from the birth rates between 1950 and 2006. The strength of this method is that it roots the future in historical experience. The weakness is that, with this method, the further into the future we try to forecast, the less certain the forecast becomes—conditions change, and some processes change quickly and repeatedly. The stability of the environment is central in determining whether trend extrapolation will be a suitable forecasting model.

So-called 'data-smoothing' methods separate historical data into trends: seasonal and random parts. Mathematical models based on the observed trends use smoothing constants, coefficients, and other features that must be chosen carefully by the forecaster. Largely, the choice of these features determines the outcome of the forecast. So, once again, the quality of the forecast depends on the expertise, experience, and intuition of the forecaster.

Forecasting complex systems often involves seeking expert opinions from more than one person. These are called *consensus methods* of forecasting. The best known 'consensus method' is the Delphi method (Jones and Hunter, 1995). In a series of iterations, experts offer judgements on the likelihood of certain outcomes, and then evaluate the answers given by their peers. This approach is intended to produce a rapid narrowing of opinions among experts. It provides more accurate forecasting than group discussions, is more reliable than judgements by individual geniuses, and makes better use of expert knowledge than mathematical trend extrapolation. However, since this method demands the co-operation of many experts over an extended period, its implementation is often impractical.

Simulation methods use analogs to model complex systems. Game analogs may be used to model the interactions of players in imagined social interactions (Walonick, 1993)—for example, in studying negotiation and bargaining.

Mathematical analogs have been successful in forecasting outcomes, especially in the physical sciences (Segall et al., 2002). Many of these models use advanced statistical techniques to model complex systems involving relationships between two or more variables (known as multivariate analyses). Multiple regression analysis is the mathematical analog of a systems approach, and it has become the primary forecasting tool of economists and qualitative sociologists.

Ironically, strong correlations between predictor variables create unstable forecasts; a slight change in one variable can have a large effect on another variable (Walonick, 1993). In a multiple regression (and systems) approach, as the relationships between the parts of the system become stronger and more numerous, our ability to predict any given part decreases. This was one of the criticisms levelled at what was perhaps the most famous future simulation in social science history: the 'limits to growth' exercise developed under the auspices of the Club of Rome (Meadows et al., 1972). It showed a variety of ways the world can come to an end, destroying humanity; all were cataclysmic but none was entirely believable.

The *scenario method* is a narrative forecast that describes a potential course of events. Recognizing the interrelationships of system components, it considers events such as new technology, population shifts, and changing consumer preferences. Scenarios, written as long-term predictions of the future, force decision-makers to ask: (1) Can we survive the *worst possible* scenario? (2) Will we be happy with the *most likely* scenario? (3) Are we able to take advantage of the *best possible* scenario? (Walonick, 1993, 2004).

Scenario modelling leads directly to a need to make choices and decisions, and this, in turn, leads to models of decision-making. *Decision trees* are graphical devices to help illustrate

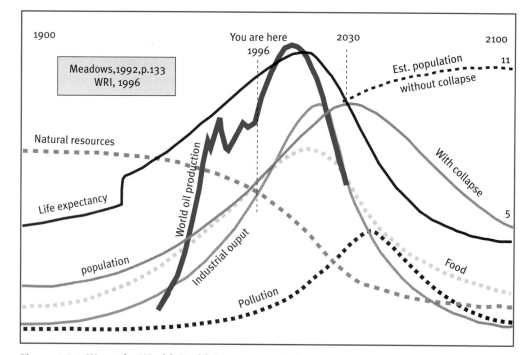

Figure 16.2 Ways the World Could Come to an End

Source: **Meadows, Randers, Meadows, 2004, *Limits to Growth: The 30-year Update*, Chelsea Green Publishing Company.**

the relationships between choices. Computer technology has made it possible to create very complex decision trees, with many subsystems and feedback loops.

Every decision can be expected to produce a variety of outcomes, some desired and some undesired, and each of these outcomes will have an assignable value for us. Decision theory, using decision trees, is based on the idea that the expected value of an outcome variable can be calculated as the average value for that variable. In other words, the value of a decision is the 'value' of the outcome it produces, calculated as the total of all estimated positive and negative outcomes in the decision tree (ibid.).

The goal of forecasting is to be as accurate as possible, and to enable social scientists, policy-makers, and the wider society to plan the use of resources efficiently and effectively. However, the usefulness of a forecast is not always related to its accuracy. The value of a forecast depends on various things, including the type of information being forecast, our confidence in the accuracy of the forecast, the magnitude of our dissatisfaction with the forecast, and the variety of ways we can adapt to or modify the forecast. The usefulness of each forecasting situation must be evaluated individually.

We predict the future based on knowledge, intuition, and logic (ibid.). Sometimes forecasts become part of a creative process, and sometimes they do not. If two people make mutually exclusive forecasts, both of them cannot be true—at least one of the forecasts is wrong. Does one person's forecast create the future while the other person's forecast does not? The mechanisms involved in the construction of the future are not well understood on an individual or social level. Because of the power of a forecast to affect the future, forecasting itself may be part of a self-interested quest for power.

If the future is a social construct, are predictions of the future a form of propaganda, designed to evoke particular behaviours? Some believe that a desire for control is hidden in all forecasts (Dublin, 1989). Since decisions made today are based on forecasts, forecasts may be attempts, whether knowingly or unknowingly, to control today's decisions. One can see this in the global warming 'debate', which has been maintained by some political and business interests long after overwhelming scientific evidence of climate change suggested there was nothing to debate. In this respect, forecasting is a type of agenda-setting, a way of forcing everyone to think about the future and to make decisions in particular ways. Since forecasts can and often do take on a creative role, is it necessary to discuss the ethics of making forecasts that involve other people's futures? Each person has the right to create his or her own future. On the other hand, a forecast can alter the course of an entire society.

Ideally, we will use forecasting to create socially desirable futures: for example, sociologists might favour peaceful coexistence, ecological sustainability, and a fairer distribution of the world's assets. However, the idea of a *desirable future* is subjective. If a goal of forecasting is to create desirable futures, then the forecaster must ask the ethical question of 'desirable for whom?' Forecasters should at least try to engage as many people as possible in the forecasting process to increase their understanding and accuracy. This would have the effect of empowering people who might be affected by the forecast. As these people are involved, they become co-creators of their own futures. In principle, according to Alexis de Tocqueville and Adam Smith, among others, such widespread engagement will yield collective well-being through the pursuit of informed personal well-being.

THEORETICAL PERSPECTIVES ON FUTURE STUDIES

Table 16.1 Theoretical Perspectives	
Theory	**Main Points**
Structural Functionalism	• Futures studies look into alternative futures and identify the most probable social trends. • Forecasting contributes to today's decision-making and planning by helping politicians to devise social policies. • Looking to the future encourages people to reflect on current patterns of events and to make adjustments in preparation for the future.
Conflict Theory	• Different forecasting and simulation methods produce different insights into the nature and probability of occurrence of certain events that may favour one population subgroup over another. • Various interest groups compete for government support by raising and perhaps exaggerating the acuity of particular concerns.
Symbolic Interactionism	• Gossip and rumour may spread misinformation and create moral panic or fear. • The rise of cyberspace and virtual communities hides many social factors (e.g., gender, race, and class) that often prevent similar people from interacting with one another.
Feminist Theory	• Despite ongoing efforts made by women to overcome gender discrimination, inequalities in wage and job opportunities will continue to persist. • Modern mothers must learn to negotiate a fine balance between work and family responsibilities as their participation in the labour force increases.
Social Constructionism	• The future is a social construct, a form of propaganda designed to evoke a particular set of behaviours. • Media portrayals of social problems and trends exert a large influence on people's perspectives of society, may spark social movements, and contribute to policy-making.

Feminist contributions to the field of futures studies have been quite limited. Male dominance in the field of futures studies has been attributed, in part, to the relative precedence that social and political activism geared towards present conditions take over theoretical work for many feminists and women's groups (Milojevic, 2008).

The almost non-existent relationship between women and futures studies is also linked to the specific limitations of futures studies, such as 'the hyper-technological and scientific orientation of professional "mainstream" futurism, the focus on "expert" opinion in the Delphi method, quantifiable trend analysis, techno-utopianism and social dystopianism, which are considered to be out of the comfortable level of knowledge for many feminists' (ibid). Furthermore, any feminist efforts in the field of futures studies are considered as special/optional issues within the field (ibid).

When predictions of alternative futures are addressed, forecasts of feminists seem to be guesses that could go either way. The more positive scenarios include women becoming more aware of their capabilities and acquiring a stronger presence in public life, while the more negative scenarios forecast a growing divide and breakdown in communication between different classes of women in our society, depending on access to education and their background (Hurley et al., 2008).

There are no clear rules involving the ethics of forecasting. For this reason, social forecasting must specifically address relevant physical, cultural, and societal values. In addition, forecasters must examine their own biases, which are likely to influence the forecasting process. As we have said, even the most rigorous forecasting techniques build on assumptions that can dramatically alter the forecast.

CHANGES IN WHAT THE PUBLIC SEES AS SOCIAL PROBLEMS

What people at one point in time consider serious social problems sometimes changes in response to changes in social, political, and economic conditions. A social problems textbook from 1898, for instance, listed 'Dumping Garbage', 'Over-Production', 'Public Debts and Indirect Taxation', and 'Slavery' among its chapter headings (George, 1898). Another text, published only 18 years later, already showed concern for some of the harmful social conditions that continue to affect the world today, including 'Unemployment', 'Crime and Punishment', 'The Liquor Problem', 'Poverty', and 'The Conservation of Natural Resources' (Towne, 1916). Many of these problems are with us today.

After the Russian Revolution in 1917, Western capitalist societies worried about Soviet Communism and the dangers of subversion and war, while Soviet Communists worried about Western capitalism and the dangers of subversion and war. Between 1917 and 1967, through two world wars and two minor wars (Korea and Vietnam), a global depression, and hunts for traitors in the Soviet Union (in the 1930s) and the United States (in the 1950s), people on both sides waited for the worst to happen—all-out, final war between Communist and capitalist nations (Mueller, 2005).

It did not, and as the risk receded, national concerns over military conflict have declined and the two political bodies have contracted to reduce and dismantle their stockpiles of nuclear weapons. The economic and political decline of the USSR, coupled with growing domestic considerations such as the economy and unemployment, replaced the fear of war with Soviet Russia. North America rode a technology-driven, record-breaking boom in the marketplace during the 1990s, and crime and other social issues became the main social problems in the public eye.

However, since the events of 11 September 2001, concerns about war and subversion have surfaced once again, especially in the United States (Davis and Silver, 2004). In the near future, we can expect to see greater concern given to terrorism, treason, and national security in the public mind.

TRENDS IN SOCIAL PROBLEMS PROJECTED TO THE NEAR FUTURE

In years to come, many predictions by today's leading futures researchers will be proven to have been wrong. Others will have come close to the reality of life as it will exist in 2100, and a few may even have hit the bull's eye (Cole, 2008).

Noted thinker Noam Chomsky is pessimistic about the prospects of futures research: 'The record of prediction in human affairs has not been inspiring, even short-range. The most plausible prediction is that any prediction about serious matters is likely to be off the mark, except by accident' (Chomsky, 1999: 30). However, the goal of futures studies is only partly to paint a picture of what life may be like for later generations. Its task is to imagine a desirable alternative future for people to work towards, a future that is actively shaped by the decisions of people living today. With this in mind, let us consider the likely future of several different categories of social problems.

Environmental Damage

The degradation of the environment is a growing social problem. Many scientists and theorists believe that even if changes are made immediately, environmental problems will become more severe and their effects more intense in the future. We need only to consider the ongoing oil-spill disaster in the Gulf of Mexico to realize this. Already, the world's temperature has increased, especially since the 1990s. This has led to more frequent droughts and famines, higher rates of skin cancer, and more extreme weather conditions throughout the year (Larsen and Gunnarsson-Ostling, 2009).

F. Sherwood Rowland, whose early warnings of the effects of chlorofluorocarbons (CFCs) on ozone depletion in 1974 earned him a Nobel Prize in chemistry, hypothesizes that:

> the global prevalence of smog will rise in the next century because more and more people will use cars. The twenty-first century will therefore begin with three major atmospheric problems firmly entrenched globally: stratospheric ozone depletion, the greenhouse effect from increasing carbon dioxide and other trace gases with accompanying global warming and urban and regional smog. My expectation in the coming decades is that the climatic consequences from continued greenhouse gas emissions will be more and more noticeable, and much more ominous. (Rowland, 1999: 209–10)

One large area where the impact of environmental damage is severely felt is Nunavut. Warmer weather has already affected Inuit hunters, forcing them to adapt their harvesting activities, hunting, use of social networks, and traditional Inuit knowledge (Ford et al., 2007). A continuation of current trends relating to differential knowledge transfer and learning of

POLICY DEBATES

Box 16.1 On the Ethics of Present and Future Social Policy Solutions

In late 2004, the Millennium Project of the American Council for the United Nations University began a double-round cycle of an international study to identify the most important ethical issues that humanity may face in the foreseeable future. The Millennium Project is a global participatory system that collects, synthesizes, and feeds back judgements on an ongoing basis about prospects for the human condition. Its annual *State of the Future*, *Futures Research Methodology*, and other special reports are used by social policy-makers and educators to add focus to important issues, clarify choices, and improve the quality of decisions. This study was intended to explore social policy and ethical issues that may arise in the future, which are not well understood today, and that may need years to fully assess and address, and it represents only a minor step in the process. The first round asked participants to add future ethical issues to an initial list, as well as to identify the values underlying said issues that are subject to change over the next 25 to 50 years. A second round follows, in which participants were asked to rate a subset of these future ethical issues and value modifications. The results of the study were published in the 2005 publication of *State of the Future*.

The issues considered for the period between 2005 and 2010 were predicted with reasonable accuracy and have been faced by social policy-makers during the time period in question; a couple of these issues have had much impact in the last decade.

— What is the ethical way to intervene in the affairs of a country that is significantly endangering its own or other people? This question has been addressed in international conflicts in the Middle East, such as with respect to the political situation and war in Afghanistan.
— Do parents have a right to create genetically altered 'designer babies'? With the progression of science in the realm of fertility and genetic testing, ethical issues concerning preferential choice of embryos and the potential for eugenics at the embryonic level have quickly arisen in the controversy that has presented itself in *the face of developing genetic screening technologies*.

The questions for the time period above were well-thought and paralleled many issues that have since faced the world. Whether or not anticipated issues for the time period of 2010 to 2050 will prove relevant, it is important to consider them, keeping in mind that throughout the course of history many issues expected to surface have yet to do so. Some issues considered in the Millennium Project's study are as follows:

— Do we have the right to genetically change ourselves and future generations into a new or several new species?
— Considering the economic and other consequences of an aging population, should we have the right to suicide and euthanasia?
— Is it ethical for society to manage the creation of future elites who have been augmented with artificial intelligence and genetic engineering?
— Do we have the right to alter our genetic germ line so that future generations cannot inherit the potential for genetically related diseases or disabilities?
— To what degree should the rights and interests of future generations prevail in decisions of this generation?
— How would you rate these potential issues? Do you think they are appropriate for consideration with respect to social policy implementations?

Sources: **Glenn and Gordon (2005, 2009).**

land-based skills in younger generations is predicted to lead to the breakdown of social networks, due to rising inequality of access to resources because of differences in the adaptive capacity of groups in the community (ibid).

Perhaps more than any other people, global warming is affecting the estimated 155,000 Inuit people in Canada, Greenland, Russia, and the United States, as the ice provides them animals to feed and clothe their families, and hunting seasons and territories have been reduced by earlier and earlier melting times each year.

Genetic Manipulation

GENETIC MANIPULATION The altering of genes to produce a more desired physical trait.

Some predictions about the future of humanity hinge on the use of genetic manipulation to improve the quality of human life. Already, scientists have mapped out the human genome, the DNA material containing the genetic instructions that determine hair, eye, and skin colour, height, physical build, susceptibility to various diseases, and, possibly, personality or temperament.

Many ethicists and researchers are worried about human cloning and the use of embryos made expressly for research purposes. The dominant concern is that without sufficient government and institutional guidelines for ethical behaviour in genetic research, humanity risks abusing this new technology in as-yet-unforeseen ways (Murray, 2002).

TECHNOLOGY The manifestation of human knowledge and ingenuity applied to the solution of a problem or need; applied science.

Negative public opinion and controversies surrounding the development of these powerful biotechnological tools are not founded on present scientific theory but rely more on potential risks and benefits of the technology in the *future*. Claims and counterclaims predicting either Utopia or dystopia play a large role in shaping the perception and attitudes of the public to the potential of such technologies (Kitzinger and Williams, 2005). For example, the careful use of language in the media constructs a perception of embryonic stem-cell research as positive or negative. Supporters of embryo stem-cell research focus on the positive outcomes, by using phrases such as 'a new medical frontier with enormous potential' and 'relief of human suffering'. Opponents of stem-cell research envision 'a dangerous and slippery path' that will 'open the floodgates' to a troubling future (ibid).

Never before have humans been able to control the future of their species to such a degree. This is a social issue—manipulating genetic code not only changes how the individual develops, but also alters the human gene pool permanently. Results could extend to parents controlling the sex and racial characteristics of their unborn children, or the ways in which genetically altered individuals interact with non-altered people. Health issues may involve redefinitions of illness and disability to include such characteristics as height, body type, skin colour, and clarity of vision. Controlling for some characteristics may create unforeseen imbalances or other unanticipated changes.

The Problem of Aging

We mentioned earlier that two kinds of forecasting are particularly common: forecasting based on changes in technology and forecasting based on changes in demography, or population structure. Changes in demography—for example, in the age composition of a society—are important because people of different ages behave differently. They buy different kinds of products, lead different lifestyles, and vote for different candidates. Age—along with sex and education—is one of the most reliable predictors of behaviour, for reasons explored previously.

The aging of the Canadian population is a result mainly of continued drops in fertility and, secondarily, of increased longevity. Whether younger generations can continue to support an aging population and whether the health-care system can cope with demands for better care for everyone remains to be seen (Raphael, 2009). How society deals with an aging population will decide future social problems associated with ageism in Canada.

Several possibilities present themselves. First, the child-bearing population could be encouraged to increase the number of children produced. This policy would likely generate only marginal effects given continuing declines over the past century, as well as socioeconomic values (such as individualism and family economics) and opportunities (such as urban careers) that work against large family sizes. Second, Canada's immigration laws could be changed to allow more young immigrants from countries with high fertility. Such a policy, however, would not be likely to win support from Canadians currently in the workforce, who would see it as increasing competition for jobs. Third, a larger portion of the national budget could be invested in health care.

TECHNOLOGY: MAKING AND SOLVING PROBLEMS

The key to future social life obviously is connected to the future of technology. In a sense, sociology itself emerged as part of the same knowledge revolution that gave us science and technology. Some say that it evolved alongside the new social problems arising from industrialization, urbanization, and political revolutions in France and other parts of Europe.

INTERNATIONAL COMPARISONS

Box 16.2 The Millennium Project's 'Rich Get Richer' Scenario

Throughout the twentieth century, the rising inequality of incomes within and between nations had been a matter of increasing concern. In 1997, the most prosperous group of workers in the world—the skilled workers of the industrial countries—earned on average 60 times more than the poorest group—the farmers of sub-Saharan Africa. Even on a national basis, taking account of all income and workers, the gap was huge; in terms of GDP per capita, by 2050 the difference between the richest country (the US) and the poorest region (Africa) was almost 50 to 1.

As one looks back from the vantage point of the mid-century [i.e., 2050], it's clear that there were two separate and distinct periods. At the beginning of the century, economic and social conditions in many of the poorer countries deteriorated—increasing the gap between rich and poor countries. In the last two decades, however, conditions in even the poorest countries have been improving and now exceed those of 50 years ago. In other words, through the last 50 years, the rich got richer, and recently—in the last two decades—conditions in even the poorest countries have improved.

It was the pace of change and the challenges of the early twenty-first century that caused some nations to stumble while others surged ahead. Regions of South Asia—Bangladesh and Sri Lanka; sub-Saharan Africa—Nigeria, Senegal and Rwanda; and Central and East Europe—Moldova, Romania, and the Russian Republic, fell behind because the institutional capacity within those regions was only partially effective at managing transition economies, integrating into the world economy, initiating institutional reform, and investing in human capital, human development, and quality education. Take these burdens and add overspending on military preparedness, soaring health-care costs, relief aid due to outbreaks of infectious disease while effectiveness of antibiotics was diminishing, environmental emergencies, and high unemployment. Corruption and organized crime made their unholy contributions to the chaos. Inevitably, some of these lagging nations lost credit worthiness, and foreign investment waned.

Relatively high population growth early in the century compounded their problems. Economic growth often promotes diminished birth rates, so the stagnation of economic growth may tend to make birth rates high. With high birth rates, labour forces grow—if the economy does not grow in parallel to population, jobs become precious, and political turmoil follows. Though birth rates were falling everywhere, even in Africa, the poorer countries dropped at a slower rate than their richer cousins [see Figure 16.3].

While the poorer countries in Africa and Asia ran into this plethora of problems, the richer countries experienced a period of robust GNP

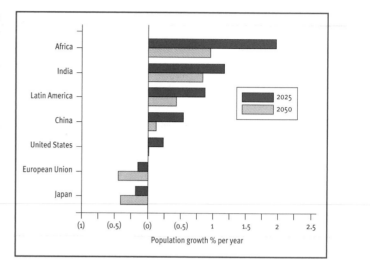

Figure 16.3 Projected Population Growth Rate: 'Rich Get Richer' Scenario

The Millennium Project's 'Rich Get Richer' scenario predicts that as economic conditions of the twenty-first century improve, population growth rates drop on a global scale.

Source: 2010 State of the Future by Jerome C. Glenn, Theodore J. Gordon, and Elizabeth Florescu, The Millennium Project. © 2009 The Millennium Project.

growth. Advancements in science led to improvements in productivity, advances in biotechnology and genetics improved agriculture, health and longevity, information technology revolutionized education and almost every industry, and new industries emerged to fuel the economic momentum. Forces for globalization worked to their benefit; their use of cheaper labour in poorer countries was welcomed by those countries because it provided needed jobs. With a few notable exceptions, their foreign investments were generally shrewd, taking advantage of local conditions and need. So, while many of the poorer countries were trapped by their own ineptitude and external circumstances, many of the richer countries achieved impressive growth. Communications technologies put the differences in living standards in bold relief and also offered tempting but elusive solutions (e.g., video-education). Nevertheless these solutions remained largely unimplemented because of low profit potential and small markets. Thus, the differences in income and living standards remained sharp: in the first two decades of the new century, the conditions in the rich countries improved while those in the poor countries deteriorated.

Source: Millennium Project (2009b).

Others place more importance on the changes associated with the Enlightenment: the rise of science, skepticism about religious belief, and a general questioning of tradition (Goldman, 2007).

Sociology—and social science more generally—arose out of a desire to explain differences and to find patterns in people's social relations, in their ways of doing things, and in their ways of living together, and the founders of sociology (as well as many sociologists today) saw their project as identifying and then providing solutions to problems in society. Some dreamed of becoming the professional managers of society just as physicians organized to become the professional arbiters of the human body. In that sense, sociology was always oriented to problem-solving: to finding better ways of living together, given the visible difficulties associated with industrialization, urbanization, poverty, political upheaval, and so on. In periods of dramatic change, such questions are motivated by a sense of urgency as well as by fascination. During the nineteenth and twentieth centuries, thinkers struggled to develop a language that could describe these new problems. Like every science, as sociology matured it spent additional time developing more precise language, theories, and methods of research. It has always developed alongside technological innovation and, today, computers are central to the sociological analysis of data.

Urban Technology

Urbanization and industrialization were main causes of the technological development from which sociology benefited. For centuries, cities have relied on sophisticated technology, for cities are built environments: humanly constructed ways of separating people from the natural environment. In the effort to improve and enlarge our built environments, innovations in various realms continue to be essential. Ask yourself what it takes to build and occupy a tall condominium, apartment, or office building—the kind of building that characterizes most cities today. Start with strong, durable, relatively lightweight, and readily available building materials and combine these with building techniques that use the materials together in easy, cheap, reliably engineered ways.

Second, the regular use of any tall building demands elevators as well as stairs, reliable heating and cooling, complex electrical wiring, and developed communication technology so people on the thirtieth floor of one building can contact people on the fiftieth floor of a building 10 km (or 10,000 km) away. There is a created need for telephones, computers, cell phones, fax machines, and so on. We are told that human messengers and snail mail are no longer good enough, which is not entirely true: large cities like New York functioned perfectly well using human messengers (and pneumatic tubes) to carry messages for more than a century before cell phones and the Internet arrived—some would say they functioned far better than today.

Technology and Toolmaking

Where did these tools and technologies come from? When and how did they make their first human appearance, and why are humans so much better at making tools than our nearest animal relatives? Likely, our first tools were sticks and stones: sticks to help us walk, to reach for high objects or fend off wild animals; stones to stun edible animals or kill our enemies (Plummer, 2004). Eventually, of course, sticks and stones became much more useful: the right, flattened stick, used with the right stone as a fulcrum, can form a lever that greatly extends the strength of the user. The invention of the lever has been incredibly important; our earliest forebears could certainly have invented it with the materials at hand. Similarly, the later invention of the wheel was far-reaching. Most of human technology prior to the twentieth century (that is, pre-electronic) was based on the use of wheels—to move heavy objects, or as toothed gears in machines or clocks (Basalla, 1988). Even today, our auto- mobiles and many other forms of transportation rely on wheels. Yet, the wheel is cognitively simple—a simple discovery, needing little prior technology. All you need do to make a wheel is to cut a slice from a cylindrical tree trunk.

In practice, however, that task is harder than it sounds. Slicing a tree trunk means you need a saw, which means you need metallurgy—a strategy for finding, refining, and crafting minerals. What is a saw but a piece of very hard metal with sharp, regular teeth? But how do you convert underground minerals into a sheet of metal that is harder than the tree trunk you are trying to cut; and how do you then shape that piece of metal to give it handles and sharp teeth? These were questions our earliest ancestors must have solved before they could make wheels and then undertake major construction or transport projects.

Of course, some would say that the greater turning point is a shift from mechanical to elec- tronic devices. Transistors are critical because they're more compact than tubes and made electronic devices more portable and convenient. But no one will deny the importance of the wheel—especially if you ride a bicycle to work, as hundreds of millions do. It seems probable that these problems were solved slowly and anonymously, building on accumu- lated knowledge over generations. Early knowledge about metal craft and other activities like wheel-making likely was passed along by word of mouth, and by example, across lifespans and between communities.

In this gradual, unheralded, and painstaking way, man the toolmaker (*homo faber*) invented his world and laid the foundations for a built environment. As anthropologist V. Gordon Childe (1936) says, 'Man made himself' through the invention of tools and tech- nologies and, in that way, created what Marx and Engels (1978 [1848]) called 'the means of production'. Each new tool further separated humanity from its animal forebears and from the natural environment. Each tool gave humanity a greater advantage over less technologic- ally advanced animals.

We can speculate that humanity enjoys a few natural advantages over other animals. One is the opposable thumb, which allows people to grasp and manipulate tools more precisely than other animals can. Another is erect posture, which gives humanity a different, less grounded, perspective on the environment and more rapid mobility: while a number of animals can outrun humans for short bursts, 'with the help of our upright stance . . . and our profuse sweating, we can outrun just about any other animal on the planet if the race extends over hours in searing midday heat' (Epstein, 2010: 56). Humanity also suffers disadvantages that made the invention of tools necessary. Relatively weak and slow over short distances, and lacking sharp teeth and claws, humans had no choice but to capitalize on their toolmaking abilities. These tools became their shields and swords, and gave them protective housing and secure food supplies; humanity could flourish.

Weapons Technology

The development of technology gave humans control over other animals; and it also gave them control over other humans. Repeatedly throughout history, superior technology has triumphed over inferior technology. Much of human history involves organized warfare, ongoing arms races involving ever bigger, better, and more deadly weapons, and strategies that use the new weapons more effectively than the old ones. The history of imperial conquest is the history of more technologically advanced nations conquering less technologically advanced nations—even though the latter nations may have other apparent advantages.

Even religious history has a military, and therefore technological, aspect: ideas have often spread on the ends of swords. Islam and Christianity did not spread around the world merely because of their spiritual merit: they also were circulated by armed zealots (for example, during the Crusades). Military concerns have been instrumental in developing tools and technology with uses in civilian life, and have also contributed significantly to improvements in medicine and health (Ponteva, 2002). Wars and technology are an integral feature of human history.

Advances in weaponry have come at an ever-faster rate in the last two centuries. In part, this is due to the increased importance of technology for warfare, industry, and global commerce. Everywhere, machines have come to supplement and even replace human labour. This rapid growth in the importance of technology was also a result of significant social and cultural change. First, it reflects capitalism's central concern with profit-making, which is often maximized by improving the mix of human labour, capital, and technology. Second, the growth of technology reflects the secular culture's concern with material improvement— with building bigger and better 'toys'—and leading more efficient, effective lives.

Technology and the Institutionalization of Science

Advances in technology—for cities, for weaponry, and for other purposes—have come about because of the scientific revolution that began in Europe 500 years ago. These advances rest on empirical, often experimental, research that obeys the 'norms of science' identified by Robert Merton as 'CUDOS' (1973 [1942]). This acronym draws out the important processes that have moved science forward: **Communalism** (the results of science are public and free for anyone to use); **Universalism** (the evaluation of scientific claims is based on universal criteria not specific to the researchers themselves); **Disinterest** (scientific knowledge is pursued and presented without hopes of personal reward or advancement); and **Organized Skepticism** (active and critical evaluation of claims; postponement of judgement until sufficient reasons for or against a claim have been presented).

The 'invention' of science represented a huge break with traditional religious thinking, and specifically between the ways science and religion carry out their inquiries. Science is a cultural and social orientation towards the search for knowledge: it focuses on the combination of empirical observation and mathematical reasoning.

Science—and therefore technology—advances largely by independent disinterested research, a public review of findings, and the application of universal criteria of judgement. And most important of all, science demands organized skepticism. Scientific claims are critically evaluated and conclusions are considered 'tentative', awaiting disproof. Without scientific norms and the social institutions (like peer review) that enforce them, technological advances would have been slow, gradual, and haphazard. In Canada, many complain of too little technological advancement, due to a relative absence of research and development work here; but compared to pre-industrial societies technology has always been a force for Canadian development.

Besides the rise of science and cities, no other social change has so transformed modern life as the development of industry and industrial working classes, a consequence of *industrial technology*. 'Classes' in sociological thinking are groups of people who share a common economic condition, interest, or, as Marx and Engels described it, relationship to the means of production. In turn, the means of production are, precisely, the combination of technology and capital. It is technology's potential to increase profitability, to improve control over labour, and even to permit the low-cost replacement of human labour that makes it both a friend and enemy of modern humanity.

The relationship of people to the means of production separates those who must sell their work, their time, or their labour to earn wages so they can survive from those who buy this work and gain profits from the goods and services that workers produce. The profit gained by the second group depends mainly on the price of the manufactured product minus the cost of labour. As a result, profit-making depends on keeping prices high and wages (and other costs of production) low.

Some have argued that this transformation—the increased significance of technology plus capital in the productive process, and the refinement of computerized production—has created a 'knowledge society' or 'information society' (Webster, 2002). This thinking, in turn, has largely transformed the ways we try to educate people for labour force participation. However, because of the greater significance of technology, many people today may be over-educated for the work they are doing (Dolton and Vignoles, 2000). Some might say that our society values conformity and consumerism above all else. Capital and technology are still important: the rest of learning and production is window dressing.

THE SOCIAL EFFECTS OF TECHNOLOGY

With the aid of technology, we have separated ourselves from nature and, most of the time, we view nature through the windows of our home, office, or car. We live inside all the secure luxury we can afford and technology can provide. Occasionally, we spend time at a cottage or camping 'in the wild' but we always return to the material environment our ancestors so gradually and painstakingly built for us. After all, it is only within this secure environment that we can carry out the 'higher' tasks that set humanity apart from raccoons, squirrels, skunks, and other animal species: activities that include reading or writing sociology textbooks, listening to the music of Beethoven, watching television, and pondering current events.

In what sense are these uniquely human activities 'higher'? That is a hard question to answer. However, two things are apparent. First, technology has set humanity socially and culturally apart from the rest of the natural world, and it has built a unique material stage for this uniquely human drama. On the other hand, it has given humanity a huge capacity for good and evil. Consider an example of a new technological evil: online bullying carried out by clique members is a new phenomenon and potentially just as damaging as the bullying that occurs face-to-face (Kowalski and Limber, 2007). With 'e-bullying', youth can constantly harass their victims over the Internet, through instant text messaging on cell phones and postings on bulletin boards and on their blogs. Thanks to technology, which makes more pervasive and unrelenting forms of bullying possible, victims are always within reach.

Consider another example of technological evil. Cultural parochialism has for centuries allowed 'developed societies' to use highly developed technology—especially, weaponry—to overwhelm less powerful, 'less advanced' societies. Modern warfare relies on unemotional killing and advanced technology. Because of advances in military technology, the modern weapons used in combat are exponentially more deadly than ever before. A single precision-guided missile released by a B-52 bomber many thousands of feet above a war zone can kill hundreds of enemy soldiers and civilians. The nuclear bomb dropped on Hiroshima more than 65 years ago in the last days of World War II is estimated to have killed 80,000 people instantly. The potential for mass destruction has grown exponentially since then.

The 'have-nots' have retaliated with terrorist threats, which have increased in developed societies. Western governments have recently made many efforts to safeguard their citizens against terrorist attacks. These measures involve tightening domestic security, sometimes at the expense of civil liberties (Gould, 2002). However, vigilance—even when combined with highly advanced technology—cannot solve what is finally a social and political problem. Improved technologies are no guarantee against future terrorist strikes or criminal sabotage. No amount of enhanced detection and counterterrorism can fully secure a country against attack.

What this means is that we must address the underlying motives of terrorists, because we cannot control their opportunities. Without understanding and changing motivation, no war against terrorism can succeed. Preventing future attacks will mean considering the historical, political, economic, and other factors that lead normal humans to see mass terror as proper and death by martyrdom as appealing.

Technology, Families, and Communities

Researchers disagree about the overall effect of information technology (IT) on family and community life. On the one hand, increased connectedness makes it easier to contact friends, neighbours, acquaintances, spouses, children, parents, and siblings—relations can be maintained even from a distance. On the other hand, the new connectedness may intrude on traditional family life, disturbing rituals and cohesion. Computers and other IT (for example, PSP) can isolate families, individuate family members across generations, separate them from one another in individual activities, and lead to addictive behaviour. Some researchers argue that extensive Internet use increases the risk of depression and loneliness by isolating the user from sources of support and sociability (Morrison and Gore, 2010). It seems clear that communication technologies will have unpredictable effects, at least for a while.

The effects of technology on intimacy seem to depend on the *type* of close relationship (Baym et al., 2004). Among strongly tied (that is, closely related) people, easy and relatively cheap technologies such as e-mail do not replace traditional communication media like face-to-face meetings or telephone calls. Closely related communicators use new as well as old technologies and communicate frequently. More communication (and more varied communication) strengthens a relationship. By contrast, weakly tied communicators rely on one medium and are less motivated to explore new technologies. Their relationships remain distant as a result.

Over the last 150 years, changes in communications and transport technologies have made contact among kin and friends, whether they live near to one another or great distances apart, less expensive, faster, and easier. As e-mail and Internet use increases, geographic constraints on social relationships decrease. Changes in technology that simplify contact among family and friends are likely to contribute to the quality and cohesion of relationships. The

The Canadian Press/AP Photo/Lee Jin-man

A South Korean consultant, left, asks students to record how many hours they use the Internet a day, during a special session for Internet addiction prevention at their school in Seoul, South Korea.

spread of easy communication shrinks distances, and we can expect this shrinking of distance to continue. Yet despite the constant changes in the technological context of social relationships, most social theory continues to assume that people will form and preserve close relationships mainly through face-to-face interaction.

One strategy for studying cross-national and cross-regional relations is to examine how technology has affected close relations in the past. New technologies rapidly traverse traditional social barriers and achieve wide adoption. Consider the history of two important communication technologies: the telephone and e-mail.

In the beginning, telephones were used mainly for long-distance calling. Commercial interests advertised the telephone as a means to link family and friends; women were shown in advertisements using it for 'kin-keeping'. The telephone improved communication: people expressed their views in their own voices, it was simple to use, and (once the private line replaced the party line) was as private as face-to-face communication. As a result, the telephone was widely adopted and used to preserve close relations, even at a distance. People quickly became dependent on this new communication instrument.

Surprisingly, the effects of the telephone on social life have been modest. There is no systematic evidence that the telephone has changed close relations. At most, the telephone helped them by keeping people in touch between face-to-face meetings.

Some of the advantages of e-mail are similar to those of the telephone. However, e-mail is not as disruptive as the telephone, nor is it dependent on both people being available at the same time. Because e-mail is written and involves computer technology and some literacy, it is not quite as simple or inexpensive to use as the telephone. Beyond that, e-mail carries a variety of dangers of its own. Faceless anonymity poses the risk of indiscretion, misunderstanding, misquoting, wide dissemination of material intended to be private, and invasion of privacy. The shield of visual and vocal anonymity may encourage blunt disclosure and misrepresentation. As well, people are more likely to express themselves intemperately and thoughtlessly through e-mail and text-messaging.

Still, the lack of temporal and spatial boundaries associated with telephone and e-mail frees relationships and makes new relationships possible. It also makes relationships with online communicators possible for people formerly prevented from socializing—for example, people housebound by illness or child care. The proven effects of e-mail on social life have been modest so far. However, the telephone and e-mail certainly have made cross-regional, cross-national, and cross-empire communication easier than ever before.

Technology and Mass Communication

Today, business success depends on finding and persuading the largest possible number of consumers. Likewise, political success depends on finding and persuading the largest possible number of voters. Finding and *rapidly* persuading large numbers of people relies on technology that simply wasn't available much more than a century ago. The radio, invented just over a century ago, really only came into widespread popular use 80 or 90 years ago. Modern mass communication—television, movie DVDs, and the Internet, for example—

are much more recent than that. So, we have to realize that the modern mass media have changed human life dramatically since the birth of our great-grandparents.

Mass communication is the communication of a message from a single source to multiple recipients who receive the message at the same time. This kind of all-at-once communication is only possible using the technology that we call 'mass media', a collection of tools including the printing press, the radio, television, the photocopier, and the camera. All of these, individually or working together, can reproduce and disseminate thousands, even millions, of copies of one original message.

The age of mass media began with the invention of the printing press around 1447 by German goldsmith and inventor Johannes Gutenberg (1398–1468). With his use of movable type, Gutenberg changed the world. By 1500 his printing technology had spread throughout Europe; in a very short space of time, ordinary people were reading the first widely distributed reading matter—the Holy Bible. The effects within the Church were revolutionary; then, in society more broadly. Since then, we have come to associate civilization with literacy, and modernity with the media. Today, communications technology is central to our culture, politics, and society.

Because of their capacity to reach millions, nothing in society is so integrative, *in principle*, as the media and the information that they carry. If anything can help us live together well, surely it is the mass media. After all, television, radio, movies, newspapers, magazines, CDs, DVDs—all are dedicated to serving society at large. However, in practice, the media can also be disintegrative. The messages that the media convey do not always serve society well. In the end, the media are only neutral vehicles that are used in as many ethical and evil ways as humans can conceive.

Communications technology has been influenced by increasingly sophisticated marketing research in recent decades. People spend their money differently, although certain commonalities are visible. Items that were once considered to be luxuries are now necessities. The mass media have played a key role in the promotion of consumerism and 'neediness'. In the influence they wield over consumers, market researchers—manipulating the mass media like orchestra conductors waving batons—are 'captains of consciousness'. In the words of social historian Stuart Ewen (1976: 70), 'They mold the desires, needs, and intentions of the spending public.'

Market research has become ever more sophisticated with repeated surveys of purchasing behaviour and the development of demographic and psychographic models. The focus is on consumer spending patterns by age, income, education, and gender across multiple market sectors. The purpose is to guess who will buy SUVs, frozen meat pies, Asian-style cooking sauces, vacations in the South Pacific, and Viagra—and with what inducements.

The Internet

INFORMATION AGE A historical time—the present—in which information of all forms is quickly and easily accessible via the Internet and computers. At the same time, there is far more information than existed only a few years or decades ago, and information drives work processes to a far greater extent than in the past.

We are living today in what some have called the **Information Age**, meaning we have more information and more ideas than ever before in history (Webster, 2002). We also make more use of this information, exchanging it and transforming it into commodities. Information is a good, to be bought and sold. What's more, the increasing spread of access to information has the potential to integrate society—to help us live together better—more than ever before.

Information truly has exploded. Five centuries ago, scholars could agree on what made up the sum total of knowledge in a literate society, whether in China or in Western Europe. It was possible for someone to imagine becoming an expert in *everything*. The Renaissance scholar Erasmus has been thought of in these terms, as a 'universal' scholar; many would see Leonardo da Vinci in the same way. Even 50 years ago, scholars could still demarcate the boundaries of knowledge, that is, the boundaries of what was known and knowable. But by then the demarcated body of knowledge was far beyond the reach of a single person, so specialization was needed even within fields (for example, within chemistry, anthropology, or literature).

This idea of a body of knowledge, of what educated people should or could know, was limited by the technology of the day and by definitions of what constituted 'knowledge'. For a long time, most knowledge was spread orally and by example and preserved by human memory. Most knowledge or information (such as how to grow food, to weave fibres, or to work with metal) was transferred from person to person. Until the invention of the printing press, there was no concept of 'authorship' as we know it today. Earlier authors participated in and extended the traditional culture, taking their own ideas from older ideas and their legitimacy from older traditions. They did not seek to reject the traditional culture as part of expressing their individual insight.

The act of writing underwent a transformation. In medieval Europe, monks copied manuscripts, believed to be the word of God. The printing press changed all this by making fast, accurate copies of what had previously taken months or years to do by hand. Knowledge became an item that could be spread among strangers. Printers sought out new material. Even so, it took several centuries for authorship to gain its modern form. The concept of knowledge that could be owned as a form of property was followed by a concept of standards. Eventually, in the popular mind, a standard of information became associated with what had been printed. Printing endowed a halo of authority or credibility.

Today, we still distinguish between knowledge producers and knowledge consumers. *Producers* are people who are seen as 'experts' and who can get their works into print. *Consumers*, by contrast, are people who use the knowledge produced in these ways. They buy 'how-to' books. They go to school and college to gain knowledge, and from there to the world of work. In the workplace, at least in theory, they use this knowledge. Often they may find that they need more knowledge and information. However, the Internet has been altering this link between consumers, producers, and knowledge. Indeed, the Internet has changed the whole way we produce information and understand the concept of knowledge; in short, it changes the relations of its production. At the same time, a wide **digital divide** exists between wealthy and poor countries, as well as between the rich and poor within countries. By 2008, an estimated 84 per cent of Canadians were using the Internet—internetworldstats.com provides comparisons: 73 per cent of Americans and 19 per cent of the rest of the world. The growth of Internet use has increased in Canada by 121 per cent since the year 2000. Most important, many of these Internet users are both information consumers *and* information producers.

DIGITAL DIVIDE The separation between those who have access to electronic technology and the Internet ('haves') and those who do not ('have-nots').

Many would argue for a distinction between the great knowledge producers of the past—for example, philosophers, writers, and scientists—and the casual, often misguided bloggers of today. Certainly much of what passes for 'information' on the Internet is dither, bluster, hot air, false, and misinformation, and for those who produce this to be considered producers of information (or knowledge) certainly shifts the understandings of past generations as to what constitutes information (knowledge). On the other hand, much of what passes for information on the Internet is valuable and true, though sometimes lacking a formal pedigree. And much of what passes for information in the commercial press or halls of academe is without much merit. So, perhaps our notions of knowledge are in a process of change, and we will need to develop new ways of assessing and controlling quality.

The revolutionary potential of the Internet is that it recreates information as something that is commonly shared and exchanged, not as a commodity to be owned. The Internet was described by Howard Rheingold as the *agora*, after the ancient Greek word for 'marketplace', the social space in which people walked and talked. In our contemporary terms, this information marketplace is huge; some see it as spinning out of control, impossible to map accurately, and used far beyond its original aims. The size and chaos of the Internet is indeed worrisome from some standpoints. Without quality checks and quality controls, we are at risk of something that we may call 'mind pollution' whenever we set foot in cyberspace.

CYBERSPACE The abstract concept of 'where' computer-stored information is exchanged.

However, the upside of cyberspace is that it gives ordinary people the chance to return to being producers or creators, rather than only consumers. Indeed, of today's Internet users, nearly half are estimated to contribute actively to *content* rather than just reading. Some of the material contributed in this way is ill-informed and ridiculous, but much of it is no worse than the material supplied by professional journalists and spin doctors, and some is contributed by educated people and by academics.

Another important aspect of the electronic agora is that it is made up of people who have probably never met each other face to face, yet share beliefs and ideologies, give one another support, and regularly exchange ideas. The result is a creation of worldwide virtual communities: communities of interest and shared viewpoint, unhampered by distance and many of the social factors (age, race, gender, class) that often keep otherwise similar people from meeting or interacting with one another.

Problems of Information Anarchy

The Internet is somewhat anarchic. There is no centralized control, including quality control, but many believe this decentralization is both good and healthy. If access to the Internet is free and open, anyone can post what he/she wants. Freedom leaves scope for new ideas to surface. But it also leaves scope for hate literature, obscenity, and pornography, plus an immense amount of sludge. Many wonder how the Internet community can control the latter without limiting free speech.

Some Internet providers have tried voluntary controls, asking that people not post offensive material on their sites. This does seem to work, to an extent. However, there have also been campaigns to censor whole categories of material, and some countries have even gone beyond this. China, for example, completely controls Internet access in and out of the country through gateways with the complicit involvement of international conglomerates. The US has tried several methods of state censorship. Some of these have been struck down. There have been challenges and counterchallenges related to spam and to free access of legal minors. It seems clear that any censorship of the Internet has the potential to prevent important ideas from being openly debated. In an **information economy**, this amounts to societal suicide.

And too much control also poses political dangers. Without vigilance by users, the Internet could be transformed from an anarchic network of information providers and communicators to a means of political surveillance. Already authorities have the potential to track the messages and website addresses of individual users, and in some countries are already doing so. The threat here is that the Internet could become a **Panopticon**: the all-seeing eye that allows those in authority to oversee people's actions, thoughts, and communications. Some Internet users are campaigning on issues of privacy and security of information, including the information they pass on when they connect to any site.

Internet communication is changing society, and it is also changing the mass media. There is no room for the traditional media to be complacent when not-for-profit information producers are making available material that is (sometimes) more entertaining, informative, honest, and insightful—for free. True, a lot of the material in cyberspace is illiterate rubbish, but at least it is (usually) honest rubbish. Will the Internet remain a free marketplace? Or will it become a forum that is ultimately controlled by a larger power, and where startling or sensitive material is excluded to protect vulnerable members of society?

Internet issues throw into clear relief the abstract issues of rights to intellectual property, liberty versus authority, geographic community versus virtual community, and technology-in-theory versus technology-in-social-use. We are faced with resolving issues democratically that, before the rise of the Internet, were mainly of theoretical interest.

Of all the changes bearing on the future of societies, and on the future of social problems, none is likely to have more impact than cyberspace and the information that resides there. In that sense, in shaping social problems of the twenty-first century, nothing will be more real in its effect than virtual reality. An information economy such as ours invests in information as a major source of wealth and power, and more and more information is coming to reside in cyberspace at little cost to the consumer.

CHAPTER SUMMARY

Knowledge is, to an important extent, empowering. Wrong information, in the form of stereotypes and **rumours**, can produce a great deal of social harm. Good information, in the form of science and technology, can shape society for the better.

One of our jobs as educated people is to learn the difference between fact and fantasy. It is our job as sociologists to learn how to understand and, if possible, control the creation of fantasy, in the belief that understanding public issues is better than not understanding them. Armed with a greater understanding of the social problems we face, we can pursue solutions

INFORMATION ECONOMY An economy in which information is treated like any other commodity and can be bought, sold, traded, and so on.

PANOPTICON An all-seeing eye of authority, as proposed architecturally for maximum prison surveillance by the English utilitarian social philosopher, Jeremy Bentham (1748–1832). A century and a half later the French social theorist, Michel Foucault, used Bentham's concept of the Panopticon as a metaphor for the modern-day surveillance society embodied in contemporary institutions.

RUMOURS Information diffusion in which the content is not pure misinformation but is conceived for a purpose with limited reliability. As information provided to solve an ill-defined problem, rumours based on stereotypes or ideal images are more likely than other rumours to gain media and popular currency and to resist denial.

through individual and collective actions. Individual solutions are easier to achieve, but in the end, collective solutions are the only road to long-lasting changes.

As this book has shown, there are a few master problems—in particular, inequality and exclusion, ignorance and misinformation—and they play out in many combinations and historical variations. Our future, as a species, will depend on our ability to understand and mitigate the more harmful versions of these problems. Cyberspace, in particular, offers us various exciting, challenging, and dangerous opportunities: to create communities that have no visible location, to participate in events almost instantaneously, to observe human life in every part of the world. Cyberspace reduces some constraints of space and time sharply; in doing so, it plunges us into a larger, more crowded pond than we have ever known. Can we face the challenge?

As with all technological advancement in the last two centuries, the development of cyberspace makes possible both a more egalitarian society and a more totalitarian society; we can cure our deadly diseases and create new ones; we can tell each other more truths and more lies—more quickly (and persuasively) than ever before. How we will survive this ordeal by information remains to be seen.

Nothing shows more clearly than cyberspace the opportunities and dangers that face humanity when new information technology produces 'new societies' without tradition or regulation. Nothing shows more clearly than futures studies the desire of humanity to imagine and, through imagination, to shape the future. Like our colleagues in the past, we must continue to imagine and struggle to create a new society.

QUESTIONS FOR CRITICAL THOUGHT

1. Can you think of a social problem (one not in the text) that will not likely be solved in the near future? Why will this be so? Can you think of one that will not be an issue in the near future? Why will it not be?

2. Future predictions are often used to determine several possible alternative futures. What are some alternative futures regarding the social issues surrounding environmental damage?

3. How has the advent of the Internet affected your life? Do you find that you have more or less information available to you? Is this information easier or harder to locate? Has its quality improved or decreased?

4. The rate at which information spreads is related to its content. Consider the daily newspaper versus tabloids. How many people, for example, know the reasons for the conflict in the Middle East compared with those who are up to date on who is dating whom in Hollywood? Can you think of any other current examples?

RECOMMENDED READINGS

Birenbaum-Carmeli, Daphna, Yoram S. Carmeli, and Rina Cohen. 2000. 'Our First "IVF Baby": Israel and Canada's Press Coverage of Procreative Technology', *International Journal of Sociology and Social Policy* 20, 7: 1–38. This article compares the Israeli and Canadian responses to IVF technologies. Using the news coverage in each country, the authors cite the difference in the two nations' cultures as an explanation of their differing levels of enthusiasm regarding IVF technology—Israeli enthusiasm is much greater, given that country's more strongly pronatalist culture.

Chappell, Neena L., and Margaret J. Penning. 2001. 'Sociology of Aging in Canada: Issues for the Millennium', *Canadian Journal on Aging* 20 (suppl.): 82–110. As Canada's population ages, one critical question is how Canadian society can cope with the new strains on our health-care system and family relations.

Cooper, Crystale Purvis, and Darcie Yukimua. 2002. 'Science Writers' Reactions to a Medical "Breakthrough" Story', *Social Science and Medicine* 54: 1887–96. After a New York Times story boosted the hopes of cancer patients, 60 science writers from the United States, Canada, and Great Britain posted e-mail messages to the discussion list of the National Association of Science Writers over a period of 12 days in a discussion on the issue of news coverage of medical 'breakthroughs'. The article analyzes these messages and finds suggestions for news coverage in the future.

Dator, Jim. 1993. 'Futures Studies and Sustainable Community Development', paper presented at the First World Futures-Creating Seminar, Renewing Community as Sustainable Global Village, Aug., Goshiki-cho, Japan. At: www.soc.hawaii.edu/future/dator.html. One of the creators of educational television in Ontario (TVOntario), Jim Dator founded the Hawaii Research Center for Futures Studies at the University of Hawaii and served as president of the World Futures Studies Federation. His long list of books and papers includes recent works on environmental and sustainability issues.

Galtung, Johan, and Sohail Inayatullah. 1997. *Macrohistory and Macrohistorians: Perspectives on Individual, Social, and Civilizational Change*. Westport, CT: Praeger. The essays in this volume focus on historians—from Ibn Khaldhun to Oswald Spengler and from Pitrim Sorokin to Arnold Toynbee—who have helped shape our way of conceiving of ourselves.

Inayatullah, Sohail, and Susan Leggett, eds. 2002. *Transforming Communication: Technology, Sustainability and Future Generation*. Westport, CT: Praeger. The contributors argue that to create sustainable futures, new ways must be found to make communication inclusive, participatory, and mindful of future generations.

Slaughter, Richard. 1999. 'A New Framework for Environmental Scanning', *Foresight: The Journal of Futures Studies, Strategic Thinking and Policy* 1, 5. At: members.ams.chello.nl/f.visser3/wilber/slaughter2.html. Current president of the World Futures Studies Federation, director and foundation professor of foresight at the Australian Foresight Institute at Swinburne University, Slaughter has been primarily interested in questions of methodology, that is, how we can know the future and how we can shape it.

RECOMMENDED WEBSITES

Environment Canada

www.ec.gc.ca

This government website offers information on current environmental issues in Canada and abroad. There are links to various programs for Canadians that can help with the environment.

Greenpeace

www.greenpeace.ca

Greenpeace is an activist organization that operates to preserve the earth's natural environment. Along with causes Greenpeace works on, this website has information about current environmental issues and discussion of their effects in the future.

NASA

www.nasa.gov

The National Aeronautics and Space Administration in the US, in addition to space exploration, also researches a wide variety of up-and-coming technologies.

World Health Organization

www.who.int

The World Health Organization is the health agency of the United Nations. It aims to achieve the highest level of health for people around the world. The site contains information about current and future health issues around the world.

World Bank

www.worldbank.org

A supporter of globalization, the World Bank helps poor and developing countries fight poverty and establish economic stability and growth based on the neo-liberal belief in free markets and private enterprise. The World Bank website has readings, statistics, and general information about globalization.

Glossary

Absolute poverty   Lack of the basic necessities (food, shelter, medicine) for basic survival. Starvation is an example of absolute poverty.

Addiction   Socially disapproved behaviour that is uncontrollable, repetitious, and possibly harmful.

Ageism   Prejudice or discrimination, mostly against seniors, but by implication against any member of society, based on their age.

Age pyramid   A graphic depiction of the age composition of a population, broken down by age and sex; pyramid-shaped if the birth rate is high but otherwise more rectangular.

Alienation   This experience involves feelings of powerlessness, meaninglessness, normlessness, estrangement, and social isolation in the workplace.

Ascribed statuses   Statuses assigned to individuals because of certain traits beyond their control.

Aversive racists   Those who sympathize with the victims of past injustice and support public policies that promote racial equality but who, nonetheless, hold prejudicial views towards other races.

Biomedical view of medicine   A medical perspective that emphasizes Western scientific principles, defines health as the absence of illness, views the human body as a machine that sometimes requires repair, and promotes the use of therapeutic intervention (e.g., drugs, surgery) to 'cure' disease and injury.

Biopsychosocial view of health and illness   A medical perspective that considers health and disease as products of the interaction between body, mind, and environment.

Bisexual   Someone who is sexually attracted to people of both the same and opposite sexes. However, the attraction to both sexes does not need to be equal in strength.

Body burden   A buildup of harmful synthetic chemicals and heavy metals in our bodies.

Body mass index (BMI)   Weight in kilograms divided by the square of height in metres (kg/m^2); 'overweight' is defined as 25 kg/m^2 and 'obesity' as 30 kg/m^2.

Bullying   Any form of repeated aggression marked by an observable power differential between individuals.

Bureaucracy   A large, complex organization employing highly specialized workers who work within the context of what Max Weber called a legal-rational authority structure.

Capitalism   The economic system in which private individuals or corporate groups own the means of production and distribution. Capitalists invest capital to produce goods and services, which they sell for profit in a competitive free market.

Chain migration   The successful migration of one family member creates a chain for the kin and community network. Migration is not random but is increasingly about networks, rational choices, and kinship relations.

Claims-making   The promotion of a particular moral vision of social life and, thus, anything people do to propagate a view of who or what is a problem and what should be done about it.

Climate change   A departure from expected patterns of temperature and other climatic properties resulting mainly from an accumulation of greenhouse gases in the atmosphere, trapping the heat reflected off the earth's surface.

Collective violence   Often organized by a group of individuals or a social movement, this type of violence is used to promote an agenda or to resist an oppressive other.

Co-morbidity   The predisposition of an individual with an illness to additional health conditions.

Conflict theory   A theoretical paradigm, derived from the writings of Marx and Engels, that emphasizes conflict and change as the regular and permanent features of society; a macrosociological research approach that focuses on processes within the whole society.

Conventional crimes   The traditionally illegal behaviours that most people think of as 'crime'. For example, homicide and sexual assault are given the most media coverage but account for only 12 per cent of all crimes.

Cornucopian view of nature   Nature is seen as an almost endless storehouse of resources that exist only for use by humans, especially by those currently living.

Credential inflation   The tendency of schools to provide and employers to demand ever-more schooling and ever-higher credentials for work that is no more demanding or complex.

Credentialism   A process of social selection that gives class advantage and social status to people who possess academic advantage.

Crime   Any behaviour that, in a given time and place, is prohibited by applicable statutory law. When a law is violated, a crime is said to have been committed.

Culture   The way of life of a society that includes dress, language, norms of behaviour, foods, tools, beliefs, and folklore. This framework of values and practices adapts to the changing socio-historical context.

Culture of poverty   Theory developed by Oscar Lewis characterizing the urban poor as having a distinct set of values and norms, including short-sightedness, impulsiveness, and a tendency to accept their marginalized status in society, and as remaining poor because they pass on these values to future generations.

Cyber-bullying   A technological extension of physical bullying occurring when an individual uses information technology (IT) to embarrass, harass, intimidate, or threaten others.

Cyberspace   The abstract concept of 'where' computer-stored information is exchanged.

Cyberterrorism   A technological and electronic attack on the enemy's technology and communications infrastructure, e.g., targeted 'virus' and 'worm' programs that collapse normal computer programming.

Demographic transition   Shift in a population or society through a series of stages from high birth and death rates to low birth and death rates.

Deterrence   A justice system based on deterrence assumes that crimes are rational acts in which the offender weighs the perceived benefits of committing the crime against the probability of being caught and the severity of the punishment. It assumes that the probability of being punished is high and that the law enforcement agencies are competent and efficient in apprehending offenders.

Diaspora   The dispersal of any group of people throughout the world; originally applied to the tribes of Israel. Almost any migrant community with some degree of international heritage is referred to as diasporic.

Differential socialization   The processes whereby individuals learn to behave in accordance with prevailing standards of culture or gender. For example, boys and men learn to be less inhibited in using aggressive and violent actions, and this may account for the disproportionate number of males involved in criminal activity.

Digital divide   The separation between those who have access to electronic technology and the Internet ('haves') and those who do not ('have-nots').

Discouraged workers   Those people who are not actively seeking employment. Specifically, they are thought to have turned their backs on the traditional work system and to have abandoned any desire to be gainfully employed.

Discriminatory unemployment   Unemployment resulting from discrimination against particular groups, such as ethnic minorities and women.

Disengagement theory   A theory that as people age, they voluntarily and normally remove themselves from activities and social contacts, to ease their passage into a less active lifestyle.

Double shift   Modern women's dual roles as breadwinner and homemaker.

Drug   Any substance that causes a biochemical reaction in the body.

Drug abuse   This concept begins with the notion of excessive or inappropriate drug use resulting in social, psychological, and/or physiological impairments. It stems from a chronic physical and psychological compulsion to continue taking a drug in order to avoid unpleasant withdrawal symptoms.

Drug dependency   The routine need for a drug for physiological and/or psychological reasons.

Drug subculture   A group of people who share common attitudes, beliefs, and behaviours surrounding drug use. These attitudes and beliefs differ significantly from those of most people in the wider society.

Economic inequality   Large differences in income and wealth across individuals and groups within a society; differences in the economic power of nations.

Entrance status   The status granted to an individual upon official entry into Canada. Statuses may be temporary (visitor visa, student authorization, live-in caregiver) or permanent (independent, professional, or skilled worker class).

Environmental racism   A type of discrimination that results in the concentration of poor racial minorities in densely packed, poorly served urban neighbourhoods, often with greater levels of pollution and located near waste dumps and heavy industry.

Epidemiology   An applied science that examines the causes, distribution, and control of disease in a population.

Extended family   More than two generations of relatives living together in a household. The arrangement often includes grandparents, aunts, uncles, and dependent nephews and nieces.

Extrinsic rewards   When work rewards the worker with money, prestige, respect, and social recognition.

Family   A group of people related by kinship or similar close ties in which the adults assume responsibility for the care and upbringing of their natural or adopted children. Members of a family support one another financially, materially, and emotionally.

Femininity   A socially constructed idea of how girls and women should act, or the various qualities that people expect to find in a typical female.

Feminization of poverty   Women are clearly over-represented among the impoverished people of the world. In the West, economic liberalization and the dominance of the market have meant that those with the least earning power—single mothers with children—have suffered most.

Filial responsibility   The sense of personal obligation or duty that adult children often feel for protecting, caring for, and supporting their aging parents; filial piety.

Futures studies   The area of research concerned with forecasting possible scenarios—technological, economic, political, social, environmental—in order to prepare for and shape what may come.

Gemeinschaft   Social situations in which those involved treat one another as ends rather than as means; primary relationships based on sentiment, found most often in rural life.

Gender   A social division referring to the social and psychosocial attributes by which humans are categorized as 'male' or 'female'. Biology is deemed somewhat irrelevant to understanding social distinctions between males and females. Gender encompasses the shared understandings of how women and men, girls and boys, should look and act. It is a label that subsumes a large assortment of traits, beliefs, values, and mannerisms, and defines how we should practise social interactions.

Gender inequality   The differential success of men and women in gaining access to valued rewards. This tends to stem from structural arrangements, interpersonal discrimination, and cultural beliefs.

Gender roles   The patterns of behaviour that a society expects of males and females and that all members of the society learn, to a greater or lesser extent, as part of the socialization process.

Gender socialization   The process by which people learn their gender-based behaviour. The socialization process links gender to personal identity in the form of gender identity and to distinctive activities in the form of gender roles. The major agents of socialization all serve to reinforce cultural definitions of masculinity and femininity.

Genetic manipulation   The altering of genes to produce a more desired physical trait.

Genocide   The deliberate, systematic, and planned killing of an entire national, ethnic, racial, or political group.

Gentrification   The restoration and upgrading of deteriorated urban property by middle-class or affluent people, often resulting in displacement of lower-income people.

Gesellschaft   Social situations in which those involved treat one another as means rather than as ends; secondary relations based primarily on calculation and individual interest, found most often in city life.

Glass ceiling   Women can have considerable success, but only up to the point of reaching top-level positions. For women at high levels of achievement, further advancement becomes especially difficult.

Globalization   The integration on a world scale of economic activities and peoples by units of private capital and improved communications technology and transportation. In other words, globalization is the trend of increasing interdependence between the economies and societies of the world.

Greenwashing   The process of promoting false ideas about the environmental friendliness of certain commercial products.

Growth ethic   A cultural or subcultural commitment to the idea that economic growth is good in itself, whatever its social effects.

Health   'A state of complete physical, mental, and social well-being' (WHO).

Heterosexism   Discrimination against homosexuals in favour of heterosexuals.

Homicide   The killing of a human being by another, directly or indirectly, by any means; includes murder, i.e., the unlawful killing of another human being with malicious intent, and manslaughter, the unlawful killing of another person without sufficient intent to constitute murder.

Homophobia   Fear or hatred of homosexuals, or behaviour that suggests such fear or hatred.

Homosexuality   Sexual attraction to people of the same sex.

Human Development Index (HDI)   A combined measure of achievement in three basic areas of human development—life expectancy at birth; literacy; and GDP per capita—used by the United Nations Development Program to monitor social and economic progress across countries.

Ideology   A system of beliefs that explains how society is, or should be; any system of ideas underlying and informing political action. In a Marxist sense, ideological ideas justify and legitimate subordination of one group to another.

Imperialism   The exercise of political and economic control by one state over the territory of another, often by military means. Developing countries are often the focus of imperialistic and exploitive activities that stifle their own development and concentrate their resources and labour for the profits of advanced capitalist countries.

Individualism   Belief in the primary importance of the individual and the need to protect individual liberty and choice against collective social or governmental restriction.

Individual racism   'Classic' form of prejudice in which a person makes unfounded assumptions about the motives and abilities of others based on a stereotypical understanding of the person's racial or ethnic group characteristics.

Infant mortality rate   Number of deaths of children under one year of age per 1,000 live births.

Information Age   A historical time—the present—in which information of all forms is quickly and easily accessible via the Internet and computers. At the same time, there is far more information than existed only a few years or decades ago, and information drives work processes to a far greater extent than in the past.

Information economy   An economy in which information is treated like any other commodity and can be bought, sold, traded, and so on.

Institutional completeness   A measure of the degree to which an immigrant ethnic group gives its own members the services they need through its own institutions.

Institutional (structural) racism   Any form of racism that occurs specifically from within an institution, such as public government bodies and private business corporations. This form of racism is considered to be 'built into' these prominent structures.

Internalized racism   When members of an ethnic or racial group accept and behave according to imposed stereotypes.

Interpersonal violence   Violent interactions occurring between individuals, such as murder, rape, and domestic and child abuse.

Intrinsic rewards   When work rewards the worker with the feeling of a 'job well done'.

Labelling   The process of defining and treating others as deviant. Labelling theory explores the effects of negative labels on individuals' self-conceptions and is interested in the development of a 'deviant identity'. Social reactions of condemnation and criminalization can lead actors to alter their individual characteristics and to adopt the values of their labelled identity.

Latent functions   Hidden, unstated, and sometimes unintended consequences of activities in an organization or institution.

Laws   Rules of conduct that may provide for the punishment of violators. In other words, the formal rules about what a society's members can and cannot do.

LGBTQ   Acronym for lesbian, gay, bisexual, transgendered, queer—often used to speak of the LGBTQ community.

Life expectancy   The average number of years remaining to a person at a particular age, given current age-specific mortality rates.

Low-income cut-offs (LICOs)   A formal definition used by Statistics Canada for measuring relative poverty based on the percentage of income devoted to daily necessities (food, shelter, clothing) and determined both regionally and by population (size of city or rural).

Low-income measures (LIMs)   A set of figures representing 50 per cent of the median 'adjusted family income'. Actual incomes are compared with LIMs to determine whether or not a family can be considered 'low-income'.

Manifest functions   The visible and intended goals, consequences, or effects of social structures and institutions.

Market-basket measure (MBM)   A way of measuring income and poverty in absolute, not relative, terms that was added in 2003 to Statistics Canada's methods of measuring income and poverty. It is based on an imaginary basket of market-priced goods and services and on the income needed to purchase the items in the basket. The determination of what goes into this imaginary basket, however, is subjective and tends to exclude all but the absolute essentials of bare survival.

Masculinity   A socially constructed idea of how boys and men should act; qualities that people in our society expect to find in a typical man.

Maternal mortality rate   The number of deaths of women due to complications during pregnancy, childbirth, or abortion, typically measured as deaths per year per 1,000 live births.

Mechanical solidarity   Durkheim's term for the kind of tight, homogeneous social order typical of a pre-industrial, primarily rural society.

Medicalization   The process through which behaviours are reconceived as instances of illness and are deemed no longer sinful since they are outside personal control; also, the process whereby the medical profession comes to be viewed as being relevant to an ever-widening range of traditionally non-medical aspects of life.

Medical sociology   The field of sociology that examines the social context of health, illness, and health care.

Mental disorder   A condition 'characterized by alterations in thinking, mood, or behaviour (or some combination thereof) associated with significant distress and impaired functioning over an extended period of time' (Health Canada).

Mental health   The capacity for individuals to feel, think, and act in ways that enhance the quality of daily functioning, the range and depth of social relationships, and the ability to adapt to both positive and negative life changes.

Mental illness   Clinical diagnosis of mental disorder requiring medical and/or psychotherapeutic treatment.

Meritocracy   The holding of power or authority by people selected because of their ability.

Moral entrepreneurs   Term coined to describe people who 'discover' and attempt to publicize deviant behaviours. Moral entrepreneurs are crusading reformers who are disturbed by particular types of evil they see in the world and who will not rest until something is done to correct the problem.

Moral panics   Public expressions of feeling and attitude typically based on false or exaggerated perceptions that some cultural behaviour or group of people (frequently a minority group) is dangerously deviant and poses a menace to society.

Morbidity rate   The extent of disease in a population, reported by incidence (the number of new cases in a given population during a given period) and/or its prevalence (the total number of cases of a disease in the population at a particular point in time).

Mortality rate   The death rate of a given disease or population, typically measured as deaths per year per 1,000 people.

Neighbourhood effects   Influences on people's lives that result from living in one type of neighbourhood (for example, rich versus poor, or dangerous versus safe) rather than another.

Normal accidents   A likely accident in a complex system of people and machines, resulting from the unanticipated interaction of multiple failures.

Norms   The rules and expectations of the society pertaining to appropriate behaviours under various social circumstances. Norms regulate behaviour in different situations and large-scale norm violation often is viewed as a social problem—a problem occurs when traditionally normative behaviour is violated.

Nuclear family   A family unit comprising one or two parents and any dependent children who live together in one household separate from relatives.

Objective elements   The measurable features of a negative social condition. Such a condition might include crime, poverty, or alcohol abuse and can be considered an objective reality.

Organic solidarity   Durkheim's term for the new social order of industrial society, which was based on interdependent, though not necessarily intimate, relationships.

Organized crime   A group or system of professional criminals who practise illegal activities as a way of life and whose criminal activities are co-ordinated and controlled through a hierarchical system of bosses.

Over-education   Having more education than is actually needed to successfully perform employment roles and functions.

Panopticon   An all-seeing eye of authority, as proposed architecturally for maximum prison surveillance by the English utilitarian social philosopher, Jeremy Bentham (1748–1832). A century and a half later the French social theorist, Michel Foucault, used Bentham's concept of the Panopticon as a metaphor for the modern-day surveillance society embodied in contemporary institutions.

Patriarchy   Male dominance that is justified in a society's system of values. This dominance is tied to the ideology of gender and can be found in practically every society.

Peak oil   The peak in global oil production, when the maximum rate of global petroleum extraction is reached, after which the rate of production goes into permanent decline.

Population density   The number of people who live within a geographic area, usually expressed as people per square mile or square kilometre.

Population health perspective   An approach to health that focuses on social determinants of health, and societal, preventive strategies and societal responses to health problems.

Positive checks   Part of Malthusian theory, these prevent overpopulation by increasing the death rate. They include war, famine, pestilence, and disease.

Post-materialist culture   A new cultural orientation that puts less emphasis on material consumption and class issues, and more on non-material (quality of collective life) benefits, such as environmental improvement.

Post-traumatic stress disorder (PTSD)   A form of psychological distress produced by a traumatic experience such as crime victimization, sexual assault, or military combat. Symptoms include nervousness, sleep disturbances, disruption of concentration, anxiety, depression, irrational fear, and flashbacks triggered by loud noises such as thunder or a car's backfiring.

Poverty line   Also called the human poverty index. It represents a usual standard of living and differs across countries. The definition of poverty varies by society, within societies, and also over time.

Precautionary principle   A tenet of environmentalism as it interfaces with economic development, which insists that when serious or irreversible damage could result from development, the wise and necessary decision is to not go ahead with that course of action, regardless of assumptions that technology could or will resolve any future problems or damage.

Prejudice   A hostile or aversive attitude towards a person who belongs to a particular group simply because of that person's membership in the group.

Preventive checks   In Malthusian theory, these prevent overpopulation by limiting the number or survivals of live births. They include abortion, infanticide, sexual abstinence, delayed marriage, and contraceptive technologies.

Primary labour market   High wage-paying jobs that provide chances to 'get ahead' and that offer job security.

Primary prevention   Proactive steps taken to prevent a disease from occurring.

Primogeniture   A system of inheritance in which only one child, the oldest son, inherits all of the family property on the death of his parents.

Professionalization   The process by which an occupation raises its standing by limiting the number of entrants and regulating their behaviour. When used to refer to the medical industry, the gradual process whereby physicians established autonomous control over the institution of health care and elevated their collective status in society to become authoritative judges of disease definitions and gatekeepers of medical services.

Queer   An umbrella term for anyone who does not identify as heterosexual.

Quid pro quo sexual harassment   The blatant demand by employers for sexual favours in exchange for promotion opportunities, salary increases, and preferential treatment.

Racial discrimination   'Any distinction, exclusion, restriction, or preference based on race, colour, descent, or national or ethnic origin that has the purpose or effect of nullifying or impairing the recognition, enjoyment of exercise . . . of human rights and fundamental freedoms' (Office of the High Commissioner for Human Rights, 1969).

Racialization   The tendency in a community to introduce racial distinctions into situations that can be understood and managed without such distinctions; in other words, the way social institutions impose racial identities on minorities.

Relative deprivation   The feelings and judgements of an individual or members of a group when they compare themselves to others who are better-off materially. People make judgements relative to standards or frames of reference. The feelings generated contribute to the formation of social movements.

Relative income hypothesis   Proposal that income inequality alone (as opposed to absolute deprivation) is enough to bring on various health problems, including premature mortality, within a population.

Relative poverty   Survival, but far below the general living standards of the society or social group in which the poor live; affects people's lives in dramatic ways.

Reporting relationships   Official hierarchical relationships established within a bureaucracy. These relationships are characterized by a power dynamic in which subordinate members adhere to a set of predetermined roles, processes, and functions.

Risk society   A society in which risk is increased by technological and economic developments, raising the need for more cautious awareness but, also, active risk-taking is considered a core element of economic and social progress.

Roles   The specific duties and obligations expected of those who occupy a specific social status.

Rumours   Information diffusion in which the content is not pure misinformation but is conceived for a purpose with limited reliability. As information provided to solve an ill-defined problem, rumours based on stereotypes or ideal images are more likely than other rumours to gain media and popular currency and to resist denial.

Secondary (marginal) labour market   High-turnover, lower-paying, and generally unstable employment. These jobs offer very little chance to get ahead and little job security.

Secondary victimization   Victimization that occurs through the response of institutions (e.g., police) and individuals (e.g., family members) to the victim's experience.

Self-reporting   The victim reports to authorities that a crime has occurred. This is the most direct method of measuring crime rates. However, it is not the most accurate, as changes in the crime rate reflect changes in victims' willingness to report.

Senescence   The biological aging of an organism as it lives beyond its maturity, usually accompanied by chemical and organic changes.

Sex   A biological concept that differentiates female and male. Most people are (mainly) male or (mainly) female from the moment of conception, with biological differences between the sexes that are anatomic, genetic, and hormonal.

Sexism   Discrimination and derogatory attitudes and beliefs that promote stereotyping of people because of their gender. Sexism and gender stereotyping are two problems for both men and women, and are most often experienced in institutions and social relationships.

Sexual harassment   Any unwanted physical or verbal conduct directed towards a person that is offensive or humiliating.

Sexual identity   How a person self-identifies—whether as straight, gay, lesbian, or transgendered.

Sexual orientation   One's sexual attraction to people of a specific sex.

Social bond theory   A type of control theory. A strong social bond prevents most people from succumbing to the temptation to engage in criminal activities.

Social capital   Sociologists call having larger, more varied, and more powerful interpersonal networks 'having greater social capital'.

Social causation   Common social factors that produce widespread health problems. Prime examples might include the effects of epidemics and other infectious diseases, and the effects of poverty, access to health care, and work-related health problems; related to social determinants of health.

Social constructionism   A sociological research approach that examines the ways people interact to create a shared social reality.

Social determinants of health   The complex causal relationships between various social, economic, and political factors and population health outcomes.

Social disorder   The uncertain and unpredictable condition in which rules are not obeyed. The environment is generally unsafe, and the boundaries of acceptable behaviour have broken down.

Social distance   Feelings of aloofness and inapproachability often felt between members of different social strata or of different ethnic or 'racial' origins.

Social group   A set of people, defined by formal or informal criteria of membership, who feel unified or are bound together in stable patterns of interaction.

Socialism   An alternative economic and political ideology that flourished in the nineteenth and twentieth centuries. It favours the public ownership of the means of production and distribution, and the investment of public capital in producing goods and services.

Socialization   The process by which people internalize and learn their culture, much of which occurs during childhood.

Social mobility   The movement of individuals from one social class to another during the course of one's lifetime.

Social movements   Broad social alliances of people who seek to affect or block an aspect of social change within a society. While they may be informally organized, they may in time form formal organizations such as political parties and labour unions. Examples of social movements include political movements, labour movements, the women's movement, environmental movements, and peace movements.

Social order   The prevalence of generally harmonious relationships; used synonymously with 'social organization'. This condition exists when rules are obeyed and social situations are controlled and predictable. Rules serve not only to indicate which behaviours are acceptable, but also to allow participants to anticipate the behaviour of others.

Social problem   A social condition or pattern of behaviour that is believed to warrant public concern and collective action.

Social selection   A correlation suggesting but not proving causation, because a third, unmeasured factor is involved; also known as 'adverse selectivity'.

Sociological imagination   A term used by sociologist C. Wright Mills in his 1959 book, *The Sociological Imagination*, that describes the sociologist's ability to connect seemingly impersonal and remote historical forces to the most basic incidents of an individual's life. The sociological imagination enables people to distinguish between personal troubles and public issues.

Strain (anomie) theory   Merton holds that strain is produced when social structure prevents people from achieving culturally defined goals through legitimate means, and, according to Durkheim, anomie is a condition characterized by a breakdown of norms and personal disorganization, which may lead to crime. Merton outlines various adaptive strategies: conformity, ritualism, retreatism, rebellion, and innovation. Innovation is most commonly associated with criminal activities, which include theft, robbery, tax fraud, embezzlement, and organized crime.

Structural functionalism   A theoretical paradigm emphasizing the way each part of society functions to fulfill the needs of the society as a whole; also called 'functionalism'; a macrosociological approach that focuses on the societal, as opposed to the individual, level.

Structural unemployment   Unemployment caused by social and economic factors that affect workers equally across all groups, such as corporate downsizing, capital flight (caused by corporate mergers and the move of operations to another geographic region—'runaway plants'), and the automation of work processes.

Subculture theory   This approach to the study of deviance investigates the norms that set a group apart from mainstream society. Specifically, it gives special insight into the subculture of the criminal, looking into the values and belief systems that may be conducive to delinquent and criminal action.

Subjective elements   People's evaluations of objective conditions and the processes that influence their evaluations. They include the moral labels that people apply to particular acts or situations, and the accounts they give for these acts and situations.

Suburbanization   The process by which housing spreads almost unhindered into once rural regions surrounding the city core. This greatly expands the geographic size of cities and takes out of production valuable agricultural land, and there is a noticed shift of the affluent out of the urban centre to these surrounding areas.

Suffrage movement   The central aim of many in the 'first wave' of the women's movement in the late nineteenth and early twentieth centuries was the right for women to vote in elections. With women's suffrage (i.e., voting rights), other goals—social reform, legal rights— would then be more readily attainable.

Symbolic interactionism   A theoretical paradigm that studies the process by which individuals interpret and respond to the actions of others and that conceives of society as the product of this continuous face-to-face interaction; a microsociological approach that focuses on individuals and small groups.

Symbols   Gestures, artifacts, and words that represent something else.

Technology   The manifestation of human knowledge and ingenuity applied to the solution of a problem or need; applied science.

Telehealth   The use of computer and communication technologies to facilitate health-care delivery across geographic space.

Tolerance   A symptom of repeated and frequent drug use. It refers to the decreased effectiveness of any given drug.

Tragedy of the commons   A market system based on the capitalist belief that economies work best when left alone, with each self-interested actor seeking what is personally best, and it leads to the situation where this agglomerated self-interest works against the common good by polluting, destroying, and exhausting common goods that are not owned by a single individual but are shared by all of us, such as bodies of water, the air, the land, ecosystems, and, especially, renewable resources such as fish and forests.

Transgendered   An umbrella term for any gender-variant person.

Under-five mortality rate (U5MR)   Number of deaths of children under five years of age per 1,000 live births.

Urbanization   The growth in the proportion of the population living in urbanized areas. There is also an increasing appearance in rural and small-town areas of behaviour patterns and cultural values associated with big-city life.

Vertical mosaic   Coined by John Porter, a socio-economic hierarchy in which French and English Canadians live at the top and other ethnic minorities are positioned below.

Vice crimes   Deviant behaviour that may be defined as immoral (for example, gambling, prostitution, drug trafficking). These crimes provide the greatest opportunity for organized crime.

Victimization surveys   Samples of people are asked how many times within a given time period they have been the victim of particular crimes.

War   Violent, usually armed conflict between states or people. This includes armed conflict, undeclared battles, civil conflicts, guerrilla wars, covert operations, and even terrorism. It is often argued that warfare is a culturally influenced phenomenon rather than simply biologically determined (instinctual aggressiveness). This would explain why some countries and cultures are more prone to warfare.

Well-being   A positive state of existence characterized by happiness, prosperity, and the satisfaction of basic human needs, and not simply the absence of negative conditions, such as illness or injury.

Whistle-blowers   Employees in a bureaucratic organization who bring forward valid information about wrongdoing or illegal conduct by their organization and who are often punished for doing so.

White-collar crimes   The crimes committed by white-collar workers and management in the course of their occupations. They always are distinguished from conventional criminal offences such as robbery or murder. White-collar crimes are performed in the course of normal work and usually occur in reputable organizations.

World system theory   A conception of the modern social world that views it as comprising one interlinked entity with an international division of labour unregulated by any one political structure. Developed by Immanuel Wallerstein (e.g., 1976), this theory seeks to explain the uneven pace of development in the world by looking at the unequal relations between different countries.

References

Preface

Beck, Ulrich. 1992. *Risk Society: Towards a New Modernity*, trans. Mark Ritter. London: Sage.

Foucault, Michel. 2000. *Power*, trans. Robert Hurley et al. New York: Free Press.

Chapter 1

Ajdukovic, Marina. 2008. 'Social Problems, Social Risks and Modern Social Work', *Revija Za Socijalnu Politiku* 15, 3: 395–414.

Alvarez, Rodolfo. 2001. 'The Social Problem as an Enterprise: Values as a Defining Factor', *Social Problems* 48: 3–10.

Anonymous. 1997. 'Youth Crime, Moral Panics, and the News: The Conspiracy against the Marginalized in Canada', *Social Justice* 24, 2: 165–84.

Becker, Howard. 1963. *Outsiders: Studies in the Sociology of Deviance*. New York: Free Press.

Berger, Peter L., and Thomas Luckmann. 1966. *The Social Construction of Reality: Treatise in the Sociology of Knowledge*. Garden City, NY: Anchor.

Blumer, Herbert. 1971. 'Social Problems as Collective Behavior', *Social Problems* 8, 3: 298–396.

Bockman, S. 1991. 'Interest, Ideology, and Claims-Making Activity', *Sociological Inquiry* 61, 4: 452–70.

Burr, Vivienne. 1995. 'What Is Social Constructionism?', in Burr, *An Introduction to Social Constructionism*. London: Routledge, 1–16.

Butler-Jones, David. 2009. *The Chief Public Health Officer's Report on the State of Public Health in Canada*. Ottawa: Public Health Agency of Canada, Publication no. HP2–10/2009E, 20 Oct. At: <www.phac-aspc.gc.ca/publicat/2009/cphorsphc-respcacsp/index-eng.php>.

Caan, Woody. 2009. 'Unemployment and Suicide: Is Alcohol the Missing Link?', *Lancet* 374, 9697: 1241–2.

Ding, Huiling. 2009. 'Rhetorics of Alternative Media in an Emerging Epidemic: SARS, Censorship, and Extra-Institutional Risk Communication', *Technical Communication Quarterly* 18, 4: 327–50.

Domenico, Desirae M., and Karen H. Jones. 2007. 'Adolescent Pregnancy in America: Causes and Responses', *Journal for Vocational Special Needs Education* 30, 1: 4–12.

Durkheim, Émile. 1951 [1897]. *Suicide*, trans. John A. Spaulding and George Simpson. New York: Free Press.

———. 1964 [1893]. *The Division of Labor in Society*, trans. George Simpson. New York: Free Press.

———. 1965 [1912]. *The Elementary Forms of Religious Life*, trans. Joseph Ward Swain. New York: Free Press.

Edwards, Craig. 2009. 'Changing Functions, Moral Responsibility, and Mental Illness', *Philosophy, Psychiatry & Psychology* 16, 1: 105.

Fine, Gary, and Corey Fields. 2008. 'Culture and Microsociology: The Anthill and the Veldt', *Annals, American Academy of Political and Social Science* 619, 1: 130–48.

Frank, J.W. 1995. 'Why "Population Health"?', *Canadian Journal of Public Health* 86, 3: 162–4.

Goffman, Erving. 1959. *The Presentation of Self in Everyday Life*. Garden City, NY: Doubleday-Anchor.

Hagan, John, and Bill McCarthy. 1998. *Mean Streets: Youth, Crime and Homelessness*. Cambridge: Cambridge University Press.

Human Resources and Skills Development Canada (HRSDC). 2010. 'Health—Self-rated Health'. At: <www4.hrsdc.gc.ca/.3ndic.1t.4r@-eng.jsp?iif=10>.

Krejci, Jaroslav. 1994. 'What Is Macrosociology About?', *Sociologicky Casopis* 30, 3: 317–28.

Krinsky, John. 2008. *Free Labor: Workfare and the Contested Language of Neoliberalism*. Chicago: University of Chicago Press.

McAndrew, F.T. 2009. 'The Interacting Roles of Testosterone and Challenges to Status in Human Male Aggression', *Aggression and Violent Behavior* 14, 5: 330–5.

McMullin, Julie. 2004. *Understanding Social Inequality: Intersections of Class, Age, Gender, Ethnicity, and Race in Canada*. Toronto: Oxford University Press.

Marx, Karl. 1990 [1862–3]. *Capital, Volume I*, trans. Ben Fowkes. London: Penguin.

——— and Friedrich Engels. 1998 [1848]. *The Communist Manifesto*, introduction by Martin Malia. New York: Penguin.

Mead, George Herbert. 1934. *Mind, Self, and Society from the Standpoint of a Social Behaviorist*. Chicago: University of Chicago Press.

Merton, Robert K. 1968. *Social Theory and Social Structure*. New York: Free Press.

Mills, C. Wright. 1959. *The Sociological Imagination*. New York: Oxford University Press.

Moore, Michael, Ho Ming Yuen, Nick Dunn, Mark A. Mullee, Joe Maskell, and Tony Kendrick. 2009. 'Explaining the Rise in Antidepressant Prescribing: A Descriptive Study Using the General Practice Research Database', *British Medical Journal* 339, 7727: 956–7.

Moran, Beverly. 2008. *Race and Wealth Disparities: A Multidisciplinary Discourse*. Maryland: University Press of America

Morgan, Stephen, David B. Grusky, and Gary S. Fields. 2006. *Mobility and Inequality*. Stanford, Calif.: Stanford University Press.

Raphael, Dennis. 2004. *Social Determinants of Health: Canadian Perspectives*. Toronto: Canadian Scholars' Press.

Reitz, G. Jeffrey. 2007a. 'Immigrant Employment Success in Canada, Part I: Individual and Contextual Causes', *Journal of International Migration and Integration* 8, 1: 11–36.

———. 2007b. 'Immigrant Employment Success in Canada, Part II: Understanding the Decline', *Journal of International Migration and Integration* 8, 1: 37-62.

Searle, John R. 2006. 'Reality and Social Construction: Reply to Friedman', *Anthropological Theory* 6, 1: 81–8.

Simmel, Georg. 1976. 'The Stranger', in *The Sociology of Georg Simmel*. New York: Free Press.

Staeheli, L.A. 2008. 'Political Geography: Difference, Recognition and the Contested Terrains of Political Claims-making', *Progress in Human Geography* 32, 4: 561–70.

Taft, Jessica K. 2009. 'Growing Up and Rising Up: Teenage Girl Activists and Social Movements in the Americas', *Dissertation Abstracts International, A: The Humanities and Social Sciences* 69, 09: 3747.

Tanner, Julian. 2009. 'Making Schools Safer: The Unintended Consequences of Good Intentions', *Education Canada* 49, 3: 12–25.

Tippelt, Hynek. 2009. 'Globalization, War and the Death Drive', *Mezinarodni Vztahy* 44, 2: 65–72.

Weir-Hughes, Dickon. 2009. 'President's Report', *International Journal of Nursing Terminologies and Classifications* 20, 3: 155–6.

Westcott, Emma. 2005. 'Equality of Opportunity and Inclusion', *Journal of Education for Teaching: International Research and Pedagogy* 31, 4: 273–4.

Wilkinson, Richard G., and Kate E. Pickett. 2007. 'The Problems of Relative Deprivation: Why Some Societies Do Better Than Others', *Social Science and Medicine* 65, 9: 1965–78.

Zazar, Kresimir. 2008. 'What Is Sociology?', *Revija Za Sociologiju* 39, 3: 205–9.

Chapter 2

Addison, Tony, David Hulme, and Ravi Kanbur, eds. 2009. *Poverty Dynamics: Interdisciplinary Perspectives*. New York: Oxford University Press.

Aratani, Yumiko. 2009. *Homeless Children and Youth: Causes and Consequences*. New York: National Center for Children in Poverty, Mailman School of Public Health, Columbia University.

Baron, Stephen W. 2006. 'Street Youth, Strain Theory, and Crime', *Journal of Criminal Justice* 34, 2: 209–23.

Bosma, Hans, Michael G. Marmot, Harry Hemingway, Amanda G. Nicholson, Eric Brunner, and Stephen A. Stansfield. 1997. 'Low Job Control and Risk of Coronary Heart Disease in Whitehall II (Prospective Cohort) Study', *British Medical Journal* 314: 558–65.

Bradley, Christopher, and Dennis J. Cole. 2002. 'Causal Attributions and the Significance of Self-Efficacy in Predicting Solutions to Poverty', *Sociological Focus* 35, 4: 381–96.

Braun, Denny. 1995. 'Negative Consequences to the Rise of Income Inequality', *Research in Politics and Society* 5: 3–31.

Breau, Sébastien. 2007. 'Income Inequality across Canadian Provinces in an Era of Globalization: Explaining Recent Trends', *Canadian Geographer* 51, 1: 72–90.

Calvano, Lisa. 2008. 'Multinational Corporations and Local Communities: A Critical Analysis of Conflict', *Journal of Business Ethics* 82, 4: 793–805.

Campion-Smith, Bruce. 2008. 'Senator Urges Debate on Plight of Poor', *Toronto Star*, 11 Feb. At: <www.thestar.com/news/canada/article/302350>.

Canadian Council on Social Development (CCSD). 2003. 'Aboriginal Children in Poverty in Urban Communities: Social Exclusion and the Growing Racialization of Poverty in Canada'. Available at: <www.ccsd.ca/research.htm>.

CBC News. 2007. 'Homelessness "Chronic" in Canada: Study', 26 June. At: <www.cbc.ca/canada/story/2007/06/26/shelter.html>.

Chitrakar, Roshan. 2009. *Overcoming Barriers to Girls' Education in South Asia: Deepening the Analysis*. Kathmandu, Nepal: United Nations Children's Fund.

Curry-Stevens, Ann. 2004. 'Income Security and Employment in Canada', in Dennis Raphael, ed., *Social Determinants of Health: Canadian Perspectives*. Toronto: Canadian Scholars' Press, 21–38.

Daniels, Norman, Bruce Kennedy, and Ichiro Kawachi. 2000. 'Justice Is Good for Our Health', in Daniels, Kennedy, and Kawachi, eds, *Is Inequality Bad for Our Health?* Boston: Beacon Press, 3–33.

Davis, Catherine. 2008. 'Book Review: J.M. Grimshaw, *Family Homelessness—Causes, Consequences and the Policy Response in England*', *Housing Studies* 23, 6: 943–5.

Defina, Robert H., and Kishor Thanawala. 2009. 'The Impact of Unemployment and Inequality in Canada', *Indian Journal of Economics and Business* 4: 17–26.

De Looper, Michael, ed. 2009. *Health Update*. Publication no. 7. Geneva: OECD, Jan. At: <www.oecd.org/dataoecd/63/18/43305158.pdf>.

Diekmeyer, Peter. 2001. 'Measuring Poverty', *CMA Management* 75, 9: 52–3.

Fisher, Gordon M. 1998. 'Using a Little-Known Body of Historical Knowledge: What Can the History of U.S. Poverty Lines Contribute to Present-Day Comparative Poverty Research?', paper presented at the annual meeting of the International Sociological Association.

Gallupe, Owen, and Stephen W. Baron. 2009. 'Street Youth, Relational Strain, and Drug Use', *Journal of Drug Issues* 39, 3: 523–45.

Gravelle, Hugh, and Matt Sutton. 2009. 'Income, Relative Income, and Self-Reported Health in Britain 1979–2000', *Health Economics* 18, 2: 125–45.

Hagan, John. 1994. *Crime and Disrepute*. Thousand Oaks, Calif.: Pine Forge Press.

Heflin, C.M., and J. Iceland. 2009. 'Poverty, Material Hardship, and Depression', *Social Science Quarterly* 90, 5: 1051–71.

Hills, John, Tom Sefton, and Kitty Stewart, eds. 2009. *Towards a More Equal Society? Poverty, Inequality and Public Policy since 1997*. Bristol, UK: Policy Press.

Hobsbawm, E.J. 1959. *Primitive Rebels: Studies in Archaic Forms of Social Movement in the 19th and 20th Centuries*. New York: Norton.

International Labour Organization (ILO). 2008. *ILO Action against Trafficking in Human Beings*. Rep. no. 978–92–2–121008–5. At: <www2.ilo.org/wcmsp5/groups/public/ed_norm/declaration/documents/publication/wcms_090356.pdf>.

Jones-Webb, Rhonda, Lonnie Snowden, Denise Herd, Brian Short, and Peter Hannan. 1997. 'Alcohol-Related Problems among Black, Hispanic and White Men: The Contribution of Neighborhood Poverty', *Journal of Studies on Alcohol* 58: 539–45.

Kanter, R.M. 1972. *Commitment and Community: Communes and Utopias in Sociological Perspective*. Cambridge, Mass.: Harvard University Press.

———. 1977. *Men and Women of the Corporation*. New York: Basic Books.

Kennedy, Bruce P., Ichiro Kawachi, Deborah Prothrow-Stith, Kimberly Lochner, and Vanita Gupta. 1998. 'Social Capital, Income Inequality, and Firearm Violent Crime', *Social Science and Medicine* 47, 1: 7–17.

Kirkpatrick, Sharon, and Valerie Tarasuk. 2003. 'The Relationship between Low Income and Household Food Expenditure in Canada', *Public Health and Nutrition* 6, 6: 589–97.

Lipset, Seymour Martin, James S. Coleman, and Martin A. Trow. 1963. *Union Democracy: The Internal Politics of the International Typographical Union*. New York: Simon & Schuster.

McMullin, Julie. 2004. *Understanding Social Inequality: Intersections of Class, Age, Gender, Ethnicity, and Race in Canada*. Toronto: Oxford University Press.

Marmot, M.G., M. Kogevinas, and M.A. Elston. 1987. 'Social/Economic Status and Disease', *Annual Review of Public Health* 8: 111–35.

———, M.J. Shipley, and G. Rose. 1984. 'Inequalities in Death—Specific Explanations of a General Pattern?', *Lancet* no. 1: 1003–6.

Marx, Karl, and Friedrich Engels. 1955 [1848]. *The Communist Manifesto*, trans. Samuel Moore. New York: Appleton Century Crofts.

Marzuk, Peter M., Kenneth Tardiff, Andrew C. Leon, Charles S. Hirsch, Marina Stajic, Laura Portera, and Nancy Hartwell. 1997. 'Poverty and Fatal Accidental Drug Overdoses of Cocaine and Opiates in New York City: An Ecological Study', *American Journal of Drug and Alcohol Abuse* 23: 221–8.

Merton, Robert K. 1957. *Social Theory and Social Structure*, rev. edn. New York: Free Press.

Michels, Robert. 1962 [1916]. *Political Parties: A Sociological Study of the Oligarchical Tendencies of Modern Democracy*, trans. Eden Paul and Cedar Paul. New York: Free Press.

Monsebraaten, Laurie. 2007. 'Guaranteed Income, Guaranteed Dignity', *Toronto Star*, 5 Mar. At: <www.thestar.com/news/article/188196>.

Mooney, Linda A., David Knox, Caroline Schacht, and Adie Nelson. 2001. *Understanding Social Problems*, 1st Can. edn. Scarborough, Ont.: Nelson Thompson.

Morgan, Stephen, David B. Grusky, and Gary S. Fields. 2006. *Mobility and Inequality*. Stanford, Calif.: Stanford University Press.

Myers, Cindy L. 2005. 'Talking Poverty: Power Arrangements in Poverty Discourse', *Dissertation Abstracts International, A: The Humanities and Social Sciences* 66, 3: 1186-A.

Nation, The. 2009. 'Ten Things You Need to Know to Live on the Streets', 289, 4: 8–9.

National Advisory Council on Aging. 2005. *Aging in Poverty in Canada*. At: <dsp-psd.

pwgsc.gc.ca/collection/H88-5-3-2005E. pdf>.

North, F.M., L.S. Syme, A. Feeney, M. Shipley, and M. Marmot. 1996. 'Psychosocial Work Environment and Sickness Absence among British Civil Servants: The Whitehall II Study', *American Journal of Public Health* 86: 332–40.

Pivot Legal Society. 2006. 'Report: Cracks in the Foundation'. At: <www.pivotlegal.org/ Publications/reportscitf.htm>.

Poliakova, S.V., and A.G. Reut. 2008. 'Evaluating the Impact of Social Protection Programs on Poverty in Ukraine', *Problems of Economic Transition* 51, 8: 21–6.

Porter, John. 1965. *The Vertical Mosaic.* Toronto: University of Toronto Press.

Prus, Steven G. 2007. 'Age, SES, and Health: A Population Level Analysis of Health Inequalities over the Lifecourse', *Sociology of Health and Illness* 29, 2: 275–96.

Putnam, Robert D. 2000. *Bowling Alone: The Collapse and Revival of American Community.* New York: Simon & Schuster.

Raphael, Dennis. 2004. *Social Determinants of Health: Canadian Perspectives.* Toronto: Canadian Scholars' Press.

Reese, Ellen. 2009. 'The Failed Welfare Revolution: America's Struggle Over Guaranteed Income Policy', *Contemporary Sociology* 38, 3: 260–1.

Reitz, G. Jeffrey. 2007a. 'Immigrant Employment Success in Canada, Part I: Individual and Contextual Causes', *Journal of International Migration and Integration* 8, 1: 11–36.

———. 2007b. 'Immigrant Employment Success in Canada, Part II: Understanding the Decline', *Journal of International Migration and Integration* 8, 1: 37–62.

Sanmartin, Claudia. 2009. *Health Services Research at Statistics Canada: It Really Does Exist!* Ottawa: Statistics Canada.

Sarlo, Chris. 2006. 'Comparing Measures of Poverty', *Fraser Forum* 1: 3–4.

———. 2007. 'Measuring Poverty—What Happened to Copenhagen?', *Economic Affairs* 27, 3: 6–14.

Shillington, Richard. 1999. 'What Do We Mean by Poverty? Or HRDC Reduces Our Obligations to Poor Children'. At: <www.shillington.ca/poverty/mbm.htm>.

Smith, George Davey, Danny Dorling, David Gordon, and Mary Shaw. 1999. 'The Widening Health Gap: What Are the Solutions?', *Critical Public Health* 9, 2: 151–70.

Statistics Canada. 2004. *Analysis of Income in Canada 2002.* At: <www.statcan.gc.ca/ pub/75-203-x/00002/4153424-eng.htm>.

———. 2009a. *Income Research Paper Series.* 75F0002MWE, 3 June. At: <www.statcan.gc.ca/bsolc/olc-cel/olc-cel?catno =75f0002m&lang=eng>.

———. 2009b. 'Income of Canadians', *The Daily*, 3 June. At: <www.statcan.gc.ca/ daily-quotidien/090603/dq090603a-eng. htm>.

Trovato, Frank. 2001. 'Aboriginal Mortality in Canada, the United States and New Zealand', *Journal of Biosocial Science* 33, 1: 67–86.

United Nations Children's Fund (UNICEF). 2005. 'Children Out of Sight, Out of Mind, Out of Reach', press release, 14 Dec. At: <www.unicef.org/media/media_30453. html>.

United Nations Development Program (UNDP). 2005. *Human Development Report 2005: International Cooperation at a Crossroads—Aid, Trade, and Security in an Unequal World.* New York: UNDP.

Watson, Pat. 2003. 'Poverty Measure Shows Nothing New', *Share* 26, 9: 8.

Wellesley Institute. 2006. *The Blue Print to End Homelessness in Toronto: A Two-Part Action Plan.* At: <intraspec.ca/TheBlueprint(final). pdf>.

Wilkinson, Richard G. 1994. 'Income Distribution and Life Expectancy', *British Medical Journal* 304: 165–8.

———. 1996. *Unhealthy Societies: The Afflictions of Inequality.* London: Routledge.

Wratten, Ellen. 2010. 'Conceptualizing Urban Poverty (1995)', in Howard Lune, Enrique S. Pumar, and Ross Koppel, eds, *Perspectives in Social Research Methods and Analysis: A Reader for Sociology.* Thousand Oaks, Calif.: Sage, 85–110.

Chapter 3

Abu-Laban, Yasmeen, and Abigail B. Bakan. 2008. 'The Racial Contract: Israel/Palestine and Canada', *Social Identities* 14, 5: 637–60.</REF

——— and Christina Gabriel. 2004. 'Selling Diversity: Immigration, Multiculturalism, Employment Equity, and Globalization', *British Journal of Canadian Studies* 17, 1: 128–30.

Adams, Michael. 2007. *Unlikely Utopia: The Surprising Triumph of Canadian Pluralism.* Toronto: Viking Canada.

Allport, Gordon. 1954. *The Nature of Prejudice.* Reading, Mass.: Addison-Wesley.

Aranda, Elizabeth M., and Guillermo Rebollo-Gil. 2004. 'Ethnoracism and the "Sandwiched" Minorities', *American Behavioral Scientist* 47, 7: 910–27.

Arkes, H.R., and P.E. Tetlock. 2004. 'Attributions of Implicit Prejudice, or Would Jesse Jackson "Fail" the Implicit Association Test?', *Psychological Inquiry* 15: 257–78.

Austin, Christopher, and David Este. 2001. 'The Working Experiences of Underemployed Immigrant and Refugee Men', *Canadian Social Work Review* 18, 2: 213–29.

Baran, Michael D. 2008. 'Race, Color and Culture: Questioning Categories and Concepts in Southern Bahia, Brazil', *Dissertation Abstracts International, A: The Humanities and Social Sciences* 68, 10: 4357.

Barbujani, Guido, Arianna Magagni, Eric Minch, and L. Luca Cavalli-Sforza. 1997. 'An Apportionment of Human DNA Diversity', *Proceedings of the National Academy of Science* 94, 9: 4516–19.

Beck, J. Helen, Jeffrey G. Reitz, and Nan Weiner. 2002. 'Addressing Systemic Racial Discrimination in Employment: The Health Canada Case and Implications of Legislative Change', *Canadian Public Policy* 28, 3: 373–94.

Best, Joel. 1989. 'Social Progress and Social Problems: Toward a Sociology of Gloom', *Sociological Quarterly* 42, 1: 1–12.

Blatz, Craig W., and Michael Ross. 2009. 'Principled Ideology or Racism: Why Do Modern Racists Oppose Race-Based Social Justice Programs?', *Journal of Experimental Social Psychology* 45, 1: 258–61.

Boyd, Monica. 2002. 'Educational Attainments of Immigrant Offspring: Success or Segmented Assimilation?', *International Migration Review* 36 (Winter): 1037–60.

Breton, Raymond. 1964. 'Institutional Completeness of Ethnic Communities and Personal Relations to Immigrants', *American Journal of Sociology* 70: 193–205.

———. 1978. 'Stratification and Conflict between Ethnolinguistic Communities with Different Social Structures', *Canadian Review of Sociology and Anthropology* 15: 138–57.

———, Jeffrey G. Reitz, and Victor Valentine. 1980. *Cultural Boundaries and the Cohesion of Canada.* Montreal: Institute for Research on Public Policy.

Bryant, Wesley W. 2009. 'African American Male Youth Violence and Internalized Racism', ProQuest Information & Learning, US.

Burns, Thomas J. 2002. 'How Claims Spread: Cross-National Diffusion of Social Problems', *Social Forces* 81, 1: 376–8.

Cea D'Ancona, Ma A. 2009. 'The Complex Detection of Racism and Xenophobia through Survey Methods. A Step Forward in Their Measurement', *Revista Espanola De Investigaciones Sociologicas* 125: 13–45.

Coleman, Joey. 2008. 'York Anti-Racism Rally Goes Off Rails', *Maclean's*, 24 Jan. At: <www. macleans.ca/education/universities/article. jsp?content=20080124_175750_5772>.

Cort, Malcolm A., Eugene S. Tull, Keratiloe Gwebu, Priscilla Dlamini, Erica Pinkney, Eundene Gramby, Shanitria Cuthbertson, Ashley Daniels, Shay Luu, and Ephraim T. Gwebu. 2009. 'Education and Internalized Racism in Socio-Political Context: Zimbabwe and Swaziland', *Social Science Journal* 46, 4: 644–55.

Coser, Lewis A. 1965. *The Functions of Social Conflict.* London: Routledge & Kegan Paul.

Costigan, Catherine, Tina F. Su, and Josephine M. Hua. 2009. 'Ethnic Identity among Chinese Canadian Youth: A Review of the Canadian Literature', *Canadian Psychology/ Psychologie Canadienne* 50, 4: 261–72.

Curtis, James, Edward Grabb, and Neil Guppy, eds. 1999. *Social Inequality in Canada:*

Patterns, Problems, Policies, 3rd edn. Scarborough, Ont.: Prentice-Hall.

D'Arcy, Carl. 1998. 'Social Distribution of Health among Canadians', in David Coburn, Carl D'Arcy, and George M. Torrance, eds, *Health and Canadian Society: Sociological Perspectives,* 3rd edn. Toronto: University of Toronto Press, 73–101.

Devine, Patricia G., and Andrew J. Elliot. 1995. 'Are Racial Stereotypes Really Fading? The Princeton Trilogy Revised', *Personality and Social Psychology Bulletin* 21, 11: 1139–50.

Ezeonu, Celestine I. 2006. 'The Social Construction of "Black-on-Black" Violence in Toronto (Ontario)', *Dissertation Abstracts International, A: The Humanities and Social Sciences* 66, 10: 3815.

Faist, T. 2000. 'Transnationalization in International Migration: Implications for the Study of Citizenship and Culture', *Ethnic and Racial Studies* 23, 2: 189–222.

Farmer, Melissa M., and Kenneth F. Ferraro. 1999. 'Who Are the "Truly Disadvantaged" in Health? A 20-Year Examination of Race, Socioeconomic Status, and Health Outcomes', paper presented at the annual meeting of the American Sociological Association.

Fenlon, Brodie. 2008. 'Canada Apologizes', *Globe and Mail,* 11 June, A2–3.

Fenton, Steve, Anthony O. Hughes, and Christine E. Hine. 1995. 'Self-assessed Health, Economic Status and Ethnic Origin', *New Community* 21, 1: 55–68.

Fleischer, David. 2009. 'Race May Shorten Housing Wait', 27 Aug. At: <www.yorkregion.com/YorkRegion/Article/550499>.

Fleras, Augie, and Jean Elliott. 2009. *Unequal Relations: An Introduction to Race, Ethnicity and Aboriginal Dynamics in Canada.* Scarborough, Ont.: Prentice-Hall.

Forgues, Éric. 2007. 'The Canadian State and the Empowerment of the Francophone Minority Communities Regarding Their Economic Development', *International Journal of the Sociology of Language* 185, 1: 163–86.

Franklin, Anderson J. 1998. 'Treating Anger in African American Men', in William S. Pollack and Richard F. Levant, eds, *New Psychotherapy for Men.* New York: Wiley, 239–58.

Frideres, J.S., and Boni Robertson. 1994. 'Aboriginals and the Criminal Justice System: Australia and Canada', *International Journal of Contemporary Sociology* 31: 101–27.

Fujiwara, Aya. 2008. 'From Anglo-Conformity to Multiculturalism: The Role of Scottish, Ukrainian, and Japanese Ethnicity in the Transformation of Canadian Identity, 1919–1971', ProQuest Information & Learning, US.

Gabbidon, Shaun L. 2010. *Race, Ethnicity, Crime, and Justice: An International Dilemma.* Thousand Oaks, Calif.: Sage.

Gaertner, Samuel L., and John F. Dovidio. 2000. 'The Aversive Form of Racism', in Charles Stangor, ed., *Stereotypes and Prejudice: Essential Readings.* Philadelphia: Psychology Press, 289–304.

Gee, Ellen M., and Steven G. Prus. 2000. 'Income Inequality in Canada: A Racial Divide', in Madeline A. Kalbach and Warren E. Kalbach, eds, *Perspectives on Ethnicity in Canada: A Reader.* Toronto: Harcourt Canada, 238–56.

Godwyn, Mary. 2009. '"This Place Makes Me Proud to be a Woman": Theoretical Explanations for Success in Entrepreneurship Education for Low-Income Women', *Research in Social Stratification and Mobility* 27, 1: 50–64.

Green, Joyce. 2001. 'Canaries in the Mines of Citizenship: Indian Women in Canada', *Canadian Journal of Political Science* 34, 4: 715–38.

Greenwald, Anthony G., Debbie E. McGhee, and Jordan K.L. Schwartz. 1998. 'Measuring Individual Differences in Implicit Cognition: The Implicit Association Test', *Journal of Personality and Social Psychology* 74, 6: 1464–80.

Haque, Eve. 2007. 'Multiculturalism within a Bilingual Framework: Language and the Racial Ordering of Difference and Belonging in Canada', *Dissertation Abstracts International, A: The Humanities and Social Sciences* 68, 01: 0054.

Harrell, Shelly P. 2000. 'A Multidimensional Conceptualization of Racism-Related Stress: Implications for the Well-Being of People of Color', *American Journal of Orthopsychiatry* 70, 1: 42–57.

Hayward, Mark D., and Melanie Heron. 1999. 'Racial Inequality in Active Life among Adult Americans', *Demography* 36: 77–91.

Henry, Frances. 1999. 'Two Studies of Racial Discrimination in Employment', in Curtis et al. (1999: 226–35).

——— and Effie Ginzberg. 1985. *Who Gets the Work: A Test of Racial Discrimination in Employment.* Toronto: Urban Alliance on Race Relations in Employment and Social Planning Council of Metropolitan Toronto.

Hong, Young-Hwa. 2008. 'Engendering Migration in the Transnational World: Highly Skilled Korean Immigrant Women in the Canadian Labour Market'. ProQuest Information & Learning, US.

Hou, Feng, and T.R. Balakrishnan. 1996. 'The Integration of Visible Minorities in Contemporary Society', *Canadian Journal of Sociology* 21: 307–16.

——— and Garnett Picot. 2004. 'Visible Minority Neighbourhoods in Toronto, Montréal, and Vancouver', *Canadian Social Trends* (Spring): 8–13.

Javed, Noor. 2010. '"Visible Minority" Will Mean "White" by 2031', *Toronto Star,* 10 Mar., A3.

Kashefi, Mahmoud. 2004. 'Racial Differences on Organizational Attachment? Structural Explanation of Attitude Differences between White and African American Employees', *Journal of Black Studies* 34, 5: 702–18.

Kent, Mike. 2009. 'Excellence Is Colour Neutral', *The Times Educational Supplement* 4867: 44.

Krieger, Nancy, Diane Rowley, Allen A. Herman, Byllye Avery, and Monol T. Phillips. 1993. 'Racism, Sexism, and Social Class: Implications for Studies of Health, Disease, and Well-Being', *American Journal of Preventive Medicine* 9, 6 (suppl.): 82–122.

Lalonde, R.N., J.M. Jones, and M.L. Stroink. 2008. 'Racial Identity, Racial Attitudes, and Race Socialization among Black Canadian Parents', *Canadian Journal of Behavioural Science* 40, 3: 129–39.

Lamarche, Lucie, Rachel Chagnon, Francine Tougas, and Martine Lagacé. 2006. 'Conflict Management and the Employment Equity Act: Visible Minorities in Canada', *Canadian Public Policy* 32, 3: 243–58.

Landrine, Hope, and Elizabeth A. Klonoff. 1996. 'The Schedule of Racist Events: A Measure of Racial Discrimination and a Study of Its Negative Physical and Mental Health Consequences', *Journal of Black Psychology* 22: 144–68.

Landry, Rodrigue, Real Allard, and Kenneth Deveau. 2007. 'Bilingual Schooling of the Canadian Francophone Minority: A Cultural Autonomy Model', *International Journal of the Sociology of Language* 185 (May): 133–62.

Laroche, Mireille. 2000. 'Health Status and Health Services Utilization of Canada's Immigrant and Non-immigrant Populations', *Canadian Public Policy* 26: 51–73.

McConahay, J.B. 1981. 'Has Racism Declined in America? It Depends on Who Is Asking and What Is Asked', *Journal of Conflict Resolution* 25, 4: 563–79.

———. 1986. 'Modern Racism, Ambivalence, and the Modern Racism Scale', in J.F. Dovidio and S.L. Gaertner, eds., *Prejudice, Discrimination, and Racism.* New York: Academic Press, 91–125.

McKown, Clark, and Michael J. Strambler. 2009. 'Developmental Antecedents and Social and Academic Consequences of Stereotype-Consciousness in Middle Childhood', *Child Development* 80, 6: 1643.

Malin, Merridy. 2000. 'A "Whole of Life" View of Aboriginal Education for Health: Emerging Models', keynote address at the Australian Medical Association, Northern Territory, Conference 2000, 'Learning Lessons: Approaching Indigenous Health Through Education'. Available at: <http://192.94.208.240/Crc/General/CRC-Pubs/Malin_AMA_2000.PDF>.

Moghissi, Haideh, Saeed Rahnema, and Mark J. Goodman. 2009. *Diaspora by Design:*

Muslim Immigrants in Canada and Beyond. Toronto: University of Toronto Press.

Moreau, Sylvie, Cecile Rousseau, and Abdelwahed Mekki Berrada. 1999. 'Immigration Policies and the Mental Health of Refugees: The Profile and Impact of Family Separations', *Nouvelles Pratiques Sociales* 11, 1: 177–96.

Morris, Theresa. 2008. 'Branch Banking and Institutional Racism in the U.S. Banking Industry', *Humanity and Society* 32, 2: 144–67.

Moya, Jose C., and Maria Bjerg. 1999. 'Cousins & Strangers: Spanish Immigrants in Buenos Aires, 1850–1930', *Urban History Review* 27, 2: 74.

Office of the High Commissioner for Human Rights. 1969. *International Convention on the Elimination of All Forms of Racial Discrimination.* At: <www.unhchr.ch/html/menu3/b/d_icerd.htm>.

Okin, Susan Moller. 1998. *Is Multiculturalism Bad for Women?* Princeton, NJ: Princeton University Press.

Omi, Michael, and Howland Winant. 2009. *Racial Formation in the United States: From the 1960s to the 1990s*, 2nd edn. New York: Routledge.

Ottaway, S.A., D.C. Hayden, and M.A. Oakes. 2001. 'Implicit Attitudes and Racism: Effects of Work Familiarity and Frequency on the Implicit Association Test', *Social Cognition* 19: 97–144.

Parmar, Alpa. 2007. 'Racial Profiling in Canada: Challenging the Myth of "a Few Bad Apples"', *Ethnic and Racial Studies* 30, 6: 1171–4.

Picot, Garnett, Feng Hou, and Simon Coulombe. 2007. *Chronic Low Income and Low-Income Dynamics among Recent Immigrants.* Publication no. 11F0019MIE. Ottawa: Statistics Canada, Business and Labour Market Analysis No. 294, Jan. At: <www.statcan.gc.ca/pub/11f0019m/11f0019m2007294-eng.pdf>.

Porter, John. 1965. *The Vertical Mosaic.* Toronto: University of Toronto Press.

Quan, H., A. Fong, C. De Coster, J. Wang, R. Musto, T.W. Noseworthy, and W.A. Ghali. 2006. 'Variation in Health Services Utilization among Ethnic Populations', *Canadian Medical Association Journal* 174, 6: 787–91.

Reed, Micheline, and Julian Roberts. 1999. 'Adult Correctional Services in Canada, 1997–98', in Canadian Centre for Justice Statistics, *The Juristat Reader: A Statistical Overview of the Canadian Justice System.* Toronto: Thompson Educational, 39–51.

Reitz, Jeffrey G. 2001. 'Immigrant Success in the Knowledge Economy: Institutional Change and the Immigrant Experience in Canada, 1970–1995', *Journal of Social Issues* 57, 3: 579–613.

———. 2007a. 'Immigrant Employment Success in Canada, Part I: Individual and Contextual Causes', *Journal of International Migration and Integration* 8, 1: 11–36.

———. 2007b. 'Immigrant Employment Success in Canada, Part II: Understanding the Decline', *Journal of International Migration and Integration* 8, 1: 37–62.

——— and Rupa Banerjee. 2007. 'Racial Inequality, Social Cohesion, and Policy Issues in Canada, " pp. 489-545 in Keith Banting, Thomas J. Courchene, and F. Leslie Seidle, eds, *Belonging? Diversity, Recognition and Shared Citizenship in Canada.* Montreal: Institute for Research on Public Policy.

———, Rupa Banerjee, Mai Phan, and Jordan Thompson. 2009. 'Race, Religion, and the Social Integration of New Immigrant Minorities in Canada', *International Migration Review* 43, 4: 695–726.

——— and Raymond Breton. 1999. 'Prejudice and Discrimination toward Minorities in Canada and the United States', in Curtis et al. (1999: 357–70).

Roberts, Julian V., and Anthony N. Doob. 1997. 'Race, Ethnicity, and Criminal Justice in Canada', in Michael Tonry, ed., *Ethnicity, Crime and Immigration: Comparative and Cross-national Perspectives.* Chicago: University of Chicago Press, 469–522.

Robertson, Lawrence. 1997. 'The Constructed Nature of Ethnopolitics', *International Politics* 34: 267–83.

Rodlandt, Theo J.A. 1996. 'Ethnic Stratification: The Emergence of a New Social and Economic Issue?', *Netherlands Journal of Social Sciences* 32, 1: 39–50.

Rodney, Patricia, and Esker Copeland. 2009. 'The Health Status of Black Canadians: Do Aggregated Racial and Ethnic Variables Hide Health Disparities?', *Journal of Health Care for the Poor and Underserved* 20, 3: 817–23.

Rollock, David, and Edmund W. Gordon. 2000. 'Racism and Mental Health into the 21st Century: Perspectives and Parameters', *American Journal of Orthopsychiatry* 70, 1: 5–13.

Rothermund, K., and D. Wentura. 2004. 'Underlying Processes in the Implicit Association Test (IAT): Dissociating Salience from Associations', *Journal of Experimental Psychology (General)* 133: 139–65.

Ruffin, Betsy. 2009. 'How Are We the Same and Different?/We Are the Earth/What Is Culture?/What Is Religion?', *Library Media Connection* 28, 2: 98.

Scottham, Krista M., and Ciara P. Smalls. 2009. 'Unpacking Racial Socialization: Considering Female African American Primary Caregivers' Racial Identity', *Journal of Marriage and Family* 71, 4: 807–19.

Segura Escobar, Nora. 2000. 'Colombia: A New Century, an Old War, and More Internal Displacement', *International Journal of Politics, Culture, and Society* 14: 107–27.

Spencer, N. 1996. 'Race and Ethnicity as Determinants of Child Health: A Personal View', *Child: Care, Health and Development* 22: 327–45.

Spinner-Halev, Jeff. 2001. 'Feminism, Multiculturalism, Oppression, and the State', *Ethics* 112 (Oct.): 84–113.

Statistics Canada. 2003. *Longitudinal Survey of Immigrants to Canada: Process, Progress, and Prospects* (Catalogue no. 89–611–XIE). Ottawa: Statistics Canada.

———. 2008. 'Aboriginal People Living Off-Reserve and the Labour Market: Estimates from the Labour Force Survey, 2008–2009'. At: <www.statcan.gc.ca/pub/71-588-x/2010001/part-partie1-eng.htm>.

Steinberg, Stephen. 1981. *The Ethnic Myth.* New York: Knopf.

Symons, Gladys L. 1999. 'Racialization of the Street Gang Issue in Montreal: A Police Perspective', *Canadian Ethnic Studies* 31: 124–38.

Tang, S.Y. 1999. 'Interpreter Services in Healthcare: Policy Recommendations for Healthcare Agencies', *Journal of Nursing Administration* 29, 6: 23–9.

Thomas, W.I., and Florien Znaniecki. 1971 [1919]. *The Polish Peasant in America.* New York: Octagon Books.

Thompson, A.C. 2009. 'New Evidence Surfaces in Post-Katrina Crimes', 11 July. At: <www.commondreams.org/headline/2009/07/11-4>.

Thompson, Venetia. 2008. 'The Masters of the Universe Have Turned to Drink', *The Spectator*, 4 Oct.

Waldram, James P., Ann D. Herring, and T. Kue Young. 1996. *Aboriginal Health in Canada: Historical, Cultural, and Epidemiological Perspectives.* Toronto: University of Toronto.

Wardman, D., K. Clement, and D. Quantz. 2005. 'Access and Utilization of Health Services by British Columbia's Rural Aboriginal Population', *International Journal of Health Care Quality Assurance* 18, 2 and 3: xxvi–xxxi.

Wen, S.W., V. Goel, and J.I. Williams. 1996. 'Utilization of Health Care Services by Immigrants and Other Ethnic/Cultural Groups in Ontario', *Ethnicity and Health* 1, 1: 99–109.

Williams, David R., Yan Yu, James S. Jackson, and Norman B. Anderson. 1997. 'Racial Differences in Physical and Mental Health: Socio-economic Status, Stress, and Discrimination', *Journal of Health Psychology* 2: 335–51.

Wockner, Rex. 2004. 'Canada', *Just Out* 21, 16: 26.

Wu, Z., M.J. Penning, and C.M. Schimmele. 2005. 'Immigrant Status and Unmet Health Care Needs', *Canadian Journal of Public Health* 96, 5: 369–73.

Yamamoto, Satomi. 2009. 'Intermediaries and Migration in the United States'. ProQuest Information & Learning, US.

Zhang, Yuanting, and Jennifer Van Hook. 2009. 'Marital Dissolution among Interracial Couples', *Journal of Marriage and Family* 71, 1: 95–107.

Chapter 4

Abbasi-Shavazi, Mohammad J., S.P. Morgan, Meimanat Hossein-Chavoshi, and Peter McDonald. 2009. 'Family Change and Continuity in Iran: Birth Control Use before First Pregnancy', *Journal of Marriage and Family* 71, 5: 1309–24.

Albelda, Randy, and Chris Tilly. 1997. *Glass Ceilings and Bottomless Pits: Women's Work, Women's Poverty*. Boston: South End Press.

Angeles, Leonora C. 2009. 'Rethinking the 'Feminisation of Poverty' Thesis,' *Sex Roles* 61, 3 and 4: 293–6.

Astor, Will. 2010. '2010 Athens Award: Wilderotter: Delivering Results Brings Rewards', *Rochester Business Journal* 25, 42: S3.

Bacchi, Carol Lee. 1999. *Women, Policy and Politics: The Construction of Policy Problems*. London: Sage.

Barreto, Manuela, Michelle K. Ryan, and Michael T. Schmitt, eds. 2009. *The Glass Ceiling in the 21st Century: Understanding Barriers to Gender Equality*, 2nd edn. Washington: American Psychological Association.

Benokraitis, Nijole V. 2008. *Marriages and Families: Changes, Choices, and Constraints*, 6th edn. Upper Saddle River, NJ: Prentice-Hall/Pearson.

Berg, J.A., and N.F. Woods. 2009. 'Global Women's Health: A Spotlight on Caregiving', *Nursing Clinics of North America* 44, 3: 375 ff.

Bloom, Adi. 2009. 'Are We Going Back to This?', *The Times Educational Supplement* 4869: 18.

Brooks, Stephen. 2007. *Canadian Democracy: An Introduction*, 5th edn. Toronto: Oxford University Press.

Campaign 2000. 2005. *Decision Time for Canada: Let's Make Poverty History, 2005 Report Card on Child Poverty in Canada*. At: <www.campaign2000.ca/rc/>.

Canadian Community Health Survey, Cycle 2.1. 2004. Available at: <http://www.statcan.gc.ca/concepts/health-sante/cycle2_1/index-eng.htm>.

Chodorow, Nancy. 1978. *The Reproduction of Mothering: Psychoanalysis and the Sociology of Gender*. Berkeley: University of California Press.

Clancy, Frank. 1994. 'When Customer Service Crosses the Line', *Working Woman* 19, 12: 36–42.

Coltrane, Scott, and Michele Adams. 2003. 'The Social Construction of the Divorce "Problem": Morality, Child Victims, and the Politics of Gender', *Family Relations* 52: 363–72.

———— and Masako Ishii-Kuntz. 1990. 'Men's Housework and Child Care: A Life Course Perspective', paper presented at the annual meeting of the American Sociological Association.

Courtenay, Will H. 2000. 'Constructions of Masculinity and Their Influence on Men's Well-being: A Theory of Gender and Health', *Social Science and Medicine* 50: 1385–1401.

Cowan, Carolyn Pape, and Philip A. Cowan. 1995. 'Interventions to Ease the Transition to Parenthood: Why They Are Needed and What They Can Do', *Family Relations* 44: 412–23.

Crespo, Stephane. 2007. 'Changes in Labor Market Participation over the Life Course of Men and Women in Canada', *Cahiers Québécois de Démographie* 36, 1: 49–83.

Crocker, J., and L.E. Park. 2003. 'Seeking Self-Esteem: Construction, Maintenance, and Protection of Self-Worth', in M. Leary and J. Tangney, eds, *Handbook of Self and Identity*. New York: Guilford, 291–313.

Crohan, Susan E. 1996. 'Marital Quality and Conflict across the Transition to Parenthood in African American and White Couples', *Journal of Marriage and the Family* 58: 922–44.

Crooks, Roberts, and Karla Baur. 1999. *Our Sexuality*, 7th edn. Toronto: Nelson Canada.

Das, Hari, and Mallika Das. 2009. 'Gender Stereotyping in Contemporary Indian Magazine Fiction', *Asian Studies Review* 33, 1:63–82.

Doucet, Andrea. 2000. '"There's a Huge Gulf between Me as a Male Carer and Women": Gender, Domestic Responsibility, and the Community as an Institutional Arena', *Community, Work and Family* 3, 2: 163–84.

D'Souza, Fahmida Z. 2007. 'Become the CEO Your Mom Wanted You to Marry: Women Who Shatter the Glass (the Social and Cultural Construction of Gender Stereotypes among a Sample of Women in Business)', ProQuest Dissertations & Theses, at: <gradworks.umi.com/32/61/3261312.html>.

Erel, Osnat, and Bonnie Burman. 1995. 'Interrelatedness of Marital Relations and Parent–Child Relations: A Meta-analytic Review', *Psychological Bulletin* 118: 108–32.

Estrich, Susan. 2007. 'Real Rape', in Barbara A. Arrighi, ed., *Understanding Inequality*. Lanham, Md: Rowman & Littlefield, 309–25.

Fargues, Philippe. 1977. 'State Policies and the Birth Rate in Egypt: From Socialism to Liberalism', *Population and Development Review* 23, 1: 115–38.

Foster, Mindi. 2009. 'The Dynamic Nature of Coping with Gender Discrimination: Appraisals, Strategies and Well-being Over Time', *Sex Roles* 60, 9 and 10: 694–707.

Fox, Bonnie. 2001. 'The Formative Years: How Parenthood Creates Gender', *Canadian Review of Sociology and Anthropology* 38: 373–90.

Gibson, Diane. 1996. 'Broken Down by Age and Gender: "The Problem of Old Women" Redefined', *Gender and Society* 10: 433–48.

Gillmore, Mary R., Steven M. Lewis, Mary J. Lohr, Michael S. Spencer, and Rachelle D. White. 1997. 'Repeat Pregnancies among Adolescent Mothers', *Journal of Marriage and the Family* 59: 536–50.

Gough, Brendan, and Paul Peace. 2000. 'Reconstructing Gender at University: Men as Victims', *Gender and Education* 12, 3: 385–98.

Gregson, Nicky, and Michelle Lowe. 1994. 'Waged Domestic Labor and the Renegotiation of the Domestic Division of Labor within Dual-Career Households', *Sociology* 28: 55–79.

Hankin, Janet R. 1990. 'Gender and Mental Illness', *Research in Community and Mental Health* 6: 183–201.

Harrison, K., L.D. Taylor, and A.L. Marske. 2006. 'Women's and Men's Eating Behavior Following Exposure to Ideal-Body Images', *Communication Research* 33, 6: 507–29.

Heath, Melanie. 2003. 'Soft-Boiled Masculinity', *Gender and Society* 17, 3: 423–44.

Hovmand, P.S., D.N. Ford, I. Flom, and S. Kyriakakis. 2009. 'Victims Arrested for Domestic Violence: Unintended Consequences of Arrest Policies', *System Dynamics Review* 25, 3: 161–81.

Humphreys, Terry P., and Ed Herold. 1996. 'Date Rape: A Comparative Analysis and Integration of Theory', *Canadian Journal of Human Sexuality* 5, 2: 69–82.

Inhorn, Marcia C. 1998. 'Infertility and the Quest for Conception in Egypt', in Robin Barlow and Joseph W. Brown, eds, *Reproductive Health and Infectious Disease in the Middle East*. Brookfield, Vt: Ashgate, 114–29.

Ishii-Kuntz, Masako, and Scott Coltrane. 1992. 'Remarriage, Stepparenting, and Household Labor', *Journal of Family Issues* 13: 215–33.

Jung, Jaehee, and Michael Peterson. 2007. 'Body Dissatisfaction and Patterns of Media Use among Preadolescent Children', *Family and Consumer Sciences Research Journal* 36, 1: 40–54.

Kaukinen, Catherine. 2002. 'The Help-Seeking Decisions of Violent Crime Victims: An Examination of the Direct and Conditional Effects of Gender and Victim-Offender Relationship', *Journal of Interpersonal Violence* 17, 4: 432–56.

Keyfitz, Nathan. 1988. 'On the Wholesomeness of Marriage', in Lorne Tepperman and James Curtis, eds, *Readings in Sociology: An Introduction*. Toronto: McGraw-Hill Ryerson, 449–62.

Knudson-Martin, Carmen, and Anne Rankin Mahoney. 2009. *Couples, Gender, and Power: Creating Change in Intimate Relationships*. New York: Springer.

Lengermann, Patricia M., and Jill Niebrugge-Brantley. 2001. 'Classical Feminist Social Theory', in George Ritzer and Barry Smart, eds, *Handbook of Social Theory*. London: Sage, 125–37.

Lillian, D.L. 2007. 'A Thorn by Any Other Name: Sexist Discourse as Hate Speech', *Discourse and Society* 18, 6: 719–40.

Lupri, Eugen. 1993. 'Spousal Violence: Wife Abuse across the Life Course', *Zeitschrift fur Sozialisationforschung und Erziehungssoziologie* 13, 3: 232–57.

——— and James Frideres. 1981. 'The Quality of Marriage and the Passage of Time: Marital Satisfaction over the Family Life Cycle', *Canadian Journal of Sociology* 6, 3: 283–305.

———, E. Grandin, and M.B. Brinkerhoff. 1994. 'Socioeconomic Status and Male Violence in the Canadian Home: A Reexamination'. *Canadian Journal of Sociology* 19, 1: 47–73.

MacDonald, Natalie C. 2007. 'Keeping the Bedroom Out of the Boardroom', *Canadian HR Reporter* 20, 18: 26.

McMullin, Julie. 2004. *Understanding Social Inequality: Intersections of Class, Age, Gender, Ethnicity, and Race in Canada*. Toronto: Oxford University Press.

McNeill, Ted. 2007. 'Fathers of Children with a Chronic Health Condition: Beyond Gender Stereotypes', *Men and Masculinities* 9, 4: 409–24.

Marshall, K. 2006. 'Converging Gender Roles', *Canadian Economic Observer* (Aug.). At: <www.statcan.gc.ca/pub/11-010-x/00806/9290-eng.htm>.

Mason, Karen Oppenheim, and Karen Kuhlthau. 1989. 'Determinants of Child Care Ideals among Mothers of Preschool-Aged Children', *Journal of Marriage and the Family* 51: 593–603.

Metropolitan Action Committee on Violence against Women and Children (METRAC). 'Stalking Statistics', 2003. At: <www.metrac.org/programs/info/prevent/stat_sta.htm>.

Monk, Timothy H., Marilyn J. Essex, Nancy A. Snider, Marjorie H. Klein, et al. 1996. 'The Impact of the Birth of a Baby on the Time Structure and Social Mixture of a Couple's Daily Life and Its Consequences for Well-Being', *Journal of Applied Social Psychology* 26: 1237–58.

Morris, Marika. 2000. 'Millennium of Achievements', *CRIAW Newsletter* 20, 1 (Winter).

Murray, Stephen O. 1995. *Latin American Male Homosexualities*. Albuquerque: University of New Mexico Press.

———. 1996. *American Gay*. Chicago: University of Chicago Press.

———. 2000. *Homosexualities*. Chicago: University of Chicago Press.

National Anti-Poverty Organization (NAPO). 1999. 'It's Time for Justice'. Submission to the Canadian Human Rights Act Review Panel. October 14. Available at: <http://www.povnet.org/node/1121>.

National Day of Remembrance and Action on Violence against Women. 2005. 'Fact Sheet: Statistics on Violence against Women in Canada', 6 Dec. At: <www.swc-cfc.gc.ca/dates/dec6/facts_e.html>.

Oakley, Ann. 1974. *The Sociology of Housework*. London: Martin Robertson.

Ontario Women's Directorate. 2009. 'Domestic Violence', 2 Oct. At: <www.citizenship.gov.on.ca/owd/english/resources/information/facts/index.shtml9>.

Orbach, Terri L., James S. House, and Pamela S. Mero. 1996. 'Marital Quality over the Life Course', *Social Psychology Quarterly* 59: 162–71.

Parsons, Talcott. 1951. *The Social System*. Glencoe, Ill.: Free Press.

Rabin, Claire, and Giora Rahav. 1995. 'Differences and Similarities between Younger and Older Marriages across Cultures: A Comparison of American and Israeli Retired Nondistressed Marriages', *American Journal of Family Therapy* 23: 237–49.

Risman, Barbara J. 2001. 'A Comment on the Biological Limits of Gender Construction: Calling the Bluff on Value-Free Science', *American Sociological Review* 66: 4.

Rodriguez-Dominguez, Luis, Isabel Gallego-Alvarez, and Isabel Maria Garcia-Sanchez. 2009. 'Corporate Governance and Codes of Ethics', *Journal of Business Ethics* 90, 2: 187–202.

Royo Vela y Otros, Marcelo. 2005. 'Gender Role and Sexism in Spanish Magazine Advertisements: An Analysis of the Twentieth Century's Last Three Decades', *Comunicacion y Sociedad* 18, 1: 113–52.

Sachs, Jeffrey D. 2005. *The End of Poverty: Economic Possibilities for Our Time*. New York: Penguin Books.

Sacco, V., and H. Johnson. 1990. 'Violent Victimization', *Canadian Social Trends* 17 (Summer): 10–13.

Schiller, Bill. 2010. 'China's Happy Two-Child Experiment', *Toronto Star*, 23 Apr. At: <www.thestar.com/.../799721--china-s-happy-two-child-experiment>.

Schoijet, M. 2007. 'Birth Control: A History's Outline', *Papeles de Poblacion* 13, 54: 115–61.

Shelton, Beth Anne, and Daphne John. 1993. 'Does Marital Status Make a Difference? Housework among Married and Cohabiting Men and Women', *Journal of Family Issues* 14: 401–20.

Statistics Canada. 2001. *Family Violence in Canada: A Statistical Profile 2001*. Ottawa: Minister of Industry, Catalogue no. 85–224–XIE.

———. 2004. *Women in Canada: A Gender-based Statistical Report*. At: <www.statcan.gc.ca/pub/89-503-x/89-503-x2005001-eng.htm>.

———. 2005a. 'Family Violence in Canada: A statistical profile', *The Daily*, 14 July. At: <www.statcan.gc.ca/daily-quotidien/050714/dq050714a-eng.htm>.

———. 2005b. 'Homicides', *The Daily*, 6 Oct. At: <www.statcan.ca/Daily/English/051006/d051006b.htm>.

———. 2005c. 'General Social Survey: Criminal Victimization', *The Daily*, 24 Nov. At: <www.statcan.ca/Daily/English/051124/d051124b.htm>.

———. 2005d. 'Pregnancy Outcomes'. At: <www.statcan.gc.ca/pub/82-224-x/2005000/5800381-eng.htm>.

———. 2009. *Family Violence in Canada: A Statistical Profile, 2009*. <www.statcan.gc.ca/pub/85-224-x/2009000/aftertoc-apre-stdm2-eng.htm>.

Staudt, K. 2009. 'Gendering the World Bank: Neoliberalism and the Gendered Foundations of Global Governance', *Choice* 47, 4: 763.

Sunden, Jenny. 2002. '"I'm Still Not Sure She's a She": Textual Talk and Typed Bodies in Online Interaction', in P. McIlvenny, ed., *Talking Gender and Sexuality*. Amsterdam: John Benjamins, 289–312.

Thetela, Puleng H. 2002. 'Sex Discourses and Gender Constructions in Southern Sotho: A Case Study of Police Interviews of Rape/Sexual Assault Victims', *Southern African Linguistics and Applied Language Studies* 20, 3: 177–89.

Tichy, Lauren L., Judith V. Becker, and Melissa M. Sisco. 2009. 'The Downside of Patriarchal Benevolence: Ambivalence in Addressing Domestic Violence and Socio-Economic Considerations for Women of Tamil Nadu, India', *Journal of Family Violence* 24, 8: 547–58.

Tilly, Louise A., and Joan W. Scott. 1987. *Women, Work, and Family*. New York: Routledge.

Tjaden, Patricia. 1997. *The Crime of Stalking: How Big Is the Problem?* Washington: US Department of Justice, Office of Justice Programs, National Institute of Justice, Nov.

Tong, Rosemarie. 2009. *Feminist Thought: A More Comprehensive Introduction*, 3rd edn. Boulder, Colo.: Westview Press.

Tremblay, Diane-Gabrielle. 2001. 'Polarization of Working Time and Gender Differences: Reconciling Family and Work by Reducing Working Time of Men and Women', in Victor W. Marshall, Walter R. Heinz, Helga Kruger, and Anil Verma, eds, *Restructuring Work and the Life Course*. Toronto: University of Toronto Press, 123–41.

Tyyska, Vappu Kaarina. 1994. 'The Women's Movement and the Welfare State: Child Care Policy in Canada and Finland, 1960–1990', Ph.D. dissertation, University of Toronto.

Vallee, Marie-Helene. 2002. 'Unaccompanied Women Immigrating to Canada during the 1920s: Laying Down a Policy Founded on "Gender"', *Recherches Feministes* 15, 2: 65–85.

Van Wingerden, Sophia A. 1999. *The Women's Suffrage Movement in Britain, 1866–1928*. London: Macmillan.

Wadsby, M., and G. Sydsjo. 2001. 'From Pregnancy to Parenthood: A Study of Couples' Relationship', *Nordisk Psykologi* 53, 4: 275–88.

Weizmann-Henelius, Ghitta, Hanna Putkonen, Hannu Naukkarinen, and Markku Eronen. 2009. 'Intoxication and Violent Women', *Archives of Women's Mental Health* 12, 1: 15–25.

Willen, Helena, and Henry Montgomery. 1996. 'The Impact of Wishing for Children and Having Children on Attainment and Importance of Life Values', *Journal of Comparative Family Studies* 27: 499–518.

Wolf, Naomi. 2009. 'Feminism and the Male Brain: Free at Last?', *Globe and Mail*, 8 June, A13.

World Health Organization (WHO). 2000. *Gender, Health and Poverty* (Fact Sheet 251). At: <www.who.int/inf-fs/en/fact251.html>.

———. 2007. *Maternal Mortality in 2005*. Rep. no. WQ 16. WHO, UNICEF, UNFPA, and the World Bank. At: <whqlibdoc.who.int/publications/2007/9789241596213_eng.pdf>.

Chapter 5

Allport, Gordon. 1979 [1954]. *The Nature of Prejudice*. Reading, Mass.: Addison-Wesley.

Alpaslan, Assim, Theresa Johnston, and Veonna Goliath. 2009. 'Parents' Experiences Regarding the Coming-Out Process of a Gay or Lesbian Child', *Maatskaplike Werk/Social Work* 45, 1: 27–46.

Bahreini, Raha. 2008. 'From Perversion to Pathology: Discourses and Practices of Gender Policing in the Islamic Republic of Iran', *Muslim World Journal of Human Rights* 5, 1 (article 2, electronic publication).

Balkin, Richard S., Lewis Z. Schlosser, and Dana H. Levitt. 2009. 'Religious Identity and Cultural Diversity: Exploring the Relationships between Religious Identity, Sexism, Homophobia, and Multicultural Competence', *Journal of Counseling & Development* 87, 4: 420–7.

Beatie, Thomas. 2008. 'Labour of Love', *The Advocate*, Apr. At: <www.advocate.com/article.aspx?id=22217>.

Berbrier, Mitch, and Elaine Pruett. 2006. 'When Is Inequality a Problem? Victim Contests, Injustice Frames, and the Case of the Office of Gay, Lesbian, and Bisexual Student Support Services at Indiana University', *Journal of Contemporary Ethnography* 35, 3: 257–84.

Biblarz, T.J., and J. Stacey. 2010. 'How Does the Gender of Parents Matter?', *Journal of Marriage and the Family* 72, 1: 3–22.

Blashill, Aaron J., and Kimberly K. Powlishta. 2009. 'Gay Stereotypes: The Use of Sexual Orientation as a Cue for Gender-Related Attributes', *Sex Roles* 61, 11 and 12: 783–93.

Bogaert, Anthony F., and Carolyn L. Hafer. 2009. 'Predicting the Timing of Coming Out in Gay and Bisexual Men from World Beliefs, Physical Attractiveness, and Childhood Gender Identity/Role', *Journal of Applied Social Psychology* 39, 8: 1991–2019.

Bonds-Raacke, J.M., E.T. Cady, R. Schlegel, R.J. Harris, and L. Firebaugh. 2007. 'Remembering Gay and Lesbian Media Characters: Can Ellen and Will Improve Attitudes toward Homosexuals?', *Journal of Homosexuality* 53: 19–34.

Brubaker, Michael D., Michael T. Garrett, and Brian J. Dew. 2009. 'Examining the Relationship between Internalized Heterosexism and Substance Abuse among Lesbian, Gay,

and Bisexual Individuals: A Critical Review', *Journal of LGBT Issues in Counseling* 3, 1: 62–89.

Bryld, M. 2001. 'The Infertility Clinic and the Birth of the Lesbian: The Political Debate in Assisted Reproduction in Denmark', *European Journal of Women's Studies* 8, 3: 299–312.

Cashore, Catherine, and Ma T.G. Tuason. 2009. 'Negotiating the Binary: Identity and Social Justice for Bisexual and Transgender Individuals', *Journal of Gay & Lesbian Social Services* 21, 4: 374–401.

Chesir-Teran, Daniel, and Diane Hughes. 2009. 'Heterosexism in High School and Victimization among Lesbian, Gay, Bisexual, and Questioning Students', *Journal of Youth and Adolescence* 38, 7: 963–75.

Chow, Pizza K., and Sheung-Tak Cheng. 2010. 'Shame, Internalized Heterosexism, Lesbian Identity, and Coming Out to Others: A Comparative Study of Lesbians in Mainland China and Hong Kong', *Journal of Counseling Psychology* 57, 1: 92–104.

Cohen, Taya R., Deborah L. Hall, and Jennifer Tuttle. 2009. 'Attitudes toward Stereotypical versus Counterstereotypical Gay Men and Lesbians', *Journal of Sex Research* 46, 4: 274-281

Concannon, Liam. 2008. 'Citizenship, Sexual Identity and Social Exclusion: Exploring Issues in British and American Social Policy', *International Journal of Sociology and Social Policy* 28, 9 and 10: 326–39.

Conlon, Deirdre. 2004. 'Productive Bodies, Performative Spaces: Everyday Life in Christopher Park', *Sexualities* 7, 4: 462–79.

Corrigan, Patrick W., Jonathon E. Larson, Julie Hautamaki, Alicia Mathews, Sachi Kuwabara, Jennifer Rafacz, Jessica Walton, Abigail Wassel, and John O'Shaughnessy. 2009. 'What Lessons Do Coming Out as Gay Men or Lesbians Have for People Stigmatized by Mental Illness?', *Community Mental Health Journal* 45, 5: 366–74.

Crandall, Christian S., Silvana D'Anello, Nuray Sakalli, Eleana Lazarus, Grazyna Wieczorkowska, and N.T. Feather. 2001. 'An Attribution-Value Model of Prejudice: Anti-Fat Attitudes in Six Nations', *Personality and Social Psychology Bulletin* 27, 1: 30–7.

Crowl, Alicia, Soyeon Ahn, and Jean Baker. 2008. 'A Meta-Analysis of Developmental Outcomes for Children of Same-Sex and Heterosexual Parents', *Journal of GLBT Family Studies* 4, 3: 385–407.

Day, Nancy E., and Patricia G. Greene. 2008. 'A Case for Sexual Orientation Diversity Management in Small and Large Organizations', *Human Resource Management* 47, 3:637–54.

DeJordy, R. 2008. 'Just Passing Through—Stigma, Passing, and Identity Decoupling in the Work Place', *Group & Organization Management* 33, 5: 504–531.

Denike, Margaret Ann. 2007. 'Religion, Rights, and Relationships: The Dream of Relational Equality', *Hypatia* 22, 1: 71–91.

DePalma, Renee, and Elizabeth Atkinson. 2009. '"No Outsiders": Moving Beyond a Discourse of Tolerance to Challenge Heteronormativity in Primary Schools', *British Educational Research Journal* 35, 6: 837–55.

Diaz, N., I. Serrano-Garcia, and J. Toro-Alfonso. 2005. 'AIDS-Related Stigma and Social Interaction: Puerto Ricans Living with HIV/AIDS', *Qualitative Health Research* 15, 2: 169–87.

Donovan, Catherine. 2000. 'Who Needs a Father? Negotiating Biological Fatherhood in British Lesbian Families Using Self-insemination', *Sexualities* 3, 2: 149–64.

Engle, M.J., J.A. McFalls Jr, B.J. Gallagher III, and K. Curtis. 2006. 'The Attitudes of American Sociologists toward Causal Theories of Male Homosexuality', *American Sociologist* 37, 1: 68–76.

Ferfolja, Tania. 2007. 'Schooling Cultures: Institutionalizing Heteronormativity and Heterosexism', *International Journal of Inclusive Education* 11, 2: 147–62.

Findlay, James F., Jr. 2006. 'Glimpses of Recent History: The National Council of Churches, 1974–2004', *Journal of Presbyterian History* 84, 2: 152–69.

Fitzgerald, B. 1999. 'Children of Lesbian and Gay Parents: A Review of the Literature', *Marriage and Family Review* 29, 1: 57–75.

Frost, David M., and Linda M. Bastone. 2008. 'The Role of Stigma Concealment in the Retrospective High School Experiences of Gay, Lesbian, and Bisexual Individuals', *Journal of LGBT Youth* 5, 1: 27–36.

Gauthier, DeAnn K. and Nancy K. Chaudoir. 2004. 'Tranny Boyz: Cyber Community Support in Negotiating Sex and Gender Mobility among Female to Male Transsexuals', *Deviant Behavior* 25, 4: 375–98.

Gebhard, Paul H., and Michael Reece. 2008. 'Kinsey and Beyond: Past, Present, and Future Considerations for Research on Male Bisexuality', *Journal of Bisexuality* 8, 3 and 4: 175–89.

Geller, Pamela L. 2009. 'Bodyscapes, Biology, and Heteronormativity', *American Anthropologist* 111, 4: 504–16.

Gillespie, Wayne. 2008. 'Thirty-Five Years after Stonewall: An Exploratory Study of Satisfaction with Police among Gay, Lesbian, and Bisexual Persons at the 34th Annual Atlanta Pride Festival', *Journal of Homosexuality* 55, 4: 619–47.

——— and Roger L. Blackwell. 2009. 'Substance Use Patterns and Consequences among Lesbians, Gays, and Bisexuals', *Journal of Gay & Lesbian Social Services: Issues in Practice, Policy & Research* 21, 1: 90–108.

Golden, Carla. 2005. 'Anatomy Is Hardly Destiny: Intersexuals, Transsexuals, Cross-Dressers', *Women & Therapy* 28, 2: 105–10.

Goldfarb, Sally F. 2007. 'Granting Same-Sex Couples the "Full Rights and Benefits" of Marriage: Easier Said Than Done', *Rutgers Law Review* 59, 2: 281–90.

Greenlee, Timothy B. 2005. 'Queer Eye for a Gay Guy: Using Market-Specific Symbols in Advertising to Attract Gay Consumers without Alienating the Mainstream', *Psychology & Marketing* 22, 5: 421–39.

Gross, Robert, and Gregory P. Bisson. 2009. 'Evaluating the President's Emergency Plan for AIDS Relief: Time to Scale It Up', *Annals of Internal Medicine* 150, 10: 727.

Halperin, David M. 1990. *One Hundred Years of Homosexuality and Other Essays on Greek Love*. London and New York: Routledge.

Hammers, Corie. 2009. 'Space, Agency, and the Transfiguring of Lesbian/Queer Desire', *Journal of Homosexuality* 56, 6: 757–85.

Hancock, Tina U. 2008. 'Doing Justice: A Typology of Helping Attitudes toward Sexual Groups', *Affilia: Journal of Women & Social Work* 23, 4: 349–62.

Harding, Rosie. 2007. 'Sir Mark Potter and the Protection of the Traditional Family: Why Same-Sex Marriage Is (Still) a Feminist Issue', *Feminist Legal Studies* 15, 2: 223–34.

Harris, Angelique C. 2009. 'Marginalization by the Marginalized: Race, Homophobia, Heterosexism, and "the Problem of the 21st Century"', *Journal of Gay & Lesbian Social Services* 21, 4: 430–48.

Haslam, Nick, and Sheri R. Levy. 2006. 'Essentialist Beliefs about Homosexuality: Structure and Implications for Prejudice', *Personality and Social Psychology Bulletin* 32, 4: 471–85.

Heath, K.V., P.G. Cornelisse, S.A. Strathdee, A. Palepu, M.L. Miller, M.T. Schechter, M.V. O'Shaughnessy, and R.S. Hogg. 1999. 'HIV-associated Risk Factors among Young Canadian Aboriginal and Non-Aboriginal Men Who Have Sex with Men', *International Journal of STD and AIDS* 10, 9: 582–7.

Hequembourg, A.L., and M.P. Farrell. 1999. 'Lesbian Motherhood—Negotiating Marginal-Mainstream Identities', *Gender & Society* 13, 4: 540–57.

Herek, Gregory M. 2004. 'Beyond "Homophobia": Thinking about Sexual Prejudice and Stigma in the Twenty-First Century', *Sexuality Research and Social Policy* 1, 2: 6–24.

Hines, Sally. 2006. 'Intimate Transitions: Transgender Practices of Partnering and Parenting', *Sociology* 40, 2: 353–71.

Hoffman, Neal D., Katherine Freeman, and Stephanie Swann. 2009. 'Healthcare Preferences of Lesbian, Gay, Bisexual, Transgender and Questioning Youth', *Journal of Adolescent Health* 45, 3: 222–9.

Jacobs, Sue-Ellen, Wesley Thomas, and Sabine Long, eds. 1997. *Two-Spirit People: Native American Gender, Identity, Sexuality and Spirituality*. Urbana: University of Illinois Press.

Kates, Steven M., and Russell W. Belk. 2001. 'The Meanings of Lesbian and Gay Pride Day: Resistance through Consumption and Resistance to Consumption', *Journal of Contemporary Ethnography* 30, 4: 392–429.

Kim, Saeromi. 2007. 'Gatekeeping and Homophobia: From Bouncers in Bars to the Macro-Social, Interpersonal, and Intrapsychological Practices of Homophobia', *Integrative Psychological & Behavioral Science* (Special Issue: 'Relating to Gender—A New Look at Gender Identity') 41, 3 and 4: 303–16.

King, E.B., C. Reilly, and M. Hebl. 2008. 'The Best of Times, the Worst of Times—Exploring Dual Perspectives of "Coming Out" in the Workplace', *Group & Organization Management* 33, 5: 566–601.

Kuntsman, Adi. 2008. 'Between Gulags and Pride Parades', *GLQ: A Journal of Lesbian & Gay Studies* 14, 2 and 3: 263–87.

Lax, Jeffrey R., and Justin H. Phillips. 2009. 'Gay Rights in the States: Public Opinion and Policy Responsiveness', *American Political Science Review* 103, 3: 367–86.

Lee, I-Ching, and Mary Crawford. 2007. 'Lesbians and Bisexual Women in the Eyes of Scientific Psychology', *Feminism and Psychology* 17, 1: 109–27.

Liu, Ting. 2009. 'Conflicting Discourses on Boys' Love and Subcultural Tactics in Mainland China and Hong Kong', *Intersections: Gender and Sexuality in Asia and the Pacific* no. 20. At: <intersections.anu.edu.au/issue20/liu.htm>.

Looy, Heather. 1995. 'Born Gay? A Critical Review of Biological Research on Homosexuality', *Journal of Psychology and Christianity* 14, 3: 197–214.

McCabe, Sean Esteban, Tonda L. Hughes, Wendy B. Bostwick, Brady T. West, and Carol J. Boyd. 2009. 'Sexual Orientation, Substance Use Behaviors and Substance Dependence in the United States', *Addiction* 104, 8: 1333–45.

McLaren, Suzanne. 2009. 'Sense of Belonging to the General and Lesbian Communities as Predictors of Depression among Lesbians', *Journal of Homosexuality* 56, 1: 1–13.

McQueeney, Krista B. 2003. 'The New Religious Rite: A Symbolic Interactionist Case Study of Lesbian Commitment Rituals', *Journal of Lesbian Studies* 7, 2: 49–70.

Madureira, Ana Flávia do Amaral. 2007. 'The Psychological Basis of Homophobia: Cultural Construction of a Barrier', *Integrative Psychological & Behavioral Science* 41, 3 and 4: 225–47.

Mamo, Laura. 2007. *Queering Reproduction: Achieving Pregnancy in the Age of Technoscience*. Durham, NC: Duke University Press.

Mattingly, Marybeth J., and Robert N. Bozick. 2001. 'Children Raised by Same-Sex Couples: Much Ado about Nothing', paper presented to Southern Sociological Society conference.

Meyer-Cook, Fiona, and Diane Labelle. 2004. 'Namaji: Two-Spirit Organizing in Montreal, Canada', *Journal of Gay & Lesbian Social Services* 16, 1: 29–51.

Miall, C., and K. March. 2005. 'Open Adoption as a Family Form: Community Assessments

and Social Support', *Journal of Family Issues* 26, 3: 380–410.

Mooney-Somers, F., and S. Golombok. 2000. 'Children of Lesbian Mothers: From the 1970s to the New Millennium', *Sexual and Relationship Therapy* 15, 2: 121–6.

Moore, M.R. 2009. 'New Choices, New Families: How Lesbians Decide about Motherhood', *Journal of Marriage and the Family* 71, 5: 1350–2.

Nell, Patricia. 2005. '"Traditional" Marriage: A Secular Affair', *Gay & Lesbian Review Worldwide* 12, 3: 10.

Oakenfull, Gillian K., Michael S. McCarthy, and Timothy B. Greenlee. 2008. 'Targeting a Minority without Alienating the Majority: Advertising to Gays and Lesbians in Mainstream Media', *Journal of Advertising Research* 48, 2: 191–8.

O'Higgins-Norman, James. 2009. 'Straight Talking: Explorations on Homosexuality and Homophobia in Secondary Schools in Ireland', *Sex Education: Sexuality, Society and Learning* 9, 4: 381–93.

Okumura, Aya. 2007. 'No Turning Back: Male to Female Transgender Journeys of Getting through Tough Times', *International Journal of Narrative Therapy and Community Work* 3: 57–66.

O'Ryan, Leslie W., and William P. McFarland. 2010. 'A Phenomenological Exploration of the Experiences of Dual-Career Lesbian and Gay Couples', *Journal of Counseling & Development* 88, 1: 71–9.

Osterlund, Katherine. 2009. 'Love, Freedom and Governance: Same-Sex Marriage in Canada', *Social & Legal Studies* 18, 1: 93–109.

Owen, Michelle K. 2001. '"Family" as a Site of Contestation: Queering the Normal or Normalizing the Queer?', in Terry Goldie, ed., *In a Queer Country: Gay and Lesbian Studies in the Canadian Context*. Vancouver: Arsenal Pulp Press, 86–98.

Peel, Elizabeth. 2008. 'De-Heterosexualising Health: Exploring Lesbian, Gay, Bisexual and Trans Health Issues and Policy in Britain', *Sex Roles* 59, 7 and 8: 609–10.

Plummer, David C. 2001. 'The Quest for Modern Manhood: Masculine Stereotypes, Peer Culture, and the Social Significance of Homophobia', *Journal of Adolescence* 24, 1: 15–23.

Popenoe, David. 1993. 'American Family Decline, 1960–1990: A Review and Appraisal', *Journal of Marriage and Family* 55: 527–42.

Potoczniak, Daniel, Margaret Crosbie-Burnett, and Nikki Saltzburg. 2009. 'Experiences Regarding Coming Out to Parents among African American, Hispanic, and White Gay, Lesbian, Bisexual, Transgender, and Questioning Adolescents', *Journal of Gay & Lesbian Social Services: Issues in Practice, Policy & Research* 21, 2 and 3: 189–205.

Próspero, M. 2008. 'The Effect of Coercion on Aggression and Mental Health among

Reciprocally Violent Couples', *Journal of Family Violence* 23, 3: 195–202.

Ragins, Belle Rose, John M. Cornwell, and Janice S. Miller. 2003. 'Heterosexism in the Workplace: Do Race and Gender Matter?', *Group and Organization Management* 28, 1: 45–74.

Ramsey, E.M., and Gladys Santiago. 2004. 'The Conflation of Male Homosexuality and Femininity in Queer Eye for the Straight Guy', *Feminist Media Studies* 4, 3: 353–55.

Reuters. 2009. 'Huge Crowd Shows Solidarity with Tel Aviv Gays', 8 Aug. At: <www.reuters.com/article/idUSL8666121>.

Richlin, Amy. 2005. 'Eros Underground: Greece and Rome in Gay Print Culture, 1953–65', *Journal of Homosexuality* 49, 3 and 4: 421–61.

Ristock, Janice. 2001. *No More Secrets: Violence in Lesbian Relationships*. London: Routledge.

Röndahl, Gerd, Elisabeth Bruhner, and Jenny Lindhe. 2009. 'Heteronormative Communication with Lesbian Families in Antenatal Care, Childbirth and Postnatal Care', *Journal of Advanced Nursing* 65, 11: 2337–44.

Rosker, Jana S. 2009. 'The Golden Orchid Relationships: Female Marriages and Same-Sex Families in the Chinese Province of Guangdong during the 19th Century', *Socialno Delo* 48, 1–3: 99–110.

Rutledge, Scott E., Neil Abell, Jacqueline Padmore, and Theresa J. McCann. 2009. 'AIDS Stigma in Health Services in the Eastern Caribbean', *Sociology of Health and Illness* 31, 1: 17–34.

Savin-Williams, R.C., and K.G. Esterberg. 2000. 'Lesbian, Gay, and Bisexual Families', in D.H. Demo, K.R. Allen, and M.A. Fine, eds, *Handbook of Family Diversity*. New York: Oxford University Press.

Seidman, Steven. 2002. *Beyond the Closet: The Transformation of Gay and Lesbian Life*. New York: Routledge.

Smith, Tom W. 1998. *American Sexual Behavior: Trends, Socio-Demographic Differences, and Risk Behavior*. Chicago: National Opinion Research Center, University of Chicago, GSS Topical Report No. 25.

Speziale, B., and C. Ring. 2006. 'Intimate Violence among Lesbian Couples: Emerging Data and Critical Needs', *Journal of Feminist Family Therapy* 18, 1 and 2: 85–96.

Stacey, J., and T. Meadow. 2009. 'New Slants on the Slippery Slope: The Politics of Polygamy and Gay Family Rights in South Africa and the United States', *Politics & Society* 37, 2: 167–202.

Taylor, Verta, and Leila J. Rupp. 2004. 'Chicks with Dicks, Men in Dresses: What It Means to be a Drag Queen', *Journal of Homosexuality* (Special Issue: 'The Drag Queen Anthology: The Absolutely Fabulous but Flawlessly Customary World of Female Impersonators') 46, 3 and 4: 113–33.

Tomassilli, Julia C., Sarit A. Golub, David S. Bimbi, and Jeffrey T. Parsons. 2009. 'Behind Closed Doors: An Exploration of Kinky Sexual Behaviors in Urban Lesbian and Bisexual Women', *Journal of Sex Research* 46, 5: 438–45.

Tomsen, Stephen. 2006. 'Homophobic Violence, Cultural Essentialism and Shifting Sexual Attitudes', *Social & Legal Studies* 15, 3: 389–407.

Towle, Evan B., and Lynn Marie Morgan. 2002. 'Romancing the Transgender Native: Rethinking the Use of the "Third Gender" Concept', *GLQ: A Journal of Lesbian and Gay Studies* 8, 4: 469–97.

Turner, William B. 2009. 'Gay Rights and Moral Panic: The Origins of America's Debate on Homosexuality', *Journal of American History* 96, 3: 928–9.

Uzzell, David, and Nathalie Horne. 2006. 'The Influence of Biological Sex, Sexuality and Gender Role on Interpersonal Distance', *British Journal of Social Psychology* 45, 3: 579–97.

Valverde, Mariana, and Miomir Cirak. 2003. 'Governing Bodies, Creating Gay Spaces: Policing and Security Issues in "Gay" Downtown Toronto', *British Journal of Criminology* 43, 1: 102–21.

VanderLaan, D.P., and P.L. Vasey. 2008. 'Born Gay: The Psychobiology of Sex Orientation', *Archives of Sexual Behavior* 37, 4: 673–4.

Walcott, Rinaldo. 2009. 'David Rayside, Queer Inclusions, Continental Divisions: Public Recognition of Sexual Diversity in Canada and the United States', *Labour/Le Travail* 64: 227–30.

Waldner, L.K., H. Martin, and L. Capeder. 2006. 'Ideology of Gay Racialist Skinheads and Stigma Management Techniques', *Journal of Political & Military Sociology* 34, 1: 165–84.

Walters, K.L., T. Evans-Campbell, J. Simoni, T. Ronquillo, and R. Bhuyan. 2006. '"My Spirit in My Heart": Identity Experiences and Challenges among American Indian Two-Spirit Women', *Journal of Lesbian Studies* 10, 1 and 2: 125–49.

Wang, Frank, Herng-Dar Bih, and David Brennan. 2009. '"Have They Really Come Out?" Gay Men and Their Parents in Taiwan', *Culture, Health and Sexuality* 11, 3: 285–96.

Weinberg, George. 1983 [1972]. *Society and the Healthy Homosexual*. New York: St Martin's Press.

Whitehead, A.L. 2010. 'Sacred Rites and Civil Rights: Religion's Effect on Attitudes toward Same-Sex Unions and the Perceived Cause of Homosexuality', *Social Science Quarterly* 91, 1: 63–79.

Winter, Sam. 2006. 'Thai Transgenders in Focus: Demographics, Transitions and Identities', *International Journal of Transgenderism* 9, 1: 15–27.

Young, Claire, and Susan Boyd. 2006. 'Losing the Feminist Voice? Debates on the Legal Recognition of Same-Sex Partnerships in Canada', *Feminist Legal Studies* 14, 2: 213–40.

Chapter 6

Alzheimer's Disease Education and Referral Center. 1995. Alzheimer's Disease Fact Sheet. At: <www.alzheimers.org/pubs/adfact.html>.

Angus, Jocelyn, and Patricia Reeve. 2006. 'Ageism: A Threat to "Aging Well" in the 21st Century', *Journal of Applied Gerontology* 25, 2: 137–52.

Antonucci, Toni C., Jennifer E. Lansford, and Lynne Schaberg. 2001. 'Widowhood and Illness: A Comparison of Social Network Characteristics in France, Germany, Japan, and the United States', *Psychology and Aging* 16, 4: 655–65.

Bélanger, Alain. 2006. *Report on the Demographic Situation in Canada 1998–1999*. Ottawa: Statistics Canada. At: <www.statcan.gc.ca/pub/91-209-x/91-209-x1999000-eng.pdf>.

———, Laurent Martel, and Éric Caron Malenfant. 2005. *Population Projections for Canada, Provinces and Territories 2005–2031*. Ottawa: Statistics Canada Catalogue no. 91–520.

Ben-Moshe, Liat. 2004. 'Juxtaposing Disability and Old Age as Constructed Identities', paper presented at meeting of the Society for the Study of Social Problems, San Francisco.

Bielby, Denise D., and William T. Bielby. 2001. 'Audience Segmentation and Age Stratification among Television Writers', *Journal of Broadcasting & Electronic Media* 45, 3: 391–431.

Blit-Cohen, E., and H. Litwin. 2004. 'Elder Participation in Cyberspace: A Qualitative Analysis of Israeli Retirees', *Journal of Aging Studies* 18, 4: 385–98.

Bonnet, Carole, and Jean-Michel Hourriez. 2009. 'Widowhood, the Survivor's Pension and Maintaining a Standard of Living after the Death of a Spouse: An Analysis of Type Cases', *Retraite et Société* 56: 71–103.

Brooke, Libby. 2009. 'Prolonging the Careers of Older Information Technology Workers: Continuity, Exit or Retirement Transitions?', *Ageing and Society* 29, part 2: 237–56.

Brown, Robert. 1991. *Economic Security in an Aging Population*. Toronto: Butterworths.

Bullard, Angela M., and Deil S. Wright. 1993. 'Circumventing the Glass Ceiling: Women Executives in American State Governments', *Public Administration Review* 53: 189–212.

CARP. 2001. 'What Is CARP?' At: <www.fiftyplus.net/CARP/about/main.cfm>.

Chatterjee, Pranab, Darlyne Bailey, and Nina Aronoff. 2002. 'Adolescence and Old Age in Twelve Communities', *Journal of Sociology and Social Welfare* 28, 4: 121–59.

Clarke, Laura H., and Meridith Griffin. 2008. 'Visible and Invisible Ageing: Beauty Work as a Response to Ageism', *Ageing and Society* 28, part 5: 653–74.

Chappell, Neena L. 1997. 'Health Care Reform: Implications for Seniors. Introduction', *Journal of Aging Studies* 11, 3: 171–5.

——— and Susan A. McDaniel. 1999. 'Health Care in Regression: Contradictions, Tensions and Implications for Canadian

Seniors', *Canadian Public Policy* 25, 1: 123–32.

Cohen, Carole A. 2006. 'Consumer Fraud and the Elderly: A Review of Canadian Challenges and Initiatives', *Journal of Gerontological Social Work* 46, 3 and 4: 137–44.

Connidis, Ingrid. 1989. *Family Ties and Aging*. Toronto: Butterworths.

Cornwell, Benjamin. 2009. 'Network Bridging Potential in Later Life: Life-Course Experiences and Social Network Position', *Journal of Aging and Health* 21, 1: 129–54.

Cullen, Jennifer C., Leslie B. Hammer, and Margaret B. Neal. 2009. 'Development of a Typology of Dual-Earner Couples Caring for Children and Aging Parents', *Journal of Family Issues* 30, 4: 458–83.

Cumming, E., and W.E. Henry. 1961. *Growing Old: The Process of Disengagement*. New York: Basic Books.

Dobbs, Debra, J.K. Eckert, Bob Rubinstein, Lynn Keimig, Leanne Clark, Ann C. Frankowski, and Sheryl Zimmerman. 2008. 'An Ethnographic Study of Stigma and Ageism in Residential Care or Assisted Living', *The Gerontologist* 48, 4: 517–26.

Dupuis, Sara B. 2009. 'An Ecological Examination of Older Remarried Couples', *Journal of Divorce and Remarriage* 50, 6: 369–87.

Elder, Glen H., Jr. 1999. 'The Life Course and Aging: Some Reflections', Distinguished Scholar lecture given at the annual meeting of the American Sociological Association. At: <www.unc.edu/~elder/asa/asacharts.pdf>.

Esping-Andersen, Gosta. 2003. 'A Model for Pension Reform in 21st Century Europe'. At: <www.socialdialogue.net/en/en_cha_key_003.jsp>.

FitzGerald, Brian A.P. 2008. 'Everything Old Is New Again: A Reflection on the State of the Defined-Benefit Pension Plan', *Canadian Public Policy* (Nov.): 23–8.

Foner, Anne. 2000. 'Age Integration or Age Conflict as Society Ages?', *The Gerontologist* 40, 3: 272–6.

Freedman, Vicki A., Lisa F. Berkman, and Stephen R. Rapp. 1994. 'Family Networks: Predictors of Nursing Home Entry', *American Journal of Public Health* 84: 843–5.

Gagliardi, Cristina, Fiorella Marcellini, Roberta Papa, Cinzia Giuli, and Heidrun Mollenkopf. 2010. 'Associations of Personal and Mobility Resources with Subjective Well-being among Older Adults in Italy and Germany', *Archives of Gerontology and Geriatrics* 50, 1: 42–7.

Gans, Daphna, and Merril Silverstein. 2006. 'Norms of Filial Responsibility for Aging Parents across Time and Generations', *Journal of Marriage and Family* 68, 4: 961–76.

Garber, Carol E., Jenifer E. Allsworth, and Bess H. Marcus. 2008. 'Correlates of the Stages of Change for Physical Activity in a Population Survey', *American Journal of Public Health* 98, 5: 897–904.

George, Linda. 1980. *Role Transitions in Later Life*. Monterey, Calif.: Brooks/Cole.

Gillen, Martie, and Hyungsoo Kim. 2009. 'Older Women and Poverty Transition: Consequences of Income Source Changes from Widowhood', *Journal of Applied Gerontology* 28, 3: 320–41.

Ginn, Jay, and Sara Arber. 1995. 'Exploring Mid-Life Women's Employment', *Sociology* 29, 1 (February): 73–94.

Gottlieb, Beatrice. 1993. *The Family in the Western World: From the Black Death to the Industrial Age*. New York: Oxford University Press.

Handel, Gerald. 1997. 'Life History and Life Course: Resuming a Neglected Symbolic Interactionist Mandate', American Sociological Association, conference paper.

Hanlon, Neil, and Greg Halseth. 2005. 'The Greying of Resource Communities in Northern British Columbia: Implications for Health Care Delivery in Already-Underserviced Communities', *Canadian Geographer* 49, 1: 1–24.

Harbison, Joan, and Marina Morrow. 1998. 'Re-Examining the Social Construction of Elder Abuse and Neglect: A Canadian Perspective', *Ageing and Society* 18, part 6: 691–711.

Havighurst, Robert, and Ruth Albrecht. 1953. *Older People*. New York: Longman, Green.

Heinz, Walter. 1996. 'Life Course and Social Change in Germany: The Interchange between Institutions and Biographies', American Sociological Association, conference paper.

Hicks, Jennifer, and Eric R. Kingston. 2009. 'The Economic Crisis: How Fare Older Americans?', *Generations* 33, 3: 6–11.

Hill, Gretchen J. 2006. 'State Policy Decisions in the 1990s with Implications for the Financial Well-being of Later-Life Families', *Journal of Aging & Social Policy* 18, 3 and 4: 211–27.

Ho, Jeong-Hwa, and James M. Raymo. 2009. 'Expectations and Realization of Joint Retirement among Dual-Worker Couples', *Research on Aging* 31, 2: 153–79.

Hughes, Mary E., and Linda J. Waite. 2002. 'Health in Household Context: Living Arrangements and Health in Late Middle Age', *Journal of Health and Social Behavior* 43, 1: 1–21.

Ikkink, Karn Klein, and Theo van Tilburg. 1998. 'Do Older Adults' Network Members Continue to Provide Instrumental Support in Unbalanced Relationships?', *Journal of Social and Personal Relationships* 15, 1: 59–75.

Johnson, Wendy, Ian J. Deary, Matt McGue, and Kaare Christensen. 2009. 'Genetic and Environmental Links between Cognitive and Physical Functions in Old Age', *Journals of Gerontology, Series B: Psychological Sciences and Social Sciences* 64B, 1: 65–72.

Jonson, Hakan, and Annika T. Larsson. 2009. 'The Exclusion of Older People in Disability Activism and Policies—A Case of

Inadvertent Ageism?', *Journal of Aging Studies* 23, 1: 69–77.

Kaestner, Robert, Jay A. Pearson, Danya Keene, and Arline T. Geronimus. 2009. 'Stress, Allostatic Load, and Health of Mexican Immigrants', *Social Science Quarterly* 90, 5: 1089–1111.

Keating, Norah, J. Frederick Fast, K. Cranswick, and C. Perrier. 1999. *Eldercare in Canada: Context, Content and Consequences*. Ottawa: Statistics Canada Catalogue no. 89–570–XPE.

Kehl Wiebel, Susana, and J. Manuel Fernandez Fernandez. 2001. 'The Social Construction of Old Age', *Cuadernos de Trabajo Social* no. 14: 125–61.

Kemmerling, A., and M. Neugart. 2009. 'Financial Market Lobbies and Pension Reform', *European Journal of Political Economy* 25, 2: 163–73.

Kim, Jeungkun. 2009. 'Early Retirement in Three Types of Welfare States', *Research on Aging* 31, 5: 520–48.

Kim, Myung-Hye. 1996. 'Changing Relationships between Daughters-in-Law and Mothers-in-Law in Urban South Korea', *Anthropological Quarterly* 69, 4: 179–92.

Lasch, Christopher. 1977. *Haven in a Heartless World: The Family Besieged*. New York: Basic Books.

Lazzarini, Guido. 1990. 'Paths of the Elderly', *Studi di Sociologia* 28: 371–85.

Lau, Denys T., and James B. Kirby. 2009. 'The Relationship between Living Arrangement and Preventive Care Use among Community-Dwelling Elderly Persons', *American Journal of Public Health* 99, 7: 1315–21.

Lennartsson, Carin. 1999. 'Social Ties and Health among the Very Old in Sweden', *Research on Aging* 21: 657–81.

Lindström, Martin. 2009. 'Marital Status, Social Capital, Material Conditions and Self-Rated Health: A Population-Based Study', *Health Policy* 93, 2 and 3: 172–9.

Litwin, Howard. 1998. 'Social Network Type and Health Status in a National Sample of Elderly Israelis', *Social Science and Medicine* 46: 599–609.

Lysaght, Patricia. 2002. Book Review of Arensberg and Kimball, *Family and Community in Ireland*, 3rd edn (2001), *Bealoideas: Journal of the Folklore of Ireland*. Clare Local Studies Project, at: <www.clarelibrary.ie/eolas/library/local-studies/clasp/publications/reviews/bealoideas_family_community_review.htm>.

Magnusson, Lennart, Elizabeth Hanson, and Mike Nolan. 2005. 'The Impact of Information and Communication Technology on Family Carers of Older People and Professionals in Sweden', *Ageing and Society* 25, part 5: 693–714.

Marshall, Barbara L. 2007. 'Climacteric Redux?: (Re)medicalizing the Male Menopause', *Men and Masculinities* 9 4(April): 509–29.

Martens, Andy, Jeff Greenberg, and Jeff Schimel. 2004. 'Ageism and Death: Effects of Mortality Salience and Perceived Similarity to Elders on Reactions to Elderly People', *Personality and Social Psychology Bulletin* 30, 12: 1524–36.

McDaniel, Susan A., and Allison L. McKinnon. 1993. 'Gender Differences in Informal Support and Coping among Elders: Findings from Canada's 1985 and 1990 General Social Surveys', *Journal of Women and Aging* 5, 2: 79–98.

McMunn, Anne, James Nazroo, Morten Wahrendorf, Elizabeth Breeze, and Paola Zaninotto. 2009. 'Participation in Socially-Productive Activities, Reciprocity and Well-being in Later Life: Baseline Results in England', *Ageing & Society* 29, 5: 765–82.

Mendenhall, Ruby, Ariel Kalil, Laurel J. Spindel, and Cassandra M.D. Hart. 2008. 'Job Loss at Mid-Life: Managers and Executives Face the "New Risk Economy"', *Social Forces* 87, 1: 187–209.

Merz, Eva-Maria, Carlo Schuengel, and Hans-Joachim Schulze. 2007. 'Intergenerational Solidarity: An Attachment Perspective', *Journal of Aging Studies* 21, 2: 175–86.

Midanik, Lorraine T., Krikor Soghikian, Laura J. Ransom, and Michael R. Polen. 1990. 'Health Status, Retirement Plans, and Retirement: The Kaiser Permanente Study', *Journal of Aging and Health* 2: 462–74.

Moody, Harry R. 2000. *Aging: Concepts and Controversies*, 3rd edn. Boston: Pine Forge Press.

Moore, Eric G., and Mark W. Rosenberg. 2001. 'Canada's Elderly Population: The Challenges of Diversity', *Canadian Geographer* 45, 1: 145–50.

Myles, John. 1989. *Old Age in the Welfare State: The Political Economy of Public Pensions*, rev. edn. Lawrence, Kansas: University Press of Kansas.

National Center on Elder Abuse. 2001. 'The Basics: What Is Elder Abuse?' At: <www.elderabusecenter.org/basic/index.html>.

Newsletter of the National Advisory Council on Aging. 2006. 9, 2 (June). At: <www.naca.ca/expression/9-2/exp_9-2_e.html>.

Novak, Mark. 1997. *Aging and Society: A Canadian Perspective*, 3rd edn. Scarborough, Ont.: Nelson Thompson.

O'Rand, Angela M., and Kim M. Shuey. 2007. 'Gender and the Devolution of Pension Risks in the US', *Current Sociology* 55, 2: 287–304.

Payling, S.J. 2001. 'The Economics of Marriage in Late Medieval England: The Marriage of Heiresses', *Economic History Review* 54, 3: 413–29.

Pew, R.W., and S.B. Van Hemel, eds. 2004. *Technology for Adaptive Aging*. Washington: National Academies Press.

Poon, Cecilia Y.M., and Bob G. Knight. 2009. 'Influence of Sad Mood and Old Age Schema on Older Adults' Attention to Physical Symptoms', *Journals of Gerontology, Series B: Psychological Sciences and Social Sciences* 64B, 1: 41–4.

Rosenthal, Carolyn J. 1997a. 'The Changing Contexts of Family Care in Canada', *Ageing International* 24, 1: 13–31.

———. 1997b. 'The Care of Canadian Families for Their Aging Members', *Lien social et politiques* 38, 78: 123–31.

Rubin, Rose M., and Shelley I. White-Means. 2009. 'Informal Caregiving: Dilemmas of Sandwiched Caregivers', *Alternative Lifestyles* 30, 3: 252–67.

Saini, Sarita, and Sushma Jaswal. 2009. 'A Comparative Appraisal of Quality of Life (QOL) of Aged Living with Sons and Living with Daughters', *The Anthropologist* 11, 2: 139–46.

Schroots, Johannes J.F. 1996. 'Theoretical Developments in the Psychology of Aging', *The Gerontologist* 36: 742–8.

Shugrue, Noreen, and Julie Robison. 2009. 'Intensifying Individual, Family, and Caregiver Stress: Health and Social Effects of Economic Crisis', *Generations* 33, 3: 34–9.

Smith, Hilda L. 2001. '"Aging": A Problematic Concept for Women', *Journal of Women's History* 12, 4: 77–86.

Statistics Canada. n.d. 'Complete Life Table, Canada, 2000 to 2002, Females'. At: <www.statcan.ca/english/freepub/84-537-XIE/tables/pdftables/caf.pdf>.

———. 1994. *Population Projections for Canada, Provinces and Territories, 1993–2016* (Catalogue no. 91–520). Ottawa: Statistics Canada.

———. 1998. *Canada Yearbook* (Catalogue no. 11–402–XPE). Ottawa: Statistics Canada.

———. 2000. 'Age Pyramid of the Population of Canada, July 1, 1974 to 2004'. At: <www.statcan.ca/english/kits/animat/pyca.htm>.

———. 2003. *The Daily*, 17 Nov. At: <www.statcan.ca/Daily/English/031117/d031117a.htm>.

———. 2004. *The Daily*, 22 July. At: <www.statcan.ca/Daily/English/040722/d040722b.htm>.

———. 2009. 'Proportion of Persons Aged 65 and over in the Canadian Population, 1956 to 2006'. At: <www12.statcan.ca/census-recensement/2006/as-sa/97-551/figures/c2-eng.cfm>.

Steinkamp, Marjorie W., and John R. Kelly. 1987. 'Social Integration, Leisure Activity, and Life Satisfaction in Older Adults: Activity Theory Revisited', *International Journal of Aging and Human Development* 25, 4: 293–322.

Ugiagbe, Ernest O., Kokunre Agbontaen-Eghafona, and Tracy B.E. Omorogiuwa. 2007. 'An Evaluation of the Principles of Primogeniture and Inheritance Laws among the Benin People of Nigeria', *Journal of Family History* 32, 1: 90–46.

Vares, T. 2009. 'Reading the "Sexy Oldie": Gender, Age(ing) and Embodiment', *Sexualities* 12, 4: 503–24.

Vincent, John. 1996. 'Who's Afraid of an Ageing Population? Nationalism, the Free Market, and the Construction of Old Age as an Issue', *Critical Social Policy* 16 (May): 3–26.

Williams, Sharon W., and Peggye Dilworth-Anderson. 2002. 'Systems of Social Support in Families Who Care for Dependent African American Elders', *The Gerontologist* 42, 2: 224–36.

Windsor, Tim. 2009. 'Persistence in Goal Striving and Positive Reappraisal as Psychosocial Resources for Ageing Well: A Dyadic Analysis', *Aging and Mental Health* 13, 6: 874–84.

Wong, Rebeca, and Deborah S. DeGraff. 2009. 'Old-Age Wealth in Mexico: The Role of Reproductive, Human Capital, and Employment Decisions', *Research on Aging* 31, 4: 413–39.

Wood, F.W., ed. 1990. *An American Profile: Opinions and Behavior, 1972–1989*. Detroit: Gale Research.

Xie, Li-Qin, Jing-Ping Zhang, Fang Peng, and Na-Na Jiao. 2010. 'Prevalence and Related Influencing Factors of Depressive Symptoms for Empty-Nest Elderly Living in the Rural Area of YongZhou, China', *Archives of Gerontology and Geriatrics* 50, 1: 24–9.

Yang, Keming, and Christina R. Victor. 2008. 'The Prevalence of and Risk Factors for Loneliness among Older People in China', *Ageing & Society* 28, 3: 305–27.

Chapter 7

Alaggia, Ramona, Cheryl Regehr, and Giselle Rishchynski. 2009. 'Intimate Partner Violence and Immigration Laws in Canada: How Far Have We Come?', *International Journal of Law and Psychiatry* 32, 6: 335–41.

Anderson, Elijah. 1994. 'The Code of the Streets: Sociology of Urban Violence', *Atlantic Monthly* (May): 80–91.

Aradau, Claudia, and Rens Van Munster. 2009. 'Exceptionalism and the "War on Terror": Criminology Meets International Relations', *British Journal of Criminology* 49, 5: 686–717.

Arnold, Robert, Carl Keane, and Stephen Baron. 2005. 'Assessing Risk of Victimization through Epidemiological Concepts: An Alternative Analytic Strategy Applied to Routine Activities Theory', *Canadian Review of Sociology and Anthropology* 42, 3: 345–64.

Bachman, Ronet, Heather Dillaway, and Mark S. Lachs. 1998. 'Violence against the Elderly: A Comparative Analysis of Robbery and Assault across Age and Gender Groups', *Research on Aging* 20: 183–98.

Betts, P., K. Henning, R. Janikowski, L. Klesges, H. Scott, and A. Anderson. 2003. *Memphis Sexual Assault Project: Final Report*. Memphis, Tenn.: University of Memphis.

Boudreaux, Edwin, Dean G. Kilpatrick, Heidi S. Resnick, Connie L. Best, and Benjamin E. Saunders. 1998. 'Criminal Victimization, Posttraumatic Stress Disorder, and Comorbid Psychopathology among a Community Sample of Women', *Journal of Traumatic Stress* 11: 665–78.

Braithwaite, John. 1993. 'Crime and the Average American', *Law and Society Review* 27: 215–32.

Britt, Chester L. 2001. 'Health Consequences of Criminal Victimization', *International Review of Victimology* 8, 1: 63–73.

Browne, Angela, Kirk R. Williams, and Donald G. Dutton. 1999. 'Homicide between Intimate Partners', in M. Dwayne Smith and Margaret A. Zahn, eds, *Studying and Preventing Homicide: Issues and Challenges*. Thousand Oaks, Calif.: Sage, 55–78.

Bush, Vanessa. 2010. 'I Don't Wish Nobody to Have a Life Like Mine: Tales of Kids in Adult Lockup', *The Booklist* 106, 11: 8.

Canadian Centre for Justice Statistics. 2005. 'Adult Correctional Services in Canada, 2003/04', *Juristat* 25, 8: 14.

Canadian Resource Centre for Victims of Crime. 2005. 'Impact of Victimization'. At: <www.crcvc.ca/en>.

———. 2006. 'Victims' Rights in Canada'. At: <www.crcvc.ca/en>.

Carrington, F., and G. Nicholson. 1984. 'The Victims' Movement: An Idea Whose Time Has Come', *Pepperdine Law Review* 11: 1–14.

CBC News. 2005. 'Indepth: Racial Profiling', 26 May. At: <www.cbc.ca/news/background/racial_profiling/>.

Cheloukhine, S. 2008. 'The Roots of Russian Organized Crime: From Old-Fashioned Professionals to the Organized Criminal Groups of Today', *Crime Law and Social Change* 50, 4 and 5: 353–74.

Church, Wesley T. II, Tracy Wharton, and Julie K. Taylor. 2009. 'An Examination of Differential Association and Social Control Theory: Family Systems and Delinquency', *Youth Violence and Juvenile Justice* 7, 1: 3–15.

Clear, Todd R. 1996. 'Backfire: When Incarceration Increases Crime', *Journal of the Oklahoma Criminal Justice Research Consortium* 3 (Aug): 7–17.

Cole, J.H., and A.M. Gramajo. 2009. 'Homicide Rates in a Cross-Section of Countries: Evidence and Interpretations', *Population and Development Review* 35, 4: 749–76.

Davis, K.E., and I.H. Frieze. 2000. 'Research on Stalking: What Do We Know and Where Do We Go?', *Violence and Victims* 15, 4: 473–87.

Dawson, Jenna. 2009. 'The Impact of Organized Crime on the Canadian Economy', *The Police Chief* 76, 1: 64.

Denkers, Adriaan J.M., and Frans Willem Winkel. 1998. 'Crime Victims' Well-Being and Fear in a Prospective and Longitudinal Study', *International Review of Criminology* 5, 2: 141–62.

Doepke, Matthias, and Michele Tertilt. 2009. 'Women's Liberation: What's in It for Men?', *Quarterly Journal of Economics* 124, 4: 1541–91.

Durkheim, Émile. 1951 [1897]. *Suicide*, trans. John A. Spaulding and George Simpson. New York: Free Press.

Elzinga, Anne. 1996. 'Security of Taxi Drivers in the Netherlands: Fear of Crime, Actual Victimization and Recommended Security Measures', *Security Journal* 7, 3: 205, 210.

Ericson, Richard. 1982. *Reproducing Order: A Study of Police Patrol Work*. Toronto: University of Toronto Press.

Farrell, G. 2010. 'Situational Crime Prevention and Its Discontents: Rational Choice and Harm Reduction versus "Cultural Criminology"', *Social Policy and Administration* 44, 1: 40–66.

Finkelhor, David, and Nancy L. Asdigian. 1996. 'Risk Factors for Youth Victimization: Beyond a Lifestyles/Routine Activities Theory Approach', *Violence and Victims* 11, 1: 3–19.

Friedrichs, David O. 1995. 'Responding to the Challenge of White-Collar Crime as a Social Problem', Society for the Study of Social Problems, conference paper.

Gartner, Rosemary. 1997. 'Crime: Variations across Cultures and Nations', in C. Ember and M. Ember, eds, *Cross-Cultural Research for Social Science*. Englewood Cliffs, NJ: Prentice-Hall.

Gaylord, Mark S., and Graeme Lang. 1997. 'Robbery, Recession and Real Wages in Hong Kong', *Crime, Law and Social Change* 27, 1: 49–71.

Gotlieb, Jennifer J. 2002. 'The Violent Crime Rate Decline: Towards an Explanation'. At: <gateway.proquest.com.myaccess.library.utoronto.ca/openurl?url_ver=Z39.88-2004&rft_val_fmt=info:ofi/fmt:kev:mtx:dissertation&res_dat=xri:pqdiss&rft_dat=xri:pqdiss:MQ76584>.

Griffin, Timothy, and Monica Miller. 2008. 'Child Abduction, AMBER Alert, and Crime Control Theater', *Criminal Justice Review* (June): 159–76.

Hannon, Lance. 1997. 'AFDC and Homicide', *Journal of Sociology and Social Welfare* 24, 4: 125–36.

Hashima, Patricia Y., and David Finkelhor. 1999. 'Violent Victimization of Youth versus Adults in the National Crime Victimization Survey', *Journal of Interpersonal Violence* 14: 799–820.

Hirschi, Travis. 1969. *Causes of Delinquency*. Berkeley: University of California Press.

Jackson, Jonathan, and Ben Bradford. 2009. 'Crime, Policing and Social Order: On the Expressive Nature of Public Confidence in Policing', *British Journal of Sociology* 60, 3: 493–521.

Jenness, Valerie. 1995. 'Hate Crimes in the United States: The Transformation of Injured Persons into Victims and the Extension of Victim Status to Multiple Constituencies', in Joel Best, ed., *Images of Issues: Typifying Contemporary Social Problems*, 2nd edn. Hawthorne, NY: Aldine de Gruyter, 213–37.

Johnson, Knowlton W. 1997. 'Professional Help and Crime Victims', *Social Service Review* 71, 1: 89–109.

Kawachi, Ichiro, Bruce P. Kennedy, and Richard G. Wilkinson. 1999. 'Crime, Social Disorganization, and Relative Deprivation', *Social Science and Medicine* 48: 719–31.

Kissner, Jason, and David C. Pyrooz. 2009. 'Self-Control, Differential Association, and Gang Membership: A Theoretical and Empirical Extension of the Literature', *Journal of Criminal Justice* 37, 5: 478–87.

Kitchen, Peter, and Allison Williams. 2010. 'Quality of Life and Perceptions of Crime in Saskatoon, Canada', *Social Indicators Research* 95, 1: 33–61.

Knight, W. Andy, and Tom Keating. 2010. *Global Politics: Emerging Networks, Trends, and Challenges*. Toronto: Oxford University Press.

Kong, Rebecca. 1999. 'Canadian Crime Statistics, 1997', in Canadian Centre for Justice Statistics, *The Juristat Reader: A Statistical Overview of the Canadian Justice System*. Toronto: Thompson Educational Publishing, 117–37.

Kupers, Terry A. 1996. 'Trauma and Its Sequelae in Male Prisoners: Effects of Confinement, Over-crowding and Diminished Services', *American Journal of Orthopsychiatry* 66: 189–96.

LaPrairie, Carol, et al. 1996. *Examining Aboriginal Corrections in Canada*. Ottawa: Solicitor General of Canada.

Lauritsen, Janet L., and Karen Heimer. 2008. 'The Gender Gap in Violent Victimization, 1973–2004', *Journal of Quantitative Criminology* 24, 2: 125–47.

Lee, Matthew R. 2000. 'Community Cohesion and Violent Predatory Victimization: A Theoretical Extension and Cross-National Test of Opportunity Theory', *Social Forces* 79: 683–706.

Lovell, Jarret. 2009. *Crimes of Dissent*. New York: New York University Press.

Lyons, Christopher J. 2008. 'Defending Turf: Racial Demographics and Hate Crime against Blacks and Whites', *Social Forces* 87, 1: 357–85.

McKee, Kevin J., and Caroline Milner. 2000. 'Health, Fear of Crime and Psychosocial Functioning in Older People', *Journal of Health Psychology* 5, 4: 473–86.

Mawby, R.I., P. Brunt, and Z. Hambly. 1999. 'Victimisation on Holiday: A British Survey', *International Review of Victimology* 6: 201–11.

Mechanic, Mindy B., Mary H. Uhlmansiek, Terri L. Weaver, and Patricia A. Resick. 2000. 'The Impact of Severe Stalking Experienced by Acutely Battered Women: An Examination of Violence, Psychological Symptoms and Strategic Responding', *Violence and Victims* 15: 443–58.

Merton, Robert K. 1938. 'Social Structure and Anomie', *American Sociological Review* 3, 5: 672–82.

Mesch, Gustavo S. 1997. 'Victims and Property Victimization in Israel', *Journal of Quantitative Criminology* 13: 57–71.

Moore, Elizabeth, and Michael Mills. 2001. 'The Neglected Victims and Unexamined Costs of White-Collar Crime', in Neal Shover and John P. Wright, eds, *Crimes of*

Privilege: Readings in White-Collar Crime. New York: Oxford University Press, 51–7.

National Research Council. 1994. *Violence in Urban America: Mobilizing a Response.* Washington: National Academy Press.

O'Donnell, Ian, and Kimmett Edgar. 1998. 'Routine Victimization in Prisons', *Howard Journal of Criminal Justice* 37: 266–79.

Paetsch, Joanne J., and Lorne D. Bertrand. 1999. 'Victimization and Delinquency among Canadian Youth', *Adolescence* 34: 351–67.

Palmer, Emma J., Clive R. Hollin, and Laura S. Caulfield. 2005. 'Surveying Fear: Crime, Buses and New Paint', *Crime Prevention and Community Safety* 7, 4: 47–58.

Peel, Elizabeth. 1999. 'Violence against Lesbians and Gay Men: Decision-Making in Reporting and Not Reporting Crime', *Feminism and Psychology* 9, 2: 161–7.

Pepinsky, Harold E., and Paul Jesilow. 1984. *Myths That Cause Crime.* Cabin John, Md: Seven Locks Press.

Pottinger, Audrey M., and Angela G. Stair. 2009. 'Bullying of Students by Teachers and Peers and Its Effect on the Psychological Well-being of Students in Jamaican Schools', *Journal of School Violence* 8, 4: 312–27.

Pratt, Carter, and Kamala Deosaransingh. 1997. 'Gender Differences in Homicide in Contra Costa County, California, 1982–1993', *American Journal of Preventive Medicine* 13 (suppl.): 19–24.

Reed, Micheline, and Julian Roberts. 1999. 'Adult Correctional Services in Canada, 1997–98', in Canadian Centre for Justice Statistics, *The Juristat Reader: A Statistical Overview of the Canadian Justice System.* Toronto: Thompson Educational Publishing, 39–51.

Roberts, Julian V., and Anthony N. Doob. 1997. 'Race, Ethnicity, and Criminal Justice in Canada', in Michael Tonry, ed., *Ethnicity, Crime, and Immigration: Comparative and Cross-National Perspectives.* Chicago: University of Chicago Press, 469–522.

Rosenfeld, Richard. 2009. 'Crime Is the Problem: Homicide, Acquisitive Crime, and Economic Conditions', *Journal of Quantitative Criminology* 25, 3: 287–306.

Ruback, R. Barry, and Martie P. Thompson. 2001. *Social and Psychological Consequences of Violent Victimization.* Thousand Oaks, Calif.: Sage.

Sanborn, Joseph B., Jr. 2001. 'Victims' Rights in Juvenile Court: Has the Pendulum Swung Too Far?', *Judicature* 85, 3: 140–6.

Scott, Bridget T. 1999. 'Chronic Community Violence and the Children Who Are Exposed To It', *Journal of Emotional Abuse* 1, 3: 23–37.

Sennett, Richard, and Jonathan Cobb. 1972. *The Hidden Injuries of Class.* New York: Vintage.

Smith, Brent L., John J. Sloan, and Richard M. Ward. 1990. 'Public Support for the Victims' Rights Movement: Results of a Statewide Survey', *Crime and Delinquency* 36, 4: 488–502.

——— and C. Ronald Huff. 1992. 'From Victim to Political Activist: An Empirical Examination of a Statewide Victims' Rights Movement', *Journal of Criminal Justice* 20: 201–15.

Statistics Canada. 2005a. *Crime Statistics, Canada, Provinces and Territories, 1977–2004.* Ottawa: Canadian Centre for Justice Statistics.

———. 2005b. 'Adult Correctional Services', *The Daily*, 16 Dec.

———. 2008. *Police Resources in Canada, 2008*, 12 Dec. At: <dsp-psd.pwgsc.gc.ca/collection_2008/statcan/85-225-X/85-225-x2008000-eng.pdf>.

Steffensmeier, Darrell, and Emilie Allan. 1996. 'Gender and Crime: A Gendered Theory of Female Offending', *Annual Review of Sociology* 22: 459–87.

Sutherland, Edwin H. 1949. *White Collar Crime.* New York: Dryden Press.

Tewksbury, Richard, Elizabeth L. Grossi, Geetha Suresh, and Jeff Helms. 1999. 'Hate Crimes against Gay Men and Lesbian Women: A Routine Activity Approach for Predicting Victimization Risk', *Humanity and Society* 23, 2: 125–42.

Tiby, Eva. 2001. 'Victimization and Fear among Lesbians and Gay Men in Stockholm', *International Review of Victimology* 8: 217–43.

Tillman, Robert, and Michael Indergaard. 1999. 'Field of Schemes: Health Insurance Fraud in the Small Business Sector', *Social Problems* 46: 572–90.

Trejos, Nancy. 2006. 'Academic Arrested in Prostitution Sting', *Washington Post*, 20 Jan., B09. At: <www.washingtonpost.com/wp-dyn/content/article/2006/01/19/AR200611903109.html>.

Turner, Heather A., David Finkelhor, and Richard Ormrod. 2010. 'The Effects of Adolescent Victimization on Self-Concept and Depressive Symptoms', *Child Maltreatment* 15, 1: 76–90.

Vaughn, Michael S., and Linda G. Smith. 1999. 'Practicing Penal Harm Medicine in the United States: Prisoners' Voices from Jail', *Justice Quarterly* 16, 1: 175–231.

Vollaard, B., and P. Koning. 2009. 'The Effect of Police on Crime, Disorder and Victim Precaution. Evidence from a Dutch Victimization Survey', *International Review of Law and Economics* 29, 4: 336–48.

Welch, Michael. 1999. *Punishment in America: Social Control and the Ironies of Imprisonment.* Thousand Oaks, Calif.: Sage.

Whaley, R.B., and S. Messner. 2002. 'Gender Equality and Gendered Homicide', *Homicide Studies* 6, 3: 188–210.

White, Jacqueline, Robin M. Kowalski, Amy Lyndon, and Sherri Valentine. 2000. 'An Integrative Contextual Developmental Model of Male Stalking', *Violence and Victims* 15: 373–88.

Whyte, William Foote. 1981 [1943]. *Street Corner Society: Social Structure of an Italian Slum*, 3rd edn. Chicago: University of Chicago Press.

Wilson, Margo, and Martin Daly. 1992. 'Who Kills Whom in Spouse Killings? On the Exceptional Sex Ratio of Spousal Homicides in the U.S.', *Criminology* 30: 189–215.

Wooldredge, John D. 1998. 'Inmate Lifestyles and Opportunities for Victimization', *Journal of Research in Crime and Delinquency* 35: 480–502.

Wortley, Scot, and Lysandra Marshall. 2005. *Bias-Free Policing: The Kingston Data Collection Project—Final Results.* At: <www.police.kingston.on.ca>.

Wrangham, Richard, and Dale Peterson. 1997. *Demonic Males: Apes and the Origins of Human Violence.* Boston: Houghton Mifflin.

Zvekic, Ugliesa. 1996. 'The International Crime (Victim) Survey: Issues of Comparative Advantages and Disadvantages', *International Criminal Justice Review* 6: 1–21.

Chapter 8

Adlaf, Edward M., Patricia Begin, and Ed Sawka, eds. 2005. *Canadian Addiction Survey (CAS): A National Survey of Canadians' Use of Alcohol and Other Drugs: Prevalence of Use and Related Harms: Detailed Report.* Ottawa: Canadian Centre on Substance Abuse.

———, Andrée Demers, and Louis Gliksman, eds. 2005. *Canadian Campus Survey 2004.* Toronto: Centre for Addiction and Mental Health.

Afifi, T.O., B.J. Cox, P.J. Martens, J. Sareen, and M.W. Enns. 2010. 'The Relation between Types and Frequency of Gambling Activities and Problem Gambling among Women in Canada', *Canadian Journal of Psychiatry* 55, 1: 21–8.

Alden, Helena, and Scott R. Maggard. 2000. 'Perceptions of Social Class and Drug Use', paper presented at the annual conference of the Southern Sociological Society.

Auerhahn, Kathleen, and Robert Nash Parker. 1999. 'Drugs, Alcohol and Homicide', in M. Dwayne Smith and Margaret A. Zahn, eds, *Studying and Preventing Homicide: Issues and Challenges.* Thousand Oaks, Calif.: Sage, 99–114.

Bailey, Ian. 2007. 'Fate of safe-injection site remains up in the air'. *The Globe and Mail.* October 3.

Bailey, Susan L. 1999. 'The Measurement of Problem Drinking in Young Adulthood', *Journal of Studies on Alcohol* 60: 234–44.

Becker, Howard. 1963. *Outsiders: Studies in the Sociology of Deviance.* New York: Free Press.

Bensley, Lillian Southwick, Susan J. Spieker, Juliet van Eenwyk, and Judy Schoder. 1999. 'Self-reported Abuse History and Adolescent Problem Behaviors, II: Alcohol and Drug Use', *Journal of Adolescent Health* 24, 3: 173–80.

Brownstein, Henry H., Sean D.Cleary, Susan M. Crimmins, Judith Ryder, Raquel

Warley, Barry Spunt. 1999. 'The Relationship between Violent Offending and Drug Use in the Pre-Prison Experience of a Sample of Incarcerated Young Men'. American Sociological Association.

Canadian Cancer Society/National Cancer Institute of Canada. 2006. *Canadian Cancer Statistics 2006*. At: <www.cancer.ca>.

Carey, Kate B., and Kelly S. DeMartini. 2010. 'The Motivational Context for Mandated Alcohol Interventions for College Students by Gender and Family History', *Addictive Behaviors* 35, 3: 218–23.

Carruthers, Cynthia P. 1992. 'The Relationship of Alcohol Consumption Practices to Leisure Patterns and Leisure-Related Alcohol Expectancies', *Dissertation Abstracts International* 52, 7-A: 2700–1.

Centre for Addiction and Mental Health. 2003. 'Do You Know . . . Cocaine'. At: <www.camh.net/About_Addiction_Mental_Health/Drug_and_Addiction_Information/cocaine_dyk.html>.

Cheung, Yuet W., and James M.N. Ch'ien. 1999. 'Previous Participation in Outpatient Methadone Program and Residential Treatment Outcome: A Research Note from Hong Kong', *Substance Use and Misuse* 34: 103–18.

Coker, Donna. 2003. 'Foreword: Addressing the Real World of Racial Injustice in the Criminal Justice System', *Journal of Criminal Law and Criminology* 93, 4: 827–79.

Colson, Tara A. 2000. *Study of Marijuana Use among Young Adults*. Knoxville, Tenn.: Southern Sociological Society.

Criminal Intelligence Service Canada. 2006. *CISC Annual Report on Organized Crime in Canada*. At: <www.cisc.gc.ca>.

Dawkins, Marvin P. 1997. 'Drug Use and Violent Crime among Adolescents', *Adolescence* 32: 395–405.

DeBeck, K., W. Small, E. Wood, K. Li, J. Montaner, and T. Kerr. 2009. 'Public Injecting among a Cohort of Injecting Drug Users in Vancouver, Canada', *Journal of Epidemiology and Community Health* 63, 1: 81–6.

———, Thomas Kerr, Kathy Li, Benedikt Fischer, Jane Buxton, Julio Montaner, and Evan Wood. 2009. 'Smoking of Crack Cocaine as a Risk Factor for HIV Infection among People Who use Injection Drugs', *CMAJ: Canadian Medical Association Journal* 181, 9: 585–90.

Delva, Jorge, Michelle L. Van Etten, Gonzalo B. Gonzalez, Miguel A. Cedeno, Marcel Penna, Luis H. Caris, and James C. Anthony. 1999. 'First Opportunities to Try Drugs and the Transition to First Drug Use: Evidence from a National School Survey in Panama', *Substance Use and Misuse* 34: 1451–67.

Dervensky, Jeffrey L., and Rina Gupta. 2004 *Gambling Problems in Youths: Theoretical and Applied Perspectives*. New York: Kluwer Academic/Plenum.

Di Nicola, Marco, Daniela Tedeschi, Marianna Mazza, Giovanni Martinotti, Desiree Harnic, Valeria Catalano, Angelo Bruschi, Gino

Pozzi, Pietro Bria, and Luigi Janiri. 2010. 'Behavioural Addictions in Bipolar Disorder Patients: Role of Impulsivity and Personality Dimensions', *Journal of Affective Disorders*.

Dishion, Thomas J., Deborah M. Capaldi, and Karen Yoerger. 1999. 'Middle Childhood Antecedents to Progressions in Male Adolescent Substance Abuse: An Ecological Analysis of Risk and Protection', *Journal of Adolescent Research* 14: 175–205.

Duster, Troy. 1997. 'Pattern, Purpose, and Race in the Drug War: The Crisis of Credibility in Criminal Justice', in Reinarman and Levine (1997: 260–87).

Ehlers, C.L., W. Slutske, D.A. Gilder, and P. Lau. 2007. 'Age of First Marijuana Use and the Occurrence of Marijuana Use Disorders in Southwest California Indians', *Pharmacology Biochemistry and Behavior* 86, 2: 290–6.

Ellickson, Phyllis L., Rebecca L. Collins, and Robert M. Bell. 1999. 'Adolescent Use of Illicit Drugs Other Than Marijuana: How Important Is Social Bonding and for Which Ethnic Groups?', *Substance Use and Misuse* 34: 317–46.

Erceg-Hurn, David M. 2008. 'Drugs, Money, and Graphic Ads: A Critical Analysis of the Montana Meth Project', *Prevention Science* 9, 4: 256–63.

Erickson, Patricia G. 1998. 'Neglected and Rejected: A Case Study of the Impact of Social Research on Canadian Drug Policy', *Canadian Journal of Sociology* 23: 263–80.

Escobar-Chaves, Soledad Liliana, and Craig A. Anderson. 2008. 'Media and Risky Behaviors', *Future of Children* 18, 1: 147–80.

Evans, Elizabeth, Suzanne E. Spear, Yu-Chang Huang, and Yih-Ing Hser. 2006. 'Outcomes of Drug and Alcohol Treatment Programs among American Indians in California', *American Journal of Public Health* 96, 5: 889–96.

French, Laurence Armand. 2008. 'Psychoactive Agents and Native American Spirituality: Past and Present', *Contemporary Justice Review* 11, 2: 155–63.

Furst, R. Terry, Bruce D. Johnson, Eloise Dunlap, and Richard Curtis. 1999. 'The Stigmatized Image of the "Crack Head": A Sociocultural Exploration of a Barrier to Cocaine Smoking among a Cohort of Youth in New York City', *Deviant Behavior* 20: 153–81.

Griesbach, Dawn, Amanda Amos, and Candace Currie. 2003. 'Adolescent Smoking and Family Structure in Europe', *Social Science and Medicine* 56: 41–52.

Griffiths, Mark. 2009. *Gambling: An Addiction?* Available at <http://www.bps.org.uk/downloadfile.cfm?file_uuid=C2B84867-E9C0-9B94-26FE-A6A958F4AF4F&ext=pdf>.

Haans, Dave. n.d. 'The Effects of Decriminalization of Marijuana'. At: <www.chass.utoronto.ca/~haans/misc/mjdcrim.html>.

Hammersley, Richard, and Marie Reid. 2002. 'Why the Pervasive Addiction Myth Is Still Believed', *Addiction Research & Theory* 10, 1: 7–30.

Hathaway, A.D., R.C. Callaghan, S. MacDonald, and P.G. Erickson. 2009. 'Cannabis Dependence as a Primary Drug Use-Related Problem: The Case for Harm Reduction-Oriented Treatment Options', *Substance Use and Misuse* 44, 7: 990–1008.

Health Canada. 1999. *Statistical Report on the Health of Canadians*. At: <www.statcan.ca/english/freepub/82-570-XIE/free.htm>.

———. 2005. 'Canada's Drug Strategy'. At: <www.hc-sc.gc.ca/ahc-asc/activit/strateg/drugs-drogues/index_e.html>.

Herzog, Benno, Esperanza Gomez-Guardeno, Rafael Aleixandre-Benavent, and Juan C. Valderrama-Zurian. 2009. 'Discourses on Drugs and Immigration: The Social Construction of a Problem', *Forum Qualitative Sozialforschung/Forum: Qualitative Social Research* 10, 1.

Hodgins, David C., JianLi Wang, Nady el-Guebaly, Harold Wynne, and Natalie V. Miller. 2008. 'Replication of Low-Risk Gambling Limits Using Canadian Provincial Gambling Prevalence Data', *Journal of Gambling Studies* 24, 3: 321–35.

Hodgson, Maggie. 1987. *Indian Communities Develop Futuristic Addictions Treatment and Health Approach*. Edmonton: Nechi Institute on Alcohol and Drug Education.

Hogan, Sean R. 2009. 'The Social Construction of Drug Policy and Its Impact on Substance Abuse Treatment Philosophies in the United States', in A. Browne-Miller, ed., *The Praeger International Collection on Addictions*, vol. 3: *Characteristics and Treatment Perspectives*. Santa Barbara, Calif.: Praeger/ABC-CLIO, 3–21.

Hutchison, Ira W. 1999. 'Alcohol, Fear, and Woman Abuse', *Sex Roles* 40: 893–920.

Inciardi, James A., Hilary L. Suratt, Hector M. Colon, Dale D. Chitwood, and James E. Rivers. 1999. 'Drug Use and HIV Risks among Migrant Workers on the DelMarVa Peninsula', *Substance Use and Misuse* 34: 653–66.

Ivis, Frank J., and Edward M. Adlaf. 1999. 'A Comparison of Trends in Drug Use among Students in the USA and Ontario, Canada: 1975–1997', *Drugs, Education, Prevention, and Policy* 6: 17–27.

Johnston, M., T. Williamson, E. Wheaton, V. Wittrock, H. Nelson, L. Vandamme, H. Hesseln, J. Pittman, and M. Lebel. 2008. *Climate Change Adaptive Capacity of Forestry Stakeholders in the Boreal Plains Ecozone*. Final Report submitted to Natural Resources Canada Climate Change Impacts and Adaptations Program. Ottawa: Natural Resources Canada.

Karp, Igor, Jennifer O'Loughlin, Gilles Paradis, James Hanley, and Joseph Difranza. 2005. 'Smoking Trajectories of Adolescent Novice Smokers in a Longitudinal Study of Tobacco Use', *Annals of Epidemiology* 15, 6: 445–52.

Kovas, Anne E., Bentson H. McFarland, Michael G. Landen, Adriana L. Lopez, and Philip A. May. 2008. 'Survey of American Indian Alcohol Statutes, 1975–2006:

Evolving Needs and Future Opportunities for Tribal Health', *Journal of Studies on Alcohol and Drugs* 12, 3: 34–48.

Kunitz, Stephen J. 2008. 'Risk Factors for Polydrug Use in a Native American Population', *Substance Use and Misuse* 43, 3 and 4: 331–9.

Kuntsche, Emmanuel, Ronald Knibbe, Rutger Engels, and Gerhard Gmel. 2010. 'Being Drunk to Have Fun or to Forget Problems? Identifying Enhancement and Coping Drinkers among Risky Drinking Adolescents', *European Journal of Psychological Assessment* 26, 1: 46–54.

Kuo, Feng-Yang, Chiung-Wen Hsu, and Rong-Fuh Day. 2009. 'An Exploratory Study of Cognitive Effort Involved in Decision Under Framing—An Application of the Eye-Tracking Technology', *Decision Support Systems* 48, 1: 81.

Leatherdale, S.T., P.W. McDonald, R. Cameron, and K.S. Brown. 2005. 'A Multilevel Analysis Examining the Relationship between Social Influences for Smoking and Smoking Onset', *American Journal of Health Behavior* 29, 6: 520–30.

Liu, Xiaoru, and Howard Kaplan. 1999. 'Role Strain and Illicit Drug Use: The Moderating Influence of Commitment to Conventional Values', paper presented at the annual meeting of the American Sociological Association.

Lozgacheva, Evgeniia A. 2008. 'Gambling Dependency: Features and Social Consequences', *Monitoring Obshchestvennogo Mneniia* 3, 87: 126–32.

McBride, Andrew J., Richard Pates, and Morfydd Keen. 1998. 'Drug Trends in Wales', *Journal of Drug Issues* 28, 1: 107–25.

McClure, A.C., S. Dal Cin, and J.D. Sargent. 2006. 'Ownership of Alcohol-branded Merchandise and Initiation of Teen Drinking', *American Journal of Preventive Medicine* 30, 4: 277–83.

McComb, Jennifer L., Bonnie K. Lee, and Douglas H. Sprenkle. 2009. 'Conceptualizing and Treating Problem Gambling as a Family Issue', *Journal of Marital and Family Therapy* 35, 4: 415–31.

McCoy, Clyde B., Lisa R. Metsch, Dale D. Chitwood, James E. Rivers, H. Virginia McCoy, and Sarah Messiah. 2000. 'Health Services for Chronic Drug Users in an Era of Managed Care: The University of Miami Community-based Health Services Research Centre', *Advances in Medical Sociology* 7: 151–74.

Mehrabadi, Azar, K.J.P. Craib, K. Patterson, W. Adam, A. Moniruzzaman, B. Ward-Burkitte, M. T. Schechter, and P.M. Spittal. 2008. 'The Cedar Project: A Comparison of HIV-related Vulnerabilities amongst Young Aboriginal Women Surviving Drug Use and Sex Work in Two Canadian Cities', *International Journal of Drug Policy* 19, 2: 159–69.

Meddis, Sam V. 1993. 'Is the Drug War Racist? Disparities Suggest the Answer Is Yes', *USA Today*, 23 July, 2A.

Merton, Robert K. 1957. 'Social Structure and Anomie', in Merton, *Social Theory and Social Structure*, rev. edn. New York: Free Press, ch. 3.

Moodie, Crawford, and Gerard Hastings. 2009. 'Social Marketing and Problem Gambling: A Critical Perspective', *Addiction* 104, 5: 692–3.

Moon, Dreama G., Michael L. Hecht, Kristina M. Jackson, and Regina E. Spellers. 1999. 'Ethnic and Gender Differences and Similarities in Adolescent Drug Use and Refusals of Drug Offers', *Substance Use and Misuse* 34: 1059–183.

Moreno, Amira Y., and Kim D. Janda. 2009. 'Immunopharmacotherapy: Vaccination Strategies as a Treatment for Drug Abuse and Dependence', *Pharmacology, Biochemistry and Behavior* 92, 2: 199–205.

Mulia, Nina, Yu Ye, Sarah E. Zemore, and Thomas K. Greenfield. 2008. 'Social Disadvantage, Stress, and Alcohol Use among Black, Hispanic, and White Americans: Findings from the 2005 U.S. National Alcohol Survey', *Journal of Studies on Alcohol and Drugs* 69, 6: 824–33.

Murphy, Jennifer. 2009. 'Therapy and Punishment: Negotiating Authority in the Management of Drug Addiction', ProQuest Information & Learning, US.

Murray, Robert P., Suzanne L. Tyas, Wanda Snow, Okechukwu Ekuma, Ruth Bond, and Gordon E. Barnes. 2010. 'Exploring the Boundary between Health Protective and Hazardous Drinking in a Community Cohort', *Addictive Behaviors* 35, 3: 278–81.

Oldham, G., and B. Gordon. 1999. 'Job Complexity and Employee Substance Use: The Moderating Effects of Cognitive Ability', *Journal of Health and Social Behavior* 40 (September): 290–306.

Patton, Travis, and Anne Baird. 2000. 'Alcohol and Interpersonal Violence: Methodological Considerations', paper presented at the annual meeting of the Southern Sociological Society.

Quann, Nathalie. 2004. *Drug Use and Offending*. Report prepared for the Department of Justice Canada. At: <www.justice.gc.ca/eng/pi/rs/rep-rap/2002/qa02_2-qr02_2/p8.html>.

Rehm, Jurgen, and Gerhard Gmel. 1999. 'Patterns of Alcohol Consumption and Social Consequences: Results from an 8-Year Follow-up Study in Switzerland', *Addiction* 94: 899–912.

Reinarman, Craig, and Harry G. Levine, eds. 1997. *Crack in America: Demon Drugs and Social Justice*. Berkeley: University of California Press.

Rush, B.R., S. Veldhuizen, and E. Adlaf. 2007. 'Mapping the Prevalence of Problem Gambling and Its Association with Treatment Accessibility and Proximity to Gambling Venues', *Journal of Gambling Issues* 20. At: <www.camh.net/egambling>.

Sample, Ian. 2008. 'Exam Cheating Alert over Brain Drugs', *The Guardian*, 22 May.

At: <www.guardian.co.uk/science/2008/may/22/drugs.medical research>.

Santolaria, Francisco, Jose Luis Perez Manzano, Antonio Milena, Emilio Gonzalez Reimers, Maria Angeles Gomez Rodriguez, Antonio Martinez Riera, Maria Remedios Aleman Valls, and Maria Joe de la Vega Prieto. 2000. 'Nutritional Assessment in Alcoholic Patients: Its Relationship with Alcoholic Intake, Feeding Habits, Organic Complications and Social Problems', *Drug and Alcohol Dependence* 59: 295–304.

Schechter, M., S. Strathdee, P. Cornelisse, S. Currie, D. Patrick, M. Rekart, and M.V. O'Shaughnessy. 1999. 'Do Needle Exchange Programmes Increase the Spread of HIV among Injection Drug Users?: An Investigation of the Vancouver Outbreak', *AIDS* 13: F45–F51.

Scott, Kathryn D., John Schafer, and Thomas K. Greenfield. 1999. 'The Role of Alcohol in Physical Assault Perpetration and Victimization', *Journal of Studies on Alcohol* 60: 528–36.

Senate Special Committee on Illegal Drugs. 2002. *Report*. Available at: <http://www.parl.gc.ca/common/committee_senrep.asp?language=e&parl=37&Ses=1&comm_id=85>.

Spillane, Nichea S. 2008. 'A Test of an Integrative Theory of Reservation-Dwelling American Indian Alcohol Use Risk', ProQuest Information & Learning, US.

Statistics Canada. 2005. 'Canadian Tobacco Use Monitoring Survey', *The Daily*, 11 Aug.

Suissa, Amnon J. 2007. 'Addiction and Medicalization: Signs and Psychosocial Issues', *Nouvelles Pratiques Sociales* 19, 2: 92–110.

Valentine, Leanne. 2009. 'Exposure to Gambling-Related Media and Its Relation to Gambling Expectancies and Behaviors', ProQuest Information & Learning, US.

Valverde, Mariana. 1998. *Diseases of the Will: Alcohol and the Dilemmas of Freedom*. Cambridge: Cambridge University Press.

Vaughan, Ellen L., William R. Corbin, and Kim Fromme. 2009. 'Academic and Social Motives and Drinking Behavior', *Psychology of Addictive Behaviors* 23, 4: 564–76.

Van Etten, Michelle, Yehuda D. Neumark, and James C. Anthony. 1999. 'Male–Female Differences in the Earliest Stages of Drug Involvement', *Addiction* 94: 1413–19.

Wagner, David. 1995. 'Historicizing Social Constructionist Perspectives: The Example of Temperance Movements', paper presented at the annual meeting of the Society for the Study of Social Problems.

Warden, Narelle L., James G. Phillips, and James R.P. Ogloff. 2004. 'Internet Addiction', *Psychiatry, Psychology and Law* 11, 2: 280–95.

Warner, Jessica, Robin Room, and Edward M. Adlaf. 1999. 'Rules and Limits in the Use of Marijuana among High-School Students: The Results of a Qualitative Study in Ontario', *Journal of Youth Studies* 2: 59–76.

————, Timothy R. Weber, and Ricardo Albanes. 1999. '"Girls Are Retarded When They're Stoned"': Marijuana and the Construction of Gender Roles among Adolescent Females', *Sex Roles* 40: 25–43.

Westphal, James. 2007. 'Emerging Conceptual Models of Excessive Behaviors', *International Journal of Mental Health and Addiction* 5, 2: 107–16.

White, Helene R., and Erich W. Labouvie. 1994. 'Generality versus Specificity of Problem Behaviour: Psychological and Functional Differences', *Journal of Drug Issues* 24: 55–74.

Wiebe, J., P. Mun, and N. Kauffman. 2006. *Gambling and Problem Gambling in Ontario 2005*. Toronto: Responsible Gambling Council (Ontario).

————, E. Single, and A. Falkowski-Ham. 2001. *Measuring Gambling and Problem Gambling in Ontario*. Toronto: Canadian Centre on Substance Abuse and Responsible Gambling Council (Ontario).

Williams, Robert, and Susan P. Gloster. 1999. 'Knowledge of Fetal Alcohol Syndrome (FAS) among Natives in Northern Manitoba', *Journal of Studies on Alcohol* 60: 833–6.

Witters, Weldon, Peter Venturelli, and Glen Hanson. 1992. *Drugs and Society*, 3rd edn. Boston: Jones and Bartlett.

Yarnold, Barbara. 1999. 'Cocaine Use among Miami's Public School Students, 1992: Religion versus Peers and Availability', *Journal of Health and Social Policy* 11, 2: 69–84.

Zerbisias, Antonia. 2007. 'Why Did Women Turn to Pills So Often', *Toronto Star*, 9 July. At: <www.thestar.com>.

Chapter 9

Altman, Lawrence. 1981. 'Rare Cancer Seen in 41 Homosexuals', *New York Times*, 3 July.

American Psychiatric Association. 1994. *Diagnostic and Statistical Manual of Mental Disorders*, 4th edn. Washington: American Psychiatric Association.

Aronowitz, Robert. 2008. 'Framing Disease: An Underappreciated Mechanism for the Social Patterning of Health', *Social Science and Medicine* 67, 1: 1–9.

Barlow, G.L. 2002. 'Auditing Hospital Queuing', *Managerial Auditing Journal* 17: 397–403.

Bartholomew, Sharon, and Rob Liston. 2006. 'Maternal Mortality: An Important Priority', *Canadian Medical Association Journal* 174, 10: 1447. At: <www.ncbi.nlm.nih.gov/pmc/articles/PMC1455436/>.

Bercovitz, K.L. 2000. 'A Critical Analysis of Canada's "Active Living": Science or Politics?', *Critical Public Health* 10, 1: 19–39.

Bern-Klug, Mercedes. 2009. 'A Framework for Categorizing Social Interactions Related to End-of-Life Care in Nursing Homes', *The Gerontologist* 49, 4: 495–507.

Caballero, Benjamin. 2001. 'Symposium: Obesity in Developing Countries: Biological and Ecological Factors (Introduction)', *Journal of Nutrition* 131 (suppl.): 866S–70S.

Cameron, Adrian J., Timothy A. Welborn, Paul Z. Zimmet, David W. Dunstan, Neville Owen, et al. 2003. 'Overweight and Obesity in Australia: The 1999–2000 Australian Diabetes, Obesity and Lifestyle Study (AusDiab)', *Medical Journal of Australia* 187, 9: 427–32.

Canadian Association of Food Banks (CAFB). 2005. *HungerCount 2005*. Toronto: CAFB.

Canadian Institute for Health Information (CIHI). 2004a. *Improving the Health of Canadians*. Ottawa: CIHI.

————. 2004b. *Overweight and Obesity in Canada*. Ottawa: CIHI.

Clarke, Alan. 2001. *The Sociology of Healthcare*. Essex, UK: Prentice-Hall.

Conference Board of Canada. 2003. *The Economic Impact of SARS*. Ottawa: Canadian Tourism Research Institute, Conference Board of Canada.

Conner-Spady, B., A. Estey, G. Arnett, K. Ness, J. McGurran, R. Bear, T. Noseworthy, and Steering Committee of the Western Canada Waiting List Project. 2005. 'Determinants of Patient and Surgeon Perspectives on Maximum Acceptable Waiting Times for Hip and Knee Arthroplasty', *Journal of Health Services Research and Policy* 10, 2: 84–90.

————, S. Sanmugasunderam, P. Courtright, J.J. McGurran, T.W. Noseworthy, and Steering Committee of the Western Canada Waiting List Project. 2004. 'Determinants of Patient Satisfaction with Cataract Surgery and Length of Time on the Waiting List', *British Journal of Ophthalmology* 88, 10: 1305–9.

Contandriopoulos, Damien, and Henriette Bilodeau. 2009. 'The Political Use of Poll Results about Public Support for a Privatized Healthcare System in Canada', *Health Policy* 90, 1: 104–12.

Currie, Janet, and Mark Stabile. 2003. 'Socioeconomic Status and Child Health: Why Is the Relationship Stronger for Older Children?', *American Economic Review* 93, 5.

Dansky, K.H., and J. Miles. 1997. 'Patient Satisfaction with Ambulatory Healthcare Services: Waiting Time and Filling Time', *Hospital and Health Services Administration* 42: 165–77.

De Man, Stefanie, Peter Vlerick, Paul Gemmel, Pieter De Bondt, Dirk Matthys, and Rudi A. Dierckx. 2005. 'Impact of Waiting on the Perception of Service Quality in Nuclear Medicine', *Nuclear Medicine Communications* 26, 6: 541–7.

Durkheim, Émile. 1951 [1897]. *Suicide*. New York: Free Press.

Eckes, Thomas B., and Hanns M. Trautner. 2000. *The Developmental Social Psychology of Gender*. Hillsdale, NJ: Lawrence Erlbaum Associates.

Engel, George L. 1977. 'The Need for a New Medical Model: A Challenge for Biomedicine', *Science* 196: 129–36.

Engels, Friedrich. 1987 [1844]. *The Condition of the Working Class in England*. New York: Penguin.

Feddock, Christopher A., et al. 2005. 'Can Physicians Improve Patient Satisfaction with Long Waiting Times?', *Evaluation and the Health Professions* 28, 1: 40–52.

Fenwick, Rudy, and Mark Tausig. 2007. 'A Political Economy of Stress: Recontextualizing the Study of Mental Health/Illness in Sociology', in W. Avison, J. McLeod, and B. Pescosolido, eds, *Mental Health, Social Mirror*. New York: Springer, 143–67.

Finamore, Sheila R., and Sheila A. Turris. 2009. 'Shortening the Wait: A Strategy to Reduce Waiting Times in the Emergency Department', *Journal of Emergency Nursing* (May): 509–14.

Fitzsimons, D., K. Parahoo, S.G. Richardson, and M. Stringer. 2003. 'Patient Anxiety While on a Waiting List for Coronary Artery Bypass Surgery: A Qualitative and Quantitative Analysis', *Heart & Lung: Journal of Acute and Critical Care* 32, 1: 23–31.

Flegel, K.M. 1999. 'The Obesity Epidemic in Children and Adults: Current Evidence and Research Issues', *Medicine and Science in Sports and Exercise* 31 (suppl. 11): S509–14.

Fox, Ashley M., and Benjamin Mason Meier. 2009. 'Health as Freedom: Addressing Social Determinants of Global Health Inequities through the Human Right to Development', *Bioethics* 23, 2: 112–22.

Frank, Lawrence D., Martin A. Andresen, and Thomas L. Schmid. 2004. 'Obesity Relationships with Community Design, Physical Activity, and Time Spent in Cars', *American Journal of Preventative Medicine* 27, 2: 87–96.

Galabuzi, Grace-Edward. 2004. 'Social Exclusion'. In Dennis Raphael and David Langille, eds, *Social Determinants of Health: Canadian Perspectives*. Toronto: Canadian Scholars Press, 235–51.

Gayle, Helene. 2000. 'An Overview of the Global HIV/AIDS Epidemic, with a Focus on the United States', *AIDS* 2 (suppl. 2): S8–17.

Goldberg, E.M., and S.L. Morrison. 1963. 'Schizophrenia and Social Class', *British Journal of Psychiatry* 109: 785–802.

Gössling, Stephan. 2002. 'Global Environmental Consequences of Tourism', *Global Environmental Change* 12, 4: 283–302.

Health Canada. 2002. *A Report on Mental Illnesses in Canada*. Ottawa: Health Canada.

Hecht, Robert, Lori Bollinger, John Stover, William McGreevey, Farzana Muhib, Callisto Emas Madavo, and David de Ferranti. 2009. 'Critical Choices in Financing the Response to the Global HIV/AIDS Pandemic', *Health Affairs* 28, 6: 1591–1605.

Hudson, Christopher G. 2005. 'Socioeconomic Status and Mental Illness: Tests of the Social Causation and Selection Hypotheses', *American Journal of Orthopsychiatry* 75, 1: 3–18.

Isaacs, Sandy, Susan Keogh, Cathy Menard, and Jamie Hockin. 1998. 'Suicide in the Northwest Territories: A Descriptive Review', *Chronic Diseases in Canada* 19, 4: 152–6.

Joint Working Group on the Voluntary Sector. 1999. *Building the Relationship between National Voluntary Organizations Working in Health and Health Canada: A Framework for Action*. Ottawa: Health Canada.

Katzmarzyk, Peter T., and Ian Janssen. 2004. 'The Economic Costs Associated with Physical Inactivity and Obesity in Canada: An Update', *Canadian Journal of Applied Physiology* 29, 2: 90–115.

Kessler, Ronald C., Wai Tat Chiu, Olga Demler, and Ellen E. Walters. 2005. 'Prevalence, Severity, and Comorbidity of 12-month *DSM-IV* Disorders in the National Comorbidity Survey Replication', *Archives of General Psychiatry* 62, 6: 617–27.

Kittell, L.A., M.P. Kernoff, and A.M. Voda. 1998. 'Keeping Up Appearances: The Basic Social Process of the Menopausal Transition', *Qualitative Health Research* 8: 618–33.

Kroll-Smith, Steven. 2000. 'The Social Construction of the Drowsy Person', *Perspectives on Social Problems* 12: 89–109.

Le Petit, Christel, and Jean-Marie Berthelot. 2005. *Obesity: A Growing Issue*. Ottawa: Statistics Canada Catalogue no. 82–618–MWE2005003. At: <www.statcan.ca/bsolc/english/bsolc?catno=82-618-M2005003>.

Lock, Margaret, and Patricia Alice Kaufert, eds. 1998. *Pragmatic Women and Body Politics*. Cambridge: Cambridge University Press.

Louria, Donald B. 2000. 'Emerging and Re-emerging Infections: The Societal Determinants', *Futures* 32, 6: 581–94.

MacIntyre, Lynn. 2004. 'Food Insecurity', in Raphael (2004: 173–86).

Mackenbach, Johan P., and Martijntje J. Bakker. 2003. 'Tackling Socioeconomic Inequalities in Health: Analysis of European Experiences', *Lancet* 362: 1409–14.

McPherson, S., and D. Armstrong. 2009. 'Negotiating "Depression" in Primary Care: A Qualitative Study', *Social Science and Medicine* 69, 8: 1137–43.

Malone, R.E., E. Boyd, and L.A. Bero. 2000. 'Science in the News: Journalists' Constructions of Passive Smoking as a Social Problem', *Social Studies of Science* 30, 5: 713–35.

Mark, D.B., et al. 1994. 'Use of Medical Resources and Quality of Life after Acute Myocardial Infarction in Canada and the United States', *New England Journal of Medicine* 331, 17: 1130.

Marmot, Michael. 2004. *The Status Syndrome: How Social Standing Affects Our Health and Longevity*. New York: Henry Holt.

———. 2005. 'Social Determinants of Health Inequalities', *Lancet* 365: 1099–1104.

Mathers, Colin D., Christina Bernard, Kim M. Iburg, Mie Inoue, Doris Ma Fat, et al. 2003. *Global Burden of Disease in 2002: Data Sources, Methods and Results*. Geneva: WHO.

Matsushita, Y., N. Yoshiike, F. Kaneda, K. Yoshita, and H. Takimoto. 2004. 'Trends in Childhood Obesity in Japan over the Last 25 Years from the National Nutrition Survey', *Obesity Research* 12, 2: 205–14.

National AIDS Control Organization (NACO). 2004. *State-Wide HIV Prevalence (1998–2003)*. New Delhi: Ministry of Health and Family Welfare.

Oermann, Marilyn H. 2003. 'Effects of Educational Intervention in Waiting Room on Patient Satisfaction', *Journal of Ambulatory Care Management* 26, 2: 150–8.

Parker-Pope, Tara. 2009. 'Kept from a Dying Partner's Bedside', *New York Times*, 19 May. At: <www.nytimes.com/2009/05/19/health/19well.html>.

Parry, Monica J.E. 2004. 'Physiologic and Psychological Responses of Men and Women Waiting for Coronary Artery Bypass Graft Surgery', *Masters Abstracts International* 39–03: 0830.

Parsons, Talcott. 1951. *The Social System*. Glencoe, Ill.: Free Press.

Phelan, Jo C., Bruce G. Link, Ann Stueve, and Bernice Pescosolido. 2000. 'A Public Conception of Mental Illness in 1950 and 1996: What Is Mental Illness and Is It To Be Feared?', *Journal of Health and Social Behavior* 41, 2: 188–207.

Pieterman, Roel. 2007. 'The Social Construction of Fat: Care and Control in the Public Concern for Healthy Behaviour', *Sociology Compass* 1, 1: 309–21.

Plakun, E.M. 2009. 'Series Epilogue: A View from Riggs: Treatment Resistance and Patient Authority', *Journal of the American Academy of Psychoanalysis* 37: 699–700.

Potter, W.J. 2003. *The 11 Myths of Media Violence*. Thousand Oaks, Calif.: Sage.

Public Health Agency of Canada. 2006. *HIV and AIDS in Canada: Surveillance Report to June 30, 2005*. Ottawa: Surveillance and Risk Assessment Division, Centre for Infectious Disease Prevention and Control, Public Health Agency of Canada.

Raphael, Dennis. 2002. *Social Justice Is Good for Our Hearts: Why Societal Factors—Not Lifestyles—Are Major Causes of Heart Disease in Canada and Elsewhere*. Toronto: Centre for Social Justice Foundation for Research and Education.

———, ed. 2004, 2008. *The Social Determinants of Health: A Canadian Perspective*. Toronto: Canadian Scholars' Press.

———. 2009. 'Poverty, Human Development and Health in Canada: Research, Practice, and Advocacy Dilemmas', *Canadian Journal of Nursing Research* 41, 2: 7–18.

Rather, L.J., ed. 1985. *Rudolf Virchow: Collected Essays on Public Health and Epidemiology*. Canton, Mass.: Science History Publications.

Rennie, K.L., and S.A. Jebb. 2005. 'Prevalence of Obesity in Great Britain', *Obesity Reviews* 6, 1: 11–12.

Ritsatakis, Anna. 2009. 'Equity and Social Determinants of Health at a City Level', *Health Promotion International* 24 (suppl. 1): 181–190.

Romanow, Roy J. 2002. *Building on Values: The Future of Health Care in Canada*. Final Report of the Royal Commission on the Future of Health Care in Canada. At: <www.hc-sc.gc.ca/english/care/romaonow/hcc0086.html>.

Ronson, Barbara, and Irving Rootman. 2004. 'Literacy: One of the Most Important Determinants of Health Today', in Raphael (2004: 155–70).

Sachs, L. 1996. 'Causality, Responsibility and Blame—Core Issues in the Cultural Construction and Subtext of Prevention', *Sociology of Health & Illness* 18, 5 (November): 632–52.

Sarmento, K.M., Jr, S. Tomita, and A.O. Kos. 2005. 'The Problem of Waiting Lines for Otorhinolaryngology Surgeries in Public Services', *Brazilian Journal of Otorhinolaryngology* 71, 3: 256–62.

Sevean, P., S. Dampier, et al. 2009. 'Patients' and Families' Experiences with Video Telehealth in Rural/Remote Communities in Northern Canada', *Journal of Clinical Nursing* 18: 2573–9.

Shah, Chandrakant P. 2004. 'The Health of Aboriginal Peoples', in Raphael (2004: 267–80).

Siciliani, Luigi, and Rossella Verzulli. 2009. 'Waiting Times and Socioeconomic Status among Elderly Europeans: Evidence from SHARE', *Health Economics* 18, 11: 1295–1306.

So, Alvin Y., and Ngai Pun. 2004. 'Introduction: Globalization and Anti-globalization of SARS in Chinese Societies', *Asian Perspective* 28, 1: 5–17.

Statistics Canada. 2003. *Canadian Community Health Survey: Mental Health and Wellbeing*. Ottawa: Statistics Canada Catalogue no. 82–617–XIE. At: <www.statcan.ca:80/english/freepub/82-617-XIE/index.htm>.

Stephens, Thomas, and Natacha Joubert. 2001. 'The Economic Burden of Mental Health Problems in Canada', *Chronic Diseases in Canada* 22, 1: 18–23.

Trauth, Martin. 2009. 'Rich Countries Corner Supplies of Swine Flu Vaccine', Agence France-Press, 26 July. At: <www.google.com/hostednews/afp/article/ALeqM5gRmFrBGwtInMVkv82AGX46Ujwz7Q>.

UNAIDS. 2005. *AIDS Epidemic Update: December 2005*. Geneva: Joint United Nations Programme on HIV/AIDS (UNAIDS and World Health Organization).

UNICEF. 2001. *Progress Since the World Summit on Children: A Statistical Review*. New York: UNICEF.

———. 2005. *The State of the World's Children 2006: Excluded and Invisible*. New York: UNICEF.

United Nations (UN). 2005. *The Millennium Development Goals Report 2005*. New York: UN.

———, Population Division. 2005. *World Population Prospects: The 2004 Revision Population Database*. At: <www.esa.un.org/unpp>.

Vermeulen, Karin M., Otto H. Bosma, Wim van der Bij, Gerard H. Koëter, and Elizabeth M. Tenvergert. 2005. 'Stress, Psychological

Distress, and Coping in Patients on the Waiting List for Lung Transplantation: An Exploratory Study', *Transplant International* 18, 8: 954–9.

Vetter, Norman J. 2004. 'What Is Epidemiology?', *Reviews in Clinical Gerontology* 14: 79–89.

Westbrook, D. 1995. 'Patient and Therapist Views of Different Waiting List Procedures', *Behavioural and Cognitive Psychotherapy* 23, 2: 169–75.

White, Peter, ed. 2005. *Biopsychosocial Medicine: An Integrated Approach to Understanding Illness.* Oxford: Oxford University Press.

Wilkinson, R., and M. Marmot. 2003. *Social Determinants of Health: The Solid Facts*, 2nd edn. Geneva: WHO.

World Health Organization (WHO). 1946. Preamble to the *Constitution of the World Health Organization* as adopted by the International Health Conference, New York, 19–22 June; signed 22 July 1946 by the representatives of 61 states (Official Records of WHO, no. 2, p. 100) and entered into force 7 Apr. 1948.

———. 2003a. 'Severe Acute Respiratory Syndrome (SARS): Status of the Outbreak and Lessons for the Immediate Future'. Geneva: WHO, 20 May.

———. 2003b. *The World Health Report 2003: Shaping the Future.* Geneva: WHO.

———. 2004. 'Global Burden of Disease Estimates'. At: <www.who.int/healthinfo/bodestimates/en/index.html>.

———. 2005a. *Health and the Millennium Development Goals.* Geneva: WHO.

———. 2005b. 'Obesity and Overweight'. At: <www.who.int/dietphysicalactivity/publications/facts/obesity/en>.

———. 2006. 'Obesity and Overweight', Sept. At: <www.who.int/mediacentre/factsheets/fs311/en/index.html>.

Chapter 10

Amnesty International. 1995. *Human Rights Are Women's Right.* New York: Amnesty International USA.

Babic, Dragutin. 2002. 'The Croatian Government and Programs Regarding the Return of War Migrants: Between Plans and Realizations—The Experience of the Brod-Posavina County', *Migracijske i etnicke teme* 18, 1: 63–83.

Bass, Gary Jonathan. 2002. 'Stay the Hand of Vengeance: The Politics of War Crimes Tribunals', *International Studies Review* 4, 1: 129–39.

Beah, Ishmael. 2007. *A Long Way Gone: Memoirs of a Boy Soldier.* Vancouver: Douglas & McIntyre.

Blanchard, Eric M. 2003. 'Gender, International Relations, and the Development of Feminist Security Theory', *Signs* 28, 2: 1289–1312.

Brown, Lester R., Christopher Flavin, and Hal Kane. 1992. *Vital Signs 1992: The Trends That Are Shaping Our Future.* Washington: Worldwatch Institute.

Buchanan, David. 2002. 'Gendercide and Human Rights', *Journal of Genocide Research* 4, 1: 95–108.

Calhoun, Martin L. 1996. 'Cleaning Up the Military's Toxic Legacy', *USA Today Magazine* 124: 60–4.

Cameron, Maxwell A., Robert J. Lawson, and Brian W. Tomlin, eds. 1998. *To Walk Without Fear: The Global Movement to Ban Landmines.* Toronto: Oxford University Press.

Cancian, Francesca M., and James William Gibson. 1990. *Making War, Making Peace: The Social Foundations of Violent Conflict.* Belmont, Calif.: Wadsworth.

CBC News. 2006. 'Women in the Canadian Military', 30 May. At: <www.cbc.ca/news/background/cdnmilitary/women-cdnmilitary.html>.

Clausewitz, Carl von. 1993 [1833]. *On War*, trans. Michael Howard and Peter Paret. New York: Knopf.

Clement, Dominique. 2008. 'The October Crisis of 1970: Human Rights Abuses Under the War Measures Act', *Journal of Canadian Studies* 42, 2: 160–87.

Coalition to Stop the Use of Child Soldiers. 2009. *Child Soldiers Global Report 2008.* London.

Coates, Colin M. 1997. 'The Culture of Rural Quebec', *Journal of Canadian Studies* 32, 1: 167–71.

Cooper, Sandi E. 2002. 'Peace as a Human Right: The Invasion of Women into the World of High International Politics', *Journal of Women's History* 14, 2: 9–25.

Cromer, Gerald. 2005. 'The Rhetoric of Victimization: An Analysis of the Coverage of Intifada El-Aqsa in the Israeli Press', *International Review of Victimology* 12, 3: 235–45.

Dhamoon, Rita, and Yasmeen Abu-Laban. 2009. 'Dangerous (Internal) Foreigners and Nation-Building: The Case of Canada', *International Political Science Review* 30, 2: 163–83.

Ehud, Ya'ari. 1991. 'Arming the Monster', *Jerusalem Report*: 11.

Enloe, Cynthia H. 1987. 'Feminists Thinking about War, Militarism, and Peace', in Beth Hess and Myra Marx Ferree, eds, *Analyzing Gender: A Handbook of Social Science Research.* Newbury Park, Calif.: Sage, 526–47.

Fanon, Frantz. 1965. *The Wretched of the Earth.* New York: Grove Weidenfeld.

Friedman, George, and Meredith Friedman. 1996. *The Future of War: Power, Technology, and American World Dominance in the 21st Century.* New York: Crown.

Gatti, Antonietta M., and Stefano Montanari. 2008. 'Nanopollution: The Invisible Fog of Future Wars', *The Futurist* 4, 3: 32–4.

Girvan, Susan, ed. 2000. *Canadian Global Almanac 2000.* Toronto: Macmillan Canada.

GlobalSecurity.org. n.d. At: <www.globalsecurity.org/military/world/israel/army.htm>.

Greenfeld, Karl Taro. 2006. 'The Long Way Home', *Sports Illustrated*, 15 May.

Harvey, David. 2005. *The New Imperialism.* Oxford: Oxford University Press.

Hudson, Valerie M., and Andrea Den Boer. 2002. 'A Surplus of Men, a Deficit of Peace: Security and Sex Ratios in Asia's Largest States', *International Security* 26, 4: 5–38.

Human Rights Watch. n.d. 'Stop the Use of Child Soldiers!' At: <www.hrw.org/campaigns/crp/index.htm>.

Kage, Tatsuo. 2002. 'War Measures Act: Japanese Canadian Experience', workshop held at a meeting on Immigration and Security, Our Voices, Our Strategies: Asian Canadians against Racism, 7–9 June, University of British Columbia, Vancouver.

Kanaaneh, Moslih, and Marit Netland. 1992. *Children and Political Violence: Psychological Reactions and National Identity Formation among the Children of the Intifada.* East Jerusalem: Early Childhood Resource Center.

Knight, W. Andy, and Tom Keating. 2010. *Global Politics: Emerging Networks, Trends, and Challenges.* Toronto: Oxford University Press.

LePoire, David J., and Jerome C. Glenn. 2007. 'Technology and the Hydra of Terrorism?', *Technological Forecasting and Social Change* 74, 2: 139–47.

McDonald, Marci. 2010. *The Armageddon Factor: The Rise of Christian Nationalism in Canada.* Toronto: Random House.

Maclean's.1990. 'The FLQ Crisis: Quebec and Canada 20 Years Later', 103, 2: 18–20.

Meyer, David S. 2009. 'Constructing Threats and Opportunities after 9/11', *American Behavioral Scientist* 53, 1: 10–26.

Miller, Kenneth E. and Andrew Rasmussen. 2010. 'War Exposure, Daily Stressors, and Mental Health in Conflict and Post-Conflict Settings: Bridging the Divide between Trauma-Focused and Psychosocial Frameworks', *Social Science & Medicine* 70, 1: 7.

Mills, C. Wright. 1956. *The Power Elite.* New York: Oxford University Press.

Moore, Barrington. 1967. *Social Origins of Dictatorship and Democracy: Lord and Peasant in the Making of the Modern World.* Boston: Beacon Press.

Moore, Colin D. 2009. 'Institutions of Empire: Information, Delegation, and the Political Control of American Imperialism, 1890–1913'. ProQuest, Ann Arbor Mich.

Moore, George, and Berwyn Moore. 2009. 'Threats to Our Nation, 1957–1959: A Public Health Retrospective', *Public Health Reports* 124, 2: 323–7.

Mowat, Farley. 1984. *Sea of Slaughter.* Toronto: McClelland & Stewart.

Petrosian, D., and N. Fatkina. 2009. '"Economic Imperialism" and Macro Theory of Management of Human Behavior', *Obshchestvennye Nauki i Sovremennost* 1: 166–70.

Porter, Bruce D. 1994. *War and the Rise of the State: The Military Foundations of Modern Politics.* New York: Free Press.

Robinson, Bill, and Peter Ibbott. 2003. 'Canadian Military Spending: How Does the Current Level Compare to Historical Levels? . . . to Allied Spending? . . . to Potential Threats?', *Project Ploughshares* 3, 1: 1–16.

Shah, Anup. 2009. 'World Military Spending', 13 Sept. At: <www.globalissues.org/article/75/world-military-spending>.

Skocpol, Theda. 1979. *States and Social Revolutions: A Comparative Analysis of France, Russia, and China*. Cambridge: Cambridge University Press.

Stockholm International Peace Research Institute (SIPRI). 2008. *TIV of Arms Exports from the Top 10 Largest Exporters.* At: <www.sipri.org/contents/armstrad/output_types_TIV.html>.

Summerfield, Derek. 2000. 'War and Mental Health: A Brief Overview', *British Medical Journal* 321: 232–5.

Thomas, Emma F., Craig McGarty, and Kenneth I. Mavor. 2009. 'Aligning Identities, Emotions, and Beliefs to Create Commitment to Sustainable Social and Political Action', *Personality and Social Psychology Review* 13, 3: 194–218.

Tucker, Robert C. 1978. 'Introduction', in Karl Marx and Friedrich Engels, *The Marx-Engels Reader.* New York: Norton.

United Nations. 1998. *50 Years of United Nations Peacekeeping Operations.* At: <www.un.org/depts/dpko/dpko/50web/2.htm>.

———. 2006. 'United Nations Peacekeeping Operations: Background Note', 28 Feb. Available at: <www.un.org/depts/dpko/dpko/bnote_htm>.

US Department of State. 2010. 'State Sponsors of Terrorism'. At: <www.state.gov/s/ct/c14151.htm>.

Vision of Humanity. 2009. 'Global Peace Index'. At: <www.visionofhumanity.org/gpi-data//2009/scor>.

Wallerstein, Immanuel. 1976. *The Modern World-System: Capitalist Agriculture and the Origins of the European World-Economy in the Sixteenth Century.* New York: Academic Press.

———. 2004. *World-Systems Analysis: An Introduction.* Durham, NC: Duke University Press.

Weber, Max. 1946. *Max Weber: Essays in Sociology*, trans. and ed. H.H. Gerth and C.W. Mills. New York: Oxford University Press.

Weimann, Gabriel. 2005. 'Cyberterrorism: The Sum of All Fears?', *Studies in Conflict and Terrorism* 28, 2: 129–49.

Wright, Quincy. 1964. *A Study of War.* Chicago: University of Chicago Press.

Zimmermann, E. 1983. *Political Violence, Crises and Revolutions: Theories and Research.* Cambridge, Mass.: Schenkman.

Chapter 11

Aguilar, Filomeno. 2009. 'Labour Migration and Ties of Relatedness: Diasporic Houses and Investments in Memory in a Rural Philippine Village', *Thesis Eleven* 98: 88.

Amato, Paul R., and Bruce Keith. 1991. 'Parental Divorce and Adult Well-Being: A Meta-analysis', *Journal of Marriage and the Family* 53: 43–58.

Ambert, Anne-Marie. 1982. 'Differences in Children's Behavior towards Custodial Mothers and Custodial Fathers', *Journal of Marriage and the Family* 44: 73–86.

———. 2002. *Divorce: Facts, Causes, and Consequences*, rev. edn. Ottawa: Vanier Institute of the Family. At: <www.vifamily.ca/cft/divorce/divorcer.htm>.

Arendell, Terry. 1995. *Fathers and Divorce.* Thousand Oaks, Calif.: Sage.

Arnup, Katherine. 1999. 'Out in This World: The Social and Legal Context of Gay and Lesbian Families', *Journal of Gay and Lesbian Social Services* 10, 1: 1–25.

Aune, Kristin. 2008. 'Evangelical Christianity and Women's Changing Lives', *European Journal of Women's Studies* 15, 3: 277–94.

Baklinski, Thaddeus M. 2009. 'Divorce Rates Down for All of Canada Except Quebec: Study', 25 Nov. At: <www.lifesitenews.com/ldn/2009/nov/09112508.html>.

Balestrino, Alessandro, and Cinzia Ciardi. 2008. 'Social Norms, Cognitive Dissonance and the Timing of Marriage', *Journal of Socio-Economics* 37, 6: 2399–2410.

Balkissoon, Denise. 2009. 'One Big Gay Family', *Toronto Life* (Feb.). At: <www.torontolife.com/features/one-big-gay-family/?pageno=1>.

Bélanger, Alain, Yves Carrière, and Stéphane Gilbert. 2001. *Report on the Demographic Situation in Canada 2000* (Catalogue no. 91–209–XPE). Ottawa: Statistics Canada.

Blanchet, Therese. 2005. 'Bangladeshi Girls Sold as Wives in North India', *Indian Journal of Gender Studies* 12, 2 and 3: 305–34.

Blosnich, John R., and Robert M. Bossarte. 2009. 'Comparisons of Intimate Partner Violence among Partners in Same-Sex and Opposite-Sex Relationships in the United States', *American Journal of Public Health* 99, 12: 2182–5.

Bould, Sally, Gunther Schmaus, and Claire Gavray. 2008. 'Welfare Regimes and the Economic Situation of Men and Women after Separation', paper presented at the International Sociological Association meeting, Barcelona.

Boyd, Monica, and Edward T. Pryor. 1989. 'The Cluttered Nest: The Living Arrangements of Young Canadian Adults', *Canadian Journal of Sociology* 14, 4: 461–77.

Brabant, Sarah. 2006. 'Metaphors as Tools in Clinical Sociology: Bereavement Education and Counseling', *Journal of Applied Sociology* 23, 2: 78–91.

Brannen, Stephen J., and Allen Rubin. 1996. 'Comparing the Effectiveness of Gender-Specific and Couples Groups in a Court-Mandated Spouse Abuse Treatment Program', *Research on Social Work Practice* 6: 405–24.

Buunk, Abraham P., Justin H. Park, and Lesley A. Duncan. 2010. 'Cultural Variation in Parental Influence on Mate Choice', *Cross-Cultural Research* 44, 1: 23–40.

Central Intelligence Agency (CIA). 2005. *The World Fact Book 2005.* Washington: CIA. At: <www.cia.gov/cia/publications/factbook/geos/ch.html>.

Chambers, Deborah. 2000. 'Representations of Familism in the British Popular Media', *European Journal of Cultural Studies* 3: 195–214.

Cheah, Charissa S.L., and V. Chirkov. 2008. 'Parents' Personal and Cultural Beliefs Regarding Young Children: A Cross-Cultural Study of Aboriginal and Euro-Canadian Mothers', *Journal of Cross-Cultural Psychology* 39: 402–23.

Cherlin, Andrew J. 1999. 'Going to Extremes: Children's Well-Being and Social Science', *Demography* 36: 421–8.

———, Frank F. Furstenberg Jr, P. Lindsay Chase-Lansdale, Kathleen E. Kiernan, Philip K. Robins, Donna Ruane Morrison, and Julien O. Teitler. 1991. 'Longitudinal Studies of Effects of Divorce on Children in Great Britain and the United States', *Science* 252 (7 June): 1386–9.

Choi, Heejeong. 2006. 'Socioeconomic Status, Marriage, and Physical Health: The Moderating Effects of Marriage on Socioeconomic Status-Health Associations', *Dissertation Abstracts International, A: The Humanities and Social Sciences* 66, 8: 3107–A.

Clark, Warren. 2007. 'Delayed Transitions of Young Adults', *Canadian Social Trends.* At: <www.statcan.gc.ca/pub/11-008-x/2007004/10311-eng.htm>.

Coleman, H.H., M.L. Weinman, and P.H. Bartholomew. 1980. 'Factors Affecting Conjugal Violence', *Journal of Psychology* 105: 197–202.

Davis, Robert C., and Barbara Smith. 1995. 'Domestic Violence Reforms: Empty Promises or Fulfilled Expectations?', *Crime and Delinquency* 41: 541–52.

Dixon, Kathrine. 2007. 'Working with Mixed Commons/Anticommons Property: Mobilizing Customary Land in Papua New Guinea the Melanesian Way', *Harvard Environmental Law Review* 31, 1: 219–77.

Dronkers, Jaap. 1996. 'The Effects of Parental Conflicts and Divorce on the Average Well-Being of Pupils in Secondary Education', American Sociological Association, conference paper.

Eichler, Margrit. 1997. *Family Shifts: Families, Policies, and Gender Equality.* Toronto: Oxford University Press.

Elton, Sarah. 2007. 'Modern Love: Rethinking the Notion of Family', *Canadian Family* (Apr.). At: <www.canadianfamily.ca/articles/modern-love/6/>.

Gavigan, Shelley A.M. 1999. 'Legal Forms, Family Forms, Gendered Norms: What Is a Spouse?', *Canadian Journal of Law and Society* 14: 127–57.

Gee, Ellen M. 1986. 'The Life Course of Canadian Women: An Historical and

Demographic Analysis', *Social Indicators Research* 18: 263–83.

Gelles, Richard, and Jon R. Conte. 1991. 'Domestic Violence and Sexual Abuse of Children: A Review of Research in the Eighties', in Alan Booth, ed., *Contemporary Families: Looking Forward, Looking Back*. Minneapolis: National Council on Family Relations, 327–40.

Geurts, Sabine, Christel Rutte, and Maria Peeters. 1999. 'Antecedents and Consequences of Work–Home Interference among Medical Residents', *Social Science and Medicine* 48: 1135–48.

Globe and Mail. 2002. At: <www.theglobeandmail.com/special/census/2001/stories/families/20021022main.html>.

Goode, William J. 1963. *World Revolution and Family Patterns*. New York: Free Press.

Grutzmacher, Stephanie K. 2007. 'Family Structure and Income Redistribution Policies: Comparing Child Poverty Outcomes in Canada, the United Kingdom, and the United States', *Dissertation Abstracts International, A: The Humanities and Social Sciences* 68, 4: 1683.

Handrahan, Lori. 2004. 'Hunting for Women: Bride-Kidnapping in Kyrgyzstan', *International Feminist Journal of Politics* 6, 2: 207–33.

Hawkins, Daniel, and Alan Booth. 2005. 'Unhappily Ever After: Effects of Long-Term, Low-Quality Marriages on Well-Being', *Social Forces* 84, 1: 451–71.

Heathcote, J., K. Cauch-Dudek, and D. Rhyne. 1997. 'The Professional Lives of Women in Gastroenterology: A Canadian Comparison Study with Men', *Gastroenterology* 113, 2: 669–74.

Hochschild, Arlie Russell. 1997. *The Time Bind: When Work Becomes Home and Home Becomes Work*. New York: Henry Holt.

Houseknecht, Sharon K., Suzanne Vaughan, and Anne Statham. 1987. 'The Impact of Singlehood on the Career Patterns of Professional Women', *Journal of Marriage and the Family* 49, 2: 353–66.

Huisman, Kimberly A. 1996. 'Wife Battering in Asian American Communities: Identifying the Service Needs of an Overlooked Segment of the U.S. Population', *Violence Against Women* 2, 3: 260–83.

Immerman, Ronald S., and Wade C. Mackey. 1999. 'The Societal Dilemma of Multiple Sexual Partners: The Costs of the Loss of Pair-Bonding', *Marriage and Family Review* 29, 1: 3–19.

Kane, Rosalie A., James Reinardy, Joan D. Penrod, and Shirley Huck. 1999. 'After the Hospitalizatioin Is Over: A Different Perspective on Family Care of Older People', *Journal of Gerontological Social Work* 31: 119–41.

Kaplan, S.J. 2000. 'Family Violence', *New Directions for Mental Health Services* 86: 49–62.

King, Michael. 2007. 'The Sociology of Childhood as Scientific Communication:

Observations from a Social Systems Perspective', *Childhood* 14, 2: 193–213.

Kline, Susan L., and Shuangyue Zhang. 2009. 'The Role of Relational Communication Characteristics and Filial Piety in Mate Preferences: Cross-cultural Comparisons of Chinese and US College Students', *Journal of Comparative Family Studies* 40, 3: 325–53.

Kunemund, Harald, and Martin Rein. 1999. 'There Is More to Receiving Than Needing: Theoretical Arguments and Empirical Explorations of Crowding In and Crowding Out', *Ageing and Society* 19, 1: 93–121.

Lee, Bong Joo, and Robert M. George. 1999. 'Poverty, Early Childbearing, and Child Maltreatment: A Multinomial Analysis', *Children and Youth Services Review* 21: 755–80.

Lehmann, Jennifer M. 1994. *Durkheim and Women*. Lincoln: University of Nebraska Press.

Longman, Chia. 2008. 'Sacrificing the Career or the Family? Orthodox Jewish Women between Secular Work and the Sacred Home', *European Journal of Women's Studies* 15, 3: 223–39.

Loveless, A. Scott, and Thomas B. Holman, eds. 2007. *The Family in the New Millennium: World Voices Supporting the 'Natural' Clan, vol. 2: Marriage and Human Dignity*. Westport, Conn.: Praeger/Greenwood.

McManus, P.A., and T.A. DiPrete. 2001. 'Losers and Winners: The Financial Consequences of Separation and Divorce for Men', *American Sociological Review* 66, 2: 246–68.

McMullin, Julie. 2004. *Understanding Social Inequality: Intersections of Class, Age, Gender, Ethnicity, and Race in Canada*. Toronto: Oxford University Press.

Mahoney, Rhona. 1995. *Kidding Ourselves: Breadwinning, Babies, and Bargaining Power*. New York: Basic Books.

Malo, Claire, Jacques Moreau, Claire Chamberland, Sophie Léveillé, and Catherine Roy. 2004. 'Parental Cognition, Emotions, and Behaviors Associated with the Risk of Psychological Maltreatment of Preschoolers', *Journal of Emotional Abuse* 4, 2: 1–26.

Marshall, Katherine. 2009. 'The Family Work Week', *Perspectives on Labour and Income* 21, 2: 21–9.

Martel, Lauren, and Jacques Legare. 2000. 'L'orientation et le contenu des relations réciproques des personnes âgées', *Canadian Journal on Aging* 19: 80–105.

Martin-Matthews, Anne. 2000. 'Gerontology in Canada: A Decade of Change', *Contemporary Gerontology* 7, 2: 53–6.

Medeiros, Marcelo, Rafael G. Osorio, and Joana Costa. 2007. *Gender Inequalities in Allocating Time to Paid and Unpaid Work: Evidence from Bolivia*. Brasília: International Poverty Centre Working Paper 34.

Mikell, Gwendolyn. 1990. 'Women and Economic Development in Ghana: Fluctuating Fortunes', *Sage* 7, 1: 24–7.

Mitchell, Barbara A. 1998. 'Too Close for Comfort? Parental Assessments of "Boomerang Kid" Living Arrangements', *Canadian Journal of Sociology* 23: 21–46.

———. 2005. *The Boomerang Age: Transitions to Adulthood in Families*. New Brunswick, NJ: Transaction.

———, Andrew V. Wister, and Ellen M. Gee. 2000. 'Culture and Co-residence: An Exploration of Variation in Home-Returning among Canadian Young Adults', *Canadian Review of Sociology and Anthropology* 37: 197–222.

Murdock, George P. 1949. *Social Structure*. New York: Macmillan.

Neher, Linda S., and Jerome L. Short. 1998. 'Risk and Protective Factors for Children's Substance Use and Antisocial Behavior Following Parental Divorce', *American Journal of Orthopsychiatry* 68: 154–61.

Nguyen, Hung V., George P. Moschis, and Randall Shannon. 2009. 'Effects of Family Structure and Socialization on Materialism: A Life Course Study in Thailand', *International Journal of Consumer Studies* 33, 4: 486–95.

Oderkirk, Jillian. 1994. 'Marriage in Canada: Changing Beliefs and Behaviours, 1600–1990', *Canadian Social Trends* 33: 3–7.

O'Farrell, Timothy J., and Christopher M. Murphy. 1995. 'Marital Violence before and after Alcoholism Treatment', *Journal of Consulting and Clinical Psychology* 63: 256–62.

Paradise, Ruth, and Barbara Rogoff. 2009. 'Side by Side: Learning by Observing and Pitching In', *Ethos* 37, 1: 102–38.

Parsons, Talcott, and Robert F. Bales. 1955. *Family Socialization and Interaction Process*. New York: Free Press.

Petten, Cheryl. 2007. 'Organizations Preparing for Impact of Compensation Money', *Saskatchewan Sage* 11, 12: 4–5.

Petts, Richard J. 2009. 'Family and Religious Characteristics' Influence on Delinquency Trajectories from Adolescence to Young Adulthood', *American Sociological Review* 74, 3: 465–83.

Phillips, Richard. 2009. 'Settler Colonialism and the Nuclear Family', *Canadian Geographer* 53, 2: 239–53.

Plambech, Sine. 2005. '"Mail Order Brides" in Northwestern Jutland: Transnational Marriages in the Global Care Economy', *Dansk Sociologi* 16, 1: 91–110.

Rao, Nitya. 2005. 'Kinship Matters: Women's Land Claims in the Santal Parganas, Jharkhand', *Journal of the Royal Anthropological Institute* 11, 4: 725–46.

Raphael, Dennis. 2009. *Social Determinants of Health: Canadian Perspectives*. Toronto: Canadian Scholars' Press.

Roeher Institute. 1999. *Labour Force: Inclusion of Parents Caring for Children with Disabilities*. Toronto: Roeher Institute.

Roizblatt, Arturo, Sheril Rivera, Tzandra Fuchs, Paulina Toso, Enrique Ossandon, and Miguel Guelfand. 1997. 'Children of

Divorce: Academic Outcome', *Journal of Divorce and Remarriage* 26, 3 and 4: 51–6.

Rosenthal, Carolyn J. 1985. 'Kinkeeping in the Familial Division of Labor', *Journal of Marriage and the Family* 47, 4: 965–74.

———. 1997. 'The Care of Canadian Families for Their Aging Members', *Lien social et politiques* 38, 78: 123–31.

Shah, Niaz A. 2005. 'The Constitution of Afghanistan and Women's Rights', *Feminist Legal Studies* 13, 2: 239–58.

Skoda, Uwe. 2007. 'The Kinship System of the Aghria: A Case Study of Peasants in Middle India', *Journal of the Royal Anthropological Institute* 13, 3: 679–701.

Spitze, Glenna, and John R. Logan. 1992. 'Helping as a Component of Parent–Adult Child Relations', *Research on Aging* 14: 291–312.

Statistics Canada. 2001. 'Changes to Family Concepts for the 2001 Census'. At: <www12. statcan.ca/english/census01/Meta/fmlycnc-pts.cfm>.

———. 2002. *2001 Census Families Time Series*, 6 Nov. At: <www12.statcan.ca/english/census01/Products/Analytic/companion/fam/canada.cfm>.

———. 2005a. 'Births', *The Daily*, 12 July. At: <www.statcan.ca/Daily/English/050712/d050712a.htm>.

———. 2005b. 'Divorces', *The Daily*, 9 Mar. At: <www.statcan.ca/Daily/English/050309/d050309b>.

———. 2007. 'Census: Age and Sex', *The Daily*, 17 July. At: <www.statcan.gc.ca/daily-quotidien/070717/dq070717a-eng.htm>.

———. 2008. 'Till death do us part? The risk of first and second marriage dissolution'. Accessed at: <http://www.statcan.gc.ca/pub/11-008-x/2006001/9198-eng.htm>.

Strohschein, Lisa, Peggy McDonough, Georges Monette, and Qing Shao. 2005. 'Marital Transitions and Mental Health: Are There Gender Differences in the Short-Term Effects of Marital Status Change?', *Social Science and Medicine* 61, 11: 2293–303.

Thomson, Elizabeth, and Min Li. 1992. *Family Structure and Children's Kin*. NSFH Working Papers No. 47. Madison: Center for Demography and Ecology, University of Wisconsin.

Trias, E.R. 2000. 'Dealing with the Economic Consequences of Divorce for Wives: Alimony under the Spanish Civil Code', *International Journal of Law, Policy and the Family* 14, 1: 45–58.

Ungar, Michael, Leslie M. Tutty, Sheri McConnell, Ken Barter, and Judi Fairholm. 2009. 'What Canadian Youth Tell Us about Disclosing Abuse', *Child Abuse & Neglect* 33, 10: 699–708.

Waite, Linda J. 2000. 'The Negative Effects of Cohabitation', *The Responsive Community* 10, 1: 31–8.

Willms, J. Douglas, ed. 2002. *Vulnerable Children: Findings from Canada's Longitudinal Survey of Children and Youth*. Edmonton: University of Alberta Press.

Chapter 12

Abrams, Burton A., Jing Li, and James G. Mulligan. 2009. 'The Steam Engine and U.S. Urban Growth during the Late Nineteenth Century', University of Delaware, Department of Economics, Working Papers.

Agence France-Presse (AFP). 2009. 'Overwork a Silent Killer in Japan', 10 Jan. At: <www.google.com/hostednews/afp/article/ALeqM5js1LZHPijMa3CVM-pVqb5QQg-GYsw>.

Aiken, G.E. 2009. 'Industrializing the Corn Belt: Agriculture, Technology, and Environment, 1945–1972', *Choice* 46, 10: 1961–2.

Ariganello, Anthony. 2009. 'Tackling Workplace Stress/S'Attaquer Au Stress En Milieu De Travail', *CGA Magazine* 43, 3: 39.

Avison, William R. 1996. 'What Determines Health? Summary of the Health Consequences of Unemployment', National Forum on Health. At: <www.nfh.hc-sc.gc.ca/publicat/execsumm/avison.htm>.

———. 2001. 'Unemployment and Its Consequences for Mental Health', in Victor Marshal, Walter R. Heinz, Helga Kruger, and Anil Verma, eds, *Restructuring Work and the Life Course*. Toronto: University of Toronto Press, 177–200.

Bamgbose, Oluyemisi. 2002. 'Teenage Prostitution and the Future of the Female Adolescent in Nigeria', *International Journal of Offender Therapy and Comparative Criminology* 46, 5: 569–85.

Bello, Deidre, Lauretta Claussen, Marvin V. Greene, and Kyle W. Morrison. 2009. 'Congressional Committees Review OSHA Enforcement Issues', *Safety & Health* 179, 6: 12.

Bernstein, Elizabeth. 2002. 'Economies of Desire: Sexual Commerce and Post-Industrial Culture', *Dissertation Abstracts International, A: The Humanities and Social Sciences* 63, 2: 778–A.

Besen-Cassino, Yasemin. 2008. 'The Cost of Being a Girl: Gender Earning Differentials in the Early Labor Markets', *NWSA Journal* 20, 1: 146–60.

Blanchflower, David G., and Alex Bryson. 2010. 'The Wage Impact of Trade Unions in the UK Public and Private Sectors', *Economica* 77, 305: 18–110.

Blendon, Robert, and John Benson. 2009. 'America's Response to a Deep Recession', *Challenge* 52, 4: 32–52.

Brumback, Gary B. 2007. 'Review of *The Modern Firm: Organizational Design for Performance and Growth*', *Personnel Psychology* 60, 1: 260–4.

Burchardt, Tania. 2000. 'The Dynamics of Being Disabled', *Journal of Social Policy* 29: 645–68.

Burke, Ronald J., and Lisa Fiksenbaum. 2009. 'Work Motivations, Satisfactions, and Health among Managers: Passion versus Addiction', *Cross-Cultural Research* 43, 4: 349–65.

Burstrom, B., M. Whitehead, C. Lindholm, and F. Diderichsen. 2000. 'Inequality in the Social Consequences of Illness: How Well Do People with Long-term Illness Fare in the British and Swedish Labor Markets?', *International Journal of Health Services* 30: 435–51.

Castaneda, Xochitl, Victor Ortiz, Betania Allen, Cecilia Garcia, and Mauricio Hernandez-Avila. 1996. 'Sex Masks: The Double Life of Female Commercial Sex Workers in Mexico City', *Culture, Medicine and Psychiatry* 20, 2: 229–47.

CBC News. 2007. 'Workplace Safety Inspections', 17 Jan. At: <www.cbc.ca/news/background/workplace-safety/>.

Chen, Shu-Peng, Cheng-Hu Zhou, and Qiu-Xiao Chen. 2003. 'Global Charm of the Changjiang River Delta', *Chinese Geographical Science* 13, 4: 289–99.

Claussen, Bjørgulf. 1999a. 'Alcohol Disorders and Re-employment in a 5-Year Follow-up of Long-term Unemployed', *Addiction* 94: 133–8.

———. 1999b. 'Health and Re-employment in a Five-Year Follow-up of Long-term Unemployed', *Scandinavian Journal of Public Health* 27, 2: 94–100.

Comino, E.J., E. Harris, D. Silove, V. Manicavasagar, and M.F. Harris. 2000. 'Prevalence, Detection and Management of Anxiety and Depressive Symptoms in Unemployed Patients Attending General Practitioners', *Australian and New Zealand Journal of Psychiatry* 34: 107–13.

Crisman, Kevin. 2009. 'Horses at Work: Harnessing Power in Industrial America', *Journal of American History* 96, 3: 838–9.

Cullen, D.O. 2009. '"They Are All Red Out Here": Socialist Politics in the Pacific Northwest, 1895–1925', *Choice* 47, 4: 752–3.

de Goede, M., E. Spruijt, C. Maas, and V. Duindam. 2000. 'Family Problems and Youth Unemployment', *Adolescence* 35: 587–601.

Desmarais, Danielle. 1991. 'Linking Unemployment, Health and Employment in Women's Accounts of Unemployment: Understanding as a Prerequisite to Social Intervention', paper presented at the annual meeting of the Sociological Practice Association/ISA Working Group in Clinical Sociology.

Druss, B.G., S.C. Marcus, R.A. Rosenheck, M. Olfson, T. Talielian, and H.A. Pincus. 2000. 'Understanding Disability in Mental and General Medical Conditions', *American Journal of Psychiatry* 157: 1485–91.

Durkheim, Émile. 1964 [1893]. *The Division of Labor in Society*, trans. George Simpson. New York: Free Press.

Edwards, Richard. 1979. *Contested Terrain: The Transformation of the Workplace in the Twentieth Century*. New York: Basic Books.

Eze, Mercy. 2009. 'A Woman on a Mission', *New African* no. 490: 26.

Fernandez Steinko, Armando. 1995. 'Technological Dualism and Regional Development: Flexible Specialization or Flexible Mass

Production?', *Revista Internacional de Sociologia* 10: 135–55.

Fillmore, Kaye Middleton, Jacqueline M. Golding, Karen L. Graves, Steven Kniep, E. Victor Leino, Anders Romelsjo, Carlisle Shoemaker, Catherine R. Ager, Peter Allebeck, and Heidi P. Ferrer. 1998. 'Alcohol Consumption and Mortality, I. Characteristics of Drinking Groups', *Addiction* 93: 183–203.

Fukuyama, Francis. 1992. *The End of History and the Last Man*. New York: Free Press.

Gaudette, Pamela, Bob Alexander, and Chris Branch. 1996. 'Children, Sex and Violence: Calgary's Response to Child Prostitution', *Child & Family Canada*. At: <www.cfc-efc.ca/docs/cwlc/00000826.htm>.

Gee, Marcus. 2009. 'Police Proud to Show Their Increasingly Multicultural Face', *Globe and Mail*, 15 Sept. At: <v1.theglobeandmail.com/servlet/story/LAC.20090915.GEE15ART2317/TPStory/TPComment/>.

Gien, L.T. 2000. 'Land and Sea Connection: The East Coast Fishery Closure, Unemployment, and Health', *Canadian Journal of Public Health* 91, 2: 121–4.

Godard, John. 2009. 'The Exceptional Decline of the American Labor Movement', *Industrial and Labor Relations Review* 63, 1: 82–109.

Golden, Timothy D., and John F. Veiga. 2005. 'The Impact of Extent of Telecommuting on Job Satisfaction: Resolving Inconsistent Findings', *Journal of Management* 31, 2: 301–18.

Gonzalez, Luque J.C., and Artalejo F. Rodriguez. 2000. 'The Relationship of Different Socioeconomic Variables and Alcohol Consumption with Nighttime Fatal Traffic Crashes in Spain: 1978–1993', *European Journal of Epidemiology* 16: 955–61.

Hanke, Steve H. 1996. 'Class Warfare', *Forbes* 157, 11: 60–1.

Heaton, C., and Paul Oslington. 2010. 'Micro vs Macro Explanations of Post-War US Unemployment Movements', *Economics Letters* 106, 2: 87–91.

Heinrich, Erik. 2008. 'Opportunity Play', *Global Finance* 22, 3: 28–30.

Henshaw, John L. 1988. 'Organization of Industrial Hygiene Management', in J.T. Garrett, L.J. Cralley, and L.V. Cralley, eds, *Industrial Hygiene Management*. Oxford: John Wiley & Sons, 89–107.

Hintikka, J., P.I. Saarinen, and H. Viinamaki. 1999. 'Suicide Mortality in Finland during an Economic Cycle, 1985–1995', *Scandinavian Journal of Public Health* 27, 2: 85–8.

Hubbard, Phil, and Teela Sanders. 2003. 'Making Space for Sex Work: Female Street Prostitution and the Production of Urban Space', *International Journal of Urban and Regional Research* 27, 1: 75–89.

Human Resources Development Canada (HRDC). 2000. *Work Safely for a Healthy Future: Statistical Analysis: Occupational Injuries and Fatalities Canada*. At: <info.load-otea.hrdc-drhc.gc.ca/~oshweb/naoshstats/naoshw2000.pdf>.

James, Jeffrey. 2002. 'The Digital Divide between Nations as International Technological Dualism', *International Journal of Development Issues* 1, 2: 25–40.

———. 2003. Bridging the Global Digital Divide. Northampton, Mass.: Elgar.

Kanter, Rosabeth M. 1977. *Men and Women of the Corporation*. New York: Basic Books.

Kelan, Elizabeth. 2007. '"I Don't Know Why"— Accounting for the Scarcity of Women in ICT Work', *Women's Studies International Forum* 30, 6: 499–511.

Kramer, Lisa A., and Ellen C. Berg. 2003. 'A Survival Analysis of Timing of Entry into Prostitution: The Differential Impact of Race, Educational Level, and Childhood/Adolescent Risk Factors', *Sociological Inquiry* 73, 4: 511–28.

Lahelma, Eero. 1992. 'Unemployment and Mental Well-Being: Elaboration of the Relationship', *International Journal of Health Services* 22: 261–74.

Lambert, Eric G., Nancy L. Hogan, and Kasey A. Tucker. 2009. 'Problems at Work: Exploring the Correlates of Role Stress among Correctional Staff', *Prison Journal* 89, 4: 460–81.

Langfred, C.W., and N.A. Moye. 2004. 'Effects of Task Autonomy on Performance: An Extended Model Considering Motivational, Informational, and Structural Mechanisms', *Journal of Applied Psychology* 89, 6: 934–45.

Langman, Lauren. 2008. 'Massive Change: The Exhibit as Apology for "New Capitalism"', *Rethinking Marxism* 20, 3: 464–71.

Li, Peter. 2003. 'Initial Earnings and Catch-up Capacity of Immigrants', *Canadian Public Policy* 29, 3: 319–37.

Liira, J., and Arjas P. Leino. 1999. 'Predictors and Consequences of Unemployment in Construction and Forest Work During a 5-Year Follow-up', *Scandinavian Journal of Work, Environment and Health* 25, 1: 42–9.

McCarty, C.A., M. Burgess, and J.E. Keeffe. 1999. 'Unemployment and Underemployment in Adults with Vision Impairment: The RVIB Employment Survey', *Australian and New Zealand Journal of Ophthalmology* 27, 3 and 4: 190–3.

MacDonald, Z., and S. Pudney. 2000. 'Illicit Drug Use, Unemployment, and Occupational Attainment', *Journal of Health Economics* 19: 1089–15.

Marx, Karl. 1936 (1887). *Capital: A Critique of Political Economy*. Trans. Samuel Moore and Edward Aveling, ed. Frederick Engels. Moscow: Progress Publishers.

Maich, Steve. 2008. 'Facts and Fairy Tales of Paulson's Bailout', *Maclean's* 121, 41: 47.

Manopaiboon, C., R.E. Bunnell, P.H. Kilmarx, S. Chaikummao, K. Limpakarnjanarat, S. Supawitkul, M.E. St Louis, and T.D. Mastro. 2003. 'Leaving Sex Work: Barriers, Facilitating Factors and Consequences for Female Sex Workers in Northern Thailand', *AIDS Care* 15, 1: 39–52.

Mathieu, Lilian. 2003. 'The Emergence and Uncertain Outcomes of Prostitutes' Social Movements', *European Journal of Women's Studies* 10, 1: 29–50.

Meadows, Donella H., Dennis L. Meadows, Jorgen Randers, and William H. Behrens III. 1972. *The Limits to Growth*. New York: Universe Books.

Montgomery, Scott M., Derek G. Cook, Mel J. Bartley, and Michael E.J. Wadsworth. 1998. 'Unemployment, Cigarette Smoking, Alcohol Consumption, and Body Weight in Young British Men', *European Journal of Public Health* 8, 1: 21–7.

———, ———, ———, and ———. 1999. 'Unemployment Pre-dates Symptoms of Depression and Anxiety Resulting in Medical Consultation in Young Men', *International Journal of Epidemiology* 28: 95–100.

Nixon, Kendra, Leslie Tutty, Pamela Downe, Kelly Gorkoff, and Jane Ursel. 2002. 'The Everyday Occurrence: Violence in the Lives of Girls Exploited through Prostitution', *Violence against Women* 8, 9: 1016–43.

Nordenmark, Mikael. 1999. 'Employment Commitment and Psychological Well-Being among Unemployed Men and Women', *Acta Sociologica* 42: 135–46.

Ooka, Emi, and Barry Wellman. 2006. 'Does Social Capital Pay Off More within or between Ethnic Groups? Analysing Job Searches in Five Toronto Ethnic Groups', in Eric Fong, ed., *Inside the Mosaic*. Toronto: University of Toronto Press, 199–226.

Ostry, Aleck, Steve A. Marion, L. Green, Paul A. Demers, Kay Teshke, Ruth Hershler, Shona Kelly, and Clyde Hertzman. 2000. 'The Relationship between Unemployment, Technological Change and Psychosocial Work Conditions in British Columbia Sawmills', *Critical Public Health* 10: 179–91.

Reitz, Jeffrey G., and Raymond Breton. 1998. 'Prejudice and Discrimination in Canada and the United States: A Comparison', in V. Satzewich, ed., *Racism and Social Inequality in Canada*. Toronto: Thompson Educational Publishing, 47–68.

Renzetti, Claire M., and Daniel J Curran, eds. 2003. *Women, Men, and Society*, 5th edn. Boston: Pearson Education.

Rodriguez, Eunice. 2001. 'Keeping the Unemployed Healthy: The Effect of Means-Tested and Entitlement Benefits in Britain, Germany, and the United States', *American Journal of Public Health* 91: 1403–11.

———, Kathryn E Lasch, Pinky Chandra, and Jennifer Lee. 2001. 'The Relation of Family Violence, Employment Status, Welfare Benefits, and Alcohol Drinking in the United States', *Western Journal of Medicine* 174,5 (May): 317–23.

Rose, Nancy E. 2009. 'Lessons from the New Deal Public Employment Programs', *Monthly Review* 61, 5: 21–32.

Rosenberg, Nathan, and Manuel Trajtenberg. 2004. 'A General-Purpose Technology at Work: The Corliss Steam Engine in the Late

19th Century US', *Journal of Economic History* 64, 1: 61–99.

Sandy, Larissa. 2009. '"Behind Closed Doors": Debt-Bonded Sex Workers in Sihanoukville, Cambodia', *Asia Pacific Journal of Anthropology* 10, 3: 216–30.

Saurel Cubizolles, M.J., P. Romito, P.Y. Ancel, and N. Lelong. 2000. 'Unemployment and Psychological Distress One Year after Childbirth in France', *Journal of Epidemiology and Community Health* 54: 185–91.

Schaufeli, Wilmar B. 1997. 'Youth Unemployment and Mental Health: Some Dutch Findings', *Journal of Adolescence* 20: 281–92.

Schildt, Gerhard. 2006. 'The Decline of the Volume of Labour in the Industrial Age', *Geschichte und Gesellschaft* 32, 1: 119–48.

Schmitt, E. 2001. 'Significance of Employment and Unemployment in Middle and Advanced Adult Age for Subjective Perception of Aging and Realization of Potentials and Barriers of a Responsible Life', *Zeitschrift fur Gerontologie und Geriatrie* 34: 218–31.

Sikora, Patricia B. 2002. 'Enlarging the View of Participation in Organizations: A Proposed Framework and Analysis via Structural Equation Modeling', *Dissertation Abstracts International* 63–02B: 1091.

Slebarska, Katarzyna, Klaus Moser, and George Gunnesch-Luca. 2009. 'Unemployment, Social Support, Individual Resources, and Job Search Behavior', *Journal of Employment Counseling* 46, 4: 159–71.

Stanton, Jeffrey M., Peter D. Bachiochi, Chet Robie, Lisa M. Perez, and Patricia C. Smith. 2002. 'Revising the JDI Work Satisfaction Subscale: Insights into Stress and Control', *Educational and Psychological Measurement* 62, 5: 877–95.

Stefansson, Claes Goran. 1991. 'Long-Term Unemployment and Mortality in Sweden, 1980–1986', *Social Science and Medicine* 32: 419–23.

Taylor, J. 2000. 'Bureaucracy and Informal Practices in the Workplace', *Sociology Review* 9, 4: 17–20.

Tombs, Steve, and David Whyte. 2010. 'A Deadly Consensus: Worker Safety and Regulatory Degradation under New Labour', *British Journal of Criminology* 50, 1: 46.

Torney, Colin, Zoltan Neufeld, and Iain D. Couzin. 2009. 'Context-Dependent Interaction Leads to Emergent Search Behavior in Social Aggregates', *Proceedings of the National Academy of Sciences of the United States of America* 106, 52: 22055–60.

Turcotte, Martin, and Grant Schellenberg. 2005. 'Job Strain and Retirement', *Perspectives on Labour and Income* 17, 3: 35–9.

Underlid, Kjell. 1996. 'Activity during Unemployment and Mental Health', *Scandinavian Journal of Psychology* 37: 269–81.

United Nations Population Fund. 2000. *State of World Population 2000: Lives Together, Worlds Apart: Men and Women in a Time of Change*. At: <www.unfpa.org/swp/2000/english/index.html>.

Viinamaki, Heimo, Kaj Koskela, and Leo Niskanen. 1993. 'The Impact of Unemployment on Psychosomatic Symptoms and Mental Well-Being', *International Journal of Social Psychiatry* 39: 266–73.

———, ———, ———. 1996. 'Rapidly Declining Mental Well-Being during Unemployment', *The European Journal of Psychiatry* 10, 4: 215–21.

Wallace, Jean E., and Fiona M. Kay. 2009. 'Are Small Firms More Beautiful or Is Bigger Better? A Study of Compensating Differentials and Law Firm Internal Labor Markets', *Sociological Quarterly* 50, 3: 474–96.

Weber, Max. 1947. *The Theory of Social and Economic Organization*, trans. A.M. Henderson and Talcott Parsons. New York: Free Press.

Williamson, Celia, and Terry Cluse-Tolar. 2002. 'Pimp-Controlled Prostitution: Still an Integral Part of Street Life', *Violence against Women* 8, 9: 1074–92.

Wood, Ellen Meiksins. 1998. 'The Communist Manifesto after 150 Years', *Monthly Review* 50 (1 May). At: <www.monthlyreview.org/598wood.htm>.

Wray, Linda A. 2000. 'Does Mental Health Affect Transitions out of the Labour Force in Older Workers?', paper presented at the annual meeting of the American Sociological Association.

Yap, Margaret, and Alison M. Konrad. 2009. 'Gender and Racial Differentials in Promotions: Is There a Sticky Floor, a Mid-Level Bottleneck, or a Glass Ceiling?', *Relations Industrielles* 64, 4: 593–619.

Yelin, E., J. Henke, P.P. Katz, M.D. Eisner, and P.D. Blanc. 1999. 'Work Dynamics of Adults with Asthma', *American Journal of Industrial Medicine* 35: 472–80.

Yoon, Sang-Chul. 2001. 'Essays on International Trade in Knowledge-Based Services'. At: <gateway.proquest.com. myaccess.library.utoronto.ca/openurl?url_ver=Z39.88-2004&rft_val_fmt=info:ofi/fmt:kev:mtx:dissertation&res_dat=xri:pqdiss&rft_dat=xri:pqdiss:3010876>.

Ytterdahl, T. 1999. 'Routine Health Check-ups of Unemployed in Norway', *International Archives of Occupational and Environmental Health* 72 (suppl.): S38–9.

——— and P. Fugelli. 2000. 'Health and Quality of Life among Long-term Unemployed', *Tidsskrift for Den Norske Laegeforening* 120: 1308–11.

Chapter 13

Anleu, Sharyn Roach, Mack, Kathy. 2008. 'The Professionalization of Australian Magistrates: Autonomy, Credentials and Prestige', *Journal of Sociology* 44, 2 (June): 185–203.

Arnot, Madeleine, Miriam David, and Gaby Weiner. 1999. *Closing the Gender Gap: Postwar Education and Social Change*. Cambridge: Policy Press.

Bennete, Neville. 1976. *Teaching Styles and Pupil Progress*. London: Open Books.

Bowlby, Geoff. 2005. 'Provincial Drop-out Rates—Trends and Consequences', *Education Matters* (Statistics Canada). At: <www.statcan.gc.ca/pub/81-004-x/2005004/8984-eng.htmc>.

——— and Kathryn McMullen. 2002. *At the Crossroads: First Results of the 18 to 20 Years Old Cohort of Youth in Transition Survey*. Ottawa: Human Resources and Development Canada, Catalogue no. H64–12/2002E.

Brinton, Mary C. 1998. 'From High School to Work in Japan: Lessons for the United States?', Social Service Review Lecture, *Social Service Review* 72: 442–51.

Brown, Louise. 2009. 'Africentric School Makes History', *Toronto Star*, 9 Sept. At: <www.thestar.com/printArticle/692804>.

CBC News. 2009. 'A Timeline of Residential Schools', 10 June. At: <www.cbc.ca/canada/story/2008/05/16/f-timeline-residential-schools.html>.

Chiswick, Barry R., and Paul W. Miller. 2008. *The Economics of Language: International Analyses*. New York: Routledge.

Cockerham, William C. 1995. *Medical Sociology*, 6th edn. Englewood Cliffs, NJ: Prentice-Hall.

Collins, Randall. 1979. *The Credential Society*. New York: Academic Press.

Colt, James P., Nancy B. Meyer, and Samuel C. McQuade. 2009. *Cyber Bullying: Protecting Kids and Adults from Bullies*. Westport, Conn.: Praeger.

Davies, Scott, and Neil Guppy. 2006. *The Schooled Society: An Introduction to the Sociology of Education*. Toronto: Oxford University Press.

Dillabough, J., and M. Arnot. 2002. 'Feminist Perspectives in Sociology of Education: Continuity and Transformation in the Field', in D. Levinson, R. Sadovnik, and P. Cookson, eds, *Sociology of Education: An Encyclopedia*. New York: Taylor and Francis.

Donnelly, Rory. 2009. 'Career Behaviour in the Knowledge Economy: Experiences and Perceptions of Career Mobility among Management and IT Consultants in the UK and the US', *Journal of Vocational Behaviour* 75, 3: 319–28.

Dorn, Richard, Gary Bowen, and Judith Blau. 2006. 'The Impact of Community Diversity and Consolidated Inequality on Dropping Out of High School', *Family Relations* 55: 105–18.

Dupuy, Max, and Mark E. Schweitzer. 1995. 'Another Look at Part-Time Employment', *Economic Commentary* (Federal Reserve Bank of Cleveland) (Feb.): 1–4.

Ekos Research Associates. 2004. *Integrated Findings: Final Report. The Dual Digital Divide IV*. Ottawa: Ekos Research.

Expert Panel on Skills. 2000. *Stepping Up: Skills and Opportunities in the Knowledge Economy*. Report presented to the Prime

Minister's Advisory Council on Science and Technology. Ottawa.

Furlong, Andy. 2008. 'The Japanese Hikikomori Phenomenon: Acute Social Withdrawal among Young People', *Sociological Review* 56, 2: 309–25.

Furniss, Elizabeth. 1992. *Victims of Benevolence: The Dark Side of the Williams Lake Residential School*. Vancouver: Arsenal Pulp Press.

Goldthorpe, John H. 1985. 'On Economic Development and Social Mobility', *British Journal of Sociology* 36, 4: 549–73.

Gomme, I. 2004. 'Education', in R.J. Brym, ed., *New Society: Sociology for the 21st Century*, 4th edn. Scarborough: Nelson Thomson, 359–81.

Good, T., B. Biddle, and J. Brophy. 1975. *Teachers Make a Difference*. New York: Holt, Rinehart and Winston.

Greening, Daniel W., and Daniel B. Turban. 2000. 'Corporate Social Performance as a Competitive Advantage in Attracting a Quality Workforce', *Business and Society* 39, 3: 254–80.

Guerra, Carmen E., Megan Krumholz, and Judy A. Shea. 2005. 'Literacy and Knowledge, Attitudes and Behavior about Mammography in Latinas', *Journal of Health Care for the Poor and Underserved* 16, 1: 152–66.

Guppy, Neil, and Scott Davies. 1998. *Education in Canada: Recent Trends and Future Challenges*. Ottawa: Statistics Canada Catalogue no. 96–321.

Halperin, Keith M. 1990. 'Helping Rising Stars Shine as Managers', *Training and Development Journal* 44, 7: 76.

Harkness, Suzan. 2001. 'Women and Work: Dynamics of the Glass Ceiling and Public Policy Perspectives', Ph.D. thesis, University of Hawaii.

Harmon, Amy. 2004. 'Internet Gives Teenage Bullies Weapons to Wound from Afar'. *New York Times*, 26 Aug. At: <www.nytimes.com./2004/08/26/education>.

Holley, Paul, Scott Yabiku, and Mary Benin. 2006. 'The Relationship between Intelligence and Divorce', *Journal of Family Issues* 27, 12: 1723–48.

Johnson, David. 2009. 'Ontario's Best Public Schools, 2005/06–2007/08: An Update to *Signposts of Success* (2005)'. Toronto: C.D. Howe Institute. At: <www.cdhowe.org/pdf/ebrief_85.pdf>.

Juvonen, J., and S. Graham, eds. 2001. *Peer Harassment in School: The Plight of the Vulnerable and Victimized*. New York: Guilford Press.

Kalichman, S.C., B. Ramachandran, and S. Catz. 1999. 'Adherence to Combination Antiretroviral Therapies in HIV Patients of Low Health Literacy', *Journal of General Internal Medicine* 14, 5: 267–73.

Lenhart, Amanda, Mary Madden, and Paul Hitlin. 2005. 'Teens and Technology: Youth Are Leading the Transition to a Fully Wired and Mobile Nation', Pew Internet and American Life Project, July. At: <www.pewinternet.org/PPF/r/162/report_display.asp>.

Li, Qing. 2005. 'Cyber-bullying in Schools: The Nature and Extent of Adolescents' Experience', paper presented at the American Education Research Association Conference, Montreal, Apr.

Livingstone, D., D. Hart, and L.E. Davie, 2003. *Public Attitudes towards Education in Ontario: The 14th OISE/UT Survey*. Toronto: Ontario Institute for Studies in Education of the University of Toronto.

McMullin, Julie Ann. 2004. *Understanding Social Inequality: Intersections of Class, Age, Gender, Ethnicity, and Race in Canada*. Toronto: Oxford University Press.

Meerkerk, Elise van Nederveen. 2006. 'Segmentation in the Pre-Industrial Labour Market: Women's Work in the Dutch Textile Industry, 1581–1810', *International Review of Social History* 51, 2: 189–216.

Murphy, Raymond. 1979. *Sociological Theories of Education*. Toronto: McGraw-Hill Ryerson.

Ng, Roxanna. 1993. 'Racism, Sexism and Nation-Building in Canada', in Cameron McCarthy and Warren Crichlow, eds, *Race, Identity and Representation in Education*. New York: Routledge, 50–9.

Nicholas, Andrea Bear. 2001. 'Canada's Colonial Mission: The Great White Bird', in K.P. Binda, ed., with Sharilyn Calliou, *Aboriginal Education in Canada: A Study in Decolonization*. Mississauga, Ont.: Canadian Educators' Press.

Organization for Economic Co-operation and Development (OECD). 2005. *Teachers Matter: Attracting, Developing and Retaining Effective Teachers*. Paris: OECD.

Pepler, Debra. 2007. 'Understanding Bullying: From Research to Practice', *Canadian Psychology* 48, 2: 86–93.

Pitts, J., and P. Smith. 1995. *Preventing School Bullying*. Police Research Group, Crime Detection and Prevention Series Paper 63. London: Home Office.

Quan-Haase, Anabel, and Barry Wellman, with Keith Hampton and James Witte. 2002. 'Internet, Social Capital, and Information Seeking', in Barry Wellman and Caroline Haythornthwaite, eds, *The Internet in Everyday Life*. Oxford: Blackwell, 291–324.

Quint, Janet, Saskia Levy Thompson, and Margaret Bald, with Julia Bernstein and Kaura Sztejnberg. 2008. *Relationships, Rigor, and Readiness: Strategies for Improving High Schools*. New York: MDRC, Oct.

Reitz, Jeffrey G. 2001. 'Immigrant Skill Utilization in the Canadian Labour Market: Implications of Human Capital Research', *Journal of International Migration and Integration* 2, 3: 347–78.

Roach Anleu, Sharyn, and Kathy Mack. 2008. 'The Professionalization of Australian Magistrates: Autonomy, Credentials and Prestige', *Journal of Sociology* 44, 2: 185–203.

Ronson, Barbara, and Irving Rootman. 2004. 'Literacy: One of the Most Important Determinants of Health Today', in Dennis Raphael, ed., *Social Determinants of Health: Canadian Perspectives*. Toronto: Canadian Scholars' Press.

Rosenbaum, James E. 2001. *Beyond College for all Career Paths for the Forgotten Half*. New York: Russell Sage Foundation.

Ross, Catherine E., and Chia-ling Wu. 1995. 'The Links between Education and Health', *American Sociological Review* 60: 719–45.

Sanders, William L., and June C. Rivers. 1996. *Cumulative and Residual Effects of Teachers on Future Student Academic Achievement*. Knoxville: University of Tennessee Value-Added Research and Assessment Center.

Santiago, Paulo. 2004. 'The Labour Market for Teachers', in G. Johnes and J. Jones, eds, *International Handbook on the Economics of Education*. Cheltenham, UK: Edward Elgar.

Sasaki, Yosei. 2000. 'Effects of Ascribed Status on Educational Attainment', *Shakaigaku Hyoron/Japanese Sociological Review* 51, 2: 33–48.

Schacter, John, and Yeow Meng Thum. 2004. 'Paying for High and Low-Quality Teaching', *Economics of Education Review* 23: 411–30.

Seeley, John R., R. Alexander Sim, and Elizabeth Loosley. 1956. *Crestwood Heights: A Study of the Culture of Suburban Life*. Toronto: University of Toronto Press.

Shariff, Shaheen. 2005. 'Cyber-Dilemmas in the New Millennium: School Obligations to Provide Student Safety in a Virtual School Environment', *McGill Journal of Education* 40, 3: 467–87.

Siggner, Andrew, and Rosalinda Costa. 2005. *Aboriginal Conditions in Census Metropolitan Areas, 1981–2001*. Ottawa: Statistics Canada Catalogue no. 89–613–MIE—Number 008.

Statistics Canada. 2005. *2001 Census: Minority Report*. Ottawa: Statistics Canada.

———. 2008. 'Aboriginal People in Canada's Urban Area—Narrowing the Education Gap', *Education Matters* (Dec.). At: <www.statcan.gc.ca/pub/81-004-x/2005003/8612-eng.htmFootnote1>.

——— and the Council of Ministers of Education Canada (CMEC). 2000. *Education Indicators in Canada: Report of the Pan-Canadian Education Indicators Program 1999*. At: <www.cmec.ca>.

Stonefish, Brent. 2007. *Moving Beyond: Understanding the Impacts of Residential School*. Owen Sound, Ont.: Ningwakwe Learning Press.

van Jaarsveld, Danielle D. 2009. 'The Effects of Institutional and Organizational Characteristics on Work Force Flexibility: Evidence from Call Centers in Three Liberal Market Economies', *Industrial and Labor Relations Review* 62, 4 (July): 573–601.

———, Danielle, Andries de Grip, and Inge Sieben. 2009. 'Industrial Relations and Labour Market Segmentation in Dutch Call

Centres', *European Journal of Industrial Relations* 15, 4: 417–35.

Watt, Douglas, and Michael Bloom. 2001. 'Brain Gain: The Economic Benefits of Recognizing Learning and Learning Credentials in Canada'. Ottawa: Conference Board of Canada, 7–20.

Weber, George. 1971. *Inner-City Children Can Be Taught to Read*. Washington: Council for Basic Education.

Wehlage, Garry, Robert A. Rutter, Gregory A. Smith, Nancy Lesko, and Ricardo R. Fernandez. 1989. *Reducing the Risk: Schools as Communities of Support*. Philadelphia: Falmer Press.

Wellman, Barry, and Bernie Hogan. 2004. 'The Immanent Internet', in Johnston McKay, ed., *Netting Citizens: Exploring Citizenship in the Internet Age*. Edinburgh: Saint Andrew Press, 54–80.

Wollstonecraft, Mary. 1997 [1792]. *The Vindication of the Rights of Women*. London: Penguin.

Wotherspoon, Terry. 1998. *The Sociology of Education in Canada: Critical Perspectives*. Toronto: Oxford University Press.

Zeitlin, Irving M. 2001. *Ideology and the Development of Sociological Theory*, 7th edn. Englewood Cliffs, NJ: Prentice-Hall.

Chapter 14

Alasia, Alessandro, Alfons Weersink, Ray D. Bollman, and John Cranfield. 2009. 'Off-Farm Labour Decision of Canadian Farm Operators: Urbanization Effects and Rural Labour Market Linkages', *Journal of Rural Studies* 25, 1: 12–24.

Ali, Abu Muhammad Shajaat. 2007. 'Population Pressure, Agricultural Intensification and Changes in Rural Systems in Bangladesh', *Geoforum* 38, 4: 720–38.

Andersson, Roger. 2008. 'Neighbourhood Effects and the Welfare State: Towards a European Research Agenda?', *Schmollers Jahrbuch* 128, 1: 49–63.

Atkinson, Rowland. 2003. 'Introduction: Misunderstanding Saviour or Vengeful Wrecker? The Many Meanings and Problems of Gentrification', *Urban Studies* 40, 12: 2343–50.

Attane, Isabelle. 2006. 'The Demographic Impact of a Female Deficit in China, 2000–2050', *Population and Development Review* 32, 4: 755–70.

Authier, Jean-Yves. 2008. 'The Urban Dwellers and Their Neighborhood. Surveys of Residents from Inner-City Neighborhoods in France' [Les citadins et leur quartier. Enquetes aupres d'habitants de quartiers anciens centraux en France], *L'Annee sociologique* 58, 1: 21–46.

Baker, Rochelle. 2009. 'Homeless in the City: Bruce Lived Here', *Abbotsford News*, 25 Sept. At: <www.bclocalnews.com/fraser_valley/abbynews/news/61562687.html>.

Bandy, Matthew S. 2005. 'New World Settlement Evidence for a Two-Stage Neolithic Demographic Transition', *Current Anthropology* 46 (suppl.): S109–S115.

Bodemann, Y.M. 1998. 'From Berlin to Chicago and Further: Georg Simmel and the Voyage of His "Stranger"', *Berliner Journal Fur Soziologie* 8, 1: 125–42.

Brint, Steven. 2001. 'Gemeinschaft Revisited: A Critique and Reconstruction of the Community Concept', *Sociological Theory* 19, 1: 1–23.

Browning, Christopher R., Lori A. Burrington, Tama Leventhal, and Jeanne Brooks-Gunn. 2008. 'Neighborhood Structural Inequality, Collective Efficacy, and Sexual Risk Behavior among Urban Youth', *Journal of Health and Social Behavior* 49, 3: 269–85.

Burdette, Amy M., and Terrence D. Hill. 2008. 'An Examination of Processes Linking Perceived Neighborhood Disorder and Obesity', *Social Science and Medicine* 67, 1: 38–46.

Button, Deeanna M. 2008. 'Social Disadvantage and Family Violence: Neighborhood Effects on Attitudes about Intimate Partner Violence and Corporal Punishment', *American Journal of Criminal Justice* 33, 1: 130–47.

Calthorpe, Peter. 1993. *The Next American Metropolis: Ecology, Community, and the American Dream*. New York: Princeton Architectural Press.

Carpiano, Richard M. 2008. 'Actual or Potential Neighborhood Resources and Access to Them: Testing Hypotheses of Social Capital for the Health of Female Caregivers', *Social Science and Medicine* 67, 4: 568–82.

Clark, Gregory, and Neil Cummins. 2009. 'Urbanization, Mortality, and Fertility in Malthusian England', *American Economic Review* 99, 2: 242–7.

Cohen, Joel. 1995. *How Many People Can the Earth Support?* New York: Norton.

Cohen, Linc. 1992. 'Waste Dumps Toxic Traps for Minorities', *Chicago Reporter* 21, 4: 6–9, 11. At: <www.chicagoreporter.com/1992/04-92/0492WasteDumpsToxicTrapsforMinorities.htm>.

Crafts, N., and T.C. Mills. 2009. 'From Malthus to Solow: How Did the Malthusian Economy Really Evolve?', *Journal of Macroeconomics* 31, 1: 68–93.

Daily Bread Food Bank. 2002, 2006. *Poorer People, Poorer Health: The Health of Food Bank Recipients, Spring Food Drive*. Toronto: Daily Bread Food Bank.

Dear, Michael. 2003. 'The Los Angeles School of Urbanism: An Intellectual History', *Urban Geography* 24, 6: 493–509.

Dickason, Olive Patricia. 2002. *Canada's First Nations: A History of Founding Peoples from Earliest Times*, 3rd edn. Toronto: Oxford University Press.

Duke-Williams, Oliver, and Nicola Shelton. 2008. 'Small Area Inequalities in Health: Are We Underestimating Them?', *Social Science and Medicine* 67, 6: 891–9.

Durkheim, Émile. 1964 [1893]). *Division of Labor in Society*, trans. George Simpson. Glencoe, Ill.: Free Press.

Ehrmann, Nicholas, and Douglas S. Massey. 2008. 'Gender-specific Effects of Ecological Conditions on College Achievement', *Social Science Research* 37, 1: 220–38.

Emerson, Michael O., George Yancey, and Karen J. Chai. 2001. 'Does Race Matter in Residential Segregation? Exploring the Preferences of White Americans', *American Sociological Review* 66: 922–35.

Fazal, Shahab. 2006. 'Addressing Congestion and Transport-Related Air Pollution in Saharanpur, India', *Environment & Urbanization* 18, 1: 141–54.

Flowerdew, Robin, David J. Manley, and Clive E. Sabel. 2008. 'Neighbourhood Effects on Health: Does It Matter Where You Draw the Boundaries?', *Social Science and Medicine* 66, 6: 1241–55.

Fong, Eric, and Kumiko Shibuya. 2000. 'Spatial Separation of the Poor in Canadian Cities', *Demography* 37, 4: 449–59.

Fortin, Andrere, Marie-Helene Villeneuve, and Martin Rioux. 2008. 'Never without My Car? Suburbanites in the Area Surrounding Quebec City', *Recherches Sociographiques* 49, 3: 447–73.

Gajdos, Peter. 2009. 'Globalization Context of Urban Development and Its Socio-Spatial Particularities', *Sociologia—Slovak Sociological Review* 41, 4: 304–28.

Galster, George C. 2008. 'Quantifying the Effect of Neighbourhood on Individuals: Challenges, Alternative Approaches, and Promising Directions', *Schmollers Jahrbuch* 128, 1: 7–48.

Gans, Herbert. 1982. *The Urban Villagers: Group and Class in the Life of Italian-Americans*, 2nd edn. New York: Free Press.

Ghitter, Geoff, and Alan Smart. 2009. 'Mad Cows, Regional Governance, and Urban Sprawl: Path Dependence and Unintended Consequences in the Calgary Region', *Urban Affairs Review* 44, 5: 617–44.

Gilbert, J., and K. Wehr. 2003. 'Dairy Industrialization in the First Place: Urbanization, Immigration, and Political Economy in Los Angeles County, 1920–1970', *Rural Sociology* 68, 4: 467–90.

Glaeser, Edward L., and Joshua D. Gottlieb. 2006. 'Urban Resurgence and the Consumer City', *Urban Studies* 43, 8: 1275–99.

Goode, William. 1963. *World Revolution and Family Patterns*. New York: Free Press.

Hoffmann, John P. 2004. 'Social and Environmental Influences on Endangered Species: A Cross-National Study', *Sociological Perspectives* 47, 1: 79–107.

Huiban, Jean-Pierre. 2009. 'Urban versus Rural Firms: Does Location Affect Labor Demand?', *Growth and Change* 40, 4: 649–72.

Johnson, Katherine M., and Charles G. Schmidt. 2009. '"Room to Grow": Urban Ambitions and the Limits to Growth in Weld County, Colorado', *Urban Affairs Review* 44, 4: 525–53.

Johnson-Hanks, Jennifer. 2008. 'Demographic Transitions and Modernity', *Annual Review of Anthropology* 37: 301–15.

Jung, Changhoon, Chul-Young Roh, and Younguck Kang. 2009. 'Longitudinal Effects of Impact Fees and Special Assessments on the Level of Capital Spending, Taxes, and Long-Term Debt in American Cities', *Public Finance Review* 37, 5: 613–36.

Kalkhoff, Will, Stanford W. Gregory Jr, and David Melamed. 2009. 'Effects of Dichotically Enhanced Electronic Communication on Crash Risk and Performance during Simulated Driving', *Perceptual and Motor Skills* 108, 2: 449–64.

Kasman, Adnan, and Evrim Turgutlu. 2009. 'Cost Efficiency and Scale Economies in the Turkish Insurance Industry', *Applied Economics* 41, 24: 3151.

Kellett, Livia, Lyla Peter, and Kelley Moore. 2008. 'The City of Saskatoon's Local Area Planning Program: A Case Study', *Social Indicators Research* 85, 1: 159–67.

Kirk, David S. 2008. 'The Neighborhood Context of Racial and Ethnic Disparities in Arrest', *Demography* 45, 1: 55–77.

Lehr, C.S. 2009. 'Evidence on the Demographic Transition', *Review of Economics and Statistics* 91, 4: 871–87.

Livi-Bacci, Massimo. 1992. *A Concise History of World Population: An Introduction to Population Processes*, trans. Carl Ipsen. Cambridge, Mass.: Blackwell.

Lutz, Wolfgang, Warren Sanderson, and Sergei Scherbov. 2001. 'The End of the World Population Growth', *Nature* 412: 543–5.

MacIntyre, Sally, Laura MacDonald, and Anne Ellaway. 2008. 'Do Poorer People Have Poorer Access to Local Resources and Facilities? The Distribution of Local Resources by Area Deprivation in Glasgow, Scotland', *Social Science and Medicine* 67, 6: 900–14.

McKenzie, Kwame. 2008. 'Urbanization, Social Capital and Mental Health', *Global Social Policy* 8, 3: 359–77.

Malmberg, Bo, and Tsegaye Tegenu. 2007. 'Population Pressure and Dynamics of Household Livelihoods in an Ethiopian Village: An Elaboration of the Boserup-Chayanovian Framework', *Population and Environment* 29, 2: 39–67.

Malthus, Thomas R. 1959 [1798]. *Population: The First Essay*. Ann Arbor: University of Michigan Press.

Millward, Hugh. 2008. 'Evolution of Population Densities: Five Canadian Cities, 1971–2001', *Urban Geography* 29, 7: 616–38.

——— and Trudi Bunting. 2008. 'Patterning in Urban Population Densities: A Spatio-temporal Model Compared with Toronto 1971–2001', *Environment and Planning A* 40, 2: 283–302.

Muhajarine, Nazeem, Ronald Labonte, Allison Williams, and James Randall. 2008. 'Person, Perception, and Place: What Matters to Health and Quality of Life', *Social Indicators Research* 85, 1: 53–80.

Ng, Shu W., E.C. Norton, and B.M. Popkin. 2009. 'Why Have Physical Activity Levels Declined among Chinese Adults? Findings from the 1991–2006 China Health and Nutrition Surveys', *Social Science and Medicine* 68, 7: 1305–14.

Nicolini, Esteban A. 2007. 'Was Malthus Right? A VAR Analysis of Economic and Demographic Interactions in Pre-Industrial England', *European Review of Economic History* 11, 1: 99–121.

Norton, William. 2010. *Human Geography*, 7th edn. Toronto: Oxford University Press.

Oakley, Deirdre A. 1999. 'Keeping Homeless Individuals Homeless: City Politics and the Zoning of Permanent Housing for Street Alcoholics', paper presented at the annual meeting of the American Sociological Association.

Oreopoulos, Philip. 2008. 'Neighbourhood Effects in Canada: A Critique', *Canadian Public Policy* 34, 2: 237–58.

Otte, Gunnar, and Nina Baur. 2008. 'Urbanism as a Way of Life? Spatial Variations in Lifestyles in Germany', *Zeitschrift Für Soziologie* 37, 2: 93–116.

Pastor, Manuel, Jr, James L. Sadd, and Rachel Morello-Frosch. 2004. 'Waiting to Inhale: The Demographics of Toxic Air Release Facilities in 21st-Century California', *Social Science Quarterly* 85, 2: 420–40.

Platt, Lucinda. 2009. 'Social Activity, Social Isolation and Ethnicity', *Sociological Review* 57, 4: 670–702.

Poulton, Michael. 2007. 'When America Became Suburban', *Canadian Journal of Urban Research* 16, 2: 182–4.

Powdthavee, Nattavudh. 2008. 'Putting a Price Tag on Friends, Relatives, and Neighbours: Using Surveys of Life Satisfaction to Value Social Relationships', *Journal of Socio-Economics* 37, 4: 1459–80.

Reading, Richard, Andrew Jones, Robin Haynes, Konstantinos Daras, and Alan Emond. 2008. 'Individual Factors Explain Neighbourhood Variations in Accidents to Children under 5 Years of Age', *Social Science and Medicine* 67, 6: 915–27.

Sahoo, Pravakar, and Ranjan K. Dash. 2009. 'Infrastructure Development and Economic Growth in India', *Journal of the Asia Pacific Economy* 14, 4: 351–65.

Sauvy, Alfred, and Paul Demeny. 1990. 'Alfred Sauvy on the World Population Problem: A View in 1949', *Population and Development Review* 16: 759–74.

Schieman, Scott. 2009. 'Residential Stability, Neighborhood Racial Composition, and the Subjective Assessment of Neighborhood Problems among Older Adults', *Sociological Quarterly* 50, 4: 608–32.

Shandra, John M., Bruce London, and John B. Williamson. 2003. 'Environmental Degradation, Environmental Sustainability, and Overurbanization in the Developing World: A Quantitative, Cross-National Analysis', *Sociological Perspectives* 46, 3: 309–29.

Simkins, Charles. 2001. 'Can South Africa Avoid a Malthusian Positive Check?', *Daedalus* 130, 1: 123–50.

Simmel, Georg. 1950 [1917]. *The Sociology of Georg Simmel*, trans. Kurt Wolff. New York: Free Press.

Simon, Julian L. 1996. *The Ultimate Resource 2*. Princeton, NJ: Princeton University Press.

Squires, Richard. 2008. 'The Interstate Sprawl System', *Society* 45, 3: 277–82.

Tönnies, Ferdinand. 1957 [1887]. *Community and Society (Gemeinschaft und Gesellschaft)*. New York: Harper and Row.

United Nations Population Division (UNPD). 2006. *World Urbanization Prospects: The 2003 Revision Population Database*. At: <esa.un.org/unup>.

Urban, Susanne. 2009. 'Is the Neighbourhood Effect an Economic or an Immigrant Issue? A Study of the Importance of the Childhood Neighbourhood for Future Integration into the Labour Market', *Urban Studies* 46, 3: 583–603.

Vortkamp, Wolfgang. 1998. 'Participation and Community: Louis Wirth's Sociology of Modernity in the Chicago School Tradition', *Soziale Welt* 49, 3: 275–94.

Wassmer, Robert W. 2008. 'Causes of Urban Sprawl in the United States: Auto Reliance as Compared to Natural Evolution, Flight from Blight, and Local Revenue Reliance', *Journal of Policy Analysis and Management* 27, 3: 536–55.

Weber, Max. 1958 [1921]. *The City*, trans. Don Martindale and Gertrud Neuwirth. New York: Free Press.

———. 1981 [1924]. *General Economic History*. New Brunswick, NJ: Transaction Books.

Weil, David N., and Joshua Wilde. 2009. 'How Relevant Is Malthus for the Economic Development Today?', *American Economic Review* 99, 2: 255–61.

Westaway, M.S. 2007. 'Life and Neighborhood Satisfaction of Black and White Residents in a Middle-Class Suburb of Johannesburg', *Psychological Reports* 100, 2: 489–94.

Whyte, William H. 1996. 'The Design of Spaces from City: Rediscovering the Center', in Richard T. LeGates and Frederic Stout, eds, *The City Reader*. New York: Routledge, 483–90.

Williams, Allison M., Nazeem Muhajarine, James Randall, Ronald Labonte, and Peter Kitchen. 2008. 'Volunteerism and Residential Longevity in Saskatoon, Saskatchewan, Canada', *Social Indicators Research* 85, 1: 97–110.

Wirth, Louis. 1938. 'Urbanism as a Way of Life.' in Richard T. LeGates and Frederic Stout, eds, *The City Reader*. New York: Routledge, 97–105.

Wright, Judith, and Nazeem Muhajarine. 2008. 'Respiratory Illness in Saskatoon Infants: The Impact of Housing and Neighbourhood Characteristics', *Social Indicators Research* 85, 1: 81–95.

Wrobel, David. 2008. 'Paradise Pondered: Urban California, 1850-2000', *Journal of Urban History* 34, 6: 1029–43.

Xu, Z.L., and N. Zhu. 2009. 'City Size Distribution in China: Are Large Cities Dominant?', *Urban Studies* 46, 10: 2159–85.

Yao, Li, and Stephanie A. Robert. 2008. 'The Contributions of Race, Individual Socio-economic Status, and Neighborhood Socio-economic Context on the Self-Rated Health Trajectories and Mortality of Older Adults', *Research on Aging* 30, 2: 251–73.

Yu, Wei-hsin. 2008. 'The Psychological Cost of Market Transition: Mental Health Disparities in Reform-Era China', *Social Problems* 55, 3: 347–69.

Yuan, Anastasia S. Vogt. 2008. 'Racial Composition of Neighborhood and Emotional Well-Being', *Sociological Spectrum* 28, 1: 105–29.

Chapter 15

ABC News. 2007. 'Extreme Green Living: New York Family Experiments with "No Environmental Impact" Lifestyle', 25 June. At: <abcnews.go.com/GMA/TenWays/Story?id=3159955>.

Abramson, Paul, and Ronald Inglehart. 1995. *Value Change in Global Perspective*. Ann Arbor: University of Michigan Press.

Anonymous. 2008. 'Nigeria: The Desert Is Fast Encroaching, but Why?', *Civil Engineering: Magazine of the South African Institution of Civil Engineering* 16, 5: 75.

Aronowitz, Stanley, and Jonathan Cutler, eds. 1998. *Post-Work: The Wages of Cybernation*. New York: Routledge.

Balaban, Oded, and A. Tsatskin. 2010. 'The Paradox of Oil Reserve Forecasts: The Political Implications of Predicting Oil Reserves and Oil Consumption', *Energy Policy* 38, 3: 1340–4.

Bandarage, Asoka. 2008. 'Control Cash Not People', *The Ecologist* 38, 8: 58.

Bartz, Sherry, and David L. Kelly. 2006. 'Economic Growth and the Environment: Theory and Facts', Working Papers 0601, University of Miami, Department of Economics.

Beck, Ulrich. 1992. *Risk Society: Towards a New Modernity*. London: Sage.

Bigano, Andrea, Francesco Bosello, Roberto Roson, and Richard S.J. Tol. 2008. 'Economy-Wide Impacts of Climate Change: A Joint Analysis for Sea Level Rise and Tourism', *Mitigation and Adaptation Strategies for Global Change* 13: 765–91.

Borek, Erika, and Stephanie A. Bohon. 2008. 'Policy Climates and Reductions in Automobile Use', *Social Science Quarterly* 89, 5: 1293–1311.

Boyd, David. 2001. *Canada vs. the OECD: An Environment Comparison*. Victoria, BC: Eco-Research Chair, University of Victoria. At: <www.environmentalindicators.com/htdocs/PDF/CanadavsOECD.pdf>.

Burra, Tara A., Susan J. Elliott, John D. Eyles, Pavlos S. Kanaroglou, Bruce C. Wainman, and Henry Muggah. 2006. 'Effects of Residential Exposure to Steel Mills and Coking Works on Birth Weight and Preterm Births among Residents of Sydney, Nova Scotia', *Canadian Geographer* 50, 2: 242–55.

At: <www.accessmylibrary.com/article-1G1-149462231/effects-residential-exposure-steel.html>.

Carter, Neil. 2001. *The Politics of the Environment: Ideas, Activism, Policy*. Cambridge: Cambridge University Press.

CBC News. 2004. 'Tracking the Tar Ponds', 6 May. At: <www.cbc.ca/news/background/tarponds/>.

———. 2007. 'Kyoto and Beyond: Kyoto FAQs', 14 Feb. <www.cbc.ca/news/background/kyoto/>.

———. 2010. 'Sydney Tar Ponds Cleanup Raises Stink', 5 May. At: <www.cbc.ca/canada/nova-scotia/story/2010/05/05/ns-sydney-tar-ponds-smell.html>.

Cizek, Petr. 2004. 'Hydro Hype, Dam Delusions: The Proposal to Dam the Deh Cho for Hydroelectricity is a Classic Case of Short-Sighted Energy Planning', *Alternatives Journal* 30, 1: 28–9.

Comim, Flavio, Pushpam Kumar, and Nicolas Sirven. 2009. 'Poverty and Environment Links: An Illustration from Africa', *Journal of International Development* 21, 3: 447–69.

Coming Clean. 2006. 'Body Burden'. At: <www.chemicalbodyburden.org>.

Copeland, Brian R., and Scott Taylor. 2004. 'Trade, Growth, and Environmental Quality', *American Economic Review* 16: 147–68.

Couchman, Robert. 1986. 'The International Social Revolution: Its Impact on Canadian Family Life', *Canadian Home Economics Journal* 36, 1: 10–12.

Coward, Harold, Rosemary Ommer, and Tony Pitcher, eds. 2000. *Just Fish: Ethics and Canadian Marine Fisheries*. St John's: ISER Books.

Curran, Giorel. 2006. 'Whither Environmentalism? Environmental Politics in the 21st Century', *Social Alternatives* 25, 2: 48–53.

Curtis, F. 2009. 'Peak Globalization: Climate Change, Oil Depletion and Global Trade', *Ecological Economics* 69, 2: 427–34.

Dalton, Russell. 1994. *The Green Rainbow: Environmental Groups in Western Europe*. New Haven: Yale University Press.

Debrovner, Diane. 2002. 'Save Your Child from Skin Cancer', *Parents* 77, 5: 108–12.

Doyle, Timothy. 2005. *Environmental Movements in Minority and Majority Worlds: A Global Perspective*. New Brunswick, NJ: Rutgers University Press.

Elena, G.d.C., and Esther Velazquez. 2010. 'From Water to Energy: The Virtual Water Content and Water Footprint of Biofuel Consumption in Spain', *Energy Policy* 38, 3: 1345–52.

Etzioni, Amitai. 2004. 'The Post-Affluent Society', *Review of Social Economy* 62, 3: 407–20.

Eriksson, Sonja. 2009. 'The Transition Initiative Comes to Cohousing', *Communities* 144: 51–3.

Gaard, Greta, ed. 1993. *Ecofeminism: Women, Animals, Nature*. Philadelphia: Temple University Press.

Giddens, Anthony. 1990. *The Consequences of Modernity*. Cambridge: Polity Press.

Gilbertson, Michael, and Andrew E. Watterson. 2007. 'Diversionary Reframing of the Great Lakes Water Quality Agreement', *Journal of Public Health Policy* 28, 2: 201–15.

Gorrie, Peter. 2007. 'Activists Sue Government over Kyoto', *Toronto Star*, 20 Sept. At: <www.thestar.com/article/258547>.

Greenberg, Michael R. 2009. 'How Much Do People Who Live Near Major Nuclear Facilities Worry about Those Facilities? Analysis of National and Site-Specific Data', *Journal of Environmental Planning and Management* 52, 7: 919–37.

Greenpeace. 2001. 'Pacific in Peril'. At: <www.greenpeace.org >.

Haalboom, Bethany, Susan J. Elliott, John Eyles, and Henry Muggah. 2006. 'The Risk Society at Work in the Sydney "Tar Ponds"', *Canadian Geographer* 50, 2: 227, 241.

Hannigan, John A. 1995. *Environmental Sociology: A Social Constructionist Perspective*. London: Routledge.

———. 2008. 'Environmental Sociology: A Social Constructionist Perspective', *Organization and Environment* 21, 4: 503–5.

Helfgott, Roy B. 1988. *Computerized Manufacturing and Human Resources: Innovation through Employee Involvement*. Lexington, Mass.: Lexington Books.

Hoag, Hannah. 2006. 'Burn, Baby, Burn?', *Canadian Wildlife* 12, 5: 30–3.

Homer-Dixon, Thomas. 1994. 'Environmental Scarcities and Violent Conflict: Evidence from Cases', *International Security* 19, 1: 5–40.

Humphrey, Craig, Tammy L. Lewis, and Fredrick H. Buttel. 2002. *Environment, Energy, and Society: A New Synthesis*. Belmont, Calif.: Wadsworth.

Inglehart, Ronald. 1977. *The Silent Revolution: Changing Values and Political Styles among Western Publics*. Princeton, NJ: Princeton University Press.

———. 1990. *Culture Shift in Advanced Industrial Society*. Princeton, NJ: Princeton University Press.

International Food Policy Research Institute (IFPRI). 1997. 'Report Finds World Water Supplies Dwindling While Demand Rises; World Food Production, Health, and Environment at Risk', press release. At: <www.ifpri.org/pressrel/030997.htm>.

Klare, Michael T. 2004. 'Crude Awakening', *The Nation* 279, 15: 35–8, 40–1.

Lamal, Peter. 2009. 'The Varied Concepts of "Epidemic" and Our Varied Reactions', *The Skeptical Inquirer* 33, 5: 58.

Larsen, Soren. 2003. 'Promoting Aboriginal Territoriality through Interethnic Alliances: The Case of the Cheslatta T'en in Northern British Columbia', *Human Organization* 62, 1: 74–84.

Li, Yi, Wen Wang, Haidong Kan, Bingheng Chen, and Xiaohui Xu. 2010. 'Air Quality and Outpatient Visits for Asthma in Adults during the 2008 Summer Olympic Games in Beijing', *Science of the Total Environment* 408, 5: 1226–7.

Luke, Timothy W. 2008. 'Climatology as Social Critique: The Social Construction/Creation of Global Warming, Global Dimming, and Global Cooling', in Steve Vanderheiden, ed., *Political Theory and Climate Change*. Cambridge, Mass.: MIT Press, 121–52.

Madeley, John. 2009. 'GM Contamination, Technology and Control', *Appropriate Technology* 36, 4: 16.

Martell, Luke. 2008. 'Beck's Cosmopolitan Politics', *Contemporary Politics* 14, 2: 129–43.

Mesic, Milan. 1998. 'Establishment and Development of the American Environmental Movement', 7, 1 and 2: 91–114.

Murphy, Raymond. 2004. 'Disaster or Sustainability: The Dance of Human Agents with Nature's Actants', *Canadian Review of Sociology and Anthropology* 41, 3: 249–67.

NASA. 2006. '2005 Warmest Year in Over a Century'. At: <www.nasa.gov/vision/earth/environment/2005_warmest.html>.

Neitzel, Richard, Robyn R.M. Gershon, Marina Zeltser, Allison Canton, and Muhammad Akram. 2009. 'Noise Levels Associated with New York City's Mass Transit Systems', *American Journal of Public Health* 99, 8: 1393–9.

Norgaard, Kari M. 2002. 'Experiencing Global Warming: The Social Organization of Awareness, Denial and Innocence', paper presented at the World Congress of the International Sociological Association, Brisbane, Australia, 7–13 July.

O'Riordan, T., and J. O'Riordan. 1993. 'On evaluating Public Examination of Controversial Projects', in H.D. Foster, ed., *Advances in Resource Management: Tribute to W.R. Derrick Sewell*. London: Belhaven Press, 19–52.

Pacione, Michael. 2001. *Urban Geography: A Global Perspective*. New York: Routledge.

Perrow, Charles. 1999. *Normal Accidents: Living with High Risk Technologies*, 2nd edn. Princeton, NJ: Princeton University Press.

Phillips, Kate. 2006. 'Report Cites Concerns over Fragrances in Lake Sediments', *Chemical Week* 168, 29: 45.

Plant, Judith. 1990. 'The Place of Women in Polluted Places', in I. Diamond and G. Orenstein, eds, *Reweaving the World: The Emergence of Feminism*. San Francisco: Sierra Club Books, 173–88.

Population Reference Bureau (PRB). 2001. *World Population Data Sheet, 2001*. Washington: Population Reference Bureau.

———. 2008. *Population Bulletin* 63, 3 (Sept.). At: <www.prb.org/pdf08/63.3highlights.pdf>.

Porter, Catherine. 2009. 'Eco-Friendly Labelling? It's a Lot of "Greenwash"', *Toronto Star*, 17 Apr. At: <www.thestar.com/news/canada/article/619936>.

Roots, Chris. 1999. 'Environmental Movements: From the Local to the Global', *Environmental Politics* 8, 1: 1–12.

Rucht, Dieter. 1996. 'The Effects of Environmental Movements: About the Difficulties of Drawing a Balance', *Forschungsjournal Neue Soziale Bewegungen* 9, 4: 15–27.

Rynbrandt, Linda J., and Mary Jo Deegan. 2002. 'The Ecofeminist Pragmatism of Caroline Bartlett Crane, 1896–1935', *American Sociologist* 33, 3: 58–69.

Scheelhaase, Janina, Wolfgang Grimme, and Martin Schaefer. 2010. 'The Inclusion of Aviation into the EU Emission Trading Scheme—Impacts on Competition between European and Non-European Network Airlines', *Transportation Research: Part D: Transport and Environment* 15, 1: 14–25.

Schoenfeld, A. Clay, Robert F. Meier, and Robert J. Griffin. 1979. 'Constructing a Social Problem: The Press and the Environment', *Social Problems* 27: 38–61.

Smith, Keith. 2001. *Environmental Hazards: Assessing Risk and Reducing Disaster*, 3rd edn. New York: Routledge.

Suzuki, David, and Holly Dressel. 2002. *Good News for a Change: How Everyday People Are Helping the Planet*. Vancouver: Greystone.

Tepperman, Lorne. 2001. 'The Postmaterialist Thesis: Has There Been a Shift in Political Cultures?', in Douglas Baer, ed., *Political Sociology: Canadian Perspectives*. Toronto: Oxford University Press, 15–36.

United States Energy Information Administration. 2001. 'World Primary Energy Consumption (Btu) 1990–1999, Table E1'. At: <www.eia.doe.gov/emeu/iea/table1.html>.

Verbruggen, A., M. Fischedick, W. Moomaw, T. Weir, A. Nadai, L.J. Nilsson, J. Nyboer, and J. Sathaye. 2010. 'Renewable Energy Costs, Potentials, Barriers: Conceptual Issues', *Energy Policy* 38, 2: 850–61.

Vogel, David. 2003. 'The Hare and the Tortoise Revisited: The New Politics of Consumer and Environmental Regulation in Europe', *British Journal of Political Science* 33: 557–80.

Windsor, J.E., and J.A. McVey. 2004. 'The Annihilation of Both Place and Sense of Place: The Experience of the Cheslatta T'En Canadian First Nation within the Context of Large-Scale Environmental Projects', *Geographical Journal* 171, 2: 146–65.

Wolfenbarger, L.L. 2002. 'Genetically Engineered Organisms: Assessing Environmental and Human Health Effects', *American Journal of Alternative Agriculture* 17, 4: 203–4.

Wood, Christopher. 1994. 'Powerhouse Politics', *Maclean's* 107: 14–21.

World Health Organization (WHO). 1997. *Health and Environment in Sustainable Development: Five Years after the Earth Summit*. Geneva: WHO.

———. 1999. *Report on Infectious Diseases*. Geneva: WHO. At: <www.who.int/infectious-disease-report/ index-rpt99.html>.

World Meteorological Organization (WMO). 2000. 'WMO Statement on the Status of the Global Climate in 1999', (WMO No. 913). At: <www.wmo.ch/web/wcp/wcdmp/statement/html/913-1999.html>.

World Resources Institute. 1998. *Climate, Biodiversity, and Forests: Issues and Opportunities Emerging from the Kyoto Protocol*. Baltimore: World Resources Institute.

Yogev-Baggio, T., H. Bibi, J. Dubnov, K. Or-Hen, R. Carel, and Boris A. Portnov. 2010. 'Who Is Affected More by Air Pollution? Sick or Healthy? Some Evidence from a Health Survey of Schoolchildren Living in the Vicinity of a Coal-Fired Power Plant in Northern Israel', *Health and Place* 16, 2: 399–408.

Zito, Anthony R. 2005. 'The European Union an Environmental Leader in a Global Environment', *Globalizations* 2, 3: 363–75.

Chapter 16

Aligica, Paul D. 2009. 'Social Predictions, Institutional Design and Prestige Loops: Richard Henshel's Contribution to Futures Studies', *Futures* 41, 3: 147–55.

Basalla, George. 1988. *The Evolution of Technology*. Cambridge: Cambridge University Press.

Baym, Nancy K., Yan Bing Zhang, and Mei-Chen Lin. 2004. 'Social Interactions across Media', *New Media and Society* 6, 3: 299–318.

Byrne, John, David E. Ingersoll, and Daniel Rich. 1981. 'Governing Utopia: The Challenge to Political Vision', *Alternative Futures* 4, 1: 136–53.

Childe, V. Gordon. 1936. *Man Makes Himself*. London: Watts and Co.

Chomsky, Noam. 1999. 'Language Design', in Griffiths (1999: 30–2).

Cole, S. 2008. 'The Zeitgeist of Futures?', *Futures* 40, 10: 894–902.

Davis, D.W., and B.D. Silver. 2004. 'Civil Liberties vs. Security: Public Opinion in the Context of the Terrorist Attacks on America', *American Journal of Political Science* 48, 1: 28–46.

Dolton, P., and A. Vignoles. 2000. 'The Incidence and Effects of Over-education in the UK Graduate Labour Market', *Economics of Education Review* 19, 2: 179–98.

Dublin, M. 1989. *Futurehype: The Tyranny of Prophecy*. New York: Plume.

Epstein, David. 2010. 'Sports Genes', *Sports Illustrated*, 17 May, 53–65.

Ewen, Stuart. 1976. *Captains of Consciousness: Advertising and the Social Roots of the Consumer Culture*. New York: McGraw-Hill.

Ford, James, Tristan Pearce, Barry Smit, Johanna Wandel, Mishak Allurut, Kik Shappa, Harry Ittusujurat, and Keven Qrunnut. 2007. 'Reducing Vulnerability to Climate Change in the Arctic: The Case of Nunavut, Canada', *Arctic* 60, 2: 150–66.

Fuller, Ted, and Krista Loogma. 2009. 'Constructing Futures: A Social Constructionist Perspective on Foresight Methodology', *Futures* 41, 2: 71–9.

George, Henry. 1898. *Social Problems*. New York: Doubleday and McClure.

Gladwell, Malcolm. 2009. *What the Dog Saw and Other Adventures*. New York: Little, Brown.

Glenn, Jerome C., and Theodore J. Gordon. 2005. *2005 State of the Future*. At: <www.acunu.org/millennium/sof2005.html>.

———— and ————. 2009. 'Ethical Issues in Society'. At: <www.docstoc.com/docs/14622155/Ethical-Issues-In-Society>.

Goldman, Lawrence. 2007. 'Foundations of British Sociology 1880-1930: Contexts and Biographies', *Sociological Review* 55, 3: 431–40.

Gould, J.B. 2002. 'Playing with Fire: The Civil Liberties Implications of September 11th', *Public Administration Review* 62 (special issue): 74–9.

Griffiths, Sian, ed. 1999. *Predictions*. New York: Oxford University Press.

Hacker, Andrew. 1955. 'In Defense of Utopia', *Ethics* 65: 135–8.

Herzog, Benno, Esperanza Gómez-Guardeño, Victor Agulló, Rafael Aleixandre-Benavent, and Juan Carlos Valderrama-Zurian. 2009. 'Discourses on Drugs and Immigration: The Social Construction of a Problem', *Forum Qualitative Sozialforschung/Forum: Qualitative Social Research* 10, 1.

Hurley, K., E. Masini, W. Boulding, R. Eisler, S. Premchander, P. McCorduck, et al. 2008. 'Futures Studies and Feminism', *Futures* 40, 4: 388–407.

Hyshka, Elaine. 2009. 'The Saga Continues: Canadian Legislative Attempts to Reform Cannabis Law in the Twenty-First Century', *Canadian Journal of Criminology and Criminal Justice* 51, 1: 73–91.

Jones, Jeremy, and Duncan Hunter. 1995. 'Consensus Methods for Medical and Health Services Research', *British Medical Journal* 311, 7001: 376–80.

Katz, Nathaniel, and Norman A. Mazer. 2009. 'The Impact of Opioids on the Endocrine System', *Clinical Journal of Pain* 25, 2: 170–5.

Kitzinger, Jenny, and Clare Williams. 2005. 'Forecasting Science Futures: Legitimising Hope and Calming Fears in the Embryo Stem Cell Debate', *Social Science and Medicine* 61, 3: 731–40.

Kowalski, Robin M., and Susan P. Limber. 2007. 'Electronic Bullying among Middle School Students', *Journal of Adolescent Health* 41, 6: S22–S30.

Larsen, K., and U. Gunnarsson-Ostling. 2009. 'Climate Change Scenarios and Citizen-Participation: Mitigation and Adaptation Perspectives in Constructing Sustainable Futures', *Habitat International* 33, 3: 260–6.

Marx, Karl, and Friedrich Engels. 1978 [1848]. *Manifesto of the Communist Party*. Moscow: Foreign Language Publishing House.

Meadows, Donella H., Dennis L. Meadows, Jorgen Randers, and William W. Behrens III. 1972. *Limits to Growth*. New York: Universe Books.

Merton, Robert K. 1973 [1942]. 'The Normative Structure of Science', in Merton, *The Sociology of Science: Theoretical and Empirical Investigations*. Chicago: University of Chicago Press.

Millennium Project. 2009a. *State of the Future 2009*. At: <www.millennium-project.org/millennium/sof2009.html>.

————. 2009b. 'Global Exploratory Scenarios'. At: <www.millennium-project.org/millennium/scenarios/explor-s.htmlCase%206.%20%20The%20Rich%20Get%20Richer>.

Milojevic, I., K. Hurley, and A. Jenkins. 2008. 'Futures of Feminism', *Futures* 40, 4: 313–18.

Morrison, Catriona M., and Helen Gore. 2010. 'The Relationship between Excessive Internet Use and Depression: A Questionnaire-Based Study of 1,319 Young People and Adults', *Psychopathology* 43, 2: 121–6.

Mueller, John. 2005. 'Simplicity and Spook: Terrorism and the Dynamics of Threat Exaggeration', *International Studies Perspectives* 6: 208–34.

Murray, Thomas H. 2002. 'Reflections on the Ethics of Genetic Enhancement', *Genetics in Medicine* 4, 6: 27S–32S.

Plummer, Thomas. 2004. 'Flaked Stones and Old Bones: Biological and Cultural Evolution at the Dawn of Technology', *American Journal of Physical Anthropology* 125, S39: 118–64.

Ponteva, M. 2002. 'The Impact of Warfare on Medicine', in: I. Taipale et al., eds, *War or Health? A Reader*. London/New York: Zed Books, 36–41.

Pourezzat, Ali A., Abdolazim Mollaee, and Morteza Firouzabadi. 2008. 'Building the Future: Undertaking Proactive Strategy for National Outlook', *Futures* 40, 10: 887–92.

Raphael, Dennis. 2009. *Social Determinants of Health: Canadian Perspectives*. Toronto: Canadian Scholars' Press.

Rheingold, Howard. 2000. *The Virtual Community: Homesteading on the Electronic Frontier*. Cambridge, Mass.: MIT Press.

Rowland, F. Sherwood. 1999. 'Sequestration', in Griffiths (1999: 208–11).

Segall, M.D., P.J.D. Lindan, M.J. Probert, C.J. Picard, P.J. Hasnip, et al. 2002. 'First-Principles Simulation: Ideas, Illustrations and the CASTEP Code', *Journal of Physics: Condensed Matter* 14, 11: 2717–44.

Towne, Ezra Thayer. 1916. *Social Problems: A Study of Present Day Social Conditions*. New York: Macmillan.

University of Houston–Clear Lake. 2001. 'What Is Futures Studies?' At: <www.cl.uh.edu/futureweb/futdef.html>.

Walonick, David S. 1993. 'An Overview of Forecasting Methodology'. At: <www.statpac.com/research-papers/forecasting.htm>.

————. 2004. *Survival Statistics*. Bloomington, Minn.: StatPac.

Webster, Frank. 2002. *Theories of the Information Society*. London: Routledge.

Wells, H.G. 1902. *Anticipations of the Reaction of Mechanical and Scientific Progress upon Human Life and Thought*. New York: Harper.

Credits

Grateful acknowledgement is made for permission to reprint the following:

Chapter 1

Photo, page 1: iStockphoto.com/Ryan Klos

Chapter 2

Photo, page 29: iStockphoto.com/Janne Ahvo
Block quote, page 39: CBC.CA
Block quote, page 40: *The Blueprint to End Homelessness in Toronto*, The Wellesley Institute, 2006.
Box 2.2: © United Nations Children's Fund 2009
Box 2.3: The Toronto Star.

Chapter 3

Box 3.2: Adapted from 'New Evidence Surfaces in Post-Katrina Crimes' by A.C. Thompson, © Copyright 2009 Pro Publica Inc.
Box 3.3: David Fleischer, © York Region Media Group (Metroland Media Group)

Chapter 4

Block quote, page 90: Wolf, Naomi, *Globe and Mail*, Monday, Jun. 08, 2009.
Box 4.2: Sachs, Jeffrey D. (2005). The End of Poverty: Economic Possibilities for Our Time. New York: Penguin Books
Box 4.3: Canadian Research Institute for the Advancement of Women (CRIAW), at: www.criaw-icref.ca/factSheets/Women%20 and%20Poverty/Poverty%20Fact%20 sheet_e.htm
Box 4.4: Adapted from: CTV, at: www.ctv.ca/ servlet/ArticleNews/story/CTVNews/2008 0105/ ski_jump_080105?s_name=&no_ads=; www.wsj2010.com/; CBC, at: www.cbc.ca/ sports/amateur/story/2009/04/22/sp-ski jumping-olympic-women.html; ctvOlympics, at: www.ctvolympics.ca/ski-jumping/news/ newsid=12786.html; *Toronto Star*, at: www. thestar.com/comment/columnists/article/ 664482; BBC, at: news.bbc.co.uk/2/hi/americas/ 8009464.stm

Chapter 5

Box 5.1: Thomas Beatie
Box 5.2: All rights reserved. Republication or redistribution of Thomson Reuters content, including by framing or similar means, is expressly prohibited without the prior written consent of Thomson Reuters. Thomson Reuters and its logo are registered trademarks or trademarks of the Thomson Reuters group of companies around the world. © Thomson Reuters 2009. Thomson Reuters journalists are subject to an Editorial Handbook which requires fair presentation and disclosure of relevant interests.

Chapter 6

Box 6.1: Review: Family and Community in Ireland. Author: Patricia Lysaght. Reviewed work: Family and Community in Ireland by Conrad M. Arensberg; Solon T. Kimball. Source: Béaloideas, Iml./Vol. 70, (2002), pp. 257–263, published by An Cumann le Béaloideas Éireann/The Folklore of Ireland Society.
Box 6.2: © Sdnet, 2001–6.

Chapter 7

Photo, page 173: iStockphoto.com/Janne Ahvo
Box 7.2: Nancy Trejos.
Box 7.3: CBC.CA

Chapter 8

Box 8.2: Reprinted with permission—Torstar Syndication Services.
Box 8.3: Ian Sample

Chapter 9

Box 9.1: Abridged from 'Rich countries corner supplies of swine flu vaccine', by Martin Trauth, Copyright © 2010 AFP. All rights reserved.

Chapter 10

Block quote, page 263: Valerie M. Hudson and Andrea Den Boes, 'A Surplus of Men, a Deficit of Peace: Security and Sex Ratios in Asia's Largest States', *International Security*, 26:4 (Spring, 2002), pp. 5–38. © 2002 by the President and Fellows of Harvard College and the Massachusetts Institute of Technology.
Block quote, page 277: Global Security, www. globalsecurity.org/military/world/israel/ army.htm.
Box 10.2: Excerpts from *A Long Way Gone: Memoirs of a Boy Soldier* by Ishmael Beah. Copyright © 2007 by Ishmael Beah. Reprinted by permission of Farrar, Straus and Giroux, LLC.

Chapter 11

Photo, page 287: iStockphoto.com/Guillaume Dubé
Box 11.1: Kline and Zhang, 2009.
Box 11.2: Adapted from 'One Big Gay Family' by Denise Balkissoon.
Box 11.3: 'Modern Love: Rethinking Family' by Sarah Elton

Chapter 12

Box 12.2: CTVglobemedia Publishing Inc. All Rights Reserved.
Box 12.3: Agence-France-Presse

Chapter 13

Box 13.2: CBC.CA
Box 13.3: Reprinted with permission—Torstar Syndication Services

Chapter 14

Box 14.2: Published with permission from The Abbotsford News, Black Press.

Chapter 15

Box 15.1: Reprinted with permission—Torstar Syndication Services

Block quote pages 410–11: 'Living Interconnections with Animals and Nature' pgs. 4–5 from *Ecofeminism: Women, Animals, Nature* edited by Greta Gaard. Used by permission of Temple University Press. © 1993 by Temple University. All Rights Reserved.

Box 15.2: Reprinted with permission—Torstar Syndication Services

Box 15.3: CBC.CA

Box 15.4: ABC News Videosource

Chapter 16

Photo, page 435: iStockphoto.com/Kelly Talele

Box 16.1: *2010 State of the Future* by Jerome C. Glenn, Theodore J. Gordon, and Elizabeth Florescu, The Millennium Project. © 2009 The Millennium Project.

Block quote, page 444: Rowland, F. Sherwood. 1999. 'Sequestration', in Griffiths (1999: 208–11).

Box 16.2: *2010 State of the Future* by Jerome C. Glenn, Theodore J. Gordon, and Elizabeth Florescu, The Millennium Project. © 2009 The Millennium Project.

Index